European Higher Education at the Crossroads

Adrian Curaj • Peter Scott
Lazăr Vlasceanu • Lesley Wilson
Editors

European Higher Education at the Crossroads

Between the Bologna Process
and National Reforms

Part 2 2012

 Springer

Editors
Adrian Curaj
POLITEHNICA University of Bucharest
Bucharest
Romania

Peter Scott
Institute of Education (IOE)
University of London
United Kingdom

Lazăr Vlasceanu
Department of Sociology
University of Bucharest
Bucharest
Romania

Lesley Wilson
European University Association
Brussels
Belgium

Printed in 2 Parts
ISBN 978-94-007-3936-9   e-ISBN 978-94-007-3937-6
DOI 10.1007/978-94-007-3937-6
Springer Dordrecht Heidelberg New York London

Library of Congress Control Number: 2012933439

Printed on acid-free paper

Springer is part of Springer Science+Business Media (www.springer.com)

Contents of Part 2: Governance, Financing, Mission Diversification and Futures of Higher Education

Contents of Part 1: Bologna Process Principles, Teaching and Learning, Quality Assurance, Mobility

Part II Teaching and Learning

Part III Quality Assurance

Part V
Higher Education Governance in the European Higher Education Area

Chapter 29
Governance Within the EHEA: Dynamic Trends, Common Challenges, and National Particularities

Robin Middlehurst and Pedro Nuno Teixeira

29.1 Introduction

It is popular to claim that higher education systems (and higher education governance specifically) have changed *significantly* in recent years – in large part in response to policy initiatives at national and regional levels. A recent analysis of governance reform in higher education points to broad reforms in Western and Eastern Europe in the 1980s and 1990s and an acceleration in the rate of change and reform since the late 1990s (CHEPS 2009). Major policy developments at the European level highlighted as part of the quickening pace of change in recent years include the Sorbonne and Bologna Declarations (1998, 1999) and the Lisbon Strategy (2000). These were two different policy processes, but have become increasingly intertwined and by 2005 (in the Bergen Communiqué) their separate goals intersected and actions linked to the Bologna Process were increasingly informed by the Lisbon targets. Underlying this convergence was recognition that higher education institutions and systems were central to the achievement of Europe's economic and social goals.

Policy developments at national or local levels, by themselves, however, do not give us the full picture. They are, as Fernand Braudel the French historian suggests, part of 'histoire evenementielle', responses on the surface to deeper structural changes (Braudel 1987). One must also pay attention to Braudel's 'longue durée',

R. Middlehurst (✉)
Kingston University, Vice-Chancellor's Office, River House, 53-57 High Street,
KT1 1LQ Kingston upon Thames, UK
e-mail: r.middlehurst@kingston.ac.uk

P.N. Teixeira
CIPES, Faculty of Economics, University of Porto, Rua 1° dezembro,
399 4450-227 Matosinhos, Portugal
e-mail: pedrotx@fep.up.pt

A. Curaj et al. (eds.), *European Higher Education at the Crossroads:*
Between the Bologna Process and National Reforms,
DOI 10.1007/978-94-007-3937-6_29, © Springer Science+Business Media Dordrecht 2012

where more powerful forces are driving deeper structural shifts at system level.[1] From this latter perspective, at least three deeper driving forces must be part of the picture of change in higher education systems: economic, socio-demographic, and technological forces. Economic developments have brought increasing prosperity to Europe since 1945; and are also associated with the growth of a global knowledge economy. The economic outlook in Europe since 2008 is no longer so positive, with recession and sovereign debt in a number of European countries causing serious concerns. This difficult financial situation has added to the pre-existing troubles of higher education funding, especially as regards public sources, which have become increasingly stretched in recent years (Teixeira 2009). Secondly, socio-demographic changes in Europe are linked to an increasing demand for higher education. Despite sometimes adverse demographic trends, the demand for higher education has not receded and we have seen a movement across the EHEA towards mass participation systems with stronger expectations of lifelong learning. Thirdly, technological developments, particularly in Information and Communication Technologies (ICT) are transforming the ways in which the core functions of higher education – teaching, research and service to society – are conducted and delivered. Each of these deeper forces has direct and indirect implications for governance in higher education. They also, of course, provide a context that has been moulding political and policy responses at the European, national and local levels under the general rubric of 'reforming' or 'modernising' higher education systems and institutions.

Bearing in mind this context, this paper aims to provide a brief portrait of the main trends in European higher education governance and the major policy and institutional challenges derived from them. We begin with an examination of the terminology of 'governance' at institutional and system level. Then, we reflect on European developments in the context both of drivers for change and wider global developments in governance. The third section briefly discusses some emerging themes and issues in higher education governance in Europe, which are explored in depth in a series of related chapters. The last section highlights a range of challenges that exist for governments, agencies and higher education providers as they seek to ensure that governance systems are responsive and appropriate for changing environmental conditions in Europe and in a global context.

29.2   Governance and Higher Education – Some Conceptual Remarks

Governance in higher education has different meanings and applications, both broad and narrow in scope (Middlehurst 2004). In addition, in theory and practice, notions of governance and ideas of what counts as effective governance in higher education

---

[1]Acknowledgement is also given here to Professor Sir Peter Scott who used Braudel's dual perspectives in a discussion paper on leadership and governance for the Leadership Foundation: "A New Deal for Higher Education: All Change, Slow Change or No Change?" (LFHE 2011).

are contested (Schofield 2009). Governance is usually defined as the structure and process for decision making at the institutional or system level. Gallagher states that "*Governance* is the structure of relationships that bring about organisational coherence, authorise policies, plans and decisions, and account for their probity, responsiveness and cost-effectiveness. *Leadership* is seeing opportunities and setting strategic directions, and investing in and drawing on people's capabilities to develop organisational purposes and values. *Management* is achieving intended outcomes through the allocation of responsibilities and resources, and monitoring their efficiency and effectiveness. *Administration* is the implementation of authorised procedures and the application of systems to achieve agreed results" (Gallagher 2001).

Like many authors studying the governance of higher education, Gallagher's focus is at the institutional level where he points to the 'structure of relationships' as being at the heart of governance. In practice, Gallagher's 'structure' involves relationships between people with specific positions and interests (executives and trustees), relationships between functions of different kinds (academic and professional services) as well as relationships between different roles, for example, representational, expert or *ex officio* roles. Gallagher's description also points to the dynamics of decision-making as a key focus of governance, with the triple purposes of bringing about 'organisational coherence', 'authorisation,' and 'accountability' for the decisions taken. He does not refer specifically to the constitutional and formal documents where the authority to make policy and take decisions at institutional level is defined (charters, statutes and other legal or statutory instruments). These are important and necessary reference points for governance, particularly where different interests and values come together, where decision-making contexts are dynamic and resources finite, and where politics and conflict are an inevitable part of the process.

Nevertheless, other authors tend to adopt a slightly broader perspective about the meanings of governance in higher education. Marginson and Considine consider that: "Governance (…) is concerned with the determination of value inside universities, their systems of decision-making and resource allocation, their missions and purposes, the patterns of authority and hierarchy, and the relationship of universities as institutions to the different academic worlds within and the worlds of government, business and community without. It embraces 'leadership', 'management' and 'strategy'" (Marginson and Considine 2000:7). For these authors, Gallagher's 'structure of relationships' for governance extend in two directions, to the staff and student communities inside the institution and the stakeholders outside it.

As George Keller states, governance is itself an ambiguous word (Keller 2001), referring to those who administer the affairs of an organization, as well as to those who manage higher education (at the system or institutional level) and also to the influence that constituents have in the decision-making processes of higher education. Thus, governance is concerned with institutional goals (strategy), purposes (mission), and also values, in other words determining what is important and what counts (Marginson and Considine 2000). This can relate to inputs to institutions (physical, human or financial), to processes (ways of operating and organising) and to outputs and outcomes (various aspects of institutional performance and contributions to wider social and economic goals). This definition reminds us that governance is a process – but can also offer a formal framework – where different values can be highlighted, where conflicts of values can be played out, and indeed, where core European values (such as academic freedom, democracy, freedom of speech or respect for diversity) can (and need to be) upheld. Hence, any overview of governance issues should recognize the diverse and sometimes sharply divergent perspectives about the topic, for example, between the academy and institutional management or between governments and institutional leaders (Stensaker and Harvey 2011; Locke et al. 2011).

Descriptions and analyses of governance arrangements in higher education refer both to institutional and system levels. Clearly, these represent two distinct zones of operation. At the system level, the players are Ministries (national or provincial), state-level agencies and university bodies. There are also bodies with an influence on governance at European level (Eurydice 2008) and also international bodies such as UNESCO, OECD or the World Bank that also have a bearing on governance at national, state and local levels. Even where the levels appear quite distinct, there is either a narrow or wide interface between levels which represents a highly political space where power and influence are debated, contested and exchanged. Responsibility for higher education within a country (or state) typically lies with a department of government led by a Minister, although in several countries, responsibilities for higher education are spread across government departments or Ministries. There may also be 'buffer or arm's length bodies' between the government and institutions. The Ministry typically oversees higher education compliance with national laws, sets national or provincial frameworks for higher education and determines national strategic priorities and policies for the system. Agencies may deal with funding, quality assurance and external policy guidance; they may also (as in the case of Rectors' Conferences or the EUA) be formal consultative, liaison or lobbying bodies for HEIs and promote collaboration, co-operation and exchange of good practice on governance. Together, these system-level functions include decision-making, advisory, operational and regulatory responsibilities (Eurydice 2007, 2008).

Several authors tend to distinguish between external and internal governance (see Rosser 2002). External governance refers to the degree of supervision by government and public authorities, which reflect not only the frequent public ownership of many higher education institutions, but also the fact that even non-public universities are regarded as having, at least to a certain extent, a public mission. The external governance of higher education is inseparable from its social purposes (see Heller 2004), namely the expected contribution of higher education regarding the advancement of knowledge, the training of qualified labour, the promotion of greater social equality, and a series of external benefits usually associated with higher education (e.g. lower crime rates, healthier habits, stronger environmental commitment, etc.) (see Weisbrod et al. 2008).

As regards external governance models, the usual types presented include the command or control model, the market model, and the autonomous model (see Kogan 1992; Clarke 1983). The first model describes a situation in which HEIs are seen mainly as an arm of government required to pursue a set of objectives mostly related to the political and social agenda. The influence of this model saw its heyday in the postwar decades of the twentieth century, but its sway significantly diminished in most European countries only in recent decades (Neave and Van Vught 1991; Neave 2009). The second model reflects a situation in which HEIs are regarded as autonomous institutions that perform certain tasks in response to a kind of contractual relationship with the government (which in turn financially compensates institutions for performing those tasks). This second model has attained increasing relevance over the last decades (for an analysis of the developments in the EHEA, see De Boer et al. 2009), following the general trend of marketization of higher education (Teixeira et al. 2004; Teixeira and Dill 2011; see also Chap. 30 by de Boer and Jongbloed in this volume). The third and final model reflects the view that HEIs are financially supported by society, namely through government funding, in order to pursue their mission (assuming that this will directly and indirectly contribute to the social good), but that in order to do this they should be autonomous from significant government (or other external) intervention. This model has been under scrutiny in recent years (Massy 2003) and presents significant tensions with either of the previous models. Whereas in most of the twentieth century the clash has mainly been with the command model, developments in recent decades have highlighted the tensions with the market model (Newman et al. 2004; Bok 2003).

As regards internal governance models, a few ideal-types are normally proposed through which universities' governance is analysed (Rosser 2002; Rhoades 1992). The first type is the bureaucratic model according to which the decision-making process of an organization is managed by a formal and complex hierarchical organization through a set of formal rules, policies, and channels of communication. A rather different mode of governance is the so-called collegial one, which emphasises the need for consensus and consultation and the role of academics and students in governance. A third type is denoted as 'political', and this highlights the primary role that power, conflict, and politics have in influencing universities' decisions and the extent to which decisions reflect the agendas of the various groups involved in governance and the potential coalitions among them. Finally, there is the so-called cybernetic type, according to which an institution is largely self-directed and where the role of leadership is mainly focused on monitoring the activity of the institution, providing feedback about its activity as well as any necessary corrections (Birnbaum 1988).

These very different views of internal or institutional governance in higher education reflect the organizational peculiarities of these institutions. Paraphrasing Weisbrod (1988), higher education institutions (like many nonprofit organizations) often combine the strengths and weaknesses of government and profit-oriented organizations. HEIs have a limited power to compel actions and are restricted in their power to use the surpluses they generate. On the other hand, they tend to be regarded as more trustworthy organizations because of their nonprofit nature. Moreover, they tend to be more flexible than many governmental organizations, due to their historical structure and the high degree of autonomy they tend to enjoy. The complex issue of institutional governance in higher education is built on the nuanced relationship between authority, influence, and power (Keller 2001).

The aforementioned complexity is also reflected in the fact that the decision-making process in many higher education institutions is based on formal and informal structures that involve (to variable degrees) each of the significant groups and interests in an attempt to build the largest compromise as possible for reaching decisions (Rosser 2002).

One of the central issues in universities' missions is their contribution to the public interest. However, serving the public interest is a complex issue and the diversity of institutions also reflects different ways of achieving this goal – potentially in different ways than how the government and policy-makers may have intended (see the background Chap. 42 by Reichert in this volume). Clearly, the financial aspect plays a major role in relation to 'mission' since public universities (and even many private ones) receive a major share of their revenues from public sources. This is particularly the case in continental European higher education (Estermann and Pruvot 2011). External governance through public or quasi-public authorities is increasingly being felt in many higher education systems through the rise of quality assessment and accreditation systems (in addition to funding arrangements) (see the background Chap. 14 by Sursock in Volume I). Other external forces influencing the governance of higher education institutions concern the role that political, social and business interests can exert in higher education, especially in those institutions that have a stronger local and regional orientation defined in their mission statement (for the potential influence of these interests, see Harcleroad and Eaton 2005). Other relevant external constituents include alumni and donors (see Schmidtlein and Berdahl 2005), both of which have been gaining more visibility in recent years in European HE due to the pressure for revenue diversification and their potential role in this respect (Teixeira and Koryakina 2011).

Among experts in models of governance, universities are often referred to as "organized anarchies" or "loosely coupled systems" (see Clarke 1983; Rhoades 1992). This reflects the complexity and specificity of these organizations and the impact of these factors in internal decision-making processes. One of the major complexities refers to the multidimensionality of higher education's objectives. This is a source of tension since universities are supposed to fulfil multiple objectives and the relevance awarded to each of these objectives will necessarily vary across each constituency. The rising marketization of recent decades has given particular prominence to this matter (Slaughter and Leslie 1997) and has shaped the political debate about how we should approach governance in higher education, including fostering important policy changes.

29.3 Symbolic Representations of HE Governance Reflecting Multiple Constituencies

The governance of higher education is a disputed territory for various reasons. One of the factors is diversity in the ownership and sponsorship of higher education institutions (Keller 2001). These range from state organizations to regional and local organizations. In the case of privately owned institutions, we find for-profit and non-profit institutions, with the latter group presenting a wide diversity of secular and religiously affiliated organizations. Another major factor is the role of multiple constituencies in HEIs' decision-making processes which results in multiple, diverse, and often conflicting views about the governance mechanisms of higher education. We can view this diversity through symbolic and historical 'lenses' as outlined below.

A classical way of looking at the governance of higher education is through an '*Academic-expert*' lens where different historical traditions coalesce. One derives from the medieval concept of a guild of masters who achieved corporate status as an *universitas* and were recognised by clerical authorities (the Pope) and by the king, as a *studium generale*. By the thirteenth century, in Paris first, followed by Oxford and Cambridge, these institutions were represented by a rector in dealing with external authorities (Shattock 2006). Clarke (1983) describes the notion of 'collegial authority' that arises from the guild arrangement where an individual master, based on his personal domain of knowledge, controlled the work of subordinates while the masters collectively exercised control over a larger territory of work. Such 'collegial authority' is also associated with 'self-governance'. The right to self-governance was claimed both on the grounds of expertise in specialist domains of knowledge (academic autonomy) and on the basis that a legitimate function of academic institutions was to act as centres of alternative opinions within a political system (Becher and Kogan 1992). University governance thus required a degree of separation from public authorities and independence from the state (institutional autonomy). Exercising collegial authority also involved a particular form of participative decision-making (see Chap. 35 by Amaral et al. in this volume). Collective decisions between the masters were to be reached through a process of discussion and consultation among peers of equal status, representing different domains of knowledge, until consensus was reached. This model of collegial (or 'professional') governance has many adherents within higher education and is part of the deliberative structures of internal governance (Senates, Courts and committees) that operate within many universities and colleges.

A quite different perspective on governance is the so-called '*Bureaucratic-civil society*' lens. A starting point for this view is a comment made by Bargh and her colleagues in their study of university governance in publicly-funded institutions, namely that "the pattern of university governance is shaped by the nature of the relationship between universities and their paymasters, generally, the state" (Bargh et al. 1996:161). Over time, universities' paymasters have extended and expanded from local communities and local benefactors to regional and national authorities, and today to a myriad of different paymasters representing public and private interests and sources of funding. In many parts of Europe in the nineteenth and twentieth centuries, concepts of university governance (at institutional level) had little meaning since universities were state institutions whose administrative (though not academic) arrangements were the same as in other parts of government (see Neave 2009). University staff, as civil servants, enjoyed security of employment but were governed by the same regulations as other civil servants. In many European countries, the appointment of professors had to be confirmed by the ministry and Rectors were often chosen by government. University buildings were typically owned and maintained by the state while the internal structures of universities were also determined by the state. Faculties and professorial chairs were established by ministries and parliaments so that overall, "oversight of the management of universities remained the responsibility of the state" (Bargh et al. 1996:165). Current modernisation and reform agendas at national and European levels are seeking to change these bureaucratic systems (although they still exist in many countries), shifting them towards autonomy and self-governance. However, autonomy is no longer to be based solely on academic primacy in governance. Instead, the emphasis is on corporate values and managerial structures of governance (Eurydice 2008; see also Chap. 31 by Paradeise in this volume).

A third way of looking at higher education governance is through the "*Student-community*" lens, which contains both historical and modern strands of development. In historical terms, the earliest medieval universities offer various examples of students' strong involvement in governance. Shades of this tradition remain enshrined to this day in arrangements for the election of Rectors in many European universities. A second historical strand refers to the idea that students are academic apprentices en route to joining 'a guild of masters' and is still expressed in degree ceremonies in a number of European universities. More recently, these ideas have become part of the notion of active 'student engagement' with their university and their own educational experience (see Chap. 34 by Klemencic in this volume). The modern strands of these ideas are strongly represented in the Bologna Process where student 'representation' is a key feature both at system-level policy discussions where the ESU is a key partner and within institutional governance where students are a formal part of both corporate and academic systems of governance at all levels of the institution. Still more recent developments bring a new strand into the frame: the student as consumer where 'the student voice' needs to be heard and to be present in institutional decision making within management and governance as well as academic arenas. This customer orientation corresponds to a view that the "only reason to create and maintain a formal organization like a business or university is to perform functions that someone – a customer – needs which cannot be done alone or in small groups" (Chaffee 1998:18).

A fourth way of looking at higher education's governance is through the "*Corporate-market*" lens. The genesis of this perspective is modern, arising from neo-liberalism and New Public Management ideologies (Pollitt 1990; Ferlie et al. 1996) and the rise of quasi-markets in higher education (see Teixeira et al. 2004).[2] One set of beliefs is that higher education institutions should be run more like

---

[2]The concept of quasi-markets was developed as a useful way of categorizing some of the more popular reforms for introducing market forces into existing publicly financed systems of education (Le Grand and Bartlett 1993). Government regulation and financing will still remain important mechanisms of coordination, but other aspects of the market, such as competition, user charges, individual responsibilities, and freedom of choice, are introduced into the system in an attempt to stimulate and simulate market behavior among (mostly) public institutions.

corporations so as to increase efficiency and productivity; a later strand is concerned with institutions operating as enterprising businesses in a global higher education marketplace. In governance terms, 'corporate' implies more executive management control within institutions, with less 'administration' and fewer committees, combined with a Board of trustees or governors with external lay (i.e. non-academic) representation that will hold the executive to account (see Chap. 35 by Amaral et al. in this volume). Where the emphasis within the corporate perspective is on efficiency and effectiveness, the market emphasis is on entrepreneurial behaviour – identifying new sources of revenue and seeking new opportunities to extend teaching and research, notably by increasing university-business links and partnerships. Both these strands are associated with more competition (within and between higher education systems) and with a much more fluid balance and set of relationships between publicly-funded institutions and private higher education providers, both non-profit and for-profit (Middlehurst and Fielden 2011; Teixeira 2009). The corporate-market perspective is visible in many parts of the world and is variously described as the 'corporatization' or 'privatization' of higher education.

These four lenses on governance highlight the range of interests and actors that are involved in institutional governance: academics, managers, students, external stakeholders including business and state representatives. The balance of power between these groups differs within institutions and countries and is generally in a state of flux. Were it to be in a state of equilibrium, one could say that 'shared governance' was operating. In an environment of scarce or constrained resources and increasing competition, there is more likely to be an unequal balance of power and more conflict between different sets of interests so that the practice of governance will be more or less politicised (Baldridge 1971; Kezar et al. 2006; Magalhaes and Amaral 2009).

29.4   European Developments in Governance in a Global Context of Change in Higher Education

European higher education has faced significant change over recent decades. One of the major features of this change has been the persistent expansion of higher education. This expansion has been increasingly linked to economic motivations and purposes. Governments have been convinced that advanced qualifications and high level skills are a key factor in promoting economic growth and development. An economic discourse has prioritised the creation of an institutional context favourable to the development of innovation and entrepreneurship and this in turn has strengthened the view that the accumulation of human capital can improve the economic prospects of different communities (Grubb and Lazerson 2004). Thus, changes in the individual and social motivations regarding higher education have had a major impact in the external and internal regulation of higher education institutions, notably by stressing the economic dimension of higher education and the potential of institutions to contribute to individual and socio-economic goals.

This shifting view about institutions and their primary purposes has led to a need to rethink and adapt the contextual framework in which these units operate. If we regard institutions as part of an industry, then the context in which they operate should promote a rational use of resources in order to maximize the social return relative to the resources allocated to the higher education sector. Hence, we have seen a reconfiguration of the sector along market rules, often through policy initiatives and government interventions that have affected funding mechanisms with a goal of promoting closer interaction between universities and industry (for examples of these policies see Chap. 30 by De Boer and Jongbloed in this volume). This has been particularly noticeable in countries with a mature HE sector. Government policies have stimulated institutions to view students as consumers and have nurtured commercial links between universities and private companies.

Changes in governance in the EHEA are therefore part of a longer-term process of modernisation of higher education in Europe that can be traced back at least as far as the 1980s in its present forms (see Chap. 31 by Paradeise and Chap. 32 by Moscati in this volume). The rationale for this 'modernisation agenda' is described in detail by the European Commission (EC, MEMO/06/190, Brussels 2006). The particular problems highlighted by the Commission include fragmentation of the European higher education system; insufficient diversity within HE systems; over-detailed and constraining national regulations; under-use of knowledge produced by universities through separation between universities and businesses' innovation systems; a lack of preparedness for competition arising from globalisation; insufficient funding for universities; and lower access rates to universities than in other leading world regions. The most recent communication from the European Commission (EC. COM (2011) 567.final) sharpens the focus on higher education's economic role, i.e. to support 'growth and jobs'.

As higher education has continued to expand, governments' responses have been to seek structural changes at system level, establishing new higher education sectors or developing private sectors still further and the promotion of new universities of applied science (see Chap. 42 by Reichert in volume 1). The boundaries between public and private sectors and vocational and professional education and levels of education are also blurring (Bjarnason et al. 2000; Middlehurst 2001). In some countries binary divides between sectors have been abolished, in others they have been maintained, but are reportedly under pressure. In several countries re-structuring has included mergers of institutions within and across higher education sectors. There are also a variety of initiatives to encourage research collaboration between higher education institutions as well as between public universities and private companies through networks, alliances and clusters. As a result of these shifts and changes, the dominant situation in European higher education seems to be that of different forms of institutional differentiation, with a large number of countries with a binary or dual system (Taylor et al. 2008) – and others with even greater levels of diversity and differentiation. Such differentiation and diversity is often a motivator for introducing changes in system and institutional governance arrangements (for an analysis of institutional responses see Chap. 31 by Paradeise in this volume).

The trend towards expansion has raised significant economic challenges both for institutions and governments alike. The fact that the number of students enrolled in higher education has multiplied several times in a few decades has called for a huge investment in hiring more academic and non-academic staff, investment in new and better equipped lecture-rooms, libraries, etc. The financial cost of the higher education system has become a significant issue in almost every country and governments have been struggling to find additional funds to sustain (and often pursue further) the process of expansion. Moreover, the financial challenges faced by higher education have been enhanced by an adverse financial situation within the wider public sector during much of the last two decades. The so-called crisis of the welfare state has challenged the sustainability of the traditional reliance of higher education on public funding (Barr 2004).

Arguably, higher education has now moved from an expanding sector to a mature industry (Levine 2001). In its expansion phase, growth was seen as a sign of improvement and HE managed to keep public and social actors satisfied by accommodating larger numbers of students. In its mature phase, external stakeholders have become more demanding and are no longer satisfied by the addition of more activities or expansion of existing ones. The rising costs of higher education cause concern among policy-makers and public opinion has encouraged increased political and social scrutiny of HE (Birnbaum and Shushok 2001). Hence, the political environment has focused increasing attention on the external and internal efficiency of the higher education system. Many governments have tried to strengthen the external efficiency of the system and have sought more responsive institutions. This has had important consequences for prescribed modes of external and internal governance, notably through a much more explicit participation of external stakeholders in formal and informal mechanisms of governance.

Another important implication of the pervasive managerial and economic dimensions of institutions has been the rising influence of academic management (Meek et al. 2010; Gumport 2001). This has challenged the traditional sovereignty of intellectual and professional expertise as the key legitimate foundation for academic management decisions (as discussed in Chap. 33 by Pechar and Chap. 35 by Amaral et al. in this volume). The internal allocation of resources within HEIs has increasingly prioritized financial and economic criteria versus intellectual, epistemological, historical or organizational ones. Furthermore, the contribution of a subject, a programme or a staff member to the ability to generate resources is increasingly used as an indirect measure to assess the social and economic relevance of that unit or individual and their effectiveness in responding to social and economic needs.

29.4.1   European Developments at the System-Level of Governance

With respect to governance reforms, the main agenda has been concerned with seeking to create real autonomy and accountability for universities (EC Memo 2006:3).

From a system perspective, the aim has been to move from a 'state control model' to a 'state supervising model' (Neave and Van Vught 1991) in which the state designs a framework of rules and policy objectives for the system as a whole and institutions have the freedom and responsibility to set their own missions, priorities and programmes, decide on their own organisation and internal management, manage their own estate and physical assets, and recruit, train and incentivise their own staff. In return, universities are to be held accountable to society for their results, including the cost-efficiency and effectiveness by which the desired outcomes are achieved. The state's role becomes 'evaluative' rather than directive (Neave 1988). At institutional level, traditional modes of academic self-governance need to shift toward new models of managerial self-governance (Eurydice 2008) that are intended to be more efficient and more responsive to society's needs and customer demands. To support greater institutional self-management, Member States should also build up and reward management and leadership capacities within universities, perhaps through national bodies dedicated to university management and leadership training (EC Memo 2006:4).

Major trends in governance reforms in the European Higher Education Area have included legislative changes (new higher education acts) and in some countries changing the legal status of institutions. As part of the shifting authority between the state and universities, new steering mechanisms have been developed. Partly inspired by the Bologna Process (but also by wider government agendas and agency action), quality assurance and accreditation systems have been established and good practice shared across networks within the EHEA (Sursock 2011; Amaral and Rosa 2011).

De Boer and File (2009) point out that shifts in system governance have become more complex and dynamic with authority and power distributed at different policy levels and with more actors involved. This is described as 'multi-level, multi-actor, or multi-vocal governance' (p10) where co-ordination increasingly takes place at inter-connected levels. Researchers illustrate that state power is moving (or being delegated) in three directions: upwards to the supra-national level (of the EU, for example), downwards towards provinces, local governments and higher education institutions themselves and outward, as some of the traditional tasks of the state are moved to the periphery (to NGOs) or are being privatized (Pierre and Peters 2000). The state's role is different across countries. In some cases, it is more 'facilitative' and 'co-operative', creating an environment aimed at delivering stronger perfor-mance outcomes rather than seeking these through detailed intervention; in other cases, the state is acting more as 'market engineer' by using mechanisms of supply and demand in governance processes (see Chap. 30 by de Boer and Jongbloed in this volume).

Research on European-wide changes in governance has also indentified the drivers underlying notions of 'less government but more governance', and this seems to be largely driven by the financial implications of larger and more costly higher education systems and institutions (de Boer and File 2009). Nonetheless, the change is also ideological, linked to pervading beliefs in the market as a co-ordinating mechanism for higher education and in 'New Public Management' as an organizational approach for modernising public services (see Chap. 32 by Moscati and Chap. 35 by Amaral et al.

in this volume). Associated with both of these ideologies is an increased emphasis on competition as a means to enhance the efficiency and quality of higher education. It is important to note, however, that although these trends were discernable across countries, they vary in extent, pace, timing and style based on very different histories, cultures and operating conditions. There are early adopters and late reformers. In some parts of Europe radical political changes were enacted in the early 1990s, in other countries, aspects of the modernisation agenda had already been a reality for many years while in others, the modernisation agenda has hardly started. So governance arrangements at system level are, in their detail, as heterogeneous as the EHEA itself – and this is also the case at institutional level. Research at the level of individual countries highlights emerging themes and issues that are highly contextual. A simple linear relationship between policy directions set at European level and governance reforms at Member State level rarely exists and socio-economic, political and historical factors are likely to be more dominant for individual countries or, indeed institutions (for an analysis of different national responses, see Chap. 31 by Paradeise and Chap. 30 by De Boer and Jongbloed in this volume).

29.4.2   European Developments in Institution-Level Governance

At the internal level, the overarching theme in governance over the last 20 years has been institutional autonomy (de Boer and File 2009). However, autonomy has different meanings in higher education and this issue has fuelled substantial debate in higher education policy and research. Researchers describe various dimensions of autonomy, for example, 'substantive' (meaning control over academic and research policy, the award of degrees, curriculum design, student selection and portfolio of programmes) and 'procedural' (meaning authority over financial management, human resource management, the deployment of physical and other assets) (Berdahl 1990). In a recent multi-country survey, it was noted that the degree of autonomy granted in recent governance reforms in different countries differed along two dimensions: 'structural freedom' (meaning the freedom to determine internal structures and organisation) and 'stakeholder involvement' (meaning the degree of internal and external stakeholder involvement in governance arrangements) (quoted in CHEPS 2009). Another major European study has also distinguished between 'organisational autonomy' (deciding on internal governance structures, internal authority arrangements, responsibility and accountability structures and ability to select the institutional leadership); 'policy autonomy' (the ability of universities to constitute themselves as academic communities – the equivalent of Berdahl's substantive autonomy); and 'financial autonomy' (the ability to decide on the internal allocation of public and private funds, to diversify sources of income, to build up reserves and to borrow funds on the capital market) (see CHEPS 2009). In the context of autonomy linked to accountability requirements, also discussed is the issue of 'interventional autonomy' and the extent to which institutions are free from accountability requirements.

Where institutions have received more autonomy and authority, the first level has been concerned with institutional strategy development, typically within a broad mission determined by national authorities. Internal governance structures may also be determined through national legislation, but institutional leadership, academics and students and to an extent, external stakeholders, are also involved. In most countries, study programmes are designed at institutional level although accreditation procedures and criteria restrict degrees of freedom. Institutions also have substantial freedom to design internal quality assurance procedures within overall national and European guidelines. Financial autonomy has increased in terms of internal budgeting and resource allocation, but does not always include extensive income diversification as yet; determining tuition fee-levels, for example, only happens in a few countries. Human resource management, staff selection and recruitment have also been devolved to institutions, typically within framework conditions set by governments. However, with regard to student selection and admissions and access policies, while there is a trend towards more autonomy, centralised national procedures and regulations are still in play. Finally, in pursuing their own priorities and in responding to a more globalised and competitive environment, institutions have engaged in a variety of partnerships at several levels.[3]

In relation to organisational autonomy, a recent EUA study found that while most countries had external regulations relating to the form and structure of decision-making bodies in universities, there was still a degree of independence available to institutions (Estermann and Nokkala 2009). There was a trend towards inclusion of external members in university decision-making processes, especially where dual governance structures existed (such as a Board/Council and Senate) – and such structures were on the rise (see Chap. 35 by Amaral et al. in this volume). In some countries there was also a clear shift towards 'CEO-type rectors' associated with greater autonomy in design of management structures; however this was not universal with a significant number of more traditional modes existing where the rector is an academic 'primus inter pares', selected by the academic community from among the professors of the university.

Trends towards greater autonomy are accompanied by various forms of accountability so that institutions are required to report on, to be audited or inspected in relation to their funding and financial management, their quality and academic management, their overall performance and their responsiveness to students and wider stakeholders. In a detailed study of accountability in different countries around the world and in trans-national contexts (including across Europe), several common trends are identified (Stensaker and Harvey 2011). Firstly, there is increasing government interest in accountability and government is a key player in new initiatives in the field; external and upward forms of accountability dominate.

---

[3]International arrangements have proliferated (associations, networks, alliances, consortia) based on historical, geographical and disciplinary ties; there are similar groupings at national and regional levels (Beerkens 2004) and public-private partnerships are also a feature of this landscape (Fielden et al. 2010).

Secondly, in many countries, special agencies set up by government are emerging charged with producing information used for accountability purposes for government itself but also for prospective students, their parents and future employers. These agencies may also have other purposes, for example dealing with aspects of the Bologna Process, internationalisation issues or providing some control over private providers of higher education. A third trend is that accountability in most countries is associated with quality assurance procedures. While there are a number of other accountability measures including funding instruments, developmental contracts, research indicators and legal obligations, the core accountability instrument is quality assurance, mainly through accreditation schemes (see Chap. 14 by Sursock in volume I).

29.4.3 Developments in Governance Beyond Europe

Despite some specificities, many of the aforementioned trends in the EHEA follow global developments in higher education's governance. In a recent survey on global trends in university governance, the main pressures on higher education systems appeared to be driving governance changes (Fielden 2008). These pressures included increasing demand for higher education and expanding participation rates, growing complexity and diversity of higher education systems and national expectations of higher education's role in economic development. Given these pressures, the old model of central control of higher education by governments is being replaced by other models based more on strategic oversight accompanied by increasingly sophisticated forms of monitoring and performance review. As in Europe, the direction of travel is from control to autonomy with accountability, and the comparison also shows a similar trajectory to Europe in terms of governments' reform agendas. Whereas reforms in the 1990s and early 2000s were concerned with legal and constitutional changes between the system and institution levels, recent reforms have been concerned with developing more complex supervisory and reporting regimes including performance against strategic objectives, performance against an agreed contract with the state and performance related to national policy objectives and targets. Accompanying these developments, governments are seeking useful performance indicators to measure the success of their own policies and also to assess comparative institutional efficiency and effectiveness. Once again, these are similar to European developments mentioned earlier (Brown 2010; Hazelkorn 2011).

At the institutional level, legislation often defines not only the relationship of the institution with the state, but also the relationship and powers of internal governance structures vis-à-vis the state. A common approach is for a higher education act to define the powers of a university board as the supreme governing body of the institution, accountable to a minister (or buffer agency), with the detailed powers of the board set out in university-level statutes and regulations. Legislation also typically defines the status of the president (rector) with accountability to the board, although processes and powers relating to the selection and appointment of the President vary quite substantially across countries (Middlehurst et al. 2010). A comparison of the characteristics of governing boards across 15 countries, including a selection from Europe, East Asia, Africa, North America and Australasia points out striking parallels (Fielden 2008). Public institutions in Europe (e.g. Denmark, Norway, Sweden, and the Netherlands) share common features of internal governance with Japan, Indonesia, Tanzania, Australia and the US. There are nevertheless differences in terms of Board composition with some countries having strong external, lay membership (Denmark, Tanzania, UK, Australia) and some retaining a majority of internal and academic membership (Hungary, Pakistan, Norway).

More theoretical studies (Huisman 2009) show parallels too in governance developments between Europe and other higher education systems globally and also highlight differences in the pace of change, cultural differences in the intent and consequences of policy as well as differences between rhetoric and reality. The comment by Paradeise et al. (2009) concerning governance reforms in Europe applies more strongly if the analysis is global, namely that "'the convergence' thesis in higher education public management reform is still at the very least partial and premature" (p93).

History matters, particularly for developments in governance, since the latter depends significantly on the timing of the creation of each higher education institution and the very particular development of each higher education system (see Chap. 31 by Paradeise and Chap. 33 by Pechar in this volume). Thus, older universities will tend to present modes of governance reflecting their medieval origins. Likewise, universities created through state initiatives and systems that were largely shaped by state intervention throughout the nineteenth and early twentieth centuries will reflect this state intervention in their modes of governance. Moreover, the same institutions will evolve in their modes of governance reflecting fashions and trends in higher education policy, which quite often leave traces even after being displaced by subsequent modes of governance. Currently, therefore, there is a certain degree of eclecticism in university governance, with many institutions com- bining historical modes of collegial and bureaucratic governance with more recent corporate-like and market-oriented ones. The symbolic representations of university governance described above illustrate the combination of historical and modern influences, interpretations and inter-connections within higher education governance arrangements and practices.

This eclecticism also reflects a contemporary tension in university governance between an institutional leadership willing to assert its power and authority and a significant resistance from traditional academic governance (see Chap. 32 by Moscati, Chap. 35 by Amaral et al., and Chap. 33 by Pechar in this volume). This tension is often solved through degrees of compromise with joint-committees and what some would call dual-governance (Keller 2001). This shared governance consists of sharing the authority among the various constituent groups and inter- ested parties (Rosser 2002). The ensuing balance has often been regarded as a major strength of university institutions, even in periods of change, since various stakeholders are involved in processes of transformation. Nevertheless, this balance seems to be shifting as a consequence of the renewed strength of institutional leadership and increasing external pressures towards greater market orientation for institutions. Despite criticisms about the ineffectiveness of more collegial modes of governance and oft-expressed fears about its crisis and replacement, a recent study (Kaplan 2004) has shown that the actual situation is far more favourable. Faculty continue to have a significant role in governance in many institutions and their participation continues to be valued. Nonetheless, the same study also confirmed that the balance of power has been changing over time, with visible advances in the power of management in decision-making. These advances have been more prominent in some institutions, especially in those with lower research intensity, where the prestige and symbolic power of faculty tends to be lower.

29.5 Concluding Remarks – Emerging Themes and Challenges in European Governance

There are, of course, a range of challenges arising for governance within and across countries in the EHEA related to the economic context within Europe and the wider global economy. Pressures on public funding of higher education exist in many countries with a range of implications, including opening up the higher education system to private providers and encouraging publicly-funded institutions to diversify their sources of income and become more 'commercial'. The consequences for governance may over the medium term be profound both at system level in terms of new regulatory frameworks and potential challenges to existing quality assurance or accountability arrangements, and at institutional level in terms of the potential for conflict between academic and commercial interests. Even were conflict not to be the key issue, increasing complexity in university operations will challenge the exercise of governance as well as the selection of governors (academics, students and lay people) capable of giving the necessary time and expertise to the role. The combination of universities becoming more permeable to external influences and the internal need to negotiate between different interests has increased tensions and the real challenge for governance will be to make this a creative tension rather than a destructive force.

Socio-demographic changes linked to increasing demand for higher education, mass participation systems and life-long learning, particularly when combined with resource and funding pressures, are likely to mean that movement towards greater institutional differentiation and system diversity will intensify (see Chap. 42 by Reichert and Chaps. 19 and 43 by Hazelkorn in this volume). Institutional efforts to build networks and consortia, including public-private partnerships, will form part of the picture, alongside mergers and acquisitions that are either orchestrated at state and system levels or form part of private sector market opportunities. If ICT developments are factored into these developments, including more distance and on-line learning provision and the emergence of new providers offering higher education in new forms, perhaps more flexibly and at lower cost, then the predictions of 'disruptive innovation' at system and institutional level will become pertinent

(Christensen 2011). ICT developments also have implications for governance operations: it is much easier to argue for transparency and accountability if data can be easily collected and reported through performance indicators and other management information processes. Trends towards system steerage through performance monitoring are likely to increase with concomitant requirements for management competence within institutions and associated governance expertise to understand and interpret the data appropriately.

Amongst many other possible governance challenges, four further issues are highlighted, some of which are beginning to be explored, but where more attention is warranted both in theoretical and practical terms. The first issue concerns networks, and may be understood in different ways. Firstly, new configurations in the landscape of higher education mean that existing boundaries are being blurred (e.g. between public and private sectors of higher education), dissolved (e.g. boundaries of time and space in the case of asymmetrical learning opportunities), traversed or re-formed (e.g. in trans-national or cross-institutional organisations). These structural developments have implications for governance in terms of challenging the forms of governance that currently operate and apply to individual sectors, individual institutions or individual, national jurisdictions. However, the concept may also be applied to people in particular roles (actors) where public policies are debated, designed and implemented through horizontally-constituted networks in a non-hierarchical, dynamic and cybernetic form (what Paradeise et al. 2009, describe as 'Networked Governance'). A third and somewhat similar interpretation involves the development and implementation of higher education policy through policy networks, for example at European level, but other international organisations could be included as well as numerous other agencies at national, regional and local levels. In this case, policy networks involve informal relationships that are needed for policy-making (and implementation) to be effective and that are created in the grey area between state and civil society (Padure and Jones 2009:108). The same authors argue that policy network analysis can be used as a theoretical framework for research to examine the effects of multi-level governance on higher education policy and practice. These different interpretations of networks – in terms of structures, processes and governance relationships – are useful areas for future exploration as they pose both conceptual and practical challenges for higher education governance.

A second challenge is associated with 'relationships,' again in both structural and process terms. In much of the policy literature (particularly at EU level) the focus is on the formal structure of relationships between actors or organisations and systems. What is needed to supplement these analyses is discussion of the dynamics of relationships at the micro-level, for example between the Rector and the Board, or the changing dynamics of power relationships between institutions (of different kinds) and governments, what de Boer and colleagues have called 'the doing of governance' (de Boer et al. 2007:6). Stensaker and Harvey's (2011) analysis of accountability regimes and relationships does explicitly focus on power and trust, while recent analyses of 'good' governance in an Australian context (Goedegebure et al. 2009) and of 'governing body effectiveness' (Schofield 2009) in a UK context get closer to the dynamics of governance. In addition, a recent Higher Education

Policy Institute report (HEPI 2011) offers an interesting personal reflection on the dynamics of power in institutional governance based on the experiences of an institutional leader. Governance is likely to become yet more challenging for those involved as tensions between competing values, ethical dilemmas, the need to prioritise interests and scarce resources dominate governance agendas.

A third area of challenge is linked to the issue of relationships, values and interests and the 'effectiveness' of governance. Once again, there are different dimensions to the issue. Goedegebure et al. (op cit.) touch on one aspect and that is the extent to which governance systems in higher education can be exercised with integrity in terms of espoused standards of public life or more particularly with reference to the Good Governance Standard for Public Services developed in the UK (CIPFA & OPM 2004). The evidence, they suggest is equivocal. Given the challenges ahead, for example, in relation to growing commercialisation of some university activities or potential ethical dilemmas arising in respect of the governance of transnational education or international research collaborations, or challenges to academic freedom in different European countries, the question of what counts as 'effective' governance with respect to particular values will grow in significance. A further dimension of 'effectiveness' arises in relation to the focus of institutional performance; what impact do particular governance arrangements have on academic performance in terms of international research and teaching excellence? In the UK, it is a point of observation that those institutions that achieve the highest levels of academic performance (Oxford and Cambridge) do not have the governance characteristics that are currently espoused in the 'corporate-hierarchical' framework for institutional governance (and nor do other highly-rated institutions such as Harvard). A recent study of governance based on the perceptions of academics of changing working practices and internal governance arrangements sheds some light on this issue (Locke et al. 2011), but more in-depth studies of the effectiveness of governance in relation to academic performance (as well as responsiveness to students or society) are needed to assess the reality as well as the rhetoric underpinning reviews of governance in European higher education.

A fourth and final challenge refers to the balance between universities' economic and non-economic dimensions and the associated implications for institutional governance. The tendency to perceive institutions as a quasi-economic organization has overshadowed the view that these are a peculiar type of economic organization (Winston 1999). Furthermore, we should not forget the fact that higher education is more than an organization. Universities are institutions, with a mission, and not merely organizations, although these terms are often used interchangeably and the latter has tended to predominate in recent times (Gumport 2001). A focus on the organization tends to (over)simplify the nature and the social role of HE and it devalues the role of history, tradition, norms, path-dependency; it also contributes to a narrower view of the scope and legitimacy of higher education as a social institution. Higher education institutions cannot escape the fact that they need resources to develop their activities. However, they can do this in very different ways. One approach may be to extinguish the institutional dimension, to become – essentially – an organiza-tion that provides academic services. Alternatively, a balance can be struck between the need to accommodate market signals and respond to short-term economic and social demands with a long-term commitment to the university's (long-term) institutional mission. HE's responsiveness to social and economic needs may not only entail benefits, but also costs and problems. Following Weisbrod (1988), we may argue that HEIs, like nonprofit organizations in general, may diverge from for-profit organizations not only because of their legal constraints (notably regarding profit-making and more specifically, the deployment of 'surpluses'), but also because the motivations and goals of their managers and directors differ. Being quite different types of organizations, HEIs tend to attract leaders and managers that have different goals and styles of leadership. However, the more the governance structure of higher education is aligned with corporate modes, the more it will attract a certain profile of leaders and managers that will reinforce that bias. Thus, more attention is needed to the analysis of the types of leadership that need to be developed in order to help in developing effective forms of governance in an increasingly diverse higher education landscape.

In looking across the EHEA, there are some common governance issues emerging, albeit they will have different implications and solutions in different countries. The research contributions prepared for this theme aim to combine attention to issues that have wide relevance across several members of the EHEA with an attention to national and regional specificities. The chapters included in this thematic track highlight some comparable trends, although they also signal important national and institutional specificities. The first two contributions address the current trends in governance in Europe. These two contributions provide a scenario in which to explore and bring into sharper focus the debates, policy changes and specific arrangements at system and institutional level. They offer insights into what is currently happening within the EHEA, providing an update on developments as well as a critical perspective on the rhetoric versus the reality of changes in governance. In the first one, Harry de Boer and Jongbloed give particular attention to the increasing role played by market forces in higher education and the changes at the system level. They highlight the fact that the government's role has changed in several ways, though it has not by any means disappeared. In the following Chap. 31, Catherine Paradeise portrays the changing landscape of governance in Europe and reflects about national and institutional differences in the response to those changes. Although the prevailing view is that much change has taken place, she points out important nuances and the need for more research to substantiate actual changes on the ground.

The following two contributions by Roberto Moscati and Hans Pechar take a more focused look into national developments regarding two very important developments in university governance in Europe, placing them within the wider European context. On the one hand, we see the growing role of middle management in higher education, and, on the other hand, the actual or perceived decline of academic power associated with shifts from an academic-collegial form of governance to a corporate-managerial mode. In the case of middle managers such as Deans and heads of department (but also those in professional support roles such as finance, marketing, human resource, enterprise management or management of student services) there has undoubtedly been an increase in workload and administrative as well as managerial responsibilities. These changes come about as much from the widening roles of universities, the expectations of accountability to a variety of external bodies and changes to working patterns associated with ICT developments as they do from changes to internal governance arrangements (although causes and effects are interrelated and difficult to disentangle). The two remaining contributions address the issue of the changing internal balances of power with the development of new structures of university governance. The decline of the academic oligarchy has been discussed by a number of authors over decades (e.g. Halsey 1992) but it needs to be nuanced according to national and institutional circumstances.

In Chap. 35 by Alberto Amaral and his colleagues, they review this wider trend and place it vis-à-vis the growing involvement of external stakeholders in university governance with examples from several European countries. They also reflect about the underpinning rationales for those changes and the way these are transforming universities' secular ethos. In the contribution by Manja Klemencic, the author addresses the theme of student participation in governance. In her chapter, she reflects on the different types of engagement that we can identify regarding higher education students, namely with the State, the University, with academics, and with Student' organizations. Klemencic reflects on important questions such as to what extent does student involvement bring with it a greater focus on high quality teaching and learning and responsiveness to students' needs or what role do students play and how different is this depending on who they are, for example, undergraduate or postgraduate, international or domestic students, part-time or full-time?

In summary, this overview has sought to capture the nature of governance changes at system and institutional levels over recent decades with reference to a wide range of studies. While governance is changing across the EHEA, the changes in train are not uniform in pace, style or impact. They are also part of much larger changes in the operating environments of higher education that will continue to have an impact on both the theory and practice of governance. Critical perspectives and different lenses will continue to be needed to keep higher education governance under the spotlight. Despite some resistance, notably by academics and students, Bologna reforms have been accepted (often – but not universally – rather passively) in many countries. This apparent passivity has created a challenge to engage internal constituencies in the implementation of substantive change and it is likely that more conflict will emerge as we move towards deeper implementation. Thus, policy-makers, institutional managers, and higher education researchers need to dialogue more to help European HEIs to develop forms of leadership and governance that promote greater degrees of engagement with internal and external stakeholders. We are confident that the breadth and depth of the contributions assembled here will be an important step in this respect by helping us to understand better the current developments in governance in the EHEA. They will also provide important insights regarding the challenges and limitations of current trends and in so doing, may help to devise modes of governance that will enable European universities to perform their missions more effectively.

References

Amaral, A., & Rosa, M. J. (2011). Transnational accountability initiatives: The case of the EUA audits. In B. Stensaker & L. Harvey (Eds.), *Accountability in higher education: Global perspectives on trust and power* (pp. 203–220). London: Routledge.

Baldridge, J. (1971). *Power and conflict in the university*. New York: Wiley.

Bargh, C., et al. (1996). *Governing universities: Changing the culture?* Buckingham: SRHE & Open University Press.

Barr, N. (2004). *Economics of the welfare state* (4th ed.). Oxford: Oxford University Press.

Becher, T., & Kogan, M. (1992). *Process and structure in higher education*. London: Routledge.

Beerkens, H. (2004). *Global opportunities and institutional embeddedness: Higher education consortia in Europe and southeast Asia*. Enschede: Centre for Higher Education Policy Studies.

Berdahl, R. (1990). Academic freedom, autonomy and accountability in British universities. *Studies in Higher Education, 15*(2), 169–180.

Birnbaum, R. (1988). *How colleges work*. San Francisco: Jossey-Bass.

Birnbaum, R., & Shushok, F. (2001). The 'Crisis' crisis in American higher education: Is that a wolf or a pussycat at the Academy's door? In P. Altbach et al. (Eds.), *In defense of higher education* (pp. 59–84). Baltimore: Johns Hopkins Press.

Bjarnason, S., et al. (2000). *The business of borderless education: UK perspectives*. London: CVCP (now Universities UK).

Bok, D. (2003). *Universities in the marketplace – The commercialization of higher education*. Princeton: Princeton University Press.

Braudel, F. (1987). *A history of civilizations*. London: Penguin.

Brown, R. (2010). *Higher education and the market*. New York: Routledge.

Chaffee, E. E. (1998). Listening to the people we serve. In W. G. Tierney (Ed.), *The responsive university: Restructuring for high performance*. Baltimore: The Johns Hopkins University Press.

CHEPS. (2009). *The extent and impact of higher education governance reform across Europe* (Final report to the Directorate-General for Education and Culture of the European Commission). Brussels: EC.

Christensen, C. (2011). *The innovative university*. Boston: Harvard University Press.

Clarke, B. (1983). *The higher education system*. Berkeley: University of California Press.

De Boer, H., & File, J. (2009). *Higher education governance reforms across Europe*. Brussels: ESMU.

De Boer, H., Huisman, J., & Meister-Scheytt, C. (2007). *Mysterious guardians and the diminishing state: Supervisors in 'modern' university governance*. Paper presented to the 29th annual EAIR Forum, 26–29 August 2007, Innsbruck, Austria.

De Boer, H., Enders, J., & Jongbloed, B. (2009). Market governance in higher education. In B. M. Kehm, J. Huisman, & B. Stensaker (Eds.), *The European Higher Education Area: Perspectives on a moving target* (pp. 61–78). Rotterdam: Sense Publishers.

Estermann, T., & Nokkala, T. (2009). *University autonomy in Europe 1: Exploratory study*. Brussels: European University Association.

Estermann, T., & Pruvot, E. B. (2011). *Financially sustainable universities II – European universities diversifying income streams*. Brussels: European University Association.

European Commission. (2006). MEMO/06/190, Brussels.

European Commission. (2011). Communique on Modernisation, MEMO/11/613, Brussels.

Eurydice. (2007). *Focus on the structure of higher education in Europe – 2006/7. National trends in the Bologna Process*. Brussels: Education and Culture DG.

Eurydice. (2008). *Higher education governance in Europe: Policies, structures, funding and academic staff*. Brussels: Education and Culture DG.

Ferlie, J., et al. (1996). *The new public management in action*. Milton Keynes: Open University Press.

Fielden, J. (2008). *Global trends in university governance* (Education Working Paper Series No. 9). Washington, DC: World Bank.

Fielden, J., Middlehurst, R., Woodfield, S., & Olcott, D. (2010). *The growth of private for-profit higher education providers in the UK*. London: Universities UK.

Gallagher, M. (2001). *Modern university governance – A national perspective*. Paper presented at "The idea of a university: Enterprise or Academy?" Conference organized by The Australian Institute and Manning Clark House, Canberra, 26 July 2001. http://www.dest.gov.au/archive/highered/otherpub/mod_uni_gov/default.htm

Goedegebure, L., et al. (2009). Good governance and Australian higher education: An analysis of a Neo-liberal decade. In J. Huisman (Ed.), *International perspectives on the governance of higher education: Alternative frameworks for coordination* (pp. 145–160). London: Routledge.

Grubb, W. N., & Lazerson, M. (2004). *The education gospel – The economic power of schooling*. Cambridge, MA: Harvard University Press.

Gumport, P. (2001). Built to serve: The enduring legacy of public higher education. In P. Altbach, P. Gumport, & B. Johnstone (Eds.), *In defense of American higher education* (pp. 85–109). Baltimore: John Hopkins Press.

Halsey, A. H. (1992). *Decline of donnish dominion: The British academic profession in the twentieth century*. Oxford: Clarendon.

Harcleroad, F., & Eaton, J. (2005). The hidden hand – External constituencies and their impact. In P. Altbach, R. Berdahl, & P. Gumport (Eds.), *American higher education in the twenty-first century: Social, political, and economic challenges* (2nd ed., pp. 253–283). Baltimore: John Hopkins Press.

Hazelkorn, E. (2011). *Rankings and the re-shaping of higher education: The battle for world-class excellence*. London: Palgrave Macmillan.

Heller, D. (2004). State oversight of academia. In R. Ehrenberg (Ed.), *Governing academia* (pp. 49–67). Ithaca: Cornell University.

HEPI Report Summary 52. (2011). *University governance: Questions for a New Era*. London: Higher Education Policy Institute.

Huisman, J. (Ed.). (2009). *International perspectives on the governance of higher education: Alternative frameworks for coordination*. London: Routledge.

Kaplan, G. (2004). How academic ships actually navigate. In R. Ehrenberg (Ed.), *Governing academia* (pp. 165–208). Ithaca: Cornell University Press.

Keller, G. (2001). Governance: The remarkable ambiguity. In P. Altbach, P. Gumport, & B. Johnstone (Eds.), *In defense of American higher education* (pp. 304–322). Baltimore: John Hopkins Press.

Kezar, A., Carducci, R., & Contreras-McGavin, M. (2006). *Rethinking the "L" word in higher education: The revolution of research on leadership* (ASHE-ERIC Higher Education Report, vol. 31, no. 6). San Francisco: Jossey Bass.

Kogan, M. (1992). Political science. In B. Clark & G. Neave (Eds.), *An encyclopedia of higher education* (Vol. 3, pp. 1926–1932). Oxford: Pergamon.

Le Grand, J., & Bartlett, W. (Eds.). (1993). *Quasi-markets and social policy*. Basingstoke: Macmillan Press.

Levine, A. (2001). Higher education as a mature industry. In P. Altbach, P. Gumport, & B. Johnstone (Eds.), *In defense of American higher education* (pp. 38–58). Baltimore: John Hopkins Press.

Locke, W., et al. (2011). *Changing governance and management in higher education: The perspectives of the academy*. New York: Springer.

Magalhaes, A., & Amaral, A. (2009). Mapping out discourses on higher education governance. In J. Huisman (Ed.), *International perspectives on the governance of higher education: Alternative frameworks for coordination* (pp. 182–197). London: Routledge.

Marginson, S., & Considine, M. (2000). *The enterprise university*. Melbourne: Cambridge University Press.

Massy, W. F. (2003). *Honouring the trust – Quality and cost containment in higher education*. Bolton: Anker Publishing Company.

Meek, V. L., Goedegebuure, L., Santiago, R., & Carvalho, T. (Eds.). (2010). *The changing dynamics of higher education middle management*. Dordrecht: Springer.

Middlehurst, R. (2001). University challenges: Borderless higher education, today and tomorrow. *Minerva, 39*, 3–26.

Middlehurst, R. (2004). Changing internal governance: A discussion of leadership roles and management structures in UK universities. *Higher Education Quarterly, 58*(4), 258–279.

Middlehurst, R., & Fielden, J. (2011). *Private providers in UK higher education: Some policy options* (HEPI Report Summary 53). London: Higher Education Policy Institute.

Middlehurst, R., et al. (2010). Leading & managing the university – Presidents and their senior management team. In E. Baker, P. Peterson, & B. McGaw (Eds.), *International encyclopaedia of education* (3rd ed., Vol. 4, pp. 238–244). Oxford: Elsevier.

Neave, G. (1988). On the cultivation of quality, efficiency and enterprise: An overview of recent trends in higher education in Western Europe, 1986-1988. *European Journal of Education, 23*(1/2), 7–23.

Neave, G. (2009). Institutional autonomy 2010-2020. A tale of Elan – Two steps back to make one very large leap forward. In B. M. Kehm, J. Huisman, B. Stensaker, et al. (Eds.), *The European Higher Education Area: Perspectives on a moving target* (pp. 3–22). Rotterdam: Sense Publishers.

Neave, G., & Van Vught, F. (1991). *Prometheus bound. The changing relationship between government and higher education in western Europe*. Oxford: Pergamon Press.

Newman, F., Couturier, L., & Scurry, J. (2004). *The future of higher education – Rhetoric, reality, and the risks of the market*. Baltimore: Jossey-Bass.

OPM, & CIPFA. (2004). *The good governance standard for public services*. The Independent Commission for Good Governance in Public Services. London: CIPFA & OPM.

Padure, L., & Jones, G. (2009). Policy networks and research on higher education governance and policy. In J. Huisman (Ed.), *International perspectives on the governance of higher education: Alternative frameworks for coordination*. London: Routledge.

Paradeise, C., et al. (2009). Reform policies and change processes in Europe. In J. Huisman (Ed.), *International perspectives on the governance of higher education: Alternative frameworks for coordination* (pp. 88–106). London: Routledge.

Pierre, J., & Peters, B. (2000). *Governance, politics and the state*. Houndmills Basingstoke: Macmillan Press.

Pollitt, C. (1990). *Managerialism and the public services: The Anglo-American experience*. Oxford: Basil Blackwell.

Rhoades, G. (1992). Governance – Models. In B. Clark & G. Neave (Eds.), *An encyclopedia of higher education* (Vol. 2, pp. 1376–1384). Oxford: Pergamon.

Rosser, V. (2002). Governance. In J. Forest & K. Kinser (Eds.), *Higher education in the United States – An encyclopedia* (Vol. 1, pp. 279–284). Santa Barbara: ABC-CLIO.

Schmidtlein, F., & Berdahl, R. (2005). Autonomy and accountability – Who controls academe? In P. Altbach, R. Berdahl, & P. Gumport (Eds.), *American higher education in the twenty-first century – Social, political, and economic challenges* (pp. 71–90). Baltimore/London: The Johns Hopkins University Press.

Schofield, A. (2009). *What is an effective and high performing governing body in UK higher education?* London: Leadership Foundation for Higher Education.

Shattock, M. (2006). *Managing good governance in higher education*. Maidenhead: Open University Press.

Slaughter, S., & Leslie, L. (1997). *Academic capitalism – Politics, policies, and the entrepreneurial university*. Baltimore: John Hopkins Press.

Stensaker, B., & Harvey, L. (Eds.). (2011). *Accountability in higher education: Global perspectives on trust and power*. London: Routledge.

Sursock, A. (2011). Accountability in western Europe: Shifting quality assurance paradigms. In B. Stensaker & L. Harvey (Eds.), *Accountability in higher education: Global perspectives on trust and power* (pp. 111–132). London: Routledge.

Taylor, J., Ferreira, J. B., Machado, M. L., & Santiago, R. (2008). *Non-university higher education in Europe*. Dordrecht: Springer.

Teixeira, P. (2009). Economic imperialism and the ivory tower: Economic issues and policy challenges in the funding of higher education in the EHEA (2010-2020). In B. M. Kehm,

J. Huisman, & B. Stensaker (Eds.), *The European Higher Education Area: Perspectives on a moving target* (pp. 43–60). Oxford: Sense Publishers.

Teixeira, P., & Dill, D. (2011). *Public vices, private interests? Assessing the effects of marketization in higher education*. Rotterdam: Sense Publishers.

Teixeira, P., & Koryakina, T. (2011). Funding diversification in the EHEA – Patterns, challenges and risks. In H.-G. van Liempd, M. Magnan, M. Söderqvist, & F. Wittmannn (Eds.), *Handbook on leadership and governance in higher education*. Berlin: RAABE Academic Publishers.

Teixeira, P., Dill, D., Jongbloed, B., & Amaral, A. (Eds.). (2004). *Markets in higher education: Reality or rhetoric?* Dordrecht: Kluwer Academic Publishers.

Weisbrod, B. (1988). *The nonprofit economy*. Boston: Harvard University Press.

Weisbrod, B., Pallou, J., & Asch, E. (2008). *Mission and money – Understanding the university*. Cambridge: Cambridge University Press.

Winston, G. (1999). Subsidies, hierarchy and peers: The awkward economies of higher education. *Journal of Economic Perspectives, 13*, 13–36.

Chapter 30
A Cross-National Comparison of Higher Education Markets in Western Europe

Harry de Boer and Ben Jongbloed

30.1   Introduction

New modes of governance have been widely reported in the literature, in higher education as well as in other public domains (Kehm and Lanzendorf 2006; OECD 2008; de Boer and File 2009; Paradeise et al. 2009; de Boer et al. 2010; Paradeise 2012; Middlehurst and Teixeira 2012; Amaral et al. 2012). For several reasons traditional modes of governance have been discussed, adapted and changed. Policy makers are reconsidering the rules of the game in higher education in order to encourage universities to deliver high quality services in an efficient way. Instead of governance via hierarchy, in combination with academic self-governance, as the traditional way of ensuring the provision of education and research services in higher education, continental Europe has seen the gradual introduction of systems of governance where elements of markets and networks play a role (e.g. Pierre and Peters 2000; Bell and Hindmoor 2009).

When it comes to higher education, nation states have been delegating some of their powers to different levels of government and they did so in three directions (de Boer and File 2009; Middlehurst and Teixeira 2012). One is an upward shift to the supranational level – as policy agendas, strategic choices and regulations are increasingly decided upon at, or influenced by, authorities such as the European Commission (despite the principle of subsidiarity) and international agreements (such as GATS). National governments keep a close eye on European Union developments and the programmes initiated at the European level. Thus, while each country has specific national (or federal) institutions and is responsible for organizing its own higher education sector, it is clearly drawing on programmes and examples from abroad. The Open Method of Coordination is a good example of the impact

H. de Boer (✉) • B. Jongbloed
CHEPS, University of Twente, Drienerlolaan 5, 7522 NB Enschede, The Netherlands
e-mail: h.f.deboer@utwente.nl

A. Curaj et al. (eds.), *European Higher Education at the Crossroads:*   553
Between the Bologna Process and National Reforms,
DOI 10.1007/978-94-007-3937-6_30, © Springer Science+Business Media Dordrecht 2012

that the European level has on the national higher education systems. A second shift is a downward one, as provinces, local governments and individual higher education institutions themselves are granted greater operating autonomy and responsibilities by their national authorities. Deregulation, though in reality often re-regulation, is a commonly employed strategy whereby the state devolves some of its powers and authorities to lower levels in its higher education system. Here, the overarching theme in higher education governance is 'enhancing institutional autonomy' (de Boer and File 2009; de Boer et al. 2010). A third shift has been an outward one, where traditional tasks of the state are moved to the periphery, such as to national agencies, or even left to private organizations (i.e. privatized). Here one can think of the establishment of accreditation agencies, advisory councils, competition watch-dogs, or a changing role for existing agencies (e.g. funding agencies). This also includes allowing private education providers to enter the market and deliver their services to meet an often rapidly growing demand for higher education.

These movements into three directions indicate that governance has not only become more complex and dynamic, but also illustrate that more actors from various levels and domains are playing a role in the higher education systems and policies. In many countries, coordination in higher education changed from a traditional state-dominated type of regulation to a mode in which various actors at different system levels play a role in the coordination of the system ('multi-level, multi-actor governance'). Coordination increasingly takes place through interconnected policy levels where a multiple actors are influencing different stages in the policy processes and shaping its outcomes. This notion of governance which comprises a variety of actors is frequently referred to as network governance (although many other terms are used to describe this mode of governance): the state explicitly involves other stakeholders such as interest groups and private organisations in developing and implementing higher education policy (Middlehurst and Teixeira 2012). Moreover, by explicitly establishing new or shaping already existing policy networks, states steer through networks. There is a growing recognition that the state is not only part of particular networks but is also steering through networks (Kickert et al. 1997).

Apart from this redistribution of authorities and responsibilities among several actors at different levels, governance also increases in complexity due to the fact that education, research and innovation are becoming increasingly intertwined. While in earlier years these areas may have been 'separated' from each other, each having its own governance structure involving different players, rules, traditions and value structures, nowadays the three areas are much more interrelated and con-stitute a 'knowledge triangle'. Governance has become multi-actor, multi-level and multi-vocal (de Boer and File 2009).

30.2   Market-Based Governance

In this dynamic playing field, states have introduced market-type instruments – prices, contracts, competition – to achieve the realization of the public goals – access, quality, efficiency (e.g. Jongbloed 2003). This market-based governance encompasses not just the delegation of authority from governmental actors to private entities, but also the introduction into public organizations of market-style management approaches and mechanisms of accountability (Donahue and Nye 2002). The state's role has become that of a market engineer; government shapes the rules of the game, intervening to safeguard competition, prevent cartels, but also protect consumers. Moreover, the state is acting as a smart buyer and be able of overseeing its contracted work. In this governance mode, new steering devices have been introduced. Market-based incentives are introduced to promote competition, which should contribute to more efficiency, higher quality and better responsiveness.

Many higher education studies leave not much doubt that there is a clear marketization in European higher education, signaled by privatization, deregulation, establishment of quasi-markets, contracting out (competitive tendering), and the establishment of public-private partnerships (e.g. see Dill 1997; Jongbloed 2003; Teixeira et al. 2004; Lynch 2006). Moreover, particularly in the 1990s when the market philosophy seriously gained ground in higher education, a rather common notion was that more market implied less state. Concepts such as a state 'steering from a distance' gave further breeding ground to such beliefs. But is a state stepping back identical to a state stepping out?

Other literature suggests that the choice between markets and hierarchies is not a zero sum game.[1] The introduction of market mechanisms does not per se imply a reduction of state interference. In other words, the state is not rolling back, nor is its role hollowed out. The shift from state control to state supervision, as described by Van Vught (1989) and Neave and Van Vught (1991), means that the state designs the framework of rules and system policy goals. According to this view, states are employing different strategies than they used to, without necessarily losing power and control. The state still puts its stamp on market-driven higher education systems. New modes of governance such as market-based governance, usually being blends of tradition and new ideas, can be seen as an extension – not as a replacement – of more traditional notions of steering (Bell and Hindmoor 2009:2). According to Keating (2004:6) the marketisation shift is an attempt of the state to maintain or increase its powers to achieve economic and social goals while minimizing efficiency loss. Reforms have been implemented as an effort to govern better rather than govern less. As Jongbloed (2003:131) states, the question is not how much government but rather what can the government do and how can it do that best.

Those arguing that more market not automatically implies less state refer to the state's responsibility for meta-governance. Ultimately, the state determines the rules, for instance on how markets should function. While some rules could leave more discretion to higher education institutions, these rules are still set by the state.

---

[1] The governance equalizer, an analytical tool to frame modes of governance in higher education systems, uses this as one of its rationales (de Boer et al. 2007). The equalizer assumes that state regulation and market mechanisms can develop hand in hand; an assumption that seems to hold in practice.

For example, in some higher education systems private providers can offer teaching programmes, or public institutions have the possibility to offer the programmes they want, *as long as* they are accredited by the state (or one of its semi-autonomous agencies). This means that changes in governance arrangements are most of all driven by changes in state preferences and strategies.

What we take from the discussion about the relationship between hierarchies and markets as presented above is that the question to which extent (the introduction of) markets have replaced traditional state-centred governance is ultimately an empirical one. Market-based steering can go at the expense of state control but not necessarily always so. We cannot rule out that market-based devices in higher education systems have led or contributed to the hollowing out of the state. Simultaneously there might be systems characterised by both high level of state regulation and market coordination. In this paper we will present a number of cases of national higher education systems to shed some further light on this relationship between hierarchies and markets.

30.3   States and Institutions in Higher Education Markets

Markets are not a playing field without any rules; there are many playing fields and states are involved. Even in perfect markets, states play an important role, for example as 'market engineer' (meta-governance, defining the rules in higher education), as upholder of justice (overseeing rule compliance) or as client (being one of the actors buying goods and services). In less perfect markets, in which higher education is perceived as a collective good (which by definition implies a more extended role of the state), states could sponsor providers or customers, set a system-wide agenda, and supervise and control system performance (see de Boer et al. 2009). The point is that in these circumstances states do not steer in a top down fashion through regulations that prescribe institutional behaviours in detail, but they certainly do play a role in shaping the arrangements allowing for the voluntary exchange of goods and services and as the result of that affect the outcomes of the system.

We can analyse markets in higher education in different ways. Following Bell and Hindmoor (2009) we may discuss market-based reforms and see to what extent these reforms have materialised in higher education. Market-based reforms refer to privatisation, internal and external markets, deregulation, contracting out, and pubic private partnerships. All these reforms address basic characteristics of markets: private property rights, competition and the price mechanism. We should ask ourselves who has ownership rights, who defines these rights and settles disputes about them. Degree awarding power is one example, intellectual property of discoveries is another. How many providers are there, are they supposed to compete with each other and what do the rules for competition look like? Do their clients, such as companies and students, pay for the services and do they pay the full costs?

Privatisation is a world-wide known phenomenon attached to neoliberal views to slim down the public sector. Privatisation as the reduction in state level provision and corresponding increase of private provision – "the sales of state services" – may imply a transferring of ownership from public to private organisations, a shifting of a sectoral balance without designating existing organisations, an increase in governmental funding and support for private organisations, and a contracting out of functions and services (Bray 1996). Though there can be various reasons for privatisation, the general rationale is that competition leads to more efficiency in service delivery.

The various forms of privatisation are readably observable in higher education around the globe (Altbach et al. 2009). The private higher education sector has gained ground, basically because of growing demand in combination with shrinking public budgets. Discussions about privatising higher education focus among other things on creating a level playing field. In an open market, every provider, public or private, should have the same opportunities to offer its services. The barriers for entering or leaving the higher education market should be the same. Are private providers allowed to offer officially recognised degrees? If this is the case, are the conditions to qualify for public funding the same for public and private providers?

The rise of privates in the public domain also results from the extension of public-private partnerships. Besides market transactions – companies pay for research and students (partly) pay for education – public and private organisations collaborate for a longer period of time to jointly achieve aims that supposedly cannot be reached by them individually at a lower cost. University-enterprise relationship have attracted much attention. Innovation agendas, loudly advocated, encourage closer cooperation between the university sector and the business world. This is for instance clearly announced in the European Commission's "Europe 2020 Flagship Initiative – Innovation Union" (COM 2010).

The issue of ownership is not just related to the question of who is entitled to provide services, but also to what kind of services are offered for what kind of market. In a real market, providers develop, offer and sell services in response to demand. In a higher education market this would mean that institutions decide what services they want to offer. They should specify the contents and objectives of programmes and curricula without restrictions. Moreover, the institutions should also control their resources such as financial means, personnel, and student selection. Without input-control the action repertoire is restricted. In higher education this means that institutions would have to be autonomous in financial and human resource matters and have the right to select their target group and to recruit their students. These issues are closely related to our next point.

Deregulation, and liberalisation, is another market-related reform that swept through public sectors everywhere (e.g. OECD 2008). Taking away legal barriers and granting organisations more decision-making powers would give organisations the opportunities to act like entrepreneurs, who in facing competition must be innovative and efficient in operating. The success of this reform, that aimed to eliminate, reduce or simplify (national) rules and to give organisations and individuals more space to take their decisions, can be questioned. However, it nevertheless has been one of the overarching trends (de Boer et al. 2010). In higher education the enhancement of institutional autonomy has clearly been one of the most visible attempts to reform the system.

Contracting-out, or competitive tendering, is another market-related trend in the public sector, including higher education (Jongbloed 2008; OECD 2008). Services are exposed to competition. This can be a competition among public institutions as well as among public and private providers. Institutions bid for the sponsor's favour, usually the government. The latter points to a specific role of the state (or one of its agencies) in market-driven systems, namely the establishment of tendering and contracting systems. Competitive tendering in higher education is found in the world of research. Third party funding of research is a competitive endeavour that has become a general phenomenon in higher education, though frequently met with scepticism ("independent and critical research will be undermined by sponsors' interests"). But still public research budgets (e.g. national research councils or Europe's framework programmes) are increasingly allocated on the basis of competition.

This competitive tendering is one of the reasons why the boundaries between public and private organisations are blurring. It seems logical that public organisations copy some modus operandi of private companies, since they are 'forced' to play a game based on 'private terms'. This business-like behaviour of public sector organisations is by the way not only a consequence of new rule systems such as competitive tendering but also the result of the implementation of a New Public Management paradigm in which 'managerialism' is seen as one of the key aspects. At the same time it has also been reported that the level of publicness of the privates, engaged in competitions that used to belong to the public domain, has increased (Bell and Hindmoor 2009:125). In being keen on winning contracts for which the terms are largely publicly set, private providers get infused by public values and procedures.

A different but related point is performance-based funding under 'zero-sum conditions'. Funding schemes based on outputs and performance and in which the total volume of the means is given, create a competitive setting. The introduction of performance-based elements is a clear observable trend in contemporary higher education (Jongbloed et al. 2010; Frølich et al. 2010). Performance as measured by means of the number of graduates, study progress, academic output (e.g. publications or citations) or successful valorisation (e.g. number of patents) may be translated into a financial reward (or sanction) for institutions. A desire for potential gains and a fear for possible losses are expected to drive institutions towards high quality and efficient service delivery.

So far the focus has been on the state and the institutions. For perfect markets also conditions on the demand side should be met (Jongbloed 2003). Just like there should be sovereignty for providers, sovereignty for consumers is also needed. This means that businesses and students as the prime examples of customers in higher education,[2] enjoy freedom of choice with respect to which provider and how much services or goods they will buy. To make conscious decisions about providers and products customers require adequate and correct information on the relationship between price and value for money (including quality). Finally, on real markets, subsidies do not exist, which implies that customers will pay cost-covering prices.

---

[2] In real markets governments are customers as well. They pick the services of some providers for which they are willing to pay a certain price.

In this section we have presented some general notions on markets that in general seem to apply to higher education as well. Because the content, timing and intensiveness of the reforms in combination with country-specific path dependencies vary across countries (e.g. see Chap. 31 by Paradeise), a more focused approach is needed to further our understanding on the relationships between states and markets. Therefore, in the remainder of this contribution, we will focus on one specific market condition in seven West European countries: England, France, Italy, the Netherlands, Norway, Portugal and Switzerland. We assume that university autonomy is a prerequisite for higher education markets. In such an ideal-type situation, universities have the ability or capacity to act and are free from external constraints, otherwise they cannot be expected to behave as 'entrepreneurs', acting independently, and pursuing the goals they have decided upon themselves. To meet the demands, they need room to manoeuvre.

30.4   Possibilities of Public Universities to Operate on Markets in Higher Education[3]

Jongbloed (2003) distinguishes eight conditions for markets: four 'freedoms' for providers and four 'freedoms' for consumers. Most of the freedoms for providers are closely related to the concept of autonomy. They refer to the possibility to define the services, to use available resources and to set prices. To operate on a higher education market, universities should be able to design and offer the programmes of their own choice, to control the borders of their organisations, and to determine the price of their services. For seven countries we systematically investigate the formal autonomy situation of their public universities. This formal autonomy gives an indication of the room for universities to operate on markets. For each of the selected countries we look at the possibilities to design and develop services (e.g. start of new teaching programmes), to control resources (e.g. recruitment of personnel, selection of students, establishing internal governance, financial autonomy) and to determine process (e.g. charging tuition fees). Moreover, we take into account external constraints such as mandatory reporting requirements (e.g. quality assessments) and financial independence.

English universities have much discretion in managing their staff: they can appoint full time senior academic staff, both in terms of deciding on how many and which type of senior posts they want to have and to take academics of their choice to these positions. Moreover, they decide, collectively that is, on the general salary levels of their academics. It is up to English universities to decide on procedures for performance assessments or appraisals as well as on procedures for promotions of

---

[3] The empirical data of this section are derived from the Governance reform project, funded by the European Commission (de Boer et al. 2010; Jongbloed et al. 2010) and the current project "Transforming European Universities (TRUE)", funded by the European Science Foundation and several national research councils.

individual academic staff. The latter reminds us to keep in mind that this concerns aspects of *formal* autonomy. Because it is up to the university, it could decide not to establish such procedures. In practice however university procedures are likely to be influenced by practices of other universities as well as by 'performance-encouraging' governmental policies. English universities also happen to have high levels of financial managerial autonomy. They can use the public grant flexibly, set their own tariffs for contract activities, have many opportunities to generate private income and they can build up reserves and/or carry over unspent resources from 1 year to the next. They are somewhat restricted in borrowing funds from the capital market (subject to ministry regulations) and also the charging of tuition fees for under-graduate programmes is not just a matter of the university (limits are set by the government). In terms of 'product specification', they are allowed to select their own Bachelors and Masters students, although capacity in terms of number of study places needs to be negotiated between the Higher Education Funding Council for England (HEFCE) and the individual university. They can start new Bachelors and Masters programmes without having ministerial approval or accreditation required. And while universities, across the board, have to take into account some national guidelines with respect to their internal governance structure (e.g. the composition or size of governing bodies), they can select their Vice-Chancellor and they can appoint the members of the governing body.

The constraints for English universities on the actual use of the decision-making competences are relatively low, which means that when looking from a formal point of view English universities are in the position to use their discretionary powers. Compared to the other countries, the English are not 'very' dependent on a public operational grant as a source of income: on average, 38% of their revenues comes from the public source – this of course is still a substantial stream of income that in practice can reduce the university's space to manoeuvre. English universities are relatively free from ex post reporting requirements. They must set up internal and external evaluation systems for their teaching, but it is up to the university if they want to do so for research. In practice universities are heavily engaged in research evaluation exercises. This does not follow from the formal obligation to do this, but because evaluation outcomes are linked to funding. Performance-based funding – linking evaluation outcomes to future funding – as a new way of state control.

In France, the public universities are in a totally different position. Compared to universities in the other countries, their capacity to take their own decisions is lim-ited. While they can decide on the number and types of posts for senior academics, and can appoint persons of their choice for these positions, there are restrictions to be taken into account. They cannot transform the operating budget into positions and an upper limit is set for each university in terms of number of positions and payroll. Moreover, salary levels of academic staff are set and paid directly by the government. The exceptions are faculty recruited on contracts; at the moment this concerns a few academics at a small number of institutions. In terms of procedures for regular individual assessments of performance and the procedures for the promotions of academic staff members the situation is unclear. A recent reform states that a regular assessment should take place every 4 years by a national committee (CNU), but is not put into practice yet. National regulation for promotions stipulates that half of the promotions are decided upon by this national committee and the other half by the university. The financial managerial autonomy of French universities is limited. The universities are allowed to use the public operational grant flexibly and can set the tariffs for their contract activities, but they are not allowed to borrow money on the capital market, the building up of reserves and/or carrying over unspent financial resources from 1 year to the next are subject to ministry regulations, and they must charge tuition fees for their Bachelors and Masters programmes and these fees are set by the ministry. The tuition for Bachelors is €174 per year and for Masters €237 per year. Another restriction is that they cannot select their own Bachelors and Masters students, with the exception of the second year Masters programme. Moreover, to qualify for public funding new Bachelors and Masters programmes are subject to an assessment of a national agency (AERES) and must be accredited by the ministry. Research programming however is a university matter. As regards governance autonomy public universities have to take into account ministerial regulations. The national Act stipulates among other things that universities must have particular governing bodies. Within the national guidelines universities develop their own bylaws. The university selects their president, but the selection procedure is set by the national Act: candidates can apply for the position and are elected by the internal members of the university council. The internal members of the university council are also elected and include students (3–5 persons), faculty members (8–17 persons) and administrative staff representatives (2–3 persons). The capacity of French universities to take their own decisions can be further hampered by the dependency of universities from the public purse (about 87% of their revenues stems from the public purse) and by the formal reporting requirements they have (i.e. their interventional autonomy is low). French universities have to take part in external quality assessments for teaching as well as for research and these processes are determined by a national agency (AERES). Moreover, French universities must establish a multi-year contract with the ministry and the format of this contract is by and large prescribed. This obligatory contractual relationship creates a new mode of control for the ministry.

The Italian picture is mixed. The formal autonomy in terms of human resources and policies is low. For appointing senior academic staff Italian universities cannot decide themselves on the number of posts they would like to see fulfilled. The number of new positions cannot exceed 50% of the turnover and may have restrictions on the type of position. The latest reform requires universities to appoint persons that have passed a national selection and are on a specific list. Salary levels are set by the ministry as are the procedures for promotions of academic staff. In terms of regular academic staff appraisals Italian universities can develop their own procedures, although this might change in the near future if the National Committee for the Evaluation of Italian Universities (ANVUR) will influence, or even regulate, this. In terms of target groups, Italian universities cannot select their own Bachelors and Masters students. They have to accept all qualified students, except for a number of subjects. This implies that the universities cannot control the number of study places. And new Bachelors and Masters programmes are subject to ministerial approval, which contains among other things a check in terms of system capacity planning.

At the same time, Italian universities enjoy considerable financial and governance autonomy. The public grant can be spent flexibly. The universities decide on tuition fees, although there is a minimum fee (set by the state) and a maximum level for student contributions to costs and services which cannot exceed 20% of state funding. The universities can decide on tariff levels for contract activities and they can borrow money from the capital market and build up reserves, although these are subject to ministerial regulations. In terms of governance they can develop their structure, but ministerial approval is required. The selection of the rector in an internal affair, but some rules must be taken into account (e.g. s/he cannot be appointed for a term of more than 4 years and can be re-elected only once). The latest reform however requires that the performances of the rector are evaluated; the rules for these evaluations are set by the National Committee for the Evaluation of Italian Universities (ANVUR). The members of the governing boards (*Senato Academico* and *Cosiglio de Administrazione*) are all appointed by the university. And although Italian universities are to a large extent dependent on public income (65% of their income comes from the public budget), they do not face many ex post reporting requirements nor is it mandatory to establish a multi-year contract with the ministry. They have to take part in external research assessments, but it is neither formally required to have internal quality assessment systems for teaching and research nor to have external quality assessments for teaching.

Dutch universities enjoy considerable financial managerial autonomy, but the governance autonomy is low. With respect to human resources management agreements made at the national level, for instance with labour unions, contain guidelines that leave some leeway to the individual university but cannot be ignored. While Dutch universities can decide themselves on the number of academic posts and select persons of their choice, the general salary levels, and many other labour conditions, are set by the national employer association and unions, followed by local negotiations between the individual university and the local unions. The Collective Labour Agreements at the national level, legally binding the universities, comprises among other things agreements about staff appraisals and procedures for promotions. The decision-making capabilities to manage financial affairs are considerable: they can decide how to spend the public operational grant, set the tariffs for contract activities, borrow money from the capital market, build op reserves and carry over unspent resources from 1 year to the next. They cannot however decide on tuition fees for Bachelors and Masters programmes: they must charge tuition fees that are fixed by the ministry (€1,732 per annum).

Dutch universities have to accept all qualified Bachelors students (with exceptions for some disciplines), although they may ask the minister to fix the number of study places for particular programmes because of limited capacity (so-called 'capacity fixus'). Universities can select their Masters students and as the result of that determine themselves the number of study places for Masters programmes (again, with some exceptions). The development of new Bachelors and Masters programmes is subject to both accreditation (by a national agency – NVAO) *and* ministerial approval. The governance structure is to some extent prescribed by law. By means of university bylaws the universities have some leeway to develop a structure to their taste, but within the legal framework. The national Act stipulates the guidelines for the selection of the rector, which by itself is a university matter (the university supervisory board appoints the rector). The members of the supervisory board, all external, are appointed by the minister. The constraints on the actual use of the university's decision-making competences are considerable. Because 66% of their income comes for the public budget, universities are seriously dependent on this income stream. Moreover, they face several ex post reporting requirements: they must have internal and external evaluation systems for both teaching and research. They have, across the board, the opportunity to decide on the methods they want to use, but these methods are evaluated by a national agency. Moreover, they have to report on their activities in annual reports and audited financial statements. They however are not required to establish a contract with the ministry.

Norwegian universities happened to have a substantial degree of autonomy on various dimensions. The autonomy of human resources management is high. They can decide on the number and type of academic posts they want to have and can select the persons of their choice. Moreover, it is up to the university to determine the procedures for individual performance appraisals and for promotions of academic staff. Salary levels however are set by employer associations and unions at the national level, followed by local negotiations between the individual university and the local unions (cf. the Netherlands).

The universities can select their Bachelors and Masters students and, with the exception of a number of subjects, decide themselves on the number of study places. For Bachelors programmes, qualified students are allocated by a national service agency (SO), but the universities have delegated this authority to this agency. They also have discretion in research and teaching programming: it is for example up to the university to decide to start new Bachelors and Masters programmes. The financial and governance autonomy is much more moderate. In terms of financial management universities are not allowed to borrow money on the capital market and they are not allowed to charge tuition fees. As regards their governance structure, universities can chose between tow legally defined models, but these 'self-determined' models must be approved by the government. The university selects its rector but the guidelines are set by the minister, i.e. the universities can choose whether the executive head should be elected by staff and students or by appointed. The internal members of the governing board are appointed by the university and the external members by the ministry.

Partially because the universities cannot charge tuition fees, they are very dependent from the public grant: 75% of the university revenues come from the public authorities. And there are a number of reporting requirements that may affect the actual use of the university's decision-making competences. They are obliged to report on their activities (annual report, audited financial statement) and must develop a strategic plan. They must have internal quality assessment systems for teaching and must take part in external quality assessment for teaching, in a process that is prescribed by a national agency (NOKUT). For research these internal and external quality assessments are not mandatory.

The public Portuguese universities show high levels of formal autonomy on the dimensions of financial management and governance. For policy autonomy and particularly managerial autonomy on human resources, this is considerably lower. As regards the financial managerial autonomy: the universities can use the public grant flexibly, can borrow money on the capital market (taking ministerial regulations into account), are allowed to build up reserves, and can decide to charge tuition fees. The tuition fees for Bachelors programmes need to take into account a minimum level – the minister decides on this minimal amount that depends on the minimal national wage rate. As regards governance, universities have to take into account the legal framework that to some extent prescribes the structure. According to procedures defined by the university (taking into account the formal requirements set by the law), the university's governing board elects the rector by majority vote. The members of the governing board, being academic staff, student representatives and (a minority of) external persons, are all selected by the university (staff and students by election and externals by co-optation). Portuguese universities have hardly any discretion on human resources: they cannot decide on the number and type of academic posts, salary levels are set by the minister, there are national rules and procedures for academic promotion procedures and the universities decide collectively on the procedures for staff performance appraisals (which gives some leeway to the individual university).

To start new Bachelors and Masters programmes accreditation is required. Moreover, Portuguese universities cannot select their own Bachelors students – qualified students are allocated to study places at different universities by a national agency and the number of Bachelors study places is fixed after negotiations between the ministry and the individual university. For Masters students the situation is different: universities select their Masters student, set the selection criteria and decide themselves on the number of study places. The universities are dependent on public income – 60% of their revenues comes from this source. There are also a number or reporting requirements: for teaching universities must have internal quality assessment systems (but they can decide on the methods they want to use) and have to take part in external teaching as well as research assessments (for which the government sets the procedures). Moreover, they must produce a strategic plan, publish their activities in an annual report, publish the outcomes of evaluations and provide an audited financial statement.

The Swiss data concern the situation of the Federal Institutes of Technology.[4] The formal autonomy of these institutes is, for many dimensions, low, compared to

---

[4] With some 600 professors, 16,000 staff (13,000 full-time equivalents) and 20,000 undergraduate and post-graduate students, the Swiss Federal Institutes of Technology in Zurich and Lausanne and the four application-oriented research institutes – the Paul Scherrer Institute (PSI), the Swiss Federal Institute for Forest, Snow and Landscape Research (WSL), the Materials Science and Technology Research Institution (EMPA) and the Swiss Federal Institute of Aquatic Science and Technology (Eawag) – produce scientific achievements of the highest calibre. Together they constitute the ETH Domain under the strategic leadership of the ETH Board as the supervisory body (ETH Act, Article 4). Appointed by the Swiss Federal Council, the ETH Board allocates funds to the six institutions within the guidelines set by the government, and administers their real-estate holdings on a fiduciary basis.

the other countries. For the six institutions federal regulations apply. The institutes require permission from the ETH board to establish academic posts. The EHT board is responsible for the nomination of professors on proposal of the university president – based on a selection of an academic commission. The ETH bard ratifies the decision of the institution. Salary levels are set by the government. Procedures for appointments and promotions are decided at the national level and codified in the law for federal institutes of technology, which means that the ETH board rules out the details. The institutes themselves can set the procedures for regular assessments of individual staff performance. The governance autonomy is also very low: the institute's governance structure is legally prescribed in detail and the government plays part in selecting the president (the institute president is appointed by the federal government based on the proposal of the ETH board). The individual institutes do not have a governing board; the functions of such a governing board are performed by the ETH board, whose members are all appointed by the federal government. The institutes have some financial managerial discretion. They decide themselves how to spend the public operational grant, the can build up reserves and/or carry over unspent financial resources from 1 year to the next and they can fix their own tariffs for contract activities. However, they cannot borrow money from the capital market, and they must charge tuition fees for Bachelors and Masters programmes. The level of these fees is set by the government (about €880 annually).

They can freely start up new Bachelors and Masters programmes and research programming is an internal matter as well. But they cannot select their own Bachelors students: they have to accept all qualified student. Regulations for access of Masters are decided upon by institutional departments. The can be more restrictive, but as a rule Bachelors degree holders get access to a Masters programme, at least in the same field. In terms of external dependencies, possibly affecting organisational decision making in practice, we see that they are rather dependent on public budgets (76% of the institution's budget is public money). They also have some reporting requirements: a strategic plan must be developed and its format is largely prescribed. This 4-year plan, to be approved by the ETH board, is the basis for financial agreements. There are also multi-year contracts, one between the government and the ETH board and one between the ETH board and the individual technological institutions. Finally, annual reports and audited financial statements must be produced. At the same time, on contrary to other countries, the technological institutions can decide themselves how they want to be engaged in matters of quality assurance, both for teaching and for research.

In Table 30.1 the main aspects for the seven countries are summarised.

Table 30.1 shows a variety related to the different aspects of autonomy. Because we argued that organisational autonomy is a prerequisite for (higher education) markets, this also implies a variety in rules framing markets in higher education. Across the board, the concept of quasi-markets seems to describe the systems best (Le Grand 1991). The introduction of market-based elements by the state as 'meta-governor' is an attempt to stimulate competition, assumed to enhance efficiency and service quality, combined with (continued) state regulation. The description of the

Table 30.1 Discretionary room for public universities in seven countries

	Staff recruitment and setting salary levels
England	Universities can appoint their staff and decide collectively on salary levels
France	Restrictions to staff appointments and salaries set and paid by the state (with some exceptions)
Italy	Restrictions to staff appointments and salary levels are set by the state
The Netherlands	Universities can appoint their staff and salary levels are given as the outcome of national collective negotiations
Norway	Universities can appoint their staff and salary levels are set by employer associations
Portugal	The state decides on number and type of academic posts and salary levels are set by the state
Switzerland	Academic posts are set by a board whose members are appointed by the state. Salaries are set by the state
	Financial discretion
England	Universities can use public grant flexibly, have the opportunity to generate private income, can build up reserves and can borrow money on the capital market (though subject to state regulations)
France	Universities can use public grant flexibly, but are not allowed to borrow money on the capital market
Italy	Universities can use public grant flexibly, have the opportunity to generate private income, can build up reserves and can borrow money on the capital market (though subject to state regulations)
The Netherlands	Universities can use public grant flexibly, have the opportunity to generate private income, can build up reserves and can borrow money on the capital market
Norway	Universities can use public grant flexibly, have the opportunity to generate private income, can build up reserves but cannot borrow money on the capital market
Portugal	Universities can use public grant flexibly, have the opportunity to generate private income, can build up reserves and can borrow money on the capital market (though subject to state regulations)
Switzerland	Universities can use public grant flexibly, have the opportunity to generate private income, can build up reserves but they are not allowed to borrow money on the capital market
	Tuition fees
England	Fees must be charged, within limits set by the state
France	Fees are set by the state
Italy	Universities decide on fees within limits set by the state
The Netherlands	Fees are set by the state
Norway	Not allowed to charge fees
Portugal	Universities decide on fees, but for Bachelors state regulations must be taken into account
Switzerland	Fees are set by the state

(continued)

Table 30.1   (continued)

	Student selection
England	Universities select their students but number of study places is set/ negotiated with national agency
France	Universities cannot select their students (with some exceptions)
Italy	Universities have to accept all qualified students (with some exceptions)
The Netherlands	Universities have to accept all qualified students (with some exceptions)
Norway	Universities can select their students
Portugal	Universities select their masters student but not their bachelors
Switzerland	Universities cannot select their bachelors
	Starting new Bachelors programmes
England	Up to the university
France	Assessment by national agency and ministerial accreditation required
Italy	Subject to ministerial approval
The Netherlands	Accreditation required and subject to ministerial approval
Norway	Up to the university
Portugal	Accreditation required
Switzerland	Up to the university
	Internal governance structure
England	Freedom but some national guidelines to be taken into account
France	Freedom but restricted by national Act
Italy	Freedom but ministerial approval required
The Netherlands	Freedom but restricted by national Act
Norway	Freedom but ministerial approval required
Portugal	Freedom but restricted by national Act
Switzerland	Legally prescribed in detail
	Dependence from state budget
England	Relatively low
France	Very high
Italy	High
The Netherlands	High
Norway	Very high
Portugal	High
Switzerland	High
	Ex post reporting requirement (accountability)
England	Formally relatively free from reporting requirements – they must set up internal and external evaluation systems for teaching
France	Severe reporting requirements – participation in external teaching and research processes that are determined by a national agency
Italy	Rather limited reporting requirements – mandatory external research evaluations
The Netherlands	Several reporting requirements – mandatory internal and external systems for teaching and research
Norway	Some reporting requirements – mandatory internal and external quality assessments for teaching; processes prescribed by a national agency
Portugal	Several reporting requirements – internal and external quality evaluations; for some of them the ministry sets the rules
Switzerland	Limited reporting requirements

seven countries in terms of items related to organisational autonomy of public universities clearly demonstrates that the (conditional) freedom of institutions is still constrained in many ways, although differences between the higher education systems exist. The universities in the West European countries have more leeway to make their decisions than the South European universities. However, in all systems the presence of the state is evident. In France, Italy, Portugal and Switzerland staff recruitment is regulated, especially regarding the setting of salary levels. While universities have financial discretion, they have not much choice on tuition fees: they are not allowed to charge fees or they must charge fees whereby levels are set by the state. This means that the 'entrepreneurs' in higher education cannot set the prices for teaching services. With respect to student selection and the starting new programmes we witness significant differences between the seven systems. In England, Norway and Switzerland universities can decide to start new Bachelors programmes; in the other countries this is subject to state-control. With the exception of Norway, universities cannot select their (Bachelors) students, or this selection by universities is subject to regulations (as is the case in England). Also the internal governance structure of universities is legally restricted. Thus, in most countries the possibilities for the university to control the 'production process', to design and develop the 'product' and to set the price for the 'products' is constrained. Moreover, in six of the seven countries the universities are very dependent on the public budget. This dependence further limits the university's possibilities to drift too far from the state.

30.5   Conclusion

Governing higher education through markets has been advocated in many countries and seems to have become one of the major governance rationales. In every European higher education system, market-based instruments and incentives to pursue of what is considered as public goals have been discussed and implemented. Market-based governance however does not automatically imply that the state is stepping back or is being hollowed out. Markets are institutionally underpinned, and states keep playing an important role in establishing and maintaining the rules for the markets. The actual shift in balance between government regulation and market governance is ultimately an empirical question.

Assuming that universities must be autonomous when operating on markets in higher education, in this paper we assessed the level of university autonomy in seven European countries. Using a number of indicators reflecting the university's formal capacity to act independently, as market-type actors are expected to do, we observe that in contemporary higher education public universities are still 'state-controlled' in several ways. Table 30.1 has shown a picture in which many state regulations are readably observable. From this we draw the conclusion that market-based governance does not tend to reduce state intervention but is rather a different strategy to pursue public goals. As argued by Van Damme (2011), states simply cannot afford it to give up, because the economic and social significance of the higher education sector is simply too important for them.

To a large extent this fits the shift from a state control to a state supervision model (Van Vught 1989). States have therefore not been disappearing but have adapted their approach and complemented their repertory of steering instruments. The introduction of more ex post accountability requirements, performance-based funding schemes and contractualisation are examples of the nation state's new steering regime. These aspects are also observable in Europe's modernisation agenda for higher education (COM 2006, 2011; SEC 2011).

Despite all the reforms over the past decade and the initiatives for future reform, we have argued in this contribution that European higher education systems are still quite far away from markets in higher education. A more market-type of governance is not very likely to emerge in the coming years, as long as institutional autonomy remains restricted (being one of the reasons). The success of market-based governance in the future will further depend on mutual trust in the institutional underpinnings of markets in higher education and on the capacity and willingness of both the state and the higher education institutions to play their respective roles as meta-governor of markets and strategic actors on markets. The state should discipline itself to resist the temptation to (again) micro-manage the sector in a different way (for example by nailing down every single detail in a contract). At the same time, higher education institutions need to further strengthen their strategic potential to successfully position themselves on education and research markets. For this, unambiguous academic commitment to the institution's strategy is required. The latter however is not something academics are known for, to put it mildly, and this makes, among other things, the realisation of markets in higher education less probable.

References

Altbach, Ph. G., Reisberg, L., & Rumbley, L. E. (2009). *Trends in global higher education: Tracking an academic revolution* (A report prepared for the UNESCO 2009 world conference on higher education). Paris: UNESCO.

Amaral, A., Tavares, O., & Santos, C. (2012). Higher education reforms in Europe: A comparative perspective of new legal frameworks in Europe. In A. Curaj, P. Scott, L. Vlasceanu, & L. Wilson (Eds.), *European higher education at the crossroads: Between the Bologna process and national reforms* (pp. 655–673). Dordrecht: Springer.

Bell, S., & Hindmoor, A. (2009). *Rethinking governance. The centrality of the state in modern society*. Cambridge: University Press.

Bray, M. (1996). *Privatization of secondary education: Issues and policy implications*. Paris: UNESCO, Division of Secondary Education.

COM. (2006). *Delivering on the modernisation agenda for universities: Education, research and innovation*. Communication from the Commission to the Council and the European Parliament, COM(2006) 208 final. Brussels: European Commission.

COM. (2011). *Supporting growth and jobs – An agenda for the modernisation of Europe's higher education systems*. Communication from the Commission to the European Parliament, the Council, the European Economic and Social Committee and the Committee of the Regions, COM(2011) 1063 final. Brussels: European Commission.

COM. (2010). *Europe 2020 flagship initiative innovation union*. Communication from the Commission to the European Parliament, the Council, the European Economic and Social Committee and the Committee of the Regions, COM(2010) 546 final. Brussels: European Commission.

de Boer, H., & File, J. (2009). *Higher education governance reforms across Europe*. Brussels: ESMU.

de Boer, H., Enders, J., & Schimank, U. (2007). On the way towards new public management? The governance of university systems in England, the Netherlands, Austria, and Germany. In D. Jansen (Ed.), *New forms of governance in research organizations – Disciplinary approaches, interfaces and integration* (pp. 137–154). Dordrecht: Springer.

de Boer, H., Enders, J., & Jongbloed, B. (2009). Market governance in higher education. In B. M. Kehm, J. Huisman, & B. Stensaker (Eds.), *The European Higher Education Area: Perspectives on a moving target* (pp. 61–78). Rotterdam: Sense.

de Boer, H., Enders, J., File, J., & Jongbloed, B. (2010). *Governance reform. Progress in higher education reform across Europe: Vol. 1. Executive summary main report*. Brussels: European Commission.

Dill, D. D. (1997). Higher education markets and public policy. *Higher Education Policy, 10,* 167–185.

Donahue, J. D., & Nye, J. S. (2002). *Market-based governance. Supply side, demand side, upside, and downside*. Washington, DC: Brookings Institution Press.

Frølich, N., Schmidt, E. K., & Rosa, M. J. (2010). Funding systems for higher education and their impacts on institutional strategies and academia: A comparative perspective. *International Journal of Educational Management, 24*(1), 7–21.

Jongbloed, B. (2003). Marketisation in higher education, Clark's triangle and the essential ingredients of markets. *Higher Education Quarterly, 57*(2), 110–135.

Jongbloed, B. (2008, October 13). *Funding higher education: A view from Europe*. Paper prepared for the seminar Funding higher education: A comparative overview organised by the National Trade Confederation of Goods, Services and Tourism (CNC). Brasiliar.

Jongbloed, B., Enders, J., File, J., & de Boer, H. (2010). *Funding reform. Progress in higher education reform across Europe: Vol. 1. Executive summary main report*. Brussels: European Commission.

Keating, M. (2004). *Who rules? How government retains control in a privatised economy*. Sydney: Federation Press.

Kehm, B. M., & Lanzendorf, U. (2006). *Reforming university governance. Changing conditions for research in four European countries*. Bonn: Lemmens.

Kickert, W. J. M., Klijn, E. H., & Koppenjan, J. F. M. (Eds.). (1997). *Managing complex networks*. London: Sage.

Le Grand, J. (1991). Quasi-markets and social policy. *The Economic Journal, 101,* 1256–1267.

Lynch, K. (2006). Neo-liberalism and marketisation: The implications for higher education. *European Educational Research Journal, 5,* 1.

Middlehurst, R., & Teixeira, P. (2012). Governance Within the EHEA: Dynamic Trends, Common Challenges and National Particularities. In A. Curaj, P. Scott, L. Vlasceanu, & L. Wilson (Eds.), *European higher education at the crossroads: Between the Bologna process and national reforms* (pp. 527–551). Dordrecht: Springer.

Neave, G., & Van Vught, F. A. (1991). *Prometheus bound. The changing relationship between government and higher education in Western Europe*. Oxford: Pergamon Press.

OECD. (2008). *Tertiary education for the knowledge society. OECD thematic review of tertiary education*. Paris: OECD.

Paradeise, C. (2012). Tools and implementation for a new governance of universities. Understanding variability between and within countries. In A. Curaj, P. Scott, L. Vlasceanu, & L. Wilson (Eds.), *European higher education at the crossroads: Between the Bologna process and national reforms* (pp. 573–598). Dordrecht: Springer.

Paradeise, C., Ferlie, E., Bleiklie, I., & Reale, E. (Eds.). (2009). *University governance. Western European comparative perspectives*. Dordrecht: Springer.

Pierre, J., & Peters, B. G. (2000). *Governance, politics and the state*. Houndmills Basingstoke: Macmillan Press.

SEC. (2011). *Commission staff working document on recent developments in European higher education systems.* Accompanying the document supporting growth and jobs – An agenda for the modernisation of Europe's higher education system. Communication from the Commission to the European Parliament, the Council, the European Economic and Social Committee and the Committee of the Rigions, SEC (2011) 1063 final. Brussels: European Commission.

Teixeira, P., Jongbloed, B., Dill, D., & Amaral, A. (2004). *Markets in higher education rhetoric or reality? Vol. 6. Higher education dynamics.* Dordrecht: Springer.

Van Damme, D. (2011, March 11). *Autonomy and connectedness: New challenges for higher education.* Presentation for the CHEPS anniversary conference, CHEPS, Enschede.

Van Vught, F. (Ed.). (1989). *Governmental strategies and innovation in higher education.* Edited by Maurice Kogen, Higher education policy series. London: Jessica Kingsley.

Chapter 31
Tools and Implementation for a New Governance of Universities: Understanding Variability Between and Within Countries

Catherine Paradeise

Since the 1960s, massification has increased the burden of public higher education costs on national budgets of Western European welfare states, while their contribution to higher education came to be considered as strategic in knowledge based advanced economies. The 1980s neo-liberal turn charged universities – as well as many other public services (Ferlie and McNulty 2002; Vigour 2008; Sikes et al. 2001) – for being professional bureaucracies, poorly efficient because loosely coupled and self-governed organizations. National governance systems were blamed for not holding national strategic orientations. Higher education reforms have been on the agenda of Western European countries for 25 years. While university systems are deeply embedded in national settings, the ex post rationale of still on-going reforms is surprisingly uniform and "de-nationalized". They all promote the "organizational turn" of universities to be rebuilt as autonomous, internally integrated, goal-oriented and accountable organizations.

Reforms were also thought as promoting better accomplishment of the various missions of universities. Better meant at lower costs and more accurately addressing social and economic needs. Diversification of universities with regard to the missions of any higher education system – that came to be identified as research, teaching, and third mission – should be favored by local autonomy of choice, orientations being selected according to locally available resources and incentives from various stakeholders – that came to be listed as national and local public authorities, students and their families, companies, etc. It has been debated whether strategic autonomy would bring along diversification or on the contrary organizational isomorphism of universities.

C. Paradeise (✉)
Université Paris Est-LATTS and IFRIS, Bâtiment Bois de l'Etang C215,
F77420 Cité Descartes, Champs sur Marne, France
e-mail: Catherine.Paradeise@univ-mlv.fr

A. Curaj et al. (eds.), *European Higher Education at the Crossroads:*
Between the Bologna Process and National Reforms,
DOI 10.1007/978-94-007-3937-6_31, © Springer Science+Business Media Dordrecht 2012

How far are the new rules of the game fitted to the (at least implicit) ambitions to diversify universities from world class to local colleges? After reviewing the major formal dimensions of Western European reforms of the last 30 years, this paper will describe and provide elements of interpretation accounting for variability between and within countries.[1]

31.1 Reforming Universities

31.1.1 Narratives and Rationale

Reforms of higher education that started in the mid 1980s can be summarized as a mix of decentralization and centralization, enhancing managerial autonomy of public institutions, on the one side, while increasing state control, on the other side. It was based on the transfer of managerial tools borrowed from private organizations, the devolution of resources that were until then managed at the public authorities' level, and distant steering. The rationale and tools of reforms – amazingly similar across countries – are based on a shared narrative: in order to improve their *performance* in *knowledge-based economies*, universities have to be rebuilt as rationalized *strategic* and *accountable organizations* by substituting mechanic to professional bureaucracies (Mintzberg 1979).

National reforms developed as endogenous initiatives at the national level. They were also encouraged by the liberal visions of a demand-driven public economy that developed in the 1980s and that were spread in particular by OECD. They were finally impacted by European institutional creations: the Bologna process led to a substantial restructuration of educational function, the European Union funding schemes pushed the networking of academics in research, and the Lisbon strategy imposed the notion of a 'knowledge-based economy' as a buzzword providing an economic meaning for change. It enhanced the new idea (Goedegebuure 1993; Van Vught 1993) that the "value for money" of investments in education and research should be measured by their returns in terms of employment and innovation, with the logical implication to link education supply with the needs of the economic system.

Before the 1960s, higher education in all countries mostly targeted general and professional education and training of elites-to-be. The expansion of universities that exploded in the 1960s and their role as Welfare institutions favoring

[1] This paper draws upon two research projects. The first part draws upon the SUN project (Steering of Universities) that involved 16 researchers in the PRIME NoE from seven Western European countries, and specifically on Chaps. 9 and 10 of its results, as published in Paradeise et al. (2009). I thank E. Reale, G. Goastellec and I. Bleiklie for letting me draw extensively upon our results. The second part draws upon the PrestEnce project (From prestige to excellence. The fabrication of academic quality), a French ANR project in process that involves 20 researchers from 4 countries using in-depth studies of 27 university departments in 3 fields and 5 countries. Some preliminary results have been published in 2011 in Paradeise and Thoenig (2011a, b). I thank Jean-Claude Thoenig for gracefully agreeing on using our common papers in this chapter.

democratization of knowledge was enhanced. The content and value of higher education used to be taken for granted, as well as the expertise of teachers as producers and diffusers of knowledge. The rise of unemployment, the decline of social deference to professionals, and the later conceptualization of advanced societies as "knowledge-based societies" converged to shift this producer-based notion to a more user-based approach of higher education. As a result, differentiation between vocational, professional and general education increased. Higher technical education was promoted: it absorbed much of the student number growth and was progressively upgraded in full-pledged higher education institutions.

Regulations or incentives developed by the Ministries of education and science encouraged the reorganization of training and research within or between universities, by offering various schemes to incite the clustering of universities, the strengthening of their ties with the economic sector, or the differentiation of their missions based on their local advantages and constraints, with the purpose to rationalize training and research, decrease relative costs by increasing efficiency and economies of scale.

Academic research originally developed inside higher education institutions as a regular and self-determined component of professorship. At the end of the twentieth century, it became a specific mission, with its dedicated budgets, organization and evaluations. The importance ascribed to innovation in economic dynamics brought about increased emphasis (and monies) on applied and strategic research over basic research (Laredo 2007).

These evolutions could not have occurred if not backed by tools to increase strategic capabilities of universities. A central property of formal organizations is to possess the jurisdiction over their own resources, such as human resources and real estate, and the possibility to develop them according to their own strategies. Until recently, no university system in Europe fitted these minimal requirements of organizations. Not even the British ones did so in spite of the traditionally high degree of autonomy of universities. Before the reforms of the 1980s, most continental European universities were ruled from the outside by administrative regulations they had to conform to, that involved administration but not purposeful management. They did not pursue collective goals as formal organizations do (Brunsson and Sahlin-Andersson 2000; Krücken and Meier 2006), their components were loosely coupled silos independent of each other, and they did not control their own performance. With few exceptions, they were funded by public subsidies to deliver free education supposed to offer equal opportunities to all citizens. Hence, their budgets were calculated by public authorities in charge on their ex ante inputs, using some formula accounting for the number, degrees and discipline of students.

From the 1970s onwards, public management developed with the purpose to ensure better "value for money" in public administrations, by deporting micromanagement towards universities, allowing them more freedom to organize and develop strategies, providing tools to rationalize their structures and processes, encouraging them to adjust to national policies by using procedural incentive rules rather than substantive prescriptive ones, and controlling them by evaluation devices. University budgets remained largely based on public money, but a rising share of it came to depend upon grants made available through public calls of funding agencies, or upon evaluation of performance in terms of various training and research outputs, treated as quasi-market devices meant to overcome outdated bureaucracy.

31.1.2   Organizational Tools

The toolbox of the reform included the usual kit of formal organizations, dealing with human resources, funding, budgeting, cost accounting and internal auditing, real estate and equipment matters.

31.1.2.1   Human Resources

Various models of university human resources administration share the floor in Europe. British universities have always acted as employers of their administrative and academic staffs. Almost everywhere else, academics were civil servants and position openings were decided at the State or regional level. Recruitment and promotion were the responsibility of national committees in certain countries; universities – or a mix of both – were in charge in others. National or regional scales ruled salaries and promotion.

As reorganized by the new forms of public management, the power to open positions and hire was devolved to universities, according to rules that may be rather complex and restricted in the many countries where civil service status were maintained. Even though civil servants and tenured positions still largely prevail today, the proportion of academics and administrative staff under contract with the university increases everywhere as well as the share of market-oriented salaries. Altogether flexibility of human resources has increased, based on temporary teaching contracts, fixed-term post-docs, part-timers and adjuncts, etc. It is not that new that short time contracts fill the lack of permanent recruitments, but public management provides a new rationale for it: flexibility favors adaptability, competition and attractiveness on an increasingly internationalized labor market. External and non-national recruitment may become a signal of quality, so that increased mobility may become an issue for institutions or disciplines facing difficulties to teep their academics leading countries or universities to develop specific programs to stabilize newcomers or to incite the return of brain-drained nationals (Metcalf et al. 2005).

31.1.2.2   Funding

Diversification of financial resources became very incrementally an issue for policymaking agendas. It was at first a pragmatic way to counterbalance the reduction of government contribution per student, which was progressively rebuilt in a rationale stressing the virtuous impact of stakeholders' contribution as a way to better fit supply of education to demand.

The relative restriction of direct research funds was a consequence of the rising competition for resources inside the public sector. It also resulted from changes in the vision of how allocation was to become more virtuous and efficient: research teams and universities should deserve these funding by competing for funds. Allocations of funds should also help solving identified economic, technical, and social issues. Thus, national, European, and local funding sources were increasingly considered as a major allocation technique, especially in research.

Tuition fees – a very hot issue – started to grow in some countries at the end of the 1990s, also based on the idea of sharing the burden of costs of higher education as its return went both to national economy and to individuals.

Regions also appeared as potential sources of diversification as university mass tertiary education, vocational training and applied research could contribute to local employment and economic dynamism. Public authorities often created new schemes to encourage regional contributions to national public service mostly on the basis of competitive grants. Regions would also develop their own policies, not only in federal countries where regions are historically in charge of universities, but also in most large countries which experienced since the 1980s some devolution of powers.

Companies were also targeted as potential sponsors of training and research programs that could feed executive education as well as specialized research responding to the innovation need of local districts, widening the so-called "third mission" of universities. In all countries, public authorities have set up various instruments – agencies, joint private–public innovation programs, new types of joint private/public legal schemes, tax deductions for investment in public or private research and innovation, encouragement of the development of company chairs in higher education institutions or investment of venture capital in "by-products" such as students' residences, etc. – to promote innovation in or with universities. Yet, in all countries, the average private funding of universities has remained marginal, with a large variance across universities (Lepori 2008).

Nevertheless, most education funds remained allocated on the basis of students' numbers, with strong historical inertia, while the increasing share of performance-based allocation in research did not lead anywhere outside UK to remove traditional criteria. But, in association with the development of strategic planning encouraged by mission statements and multiannual contracts, it contributed to irrefutable differentiation.

Diversification meant achieving a better fit between resources and missions, thus a more incisive characterization of universities in training and research. In other words, diversification of funding also meant diversification of universities with resulting effects in terms of disciplinary specialization (especially in small countries) or emerging differentiation between those universities which were meant to become research vs. teaching-oriented.

31.1.2.3 Budgeting

Besides encouraging resources growth through diversification, public authorities became convinced that rationalization of the production process was needed in order to reduce costs. Reforms were to eliminate weak efficiency in professional bureaucracies. This implied important innovations to sustain strategic behavior by building instruments to inform objectives, rationalize allocation choices, allow diversification and provide insight into the use of resources.

Universities historically provided a rather uniform public good in higher education with rather uniform means decided by ministries in charge. Hence, budgets were itemized and dependent upon various rather hermetical silos. The lack of budgetary autonomy echoed the collegial vision of universities in the framework of (national or regional) administrations. They were not considered as problem solving organizations nor were they strategic actors free to allocate and manage their own resources according to their own strategies. They were the last step of a top-down administrative ladder that took advice from the academic communities in various institutionalized committees. Core budgets were most often computed through student numbers based formula, in which parameters took care of differential costs of education along disciplines and steps in the curricula. They did not differentiate teaching from research and considered quality of teaching or research only by ex ante accreditations they most of the time delivered themselves by consulting ad hoc committees. Funding of functional departments and real estate was itself based on line-item budgeting. The budgetary allocation process left no room to university strategies: budgetary inputs were based on central bureaus' definitions of local needs and expenses, and they were submitted to ex ante controls of legality. Universities had no much choice but passively registering and spending input monies with the obligation of balancing each item.

Over the last decade, itemized budgets have been substituted by lump-sum funding and global budgeting at the university level. Financial resources were transferred from the state to universities. Global budgets were credited under large chapters – typically public salaries, operations and investment. Expenses were usually free within the global budget, except for a ceiling limiting global public salary costs and various obligations dealing with public regulations. This process usually came with the introduction of indicators, incentives and evaluation, with the purpose to better articulate allocation and performance.

31.1.2.4 Cost Accounting and Internal Auditing

A decreasing number of universities still function with accounting schemes that are characteristic of professional bureaucracies. Global budgeting and management decentralization require (and allow) shifting to cost accounting and ex post control of each individual university as a whole. The share of full costs of the whole organization dedicated to each of its components can be computed. Cost accounting creates transparency and commensurability of investments, allocations and returns. It carries along an ideal of rationalized formal organization. Each strategic action can be evaluated by comparing full costs, its expected returns (in terms of publications, patents, public goods delivery) and accepted risks.

The shift to cost accounting was usually complemented by internal and external audit and assessment systems which first and most extensively were created in the 1980s in the UK with the well-known British Research Assessment Exercise. Cost accounting drew universities towards a more managerial culture by developing a norm of accountability, where global revenues must cover global costs and be understandable in terms of organizational strategy: therefore, every action can be evaluated through its outputs. Cost accounting also informs on all internal interdependencies within the organization and can be used as a tool for internal audits. Hence, it requires internal political leadership to settle which options are going to be taken considering short-term returns as well as middle range strategic investment.

31.1.2.5 Real Estate and Equipment Matters

Most universities in Continental Europe did not own their buildings until quite recently. Depending upon the degree of actual delegation to universities in decision-making on construction and administration, consequences could be more or less unfortunate. In certain cases, universities were not even allowed to create provisions for depreciation in their budgets. Things have now changed in most countries, where all real estate has been devolved to universities or are in the process to be. More private property is also allowed and schemes bringing in private monies and management in university buildings develop in several countries.

31.1.3   Governance Tools

31.1.3.1   Internal Governance

From Weak and Subordinated Organizations...

Shifting from administrative bodies to strategic actors requires as a key initial prerequisite to reinforce individual universities' internal steering capabilities. Whether they benefited from a large degree of autonomy as in the UK or they were directed by a large number of laws defining detailed substantive rules implemented top-down by Ministries in charge as in France or Italy, universities came to be conceptualized during the two last decades of the twentieth century as loosely coupled professional bureaucracies (Cohen et al. 1972; Weick 1976) lacking major properties of formal organizations such as strong principal agent relationships.

On the continent, the roughly common pattern was based on dual leadership at each organizational level, where administratively appointed staff shared the floor with elected academic leaders. Their respective jurisdictional divide was often unclear, in particular at the top level. While administrative staffs were small in numbers, weak and formally confined to operating bureaucratic rules, it might occur that the head of administrative staff gained much power by handling relationships with the ministry and politicians. It might also happen that elected academics captured the floor even though their authority was limited. Yet neither of them usually had much strategic leadership capacity since they both lacked the tools of strategic decision-makers. Consequently, presidential functions were usually restricted to public relations and internal consensus building across disciplinary powers. Rather than a CEO heading a big organization, the President or Rector, usually backed by an elected governing Board, was an institutional integrator among colleagues rather than a boss. Major decisions were taken by faculties or prominent professors often in direct interaction with the Ministry, discussed in Scientific boards acting as elected non executive university councils and ratified by the executive Board.

In countries where university structures were the strongest, leaders were more often appointed than elected. Nevertheless, appointment was most often a confirmation of the nomination by the university. Leaders worked in close connection with the Ministry of Education. Being appointed, they had more power to buffer the relationship between disciplines or faculties and the Ministry. They might even succeed in building national associations that mediated the relationship between academic institutions and public authorities.

… To Emerging Formal Organizations…

The development of organizational tools helped reinforcing the organizational density of universities. By strengthening leadership and senior management and by internalizing arbitration and decision-making, the rise of self-government tools attempted to increase the subjective and objective belongingness of university members.

In several countries, leadership was first strengthened by the repudiation of the notion of academic collegiality and election rules of Presidents or Rectors that came with it. It led to concentration of power, weakening of the representative bodies, and increased power of the managerial hierarchy based on strategic planning. Presidents or rectors became principal negotiators and inescapable gatekeepers for reaching the outside world of Ministries and stakeholders (see Chap. 33 by Pechar and Chap. 35 by Amaral et al.).

The introduction of management instruments also enhanced the role of senior management: on the one side, they tended to explicitly place faculties under scrutiny of new instruments measuring performance; on the other side, they sustained the professional claims of an increased numbers of qualified managers. As a consequence, power came to be redistributed between presidential teams and senior management on one hand, between management and academics on the other.

... Based on Strategic Planning

A common feature in all countries is the promotion of strategic planning at the level of individual universities, most often as a basis for negotiating the allocation of resources, using university contracts as in France or mission statements as in Germany. At first, budget shares related to the negotiation of such plans may have remained limited and the impact of ex post evaluation on next year's budgets weak. But they have constrained universities to make plans before budgetary negotiations, stimulating identity assertion, development of common frames for internal operation, external communication and elaboration of prospective visions of their future, and finally opening the way to the building of a shared interest by negotiating institutional projects. They have often led universities to get a better knowledge of their internal landscape and external networks, of their strengths and weaknesses, of their actual and expected resources and performance. Therefore, much more than technical tools, they proved to be governing instruments with structuring effects on the higher education system organization.

31.1.3.2   External Governance: Steering at a Distance

Steering tools have a double face. They strengthen the internal strategic capability of universities. They also enable ex post external evaluation of performance by scrutinizing outputs and budgetary efficiency. Thus they are ambiguous. On the one hand, they afford a common language of accountability that may serve internal steering and strategic autonomy. On the other, they serve relationships between national policies and universities as potential fabrics of strategies. Altogether, these tools help articulating centralized steering by public authorities and decentralized micro – management in the universities.

New Funding Tools, New Allocation Models

Public funds remain largely dominant in university budgets of all countries, even though private contributions to funding have more than marginally increased. The major innovation is more to be found in the restructuring of public money allocation methods than in changing sources of funding. The striking common feature in all countries is the development of public competitive centralized basic funding, its dramatic rise in volume and share even though it has not replaced the large input base of public funding, and the separation between research and teaching funding. Departments and research centers are encouraged to look for competitive public money, with possible incentives in terms of teaching loads, positions, salaries, fringe benefits, promotions, etc.

The rise of competitive money came with the diversification of funding tools and the development of coordination mechanisms of steering functions between local and national authorities and between branches of government, and the generalization of the notion of public agency as a funding institution.

Indicators

The share of competitive money won by departments or research centers contribute more and more to their evaluation and public allocation of resources, based on more or less complex measures of performance. Indeed, as a counterpart of increased autonomy, public controls of legality and efficiency are shifting from ex ante to ex-post. The assumption that resources dedicated to carry out public services were accurately allocated through vertical channels from Ministries at the top to delivering agencies such as universities comes gradually to be contradicted in the on-going process of rationalization.

Indicators may be built and used in various ways in the external steering process. They may either be imposed as a top-down rule, or by negotiation at the level of each individual university or even of each research center or teaching department. They may be imposed as steering tools through quasi-market mechanism strictly coupling resources to performance in a principal-agent perspective, by linking impersonally and non-ambiguously central resource allocation to a complex measure of output. They may back up the allocation process in a much looser manner, by contributing to build a set of multidimensional strategic tools anchoring strategic debates within universities as well as between universities and their stakeholders. In all cases, they aim at providing visibility and accountability of universities in terms of costs, performance and efficiency. Whatever their characteristics, indicators obviously carry the hopes of governments (and, in a fractal process, of university leadership) to increase transparency by building systemic information, and to monitor coordination between university strategies and national or regional policies.

Assessment, Quality Auditing and Ranking

Assessment and evaluation of careers, curricula, research, universities, etc., are an old story in several countries. Auditing emerged in the mid 1980s and spread in the 1990s, as a standardized process largely forced from the outside, with little cooperation from inside many higher education institutions (Perellon 2003; Schwarz and Westerheijden 2004). Over the last two decades, internationalization of teaching programs combined with rising competition for international students have generated new international accreditation agencies assessing quality of degrees on a voluntary basis. As it was explicit in the 2003 and 2005 follow-up conferences, the Bologna process reinforced the need for national evaluation and accreditation agencies to build comparable degree structures which have been built in several European countries. Altogether, assessment and audits contributed to the organizational turn of universities over the last 30 years, by nurturing identity and strategy building.

31.2   From Formal Tools to Implementation

Recent reforms of higher education in European countries share a common repertoire of reform instruments that aimed at developing a new pattern of governance in public institutions, based on three principles, usually (even if abusively) summed up under the banner of New Public Management. (1) Decentralization of micromanagement at the bottom-line level of universities, sometimes understood as a downgrading of universities from knowledge institutions to "productive organizations". (2) Centralization of distant steering by public authorities based on a retroaction loop between central incentives, performance measurement and funding. (3) Fractal expression of this pattern from the top level of public authorities to the bottom-line of universities: at level n, universities are to public authorities what departments are to universities at level n − 1. The narrative of reforms was most often built and clarified incrementally in their process and ex post rationalized in principles justifying the creation of steering and management tools actually invented incrementally or transferred by benchmarking.

This governance pattern implicitly or explicitly enhances the virtues of quasi-market regulations in bureaucracies as compared to collegial ones (see Chap. 29 by Middlehurst and Teixeira and Chap. 30 by De Boer and Jongbloed). It aims at substituting the prevalence of quasi-clients to the sovereignty of the supply-side on the determination of which outputs – research, curricula and service should be selected. Yet observation of reforms implementation provides evidence that such a program never proved that radical, nor brought along uniform changes. This section explores variations across and within countries and provides some elements of interpretation.

31.2.1   What Observation Tells Us

31.2.1.1   Diversification and Concentration of Universities

Before the reforms started, public European universities visibility differed within the same country, in spite of the fact that they were generally placed under the same national regulations and were expected to fulfill the same missions. Reputation was what made the difference. It brought back to the historical splendor of Europe, without telling much about what was to be found in the black box of universities as organizations. Some timid structural differentiation started in the 1980s, when funding became less unconditional and a bit more competitive in one way or the other.

Certainly, the hidden agenda of reforms included clarification and differentiation of university missions as well as concentration of research resources, based on several assumptions. (1) The growth in number and size of universities since the 1970s was based on education rather that research. It mechanically induced the development and dissemination of research forces, very unequal though in terms of their quality. (2) All universities cannot pretend to be research-driven and yet, all are submitted to uniform rules regarding recruitment, funding, management and governance. (3) Research costs increase while relative public budgets shrink and are allocated without consideration of their productivity in terms of research outputs. (4) Because money becomes relatively scarcer, it has to be directed, not only towards good research teams, but also towards the highest priorities in science as defined by policy-makers enlightened by scientific elites (5) Therefore, universities organization should be given the possibility to diversify, because what is good for research is not necessarily good for undergraduate teaching, or service to the local communities, etc. (6) Concentration of resources should be favored since resources attract resources (Merton 1988/1968), as demonstrated by the huge success of American research universities after World War II (Graham and Diamond 1997; Picard 1999). The influence of post World War II dominating scientific elites contributed to deeply root this vision in policy-makers minds, even though concentration in US research money allocation form the 1950s to the 1970s was followed in the 1980s by more dispersion across more research universities, also as biology became more of a priority implying lesser costs than nuclear physics (Graham and Diamond 1997; Geiger and Feller 1995).

Based on this agenda, national as well as European public authorities developed increasingly elitist schemes of research money allocation in the 2000s: more money for fewer teams; more money for prioritized domains. It was the meaning of the creation of new competitive schemes developed under the umbrella of national research agencies and European framework programs. This process was accelerated in the 2000s with a whole range of schemes increasing selectivity and allocation amounts for the happy few at the national level – such as Excellenz Initiative in Germany, various schemes culminating in the "Investissements d'avenir" in France – and at the European level of the ERC with for instance Excellence chairs. All this implied that universities should not only run for the best, but also that they develop organizational efforts to carry their best teams' applications and manage the big amounts of money they might win. In other words, competition for resources translated into rising differentiation between scientific and teaching activities, but also in organizational densification of universities when they ambitioned to become or remain part of the elite. It also tended to undermine the status of teaching as a second range activity, with on-going impacts on the fragmentation of academics identities (Henkel 2000).

Indeed, observation shows that in all countries differentiation comes progressively to rely more on strategies and less on status, even if there is still a long way to go since status remains as such a strong source of attractiveness with the consequence to favor winning strategies. But, until now, implementation of reform has not led European higher education systems and universities within each of them to converge towards a unified pattern that would progressively erase borders with the help of European level policies and intergovernmental actions. Major changes are on their way, but they exhibit international as well as intra-national differences in terms of dynamics and acceptance: the same supply of values, norms and rules provided by reforms induces different impacts from one country to the other, but also across universities in the same country.

31.2.1.2   International Variations

Change did not develop at the same pace and did not follow the same path in all countries. The reason is threefold. First, financially and politically, reform was largely resource driven: reformers determination was very much linked to how urgent they felt the problem was, and what corridors of political action they felt were open. Second, action was incremental (Lindblom 1959) rather than ex ante planned – with the possible exception of the UK – as we amply exemplified in our recent exploration of reforms in seven Western European countries (Paradeise et al. 2009). Its development was constrained by local conditions in the organization of central public administrations and universities as well as the reactivity of academics as a profession, so that reformist intentions tended to be brought back into traditional national trajectories. In many countries, general legislation would typically pile up without offering operational tools efficient enough to rearrange power positions. Third, in most countries, foreign experiences were either ignored or rejected as inadequate.

The impact of the development of a 'European space' on national reforms came quite late. Benchmark and diffusion effects certainly increased with the role of EOCD, with the development of the European dialogue in associations like EUA, during EU working groups, in agencies such as ENQA, or thanks to intergovernmental processes on higher education and research. Benchmarks have become an explicit part of the Bologna process, the EU's Lisbon strategy and the Open Method of Coordination. They have also been favored by the huge development of international rankings that – out of states control – put national systems under pressure of international competition.

Two broad groups of countries can be distinguished, cutting across the usual typology used to characterize European universities which opposes the internal consistency of British and "Humboldtian" individual universities in Northern Germanic countries to the vertical dominance of the nation-state in the Southern "Napoleonic" ones. The first group includes early movers, UK starting at the very end of the 1970s (Ferlie et al. 1996; Ferlie and Andresani 2009) and Netherlands in the 1980s (van Vught 1989; Westerheijden et al. 2009). The UK early on systematized the rationale of reform and was imitated a few years later by the Netherlands. Although the Netherlands was less efficient in implementation, both countries went far and strong in reorganizing forcefully and systematically the entire multilevel governance system according to a general reform plan. The second group includes countries severely burdened by massification and budgetary limitations in the 1970s (France, Germany, Italy) (Musselin and Paradeise 2009; Schimank and Lange 2009; Reale and Potì 2009 and Chap. 32 by Moscati), as well as countries where a lower degree of massification induced less of a financial burden (Bleiklie 2009; Baschung et al. 2009). These late or slow movers developed mostly incremental approaches to reform. They used bits and pieces of a global instrumental repertoire or even reinvented parts of it.

Thus, the degree of advancement, speed and processes enacted to deploy the reforms, as well as the manner in which they have been taken up, varies enormously from one country to another. Ultimately, while the academic landscape has definitely changed, the picture is one of strong international diversity, a long way from the homogenized vision of convergence theory. Next section suggests that diversity is not only international but also intra-national.

31.2.1.3 Cross-Country Variations in University Acceptance of Reform

Moving down from the macro-level of states to the meso level of universities, observation exhibits considerable variations in the way universities engaged in reforms, based upon their historical power relationships with public authorities, and their internal working arrangements across disciplines and with managerial actors. Some seized upon the available tools of internal reform as new development resources, others put up with them as mutilating constraints. Hence, three decades after reforms started, empirical analysis of the way universities actually position themselves in their day-to-day management demonstrate that they are not passive agents subjected to the demands of an exogenous principal, but more or less autonomous actors pursuing more or less consistent ends, trying to use resources and faced with constraints.

Four types of universities distinguish according to where they stood ahead of reforms and to which degree, as a social system, they have been supportive of reforms and able to take advantage of new tools and schemes to position on university missions (Paradeise and Thoenig 2011).

Top of the Pile

The top of the pile gathers some extremely prestigious international institutions consistently placed over time at the very top of universities in national and international benchmark, either in terms or formal excellence as expressed in rankings or in terms of informal social reputation. Even when new forms of evaluation are used, they appear not to have to make any great effort to stay at the top of the status-related pyramid. There is not even a handful of them in Europe and they are concentrated in the UK. Their leadership would appear to be protected by a sort of ongoing benefit that they reap from their situation. They are prestigious and excellent in equal measure – paragons of academic virtue (Nedeva 2008).

They rapidly adapt to national and international developments in quality-based judgment criteria and developments among their key publics by juggling between basic and applied research, providing training at various different levels and engaging in disinterested and commercial leveraging of their products. While their performances are also evaluated by key external stakeholders, they are able to efficiently pay close attention to the manner in which they endogenously produce and maintain the sources of quality that underpin both their prestige and their excellence.

Wannabes

Higher education institutions may have attained genuine local or national prestige and suddenly disappear from the radars when compared on a set of formal international and/or national indicators: too small, insufficient focus on publications, insufficient exposure for their offering, teaching staff not cosmopolitan enough, low degree of international attractiveness, etc. They may as well have remained out of sight of reputation radars in spite of decent outputs for instance because they are newcomers. Wannabes consider reforms as an opportunity to convert – as quickly as possible – their national prestige capital into international formal excellence, or simply to emerge on the globalized scene, by using organizational and political resources embedded in reforms and oppose their actual performance to socially long established reputations (Porter 1995).

To improve their position, they stick to reforms by playing the rules and gluing on formal assessment indicators used by their principals. They pour all their energy and resources into boosting their performances according to the standards laid down by the league tables currently in vogue or the indicators basing public authorities funding decisions. They deploy radical upgrading strategies to rebuild in a way that involves clean breaks with their past notwithstanding their effects on their internal social structure and the nature of their outputs. They do not give much thought to their university as a social institution with its specific affectio societatis, often because they do not see any way out of the logics imposed by their changing conditions of action (Tuchman 2009).

Missionaries

The *missionaries* actively disapprove on-going reforms. In their opinion, they promote the mutation of universities from professional to mechanic bureaucracies, by de facto reinforcing centralization of the higher education and research system while they pretend to decentralize and redistribute power. They increase heteronomy of research and education orientations under cover of rising managerial autonomy of universities, hence downgrading academics to knowledge workers and perverting the very notions of free research and education (Christensen 2011).

As wannabes, they believe in the straightforward efficiency of reforms, but in opposition to them, they denounce this drive as a dangerous one. Instead of joining the game, they claim to resist its rules. Prestige is a not a relevant issue. Content matters more than signal. The pursuit of excellence based on impersonal and a-contextual criteria can only exacerbate costly competition in exchange for dubious social benefits, increase inequality, hamper the integrative mission of education and ultimately say little about the intrinsic quality of their activities.

They see universities as institutions in charge of public service missions carried out by personnel subject to the same status and regulations and offering same-type services in a spirit of selflessness. They sing the praises of the continuity of the public service function of higher education and refuse to consider education as the "dirty work" of academia whose noblest elements are given over to research. They disregard indicators as management tools as they consider them as a way to impose exogenous definitions of academic work as well as its exogenous evaluation, failing to take account of the different missions academics are in charge of, depending on their publics and disciplines.

Venerables

The *venerables* enjoy considerable local prestige and are loathe playing the whole "excellence" game, which they deem to be absurd given the singular nature of all academic institutions. Unlike the nouveau riche wannabes who seek to win status within a larger space by converting their prestige into excellence, the *venerables* behave like an established aristocracy whose prestige reflects an intrinsic quality founded on history and carefully preserved by the wisdom of the academic corps. While they are well aware of the exogenous criteria driving comparisons between universities, they remain splendidly aloof or overtly hostile. They deem such comparisons to be unfounded in epistemological terms and to undermine their own institutional integrity. They counter this bean-counting logic of the uninitiated – journalists, bureaucrats, international institutions, etc. – with the capital of a prestige built around the preservation of a collegial approach to producing knowledge and a quality they consider to be intangible. The initiation rites for new entrants to their exclusive club that keeps outsiders at a distance ensure pacific coexistence and cooperation between equals rather than the competition that is rife in the world of the wannabes. Venerable institutions are founded on the elective affinities between elites who are disdainful of conventional academic ideas and confident of the intrinsic value of their products – publications, courses, diplomas, etc. – and of the vulgarity of competition. They give little thought to how relevant their content is for their public. Unlike the wannabes who bend over backwards to meet all excellence-related criteria, the *venerables* are resolutely attached to an offering whose quality they and they alone are qualified to judge. They attempt to counter the fallout from any policies likely to challenge their traditional pre-eminence in their own field, particularly the introduction of performance analysis tools that could undermine their status and their ability to sustain their social network, with the risk of being downgraded for not being accountable.

The next section provides some interpretations of diversity by underscoring a series of factors that contribute to build each case as a specific one, depending on how reform hits its formal structures (internal organization, relation to public authorities), its administrative culture and its underlying norms and values, and its technical and institutional environment (tools sustaining performance and visions embedded into models, prescriptions and standards) (Christensen 2011).

31.2.2 Accounting for Variety

31.2.2.1 From a Macro-determinist Vision to Local Orders

Macro-determinist interpretations of change are based on the vision of an iron cage dynamic process. A single framework is postulated to impose its global hegemony that is driven by incentive and remote control processes, that is promoted by external bodies and is postulated to be applicable to all local actors. All stakeholders in a given domain are thereby supposed to refer to the same body of normative and cognitive standards, thus resulting in identical practices in all local spheres within a relatively short time. As tempting as they may seem at first sight, such interpretations obviously do not fit observation that exhibit inter- and intra-national variations in pace, methods and extent of implementation of reforms that nevertheless share approximately the same rationales and tools. Even though they have much in common, reforms remain path dependent and most often incremental: patterns imposed from the outside by coercive public authorities combine with renegotiation between public authorities, universities, academic professions, and civil society at large. The concept of local order helps (March 1962) grasping the instrumental dimension that characterizes the actual organization of resources in a given space of action rather than the impact of incentives *per se*.

Thus, a national higher education and research system – as well as a given university or a given component in a university – can be considered as a specific social space, in which actors manage conflicts between different approaches to which they are subjected on a day-to-day basis, building up their resources by leveraging different, extremely diverse environments at different times (Serow 2000) and valuing various perspectives – serving this local community, serving distinct national job markets, being ranked as an international scientific body, simply continuing to do their own thing, etc.

The basic tenet of such an approach is that resources are built up by concrete organizational arrangements that affect performance processes and levels. Local orders are forged by action and may be analyzed in terms of the fit between decisions taken at various levels of higher education systems, not all of which simply follow on mechanically, one from the other. Thus, diversification may be a result of unequal ability, interest or will of individual universities to capture new norms and rules as strategic resources. Some will treat new rules as formal administrative requirements forced upon universities by bureaucrats, thus refusing to make sense of the new organizational tool offered to them and, by the same token, weakening their position in terms of accountability. On the contrary, others will use them as internal resources to enhance shared identities among university members and to sustain legitimate global organizational strategies, thus appearing as responsive and accountable from the point of view of new values, and deserving more delegation of resources or better allocation of money.

31.2.2.2 Implementation of Reforms: Macro-level Structures

Organizational structures and resources frame the action-set and social-economic space in which universities can move. Despite the common identity of the basic repertoire, variations in political, technical and social environment of reforms express path-dependency of national trajectories as well as they prolong them. The drive to move of each actor of the higher education and research system – central administration, the academic professions and universities – is conditional to the preexisting distribution of power between them and their alliances with prominent actors in the political system at large.

Anticipations and Implicit Social Negotiations

All countries provide many good examples of how local interpretation may lock intended reforms into national paths. The basic cybernetic loop linking incentives, performance and awards was and remains quite weak in many places. In several countries, direct basic public funding long remained disconnected from evaluation or the share of performance-based funding remained limited and had only very indirect influence on supply. Funding formulae were transformed to incorporate a proportion of performance-based budgeting but its share varied enormous across countries, from very small to half of the global allocation. Decision-making competencies of rectors and deans have been extended in many countries, yet academic self-governance remains very strong in most, because daily operations are based on informal long lasting and non-hierarchical peer relationships. The rise of competitive money is advocated as encouraging excellence, but it also implies heavy costs of reorganization and maintenance within universities, which it takes time and internal authority to achieve. Differentiation by excellence may induce counterproductive effects such as demoralization and stress among teachers devalued by this increasing emphasis, so that public authorities may act carefully in anticipation of unionized resistance.

Hence, old patterns seem often to reassert themselves and slow down the process of planned policy change, taking advantage of situations characterized by localism and incrementalism. Path dependency is in control of change dynamics. Research programs may be developed, but so vaguely formulated that they can catch in a harmless way all disciplinary traditions and interests. Peer review can develop some tricks as a protection against outside interference threatening the established distribution of power within academia. On the other side, it also happens that central administration, under the pressure of scientific or political lobbies, interferes more or less openly with peer judgments to protect such or such project. Thus, slow adaptation seems to be the rule in most countries, both on the side of central authorities, academic professions and higher education organizations.

Public Service Culture

Variation relates to national visions of desirable change, political voluntarism and capability to shape rearrangements of power distribution within universities, and between the universities and their stakeholders. National dominant cognitive frames also play their part. The Benthamite British political and social philosophy clearly helped promoting reforms based on economic views of society, where quasi-markets and principal-agent relationships appeared to be the best substitute regulatory instruments to bureaucracy. The economic crisis in the UK also bolstered the will to undertake radical innovation, with huge consequences that broke the path dependence built into a century long history. Continental European Welfare states have been more reluctant to deregulation by the market, fearing that competition might be, at the end of the day, more destructive than regenerative, and very costly in terms of social unrest.

How public servants were linked to the outside world is also of much importance on their ability to learn lessons from foreign experiences. In most European countries, in particular the largest ones, they long remained largely isolated inside self-sufficient frontiers. They sometimes came to invent their own solutions, discovering ex post, sometimes many years later, how similar they were to the ones used elsewhere.

How reforms position has also to do with the degree to which civil servants in the administration of higher education and research are interweaving with the academics profession and academic national and international elites (Whitley 2008; Edler et al. 2012). Where the link is very strong and long-standing, the administration is very likely to so to speak become an hostage of specific academic lobbies well connected to political power arenas, as often is the case in fields such as law, medicine or economics. In such cases, conflicts on the front stage of administrative organization and tools often hide backstage conflicts on the redistribution of power between national scientific elites.

Regulatory Traditions and the Strength of the Academic Profession

Academics may be hostile or enthusiastic towards reforms (see Chap. 32 by Moscati and Chap. 33 by Pechar). Most of the time, they are ambivalent. They fear that organizational-based reform weakens their professional identity, as if organizational and professional strength were necessarily mutually exclusive. As noticed by Freidson (2001), the capacity of professional social regulations to counterbalance bureaucratic authority or the law of the market is very uneven across countries. They more easily play the role of alternative regulations in countries where public authorities are coordinators rather than they exert a hierarchical authority (Paradeise 2011). In the first case, they coordinate with existing professions to make and implement decision and develop reactive and procedural policies, while in the second one strong administrative bodies impose decisions in an interventionist perspective embedded in substantial policies.

The reforms in process are supposed to handle asymmetry between administrative and organizational actors by relaxing the domination of the administrative hierarchy on organizations and professions, so that each partner may gain based on a symmetrical relationship maintained by negotiation between equal players. But this would suppose that public authorities actually move from substantial to procedural rules in all their fields of action and effectively transfer their control over resources to other actors, for instance international scientific elites as far as competitive allocation of resources is concerned. It would also suppose that managerial and academic components of universities find some way to institutionalize internal checks and balance. Achieving organizational and strategic autonomy of universities requires the withdrawal of strategy-driven administrations from finicky rules that secure their on-going control.

31.2.2.3   Implementation of Reforms: Meso-level of Universities

Relaxation of tight bureaucratic substantive rules allow for strategic diversification of individual universities, while the expansion of incentives built into procedural rules may encourage institutions to imitate the new structures introduced by pioneering institutions. Actually, both trends can be observed. On the one hand, the requirement to build a profile according to a specific strategy in mission-based contracts often leads universities to try to copy those that are seen as especially successful (DiMaggio and Powell 1983). This trend results in the repetition of strategic orientations from one individual university to the other, so much so that research programs at all levels, from regions to country to Europe, encourage repetitively the same fields of specialization. On the other hand, diversification is rooted in direct efforts by public authorities to increase specialization of universities in terms of concentration of resources in specific disciplinary or functional activities.

Until now, we have simplified our argument on universities by considering them as internally homogenous. But they are themselves loosely coupled social systems. At best, they articulate one organizational agenda with multiple academic agendas. As a totality, they thus have to fit into several reference frames: the first ones link faculty members with their scientific communities; the second one links faculty members with each other across disciplines within the university as an organization.

This double requirement is rarely satisfied. The various components are unequally strong to impose their vision or to compromise with others in the organization. It can be argued though that top of the pile universities described above own a social capital that enables them to benefit from a productive tension at a very high level between the professional and administrative spheres on the one hand, and the individual and collective spheres on the other (Paradeise and Thoenig 2011b). They can act as "agile elephants" because they can face a strong drive for administrative rationalization without shackling strategies based around a professional approach; they have explicitly incorporated professional standards into their organization and safeguarded them by their internal governance, avoiding common bureaucratic scourges such as rampant centralization or silo effects. They benefit from long-lasting effects of diverse material and institutional resources that consolidate their internal instrumental quality without destroying their assets as institutions based on shared values and negotiated compromise on major issues, while they can respect the quality regime of each discipline. Shared and often implicit rules regulate the room for maneuver and content of roles vis-à-vis the centre and the grass roots, and between the administrative and the academic spheres. They can focus at length on developing and enhancing their – already excellent – internal institutional arrangements and forge a virtuous circle in which their instrumental quality bolsters their status-related quality. There is a legitimate means of social regulation based around rules that underpin shared knowledge and a space for common interpretation of situations. There is also strong pressure to act collectively on the different components, departments, research centers and members of the academic corps, because the inconsiderable resource of a recognized brand also entails an obligation to produce a result that, aside from formal obligations, is based on a shared perception of a moral duty to contribute to the collective good and maintained by practical rules that make sense for the academic corps concerning the allocation of research subsidies, the creation of chairs or promotion of the establishment's reputation. In other words, these universities are well managed, internally integrated around common scientific and managerial values but respectful of their internal diversity. Their reputation and their wealth make them very attractive for stakeholders, which in turn bring them more resources. They do not really fear reforms because they can take the best of them, especially in terms of resource concentration, while their internal organization and external reputation protects them from the risk of managerialism.

At the other extreme of the spectrum one finds universities that are weak on both dimensions of professions and organization. It is often the case of "missionaries", where management is relatively undeveloped and is not given much consideration, hierarchical authority is poor as it is suspect of being abusive and organizational structure juxtaposes specialized professional silos, each differentiated around a specific domain with very little direct spontaneous inter-component cooperation. Apart from tinkering at the margins, the central hierarchy struggles to arbitrate between different missions. Hence, any strategic change is perceived as a risk both in itself and for the institution. It makes it very difficult and sometimes impossible to redeploy resources on the basis of strategic arbitration as this is seen as a major infringement of the professional values. A tacit acceptable goal is for everyone and every component to keep on doing what they do. Components evolve in a context of affective power relationships that veer between trust and mistrust. This produces relatively opaque forms of decision-making and the collective is subject to centrifugal forces. Priorities are formulated by 'localist' professionals, whose references are endogenous to the local institution. Their power resources come from local experience that is not easily transposable elsewhere and who devise ad hoc expertise and solutions in local functional networks. Each person or group has one's own internal field of action, one's own local network and its own agenda. Egalitarianism is a basis of instrumentation that gives everyone equal priority in terms of treatment, even though subtle or informal differences can creep in as this allocation process does not specifically refer to selection criteria – as if one priority was just as important as any other – while allowing for the perpetuation of specialist niches accorded a large degree of *de facto* functional autonomy. The weakness of collective governance precludes the spontaneous emergence of any strong bargaining process that would be tolerated by mutual consent. Consequently, instrumentation increases the establishment's degree of disconnection, reduces its ability to keep pace with developments in society and in education and research demands.

Cumulating poor management, weak internal and external integration, little scientific recognition and faculty members essentially dedicated to local teaching and service missions, such universities are defenseless in front of reforms. They lack strategic agility and they lack top publications. The most research-driven faculty members are internally perceived as not enough committed to the "real issues" of teaching and administrating day-to-day activity. They are also perceived threatening in terms of internal allocation of resources and organizational restructuration. And they are seen as arrogant members of the organization who prefer to work with doctoral students and colleagues abroad rather than sustain the humble and equalitarian mission of their own university.

Taking advantage of reforms is thus very difficult for such institutions, even though their presidential team may try hard and strengthen its management, because prevailing informal arrangements deeply embedded into the internal organization fade ambitions developed at the top level – regarding for instance recruitment. In such circumstances, there seems to be only two possible futures. Either the university looses foot in terms of those outcomes valued by performance indicators, its resources regresses and it stabilizes as a possible good teaching college, or the presidential team and top management find resources to behave as enlightened despots and centralize power as to sustain ambitious projects, drawing new faculty members and redistributing resources and structures, with a high risk to lose legitimacy and face major resistance.

The third case deals with professional bureaucracies with strong scientific links and reputation, which professionals are not always strongly integrated internally except for sharing special attention paid to their prestige. They perceive the overall establishment as the sum of self-sufficient parts distinct from the hierarchical line of management. The president and management have too little influence and hierarchical legitimacy to develop or impose an overall strategy, or to impulse debate on strategies among faculty members. The internal governance draws upon the implicit trust in interpersonal peer relations. Administrative services are considered as second-class tasks to be staffed by good, loyal servants who are requested not to interfere in academic policies and to remain subordinated to the academic world. The organization is conceived as a receptacle deployed to serve its members' prestige, rather than as a proactive principle driving a collective dynamic. Debating on the organization of resources or bargaining are all forms of bad manners. There is no strategy except as the culmination of organizational forms accumulated over time that favor a distributive policy tending to preserve vested positions since resources are allocated based on acquired rank, prestige and status. Managing the organization consists primarily of incident management.

The benchmark community is disciplinary and cosmopolitan. It is the scope and quality of the professional networks rather than membership in the local institution that confers visibility and power upon the institution. Thus, the internal strength of a sub-community – and of its members – derives in large part from the degree of exclusivity of the control it exercises over the selection, training, placement and careers of its members throughout their lives, and from its ability to impose distinguishing social and professional criteria in its domain at both national and international level.

In other words, the local institution outsources its human resource management function, its scientific policy and its operating definitions of relevance and excellence to outside professional communities. It serves as a host structure for professionals distinguished by their community. Each profession or discipline is governed by inherently intractable criteria in terms of the type of research or courses provided, or the social regulation of its members. The local institution has to trust the ability of the professionals present in its midst to promote its image and reputation in larger external arenas. This does not mean that the reputation of the institution is indifferent to the prestige of its faculty members. This is why they resist developments that could affect the image of the most prestigious local institutions in which they are established. As a guiding principle for action, collegiality facilitates the alliance between the local and the cosmopolitan, and between the establishment and the profession. It enables both governance of a peer group by importing external standards of legitimate power, such as length of service and grade, and coexistence of different professional communities by not imposing uniform, rigid criteria for arbitrating between them.

Such aristocratic organizations are allergic to the type of reform that is imposed upon them. They may have good scientific assets, their poor internal integration capacity, their weak level of professional management, and their reluctance towards organizational leadership and collective strategy, put them into a difficult position to face the challenges of reforms impacts. The organization as such is unable to back up its members in the competition that rebuilds reputation by formal performance, such as grants and rankings.

Like missionaries, *venerables* have two ways out.

One is to stiffen their position with the risk to weaken their reputation by progressively downgrading their resources of all sorts. The other one is to enter a revival scenario by building up a strong managerial leadership that reorganizes the whole institution top-down from the inside. In that last case, typical of wannabes they will centralize managerial power, dilute internal rules that used to give a strong say to academics, renew their faculty by buying them at their fair price on the labor market, and develop incentives as to have them contribute to the collective formal performance just by summing up individual contributions (based on their gender, nationality, publications), encouraging normal science – more productive in terms of publication – over scientific exploration activity and paying less attention to their education mission than to their ranking. They will find ad hoc solutions to issues raised by this reconstruction of their labor force, such as recruiting high standing professionals as part-time lecturers to face the need of high level ongoing education courses that young intensive article producers cannot fill adequately and replace the ranks of permanent staff depleted by publication incentives. In other words, managers will reestablish the organization from the top, based on a shared value of opportunistic utilitarianism, with the premise that an academic institution can be managed sustainably just like a kit, by reducing the academic activity to a market commodity that reconciles individual interests with the collective good through the individualistic behavior of staff driven by short-term material success incited by an authoritarian management that can and will tread on the academic ethos.

31.3 Conclusion

The first part of this paper details why and how European countries, with predominant public higher education based on funding by welfare states, are experiencing the same trend of reforms since the 1980s and more intensively since the turn of the twenty-first century. Ongoing reforms aim at reinforcing the intra-organisational link. Academics fear, with some lapses of memory and for some good reasons, that these reforms might weaken their professional links and convert professional bureaucracies into mechanic bureaucracies by enhancing exogenous governance mechanisms based on new ways of setting research priorities, reinforcement of presidential power and formal accountability of universities, all these orientations converging towards tighter coupling of constituents within the university organization.

We have shown that the same reform repertoire gives birth to interpretations that vary from one country and from one university to the other. Countries and universities face these reforms in highly variable manners, with varying impact on the academic professions, depending upon where they come from, how scientific elites relate to society and political power at large, and how much stress is put on their constituents.

Hence, reforms are in the process of differentiating European universities. Whether they will produce wannabes or top of the pile institutions remains to be discovered in the future.

References

Baschung, L., Benninghoff, M., Goastellec, G., & Perellon, J. (2009). Switzerland: Between cooperation and competition. In C. Paradeise, E. Ferlie, I. Bleiklie, & E. Reale (Eds.), *University governance: Western European comparative perspectives* (pp. 153–177). Dordrecht: Springer.

Bleiklie, I. (2009). Norway: From tortoise to eager beaver? In C. Paradeise, E. Ferlie, I. Bleiklie, & E. Reale (Eds.), *University governance: Western European comparative perspectives* (pp. 127–152). Dordrecht: Springer.

Brunsson, N., & Sahlin-Andersson, K. (2000). Constructing organisations: The example of public reform sector. *Organisation Studies, 21*(4), 721–746.

Christensen, T. (2011). University governance reforms: Potential problems of more autonomy? *Higher Education, 62*, 503–517.

Cohen, M. D., March, J. G., & Olsen, J. P. (1972). A garbage can model of organizational choice. *Administrative Science Quarterly, 17*(1), 1–25.

DiMaggio, P. J., & Powell, W. W. (1983). The iron cage revisited: Institutional isomorphism and collective rationality in organizational fields. *American Sociological Review, 48*(2), 147–160.

Edler, J., Frischer, D., Glanz, M., & Stampfer, M. (2012, July). *The impact of ERC on universities. Conceptualising and exploring the organisational reactions to a new European funding instrument.* Paper to be presented to the EGOS Colloquium 2011 Gothenburg. Subtheme 45: Reconstructing Universities as Organizations: Increasing Authority with Limited Strategic Capabilities.

Ferlie, E., & Andresani, G. (2009). United Kingdom from bureau professionalism to new public management? In C. Paradeise, E. Ferlie, I. Bleiklie, & E. Reale (Eds.), *University governance: Western European comparative perspectives* (pp. 177–196). Dordrecht: Springer.

Ferlie, E., & McNulty. (2002). *Reengineering health care: Complexities of organizational transformation.* Oxford University Press, Oxford.

Ferlie, E., et al. (1996). *The new public management in action.* Oxford: Oxford University Press.

Freidson, E. (2001). *Professionalism, the third logic: On the practice of knowledge.* Chicago: University of Chicago Press.

Geiger, R., & Feller, I. (1995, May–June). The dispersion of academic research in the 1980s. *The Journal of Higher Education, 66*(3), 336–360.

Goedegebuure, L. (1993). *Higher education policy: An international comparative perspective.* Oxford: Pergamon Press.

Graham, H. D., & Diamond, N. (1997). *The rise of American research universities. Elites and challengers in the postwar era.* Baltimore: The Johns Hopkins University Press.

Henkel, M. (2000). *Academic identities and policy change in higher education.* London: Jessica Kingsley Publishers.

Krücken, G., & Meier, F. (2006). Turning the university into an organizational actor. In G. Drori, J. Meyer, & H. Hwang (Eds.), *World society and the expansion of formal organization.* Oxford: Oxford University Press.

Laredo, P. (2007). Revisiting the third mission of universities: Toward a renewed categorization of university activities. *Higher Education Policy, 20*, 441–456.

Lepori, B. (2008). Options et Tendances dans le Financement des universités en Europe. *Critique internationale, 39*, 25–40.

Lindblom, C. E. (1959, Spring). The science of muddling through. *Public Administration Review, 19*(2), 79–88.

March, J. G. (1962). The business firm as a political coalition. *Journal of Politics, 24*, 662–678.

Merton, K. R. (1988/1968). The Matthew effect in science, II cumulative advantage and the symbolism of intellectual property. *ISIS, 79*, 606–623.

Metcalf, H., et al. (2005). *Recruitment and retention of academic staff in higher education.* London: Department of Education and Skills Research Report.

Mintzberg, H. (1979). *The structuring of organizations.* Englewood Cliffs: Prentice Hall.

Musselin, C., & Paradeise, C. (2009). France: From incremental transitions to institutional change. In C. Paradeise, E. Ferlie, I. Bleiklie, & E. Reale (Eds.), *University governance: Western European comparative perspectives* (pp. 21–50). Dordrecht: Springer.

Nedeva, M. (2008). New tricks and old dogs? The 'Third Mission' and the re-production of the university. In D. Epstein, R. Boden, R. Deem, F. Rizvi, & S. Wright (Eds.), *The world yearbook of education 2008: Geographies of knowledge/geometries of power: Framing the future of higher education* (pp. 85–105). New York: Routledge.

Paradeise, C. (2011). *La profession académique saisie par la nouvelle gestion publique.* Sociologie du travail, Dossier « Nouveau management public dans l'Etat », sous la direction de Ph. Bezes et D. Demazière, no. 3, pp. 313–321.

Paradeise, C., & Thoenig, J.-C. (2011a). Réformes et ordres universitaires locaux. In G. Felouzis & S. Hanhart (dir.), *Gouverner l'éducation par les nombres? Usages, débats et controverses.* Bruxelles: Éditions de Boeck, collection Raisons Éducatives (pp. 33–52). English version available.

Paradeise, C., & Thoenig, J.-C. (2011b, May 25–27). *The road to world class university. Elites and wannabes*. Organization studies workshop, 'Bringing public organizations back in'. Les Vaux de Cernay.

Paradeise, C., Ferlie, E., Bleiklie, I., & Reale, E. (Eds.). (2009). *University governance: Western European comparative perspectives*. Dordrecht: Springer.

Perellon, J. F. (2003). *La qualité dans l'enseignement supérieur. Reconnaissance des filières d'études en Suisse et en Europe: analyse d'une révolution* (Le Savoir Suisse). Lausanne: Presses polytechniques et universitaires romandes.

Picard, J.-F. (1999). *La fondation Rockefeller et la recherche médicale*. Paris: PUF.

Porter, T. M. (1995). *Trust in numbers*. Princeton: Princeton University Press.

Reale, E., & Potì, B. (2009). Italy: Local policy legacy and moving to an 'In Between' configuration. In C. Paradeise, E. Ferlie, I. Bleiklie, & E. Reale (Eds.), *University governance: Western European comparative perspectives* (pp. 71–102). Dordrecht: Springer.

Schimank, U., & Lange, S. (2009). Germany: A latecomer to new public management. In C. Paradeise, E. Ferlie, I. Bleiklie, & E. Reale (Eds.), *University governance: Western European comparative perspectives* (pp. 51–70). Dordrecht: Springer.

Schwarz, S., & Westerheijden, D. (2004). *Accreditation and evaluation in the European Higher Education Area*. Dordrecht/Boston/London: Kluwer.

Serow, R. (2000). Research and teaching at a research university. *Higher Education, 40*, 449–463.

Sikes, R. S., Prior, P., & Palier, B. (2001). *Globalization and European welfare states. Changes and challenges*. London: McMillan.

Tuchman, G. (2009). *Wannabe U: Inside the corporate university*. Chicago: The University of Chicago Press.

van Vught, F. (Ed.). (1989). *Governmental strategies and innovation in higher education* (Higher education policy series no. 7). London: Jessica Kingsley.

van Vught, F. (1993). *Patterns of governance in higher education*. Paris: UNESCO.

Vigour, C. (2008). Ethos et légitimité professionnels à l'épreuve d'une approche managériale: le cas de la justice belge. *Sociologie du travail, 50*(1), 71–90.

Weick, K. F. (1976). Educational organizations as loosely coupled systems. *Administrative Science Quarterly, 21*, 1–19.

Westerheijden, D. F., de Boer, H., & Enders, J. (2009). Netherlands: An 'Echternach' procession in different directions. Oscillating steps towards reform. In C. Paradeise, E. Ferlie, I. Bleiklie, & E. Reale (Eds.), *University governance: Western European comparative perspectives* (pp. 103–126). Dordrecht: Springer.

Whitley, R. (2008). Universities as strategic actors: Limitations and variations. In L. Engwall & D. Weaire (Eds.), *The university in the market* (pp. 22–37). London: Portland Press.

Chapter 32
University Governance in Changing European Systems of Higher Education*

Roberto Moscati

32.1   New Mission for Higher Education

In the last decades it has become the more and more clear that the national economies based on the use of knowledge – the one in the USA in particular – have been affected by a rate of development much higher than the others. This model rapidly spread out in the developed world starting an economic model strictly related on knowledge and specifically on knowledge as a commodity. This evolution has produced substantial consequences particularly on the relationship between states and higher education systems as well as inside the academic world. Among other things, the "humboldtian" university model turned out not to be in tune with the new functions given to higher education while the university tasks have progressively changed because of the multiple use of scientific research and thanks to the development of new kind of relations with several sectors of society globally included in the so called "university third mission (or third stream)".

As it is well known, the development of the economy based on the use of knowledge received in the 1980s its ideological subsistence in Great Britain and the United States with the government led by Thatcher and Reagan which were representing a neo-liberal vision of the virtue of individual freedom and of free market. This political and cultural position could be considered as a global project of modernization based on the "great narration" of the market and of the competitive individualism as instruments of cultural renewal. As a consequence, the Western economies have to adapt themselves to a unique process of economic globalization which involves – among

*Paper presented at the Conference on the Future of Higher Education
17–19 October 2011 – Bucharest, Romania

R. Moscati (✉)
Department of Sociology and Social Research, Università di Milano Bicocca,
via bicocca degli arcimboldi 8, I-20126 Milan, Italy
e-mail: roberto.moscati@unimib.it

A. Curaj et al. (eds.), *European Higher Education at the Crossroads:*
Between the Bologna Process and National Reforms,
DOI 10.1007/978-94-007-3937-6_32, © Springer Science+Business Media Dordrecht 2012

other things – the transformation of the role of the state. In fact, the state has to remain as far as possible away from the citizens' life while it has to exercise several forms of control on the institutions of education. From their side, these institutions are supposed to compete one against the others and to improve their performances through this competition.

It is also worth to notice a significant change introduced in this process as far as the idea of mission is concerned. In fact, traditionally the classic concept of mission did not apply to individual institutions of higher education. Rather it applied to the sector as a whole. Institutional mission and identity were conceived as collective terms that applied to a particular segment of the Nation's provision, not in terms of an identity specific to an individual establishment. Therefore, both institutional identity and mission derived from being one of a species, as one of a broad type of establishment rather than the individual activities of a particular establishment (Teichler 1996).

32.2 University Governing Systems Affected by Autonomy and Competition

Changed social and economic conditions have therefore created the premises for a greater autonomy of universities and have put them in various ways in competition with one another to obtain recognition and to increase funding.

University autonomy has taken different aspects and reached different levels in various European systems of higher education.

In **Germany**, for instance, a series of federal and state laws has substantially increased the individual university autonomy, although *Länder* bureaucracies are inclined to keep a certain degree of direct control. In addition, the political coalitions' dynamics may push forward or slow down the drive toward autonomy. All in all, the on-going transformation seems relevant with special emphasis on (i) introduction of global budget, (ii) staff recruitment, (iii) definition of teaching supply, (iv) student fees.

In **France** – on the other end – a larger autonomy from the ministerial "*tutelle*" doesn't seem near. System of contractualisation created in the 1980s remains a key element of the ministerial control although the universities have obtained relevant degrees of autonomy and responsibility through recent laws like the LRU (or Law Pécresse).

In **Italy** the ministerial control over the structure of the teaching activities has recently become more severe with the introduction of "requisites" for the creation of academic courses which include a minimum numbers of academic staff and the stop of academics' recruitment. Together with the reduction of the state financial support to the all system these measures reveal the purpose to shrink the global offer of education at tertiary level and to limit the autonomy of universities' activity.

In **Great Britain** are well known the procedures of assessment made by public institutions like HEFCE with an impact on the amount of resources provided to the universities by the government. A typical characteristic of the British universities is the dialectic between structures of governance (the Council) and executive teams which is related to the traditional legal autonomy of the universities even if they receive a substantial economic support from the state.

On the other hand, in **Spain** it seems emerging a "new regulated autonomy" provided by the government with limits including the legal value of degrees granted to the accredited courses. Thus the government has the right to decide on new curricula and it seems refraining the creation of new courses and universities (somehow in a similar way as in Italy). Also as in Italy, governmental decisions are not based on a national system of evaluation as on a pure political will.[1]

Autonomy and competition have inevitably exerted a strong influence over the values characterising higher education, and particularly on the governing systems of the universities. In other words, the need has been developed to justify the transformation of higher education systems. Specifically, the traditional values of collegiality, individual freedom of academics, just as the autonomy of research and courses offered which characterised the academic community are being replaced by new models described as positive (therefore considered in terms of value), like responsibility being taken for professional tasks and activity (accountability) towards the subjects involved (stakeholders), together with a passage from an administrative to a managerial organisation of teaching and research establishments, now in competition with one another.

In particular, the diffusion of new interpretative models for the objectives of higher education and training systems is presented as necessary because it is just. And just (therefore enhanced with value) because it is useful to society as a whole.

In this perspective, competition between universities represents the logic of the market and is applied at various levels: at a local level, where moreover it is called to coexist with the symmetric value of cooperation, often in order to create the synergies essential for reaching a critical mass useful for international competition (see here the PRES phenomenon in France). But also at a national and indeed international level towards the establishments and subjects who want to/have to utilize the products of the academic world. At the same time, competition between subject areas has been facilitated within the same establishment, to respond to outside requests (expressed or even only potential). In this way finding extra funds is interpreted according to the same market logic, under the form of the offer of services linked to knowledge. Therefore for the university the opening to the outside world, in this perspective, means a greater dependence on logics which are different from its own, especially because are characterised by temporariness. A market relationship, in fact, implies a greater flexibility, a capacity for adaptation in functioning and fewer binding regulations.

---

[1] These and the following comparative analysis are derived from a research carried out on the governance in universities of Germany, France, Great Britain, Spain and Italy (Boffo and Moscati 2011; Moscati et al. 2010).

It also calls for the development of new qualities in university teaching, research and technical-administrative personnel. Competition, it is said, calls for speed in decision-making, which influences individual behaviour patterns, but especially the mechanisms of decision-making and the structures involved in the process of elaborating university policies.

Hence, the increasing importance of the themes tied to governing universities and the characteristics needed for leadership. The latter, in turn, appear to be strictly linked to the image the individual university assumes in distinct moments in history and in different societies.

In this perspective, a typology elaborated by Robin Middlehurst (1995) proposes a link between the way of perceiving universities and the relevant features of leadership. If we look at the new models of university, we see that leadership becomes inevitably more widespread and involves different subjects at different levels within the establishment, justifying in this way – among other thinks – the use of the term "governance".

32.3   Development of University Governance

The term "governance" is identified with the structure of relations holding up the organisational coherence, and therefore authorizes policies, programming, decisions and also furnishes controls over their correctness, coherence and suitability.[2] Governance therefore refers to the context in which universities operate and also to the structures via which the fixed results are reached or are sought. Consequently, it can be held that the concept of governance incorporates those of management, administration and institutional leadership.

According to Renate Mayntz, in fact, the term "governance" includes a system of rules and also the way in which the system works. In its turn the system of rules is to be considered a description of the institutional framework according to which the actors in a particular field of policies orient their activities (Mayntz 2004, cit. in Kehm and Lanzendorf 2006, 15).

A well-known reference model for defining the dimensions of governance is the "triangle of coordination" elaborated by Burton Clark, consisting in a system of rules concerning the behaviour of the actors in the academic world and variously influenced by the market, state or academic oligarchy (to which Clark himself later added academic hierarchical and entrepreneurial leadership as a fourth basic element). It forms a "power parallelogram" representing a regime of governance in which – in different circumstances – one of the four components prevails (Clark 1983, 1997, 1998).

---

[2]In contrast "management" consists in reaching the established goals by attributing responsibility and resources as well as monitoring their efficiency and efficacy; While "administration" can be understood as the process of interpreting and pursuing the objectives of the organization, in line with the established policies and procedures (Gallagher 2001; Meek 2003, 12).

A further development of the Clark model was elaborated later on by Schimank who identifies five dimensions of governance.

- State regulation which refers to the top-down notion of authority represented by the national government.
- The guide of stakeholders, which is to be found in the definition of the aims and objectives as well as suggestions and advice (the national government may be the main stakeholder, but not the only one).
- Academic self-government, composed of the professional communities with their mechanism for reaching consensus, based on a strong egalitarianism balanced by the authority of reputation, as well as on self-evaluation and the control of activity by means of the "peer-review".
- Managerial self-government, featuring a hierarchical classification of universities with a series of hierarchically well distinguished roles, leaderships aiming at reaching objectives, and where there is a prevalence of rectors/chancellors and deans who are required to have decision-making capacities.
- The dimension of competition which refers to the distribution of the scarce resources – in particular identified with public funds and academic prestige – as an object of competition between universities and within a single establishment (Kehm and Lanzendorf 2006, 15; Enders et al. 2008, 115)

It can be held that it is along these lines that modern forms of government in higher education systems and in particular individual universities are developed.

Therefore, it becomes of interest to enquire how and why these new forms of governance are emerging.

First of all, we see how some features of the context like the high level of public spending on higher education coupled with the relatively low position of higher education in the list of national government priorities has contributed to the move for changes in governance.

At the same time, globalization and internationalization accelerated by the processes of production and distribution of knowledge have started off a contrast between different actors (politicians, intellectuals, students, economic operators) about the real nature of knowledge and its applications. New power struggles breaking out between different groups in political and economic spheres, about the functions of teaching-learning structures and knowledge producers, have seen the increased application of neo-liberal thought as in the "New Public Management" theory. According to this theory, universities need to be transformed from loosely-coupled institutions to solidly structured organizations in order to insert themselves efficiently in market dynamics, sustain the mechanisms of competition and respond to the requests for reliability by means of evaluation.

Specifically, in European universities changes are signalled in the forms of governance, which have shifted the balance of power and authority towards new central structures. The central administration is reinforced and acquires a crucial role. The traditional bicameral systems (academic senate and council of administration) are evolving towards a reinforcing of administrative capacities. There is an increasing presence of outside subjects bearing interests (known as "*stakeholders*") in decision making bodies. Criticism grows over the collegiality of the decision making processes, with a trend towards the centrality of decisions and a consequent reduction in some cases (France) of decisions at a disciplinary level. Chancellors/rectors in some cases are appointed rather than elected, while deans and department head (middle managers) are seen as administrative professionals and can be appointed by the rector/chancellor. In certain cases they can form – together with some of the higher levels of the administration – a kind of informal steering committee (Amaral et al. 2002b, 287).

32.4 Evolution of the University Governance and Academics' Reaction

More broadly it can then be asked whether the managerial revolution is really taking hold of the university governance structures or managerialism is only a political tool of a rhetoric nature, useful for encouraging adaptation to the new conditions of functioning of academic institutions. In effect, managerialism is not convincing as the only paradigm for the government of public institutions and the traditional model of government still finds applications in particular in the sector of higher education where there are no pure forms of management and academic self-government and state regulations still carry considerable weight.

It also must not be forgotten that there is a whole series of negative effects partly produced or at least encouraged by the application of the new forms of governance and management. We are witnessing the progressive transformation of academics into workers dealing with knowledge with a growing proletarization of their profession. The decline of the dons' dominion seems to coincide with the decline of the institutional autonomy of the universities (by means of the increasing control of the state through evaluation) (Halsey 1992). And nevertheless it should also be remembered how the crisis of academic collegiality as guide to university life was already apparent before the arrival of neo-managerial theories.

It seems rather that the New Public Management pushes universities towards a situation of "scarce faith and strong control" which appears to be the consequence of the newly regulated autonomy. The traditional faith on which the social dynamic of the university was founded is being progressively substituted by verifying reliability – accountability. It follows that the increasing bureaucratic and managerial control comes to signify *de facto* doubt in the moral probity of the teaching staff. Nevertheless, according to much evidence, efficient organizations are based on trust. It can consequently be asked what institutional conditions favour trust or mistrust.

The question is linked to the issue of coherence between the central organization of academic institutions (managerial approach, hierarchical power structure) and the concrete functioning of the basic structures for teaching and research. If academic values and dynamics survive, are collegial practices indispensable or not for the survival of university institutions? If they are, a reflection needs to be made on possible hybrid forms of academic organizations (Amaral et al. 2002a, 294).

It also needs to be said that in the present situation of uncertainty on the level of identifying decision-making processes, many academics are hostile to collective bodies ("too many meetings and too few decisions taken"), and if they are involved in forms of academic capitalism (in the sense that their professional interest are concentrated outside the university) they seem to favour power being concentrated at a central level! (Amaral et al. 2003, 277).

At the same time, the strong opposition to the implementation of the Bologna Process among academics in several countries like Italy, Germany and Austria has been often linked to the criticism of New Public Management approach, sometimes in the name of Humboldtian values, as Hans Pechar pointed out for German countries (Pechar 2011).

32.5   Evolution of University Governance in Different Higher Education Systems

Different forms of governance which are developing in various universities are affected – among other thinks – by the kind of relations between public authorities and individual institutions.

For example in **France** the 4 year agreements with the ministry require the elaboration of institutional plans which the *Président* of the university has to organise and support, in this way acquiring a greater power over the representatives of different disciplinary areas. A number of researches have underlined the relevance of the *Président's* personality on the actual realisation of the governance in French universities. (Mignot-Gérard and Musselin 1999, 2002; Boffo et al. 2008).

On the other end, in **Germany** it seems that the model of university-enterprise is becoming the more and more appealing with strongest functions of the *Rektors* and the weakening of the collegial structures in order to speed-up the decision-making processes through an influential leadership. This trend is justified in particular by the introduction of measures enhancing competition among universities like the *Exzellenzinitiative*. Thus the Rektor (the more and more called perhaps not by chance "President") is supported by an executive committee in order to elaborate an institutional multi-year plan useful to participate to the *Exzellenzinitiative* and in some way reminding the French plan.

Nothing similar characterises at the moment the situation in **Italy** and **Spain** although there are attempts to strengthen the power of the top university administration. In both cases rectors are elected by the academic staff and the central national government is not willing to weakening its control (as mentioned before).

In this last respect – as it is well known (and as it will be treated in the following pages)- the situation in **Great Britain** is very different and is reflected by the different system of governance traditionally based on a dialectic between Boards, Vice-Chancellor and Senate.

In any case, the pressure to consider (and somehow accept) the rules of the market pushes the universities of all systems of higher education to improve the efficiency of their decision-making processes. The effort to achieve this result has to take into consideration from one side, the different traditions of distinct scientific areas as well as the democratic procedures and the equalitarian values of the university in history, but also, on the other, the new appeal of the managerial models. The result of this effort in terms of trends of university governance seems – at least in theory – not to be very different in various HESs.

In **France**, the *bureau* of the *Président* becomes a sort of chief executive group operating as a buffer structure between *Président* and central councils. Members of this group can be Vice-*Présidents* and head of departments, together with representatives of administrative staff and students.

In **Great Britain** Executive teams can include pro-vice-chancellors, the registrar, deans of faculties and the president of the Student Union. And it is at this level that final decisions are taken.

In **Spain** the rector can count on a similar group (*equipo rectoral*) made by a number of vice-rectors nominated by the rector himself, together with a *Segretario General* also nominated by the rector and the *Gerente* who is the representative of the national government. This *Junta de Gobierno* represents an effort to provide more power to the rector vis-à-vis the peripheral structures, but the policy applied by the central structure toward the peripheral ones (faculties and departments) is characterised by a very equalitarian attitude with the purpose to achieve a general consensus even at a cost of slowing down the timing of the decision-making process.

Somehow similar is the situation in **Italy** where the decision-making process appears to differentiate multidisciplinary universities from the technological ones. In the former a sort of centralised system of running the institution is blended with a process of achieving consensus through a combination of formal and informal processes of consultation with a relevant number of disciplinary and scientific committees; while in the latter (the Polytechnics) strategic decisions are taken by the rector and his team having granted a large mandate of confidence from the internal structures (faculties, departments).

From a comparative point of view, though faced by a series of signals at times contradictory and keeping well in mind the differences in the national systems of higher education, some tendencies can be identified which are common or at least similar in various institutional realities.

No sole definition of governance holds way, even though a series of innovations have been spreading: controls and forms of incentives/sanctions have increased; the operative autonomy of individual institutions has grown, as have government mandated rules while the search for legitimization has expanded by means of the mechanism of accountability.

Even if the self-government of universities has been weakened its disappearance is not foreseen. As regards its impact, much seems to depend on the type of leadership orchestrated by those in command. Besides, more and more frequently situations are occurring where the academic leaders appear to be pushed into carrying out the intermediary roles between academic values and outside requests (Kehm and Lanzendorf, cit., 207).

32.6   New Government and Relevance of the Middle Management

Basically for these reasons roles dealing with university government are being modified, although in reality there is no complete replacing of one model to another. Thus the role of *primus inter pares*, traditionally attributed to leaders in the various positions (rectors. vice-chancellors, deans, department or degree course heads) cannot be said to have disappeared, but to be merged into others, for which, however, academic leaders in most of the cases have had no training (in, for example, managerial, evaluation and programming skills) (Musselin 2002).

As for the governance, the problem arises of constructing a sufficiently united collective leadership, although based on different dynamics from the traditional ones. The usual principles of collegiality, in fact, destined to construct forms of consensus do not appear to be so suitable for identifying priorities and implementing decisions taken. Thus, new modalities of consensus and forms of cooperation need to be developed in what is generally a top-down decisional process coming from vice-chancellor (*rektor/rettore/président*) and having to find agreement at the level of deans/department heads and from there to the shop floor.

As a consequence the role of "middle management" has become crucial. To deans and heads of departments are attributed academic as well as managerial roles, which are difficult to combine, and thus becoming a source of uneasiness for the actors fulfilling roles of leadership directly as well as for the members of the "academic estate" (Neave and Rhoades 1987). The former often feel overwhelmed by organisational assignments difficult to reconcile with their traditional duties of teaching and research. In fact, they have to interpret and reproduce the ethos of their institution reflecting its priorities and strategies. This task has become, at the same time, more relevant and more difficult to undertake due to the transformations higher education systems are experimenting in recent times. As it is well known, structures in higher education as well as the entire shape of the higher education system may change rather rapidly while academic staff attitude in general will not follow the changing process at the same pace (Bleiklie and Kogan 2006).

In particular, the growing process of scrutiny and objective assessment of performance of academic staff as well as sections of the university or the entire institution made by internal and external structures has produced the already well known process of bureaucratization and visualization of academic work (Bleiklie et al. 2000). In addition, individual members of the academic staff have been the more and more "invited" to engage themselves outside their institutions (the so called "academic capitalism" process) (Slaughter and Leslie 1997).

Thus, middle managers have to face the contradictory pressures coming from a growing relevance of the universities' policy which are competing for resources and striving to achieve positive evaluation in the assessment exercises and – at the same time – from the traditional (but the more and more diffuse) mixture of academic activities "divided and grouped in two basic ways: by discipline and by enterprise" (Clark 1983, 28). Operationally, they have to vertically transfer the top leaders' policy to the academics as well as to mediate between the strategies of faculties and departments which strive to maintain their autonomy with the general institution plan.

The uneasy duty of middle managers is to combine all these elements pursuing a set of shared objectives and making progressively evident common interests and mutual benefits. Perhaps, this is why leadership qualities are more important than managerial ones for deans and head of departments. In fact, it has been suggested that management should be largely delegated to non-academic staff (provided the quality of the latter allows it).

In any case, the role of middle managers appears to have progressively acquired a different relevance according to the systems of higher education.

In **Germany** deans seem to have experienced a little improvement in their prerogatives. Their role basically remains linked to the mediation with rectors while their power is based on the cleverness to create a high level of agreement among colleagues. At the same time, departments are becoming the more and more relevant and independent (therefore more resistant toward forms of coordination). As a consequence deans' role is not terribly wanted.

A somehow similar trend emerges in **Italy** where the transformations in the university structure with the merging of faculties and departments from one side and the re-centralisation policy activated by the state from the other should reduce – at least in principle – the relevance of the middle managers while rectors should reinforce their role. It is worth to remember that traditionally deans and heads of department have represented more the interests of their fellow academics (bottom up process) then the general policy of the institution (top down process).

Even more clearly in **Spain** middle managers represent their electorate, which means members of faculties for deans, of departments for their heads. Their impact on the decision-making processes is very much related to the relevance of the structure (faculty, department) they are representing inside the university.

In **France** deans of the "*Unité de Formation et Recherce*" (UFR) seem to become more powerful as much as they are able to detach themselves from the control of their colleagues and become part of a general strategy created by the top management of the university.

In all the cases mentioned so far – which are belonging to continental European systems of higher education – representatives of the middle management have difficulties in playing a clear role since the governance of their universities is still very much related to the traditional way of achieving consensus through a balance (often complicated and difficult to achieve) of different disciplinary interests. In that scenario a well-designed institutional policy finds difficulties to emerge. In addition, deans and heads of department are elected (as the rectors/presidents) and have to take into very serious consideration the will of their electorate.

Different conditions are characterising the management of the universities in **Great Britain** where autonomy and competition among universities are concepts largely accepted by the academics, and managerial roles mostly acquired by nomination and not through election. Together with the relevant role of lay members (in the University Boards) these characteristics give rise to a different decision-making process, as well as to a middle management with a better defined role. But what is perhaps worth to notice is that decision-making processes in British universities are not reproducing in actual terms those considered typical of firms (as instead it is frequently perceived by the public opinion throughout Europe). If – as it is usual – the proposal of an initiative will come from the top (vice-chancellor and its team), then a circular mechanism will start in order to verify the degree of acceptability down to the different layers of the university organisation which in turn will send back to the top their reactions and proposals in order – among other thinks – to avoid for the vice-chancellor the accusation of not having involved the various structures in the process. Of course, these processes are based on a diffuse awareness among the university academic and administrative staff of the common interest in the success of the institutional policy. The absence or the weakness of this "cultural" pre-condition perhaps represents the basic difficulty for continental universities in their effort to answer to the new (not always coherent) requests coming from the contemporary economy and society.

32.7   Concluding Remarks

For what has been summarised so far it becomes rather clear the relevance acquired by academic leadership and the key role of middle management in the changing role of higher education in contemporary society.

Unfortunately, in many higher education systems (of continental Europe in particular) one of the aspects highlighting the difficulties in perceiving the transition process can be found in the scarce attention given to the development of academic leadership. The aversion to the concept of managerial skills is probably one of the main reasons for the recourse to stereotypes and common places holding that leadership is a natural gift, or an art or a skill acquired through experience. Similar attitudes automatically exclude the necessity for a specific professional training, with the risk however of finishing with being forced to adopt models applied in other contexts. This seems to be particularly true for systems where academic leaders are elected (and not nominated) by academic staff members.

The decision-making process has never been an easy task but – in recent times – the combination of traditional and new goals in the same institution has made the running of the university more articulated and compelling. The governance has therefore become a relevant subject of analysis.

As we have seen, this attempt to realise a more entrepreneurial attitude inside the universities has its justifications and is certainly relevant but it is far from representing a homogenous model. Too many aspects of the transformation of the higher education system and of its mission (as well as the mission of each individual university) have to be clarified. Meanwhile, the effective working of university governance will vary according to a number of variables related to the external environment as well as to the combination of scientific disciplines inside the institution and – more than anything else – to the quality of academics involved in the governance itself.

This is particularly true when one considers the middle management which the more and more seems to represent an essential cross-road for the success (or failure) of the university governance. Here the organizational responsibility more than everywhere else requires some special professional skills the academics involved not always are ready to show.

References

Amaral, A., Jones, G. A., & Karseth, B. (Eds.). (2002a). *Governing higher education: National perspectives on institutional governance*. Dordrecht: Kluwer Academic Publishers.

Amaral, A., Jones, G. A., & Karseth, B. (2002b). Governing higher education: Comparing national perspectives. In A. Amaral, G. A. Jones, & B. Karseth (Eds.), *Governing higher education: National perspectives on institutional governance* (pp. 278–298). Dordrecht: Kluwer Academic Publishers.

Amaral, A., Fulton, O., & Larsen, I. M. (2003). A managerial revolution? In A. Amaral, V. L. Meek, & I. M. Larsen (Eds.), *The higher education managerial revolution?* (pp. 275–295). Dordrecht: Kluwer Academic Publishers.

Bleiklie, I., & Kogan, M. (2006). Comparison and theories. In M. Kogan, M. Bauer, I. Bleiklie, & M. Henkel (Eds.), *Transforming higher education: A comparative study* (pp. 3–22). Dordrecht: Springer.

Bleiklie, I., Høstaker, R., & Vabø, A. (2000). *Policy and practice in higher education. Reforming Norwegian universities*. London: Jessica Kingsley.

Boffo, S., & Moscati, R. (2011). How growing pressure to be competitive at national and international level affects university governance: Some preliminary remarks from a comparative analysis of fifteen European universities. In P. N. Teixeira & D. D. Dill (Eds.), *Public vices, private virtues? Assessing the effects of marketization in higher education* (pp. 141–155). Rotterdam: Sense.

Boffo, S., Dubois, P., & Moscati, R. (2008). *Gouverner les universités en France et en Italie*. Paris: L'Harmattan.

Clark, B. R. (1983). *The higher education system. Academic organization in cross-national perspective*. Berkeley: The University of California Press.

Clark, B. R. (1997). *The entrepreneurial university: Demand and response*. Paper presented at 19th EAIR Forum, University of Warwick, UK.

Clark, B. R. (1998). *Creating entrepreneurial universities. Organizational pathways of transformation*. Kidlington: Pergamon.

Enders, J., De Boer, H., & Leisyte, L. (2008). On striking the right notes: Shifts in governance and the organisational transformation of universities. In A. Amaral, I. Bleiklie, & C. Musselin (Eds.), *From governance to identity. A festschrift for Mary Henkel* (pp. 113–129). Dordrecht: Springer.

Gallagher, M. (2001). *Modern university governance. A national perspective*. Paper presented at conference "The Idea of a University: Enterprise or Academy?", The Australian Institute and Manning Clark House, Canberra.

Halsey, A. H. (1992). *Decline of donnish dominion. The British academic professions in the twentieth century*. Oxford: Clarendon Press.

Kehm, B. M., & Lanzendorf, U. (Eds.). (2006). *Reforming university governance. Changing conditions for research in four European countries*. Bonn: Lemmens.

Mayntz, R. (2004). *Governance Theory als fortentwickelte Steuerungstheorie?* (MPIfG Working Paper 04/1). Köln: MPIfG.

Meek, V. L. (2003). Introduction. In A. Amaral, V. L. Meek, & I. M. Larsen (Eds.), *The higher education managerial revolution?* (pp. 1–29). Dordrecht: Kluwer Academic Publishers.

Middlehurst, R. (1995). Changing leadership in universities. In T. Schuller (Ed.), *The changing university?* (pp. 75–92). Buckingham: SRHE-Open University Press.

Mignot-Gérard, S., & Musselin, C. (1999). *Comparaison des modes de fonctionnement et de gouvernement de quatre universités*. Paris: Rapport Cso/Amue.

Mignot-Gérard, C., & Musselin, C. (2002). *Enquete quantitative sur les modes de gouvernement de 37 universités françaises*. Paris: Rapport Cso/Amue.

Moscati, R., Regini, M., & Rostan, M. (Eds.). (2010). *Torri d'avorio in frantumi? Dove vanno le università europee*. Bologna: Il Mulino.

Musselin, C. (2002). Editorial. *European Journal of Education, 37*(1), 1–6.

Neave, G., & Rhoades, G. (1987). The academic estate in Western Europe. In B. R. Clark (Ed.), *The academic profession. National, disciplinary & institutional settings*. Berkeley: University of California Press.

Pechar, H. (2011, October 17–19). *The decline of an academic oligarchy: The Bologna process and 'Humboldt's last warriors'*. Paper presented at the Conference on Future of Higher Education, Bucharest.

Slaughter, S., & Leslie, L. (1997). *Academic capitalism: Politics, policies and the entrepreneurial university*. Baltimore: Johns Hopkins University Press.

Teichler, U. (1996). Comparative higher education: Potentials and limits. *Higher Education, 32*(4), 431–465.

Chapter 33
The Decline of an Academic Oligarchy. The Bologna Process and 'Humboldt's Last Warriors'

Hans Pechar

33.1 What Explains the Strong Resistance to Bologna in Austria and Germany?

All over Europe student representatives voiced some criticism about Bologna. For example, the European student union (ESU) criticized that they were only marginally included in the decision making process. But this organization is not fundamentally opposed to the Bologna philosophy. ESU is concerned that in many countries the level of attention given to employability is not yet sufficient (ESU 2009, 137). In contrast, German and Austrian student representatives reject the Bologna process in principle. They are in particular opposed to the very concept of employability which in their view subordinates universities to the demands of the labor market. This paper will discuss the connections between this fundamentalist opposition and the Humboldtian legacy.

In 2009, Austria and Germany experienced strong student protests over several weeks. The Bologna process was a key target of criticism ('Bologna burns'). The mood of this opposition is aptly symbolized by a slogan at student protest rallies, claiming: 'In former times I was a poet and a philosopher[1]; now I am a Bachelor'. Another popular slogan juxtaposes the spiritual sphere of cultivation with the vulgar sphere of commerce; the Bachelor, of course, is associated with the vulgar: 'rather a poet and a philosopher than a banker and a Bachelor'.

Many academics in Germany and Austria – at least those who actively participate in the debate about Bologna – join the criticism of students. According to

---

[1] Germany used to praise itself as 'the country of poets and philosophers'.

H. Pechar (✉)
Institute for Science Communication and Research in Higher Education,
University of Klagenfurt, Schottenfeldgasse 29, Wien 1070, Austria
e-mail: hans.pechar@uni-klu.ac.at

A. Curaj et al. (eds.), *European Higher Education at the Crossroads:*
Between the Bologna Process and National Reforms,
DOI 10.1007/978-94-007-3937-6_33, © Springer Science+Business Media Dordrecht 2012

Wolfgang Frühwald, the former president of German research Council said the "mental resistance to this reform is huge. I hardly know anyone – to be honest, no one – who is inspired by the change to Bachelor and Master courses. (…) The reforms are pushed by university managers, higher education organizations, and policymakers. The gap between those who design the reform and academics at the bottom is huge" (DIE ZEIT, 17.01.2008).

Opponents claim that Bologna has resulted in a substantial deterioration of study conditions. They argue that many outcomes of the reform are the exact opposite of its original goals. This criticism refers to the workload for students, to academic mobility of students, and to employability of Bachelors.

- Instead of making the workload for students more transparent, the Bologna process has increased the workload and thus intensified the 'time burden' on students.
- Instead of facilitating mobility of students, the new study architecture has resulted in a decrease of student mobility.
- Instead of improving the employability of graduates, Bologna has created a new degree that is not accepted in the labour market.

Each of these claims is disputed. A recently published study (Schulmeister and Metzger 2011) provides empirical evidence to the factual workload in bachelor programs. Schulmeister, a sceptical of Bologna himself, originally intended to prove that Bologna has increased the workload of students. The empirical bases of his study are very detailed diaries of students in which they report all their activities (those related to studies and others) during a day. The results surprised researchers and participating students alike. It turned out that there was a huge gap between the general estimate of students of the time they spent for their studies and the detailed accounts of their time protocoled in their diaries. The latter were significantly lower than the former. In other words, students consistently overestimate the time they devote to their studies. The subjective feeling of being burdened is much stronger than the objective time they spend either at the university or studying at home. Schulmeister and his co-authors voice a lot of criticism to the organization of the study courses. But the problems they point to can hardly be attributed to the Bologna philosophy.

The amount of student mobility is equally controversial. A recent mobility study by the German Hochschul-Informations-System (HIS) was a subject of dispute before it was published.[2] Critics of Bologna assert that the study provides evidence for a decline in student mobility. The authors themselves say that the overall mobility in the new bachelor's and master's programs is as high as it was in the pre-Bologna study courses. It is undisputable, however, that student mobility at the bachelor level is low.

An important goal of Bologna is the improvement of employability of graduates. So far, the status of the Bachelor's degree is still vague and employers are rather sceptical. Ironically, although employers' associations are among the most vigorous

---

[2] Cf. http://www.zeit.de/wissen/2011-08/studie-mobilitaet

advocates of the new study architecture – because they strive for shorter study duration – individual employers still tend to prefer a master's degree. It does not help to overcome this scepticism that the government, which is one of the most important employers of graduates in Austria, gives a bad example by not recognizing the Bachelor's degree for high level civil service positions. It is equally counterproductive that representatives of academics and students frequently downgrade the value of the Bachelor in the public debate. It is often presented as an "intermediate degree" on the way to the master's degree, not as a degree in its own right. This dismissive assessment by significant parts of the academic community functions as a self-fulfilling prophecy. Many employers believe that only the master is a 'real' academic degree. Students act accordingly: the huge majority continues with a master program to complete their bachelor's degree.

33.1.1 Mistakes in the Implementation of Bologna

Even the advocates of Bologna admit that the implementation of the reform was overshadowed by many mistakes and that there is need for improvement ('Bologna reloaded'). It would be naïve to believe that a reform of this magnitude could be implemented without start-up problems. Furthermore, many of the actors responsible for implementing Bologna had either an indifferent or even negative attitude to the reform; or they had second motives that were unrelated to the creation of an EHEA. By some governments Bologna was used to push national policies, for instance, the ambition of the Austrian government to reduce the duration of studies resulted in a rigid legal regulation allowing only Bachelor courses with the duration of 3 years.

It should be no surprise, that implementation of a policy is likely to fail when those who are in charge reject that policy – in many cases the content of the former 4 years course was squeezed into a 3 years Bachelor course. The opponents were quite successful to assimilate the new degree to the traditional one tier framework. In many cases the reform was implemented in a way that contradicts the spirit of the Bologna declaration. In some cases, Bachelor's programs are set up by simply dividing a "Diplomstudiengang" (the old type of one tier master's program, taken after completion of secondary school) into two parts. The curriculum of the Bachelor's program is not shaped by the logic of a two tier system, but remains rooted in one tier logic.

33.1.2 A Clash of Values

However, such mistakes cannot fully explain the strong emotional and ideological resistance of many academics and students. This paper will focus on the normative tensions between Bologna and the Humboldtian values that are still present (if only as jargon) in the higher education debate in the Germanic countries (cf. Schultheis et al. 2008).

Schimank (2009) has interpreted this conflict as a battle between the educated elite (*Bildungsbürgertum*) that tries to maintain its privileges on the one hand, the lower middle classes that are interested to use higher education for upward mobility on the other hand. The former do not worry about employability because they occupy positions in the cultural sector of society – or so they hope. This is an occupational sector that used to be generously supported and funded by various levels of government. This support declined during the last few decades, due to (a) cuts as a result of fiscal austerity and (b) a more severe and fundamental policy shift towards new public management. It goes without saying that the educated elite is strongly opposed to any decline in governmental support of high culture and to the abandonment of governments from their cultural mission. From their view Bologna is strongly linked to new public management approaches. Both are utilitarian approaches that threaten the cultural profile and identity of the Germanic tradition.

The controversy over Bologna is not the first 'clash of values' of this kind. For more than a hundred years the guardians of the Humboldtian tradition in the German speaking countries are in defence against modernization of their education system. The campaign of universities and *Gymnasien* against technical schools and higher education institutions during the second half of the nineteenth century provides a striking parallel to the present controversies. Ringer's classic study about the decline of the German mandarins (1969) is an impressive account of the ideological motives that form the basis of this defence against modernization. Ringer's analysis focuses on the period between 1890 and 1933. In the next section I will summarize his argument and will then analyze how the Mandarin ideology advanced after 1945.

33.2 The Rise and Decline of the Mandarin Ideology

Ringer's book is a contribution to the extensive literature on "German exceptionalism" – the "special path" (*Sonderweg*) that eventually led to the political catastrophes of the twentieth century. One aspect of exceptionalism that is emphasized by Ringer is the unparalleled social standing of the educated middle classes in nineteenth century Germany. This class is called '*Bildungsbürgertum*' – a term without equivalent in any other language. This educated middle class was shaped by the neo-humanist concept of *Bildung*, which emphasizes the non-utilitarian self-cultivation of the mind. Inspired by Max Weber's portrait of the Chinese literati, Ringer calls this group 'mandarins' and defines them as a "social and cultural elite which owes its status primarily to education qualifications, but rather than to hereditary rights or wealth. (…) The 'Mandarin intellectuals', chiefly the university professors, are concerned with the educational diet of the elite. They uphold the standards of qualification for membership in the group, and they act as its spokesmen in cultural questions" (Ringer 1969, 6).

Ringer and other historians have pointed to the links between Pietism – a religious reform movement within the Lutheran church, emphasizing 'inner growth' – and the quasi religious character of the idea of cultivation. Accordingly, universities were not considered significant to society because they trained practically skills but because they fostered 'inner growth' at cultivated citizens. It is also noticeable that a "striking number of scholars came from clerical families and had originally planned to study theology"; they experienced a "transition from love and service of God to love and service of knowledge (...); this religious element helped to raise professorial status as against the nobility, insofar as it laid stress on the belief that the scholars served God rather than men" (O'Boyle 1983, 10).

The emphasis on non-utilitarian values endorsed the pretension of the educated middle class to be an aristocracy of the mind. The ideal of cultivation for its own sake helped "to move from a lowly class of origin to a position of alliance with a governing class of aristocrats and patricians. (...) association with manual labor and the kinds of material reward satisfying to lesser men was eliminated. (...) the focus on abstract principles and forms in the philological disciplines was viewed as a concern with the general (...) as parts of a whole rather than as isolated facts of the sort that distracted most men and indeed absorbed their lives" (O'Boyle 1983, 8).

33.2.1 A Historic 'Window of Opportunity'

Ringer explains this uniqueness of the *Bildungsbürgertum* as a result of a peculiar historic situation: an "intermediate stage" of economic development, in which "the ownership of liquid capital has not yet become either widespread or widely accepted as a qualification for social status, and hereditary titles based on landholding, while still relevant, are no longer absolute prerequisites" (Ringer 1969, 7). The relative economic and political backwardness of Germany compared to Western Europe limited the sphere of action for ambitious young men to the field of culture. Governments in the German states were large and in need of qualified bureaucrats. This specific constellation opened the opportunity for social upward mobility for the educated middle class.

The early 1800s were an area of modernization and reorganization of the social order. The feudal social estates based on birth (*Geburtsstände*) lost their significance as the principal criterion of societal order and hierarchy; they were gradually replaced by social estates based on vocation (*Berufsstände*). "A new division of society by profession and education and thus came to run parallel to the traditional stratification by birth" (Ringer 1969, 16). The educated middle classes achieved to establish themselves as the leading estate (*Bildungsstand*=cultivated estate) with the highest social prestige and considerable privileges. Because this cultivated estate was strongly interconnected with the state bureaucracy (gradually replacing aristocracy) Ringer describes it as a functional ruling class. The neo-humanist philosophy is the ideological fundament, the educational infrastructure (Humboldtian Gymnasium and university) are the institutional basis of their hegemony.

Governance of universities was based on the concept of a 'cultural state' that gave universities the financial stability of a state agency but limited the interference of the government to 'external affairs' while leaving the internal governance to the academic oligarchy. The academic culture at universities strongly accentuated freedom of teaching and learning thus underlining the independence of both, academics and students, from formal rules. Both aspects – governance and the culture of teaching and learning – will be discussed in more detail in the next section.

The early 1800s were the period when the cultivated elite rose in social status; it established a hegemonial position in culture and it represented the political interest of all classes that were opposed to the landed aristocracy. The claim of social leadership based on cultivation was broadly accepted among the emerging bourgeois society. Academics and other professional men played a decisive role in the revolution of 1848. The political goal of that period was to abolish the aristocratic privilege of birth.

This was also the time when the German research university rose to its preeminence and became a global role model. The new paradigm – research being no longer an off time and part time activity, but an integral part of the academic vocation – unleashed unprecedented scientific growth. It is worthwhile to note, however, that this success was mainly based on developments that were in contradiction with neo-humanist principles. German universities in the mid-1800s became the home of specialized research, most visibly in the sciences. That was in conflict with the neo-humanist principles of 'unity of research' and its preference for the humanities.

33.2.2   Horizontal Segmentation of the Middle Classes

In all European societies of that time there was a differentiation between commercial and educated middle classes. But in Germany the difference between these groups was more accentuated than elsewhere. In his later work that focused on the comparative history of education Ringer found that in France the education system could be characterized as 'vertical segmentation' with the whole bourgeoisie attending the same type of school whereas in Germany he found a 'horizontal segmentation' with educated and commercial middle classes attending different types of school (Ringer 1969, 1979). Max Weber's distinction between social class and social status (Weber 1972, 177) is an important sociological concept that helps to understand this segmentation. Class refers to the position in the system of economic production; status (social estate) refers to the distinctive style of life with a corresponding code of honour. The ideal of non-utilitarian cultivation emphasizes the status dimension. The educated middle classes in Germany succeeded in appropriating the education system for the reproduction of social status based on cultivation. "In democratic and highly industrialised societies a university degree or position competes with several other measures of social value and esteem, the most important of them being political and economic in origin. In Germany before 1890, by contrast, academic values bore the stamp of public and official recognition" (Ringer 1969, 38).

Weber himself has characterized the neo-humanist ideals as a mechanism of social distinction. "Differences of education are one of the strongest social barriers, especially in Germany, where almost all privileged positions inside and outside the civil service are tied to qualifications involving not only specialized knowledge but also 'general cultivation' and where the whole school and university system has been put into the service of this ideal of general cultivation" (quoted by Ringer 1969, 35).

The unique social standing of the cultivated elite is confirmed by Friedrich Paulsen, the authoritative historian of German education in the early 1900s. "The academically educated constitute a kind of intellectual and spiritual aristocracy. (…) Conversely, anyone in Germany who has no academic education lacks something which wealth and high birth cannot fully replace" (Ringer 1969, 35). There is no other country where the following statement of Paulsen would make any sense: "Educated and uneducated, these are the two halves into which society is at present divided. They have gradually caused older divisions to be forgotten" (quoted by O'Boyle 1978, 246).

33.2.3   The Decline of the Mandarins and the First Wave of 'Humboldt Myth'

However, at the turn of the century, when Paulsen celebrated the social status of the *Bildungsbürgertum*, its hegemony was already in peril. Central to Ringer's argument is the shift of power between the different factions of the middle classes and a corresponding change in the political mood of the cultured elite. As long as the Humboldtian model was in line with the overall social and economic development, the mood of the mandarins was optimistic, politically progressive (liberal), and socially inclusive. This was the historic era that Ringer calls the 'early industrial phase'. During the 'high industrial phase', starting in the 1860s according to Ringer, the neo-humanist model reached its limits. Notwithstanding the high social standing of the mandarins at the late 1800s – at this time their prestige reached its peak – they could witness that new social groups – the 'industrial classes' – were on the rise and they could anticipate that in the long run their status would decline.

The late 1800s was a time of remarkable economic growth. The transformation of Germany to a strongly industrialized capitalist society was accompanied by substantial social change. On the one hand, the growing group of wealthy industrialists gained political power; on the other hand, the working and lower middle classes demanded social and political rights. The cultivated elite was squeezed between the two opponents of the industrial age. It experienced a status contest and the danger of downward mobility. Modernization, fuelled by economic growth and the political organization of the lower classes threatened to undermine the stable order of social estates in which the educated middle classes enjoyed cultural hegemony.

From the mandarins perspective these developments constituted a 'cultural crisis'. Their ideology now turned defensive, backward looking, politically conservative, and socially exclusive (cf. Bollenbeck 1996). Moreover, it became increasingly chauvinistic. The distinction of a 'spiritual German culture' from the 'shallow civilization' of the western countries, in particular England, provided ideological support for the aggressive imperialistic politics of Germany at the turn of the century.

Most disturbing for the mandarins were the growing tensions between the neo-humanist emphasis on non-utilitarian values and new social and economic demands on education. Technical schools and institutes that had for a long time subordinated to Mandarin hegemony requested equal standing with *Gymnasien* and universities. The mandarins refused claims for more practical and utilitarian forms of education as 'usefulness in the vulgar sense'. The non-classical schools were downgraded as 'schools of useful junk' (Ringer 1969, 29). The quest for academic standing of technical institutes was rejected. Moreover, the mandarins attacked specialized research at universities.[3] "The universities had lost their moral and cultural leadership in a society that was increasingly dominated by shallow utilitarianism and materialism, by the unprincipled interest politics of the mass parties, by the power of money, and by the monotony of the machine age. What was needed was a revitalization of German learning, and a recovery of its philosophical roots in the German neo-humanist and idealist tradition" (Ringer 1986, 157).

The first wave of 'Humboldt myth' (Ash 1997) played an important role in this quest for revitalization. At the turn of the century a Humboldt's essay 'On the internal and external organization of higher academic institutions in Berlin', unpublished and unknown until then, was discovered.[4] This document hit the nerve of the time and triggered the 'invention of Humboldt'. Under reference to Humboldt the mandarins called not only for a renewal of the university. They aimed for a 'spiritual rebirth' of the nation (themselves being the midwives) that would re-establish their hegemony.

33.2.4   Weimar Republic: Climax of the 'Cultural Crisis'

The First World War did not lead to a spiritual rebirth of the nation, but to an unprecedented humiliation of Germany. The home of poets and philosophers was defeated by the powers of shallow civilization. Even worse, the material well-being of the middle classes – simply taking for granted notwithstanding all polemics against

---

[3] It is remarkable that the mandarins were alarmed by a cultural crisis just at the time when their core institutions, the German research universities were at the peak of their international reputation. Global university rankings did not exist in those days but on the bases of the Noble prices that were already awarded it is obvious that the reputation of the leading German universities were comparable to today's American Ivy League institutions.

[4] "Throughout the nineteenth century the term 'Humboldtian university' was not used to characterize the German university system. In the definitions of *Universität* in encyclopaedias, books or speeches of that time, the name of Wilhelm von Humboldt does not even appear. The idea of a new humanistic university appears only marginally, if at all" (Paletschek 2001, 38).

materialism – severely deteriorated. With the exception of a few wartime profiteers the whole country was negatively affected by the economic crisis of the post-war years. But in relative terms the middle classes were hit especially strong. "In 1913 a German higher official earned seven times as much and in 1922 only twice as much as an unskilled labourer. (...) The German government were forced to restrict very severely their expenditures for cultural purposes" (Ringer 1969, 64).

Fiscal crisis led to a deterioration of academic salaries and working conditions at Universities. Prospects for graduates who hoped for employment in the civil service were bleak. The response of academics and students was a fierce opposition to the new government. Right wing extremism spread among students. Mandarins were less radical but they contributed to delegitimize the Democratic regime – of course by referring to Humboldt and the spiritual power of cultivation that was irreconcilable with democracy.[5] "Until 1933, the difference between the intellectual elite of Germany and the extremist right-wing intellectuals was largely a matter of style and tone – for example, the mandarins' main objection to the nationalistic students was that they politicized the university. They regarded the heart of the national movement as "sound". If the anti-intellectual forces had not appeared in jackboots, the mandarins would have appreciated (and misunderstood) them as sharing their own outlook" (Habermans 1971, 426).

33.2.5   The Mandarin Ideology After 1945

Ringer's narrative ends at 1933. But, as Habermas (1971) emphasized in his review of Ringer's book, this was not the end of the Mandarin ideology. Rather 1945 was the birth of the new wave of the "Humboldt myth". The very fact, that the Nazi regime politicized the universities and brutally interfered into academic affairs gave the mandarins ammunition in their request to re-establish the old academic regime.

Although the Mandarin ideology played an important role in undermining the democratic government of the Weimar Republic, it reappeared virtually undamaged after the war and gained hegemony in academe for another two decades. The mandarins successfully downplayed their antidemocratic attitudes during the Weimar Republic and portrayed themselves as victims of the Nazi regime.[6]

---

[5] According to the educational philosopher Eduard Spranger, "the German universities had been disrupted by the 'accelerated speed of the industrial and technological era'. In his opinion, the university crisis could also be attributed to the democratization of education and the 'inevitable reduction in quality associated with it'" (Paletschek 2001, 42).

[6] "According to Jaspers 'it has not yet been possible to destroy the academic spirit'. Until the 1960s and in some aspects until the 1900s, this idea prevented further questions about the previous academic alignment with National Socialism and with racist and völkisch premises. Though many professors had conformed to National Socialism during the Third Reich, they could now hide behind the 'timeless' ideal of Humboldt" (Paletschek 2001, 53).

The Humboldt myth helped to reject the attempts of the occupational powers, in particular the Americans, to democratize the German education system. During the first years after the war the policy of 're-education' had a high priority because the Allies emphasized the connection between the authoritarian and social selective education system and the antidemocratic features of German society (Schildt and Siegfried 2009, 45). In the late 1940s this policy was discontinued, first because the Allies could not overcome the strong resistance of the Mandarin intellectuals; second because the beginning of the cold war changed the political priorities.

Thus the mandarins successfully re-established the old regime of higher learning at the *Gymnsasium* and the university. Habermas – in the review of Ringer's book – confirmed that the Mandarin culture was "still in existence and taken for granted when I was a student in the early 1950s" (Habermas 1971, 423). The post-war years were characterized by a tension between a dynamic political and economic development on the one hand and a cultural stagnation on the other hand. The transformation of Germany and Austria to democracies and welfare economies raised the level of political participation and affluence of the general population. But in the cultural sphere the Mandarin hegemony led to the persistence of an elite pattern that reserved higher learning for an aristocracy of the mind. It took two more decades to leverage mass participation in higher education.

33.3   NPM, Bologna, and the 'Death of Humboldt'

The 1960s marked a definitive turning point in the academic culture of the Germanic countries. The long perseverance of Mandarin hegemony came to an end. This was partly caused by legal reforms, such as the reform of university governance that weakened the dominance of the academic oligarchy by including junior faculty and students into collegial bodies. Most important, however, was the rapid expansion of student enrolments that inevitably eroded the elite model aiming for an intellectual aristocracy. Although massification of higher education was slow in Germany and Austria compared to most other OECD countries, it was sufficient to irreversibly change the teaching conditions.

And yet the neo-humanist model did not disappear completely. It survived in a paradoxical form, as an ideologically façade, increasingly being in contradiction with the realities of mass higher education, but nevertheless influencing the teaching conditions. It served as an ideology that denied the need for change and delayed structural reforms. The concept of the cultural state, a key factor of the neo-humanist model, was maintained although the premises and prerequisites of that concept were no longer valid. Governments were no longer benevolent patrons that funded universities without any strings attached but they increasingly demanded economic relevance. However, the majority of academics (in particular at humanities and social sciences) still insisted that Universities are institutions of non-utilitarian cultivation. It was easy to ignore external requests for relevance as long as the old governance model was maintained. Policy makers and state bureaucrats had no power to enforce their demands because they had no effective influence on internal academic decisions. Tensions increased[7] but that individual autonomy of academics was still protected by constitutional law.

The consequence was an increasing alienation between the academic and the political sphere and an erosion of mutual trust. Trust, however, is the indispensable prerequisite for the functioning of the cultural state model. Austria and Germany thus entered the period of mass higher education with a governance model that has lost its functionality.

It was only in the 1990s when a new wave of governmental reforms seriously challenged the core concept of the neo-humanist ideology. There were two main roads of reform that are, however, closely interconnected: a new governance regime that ended a 200 years dominance of the cultural state and introduced new public management (NPM) to the world of higher learning. And a fundamental reform of the "study architecture" that was undertaken at the European level (Bologna process). Both reforms were and are strongly rejected by the majority of academics and also by most of those students who are actively involved in higher education policy (which is, however, a minority of students). This resistance triggered a new wave of the "Humboldt myth". The following sections will discuss why NPM and Bologna are regarded as a violation of traditional academic values.

33.3.1   NPM – A Farewell to the 'Cultural State'

In the neo-humanist concept, governance of universities is based on the idealist notion of a benevolent state paternalism. Academic freedom has not to be defended against the state but is guaranteed by the state. The cultural state is not a threat to academic autonomy, but rather its guardian. "The important point is that the nation and, through it, the state were defined as creatures and as agents of the mandarins' cultural ideas" (Ringer 1969, 117). The claim by neo-humanists is that funding universities by public money without any strings attached is ultimately in the best interest of the state. "It would become a vehicle, a worldly agent of form for the preservation and dissemination of spiritual values. Indeed, it would seek its legitimacy in this action, and it would be rewarded by finding it there. The state earns the support of the learned elite, who would serve it not only as trained officials but also as theoretical sponsors and defenders" (Ringer 1969, 116). The autonomous university protected by the enlightened government against interference of particularistic interests (meaning utilitarian goals) gives legitimacy to the state and trains its civil servants and teachers.

Humboldt originally favoured a different concept. He suggested that the university should be made financially independent from the state. The state should

---

[7] "The clash of cultures could not be stronger: what one side views as a necessary condition for work that benefits society at large, the other interprets as a profound lack of interest in the needs of society. Deeply distrustful, policy-makers have come to read 'autonomy' as 'irresponsibility'" (Schimank 2005, 372).

provide a grant and the university should subsequently be able to administer this endowment autonomously. This liberal concept that has great affinity with the funding arrangements for public universities in North America was rejected by the Prussian minister of the interior on the grounds that it would be too dangerous for the government to grant academic and financial autonomy at the same time. In his words: "However exalted the heads may be, the stomachs we always maintain their rights against them .... He who rules the latter will always be able to deal with the former" (Ringer 1969, 112). For Humboldt – whose liberal attitudes were similar to those of Adam Smith – the paternalistic concept of the cultural state was a 'plan B' after his original proposal of a financially autonomous university failed. Nevertheless the cultural state has become one of the cornerstones of every version of the Humboldt myth that has evolved since the early 1900s.

Based on this concept the university had a dual nature: it was a state agency, subject to political regulation, and at the same time an autonomous corporation, governed by the academic oligarchy. "The Universities had the statutory right to manage their own purely academic affairs; but only full professors participated in the exercise of this partial autonomy. From among themselves, the professors at each institution elected a rector and a Senate every year. Neither had anything like the powers of an American college president or faculty; but the Rector did function as a general representative and spokes man for the university and the Senate ruled in matters of academic discipline" (Ringer 1969, 36).

This governance pattern requires a high level of trust between state and universities. This prerequisite was not always fulfilled. During the first half of the nineteenth century government officials were quite suspicious of politically progressive academics. After all, the leaders of the revolution of 1848 came predominantly from the educated middle classes, many of them being academics. At the end of the nineteenth century, the Mandarin culture has by and large embraced the values of the authoritarian government, resulting in a high level of mutual trust. There was no need for governments to violate academic freedom because academics on their own discriminated against Jews and Social Democrats.[8] One of the very few academics who openly addressed this hypocrisy was Max Weber who declared in an open letter that "the freedom of learning exists only within the limits of officially accepted political and religious views" (cf. Ringer 1969, 143). During the Weimar Republic the trust between the new Democratic government and the majority of academics eroded. The rejection of democracy by the Mandarin culture significantly contributed to the weakening and undermining of the new political regime. After the war, relationships improved and it seemed that governments again acted as benevolent patrons. Starting with the late 1960s, the initiatives by governments to increase postsecondary participation and to democratize universities created new fields of conflict. These contradict eventually led to the substitution of the cultural state model by NPM.

---

[8] Ringer (1969) has documented several 'cases' of that kind: Valentin case (p. 57), Arons case (p. 141), Spahn case (p. 142), Michels case (p. 143).

NPM introduced two kinds of radical change: firstly, a reconstruction of the relationship between state and universities. Funding is no longer based on state paternalism but on performance contracts. Secondly, a modification in internal governance. The old type of rector who was a 'primus inter pares' without decision making power was substituted by a university management similar to that of public universities in North America (Pechar 2005). NPM was implemented more radical in Austria than in Germany (Lanzendorf 2006) but the direction of the reform is the same in both countries.

Academics and students strongly oppose to this reform. Obviously NPM violates the neo-humanist principles of cultivation for its own sake. For academics, in particular for full professors, NPM means a limitation of individual autonomy. In the old regime "institutional autonomy of the university is low, whilst the autonomy of individual professors is high. (...) With their 'freedom of teaching and research', chairholders are comparable to small businessmen with staffs of subordinates. But as civil servants, they also enjoy the special rights of an occupational group that has complete job security. To put it in a nutshell, chair-holders are small businessmen who cannot go bankrupt" (Schimank 2005, 363). In NPM, institutional autonomy is increased at the expense of individual autonomy. The management increasingly concludes performance contracts within the institution and enforces a culture of accountability.

From the perspective of students the new governance model is ambiguous. On the one hand it will increase the service orientation of universities with students being the main beneficiaries. On the other hand the new university management is eager to abolish the laissez-faire culture of teaching and learning that is legitimized with reference to Humboldt. While it is questionable whether this culture really serves the interests students (after all it results in an excessive duration of studies and high dropout), many students love it because it allows procrastination. The Bologna process can be regarded as the intersection of these two strands of reform.

33.3.2 The Bologna Philosophy: Laissez-Faire Culture Under Attack

The lack of effective leadership in universities – due to the perseverance of the traditional governance model – retarded structural reforms that would allow to cope with the new realities of mass higher education. The mandarins could not prevent massification of universities but they were successful in maintaining a culture of teaching and learning that is inadequate for mass participation. It is the neo-humanist laissez-faire approach[9] for teaching and learning that was tailored for small elite universities.

---

[9] This laissez-faire approach is equally attractive to left wing academics and students. They have a completely different notion of 'cultivation' – not to immerse oneself in classical cultures, but to sharpen 'critical thinking'; but like the Mandarins they regard the non-utilitarian character of the curriculum as a safeguard for academic freedom.

Ringer describes the culture of teaching and learning during the nineteenth century as follows: universities "did not supervise their students programs of study, nor did they test or grade class performance. They had to enrol any applicant who had earned the privilege on the basis of the classical Abitur (…). Once registered, a student could prepare himself in whatever way he chose for the next step along the road of examinations and privileges. Usually, his first concern was to pass one of the standard state examinations and thus to earn the official "diploma" in his field of study" (Ringer 1969, 32).

The laissez-faire culture provided a splendid environment for intellectual growth for a few highly talented students; it is not suited for less able students. As long as universities where elite institutions that were supposed to cater only for the very best, the laissez-faire culture was consistent with the profile of universities and the societal expectations upon them. With the advent of mass higher education, universities were confronted with new demands and expectations. Even at a time when the substance of the neo-humanist concept of higher learning was eroded by the pressures of mas-sification, the façade that was still left served as an excuse for avoiding structural reforms (in course structure and in the delivery of content) that would adjust the Germanic universities to the requirements of mass higher education.

The Humboldtian narratives serve as a powerful legitimation for resistance of struc-tural reforms. This of course did not prevent structural change, but this change hap-pened in rather chaotic form, it was an unwelcome by-product of ever growing student's enrolment. In particular the formula of "unity of teaching and research" is used as a defence against initiatives to improve the quality of teaching. It serves as an excuse for regarding teaching as a by-product of research that does not deserve special attention in its own right. This is most obvious in the refusal of didactics at universities, which is regarded as a mechanism of making the curriculum more school like. From a Humboldtian view, however, it is the very nature of higher learning that students must acquire the full scholarly content without "artificial" didactical auxiliary means.

We should, however, not over emphasize the neglect of teaching as a special feature of the Germanic academic culture. In all countries academics at research universities typically value research higher than teaching – not only due to their intrinsic interest and curiosity, but also due to the reward structures of this profes-sion. For that reason, complaints of students, policymakers, and the general public about universities neglecting their teaching duties sound familiar all over the world. However, in many other countries there are counter-forces that balance the aca-demic preference for research: universities compete for students rather than trying to avoid them; and this competitive struggle is endorsed by a strong management. All these factors were missing in the traditional Humboldtian university. The Humboldtian tradition provides exceptionally strong ideological ammunition against structural reforms.

Let us – as one example – look to the resistance against the modularization of study courses in the Bologna study architecture:

• Modules have to be organized in a meaningful structure; typically this structure serves as a guideline for the sequence in which the single modules should be taken. This contradicts the emphasis on individual freedom and responsibility of students in the Humboldtian concept. Hence the refusal of structured curricula, which regarded as "school-like", is one source of opposition against modularization.

- Modularization is regarded as a destruction of a holistic and integrated form of cultivation of the mind. It is viewed as disintegrating the content of higher learning into unrelated little bits and bytes that prevent a deeper understanding of the knowledge base.
- The hidden implication of this view is a confirmation of the elite nature of higher education. The opposition to modularization is fully consistent with the idea that only a small elite can achieve a truly cultivated mind. This elitist concept is not compatible with the idea of incremental steps (= accumulation of credits), it is based on that assumption that one either can have a full education or no education at all (either the whole thing or nothing). In this way, it significantly raises the risk of an investment in higher education and thus protects the educated upper middle class against upward mobility from the lower social strata.

Equally strong is the resistance against a clear structure of study courses at the bachelor level that limits the freedom of students to decide when they take exams, how long they stay enrolled etc. "Humboldtian values encompass two freedoms: those of teaching and learning. The professors must be free to teach truth and knowledge as they see it, and the students must be free to learn independently and grow without being spoon-fed (verschult) or constantly tested. Allegiance to the Humboldtian concept of freedom underlies the academic conventions of allowing students to take their examinations when they feel ready to do so (rather than at times set by the university), and of being reluctant to present them with fixed course length, content and timetables" (Pritchard 2006, 510).

The Bologna architecture is not compatible with this concept of freedom. To a large extent students' resistance to Bologna is due to this 'clash of values'. A good example is the present controversy in the German, universities about the forced exmatriculation of long-term students. In Germany about 40,000 students, that is 3% of the whole students enrollment, is enrolled for more than 20 semesters.[10] By increasing efficiency and complying with the regime of performance contracts most universities try to get rid of these 'dinosaurs'. Many students see the freedom of teaching and research endangered by this movement. Recently a student who is enrolled for 48 semesters lost a lawsuit against his University that has exmatriculated him.[11] The most extreme case is the student who is enrolled for 108 semesters.[12]

---

[10] http://www.spiegel.de/unispiegel/studium/0,1518,764373,00.html

[11] http://www.spiegel.de/unispiegel/studium/0,1518,787449,00.html

[12] http://www.spiegel.de/unispiegel/studium/0,1518,784016,00.html

33.4 Conclusion

In all academic cultures educational institutions, universities in particular, mostly react with delay and opposition to social and economic change. And yet the resistance of the higher education community in German-speaking countries against the Bologna process and governance reforms stands out due to its fundamentalist nature fueled by the Humboldtian legacy. This paper has argued that the realities of mass higher education in Austria and Germany are in sharp contrast with the neo-humanist concept of higher learning. But despite this, the Humboldtian concept has survived in the odd form of a jargon that has developed a life on its own. It constitutes a parallel universe in order to escape the pressures of mass higher education.

The core of the Humboldtian ideology is the insistence on the exceptional nature of cultivation in universities that is supposedly incomparable to any other form of learning. The learning experience in universities is not interpreted in terms of gradual differences to other types of education, but as something qualitatively unmatchable. Today it would be politically unacceptable to express this view in the phrase of an 'intellectual aristocracy'. But the connecting line to this ideology of the nineteenth century is obvious. The Humboldtian ideology will neither acknowledge that academics in mass higher education systems can no longer act as 'god among the angels' (cf. Amaral et al. 2012), nor that student exceptionalism disappears when the participation rate exceeds a certain threshold (cf. Klemenčič 2012).

This ideology is incapable to deal with the trade-offs with which decision makers in complex higher education systems are necessarily faced. As a consequence, many controversial issues in higher education policy are over many years caught in a deadlock, characterized by irreconcilable fronts. Examples are the fundamentalist debates on tuition fees in Germany and Austria or the heated conflict on admission policy in Austria (Pechar 2009). In each of these cases higher education appears as an unmatchable good for which the ordinary rules of social and economic life are invalidated.

The opposition to the Bologna process and to governance reforms is just another example of this pattern. Complex policies of that kind require a balance of pros and cons. Recent research has pointed to some negative side effects and unintended consequences of these reforms (cf. Amaral et al. 2012; Moscati 2012). A productive theoretical discussion of such problems that eventually might result in policy measures requires a balanced approach, not a fundamentalist opposition.

Will the Humboldt myth resist the present wave of policy reforms? This ideology was often pronounced dead and yet has surprised by its longevity. Nevertheless one might argue that the controversy about Bologna and NPM could be the final battle of the 'Humboldt warriors'. It could be that the abolition of the 'cultural state' by the NPM reform has dispossessed the institutional base for advocates of the Humboldtian ideology. After all the cultural state – separating external and internal academic affairs – was a precondition for the neo-humanist façade that has for many years obscured the realities of mass higher education. The state bureaucracy micro-managed the external affairs (financial and administrative matters) while academics maintained the laissez-faire culture of teaching and learning. The new governance pattern that internalizes the financial and administrative responsibility is less conducive to this laissez-faire culture. The new rectors who no longer feel 'first among equals' but have managerial power are interested in increasing the efficiency of teaching and in reducing drop out and the duration of studies. Unlike the state bureaucracy that had the same interest during the old governance regime, the new rectors have much more influence on the internal academic affairs and are able to change the culture of teaching and learning.

It is this change in the academic culture that has triggered a new wave of the Humboldt myth. However, it the older cohorts of academics who predominantly oppose to these reforms with reference to the Humboldtian legacy. For the professional socialization of these cohorts the neo-humanist jargon was much more influential than for younger academics. Furthermore, a higher percentage of these younger academic cohorts has international experience (e.g. as post-docs) and is acquainted with other academic cultures. They have on average a more positive attitude to Bologna and the new governance regime and are less in favour of the Humboldt myth.[13] As the attitudes of students are strongly influenced by their academic teachers, one might expect that the impact of the Humboldtian legacy on higher education policy will decline in the years to come.

References

Amaral, A., Tavares, O., & Santos, C. (2012). Higher education reforms in Europe: A comparative perspective of new legal frameworks in Europe. In A. Curaj, P. Scott, & L. Vlasceanu (Eds.), *European higher education at the crossroads: Between the Bologna process and national reforms*. Dordrecht: Springer.

Ash, M. G. (Ed.). (1997). *German universities – Past and future: Crisis or renewal*. Providence: Berghahn Books.

Bollenbeck, G. (1996). *Bildung und Kultur. Glanz und Elend eines deutschen Deutungsmusters*. Frankfurt/Main: Suhrkamp.

ESU. (2009). *Bologna with students eyes*. Brussels: ESU.

Habermas, J. (1971). The intellectual and social background of the German university crisis. *Minerva, 9*, 422–428.

Klemenčič, M. (2012). The changing conceptions of student participation in higher education governance in the EHEA. In A. Curaj, P. Scott, & L. Vlasceanu (Eds.), *European higher education at the crossroads: Between the Bologna process and national reforms*. Dordrecht: Springer.

Lanzendorf, U. (2006). Austria – from hesitation to rapid breakthrough. In B. Kehm & U. Lanzendorf (Eds.), *Reforming university governance. Changing conditions for research in four European countries* (pp. 99–134). Bonn: Lemmens.

Moscati, R. (2012). University governance in changing European systems of higher education. In A. Curaj, P. Scott, & L. Vlasceanu (Eds.), *European higher education at the crossroads: Between the Bologna process and national reforms*. Dordrecht: Springer.

O'Boyle, L. (1978). A possible model for the study of nineteenth-century secondary education in Europe. *Journal of Social History, 12*(2), 236–247.

---

[13] A recent survey among Austrian academics reveals strong differences in the attitudes towards the new governance model. Older academic cohorts (who are still civil servants) are more likely to dismiss this model than younger cohorts with private employment contracts.

O'Boyle, L. (1983). Learning for its own sake: The German university as nineteenth-century model. *Comparative Studies in Society and History, 25*(1), 3–25.

Paletschek, S. (2001). The invention of Humboldt and the impact of national socialism. The German University idea in the first half of the twentieth century. In M. Szöllösi-Janze (Ed.), *Science in the Third Reich* (pp. 37–58). Oxford: Berg.

Pechar, H. (2005). Backlash or modernisation? Two reform cycles in Austrian higher education. In A. Amaral, M. Kogan, & A. Gornitzka (Eds.), *Reform and change in higher education. Analysing policy implementations* (pp. 269–285). Dordrecht: Springer.

Pechar, H. (2009). Can research universities survive without control over admission? Reflections on Austria's exceptionalism in higher education policy. *Journal of Adult and Continuing Education, 15*(2), 142–154.

Pritchard, R. (2006). Trends in the restructuring of German universities. *Comparative Education Review, 50*(1), 90–112.

Ringer, F. (1969). *The decline of the German mandarins. The German academic community 1890–1933*. Cambridge: Harvard University Press.

Ringer, F. (1979). *Education and society in modern Europe*. Bloomington: Indiana University Press.

Ringer, F. (1986). Differences and cross-national similarities among mandarins. *Comparative Studies in Society and History, 28*(1), 145–164.

Schildt, A., & Siegfried, D. (2009). *Deutsche Kulturgeschichte*. Die Bundesrepublik von 1945 bis zur Gegenwart, München, Hanser.

Schimank, U. (2005). 'New public management' and the academic profession: Reflections on the German situation. *Minerva, 43*, 361–376.

Schimank, U. (2009, April). *Humboldt: Falscher Mann am falschen Ort* (FAZ, 17). http://www.faz.net/artikel/C30901/hochschulreform-humboldt-falscher-mann-am-falschen-ort-30127687.html

Schulmeister, R., & Metzger, C. (Hrsg.). (2011). *Die Workload im Bachelor. Zeitbudget und Studierverhalten*. Münster: Waxmann.

Schultheis, F., Cousin, P. F., & Escoda, M. R. (2008). *Humboldts Albtraum. Der Bologna-Prozess und seine Folgen*. Konstanz: UVK.

Weber, M. (1972). *Wirtschaft und Gesellschaft*. Tübingen: Mohr.

Chapter 34
The Changing Conceptions of Student Participation in HE Governance in the EHEA

Manja Klemenčič

34.1 Introduction

Student participation in HE governance is considered one of the foundational values in European HE. Different models of student participation can be traced back to medieval universities. In the Bologna University students were organised in a federation of student guilds and were in control of the organisation – not curriculum – of their studies and 'supervised' the professors to the extent that professors needed to make a financial deposit from which fines could be deducted if professors defected on certain agreed aspects of teaching or left town without permission (Haskins 1923: 1–36). A different model of student involvement evolved in Paris where the guild of professors – the masters – shared control over university with a student rector – a young master – elected by the students (ibid.). Student participation in governance resurges again prominently in 1960s and 1970s as part of student revolts resulting in significant governance reforms encompassing also new provisions on student participation. Perhaps the most significant changes were achieved in Germany with *Gruppenuniversitäten* emerging depicting a tripartite model of governance with the professoriate, non-professorial academics, and students represented in equal numbers in most institutional decision making bodies (de Boer and Stensaker 2007). Other countries in continental Europe also reformed their HE legislation towards a democratic governance model, which stipulates that universities as public institutions ought to be governed democratically, and that this implies the participation of all politically significant constituencies, including – and especially – students. Consequently, students as a collective body are in some way represented in the HE governance in basically every European country (Bergan 2004; Persson 2004).

M. Klemenčič (✉)
Faculty of Education – Centre for Educational Policy Studies, University of Ljubljana,
Kardeljeva ploščad 16, SI-1000 Ljubljana, Slovenia
e-mail: manja.klemencic@guest.arnes.si

A. Curaj et al. (eds.), *European Higher Education at the Crossroads:*
Between the Bologna Process and National Reforms,
DOI 10.1007/978-94-007-3937-6_34, © Springer Science+Business Media Dordrecht 2012

Accordingly we can find advanced – but also highly diversified – systems of student representation.

The issue of student participation in HE governance has featured prominently in policy making within the Bologna Process. The European Ministers referred to student participation in affirmative terms in every Communiqué after the Prague Ministerial Summit in 2001. European Students' Union [ESU], the representative platform of the European national unions of students, was granted a consultative membership and has participated in the governing structures of the Process. Yet, despite this intense political involvement on the European level, ESU continues to report deteriorating student influence when it comes to institutional governance (ESU 2009, 2011a, b). This raises questions about the interactions and interrelations between student participation as a concept and social phenomenon and EHEA policy developments.

The chapter addresses the ideational and normative foundations of student participation emerging from the two – intertwined – policy developments: the Bologna Process and the 'modernisation agenda for universities'. The factors influencing the governments' and institutional choices regarding HE policy and strategy are no longer bound to the national context. Prior to the Bologna Process the national HE policies were formulated using international cross-country comparisons as a tool for reflection (Huisman et al. 2001). After the initiation of the Bologna Process, a new forum evolved providing a space for various policy issues to emerge, develop and possibly diffuse into the national and institutional levels (Kehm et al. 2009). Indeed, the Bologna Process transformed HE policy making 'from an almost exclusively national affair with some international influences to one where national policy is systematically considered within a Europe-wide framework' (Westerheijden et al. 2010: 38). During the same time, the adoption of the Education and Training 2010 Programme (Council 2001), which was linked to the Lisbon Agenda, created enabling conditions for deeper HE policy making within the European Union. HE became to be seen as one of the key drivers of the economic competitiveness stipulated by the Lisbon Agenda, and the policy recommendations called for HE reforms to serve this role better. A series of influential policy documents followed referred to collectively as the 'modernisation agenda for European HE' (EC 2003, 2005, 2006, 2008a, b). Both, policy developments have become closely intertwined. In fact, scholarly work suggests that Bologna initiatives had been 're-addressed in the light of the Lisbon Agenda' (Capano and Piattoni 2011: 586; Keeling 2006).

In view of these policy developments, this chapter poses the question as to what conceptual and normative foundations regarding student participation emerge from the Bologna recommendations and the modernisation agenda for universities. The investigation focuses on the changes to the four main relationship constellations involving students: between the state and students, between university and students, between the academics and students, and between student representatives and students. The chapter suggests that the analysis of these interdependent relationships can give us a more comprehensive explanation of the changes in the conception of student participation in the development within the EHEA.

In the following sections, this chapter first (Sect. 34.2) develops and analytical approach to investigation of student participation in the EHEA. The analytical approach takes into account the diverse domains, the varying degrees and the multilevel character of student participation. The following section (Sect. 34.3) focuses on the ideational and normative foundation regarding student participation as constructed within the policy space of the EHEA. Concretely, the chapter reviews how student participation has featured within the Bologna Ministerial Communiqués and who the key protagonists of these ideas were. The next section (Sect. 34.4) describes the changes in European HE systems stemming from the European Union's 'modernisation agenda for universities'. The subsections depict the implications of this policy development on the four relationship constellations involving students: (Sect. 34.4.1) state/students – (Sect. 34.4.2) university/students – (Sect. 34.4.3) professoriate/students – (Sect. 34.4.4) representative student organisations/students. The concluding section analyses how these evolving relationships interact and impact on the changing notions of student participation in HE governance.

34.2   Analytical Approach to Investigation of Student Participation in the EHEA

Within the EHEA policy discourse (as well as in the majority of scholarly literature), student participation has tended to be addressed as a simple, undifferentiated phenomenon referring to student influence in the institutional governance. This chapter proposes a more comprehensive analytical approach to the investigation of student participation. It adopts the basic – common-sense – definition of student participation as students' formal and/or actual ability to influence decisions made in the context of a HE institution or administration; but it qualifies it in terms of (a) the multilevel nature, (b) the extent, and (c) the degree arguing that student participation is – inevitably – a complex, multifaceted phenomenon.

(a) The multilevel nature of student participation comes from the observation that both HE governance and student representation are conducted within multilevel systems. As discussed earlier, the European-level policy making have stretched previously nationally governed HE policy making to be conducted also on the supranational level. At the same time, subnational levels – both regional and institutional – are also gaining strength in HE governance (de Boer and File 2009). And, in any case, the most vital decisions regarding the conduct of HE – on teaching and learning and research – still take place on the departmental level (Lizzio and Wilson 2009; Pabian and Minksová 2011). Such multilevel governance of HE inevitably induces multilevel student representation.

ESU congregates the national representative student organisations. These are the ones recognized to represent student interests on the national level, either through legal provisions or informally by the governments. In a majority of cases the line of organizing goes from individual students who elect their representatives – directly or via faculty – to institutional representative student organisations. On the national level, these come together in a national student union or a network of regional or institutional organisations. Just as the models of HE governance vary across countries, regions and institutions (Paradeise et al. 2009; de Boer and File 2009) so do also models of student representation and concomitantly their participatory mechanisms. Both models are embedded in the national legislative and historical context, and the closer one investigates them, the more evident are the differences.

That there is a great variety of national models of student representation is well known in practice, but largely absent from scholarly literature (Klemenčič 2011a, b). All representative student organisations are similar in that their representatives participate in HE governance on national and institutional level, they provide student services, and they congregate within the European Students' Union. Yet there are significant differences among them in terms of their governance – even on basic parameters such as whether their existence is stipulated in primary legislation or not; whether their membership is automatic, compulsory or voluntary; what and how stable their sources of financing are; and what their political structures are (council, union or both). These differences reflect the different models of student interest intermediation and they effect the various relationship constellations involving students, and hence student participation.

(b) The 'domain' of student participation in this chapter is extended to include, in addition to the formal area of governing and management, also the areas of quality assurance [QA], and student-centred learning. Typically, the studies of student participation refer only to the various areas of governing and the underlying regulative decisions (e.g. regarding institutional mission and profiles, budgetary and financial, study programmes and curriculum), i.e. the areas of *'formal participation'* (Persson 2004). There is, however, an emerging awareness that *'informal participation'*, such as in QA and student centred learning, may be equally important from the standpoint of achieving 'academic democracy' since these domains too create opportunities for and experiences of democratic involvement (Molander 2002; Boland 2005; Menon 2003, 2005; Bartley et al. 2010; Klemenčič 2010).

In fact, all of these different domains of student participation are interlinked and may be mutually reinforcing. Biesta (2007: 4) argues that HE institutions 'always already are sites of citizenship, simply because they are part of the lives of those who 'inhabit' such institutions, either as students or as staff, and as such provide a range of experiences that are potentially significant for civic learning […]'. At the same time, 'the most significant "lessons" in citizenship actually are the result of what people learn from their participation (or for that matter: nonparticipation) in the communities and practices that make up their everyday life' (ibid.). According to these notions, academic democracy does not include only the student involvement in university senates and boards, but also individual students' participation in, for example, course evaluations, and in the great variety of student-led 'extracurricular' activities that compose the overall student experience. Institutions can create enabling conditions for such involvement, and link it to the curricular activities, and thus not only offer practical opportunities for active democratic participation, but they also transmit norms, values and attitudes to this effect.

The Bologna Process has made significant advances in the area of QA, and student participation has been affirmed as an integral aspect of it (Brus et al. 2007; Gibbs and Ashton 2007; Bologna Process 2003, 2005b). Similarly, modernisation agenda also propagates QA and highlight involvement of all stakeholders, including students. Student participation is specifically mentioned both in the external procedures and in the internal QA of programmes and awards, as well as in the evaluation of the QA agencies which need to show that they have a 'strategy for student participation' (Bologna Process 2005b: 16, 21, 37). The terms of student involvement in QA vary from being consulted in surveys, institutional self-assessment reports and external reviews to being involved as members (with varying degrees of responsibilities) of internal self-evaluation groups, external review panels and consultative bodies of national QA agencies. Finally, students can also be involved in the governing aspects of QA within institutions and within external QA bodies.[1]

Related to QA, we are also witnessing development of informal student participation in the context of institutional efforts to enhance the 'total student learning experience'. The UK is at the forefront of this development with the National Student Survey[2] conducted annually across all publicly funded HE institutions surveying students' learning experience in terms of teaching, assessment and feedback, academic support, learning resources, and also personal development. Another related survey is the Times Higher Awards for 'Best Student Experience' which evaluates HE institutions also on indicators such as good community atmosphere, extracurricular activities and societies and good student union.[3] It is not surprising that HE institutions striving to improve their ratings in such surveys seek to involve more systematically individual students and student groups and organisations into institutional efforts to enhance student experience. The emphasis is on amplifying 'student voice' through a new style of student engagement that would ultimately lead to enhanced student learning experience and better met student expectations. The idea is to develop institutional and student union processes and practices, such as those relating to student representation, student feedback and student services, to 'enhance the collective student learning experience, as distinct from specific teaching, learning and assessment activities that are designed to enhance individual students' engagement with their own learning' (Little et al. 2009: 3).

Finally, the renaissance of student centred learning in the EHEA implies enabling conditions for informal student participation in the organisation and the processes and contents of teaching, and thus increased control over own

---

[1] For more details see Chap. 20 by Palomares.

[2] See http://www.thestudentsurvey.com/. Accessed 25 Oct 2011.

[3] See http://www.timeshighereducation.co.uk/story.asp?storycode=415180. Accessed 25 Oct 2011.

learning (Bologna Process 2009).[4] In terms of the domains, student involvement in student centred learning takes place in the micro-environment of the classroom in the interactions between professors and students; it is, however, not confined to this domain. Similarly as in the case of QA, a systematic institutional approach is required and that needs to be supported by appropriate institutional polices (ESU and EI 2010). Hence students participate in the consultative role feeding into the design of practices; and formally in the governing structures deciding on policies and strategies regarding student centred learning on all levels of HE governance.

(c) The degree of participation is another defining element in the social meaning and effects of student participation. The degree of participation ranges from access to information as the basic degree of participation, to consultation and dialogue, and finally to partnership as the highest degree (Klemenčič 2011a: 12–13). Access to information is the basis for all subsequent levels of participation. It implies a one-way provision of information from the administration to representative student bodies. At the level of consultation, the administration solicits student representatives' opinion on specific issues. The (structured) dialogue is a more advanced form of participation since student representative bodies and administration hold regular (formal or informal) exchange of views built on mutual interests and potentially shared objectives. Practically this means that student representatives are involved in various consultative committees where they perform advisory functions or are informally consulted on a regular basis. They have opportunities to launch their own agenda issues. They do not, however, have formal decision-making powers, i.e. voting or veto rights. This degree of participation is reached only through partnership which implies shared responsibilities in each step of the institutional decision-making process: agenda setting, drafting, decision-taking, implementation and monitoring of institutional decisions. While most of the policy references in the Bologna Process are concerned with the question whether there should be student involvement, the profound differences between the different degrees of participation point to the need to qualify how student participation should be exercised.

While we cannot ignore the diversity of HE governance structures, nor the diversity of forms of student representation across Europe, there is, however, evidence of overarching reform processes with profound effects on the conception of students' role and on the key relationship constellations involving the students: with the state, university and academics, and within the student body itself. The EHEA policies offer one impetus for reforms. The other impetus comes from the modernisation agenda for universities containing the paradigm of a new public management approach to university governance and implying changes in the relationship between the state and HE institutions. The mechanisms and instruments that follow from this approach have – so this chapter

---

[4]For more details see Chap. 9 by Attard and Geven.

argues – significantly transformed the conceptions of students, the various relationship constellations involving students, and ultimately the conceptions of student participation in HE governance.

34.3   Student Participation as an EHEA Principle

In the context of the Bologna Process, there has been virtually unprecedented political affirmation of student participation in HE governance by European Ministers. The Ministers have spoken in favour of both: student involvement in the policy making towards the emerging EHEA (Bologna Process 2001), and student participation in the HE decision-making on all levels: institutional, national and European (Bologna Process 2001, 2010). In fact, student participation emerged as one of the EHEA principles, and in several variations as: (a) a procedural principle, (b) a substantial value and (c) a policy objective.[5]

(a) Student representation was 'neither foreseen nor much talked about at the Bologna Conference' (Bergan 2004: 3; see also Klemenčič 2011b). ESU[6] – not formally involved with drafting Bologna Declaration – expressed regret and hope 'that in future discussions, NUSes will be consulted at the national level and that ESIB will be consulted at the European level' (ESU 1999). ESU's demands fell on fruitful ground as there was a shared concern among the participants to adopt a more participatory approach to the Process governance.[7] Representatives of stakeholders that would be affected by the policies were invited to participate in the Process to contribute to effective policy-making and implementation as well as for the legitimization of the Process. Some Ministers – especially from the countries with corporatist tradition of student interest intermediation – actively pushed for it (Bergan 2004; Klemenčič 2011b). The more reluctant ones – from countries will less developed structures and traditions of student representation – could be persuaded on the account that students, which appeared in favour of the reforms, could be an important ally to governments requesting changes where institutions may be more reluctant to implement them. Ultimately, given the predominant model of participatory HE governance across Europe, to involve students (and other stakeholders) effectively meant that 'the Bologna Process would be in better conformity with the situation in most of its constituent parties' (Bergan 2004: 3).

---

[5] For more on EHEA principles guiding the discussion below see Chap. 2 by Zgaga.

[6] At that time, ESU still went by its previous name ESIB-The National Unions of Students in Europe.

[7] Notably, at the same time the European Commission's – also participating in the Process – was developing a new approach to its own governance which among several other issues has highlighted participation of civil society in all stages of the policy process (EC 2001).

Student participation began to emerge as a procedural principle with the Prague Communiqué (Bologna Process 2001) which paved the way for formal student participation: '*the involvement of universities and other HE institutions and of students as competent, active and constructive partners in the establishment and shaping of a European HE Area is needed and welcomed*'. ESU was acknowledged as the sole representative of the students and, in 2003, together with several other stakeholders obtained consultative membership (Bologna Process 2003). Effectively this meant that ESU and other consultative members were involved in a structured dialogue with governments (and the European Commission); with speaking, but no formal decision making rights or rights to veto, and no possibility to assume formal positions of a chair of the governing bodies. Given the consensual nature of Bologna Processes' decision making such status implies *de facto* considerable influence. The relative weakness of ESU compared to the full members comes perhaps from the lack of competences to assume the chairing role. The role of a chair in consensual negotiation settings has been shown to carry a considerable leverage by the way of agenda setting and brokerage (Tallberg 2004).

At the same time, there were new opportunity structures opening up for ESU within the EHEA. ESU assumed a role also in several 'spin-off' initiatives within EHEA. For example, ESU became a formal partner in the new European Network of Quality Assurance Agencies. An informal 'E4 Group' was formed within the Process consisting of ESU, ENQA, EUA and EURASHE to represent the views of the stakeholders and to offer expert participation within the various Bologna-related processes, such as the developments of the European Qualifications Framework, and the European Register for Quality Assurance Agencies in HE. There has also been a visible increase in ESU's participation in EU-funded projects, both as a lead coordinating party and as a partner in joint projects (Klemenčič 2011b).

ESU strengthened its organisational capacity and further professionalised maintaining quality input into the process (Klemenčič 2011b). It used its role to bring several of its most salient policy issues onto the agenda of the Bologna Process. One of them has been strengthening student participation in institutional and national HE governance, and others include the recognition of the multiple purposes of education, the social dimension in HE including consolidation of the principle of education as a public good and public responsibility. The real strength of ESU in the Bologna Process has been, as Sjur Bergan of the Council of Europe suggests, that 'student representatives [...] certainly stood up for student rights but [...] have not seen their mission only as engaging on a limited range of issues' (Bergan 2011: 264).

(b) Largely to the credit of ESU prominent role in the Process, the issue of student participation in the institutional and national HE governance was also affirmed as a 'substantial value' and as a 'policy objective' of the EHEA. The Ministers stated that students '*should participate in and influence the organisation and content of education at universities and other HE institutions*' (Bologna Process 2001), that they '*fully support staff and student participation in decision-making structures at European, national and institutional levels*' (Bologna Process 2010) and that students are '*full partners in HE governance*' (Bologna Process 2003). As such, they have expressed to judge student participation as important and as a value guiding our understanding, acting, governing (cf. Chap. 2 by Zgaga).

(c) Furthermore, student participation gradually emerged as a 'commonly agreed Bologna objective', i.e. as an objective that ought to be pursued in the construction of the EHEA, and, accordingly, as a 'standard' by which EHEA and its underlying policy actions will also be evaluated and judged (cf. Chap. 2 by Zgaga). The strongest wording towards such normative goal was visible in the Berlin Communiqué (Bologna Process 2003), where the Ministers called on institutions and student organisations '*to identify ways of increasing actual student involvement in HE governance*' (Bologna Process 2003). Still, student participation was left largely undefined, even ambiguous in terms of the extent and degree of student participation advocated. The ambiguity in wording allows each government and institution to interpret it and to organise it within its own national and institutional context and interests. In other words, the full meaning and its impact depends on the negotiated interpretation between the policy actors involved. Given the consensual nature of the Bologna Process, such conceptual and normative ambiguity indicates a policy formulation strategy which was 'in offensive' against potential opposition or rejection by individual governments or HE institutions.

Less contentious – and hence stronger in wording – has been the reference to student participation in the area of QA. Standards and Guidelines for Quality Assurance (ESG) adopted within the Bologna Process basically made student participation in external and internal QA procedures mandatory (Bologna Process 2005a, b). Following the adoption of ESG, it was noted already in London Communiqué (Bologna Process 2007) that '*[t]he extent of student involvement at all levels has increased [...], although improvement is still necessary*'. Furthermore, student involvement was highlighted also in relation to the student centred learning (Bologna Process 2009): '*Academics, in close cooperation with student and employer representatives, will continue to develop learning outcomes and international reference points for a growing number of subject areas*'.

All in all, student participation has been fully consolidated in the Bologna Process as a procedural and substantial principle. It features also as a policy objective; however, as such it is neither fully defined nor qualified. The EHEA political endorsement of student participation has been used by national representative organisations as a leverage to consolidate or strengthen their participation in the national policy processes (Moscati 2009). The effects vary, however, among the countries depending on the pre-existing models of student interest intermediation. In countries with strong corporatist tradition, such as for example in the Nordic states, there was not much change since in these countries there already exists structured dialogue between national student unions and governments. In some parts of Europe, such as Central and South

Eastern Europe, the political endorsement arguably led to an improved student participation in national-level HE policy making (ESU 2009). In other countries, like for example Spain, the European developments created enabling conditions for the institutional-level student organisations to further their cooperation on the national level, and thus strengthen their ability to influence national HE policy making. In sum, the general tendency across EHEA has been to involve student representatives in the national-level Bologna-initiated policy processes and implementation. Yet, there are also profound differences on national and institutional levels as to the extent and degree of student participation. The reasons for why more convergence in this regard cannot be seen are several. One is in the profound differences in structures and traditions of student representation. Related to the above discussion, the reason could be also in the normative ambiguity of the Bologna documents when it comes to the questions of the extent and degree of student participation. Finally, as it will be discussed in the next section, there is another powerful source of prescriptive policies emerging from the EU modernisation agenda, which has implications on student participation even if it does not tackle it in explicit terms.

34.4   Modernisation Agenda and the HE Reforms Across EHEA and the Evolving Relationship Constellations Involving Students

HE reforms are sweeping across Europe. In the early stages of the Bologna Process, it was effectively Bologna recommendations that 'captured' HE reform agenda across EHEA (Gornitzka 2010: 11). Those recommendations have largely focused on the structural convergence and convergence in terms of QA systems in order to support mobility. Just with a couple of years of delay, in the – subsumed – policy arena of the European Union, HE become highlighted as one of the key drivers of the economic competitiveness, a goal determined in the Lisbon Agenda, an influential action and development plan for the European economy. Lisbon Agenda paved the way for a deeper HE policy to be proposed by the European Commission. From 2003, a series of influential policy documents and related financial instruments were developed under a general heading of 'HE modernisation agenda'. Both Bologna and European Union HE reform discourses became increasingly intertwined. Scholarly work suggests that the Bologna Process has been absorbed into the more general 'stream' of the Lisbon Agenda through a progressive convergence of documents (Capano and Piattoni 2011: 586). Specifically, the strategic role of HE in the promotion of competitiveness of European economy set out in the Lisbon Agenda has had implications on certain emphasises within the Bologna documents, and, more broadly, on the governance and funding reforms within the EHEA.

HE modernisation agenda has obvious ideational foundations in the new public management approach to HE governance (de Boer and File 2009).[8] By incorporating management practices from the private sector to public services, the aim is to increase the efficiency and effectiveness of institutions by giving them more autonomy while demanding more accountability. There is an emphasis on a more indirect role of governments in steering the HE system. The principle of institutional autonomy implies granting institutions the right to decide by themselves on their internal organisation and conduct of their operations, while remaining accountable to their main stakeholders. In view of the quest for universities to be more responsive to the socio-economic demands, this approach favour participation of external stakeholders – especially from industry and government – to increase accountability and cultivate links with the broader environment (Teichler 2006; Bleiklie and Kogan 2007). These are typically included in the external university boards, as part of general tendency towards the creation of managerial infrastructures parallel to academic ones, leading to a shift in decision-making from the collegiate governing bodies to managerial bodies (de Boer et al. 2007; Amaral et al. 2003; Maassen 2003). The underlying expectation is for universities to act more as corporate institutions (Shattock 2009).

The increased autonomy of HE institutions does not mean that these are no longer accountable to the public. There has been a rise in external and internal evaluation and accountability mechanisms to this effect (Stensaker and Harvey 2011). Accountability means that HE institutions have to use public funds granted to them responsibly and pursue their operations in line with the governmental and general public expectations. The institutions need to demonstrate this through various performance evaluations and other control mechanisms. While the relationship between the state and institutions shifted from state control to state supervision (van Vught 1989), the state remains interventionist in an evaluative sense (Neave and van Vught 1991). The evaluative state has developed more procedural policies (Musselin 2009), and delegated evaluative competencies onto independent agencies, such as quality assurance and accreditation agencies, research funding agencies, education councils (de Boer et al. 2007).

The modernisation discourse also highlights that more funding is needed for European HE if it is to serve effectively the envisaged European knowledge economy and society and compete with the rest of the world. While the financing formulas continue to be debated across Europe, the overall trend is towards shifting the burden of financing public HE from the governments to the institutions. The public spending crisis across Europe – reflecting the global financial crisis – has largely reinforced this trend (Teixeira 2009). Institutions bearing a rising burden of self-financing are trying to compensate by strengthening links to business and industry, and especially by increasingly passing the cost burden onto students. The emerging discourse within the EHEA – accepted with varying degrees nationally and countered

---

[8] For more on new public management approach and for examples of reform changes in governance see Chap. 35 by Amaral et al.

by several actors, most notably students – includes a shift in the conviction that the burden of HE financing lies exclusively or predominately with governments and thus taxpayers, to that of cost-sharing. For example, in Germany tuition fees were gradually introduced across the *Bundesländer* between 2006 and 2008, while in the United Kingdom (except in Scotland) tuition costs increased significantly in 2006, under the label of top-up fees (Eurostudent 2008: 83). The current trend is towards introduction of or increase in tuition fees (Eurydice 2007: 25–27). The notions of education as a public good and public responsibility, which implied tuition-free provision of HE has thus come under question.[9] All in all, the diffusion of the modernisation agenda for universities into the Bologna Process brought forward two major tensions. One is regarding the priority purposes of HE: Does it performs a purely educational function or fulfils a social role? The other is concerning the role of HE: Is HE a public good or a service? The underlying tension is that of the role of students: Whether students are or should be conceived as costumers or full partners? Each conception implies a particular mode of relationships between institutions and students, and a correspondingly different narrative as to the justifications in favour or against student participation.[10]

While Bologna documents repeatedly declared that HE serves multiple purposes, it is public good and public responsibility, and students are full partners in HE governance, the modernisation discourse inherently challenges these notions. The following sections discuss the implications of the modernisation agenda on the various relationships involving students, and the conception of students.

34.4.1   Transformations in the Relationship Between the State and Students

Perhaps the key observation regarding the relationship between the state and the students is in that of the further erosion of 'student exceptionalism' as the governments subscribe to the new public management ideologies.[11] Introduction of plurality of stakeholders at all levels of HE governance – in interest of effective policy formulation, legitimisation of adopted policy and accountability – implies more governments' coordination among diverse interests of multiple actors in the interconnected policy levels (de Boer et al. 2007; Olsen 2005). Students and academics no longer have the privileged access to the governments' HE policy process. They have to share these privileges with other stakeholders, namely from the industry and

---

[9]For more see Chap. 5 by Hackl.

[10]For an extensive discussion on arguments in favor and against student participation based on different conceptions of students within European context see Klemenčič (2011a), and more generally see Luescher-Mamashela (2010).

[11]Indeed, as Hans Pechlar noted during the FOHE-BPRC, student exceptionalism began to deteriorate already as HE has moved into mass and towards universal provision.

employers. These actors have specific interests in HE provision, especially in terms of expected graduates' competences and research outputs. They also tend to be sympathetic to the managerial ideologies applied to HE setting. In fact, their sheer presence and political leverage based on the economic weight contribute to consolidation of corporate values into HE. Students and academics continue to be inherently relevant constituencies, and cannot be – at least in principle – ignored from the policy process. However, their relative weight decreases with increasing number of actors involved in the policy process. In view of this, representatives of students and academics may emerge as 'advocacy coalitions' defending the predominance of educational purposes of HE as opposed to serving the needs of the industry.

While students' influence may be deteriorating with involvement of external stakeholders in policy making, they are gaining influence as governments have passed the task of evaluative procedures onto independent quality assurance and accreditation agencies. QA is a powerful element of the new public management agenda, and student participation along with participation of other stakeholders is its vital element. In addition, the various 'transparency and performance measuring tools' promoted by the European Commission (2008b) and acknowledged by several governments are intended at empowering students to exercise an informed and effective choice of education provision.

As corporate culture increasingly permeates policy interactions within HE governance on national level, the representative organisations of students (and academics and staff) need to become more professionalised if they are to represent the interests of their constituencies effectively. Professionalisation of student unions is also desired by the governments for student representatives to contribute competently and constructively in the advisory and evaluative role they have been solicited to within quality assurance agencies and external reviews. Some governments, such as for example the Dutch, have increased funding of representative student organisations on national level (i.e. LSVb and ISO) with explanation that it wanted them to be more professionalised.

With similar intentions to 'strengthen and vitalise student influence and strengthen the legitimacy of student unions' the government of Sweden in 2010 abolished compulsory membership of student unions.[12] The government's argument goes that each student ought to choose voluntarily whether to join the union or not; and having to recruit students into membership would ultimately professionalise the unions, and thus make them more effective. The governments allocated an annual grant to be distributed to student unions to ensure their participation 'in the quality assurance procedures' of both public and private HE institutions. The grant typically suffices to finance several union officers, but not to sustain the same extent of services and activities. For conducting these services and activities student union will need to fundraise from the institutional management and using membership fees. Such arrangement will inevitably transform the nature of student representation from more political to more entrepreneurial. Student unions ultimately assimilate

---

[12] See http://www.sweden.gov.se/sb/d/11815. Accessed 29 Oct 2011.

into the managerial norms of conduct and corporatist practices at institutions depicted in the new public management approach (cf. Luescher-Mamashela 2010).

Finally, the social contract between the state and students in terms of the public funding of HE is – with different degrees in different national contexts – also being challenged. Here student exceptionalism in terms of their right to free tertiary education is challenged when compared to the rights of those not seeking such education. The justification for cost sharing is based on the argument of the private benefits to individuals for obtaining a HE degree in the form of higher earnings deriving from investment in their human capital – an argument that appear today much more in vogue than it was only 10 years ago. The introduction of or substantial increase in tuition fees in some countries have significant implications for student-university relations. Paying students conceived as customers rather than partners fits well into the emerging ideal of the modern corporate university.

34.4.2 Transformations in the Relationship Between the University and Students

As the European HE institutions assert their organisational autonomy towards the creation of managerial infrastructures parallel to academic ones, this has significant implications on the university-student relationships. First, there is a shift in decision-making from the collegiate governing bodies – where students tend to be formally represented – to managerial bodies where students are represented less or not at all. Strong executive leadership has come to be seen as a new ideal supplanting the representative democracy model. The composition of the university boards typically favours participation of external stakeholders. In case of Portugal, for example, the new provisions stipulate student participation in the *Conselho Geral*, but the minimal share of student representatives is not specified. The arguments given for the change revolved around disturbance of student representatives (in view of the fights over tuition fees) and the effectiveness of decision making. Concomitantly, the relative political weight of student representatives (as well as that of academics and staff) in these boards has decreased. Along with other internal stakeholder representatives, student representatives are increasingly being eclipsed by the executive leadership. Such reforms thus evince a trend away from the ideal of partnership, which implies that students are involved in all stages of the decision making, on all vital policy and strategy decisions, and that they act in decision-making capacity.

A combination of managerial organisational arrangements with introduction of (or increase in) tuition fees brings the institutions closer to the model of corporate university. In such model, students are conceived as costumers and academics as employees (Pabian and Minksová 2011). In the consumerist view of educational provisions, there is a contractual relationship between the institution as a provider of educational services and students as costumers of these services who are expecting value-for-money. Conceiving students as costumers appears to empower each student individually while representation of collective student body withers.

Individual student is actively recruited by institutions competing on the education market. The transparency tools help the student to make an informed choice. Institutions seeking to meet student expectations develop internal quality assurance procedures to secure 'customer satisfaction'. They are eager to obtain individual student feedback on the various aspects of services they offer in order to avoid complaints and maintain reputation for further recruitment. Indeed, an individual student as sovereign customer has a right to complain and demand better service; and if his complaints not remedied has an option to change institutions. However, as it has been often argued, customer rights are more difficult to enact in educational services than this may be the case in other industries (e.g. Bergan 2011: 263–264).[13] There is significant time and financial investment involved in choice of HE provision.

Conceiving students as customers does not preclude student participation but it fundamentally transforms it. The contemporary institutional preference for student participation is clearly towards an advisory rather than decision making model, i.e. student participation in a form of consultation and quality assessment rather than partnership. Indeed, the institutional strategic emphasis on quality assurance and enhancing total student learning experience opens up new opportunity structures for student representatives. These informal forms of student involvement – where student representation is 'instrumentalised' in pursuit of the institutional quality agenda – may supplement full formal student participation in governing. Informal student participation can serve institutional leadership as an argument against student requests for more participation in governing. By involving students in QA, institutional management can argue the case that student participation exists and that this no longer needs to be a cause for political struggle. In other words, informal forms of student participation are convenient evidence for acceptance of student participation in principle. At the same time, students influence in governing is accommodated only to the extent that it does not compromise management control over the governing bodies and decisions. From the point of efficiency of decision making this is desirable for the leadership as students are assumed to hold adversary positions, and thus potentially disrupt or stall the decision making process.

Institutional leadership in corporate institution is more interested in student representatives' expertise and ability to perform various student services and manage student facilities then their representativeness. Student unions tend to adapt to these changing institutional structures, practices, norms of appropriateness and the leadership expectations as to the student role. The corporate culture permeating institutional governance ultimately spills over to the student governance – perhaps not immediately, but gradually as new generations of student leaders join ranks. More political student groups within student governance become increasingly marginalised within the corporate university. The trend of entrepreneurialism in student representation

---

[13]This is but one reason why an external consumer protection agency cannot replace the function of a student union defending not only an individual student's interests, but also interests of the collective student body.

is stronger where student governance is already more service-oriented rather than political (e.g. in the UK, Netherlands as opposed to typical French, Swiss, Italian unions). The less financial autonomy the institutional unions have, the quicker and more ideal is such transformation likely to be.

In sum, modernisation agenda is leading not only to re-conception of students, but also to a transformation of student representation. The trend is towards conceiving students as customers and professionalising and de-politicising student representation to play a role in institutional quality assurance and student services.

34.4.3 Transformations in the Relationship Between the Academics and Students

The changing organizational arrangements that appear to be weakening the influence of internal stakeholders may result in strengthened cooperation between students and academics in the formal governance. Both tend to agree on the importance of educational purposes of HE and the need to moderate the demands coming from the industry. Academics in general tend to be less supportive of the view that students should be regarded as customers than institutional leadership (Lomas 2007: 42). Such conception reinforces the conception of academics as employees in the educational enterprise whose role is to transmit course content. Their self-perception tends to be more all-encompassing and conceived within the notions of multiple purposes of education including that of serving the intellectual needs of their societies (Henkel 2000). Hence, there exists ground for advocacy coalitions between representatives from these two internal constituencies, assuming that these will continue to defend – as they have so far – the multiple purposes of HE.

In addition, a new cooperative relationship between the student and academic 'estates' may be developing within the student centred learning approach. As we are moving from teacher-centred towards learner-centred approach, the academics' control over the curriculum contents and methods weaken while individual student's autonomy and active involvement strengthens. Empirical studies show that students typically are interested in being involved in shaping the 'content, curriculum and design' of their courses (Bols and Freeman 2011), and thus this type of informal student participation is not subject to the same trend of weakening of political participation as we see in low turnouts in student elections. Conceptually, student centred learning appears to be more convergent with the conception of students as partners in a joint teaching and learning and research endeavour than that of students as customers which implies external and passive student role.

At the same time, academics are subject to more pedagogical and scientific evaluation within the QA frameworks. The results of these evaluations bare repercussions on reputation and financial rewards of academics. Students are involved in these frameworks as evaluators which somewhat undermines the traditional power imbalance between students and academics stemming from the academics' role in the testing and certifying students' acquisition of knowledge.

In sum, as academics autonomy may be weakened with various performance measures and students autonomy strengthened through student centred learning, these two estates might find more ground for cooperative arrangements not only within the classroom, but also within the governing structures.

34.4.4   Transformations in the Relationship Between Representative Student Bodies and Students

While on the one hand the representative student organisations across EHEA continue to pledge the case for more participation in institutional governance, they are on the other hand struggling to elicit participation in their own organisations. A major cross-national survey of student participation in university governance in Europe conducted by the Council of Europe (Bergan 2004; Persson 2004) suggests that although voter turnout in student elections varies considerably across Europe, it tends to be low: most of the time, less than half the student population elects those representing the whole student body, and in most cases voter turnout is actually one in three or less. Recruiting student representatives is generally less difficult. More challenging is, however, for student governments to effectively engage and represent interests of increasingly diverse body of students: lifelong learners, distance education students, those enrolled in transnational HE operations, and minority students according to religion, language/ethnicity, race, sexual orientations, etc. Involving these students requires special effort and makes policy making among groups with diverse and often conflicting interests more difficult.

The modernisation discourse eliciting the sense of higher education as a market place is also transmitting the notion of students as customers with choice of a higher education provider, right to complain over the quality of service provision and obligation to share a burden of cost of this provision. Such notions are intertwined with and reinforce the rising vocationalist orientations of contemporary student body as well as the culture of individualism. We can observe among students today a growing culture of individualism, a pre-eminence of self-interest and a preference for the benefit to the individual over concerns for the common good, and students appear increasingly concerned with prioritising personal advancement and gratification over moral and social meanings (Colby et al. 2007). Such orientations are typically not conducive to student political activism, be that in a form of active involvement in student unions (unless this is considered a way of improving career prospects) or in other forms of social engagement. Such orientations also do not fare well for these students' active participation in our societies' democratic processes and institutions. If higher education institutions do not act as 'sites of citizenship and democratic participation' and develop ample opportunities for academic democracy, they yield high opportunity costs of not contributing to sustaining and developing democratic societies (Klemenčič 2010). Student governments also have a key role to play in terms of capacity building of their own structures and raising student awareness.[14]

While the student body typically remains relatively dispassionate in the course of strictly educational reforms, it continues to be willing to engage in mass action when issues at stake tackle student welfare and financing, such as the introduction of or increase in tuition fees. While student protests are a permanent feature in HE space (Altbach 2006), we are witnessing expansion and strengthening of student movements across EHEA in the last decade. The common denominator of these student movements is a reaction to – what is broadly labelled as – the neoliberal approach to the HE reforms across Europe. The opposition to GATS in education, which used to be the most salient issue of student protests within the general opposition to commodification and commercialisation of HE, is now overshadowed by other issues: rising tuition fees, decreasing public spending on HE and the focus on the commercially-driven research and university-industry partnerships. Many of the protests are connected – at least virtually – through the initiatives called '*unibrennt*' [university burns], and '*unsereuni*' [our university].[15] There are very different examples across Europe of how student representative organisations relate to the movements. In some countries – such as, for example, Austria – the formal student representative organisation acknowledges and participates in the movement. The growth in student movement depicts, however, the growing distance between the political decisions taken by the student political elites and those of their constituency. This trend is not only pertinent to student politics, but indeed also to nation politics. Taken together, the low turn-outs in student elections and the rise in student movements perhaps signal a growing detachment of the student body from the representative student organisations, their politics and policies.

34.5   Conclusion

The conceptions of student participation in HE governance in the context of the EHEA are caught in the two major tensions underlying the HE reform processes: that of the purposes of HE and that of its role. The Bologna Process policy documents declaratively affirm the equal importance of the multiple purposes of HE and qualify HE as a public good and public responsibility. The European Union's modernisation agenda challenges these declarations by putting an emphasis on the HE's service to the knowledge economy and of the private benefits to the individuals. While the Bologna documents do not offer prescriptive advice on governance

---

[14]ESU (2011a, b) is aware of these challenges and seriously working on capacity-building of student representation at all levels including raising awareness of the role of student representatives and developing principles of good governance of student organisations.

[15]For more information see http://www.unsereuni.at; http://www.unsereuni.ch/; http://www.unsereunis.de/vernetzung/. Accessed 20 Oct 2011.

reforms specifically, the European Commission's contributions are elaborate and with distinct ideological underpinnings – those of the new public management in HE. The governments and HE institutions are subscribing to these recommendations near universally albeit with varying degrees and nuances based on national and institutional idiosyncrasies.

The new public management-based governance reforms of institutional structures, procedures and practices inevitably have implications on the relationships and balance of power between the key HE constituencies.[16] The ideological underpinnings of the reforms construct within institutions new shared meanings, social norms and rules, which consequently influence not only actors' behavioural choices, but also their interests and identities (cf. March and Olsen 1995: 30; Risse and Wiener 1999: 778). These interests and identities are learned and sustained through the iterative interactions within governance processes (Wendt 1999: 331). Gradually, but inevitably, students and student representatives (as well as other stakeholders) internalise the norms which then influence how they see themselves and what they perceive as their interests. The process of socialisation of student representatives is perhaps faster due to the volatile nature of student representation, and because the reforms offer new opportunity structures for student involvement (and not only curb the formal participation in governing, which would typically cause revolt).

Entailed in these reforms is an emerging conception of students as customers, which is supplementing or complementing the existing notions of students as core constituency and thus partners in democratic model of HE governance. Looking closely at the national and institutional realities across EHEA the changes in conception of students reflect the intensities of adoption of managerial approaches as well as the tradition and strength of student representation. In corporatist countries, such as the Nordic states, with mature and highly developed forms of student representation and with strong channels of student influence to HE governance, attempts are made to combine both conceptions. In contexts of weak student representation and enthusiastic managerial reforms of institutions, the conception of costumers may well be overriding the 'traditional' conception – based on participatory governance model – of students as partners.

Correspondingly to the changes in conception of students, the modes of student representation are being transformed. Student unions appear to be shifting from political role – where student representatives defend interests of the collective student body in relation to other constituencies within institutional governance – to professionalised, even entrepreneurial, role focusing on performing advisory function for quality assurance and delivering student services. The trend to professionalisation is reinforced by the new opportunity structures for student involvement emerging in the context of quality assurance especially. In line with new public management ideology, institutional leadership and governments have growing interest in professional student representative groups that can contribute competently

---

[16]For an elaborate discussion on HE governance as a concept see Chap. 29 by Middlehurst and Teixeira.

and constructively in consultative, evaluative and service role; while they are less interested in these organisations' representativeness.

The emerging *modus operandi* of student participation within EHEA is that of *weakening formal student participation* – as decision making powers in institutional governing bodies – and *strengthening informal student participation* through their involvement in quality assurance, activities related to enhancing student experience, and through student centred learning.

Acknowledgments The author would like to thank Pedro Teixeira and Robin Middlehurst for their valuable input in the preparation of this chapter, and Harry de Boer and Hans Pechar for their helpful comments to the first draft.

References

Altbach, P. G. (2006). Student politics: Activism and culture. In J. F. J. Forest & P. G. Altbach (Eds.), *International handbook of higher education*. Dordrecht: Springer.

Amaral, A., Meek, V. L., & Larsen, I. M. (Eds.). (2003). *The higher education managerial revolution?* Dordrecht: Springer.

Bartley, K., Dimenäs, J., & Hallnäs, H. (2010). Student participation in higher education: A question of governance and power. *Nordic Studies in Education, 30*, 150–165.

Bergan, S. (2004). Higher education governance and democratic participation: The university and democratic culture. In S. Bergan (Ed.), *The university as Res Publica: HE governance, student participation and the university as a site of citizenship* (pp. 13–30). Strasbourg: Council of Europe Publishing.

Bergan, S. (2011). *Not by bread alone*. Strasbourg: Council of Europe Publishing.

Biesta, G. J. J. (2007, November 30–December 1). *Higher education, democracy and European citizenship*. Invited plenary presentation at the conference of the European Education Policy Network, Brussels/Leuven, Belgium, pp. 1–6.

Bleiklie, I., & Kogan, M. (2007). Organization and governance in universities. *Higher Education Policy, 20*, 477–493.

Boland, J. A. (2005). Student participation in shared governance: A means of advancing democratic values. *Tertiary Education and Management, 11*(3), 199–217.

Bologna Process. (2001, May 19). [Prague Communiqué]. *Towards the European Higher Education Area*. Communiqué of the meeting of European Ministers in charge of Higher Education, Prague.

Bologna Process. (2003, September 19). [Berlin Communiqué]. *Realising the European Higher Education Area*. Communiqué of the Conference of Ministers responsible for Higher Education, Berlin.

Bologna Process. (2005a, May 19–20). [Bergen Communiqué]. *The European Higher Education Area – Achieving the goals*. Communiqué of the Conference of European Ministers Responsible for Higher Education, Bergen.

Bologna Process. (2005b). *Standards and guidelines for quality assurance in the European Higher Education Area*. Helsinki: European Association for Quality Assurance in Higher Education.

Bologna Process. (2007, May 18). [London Communiqué]. *Towards the European Higher Education Area: Responding to challenges in a globalised world*, London.

Bologna Process. (2009, April 28–29). [Leuven/Louvain-la-Neuve Communiqué]. *The Bologna Process 2020 – The European Higher Education Area in the new decade*, Leuven/Louvain-la-Neuve.

Bologna Process. (2010, March 12). *Budapest-Vienna declaration on the European Higher Education Area*, Budapest-Vienna.

Bols, A., & Freeman, R. (2011). Engaging students in shaping their curriculum. *Education Developments Issue, 12*(2), 5–9.

Brus, S., Komljenovič, J., Sıthigh, D. M., Noope, G., & Tück, C. (2007). Student participation in QA: Strengths and challenges. In L. Bollaert, S. Brus, B. Curvale, L. Harvey, E. Helle, H. T. Jensen, et al. (Eds.), *Embedding quality culture in HE* (pp. 53–58). Brussels: European University Association.

Capano, G., & Piattoni, S. (2011). From Bologna to Lisbon: The political uses of the Lisbon "script" in European higher education policy. *Journal of European Public Policy, 18*(4), 584–606.

Colby, A., Beaumont, E., Ehrlich, T., & Corngold, J. (2007). *Educating for democracy: Preparing undergraduates for responsible political engagement.* San Francisco: Jossey Bass-Carnegie Foundation for the Advancement of Teaching.

Council of the European Union. (2001). *Detailed work programme on the follow-up of the objectives of education and training systems in Europe.* Official journal of the European Communities. C 142/1. 14.6.2002. (2002/C 142/01).

de Boer, H., & File, J. (2009). *Higher education governance reforms across Europe.* Brussels: ESMU.

de Boer, H. F., Enders, J., & Schimank, U. (2007). On the way towards new public management? The governance of university systems in England, the Netherlands, Austria, and Germany. In D. Jansen (Ed.), *New forms of governance in research organizations – Disciplinary approaches, interfaces and integration* (pp. 137–154). Dordrecht: Springer.

de Boer, H., & Stensaker, B. (2007). An internal representative system: the democratic vision. In P. A. M. Maasen, & J. P. Olsen (Eds.), *University dynamics and European integration* (pp. 137–163). Dordrecht: Kluwer.

EC. (2001). *European governance* (A White Paper). Brussels, 25 July 2001. COM(2001) 428.

EC. (2003). *The role of the universities in the Europe of knowledge.* Commission Communication.

EC. (2005). *Mobilising the brainpower of Europe: Enabling HE to make its full contribution to the Lisbon strategy: Resolution of the council and of the representatives of the governments of the member states.* Official Journal C 292, 24/11/2005 pp. 0001–0002.

EC. (2006, May). *Delivering on the modernisation agenda for universities: Education, research and innovation.* Communication from the Commission to the Council and the European Parliament. COM(2006) 208 final.

EC. (2008a). Report from the Commission to the Council on the Council Resolution of 23 November 2007 on Modernising Universities for Europe's competitiveness in a global knowledge economy. COM(2008) 680 final.

EC. (2008b). Commission staff working paper accompanying document to the report from the Commission to the Council on the Council Resolution of 23 November 2007 on Modernising Universities for Europe's competitiveness in a global knowledge economy. SEC(2008) 2719.

ESU [ESIB]. (1999, June 17). *Bologna Student Declaration.* Bologna.

ESU. (2009). *Bologna with student eyes.* Brussels: European Students' Union.

ESU. & EI. (2010). Student Centered Learning. An Insight into Theory and Practice. Bucharest: European Students' Union and Education International.

ESU. (2011a, February 15–19). *Budapest Declaration: Governance and student participation.* 21st ESU European Student Convention. Budapest.

ESU. (2011b). *No student left out: The do's and don'ts of student participation in HE decision-making.* Brussels: European Students Union.

Eurostudent. (2008). *Social and economic conditions of student life in Europe. Synopsis of indicators* (Final Report). Eurostudent III 2005–2008. Bielefeld: W. Bertelsmann Verlag GmbH & Co.

Eurydice. (2007). *Key data on higher education in Europe – 2007.* Brussels: Eurydice.

Gibbs, A., & Ashton, Ch. (2007). Student involvement in university life and quality processes: Results of thematic audit on student involvement in university governance and decision-making. In L. Bollaert, S. Brus, B. Curvale, L. Harvey, E. Helle, H. T. Jensen, et al. (Eds.), *Embedding quality culture in higher education* (pp. 48–52). Brussels: European University Association.

Gornitzka, Å. (2010). Bologna in context: A horizontal perspective on the dynamics of governance sites for a 'Europe of Knowledge'. *European Journal of Education, 45*(4), 535–548.

Haskins, C. H. (1923). *The rise of universities*. New York: Henry Holt and Co.

Henkel, M. (2000). *Academic identities and policy change in higher education* (Vol. 46). London: Jessica Kingsley Publishers.

Huisman, J., Maassen, P., & Neave, G. (Eds.). (2001). *Higher education and the nation state*. Oxford: Pergamon.

Keeling, R. (2006). The Bologna Process and the Lisbon Research Agenda: The European Commission's expanding role in HE discourse. *European Journal of Education, 41*(2), 203–223.

Kehm, B., Huisman, J., & Stensaker, B. (2009). *The European Higher Education Area: Perspectives on a moving target*. Rotterdam: Sense Publishers.

Klemenčič, M. (2010). Higher education for democratic citizenship. In E. Froment, J. Kohler, L. Purser, & L. Wilson (Eds.), *EUA Bologna handbook. Making Bologna work* (pp. 1–25). Berlin: RAABE Academic Publishers.

Klemenčič, M. (2011a). Student representation in European HE governance: Principles and practice, roles and benefits. In E. Egron-Polak, J. Kohler, S. Bergan, & L. Purser (Eds.), *Handbook on leadership and governance in HE. Leadership and good governance of HEIs. Structures, actors and roles* (pp. 1–26). Berlin: RAABE Academic Publishers.

Klemenčič, M. (2011b). Europeanisation of the "European Student Movement". In *EUSA 2011: Papers archive from the Network of European Union Centres of Excellence*. Washington, DC: Network of European Union Centres of Excellences, EUCE. http://euce.org/eusa/2011/papers/7c_klemencic.pdf. Accessed 20 Oct 2011.

Little, B., Locke, W., Scesa, A., & Williams, R. (2009). *Report to HEFCE on student engagement*. London: Centre for Higher Education Research and Information, The Open University.

Lizzio, A., & Wilson, K. (2009). Student participation in university governance. The role conceptions and sense of efficacy of student representatives on departmental committees. *Studies in Higher Education, 34*(1), 69–84.

Lomas, L. (2007). Are students customers? Perceptions of academic staff. *Quality in Higher Education, 1*(3), 31–44.

Luescher-Mamashela, T. (2010). From university democratisation to managerialism: The changing legitimation of university governance and the place of students. *Tertiary Education and Management, 16*(4), 259–283.

Maassen, P. (2003). Shifts in governance arrangements. An interpretation of new management structures in higher education. In A. Amaral, V. L. Meek, & I. M. Larsen (Eds.), *The higher education managerial revolution?* (pp. 31–53). Dordrecht: Kluwer Academic Publishers.

March, J. G., & Olsen, J. P. (1995). *Democratic governance*. New York/London: Free Press.

Menon, M. E. (2003). Student involvement in university governance: A need for negotiated educational aims? *Tertiary Education and Management, 9*(3), 233–246.

Menon, M. E. (2005). Students' views regarding their participation in university governance: Implications for distributed leadership in higher education. *Tertiary Education and Management, 11*(2), 167–182.

Molander, B. (2002). Politics for learning or learning for politics? *Studies in Philosophy and Education, 21*(4–5), 361–376.

Moscati, R. (2009). The implementation of the Bologna Process in Italy. In A. Amaral, G. Neave, C. Musselin, & P. Maassen (Eds.), *European integration and the governance of higher education and research* (pp. 207–225). Dordrecht: Springer.

Musselin, C. (2009). The side effects of the Bologna Process on national institutional settings: The case of France. In A. Amaral, G. Neave, C. Musselin, & P. Maassen (Eds.), *European integration and the governance of higher education and research* (pp. 181–207). Dordrecht: Springer.

Neave, G., & van Vught, F. A. (1991). *Prometheus bound. The changing relationship between government and higher education in Western Europe*. Oxford: Pergamon Press.

Olsen, J. P. (2005). *The institutional dynamics of the (European) university* (Working Paper No.15). Oslo: Arena. http://www.arena.uio.no. Accessed 20 Oct 2011.

Pabian, P., & Minksová, L. (2011). Students in HE governance in Europe: Contrasts, commonalities and controversies. *Tertiary Education and Management, 17*(3), 261–273.

Paradeise, C., Reale, E., Bleiklie, I., & Ferlie, E. (Eds.). (2009). *University governance. Western European comparative perspectives*. Dordrecht: Springer.

Persson, A. (2004). Student participation in the governance of HE in Europe. In S. Bergan (Ed.), *The university as Res Publica: HE governance, student participation and the university as a site of citizenship* (pp. 13–30). Strasbourg: Council of Europe Publishing.

Risse, T., & Wiener, A. (1999). 'Something Rotten' and the social construction of social constructivism: A comment on comments. *Journal of European Public Policy, 6*(5), 775–782.

Shattock, M. (Ed.). (2009). *Entrepreneurialism in universities and the knowledge economy: Diversification and organizational change in European HE*. Maidenhead: Open University Press.

Stensaker, B., & Harvey, L. (2011). *Accountability in higher education: Global perspectives on trust and power* (International studies in higher education series). Oxon/New York: Routledge/Taylor & Francis.

Tallberg, J. (2004). The power of the presidency: Brokerage, efficiency and distribution in EU negotiations. *Journal of Common Market Studies, 42*(5), 999–1022.

Teichler, U. (2006). Changing structures of HE systems: The increasing complexity of underlying forces. *Higher Education Policy, 19*(4), 447–461.

Teixeira, P. (2009). Economic imperialism and the Ivory Tower: Economic issues and policy challenges in the funding of HE in the EHEA (2010–2010). In B. M. Kehm, J. Huisman, & B. Stensaker (Eds.), *The European HE Area: Perspectives on a moving target* (pp. 43–60). Rotterdam: Sense Publishers.

van Vught, F. (Ed.). (1989). *Governmental strategies and innovation in higher education* (HE policy series). London: Jessica Kingsley.

Wendt, A. (1999). *Social theory of international politics*. Cambridge: Cambridge University Press.

Westerheijden, D. F., Beerkens, E., Cremonini, L., Huisman, J., Kehm, B., Kovac, A., et al. (2010). *The first decade of working on the European HE area: The Bologna process independent assessment – Vol. 1 detailed assessment report*. Brussels: European Commission, Directorate General for Education and Culture.

Chapter 35
Higher Education Reforms in Europe: A Comparative Perspective of New Legal Frameworks in Europe

Alberto Amaral, Orlanda Tavares, and Cristina Santos

35.1 From the Middle Ages to the Modern University

Walter Ruegg (1996) considers the University is a European institution, a creation of medieval Europe, of the Europe of the Roman Catholic Church. In its early days, the university was in general "a guild organisation of masters or students or of masters and students combined, having a high degree of juridical autonomy, the right to elect its own officers, statutory making powers, and a communal seal" (Cobban 1975: 32). Oxford and Cambridge offer a good example of this type of organisation, both universities being self-governing communities of scholars that had the right to remove unsuitable masters and to co-opt new members using the equivalent of peer review mechanisms. However, there were other models, such as the University of Paris, where the chancellor of the Notre Dame cathedral had power to decide about the content of studies thus ensuring a higher degree of external accountability. And there was the model of the University of Bologna, ruled by students who hired the professors on an annual basis, controlling their assiduity and the quality of teaching, an extreme example of the present principles of customer satisfaction.

Giovanni Agnelli (1988), in his keynote speech at the celebrations of the 900th anniversary of the University of Bologna, emphasised the international character of the universities "…that from the very beginning were international in spirit. Even in the most difficult and intolerant times they defended that knowledge should be free and universal" (1988: 11). Guy Neave associates the universal character of the medieval universities with the role of the Pope in their recognition: "in so far as Christianity was universal, universities could be considered as an organised expression of that universality" (2001).

A. Amaral (✉) • O. Tavares • C. Santos
CIPES, Rua 1.º de Dezembro, 399, 4450-227 Porto, Portugal
e-mail: aamaral@cipes.up.pt

A. Curaj et al. (eds.), *European Higher Education at the Crossroads:*
Between the Bologna Process and National Reforms,
DOI 10.1007/978-94-007-3937-6_35, © Springer Science+Business Media Dordrecht 2012

The modern university is the result of reforms that have taken place since the mid seventeenth century (Neave 2001: 10), the most remarkable being the French Napoleonic reforms (1806–1808) and the implementation of von Humboldt research university (1807). This was the consolidation period of the 'nation-state' in Europe, when universities played an important role by producing the highly trained people necessary for the modernisation of society by means of a modern public administration (Neave and van Vught 1994).

The important role played by the modern university in the construction and reinforcement of the nation-state and as "an agent of national reconstruction allied with the overhaul of recruitment to the apparatus of the state" (Neave and van Vught 1994: 268) led to its assimilation "into a national system of oversight and control exercised through legislative enactment, ministerial decree and circular... and the incorporation of academia into the ranks of public service, thereby placing upon it the implicit obligation of service to the national community" (Neave 2001: 26).

Academic autonomy in the Napoleonic University was rather restrictive (Neave and van Vught 1994) as the state exercised close control over appointments and promotions, and over the design of study programmes (Carrier and van Vught 1989). The von Humboldt model is more interesting as the idea of the Humboldt University "is still today re-cycled and revered at almost every academic ritual and ceremony" (Nybom 2003: 26).

Nybom (2003) argues that the central political problem faced by von Humboldt was how to ensure the necessary autonomy to modern science and the pursuit of research and to prevent its progressive corruption or even destruction by other powerful societal forces such as politics, economy and religion. To solve the problem, von Humboldt created what "has gradually become one of the most popular and frequently used degrading metaphors for the supposed societal and even cultural irrelevance of the university" (Nybom 2003: 19): an ivory tower. "It was to use Wilhelm von Humboldt's own famous expression, only in *"Einsamkeit und Freiheit"* that the pursuit of qualified knowledge could be achieved and prosper" (Nybom 2003: 20). The individuals devoted to this most noble and most "virtuous" of all human tasks should also enjoy the most extended form of autonomy and freedom. In the words of Jürgen Mittelstrass: "What God was among the angels, the learned man should be among his fellow men" (Mittelstrass 1994: 83).

The von Humboldt model of academic autonomy, or more precisely of academic freedom, was individual not institutional. Indeed, mainly for political reasons, von Humboldt abandoned his original idea of a totally autonomous institution and instead accepted the "conservative compromise" of a reformed university within and under the legal framework of the state (Mittelstrass 1994: 21 and 41, cited by Nybom 2003: 19; see Chap. 33 by Pechar).

Over this initial period, the relationship between government and higher education institutions corresponded to the model of state control. The state was the sole regulator of the higher education system and used traditional regulation mechanisms such as legislation (the daily life of institutions was strongly regulated by laws, ministerial decrees, circulars and regulations), funding, approval of study programmes, and in many cases the appointment of professors. This was the prevailing model in the European continental systems of higher education, and was built around the principle of legal homogeneity to ensure similarity of educational standards and programmes, aiming at granting all individual citizens were on an equal footing when applying to public employment.

To guarantee the complete fulfilment of the university's mission, the state assumed as its task to protect individual academic freedom (see Chap. 33 by Pechar) against the undesirable influences of all external factions and sometimes even conflicting interests, including those arising from professions, religions or politicians. Neave and Van Vught consider the state control model was character-ised by "the state's underwriting of non interference by external interests in the individual freedom to teach and to learn, as a monopoly of access to curricular pathways leading to public service or as the administrative subordination to a pow-erful central ministry" (1994: 271).

This was in essence the idea of the modern university, based upon the concept of individual academic freedom but not of institutional autonomy. The state was responsible for the protection of individual academic freedom to allow academics a proper environment for knowledge production without any outside interference. And the university (Neave 2001) "was to act as the highest expression of cultural unity, the independence of which was upheld by the legislative framework the state provided".

35.2   Massification of Higher Education

Amaral and Magalhães (2003) argue the traditional model of the modern university subsisted without loss of legitimacy until the end of the 1960s, while the traditional welfare state survived. They consider the development of the 'secondary' welfare state – which corresponds to the mobilisation of political, social and educational institutions for promoting democracy and for encouraging social mobility (Peter Scott 1995: 15) – was coterminous with the movement of higher education systems towards massification in most European countries.

In this new phase, the model of state control came under pressure due to several factors: massification of higher education systems increased their diversity and complexity, making detailed state control of the daily life of institutions impossible or at least inefficient; the emergence of the 'private sector' as the main employer of graduates weakened the arguments in favour of the legal homogeneity principle; the idea that massification implied a more diversified higher education system and that institutions should compete in a market were incompatible with a state control model supported by the legal homogeneity principle (Neave and van Vught 1994: 273–274).

As a result, the model of state control was replaced with the model of state supervision. In the state supervision model, central government administration downsizes its interference in the daily decisions of institutions, which are given "autonomy", and tries to promote the self-regulatory capacities of institutions, limiting government activities to long distance steering. Neave (1995: 61) considers the supervisory state seeks to improve the strategic oversight over national policies by shedding the functions of detailed control in favour of defining, monitoring, and evaluating, *post hoc*, the performance of individual institutions.

Institutional autonomy is different from the Humboldt concept of individual academic autonomy. Institutions are supposed to self-regulate in order to promote public good, while the new more competitive environment increases the diversity of the system. The implementation of markets needs that providers and consumers have a number of freedoms (Jongbloed 2003); for instance, providers need to be free to enter the market, to determine prices and to specify the products, while consumers should be free to choose the product and the provider and have adequate information on prices and quality. Therefore, the implementation of markets in higher education was accompanied by increasing institutional autonomy that allowed institutions to compete by deciding what programmes to offer, their characteristics and eventually the level of fees, although in practice, the state still regulates heavily some of these institutional freedoms (see Chap. 30 by de Boer and Jongbloed).

Ben Jongbloed (2004: 89–90) used a traffic metaphor to clarify the differences between the model of centralised command and control (similar to traffic signals) and the adoption of market-based regulation (similar to a roundabout). In Ben Jongbloed's metaphor, traffic lights condition heavily drivers' decisions, the same way that government regulation conditions the behaviour of institutions. On the contrary, a roundabout, while influencing traffic behaviour, delegates decision-making authority to the drivers (Dill et al. 2004: 329) that need to self-regulate their trajectories to avoid bumping against others:

> Drivers in a roundabout are awarded greater discretion (and more immediate forms of accountability!) than when traffic is controlled centrally by signals. This coordination by 'mutual adjustment' supposedly increases the efficiency of the traffic flow. The challenge confronting those experimenting with market-based policies in higher education therefore is to discover the institutional framework of rules and incentives that produces welfare maximising competition among (mainly) publicly subsidised, but autonomous, academic institutions. (Dill et al. 2004: 329).

However, increased institutional autonomy combined with market competition may lead to market regulation problems, as autonomous institutions competing in a market may follow strategies aiming at ensuring their own development and survival, which may be contrary to the public good or the government's objectives. Therefore, despite a rhetoric of autonomy and market regulation, the government arbitrarily intervenes forcing institutions to adapt their behaviour to government objectives, for instance by using compliance tools such as arrays of performance indicators and measures of academic quality, or performance-based contracts (see Chap. 30 by de Boer and Jongbloed and Chap. 31 by Paradeise). As recognised by the OECD:

> Thus the governance of higher education faces some difficult challenges. If higher education is indeed an important strategic lever for governments in seeking to pursue national objectives, can governments achieve those ends without compromising the independence of universities, or their dynamism in catering for new markets? (OECD 2003)

At this point it is important to emphasise that over this period collegiality dominated the governance modes of higher education institutions. There was a generally accepted idea that only professional experts – the academics – could run these very complex institutions, characterised by strong emphasis on professionalisation along the lines of distinct 'disciplinary specialisms' (Clark 1983).[1]

Others considered the need to protect academic freedom, thus echoing the fundamental idea behind the Humboldt model, and the danger that when "an external control is imposed, it should be realised that the professional tasks these institutions perform may be severely damaged" (Van Vught 1989: 54). Karl Jaspers, as cited by Kenneth Wilson (1989: 38), argues:

> The university is a community of scholars and students engaged in the task of seeking truth. It derives its autonomy from the idea of academic freedom, a privilege granted to it by state and society, which entails the obligation to teach truth in defiance of all internal and external attempts to curtail it.

The ideas of "academic freedom and the right of academic self-government" (Fulton 2002: 206) were the basis of a strong recommendation by the UK's Robbins Committee:

> We are convinced also that such freedom is a necessary condition of the highest efficiency … and that encroachments upon their liberty, in the supposed interests of greater efficiency, would in fact diminish their efficiency and stultify their development (Robbins Report 1963: 228).

And in 1975 Moodie and Eustace defended academics' predominance in university management on the basis of their very specific professional qualifications:

> The supreme authority, providing that it is exercised in ways responsive to others, must therefore continue to rest with the academics, for no one else seems sufficiently qualified to regulate the public affairs of scholars. (Moodie and Eustace 1974: 233)

A view later endorsed by Clark (1983), among others, in a classical Mertonian formulation suggesting, "universities firmly based on the development of disciplinary specialisms could only be effectively governed by experts in those disciplines" (Fulton 2002: 207). Therefore, until the last few decades, university governance was in general based on collegiality. The legitimacy of those in charge was ensured by democratic elections, a characteristic that was reinforced by influence of the May 68 student uprising. Collective decision making bodies were dominated by academics although students and even non-academic staff were present. The power of the central administration was rather weak, the rector being only a "primus inter pares".

---

[1] It is interesting to note that Adam Smith did not agree with the authority of academics over the university arguing if authority resides in the body corporate in which the majority of members are also academics, "they are likely to make a common cause, to be all very indulgent to one another, and every man to consent that his neighbour may neglect his duty, provided he himself is allowed to neglect his own" (Smith 1976, 1978: 343).

35.3 New Public Management

It has been argued that any specific discussion of higher education management needs to be set within the broader context of NPM and of policies for the public sector taking place over the last decades (Meek 2003). NPM and related concepts, such as new managerialism and reinventing government (Osborne and Gaebler 1992), have dominated public sector reform over the last decades. Pollitt considers NPM as a two level phenomenon:

> ... at the higher level it is a general theory or doctrine that the public sector can be improved by the importation of business concepts, techniques and values, while at the more mundane level it is a bundle of specific concepts and practices ... (Pollitt 2007: 110)

A paper by Tolofari (2005) offers a better understanding of the theories supporting NPM and of the drivers that promoted its rather generalised implementation. Boston et al. (1996) consider the main theoretical foundations of NPM are public choice theory, transaction cost economics and principal-agent theory. Ferlie et al. (1996) add microeconomic theory and the new economic sociology to the three previous theories. Tolofari (2005) argues the drivers of NPM were economic, political, social, intellectual and technological.

Economic drivers: The success of the welfare state has resulted in the accumulation of a huge public debt to meet the increasing financial burden of social benefits. This led to a crisis as governments were faced with the contradiction between promoting economic competitiveness and enhancing social cohesion. This contradiction was exposed in the 1970s by several authors as the "overloaded government" (Crozier et al. 1975), the "legitimation crisis" (Habermas 1973) or the "fiscal crisis of the state" (O'Connor 1973). Tolofari quotes Bovaird and Löffler and Larbi to support the idea that economic and fiscal problems were one of the major drivers of NPM. Bovaird and Löffler (2001) argue that NPM was born out of economic recession, Larbi considers:

> ... the common feature of countries going down the NPM route has been the experience of economic and fiscal crises, which triggered the quest for efficiency and for ways to cut the cost of delivering public services (Larbi 1999: iv).

Political drivers: The repudiation of welfare policies was not only financial or efficiency grounded; it was also and mainly ideological. For Ferlie et al. the NPM reforms of the public sector, driven by persistent political will were not:

> ... socially neutral, but reflect the rise of some constituencies and fall of others. In effect, as the balance of power shifted during the 1980s so a new political economy of the public sector emerged. (Ferlie et al. 1996: 4)

The implementation of NPM was coterminous with the emergence of the political New Right that won elections in the US (Reagan in 1978) and UK (Thatcher in 1979). The fiscal crisis of the welfare state provided the New Right with strong arguments: the welfare state was accused of being a big spender, responsible for wasting financial resources on inefficient and unfair social policies. Neo-liberal theorists promoted the idea that markets and private management approaches were more effective to solve the problems that governments were dealing with: declining economic performance, fiscal deficits, changes in the patterns of demand for government services, greater consumer expectations about quality of service, and reduced community confidence in the ability of government to deliver services (Meek 2003).

Social drivers: The increased demands of citizens for transparency and accountability for performance by governments also played a role:

> One of the arguments of the New Right was the lack of openness on the part of governments; the ordinary man hardly knew how the government functioned. There was no involvement of the citizen in the processes that involved him as a service user, and there was no choice or voice. (Tolofari 2005: 78)

To preserve the individual freedom of citizens presumed to be under attack by public bureaucracy, market mechanisms were imposed on civil servants that should regard the public as clients to whom satisfactory services were to be provided (Meek 2003: 10). The inefficiency and unresponsiveness of public services was to be met by a combination of two kinds of measures: the use of market or quasi-market concepts and disciplines in the public sector, and by transferring some tasks to the private sector (Self 2000). On the one hand, it was "assumed that efficiency and effectiveness of service delivery would be achieved through the use of private sector management techniques, such as specifying service objectives and competition for customers, performance measurement, decentralization of decision making and the use of markets to deliver services" (Meek 2003: 8). On the other hand, with exclusion of functions such as legislation, taxation, security and justice, many activities should be developed in partnership with the private sector and civil society's bodies where the role of the state would be reduced to formulation, implementation and evaluation of policies (Cunha 1999).

Tolofari also associates the development of NPM with the development of new managerial ideas and beliefs resulting from intellectual work (intellectual drivers) and argues ICT "has promoted the rapid spread of the philosophy and processes of NPM around the world" (technological drivers) (Tolofari 2005: 79).

35.4 NPM and Higher Education

Over the last decades, the intrusion of the rhetoric and management practices of the private sector into higher education resulted in important changes in the operation of higher education institutions (see Chap. 31 by Paradeise and Chap. 32 by Moscati). This phenomenon, which has been interpreted by several authors using concepts such as "managerialism" (Miller 1995; Amaral et al. 2003a) "new managerialism" or "new public management" (Meek 2003; Deem 1998, 2001; Reed 2002), is associated with the emergence of market or quasi-market modes of regulation (see Chap. 32 by Moscati).

Under NPM, students are seen as customers or clients, (see Chap. 34 by Klemenčič), and quality assurance and accountability measures are used to ensure that academic provision meets client needs and expectations. One consequence of NPM policies was a strong attack on professions, and specifically on the academic profession:

> ... the ideology of 'new managerialism' attempted to destroy, or at least weaken, the regulatory structures that had protected unaccountable professional elites and their monopolistic labour market and work practices across the full range of public sector service provision throughout the 1980's and 1990's (Reed 2002: 166).

The academy no longer enjoys great prestige on which higher education can build a successful claim to political autonomy (Scott 1989). There was a gradual proletarianisation of the academic professions – an erosion of their relative class and status advantages (Halsey 1992). The development of academic capitalism (Slaughter and Leslie 1997) and institutional patent policies also made faculty more like all other workers... whose discoveries are considered work-for-hire, the property of the corporation, not the professional.

The emergence of NPM and the attacks on the efficiency of public services, including higher education, resulted in loss of trust in institutions (Martin Trow 1996) and demands for more accountability. Governance models were imported from the private sector to replace the slow, inefficient decision making processes of academic collegiality by the "fast, adventurous, carefree, gung-ho, open-plan, computerised, individualism of choice, autonomous enterprises and sudden opportunity" (Ball 1998). The reinforced presence of external stakeholders in the governance bodies of universities was another step towards the creation of responsiveness to the 'external world' (Magalhães and Amaral 2000). Appointed Presidents and Rectors with sound managerial curricula are replacing elected academics (see Chap. 32 by Moscati).

The changes taking place are not only structural adjustments. There are changes of ideology and values, and significant changes in the relationship between higher education institutions and the state and society. These changes are without parallel since the foundation of the medieval university: instead of revering the unique capacity of academics to run the complex universities they are increasingly considered as incapable of efficient management, being replaced by lay members of the private sector; the multi-secular tradition of collegial governance became considered inefficient and corporative; the state, instead of protecting institutions from external intervention and influence, takes measures (if necessary through legal enactment) to guarantee that external parties, through the presence of stakeholders, intervene; the State, instead of protecting the individual freedom to teach and to learn from interference by external interests, opens the governance structures of universities to the outside world while the "Ivory tower" is denounced as a major flaw of traditional university governance.

The emergence of NPM in higher education has changed the role of academics and students, the former becoming increasingly seen as employees or work for hire while the later are being assumed as clients or customers (see Chap. 34 by Klemenčič). Unlike students, academics are not directly represented in the Bologna process and the increasing privatisation of higher education may reflect on the loss of traditional tenure or on the introduction of performance based salaries.[2] Klemenčič (Chap. 34) recognises the autonomy of academics may suffer with performance measures while the autonomy of students was improved by the student centred learning paradigm. And Klemenčič suggests that the two constituencies might increase their cooperation in governance matters.

In the two next sections reforms in a number of European countries (UK, Austria, Denmark, Sweden, Norway, Finland, the Netherlands, France and Portugal) are analysed for changes in governance and in the legal status of higher education institutions. The comparative analysis confirms that the rationale and tools of higher education reforms in Europe are surprisingly uniform and denationalised (see Chap. 31 by Paradeise).

35.5   Examples of Reform – Changes in Governance

In UK, change took place in the period of the 1988–1992 reforms, much earlier than in most European countries. Traditionally:

> British universities (other than Oxford and Cambridge) operate on the familiar bicameral principle. The Senate is... the body with responsibility for decision-making on all academic issues...; the Council is the supreme decision-making body with responsibility for finance and resources, [non-academic] terms and conditions of employment of staff, etc. The Council contains both external members and academic staff; the Senate, mainly academic staff, normally contains very few external and no strictly non-academic members. Both Senate and Council may include students. (Fulton 2002: 208–209).

The main changes were the establishment of a small *executive board*, half of whom must be from outside the university with experience in industrial, commercial or employment matters, a reinforcement of the power of the chief executive position and the subordination of the Academic Board to the Board of Governors. The 1997 Dearing report recommended that "as a general rule in the interests of effectiveness, membership of a governing body should not exceed 25" (Dearing report 1997). While in the new universities (former polytechnics) the board of governors comprises about 12–14 members (OECD 2003), the great majority of pre-1992 universities have boards with an average between 30 and 34 members (Shattock 2001).

---

[2] Performance related salaries were proposed by Adam Smith: "It is the interest of every man to live as much at his ease as he can; and if his emoluments are to be precisely the same, whether he does, or does not perform some very laborious duty, it is certainly his interest... either to neglect it altogether, or, if he is subject to some authority... to perform it in as careless and slovenly a manner as that authority will permit" (Smith 1776: 343). A view also shared with Bernard Mandeville: "Professors should, besides their Stipends allowed 'em by the Publick, have Gratifications from every Student they teach, that Self–Interest as well as Emulation and the Love of Glory might spur them on to Labour and Assiduity . . . Universities should be publick Marts for all manner of Literature . . ." (Mandeville 1924, pt.i.335, ed. Kaye i.293–4).

In Austria, the 2002 reforms introduced as main university boards the University Board or University Council (with 5, 7 or 9 members), the Senate (with 12–24 members) and the 'rectorate' (rector and up to 4 vice-rectors). The University of Vienna has a 9-member university board, 4 members being appointed by the senate, 4 being appointed by the federal government and 1 co-opted by the other members. The University Board has both strategic and supervision functions and appoints the rector (from a short-list of three names proposed by the senate) and the vice-rectors and dismisses them, approves the development plan, the university organisation and drafts the performance agreement to be signed with the federal authorities, supervises the legality of decisions and prepares the performance report. The Senate has mainly academic functions such as dealing with the curricula for degree programs and university courses.

In Denmark the highest university authority is the University Board with a majority of external members, the chairman being one of the external members. The Board manages the general interests of the University and appoints the rector and pro-rector to head the daily management, and both respond to the Board. The Boards of the University of Copenhagen and of the Aalborg University comprise 6 external and 5 internal members. Two of the internal members represent the scientific and academic staff, one represents the technical and administrative staff and two represent students. The Rector, the Pro-rector and the University Director participate in board meetings as observers. The University Board has signed a performance contract with the Ministry, which formulates the University's objectives and intended progress for a fixed period of time. The Technical University of Denmark has a 15-member Board of Governors with 9 external members and 6 internal members (2 representing the scientific and academic staff, 2 representing the technical and administrative staff and 2 representing students). The board approves the University's strategy as well as budget and action plans, enters into Development Contracts with the Minister for Science, Technology and Innovation, appoints the Rector and makes decisions on new building projects, etc. The rector is responsible for the daily running and answers to the Board.

In Sweden the University Board is the main governing body and has a majority of external members representing community and business interests, all of them appointed by the Minister who also appoints the chairman. The internal members are the vice-chancellor and representatives of staff and students. At Umeå University and at Gothenburg University the Board has 8 external members, the vice-chancellor, 3 representatives of the academic staff and 3 representatives of students. Representatives of employees, i.e. three union representatives, have the right to attend and express views at board's meetings. The board has "supervision over all the university's affairs, and is responsible that its duties are fulfilled".

In Norway there is a small University Board with 11 members but there are two possibilities. In cases such as the University of Trondheim, the University of Oslo or the University of Tromsø, the Board is composed of 3 representatives of tenured academic and scientific staff, 1 representative of contracted academic and scientific staff, 1 representative of technical and administrative staff, 2 representatives of students and 4 external members, including the chairman. The Board is responsible for running university activities and for ensuring that it operates within the framework and guidelines stipulated by the Ministry of Education and Research, and the Storting. The Board decides strategies, objectives and expected results from the university. It also presents the accounts, financial statements and budget proposals and appoints the Rector that answers to the Board. The University of Bergen opted for the alternative version of the law. The rector is elected (not appointed by the Board) and presides over the Board that includes 10 additional members, comprising 3 representatives of tenured academic and scientific staff, 1 representative of contracted academic and scientific staff, 1 representative of technical and administrative staff, 2 representatives of students and 4 external members.

In Finland the statutory bodies of public universities are the university board, the rector and the university collegiate body. The board has 7 or 9–14 members, its number being determined by the university collegiate body that also decides on the number of members representing the university estates. At a minimum, 40% of the members must be persons external to the university and are elected by the university collegiate body. The rector, vice-rector, deans, members of the university collegiate body may not be a member of the board. The chair of the board is elected from amongst the external members. The board elects the rector, decides on the main aims of the activities, the strategy and the principles governing the steering of operations and adopts the regulations governing the organisation of the university. It is also responsible for the finances. However, the disposal of real property is dependent of the ministry.

In the Netherlands a 1995 bill, Modernising Universities' Governance Structure (MUB), introduced a new form of *executive leadership*, aiming to increase the efficiency of university governance while promoting more effective interactions with society. The MUB created a new governing body, the *Raad van Toezicht* (a Supervisory Board comparable to a Board of Trustees) (de Boer et al. 1998). The Supervisory Board consists of five members, external to the university, nominated by the university but appointed by the Ministry. The Board represents external interests in the university governance process and is accountable to the Minister but not to the University. The Board approves the strategic plans and the budget plans of the university and will arbitrate disputes between the executive board and the council.

The executive board (*college van bestuur*) consists of three members, appointed by the Supervisory Board, one of them being the *rector magnificus*. Academic and management matters are concentrated in a single body, abolishing the old system of 'co-determination' by board and council. The executive board also appoints the deans (*decaans*) that are no longer elected at faculty level. Thus, a new hierarchical management system based on appointments replaced the old democratic system.

The university council still exists but has become an advisory body (with students and staff as members). One of its most powerful rights (approval of the budget) was removed. Both the legislative and the executive powers were centralised and collegial decision-making was suppressed, for the sake of increasing personal responsibility (apparently absent in collegial decision-making), avoiding dispersal of authority and the inadequacy and incoherence of communication between organisational levels (de Boer 2003: 95).

In France, the 2007 Pécresse Law reduced the membership of the management board by 50% (from 30–60 members to 20–30 members). The board is responsible for defining the institutional policies for research and education and the elected members of the board elect the President of the institution. The external participation was increased to 7 or 8, being nominated by the president of the board and appointed by the board, except for the 2 representatives appointed by the territorial authorities. The President was given real authority over all the staffs of the institution and the scientific council has only an advisory role.

In Portugal, the Parliament (2007) defined a new legal framework of higher education institutions. The act creates a university board – the General Council – with 15–35 members, depending upon the size of each institution and the number of schools and research units. At least half of the members are elected from among teachers and researchers of the institution and at least 15% are elected among students. The elected members will co-opt external members up to at least 30% of the total membership of the Council, one of the external members being elected chairman. The Council elects the Rector and approves strategic and action plans, budget proposals, annual consolidated accounts, student fees, authorises the purchase or sale of the institution's assets and its credit operations, etc.

35.6   Examples of Reform – Changes in the Legal Status

Another important element is the legal status of public universities:

> In broad terms, institutions can be considered either a State agency or as a legal independent person. In the former case, institutions are treated in a similar way to other State agencies… Granting independent legal status (ILS) is one means of giving greater autonomy to institutions. Having ILS means an institution is legally responsible for its functioning. One of its forms is that of a foundation. (OECD 2008: 82)

There is a recent trend to grant independent legal status to public universities. In Austria, the 2002 act gave universities "independent legal status", and, although they remained in the domain of public law, they are no longer state agencies without legal capacity (Pechar 2005; Sporn 2002). Universities became "free to decide on employment conditions, academic programmes, resource allocation without government approval (Sporn 2002), and to borrow funds" while "all academic personnel are to be employed by the university on the basis of private contracts" (Pechar 2005: 10).

Another development is the establishment of universities as foundations under private law. The Chalmers Technical University was the first well-known initiative in this area. In 1994 Chalmers became a semi-private foundation-owned university founded by the Swedish State with an initial endowment capital of €170 million. The university is run as a limited company. In the same year the University College of Jönköping also became a private foundation.

This model is starting to spread across Europe. In 1998, an amendment of the German Federal Framework Act for Higher Education, allowed the sixteen Länder (the German states) to establish a modified legal status for their universities (Palandt 2003: 182). Lower Saxony was the first "land" to take advantage of this possibility and its parliament passed the Lower Saxony University Reform Act, of 24 June 2002, allowing universities to become public foundations as legally self-administered public bodies (Palandt, ibid.). The decision of the university to become a foundation is taken on a voluntary basis.

Several universities in Lower Saxony, including the University of Göttingen and Fachhochschule (university of applied sciences) Osnabrück. – were transformed into foundations with effect from 1 January 2003. The new legal status grants institutions substantial autonomy, being expected this will allow for more effective and economic resource management, while there is hope that increased private and social funding will be attracted. Foundation universities can hire staff without state intervention, although keeping their status as civil servants and leaving public wage scales untouched (ibid.: 187). The new institutions will continue to receive financial support from the state, regulated by a contract negotiated with the state. The contract sets development and achievement targets that are the basis for calculating the level of financial support and the basis for future financial agreements. However, as the state of Lower Saxony does not have enough money to create an initial endowment, "the Reform Act authorises the government of Lower Saxony to transfer the property holdings of universities to them to form the basic capital of their foundations" (Palandt 2003: 184), although it cannot be used as security for bank credit.

In Finland a new university was created in Helsinki by merger of existing institutions into a new institution that is a foundation. The official inauguration of the new Aalto University, created by the merger of the Helsinki School of Economics, Helsinki University of Technology and the University of Art and Design took place on 8th January 2010.

In Portugal, the new legal framework for higher education institutions allows public universities to become "public foundations under private law" and three universities decided to immediately use this possibility – the University of Porto, the University of Aveiro and the ISCTE (Instituto Superior de Ciências do Trabalho e da Empresa). More recently a fourth institution, the University of Minho, has decided to apply to become a foundation.

The advantage of foundations is allowing its leaders more freedom to run the institution, with a minimum of external interference. However, transforming a public university into a foundation presents difficulties in restructuring internal management and staff may resist moving from a public service status to a foundation employee. However, it is very uncertain how future governments will be favourable to the foundation. This was apparently the case of Chalmers where the new government was against the idea of foundations and did not transfer the property holdings to Chalmers. In Portugal, the new government decided to integrate again foundation universities in the public budget, thus eliminating the main advantages of the new model.

35.7   Final Comments: International Bodies, Isomorphism and Path Dependency of Reforms

The empirical data collected on a number of European higher education systems shows there is an apparent convergence to a new governance model under the influence of new public sector policies. Paradeise (Chap. 31) argues the rationale and tools of reforms are amazingly similar across countries.

Governance models imported from the private sector are replacing traditional university models while there is a strong attack on the academic profession and the capacity of academics to run their institutions. There is concentration of power at top-level administration; collegial decision-making is becoming a souvenir from ruined Ivory towers; external constituencies are playing increasingly important roles in university governance; academics are no longer considered as being suitable to run their own institutions.

At "macro level" higher education systems are apparently converging all over the world, although at meso and micro level strong local and national characteristics play against uniformity. Dill and Sporn consider that "the contexts and organisational challenges confronting major universities in different countries are beginning to converge" (1995: 2) while for Halpin and Troyna "countries seem to be doing similar things, but on closer examination they are not as similar as it first appeared" (1995: 304). Levy argues "the literature on educational assistance (Ilchman and Ilchman 1987) and probably most of the literature on educational dependency (Altbach and Kelly 1978) and 'world systems' or hegemony (Meyer and Rowan 1977) can be cited for evidence of international isomorphism, some of it mimetic and normative but some of it coercive" (1999: 27).

The "macro" convergence of higher education systems can be explained in terms of globalisation and the emergence of neo-liberal policies (see Chap. 30 by de Boer and Jongbloed, Chap. 31 by Paradeise and Chap. 32 by Moscati). Ball (1998) explains the dissemination of these "universal" influences internationally – what Popkewitz (1996) calls the 'inter-national circulation of ideas' where some countries (UK, New Zealand, Chile) act as laboratories for political reform – using Levin's (1998) medical metaphor that considers international experts, policy entrepreneurs, and representatives of organisations selling tailor-made miraculous solutions for national problems as the analogues of infectious agents moving from country to country looking for suitable hosts to be infected, and by the sponsorship or even enforcement of particular policy solutions by international agencies (Jones 1998). International organisations, when they hold the 'power of the purse' as is the case with the Bretton Woods' offspring (WB and IMF) can originate strong isomorphic pressures. Other international agencies such as OECD and UNESCO can influence governments by means of international surveys and analyses (see Chap. 30 by de Boer and Jongbloed, Chap. 31 by Paradeise and Chap. 32 by Moscati). The European University Association through its Institutional Evaluation Programme has also been influencing changes in university governance towards a preferred model (Tavares et al. 2010).

National characteristics still play an important role, even when internal reforms of the systems are legitimated, at least at rhetoric level, by the country's need of assuming a position in the increasingly globalised world. Therefore, the degree and speed of reform implementation varies substantially from country to country (see Chap. 31 by Paradeise). This apparent paradox between the external weakening of sovereignty and internal strengthening of the state can be seen in the implementation of Bologna process in which national interests mask the European political objectives as each country reverts to a national logic to fulfil national objectives.

At meso level there is a very different picture, as "reforms remain path dependent and most often incremental" (see Chap. 31 by Paradeise), which may result in increasing institutional diversification.

However, there are conflicting pressures bearing on institutions. On the one hand, the recent emphasis on strategic planning and mission statements and the use of market regulation (see Chap. 32 by Moscati) may result in the definition of institutional identities that will protect diversity. The role of markets may produce contradictory effects. Institutions may diversify to occupy market niches or, on the contrary, they may be influenced by mimetic isomorphism and emulate successful competitors.

On the other hand, there are strong isomorphic pressures acting both at global level (globalisation, international organisations, networking) and at national level (mainly governments and traditional institutions with strong academic traditions and prestige). Some activities imported from the business world such as benchmarking, quality evaluation and accreditation, as well as competitive funding mechanisms may reinforce isomorphic pressures, namely if some of these activities assume an international character. The decision of the Ministers to support multi-dimensional transparency tools, creating a classification of European universities (U-Map) to be followed by a ranking system (U-Multirank) may also have consequences as institutions try to improve their classification or jump a few places in rankings.

Not being a "seer" it is difficult to guess what the future will be. Path dependency explains that reforms should not produce the same effects on every institution, as Paradeise argues in her chapter in this book. An important development with unforeseeable consequences is the investment made by a number of European countries to establish "research universities" capable of competing at world level. This may lead to very stratified national higher education systems – and to a stratified European Higher Education Area – with what Guy Neave suggests will be "a highly focused and selective 'Guardian Relationship' resurrected and built around a few highly performing establishments" or, a variant alternative would be "the emergence in Europe's higher education systems of a 'temporarily protected' sector, consisting of highly-performing research universities at the apex and at the base a 'market-driven' mass sector" (Neave 2009).

It is also too early to elaborate on the consequences of a growing influence of external forces and stakeholders on the internal governance of HEIs. This development may be seen as an attempt of governments to regulate higher education institutions that were given some level of autonomy for competing in a market. Institutions may follow strategies aimed at ensuring their own development and survival, to the detriment of the common good or the government's objectives.

The presence of 'external stakeholder' refers to a third party acting between the community of scholars and the society. This third party aims at articulating the interests of society within the institution, ensuring that the institution is 'relevant'. And it is anti-Humboldtian by nature as opposes the Humboldtian principle that third parties should not interfere with the institutions' pursuit of its mission.

On the one hand, external stakeholders may represent outside interests in the same way that stockholders have a role in the management of firms and companies. This corresponds to a vision of the university as mere service provider, inducing quick-fix attitudes from the institutions and may result in what Cardinal Newman called 'utilitarism'.

On the other hand, external stakeholders may represent the broader and long-term interests of society upholding the notion of higher education as a public good. Their role is not to promote market values *à outrance,* but to ensure that externalities and the core values of the university are not jeopardised by institutional attitudes that emphasise short-term market values while ignoring the university's social role (Amaral and Magalhães 2002).

References

Agnelli, G. (1988). Industry's expectations of the university. *CRE-Action, 83,* 11–17.

Altbach, P., & Kelly, G. (Eds.). (1978). *Education and colonialism.* New York: Longman.

Amaral, A., & Magalhães, A. (2002). The emergent role of external stakeholders in European higher education governance. In A. Amaral, A. G. Jones, & B. Karseth (Eds.), *Governing higher education: National perspectives on institutional governance* (pp. 1–21). Dordrecht: Kluwer Academic Publishers.

Amaral, A., & Magalhães, A. (2003). The triple crisis of the university and its reinvention. *Higher Education, 16*(2), 239–253.

Amaral, A., Magalhães, A., & Santiago, R. (2003a). The rise of academic managerialism in Portugal. In A. Alberto, L. Meek, & I. M. Larsen (Eds.), *The higher education managerial revolution?* (pp. 101–123). Dordrecht: Kluwer Academic Publishers.

Amaral, A., Fulton, O., & Larsen, I. M. (2003b). A managerial revolution? In A. Amaral, L. V. Meek, & I. M. Larsen (Eds.), *The higher education managerial revolution?* (pp. 275–296). Dordrecht: Kluwer Academic Publishers.

Ball, S. J. (1998). Big policies/small world: An introduction to international perspectives in education policy. *Comparative Education, 34*(2), 119–130.

Boston, J., Martin, J., Pallot, J., & Walsh, P. (1996). *Public management: The New Zealand model.* Auckland: Oxford University Press.

Bovaird, T., & Löffler, E. (2001). Emerging trends in public management and governance. *BBS Teaching & Research Review, 5*(Winter 2001), 1–9.

Carrier, D., & van Vught, F. (1989). Government and curriculum innovation in France. In F. van Vught (Ed.), *Governmental strategies and innovation in higher education.* London: Jessica Kingsley Publishers.

Clark, B. R. (1983). Governing the higher education system. In M. Shattock (Ed.), *The structure and governance of higher education* (pp. 19–42). Guilford: Society for Research into Higher Education.

Cobban, A. B. (1975). *The medieval universities: Their development and organization.* London: Methuen.

Crozier, M., Huntington, S. P., & Watanuki, J. (1975). *The crisis of democracy.* New York: New York University Press.

Cunha, L. A. (1999). O público e o privado na educacão superior brasileira: uma fronteira em movimento. In H. Trindade (Ed.), *Uma Universidade em Ruínas – Na República dos Professores* (pp. 39–56). Petrópolis: Editora Vozes.

de Boer, H., Denters, B. & Goedegebuure, L. (1998). On boards and councils; shaky balances considered. The governance of Dutch universities. *Higher Education Policy, 11*, 153–164.

de Boer, H. (2003). Who's afraid of red, yellow and blue? The colourful world of management reforms. In A. Amaral, L. V. Meek, & I. M. Larsen (Eds.), *The Higher Education Managerial Revolution?* (pp. 89–108). Dordrecht: Kluwer Academic Publishers.

Dearing report. (1997). *Report of the National Committee of Enquiry into Higher Education,* London.

Deem, R. (1998). New managerialism in higher education: The management of performances and cultures in universities. *International Studies in Sociology of Education, 8*(1), 47–70.

Deem, R. (2001). Globalisation, new managerialism, academic capitalism and entrepreneurialism in universities: Is the local dimension important? *Comparative Education, 37*(1), 7–20.

Dill, D., & Sporn, B. (1995). The implications of a postindustrial environment for the university. In D. Dill & B. Sporn (Eds.), *Emerging patterns of social demand and university reform: Through a glass darkly.* Oxford: Pergamon Press.

Dill, D., Teixeira, P., Jongbloed, B., & Amaral, A. (2004). Conclusions. In P. Teixeira, B. Jongbloed, D. Dill, & A. Amaral (Eds.), *Markets in higher education: Rhetoric or reality?* (pp. 327–352). Dordrecht: Kluwer Academic Publishers.

Ferlie, E., Pettigrew, A., Ashburner, L., & Fitzgerald, L. (1996). *The new public management in action.* New York: Oxford University Press.

Fulton, O. (2002). Higher education governance in the UK: Change and continuity. In A. Amaral, G. A. Jones, & B. Karseth (Eds.), *Governing higher education: National perspectives on institutional governance* (pp. 187–211). Dordrecht: Kluwer Academic Publishers.

Habermas, J. (1973). *Legitimations probleme im Spatkapitalismus.* Frankfurt: Suhrkamp.

Halpin, D., & Troyna, B. (1995). The politics of policy borrowing. *Comparative Education, 31*(3), 303–310.

Halsey, A. H. (1992). *Decline of donnish dominion: The British academic professions in the twentieth century.* Oxford: Clarendon Press.

Ilchman, W., & Ilchman, A. (1987). Academic exchange and the founding of new universities. *Annals AAPSS, 491*, 48–62.

Jones, P. W. (1998). Globalisation and internationalism: Democratic prospects for world education. *Comparative Education, 34*(2), 143–155.

Jongbloed, B. (2003). Marketisation in higher education: Clark's triangle and the essential ingredients of markets. *Higher Education Quarterly, 57*(2), 110–135.

Jongbloed, B. (2004). Regulation and competition in higher education. In P. Teixeira, B. Jongbloed, D. Dill, & A. Amaral (Eds.), *Markets in higher education: Rhetoric or reality?* (pp. 87–111). Dordrecht: Kluwer Academic Publishers.

Larbi, G. A. (1999, September). *The new public management approach and crisis states* (United Nations Research Institute for Social Development (UNRISD) Discussion Paper 112). Geneva: UNRISD.

Levin, B. (1998). An epidemic of education policy: (What) can we learn from each other? *Comparative Education, 34*(2), 131–141.

Levy, D. C. (1999). When private higher education does not bring organizational diversity. In P. G. Altbach (Ed.), *Private Prometheus. private higher education and development in the 21st century.* Westport: Greenwood Press.

Magalhães, A., & Amaral, A. (2000). Portuguese higher education and the imaginary friend: The stakeholders role in institutional governance. *European Journal of Education, 35*(4), 439–448.

Mandeville, B. (1924). *The fable of the bees: Or private vices, publick benefits with a commentary critical, historical and explanatory by F.B. Kaye*. Oxford: Clarendon Press.

Meek, V. L. (2003). Introduction. In A. Amaral, V. L. Meek, & I. Larsen (Eds.), *The higher education managerial revolution?* (pp. 1–29). Dordrecht: Kluwer Academic Publishers.

Meyer, J. W., & Rowan, B. (1977). Institutionalized organizations: Formal structure as myth and ceremony. *The American Journal of Sociology, 83*(2), 340–363.

Miller, H. D. R. (1995). *The management of changes in universities*. Buckingham: SHRE/Open University.

Mittelstrass, J. (1994). *Die unzeitgemässe Universität*. Frankfurt am Main: Suhrkamp.

Moodie, G., & Eustace, R. (1974). *Power and authority in British universities*. London: Allen & Unwin.

Neave, G. (1995). The stirring of the prince and the silence of the lambs: The changing assumptions beneath higher education policy, reform and society. In D. Dill & B. Sporn (Eds.), *Emerging patterns of social demand and university reform: Through a glass darkly*. Oxford: Pergamon Press.

Neave, G. (2001). The European dimension in higher education – An excursion into the modern use of historical analogues. In J. Huisman, G. Neave, & P. Maassen (Eds.), *Higher education and the nation state*. Oxford: Pergamon.

Neave, G. (2009). Institutional autonomy 2010 – 2020 The tale of the Elan – Two steps back to take one very large leap forward. In B. Kehm, J. Huisman, & B. Stensaker (Eds.), *The European Higher Education Area: Perspectives on a moving target* (pp. 3–22). Rotterdam: Sense Publishers.

Neave, G., & van Vught, F. (Eds.). (1994). *Government and higher education relationships across three continents, The winds of change*. London: Pergamon Press.

Nybom, T. (2003). The Humboldt legacy and the contemporary European university. In E. De Corte (Ed.), *Excellence in higher education* (pp. 17–32). London: Portland Press.

O'Connor, J. (1973). *The fiscal crisis of the state*. New York: St. Martin's.

OECD. (2003). Changing patterns of governance in higher education. In *Education policy analysis 2003*. Paris: OECD.

OECD. (2008). *Tertiary education for the knowledge society*. Paris: OECD.

Osborne, D., & Gaebler, T. (1992). *Re-inventing government: How the entrepreneurial spirit is transforming the government*. Reading: Addison-Wesley.

Palandt, K. (2003). Universities as foundations – The new model of Lower Saxony. *Higher Education in Europe, XXVIII*(2), 181–187.

Pechar, H. (2005). *University autonomy in Austria* (HOFO Working Paper Series: IFF_hofo.05.001).

Pollitt, C. (2007). The new public management: An overview of its current status. *Admnistratie SI Management Public, 8*, 110–115.

Popkewitz, T. (1996). Rethinking decentralisation and state/civil society distinctions: The state as a problematic of governing. *Journal of Education Policy, 11*(1), 27–52.

Reed, M. (2002). New managerialism, professional power and organisational governance in UK universities: A review and assessment. In A. Amaral, G. A. Jones, & B. Karseth (Eds.), *Governing higher education: National perspectives on institutional governance* (pp. 163–186). Dordrecht: Kluwer Academic Publishers.

Robbins Report. (1963). *Higher education: Report of the Committee appointed by the Prime Minister under the chairmanship of Lord Robbins 1961–63* (Cmnd. 2154). London: HMSO.

Ruegg, W. (1996). Prólogo. In H. Ridder-Symoens (Ed.), *As Universidades na Idade Médi* (pp. XVII–XXIV). Lisbon: Imprensa Nacional Casa da Moeda.

Scott, P. (1989). The power of ideas. In C. Ball & H. Eggins (Eds.), *Higher education into the 1990s: New dimensions* (pp. 7–16). Buckingham: Society for Research into Higher Education and Open University Press.

Scott, P. (1995). *The meanings of mass higher education*. Buckingham: SHRE and Open University Press.

Self, P. (2000). *Rolling back the market: Economic dogma and political choice*. New York: St. Martin's Press.

Shattock, M. (2001, October 30). *The governance of UK universities in the post-dearing era*. Paper presented at the UK Society for Research in Higher Education Seminar, London.

Slaughter, S., & Leslie, L. (1997). *Academic capitalism: Politics, policies and the entrepreneurial university*. Baltimore: John Hopkins Press.

Smith, A. (1776). *An inquiry into the nature and causes of the wealth of nations* (2nd ed., Vol. 2). London: Strahan & Cadell.

Sporn, B. (2002). World class reform of universities in Austria. *International Higher Education*, Boston College, *29*(Fall), 18–19.

Tavares, D., Rosa, M. J., & Amaral, A. (2010). Does the EUA institutional evaluation programme contribute to quality improvement? *Quality Assurance in Education, 18*(3), 178–190.

Tolofari, S. (2005). New public management and education. *Policy Futures in Education, 3*(1), 75–89.

Trow, M. (1996). Trust, markets and accountability in higher education: A comparative perspective. *Higher Education Policy, 9*(4), 309–324.

Van Vught, F. A. (1989). Innovations and reforms in higher education. In F. A. van Vught (Ed.), *Government strategies and innovation in higher education* (pp. 47–72). London: Jessica Kingsley Publishers.

Wilson, K. (1989). The pattern, range and purpose of higher education: A moral perspective. In C. Ball & H. Eggins (Eds.), *Higher education into the 1990s: New dimensions* (pp. 38–50). Buckingham: Society for Research into Higher Education and Open University Press.

Part VI
Funding of Higher Education

Chapter 36
A Policy Gap: Financing in the European Higher Education Area

Liviu Matei

36.1 The European Higher Education Area as a Knowledge Society Project and Its Unexpected Success

We are witnessing a fascinating phenomenon at the beginning of the twenty-first century. Ambitious initiatives have been put forward as mere blueprints or as actual, implemented projects, attempting to address, occasionally even to completely "solve", large societal issues at local, national, regional or global levels. Such projects, so ambitious that they may appear utopian, try to take advantage of new opportunities brought about by "the knowledge society". They represent what the author of this paper calls "knowledge society projects". There are hundreds, perhaps even thousands of knowledge society projects around the world.

The Millennium Development initiative of the United Nations (UN), for instance, could be defined as a knowledge society project on a *global* scale.[1] It aims primarily at the eradication of extreme poverty – by putting together "building blocks of a global knowledge society" (Understanding Knowledge Societies 2005). The project of an African Renaissance launched by the former South-African president Thabo Mbeki is an example of a *regional* knowledge society project. This complex initiative attempted to set off the overall economic and cultural revival of an entire continent, Africa, specifically and explicitly by taking advantage of the new opportunities brought about by the knowledge society[2] (see for example, Mbeki 1998). A similar attempt to develop a blueprint for a *regional* knowledge society project has been made in the Arab world, as illustrated by the Arab Human

---

[1] See for example Understanding Knowledge Societies (2005), for arguments in favour of characterising the UN Millennium Development project as a knowledge society project.

[2] see for example, Mbeki 1998.

L. Matei (✉)
Department of Public Policy, Central European University, Nador str. 9, 1051 Budapest, Hungary
e-mail: mateil@ceu.hu

A. Curaj et al. (eds.), *European Higher Education at the Crossroads:*
Between the Bologna Process and National Reforms,
DOI 10.1007/978-94-007-3937-6_36, © Springer Science+Business Media Dordrecht 2012

Development Reports.[2] In Europe, we have our own knowledge society project, developed in the framework of the Lisbon strategy of the European Union (EU) since 2000, aiming at building a knowledge society which would in turn help Europe/the European Union achieve ambitious economic, political, and social goals. Two of the original objectives of this *regional* knowledge society project (Presidency Conclusions. Lisbon European Council 2000) were to make the EU the most competitive economy in the world by 2010, and to achieve no less than full employment by the same deadline (none of these objectives was achieved as such, as it is well known by now). The Lisbon strategy of the EU could be considered an all-encompassing knowledge society project. Although it did not initially intend to cover the area of higher education, its focus on knowledge and on the knowledge society lead to significant interest in higher education. In fact, the overall project had a major influence on higher education policies in the EU and in Europe, in particular through two of its distinct policy initiatives, the European Research Area and the European Area of Lifelong Learning.

What is remarkable about knowledge society projects is that they are intended to be, and sometimes indeed are, **real projects**. The term "project" attached to such initiatives is not just a metaphor. Despite the extraordinary scope of ambitions and their vast complexity, such endeavours are designed, and sometimes implemented, using an unmistakable managerial perspective: they have explicit targets and indicators (numerically expressed), detailed roadmaps, implementation calendars, evaluation mechanisms, human resources/taskforces, detailed organisational implementation infrastructures, etc. Sometimes they also contain detailed provisions regarding financial resources necessary for implementation (every proper project must have a budget).

Knowledge society projects have emerged in particular sectors as well; they are not always as all-encompassing as the initiatives mentioned briefly above. It is possible, for example, to define the Bologna process as a regional, pan-European knowledge society project restricted to the area of higher education. One of the declared original goals of the process, as stated in its founding document, the Bologna Declaration of 1999, was to contribute to the creation of a **European knowledge society** as a means of advancing a specific political, economic and social agenda for the European continent:

> A Europe of Knowledge is now widely recognised as an irreplaceable factor for social and human growth and as an indispensable component to consolidate and enrich the European citizenship, capable of giving its citizens the necessary competencies to face the challenges of the new millennium, together with an awareness of shared values and belonging to a common social and cultural space (...) The course has been set in the right direction and with meaningful purpose. (The Bologna Declaration 1999)

It could be argued that when analysed as a project (a **knowledge society project**, more precisely) in a historical perspective, the Bologna process appears to be a

---

[2] See for example Arab Knowledge Report: Towards Productive Intercommunication of Knowledge (2009); Arab Knowledge Report: Building a Knowledge Society (2003).

surprising success. It is not so because it has fully achieved its original or subsequent objectives (it has not), nor because it has helped to build an impeccable European Higher Education Area (EHEA), with flourishing, problem-free national higher education systems and institutions (far from that). Rather, the Bologna process can be seen as a success for two different reasons. First, it has stimulated real and perhaps unexpected progress in several areas in European higher education, such as degree structures, quality assurance or international mobility. Second, the Bologna process has evolved as a specific European answer to the challenges of globalisation, displaying a remarkable European capacity to innovate in higher education.

Various authors, scholars or other observers of recent developments in European higher education point to different aspects of the Bologna process that make it a singular and, at least partially, also a success story. One could ask how this was possible. What made the Bologna process/project a success story? Why significant progress can be reported in some areas while nothing really relevant happened in others.

When analyzing Bologna as a knowledge society project what is possibly the most salient and remarkable aspect is its political and cultural geography, the fact that almost all countries of the continent (47 at present) joined it. It is indeed unprecedented in the history of higher education and unheard of in any other part of the world in our time to have first 29, then increasingly more until the current 47 countries, with their copious diversity of cultures, languages, levels of economic development, constitutional systems and traditions *agreeing* to work together and, moreover, *actually working* together towards the creation, with program and method, despite back and forth, of a common Higher Education Area. Launched formally in 2010 by the responsible ministers from the Bologna countries, although not exactly complete or final, the European Area of Higher Education is indeed today more than just a blueprint or a nominal knowledge society project. Most probably when the Bologna Declaration was signed in 1999 very few expected that it would ever come into being in any significant form. Today it appears that the project has been successfully "implemented" to a surprising extent. The success of the project is in part reflected in the development of innovative, European concepts, tools, instruments and new approaches to policy making. Such developments were made possible to a large extent by the emergence of a new, unique type of **space for dialogue in higher education that has been created within the European Higher Education Area**. This is at the same time a professional space, and intellectual space, a policy space, and a political one.

It should be noted that the European space for dialogue is not the result of the Bologna process alone. The emergence of a European Research Area, as part of the Lisbon strategy of the EU, brought additional elements to this space, as the two areas, the European Research Area (promoted by the EU Lisbon strategy) and the European Area of Higher Education (the creation of which was the objective of the Bologna process) become intertwined in a variety of ways, showing both significant complementary aspects, as well as occasional incongruities.

The new space for dialogue in higher education is extraordinary not only given its remarkable geographic spread, or its cultural and linguistic diversity. It is also unique as it has made it possible for new actors to emerge and for old and new actors in higher education to interact in new ways. For example, the traditional room for interaction between the State and the university, or higher education institutions more generally, has been significantly altered by the emergence of a trans-national, European policy arena. New actors have emerged or old actors have acquired new roles. EU institutions, such as the Commission (a full member of the Bologna process, together with national governments) or the Parliament are an example of new actors in the larger European higher education policy arena. Other examples include university and professional associations, student organisations, or organisations of the employers, acting locally, nationally, or interacting with each other at European level in unprecedented ways, under the auspices of a set of common, goals, be they occasionally vague and in flux. Universities, academics and students have noticed new possibilities and learned to interact with each other and with the authorities in new ways, within a given institution, country or across borders.

While Bologna is rightly described as a fundamentally top-down process, and possibly not exactly democratic, it should be acknowledged at the same time that it has created unprecedented possibilities for action, a new "freedom" or "freedoms" for universities, academics, and students, within a European space for dialogue in higher education with a set of unique characteristics.

The emergence of **a common European space for dialogue** in higher education stretching all the way from Greenland to Vladivostok and from Trondheim to La Valletta is remarkable in itself, even before identifying any concrete elements of innovation it has made possible and helped put in practice. It is impressive, for example, that a common qualifications framework for the entire European Higher Education Area has been adopted by the ministers responsible for higher education from the Bologna countries (Bergen 2005). Even though this framework is still more of a nominal policy tool at present and even before various countries will eventually implement it and transfer into national qualifications frameworks, it is extraordinary that they could discuss and eventually agree on a very short set of common descriptors and definitions for all higher degree levels expected to be valid for all these countries, despite their abundant diversity (the document itself with the qualifications framework adopted in Bergen is no longer than two pages). The same could be said about the adoption in 2005 of European Standards and Guidelines for Quality Assurance (ENQA 2005). In a way that is indicative for how the new space for dialogue works, the development of the Qualifications Framework for Higher Education and of the Standards was the result of complex interactions, involving several European organizations representing universities, students, quality assurance agencies, and also of university administrators, experts, politicians from various countries, national governments and the EU Commission. These are two examples showing that a European space for dialogue in higher education does exist and that it creates conditions for innovative policy developments.

As a regional integration project, the Bologna process is also remarkable in that it was initiated and has progressed in connection with the larger process of European integration. Bologna illustrates how a higher education project can contribute, with all related difficulties and shortcomings, towards a continental effort aiming at economic and political integration. The Bologna process, on the other hand, is more than just a case of a regional higher education project contributing to a "superordinate" project of political and economic integration. If that were the case, it would mean that it only contributes to subordinating higher education to higher-level political aspirations and imperatives. In fact, Bologna is also an example of how higher education itself came to the forefront of the political and public policy agenda. As put by Elkana and Klöpper (2012):

> In the present atmosphere of ferocious attacks on Bologna – perhaps the strongest in Germany – one should not overlook the enormous achievements. One of them surely is that the Bologna process managed to put higher education at the top of the European policy agenda. Therefore, justified as many of the individual complaints may be, going back to square one and unthinking the whole process is neither feasible, nor desirable.

Other than developments and even achievements at political or public policy level, the Bologna process and the new space for dialogue have stimulated the creation of new concepts, practical instruments and tools which are directly related to the work of universities and are meant to instrumentally support the more operational objectives of the project, such as increased intra-European mobility, easier recognition of degrees and qualifications, or quality improvements. Such "European" tools, instruments and concepts are relatively well-known: the new BA-MA degree structure (completed by the addition of a doctoral layer since 2003) now implemented in many European countries and leading to a relatively homogenous academic degree landscape in Europe, as opposed to the previous wide diversity; the development and implementation of the European credit system, ECTS, which pre-dates Bologna but acquired a new role and prominence; the diploma supplement; the European Quality Assurance Register for Higher Education; the Tuning project (Tuning Educational Structures in Europe); the European Qualifications Framework for Higher Education; the emerging new European model of doctoral education (based on the "Salzburg principles"), etc. Some of these concepts and tools already have a major impact on European dynamics in higher education (e.g. structure of degree, diploma supplement). Other, such as the Qualifications Framework or the Quality Assurance Register has the *potential* to produce tectonic shifts in European higher education.

It could be stated that it is through all these developments and achievements, and without ignoring many shortcomings and difficulties, that the Bologna process acquired international prominence. Researchers, university administrators and policy makers, organizations active in higher education in all parts of the world became interested in the Bologna model or its certain elements. Such interest is not only a scholarly or theoretical one, but it involves looking for eventual sources of inspirations for practical initiatives. Occasionally, Bologna-stimulated developments, such as Tuning, are "imported", almost as if they were a "product" that could immediately be put to use, as it is the case already in the United States, in countries of Africa and Latin America. Bologna became so influential and "present" outside Europe that it is even perceived sometimes as a new form of Eurocentric imperialism (Espinoza Figueroa 2010). Governments of non-European countries became interested in Bologna and one country (Israel) even formally applied to become a member despite not being on the European continent.

The Bologna process had an impact on Europe and attracted significant international interest and prominence both as a model of a bold regional knowledge society project in the area of higher education (with important political and economic ramifications), and through its direct contributions to changing higher education realities in Europe.

There is a lot of criticism about Bologna as well, which should not be ignored. For example, it is generally accepted that if the Bologna process was a success story (compared to expectations even if not with all declared goals at various moments), the success, its real positive contribution, was more in terms of creating innovative and promising **structures and instruments**, rather than new and positive **content** within the European Higher Education Area. There is increasing interest, however, in what Bologna could contribute in terms of content as well, in a variety of ways, and there is hope that Bologna could facilitate new developments in higher education in terms of student learning, for example, and not only in terms of student mobility or reforms of the degree structures. To quote again Elkana and Klöpper, the Bologna process stimulated that

> university communities across Europe have begun to think about the aims of the university and begun to wonder about what it is that should be taught in order to achieve those aims. (…). If the current dissatisfaction with the reform can give birth to a new unity of purpose within the European higher education community, the Bologna reform may ultimately prove to have been a first step not just towards its structural, but also its intellectual renewal.

36.2 Financing as a Dimension of the EHEA Project

This paper does not intend to pursue a systematic analysis of the contributions of the Bologna process action line by action line, or priority by priority. It does argue, however, that significant, and often innovative, developments in various sub-areas or dimensions of European higher education have been made possible by the Bologna process, in particular by the fact that the process has helped to create a new, special type of space for dialogue in higher education.

A particular observation to be considered in the context of the present analysis is that although the Bologna process is a **project**, there was very little work, or even talk regarding how this project was supposed to be financed. In addition, although the project was about a specific model of reform of higher education at European scale and such a reform could not possibly succeed without effectively addressing issues of funding of universities, to date there has been very little programmatic reference to funding of higher education and very few efforts to conceptualize challenges that the project has brought or has to face in terms of funding. There is a double "neglect" of financing of higher education as part of the Bologna project. First, there are no clear views or projections about how the project itself was to be funded. Second, and perhaps more importantly, there are no major or systematic efforts to develop new tools in Europe in the area of financing, corresponding to the new, unprecedented ambitions of the project, so that to allow in the end better work of individual universities in the European Higher Education Area.

In all fairness, it should be said that innovation in the area of financing of higher education is rare anywhere in the world (Salmi 2009). On the other hand, evolutions in European higher education stimulated by the project of the European Research Area (a policy area within the Lisbon strategy of the EU that is outside of, but not too far from, the Bologna process), show that innovation in financing is not only necessary but also possible, in order to address new challenges and ambitions.

A central argument advanced in this paper is that despite its ability to encourage innovation in several areas of higher education, the Bologna process has not directly stimulated or produced any specific European tools, approaches, or concepts related to financing. A major reason for this "incapacity to innovate" in the area of funding in the context of the Bologna process could be that funding has not been included in the new "European space for dialogue" created by the Bologna process, which in turn has contributed decisively to make possible many other new, innovative developments in those areas that have been part of this space (mobility, structure of degrees, quality assurance, etc.).

The inclusion of the area of funding into the European space for dialogue in higher education has not happened despite the efforts in this direction made by the European Commission (EC). The EC not only openly attempted to stimulate a discussion at EU/European level regarding funding of universities, to propose policy analyses and new approaches with regard to funding, but it has actually developed and put in practice funding policies and policy instruments that had a direct and significant impact within the EU and also in the larger Europe (including by linking directly such efforts with Bologna objectives) and even outside Europe. The most significant of these instruments are the Erasmus programs, both the so-called Erasmus bilateral (to support intra-European mobility of students and staff), and the Erasmus Mundus, to support collaborative work of EU and non-EU universities, student mobility and increased attractiveness of the European Higher Education Area outside the EU. The EC efforts in this area can be tracked down in a series of *communications* regarding the role of universities in Europe issued within the framework of the Lisbon strategy and its extension, the Europe 2020 strategy (European Commission 2011; Commission of the European Communities 2003, 2005, 2006). All these communications attempt to address the issue of funding, sometimes by making direct reference to the Bologna process and the European Higher Education Area, which are otherwise outside the legal mandate of the EC, both as a policy area and geographically. The most recent of these communications (2011) deals extensively with funding as linked with governance of universities. Traditionally, the proposals of the EU in this area are rather vague and often devoid of practical substance (more funding for European university is needed to make them more competitive globally, more funding from private sources, etc.). The 2011 Communication, for a change, indicates very concrete and daring possible commitments of the EU to support a more systematic discussion about funding of higher education within the Union, new policy arrangements in the area of funding, and also significantly increased future funding for higher education, from older and new European sources.

Why have such efforts not succeeded in making financing an integral part of the new European space for dialogue in higher education, despite at least some very good initiatives and even major achievements (the Erasmus Mundus program launched and funded by the EU being the most significant)? It is possible that this has to do with the fact that the Bologna process and the Lisbon strategy do not overlap as policy arenas, the EC has limited possibilities to influence higher education policies within the EU itself and only very limited outside the EU, in the larger European Higher Education Area.

36.3 The Bologna Process and Financing of Higher Education: A Money Gap or a Policy Gap?

The existence of a "funding gap" in the European higher education has become everyday talk, almost like a mantra. It is openly and frequently mentioned by students, academics and university administrators, by professional associations of various kinds active in higher education, even by politicians, both at national and at European level. However, the exact understanding of the nature of this gap varies.

A programmatic policy paper on **Financing of Higher Education** published in 2005 by ESIB – The Unions of Students in Europe (currently ESU – European Students' Union) addresses the nature of the funding gap in European higher education explicitly, mainly from a students' perspective. The paper appears to correctly identify the funding gap not only as a matter of insufficient financial resources, as amounts mobilized for higher education, but also as a policy issue reflecting Europe's inability to innovate in this area. Following the policy line of thinking, ESIB points to a kind of incapacity in Europe to imagine solutions (that is new, adequate solutions) to contemporary challenges regarding financing of higher education. These challenges appear to be, in ESIB's view, not necessarily linked to the Bologna process, but rather to generic developments in higher education:

> In recent decades, public funding for HE has not adequately reflected the massive growth in student numbers, resulting in a gap in financial resources. Among the developments that have dramatically influenced the level of required financial support are internationalisation of higher education and research, the urge for quality and new teaching methods, the increasing and different economic interests in HE, and the diversification of places where knowledge is created, disseminated and transferred.
>
> The funding gap is a priority issue of both national and international concern, and has never been as present as it is today. It has proved difficult to find innovative and adequate solutions to the increasing demand for financial resources. Developments in society, together with extensive changes in higher education, call for a renewal of financing policies. However, these policy changes must not take place without accurate and extensive research and analysis of their long-term effect on students, HEIs and society (ESIB 2005).

As another example, the European Commission also talks about a "funding gap" in several documents referring to higher education (see above). The EU's perspective is chiefly informed by concerns regarding the potential role of universities in enhancing the economic competitiveness of the EU, as well as social cohesion. The EU communication on the Modernisation Agenda for Universities (EU Commission 2006) identifies a funding gap defined in terms of insufficient funding that is available to ensure that European universities become or remain globally competitive. The communication goes on to propose a kind of theoretically possible solution, pointing in the direction of increased private funding, but without any elaboration on how this could happen.

> Structural and cultural problems (…) are exacerbated by the huge dual funding deficit which affects universities on both the education and research sides. While there has been welcome growth in student enrolments, this has not been matched by growth in public funding, and universities in Europe have not been able to make up the difference from private sources. The average gap in resources for both research and education activities compared with their US counterparts is some EUR 10 000 per student per year. At the same time high-quality education and research are becoming more expensive and, with public finances tight, public authorities are attaching increasingly stringent conditions to support for university-based research. For the future, it seems likely that the bulk of resources needed to close the funding gap will have to come from non-public sources.

Similarly to student representatives or EU experts, scholars in the field of higher education policy are also aware of the existence of a "funding gap". In the same way as the European Commission, Jo Ritzen writes about the negative impact of insufficient funding, following from the reduction of public funds for higher education, on the universities' capacity to fulfil their potential, and about alternative solutions. His focus, however, is not that much and not directly on the mere competitiveness of Europe, but rather on how to support quality work (excellence) of universities:

> The finance needs to be rebalanced so that public budget cuts of the past decades can be met by private sources. The 2008/2009 economic crisis (never waste a good economic crisis) is an excellent opportunity for a paradigm shift all over Europe to promote excellence together with emancipation (Ritzen 2009).

Other researchers, like Marcel Gerard, point out, same as ESIB, the inadequacy of the current funding mechanisms to meet new challenges and to support new ambitions in Europe, such as student mobility, which is otherwise at the very core of the Bologna project (Gerard 2008).

A careful examination of Bologna developments appears to indicate that what is happening in the area of financing of higher education is not only a money gap (the usual mantra: insufficient budgets allocated to universities, insufficient financial resources mobilized by universities themselves). It is important to recognize that there is also a **policy gap in this area**. This is reflected in the fact that there is no systematic thinking, let alone real action, as part of the Bologna process to address the issue of funding. There is no systematic discussion at the level of the European Higher Education Area to try to identify and conceptualize challenges in the area of funding, and there are no organized efforts to develop solutions. A rare counter-example is the project of the European University Association (Estermann and Benetton Pruvot 2011) shedding light on issues related to diversification of funding of higher education in Europe and trying to promote a discussion on this subject.

Although funding is a formal Bologna priority since the 2009 Leuven ministerial conference, there are no elaborations about how to address this priority. Beyond the recognition of funding as a Bologna priority, there is almost no work to address it as part of the "project support infrastructure". The mention regarding the importance of funding in the Leuven/Louvain-la-Neuve communiqué (2009) appears to be more a place-holder than a policy statement intended to or capable of generating practical consequences. Symptomatically, participants to an international conference dedicated to the issue of financing of higher education, organized by the co-presidents of the Bologna process in Yerevan, Armenia, in September 2011 came to the conclusion that this was the first time ever, 12 years after the launch of the project, that a major Bologna conference on funding was organized.

The final report of the conference (Matei 2011) put forward conclusions that are directly relevant for the understanding of the "funding policy gap" in the European Higher Education Area, as well as recommendations regarding how to address the present situation.

As a policy area, funding of higher education appears to be a severely underdeveloped dimension of the Bologna Process. While remarkable progress has been made in other areas/Bologna action lines, it is very difficult to identify any initiatives in the area of funding of higher education that were meant to support or were derived from the overall objectives of the Bologna process (except initiatives of the EC, such as the Erasmus programs mentioned above).

It is this circumstance that points to what could be called a "funding policy gap", rather than only a "funding gap": while the Bologna project put forward many European-wide objectives and initiatives in higher education, the existing policies and mechanisms regarding funding in the European Higher Education Area remain almost exclusively national, or sub-national. There is a widening gap between the increasing European scope of the developments in higher education stimulated by the Bologna process (such as trans-national student mobility, joint degree programs, etc.) and the mostly scattered, national efforts to support or respond to these developments and associated challenges by putting in place appropriate funding policies and mechanisms. Finally, systematic efforts to understand conceptually this policy gap are also largely absent.

36.4 A Possible Way Ahead: Making Financing a Part of the European Space for Dialogue in Higher Education?

In order to ensure continuing progress of the Bologna process, for the benefit of all member countries and in full respect of their diverse models and national realities, it is important to start addressing this funding policy gap.

At this stage in the evolution of the European Higher Education Area, it appears important to make a strong and also substantive statement regarding the relevance of funding of higher education in the framework of the Bologna Process; it is important to move beyond the vague, place-holder recognition of funding as an "ingredient" of the process, and attempt to provide guidelines to orient practical future efforts.

To help achieve this, two recommendations were put forward at the Yerevan 2011 conference on funding of higher education (Matei 2011):

1. Re-affirm public responsibility for funding of higher education in the context of the Bologna process.
2. Stimulate the creation of a European space for dialogue in the area of financing of higher education.

Public responsibility does not mean that funding must come exclusively from public/state sources. Rather, it means that the state should be responsible for a regulatory framework that ensures efficient mobilisation, allocation, and use of financial resources in higher education, consistent with larger policy goals and principles. While Europe has at present and will preserve in the future a large diversity in the area of funding of higher education, in terms of national situations, specific challenges, approaches, and solutions (e.g. share of private vs. public provision in higher education), it is also possible to identify common public policy principles and goals to be considered when designing regulatory frameworks for financing of higher education. Such goals and principles include among others: education as a public good; concern for equity, access, and quality; need to consider the multiplicity of goals promoted by higher education policies (economic, social, national, European, etc.); sustainability; accountability and transparency.

The creation of a European space for dialogue in the area of financing of higher education, or the inclusion of financing in the existing European space for dialogue in higher education, could help bridging the funding policy gap. Such efforts could draw inspiration from the good precedent in the area of quality assurance. While 10–12 years ago the quality assurance landscape in Europe was totally scattered, a common European space for dialogue in this area has emerged, respecting diversity while making possible and stimulating joint work and advancement. This sub-"space" consists of a European Quality Assurance Register for Higher Education, the European Standards and Guidelines on Quality Assurance in the European Higher Education Area, and, not less important, an increasingly common European quality assurance vocabulary. Clearly, funding of higher education is in many ways different from quality assurance, if we consider only the fact that holders of the purse strings are ministries of finance, rather than educational authorities. Still, using the model of a "European space for dialogue" in this area is possible. This would mean systematic and coordinated efforts that would not put in danger existing prerogatives of national authorities to decide on the use of public money or, more generally, on regulatory frameworks for funding. Such activities would instead consist of: collecting and exchanging data and information on funding; sharing of good practices and success stories; learning from unsuccessful efforts and initiatives; joint efforts to conceptualize challenges (national, European, global) regarding funding of higher education; developing eventual common benchmarks; generating ideas for designing new funding mechanisms to support the advancement of the European Higher Education Area (e.g. jointly developing new, better mechanisms for funding mobility); developing and testing new concepts and tools (e.g. student vouchers).

The other papers included in the financing section of the present volume provide direct examples of what the discussion regarding financing in the European space for dialogue could be about, who could participate, and with what potential practical benefits.

The paper by Kata Orosz is a strong illustration of the need for an informed discussion, based on solid research, regarding particular methods of funding allocation. The author shows through a comparative study of experiences in the US and in Europe that, most surprisingly, performance-based funding has a very limited impact, eventually a small negative impact. This is a rare piece of research showing that policy makers can make monumental mistakes by using principles that appear simple and unproblematic ("performance funding does perform"). A European discussion of principles and experiences regarding performance funding, largely absent at present, is possible and could be very useful, also considering the fact that performance-based funding methods are usually expected to contribute to more accountability. What if they do not, in fact? How could they be made effective? How could powerful policy myths with regard to funding, performance, and accountability be avoided?

The paper by Enora Pruvot and Thomas Estermann is based on the study they conducted for the European University Association regarding the diversification of funding in the European Higher Education Area. This paper illustrates the need for data in the area of funding and how it can be gathered, in this case by a university association, in order to support informed policy discussions, at institutional, national, or European levels. Absent accurate and systematic information about the situation with regard to funding in EHEA, we are left with mostly guessing about what institutions or government do or should do. One particularly interesting finding is that a major gap exists between expectations of universities for new sources of funding in the near future and actual trends regarding new funding (universities unrealistically expect more funding from unlikely sources). This finding could help to orient both institutional approaches to diversifying funding and national or European initiatives in the area. The paper illustrates how focused research can facilitate a productive European discussion regarding more efficient approaches to diversifying funding.

The paper by James Powell provides conceptual, as well as practical guidelines, for institutions and for policy makers in the area of funding. It is based on the results of a comparative research conducted by the author involving Bologna countries and countries from other parts of the world. His paper points to the surprising capacity of higher education institutions to generate funding through engagement with their communities, with very little being needed by way of support from regulators and public policy makers.

Marcel Gerard writes about the inadequacy of current funding methods to support national and European-wide ambitious with regard to student mobility or to solve problems created by student mobility. Moreover, he points to the need for a sophisticated, European approach at two levels: conceptualizing the challenges and finding policy solutions. He uses advanced modelling to show that a solution to national concerns regarding mobility can only be found through of European joint work, taking into account legal, fiscal, and ethical aspects.

Lazar Vlăsceanu and Adrian Miroiu present lessons from the Romanian policy experiences of the last 10 years trying to link performance and funding. Their findings would certainly be interesting for colleagues in other countries preparing to introduce similar policies, should there be possible to discuss such issues in a European space, in order to avoid repeating mistakes.

36.5   Conclusions

The paper puts forward arguments to characterize and analyze the Bologna process as a knowledge society project. It argues that the Bologna process is a particular, in fact unique example of a regional knowledge society project, carried out in the area of higher education, in connection with a larger "European construction project". The Bologna process is a surprising success story. Several developments brought about by the Bologna process are indeed uniquely European, innovative, and they attracted a lot of attention outside Europe. The project displays, at the same time, many difficulties and shortcomings. The only one that is discussed here is related to funding. The paper argues that the Bologna process, as a knowledge society project in the field of higher education, shows a two-fold funding policy gap: no systematic provisions have been developed to ensure that the project itself would be properly funded; and no systematic work has been undertaken to date to advance the understanding of challenges that have to be addressed. Moreover, there have been no systematic efforts as part of the Bologna process to develop solutions in the area of funding, so that European universities could improve their work and performance as actors in the European Higher Education Area. The fact that financing is a severely underdeveloped dimension of the European Higher Education Area may be linked to the fact that financing has not been made a part of the space for dialogue brought about by the Bologna process. Finally, recommendations from a recent conference on funding of higher education in Europe are summarized as a possible way forward. The papers included in the financing section of the present volume are shortly reviewed with a view to indicate how financing could be effectively included in the European space for dialogue in higher education.

References

Arab Knowledge Report: Building a Knowledge Society. (2003). United Nations Development Program. Arab Fund for Economic and Social Development.

Arab Knowledge Report: Towards Productive Intercommunication of Knowledge. (2009). Al Maktoum Foundation, United Nations Development Program.

The Bologna Declaration of 19 June 1999. Joint declaration of the European Ministers of Education. Accessed at http://www.ehea.info/Uploads/Declarations/BOLOGNA_DECLARATION1.pdf.

Bergen (2005). The framework of qualifications for the European Higher Education Area. Adopted at the Bergen Conference of European Ministers Responsible for Higher Education 19-20 May 2005. Accessed at http://www.bologna-bergen2005.no/EN/BASIC/050520_Framework_qualifications.pdf.

Commission of the European Communities. (2003). Communication from the Commission – *The role of universities in the Europe of knowledge*.

Commission of the European Communities. (2005). Communication from the Commission – *Mobilising the brainpower of Europe: Enabling universities to make their full contribution to the Lisbon Strategy*.

Commission of the European Communities. (2006). *Communication from the Commission to the Council and the European Parliament.* Delivering on the Modernisation Agenda for Universities: Education, Research, and Innovation.

Elkana, Y., & Klöpper, H. (2012). *The university in the 21st century: Teaching the enlightenment at the dawn of the digital age* (pre-print draft version made available by the authors).

ESIB – The National Unions of Students in Europe. (2005). Policy Paper "*Financing of higher education*". Accessed at http://www.esib.org/index.php/documents/policy-papers/301-policy-paper-qfinancing-of-higher-educationq.html

Espinoza Figueroa, F. (2010). The Bologna Process as a hegemonic tool of Normative Power Europe (NPE): The case of Chilean and Mexican higher education. *Globalization Societies and Education, 8*(2), 247–256.

Estermann, T., & Benetton Pruvot, E. (2011). Brussels: *European universities diversifying income streams. Financially Sustainable Universities.* European University Association.

European Association for Quality Assurance in Higher Education (ENQA). (2005). *Standards and Guidelines for Quality Assurance in the European Higher Education Area.* Helsinki: ENQA.

European Commission. (2011). Communication from the Commission to the European Parliament, the Council, the European and Economic and Social Committee and the Committee of the Regions. *Supporting growth and jobs – An agenda for the modernisation of Europe's higher education systems*.

European Council. (2000). *Presidency conclusions, Lisbon European Council 23 and 24 March 2000.* Brussels: General Secretariat of the European Council.

Gerard, M. (2008). Higher education, mobility and the subsidiarity principle. In G. Gelauff, I. Grilo, & A. Lejour (Eds.), *Subsidiarity and economic reform in Europe*. Berlin: Springer.

Leuven/Louvain-la-Neuve communiqué (2009, April 28–29). *The Bologna Process 2020 – The European Higher Education Area in the new decade.* Communiqué of the Conference of European Ministers Responsible for Higher Education, Leuven/Louvain-la-Neuve. www.ond.vlaanderen.be/hogeronderwijs/bologna/conference/documents/Leuven_Louvain-la-Neuve_Communiqu%C3%A9_April_2009.pdf

Matei, L. (2011, September 8–9). Conference report. International conference on Funding of Higher Education Yerevan, Armenia. Accessed at http://www.ehea.info/news-details.aspx?ArticleId=253

Mbeki, T. (1998, August 13). The African Renaissance Statement of Deputy President, Thabo Mbeki, SABC, Gallagher Estate. Accessed at http://www.dfa.gov.za/docs/speeches/1998/mbek0813.htm

Ritzen, J. (2009). *A chance for European universities*. Amsterdam: Amsterdam University Press.

Salmi, J. (2009). Scenarios for financial sustainability in higher education. In *Higher education to 2030, Vol. 2: Globalisation*. Paris: Centre for Educational Research and Innovation. OECD.

Understanding Knowledge Societies. (2005). *In twenty questions and answers with the index of knowledge societies*. New York: United Nations.

Chapter 37
Accountability and the Public Funding of Higher Education

A Comparison of Stakeholder Views and Institutional Responses in the US and Europe

Kata Orosz

37.1 Higher Education Accountability in the US and Europe

The term "accountability" has enjoyed a remarkably ubiquitous status in higher education policy discourse in the US and Europe alike. Its widespread usage is dated to late 1980s, early 1990s in the US (Zumeta 1998) and around the same time, perhaps with a little lag, in Europe (Rhoades and Sporn 2002). Despite its frequent occurrence in policy documents and scholarly literature alike, its meaning has been far from unambiguous. Many have attempted to define "accountability" as a concept for public policy in general, and for higher education policy in particular.

Trow (1996) defined accountability as "the obligation to report to others, to explain, to justify, to answer questions about how resources have been used, and to what effect" (p. 2). Romzek (2000) differentiated between four types of accountability in the public sector: hierarchical, legal, professional and political; Huisman and Currie (2004) argued that in the state–higher education sector relationship, professional and political accountability figures most prominently.

Metz (2011) offers a comprehensive theoretical framework for describing accountability systems; he argues that each accountability concept can be described as a matrix of three distinct duties: the duty to act responsibly, the duty to report on succeeding or failing to act responsibly, and finally the duty to respond to infraction to responsible behaviour. For example, accountability in a national higher education system may be characterized by the higher education institutions' duty to contribute to the national knowledge economy, the duty of the institutions' leaders to report on how their activities relate to the achievement of this goal, and finally the duty of the national government to respond to failures in achieving this goal.

K. Orosz (✉)
Teachers College, Columbia University, New York, NY, USA
e-mail: ko2270@columbia.edu

A. Curaj et al. (eds.), *European Higher Education at the Crossroads:*
Between the Bologna Process and National Reforms,
DOI 10.1007/978-94-007-3937-6_37, © Springer Science+Business Media Dordrecht 2012

Scholars of higher education policy pointed out that some concept of accountability emerged at approximately the same time in the US and Europe, two "core" regions of higher education policies (Rhoades and Sporn 2002). There have been attempts to explore the similarities and differences between the way various states in the US and countries in Europe embraced the concept of accountability. A comparative inquiry (Huisman and Currie 2004) argued that in both regions, "the changing relationship between government and universities [was] the most important factor affecting the rise of accountability" (p. 547). However, the change in the state–higher education sector relationship played out very differently in the US and Europe – which likely have affected the way each regional policy discourse made use of the concept (Herbst 2007).

Arguably, the emergence of increasing calls for accountability was associated with the "retreat of the state" in Europe (Huisman and Currie 2004). A summary of European higher education reform trends in the past two decades offers the following chronology: "The first wave of [higher education reforms in Europe] comprises elements such as market, participation, flexibility and *deregulation*, while the second wave encompasses concepts such as coordination, *accountability*, regulation and performance management" (Frøhlich et al. 2010, p. 17, emphasis added). Since the retreat of the state implies increasing institutional autonomy, European concepts of accountability often make use of Romzek's category of professional accountability, with the focus on quality of teaching and research (Rhoades and Sporn 2002; Huisman and Currie 2004).

Accountability appears to have been rooted in a very different ground in the US. Calls for accountability accompanied not the retreat of the state, but the advent of increasing state oversight of higher education institutions. Zumeta (1998) argued that while historically state governments in the US were content to leave the public oversight of public higher education institutions to two intermediary institutions, the lay board of trustees and the state higher education boards or commissions, this dynamic started to change in the late 1980s. The economic downturn and a political shift to the right in many states resulted in cuts to higher education budgets, which in turn contributed to increasing tuition in public institutions. State governments facing budget pressures and an electorate largely opposed to tax increases, as well as parents of college-aged students facing tuition increases that surpassed inflation, started demanding that public higher education institutions operated more efficiently. Given that the US accountability concept seems to be the product of political pressures to increase the productivity of higher education institutions (Harnisch 2011), state accountability policies in the US may be characterized as predominantly political.

Usage of the same, or similar, terms (e.g. transparency, the "right to know") may give the impression that higher education policy developments in the US and in certain European countries have been on a very similar trajectory over the past two or three decades. Research lends support to the view that some policy borrowing from the US has taken place in Europe, either directly, or through the mediation of international organisations, which may partially explain similarities in accountability policies (Rhoades and Sporn 2002). Nevertheless, any transatlantic study of higher education policies should be aware of the differences in the economic and political origins of the accountability concept, and be on the lookout for how these differences may impact the way accountability systems are designed, implemented and evaluated in the US and Europe.

Accountability systems, including performance funding policies, are not a new phenomenon. The fact that they have been around for some time now (especially in the US) makes them attractive research subjects: policies that have been implemented for over two decades can reasonably be assumed to have had some effects, intended or unintended. Indeed, the past few years have shown a renewed interest in performance funding among policy makers and researchers alike. This paper offers a review of recent empirical research evidence on state-level (in the US context) and national (in the European context) accountability systems, with a special focus on performance accountability.

Following a review of theoretical literature on performance accountability, and specifically, performance funding, the paper compares and contrasts empirical studies of performance accountability systems from the US and Europe. Given the immensity of the subject, as well as the relatively autonomous developments of performance accountability policies for teaching and for research (Herbst 2007; van Damme 2009), present paper focuses on performance accountability for teaching (i.e. performance accountability policies designed for university research will not be discussed). Some studies covered in the paper explored stakeholder perceptions of performance accountability systems; others assessed the impact of specific accountability systems on institutional behaviour and performance. Using the method of content analysis, the paper attempts at highlighting common patterns as well as dissimilarities in performance accountability policies in the US and Europe, as manifest in the findings of recent empirical research.

37.2 A Popular System of Accountability – Performance Funding

Since the adoption of the first explicitly performance-based higher education accountability system in Tennessee in 1979, performance accountability policies have taken various forms. This section offers a brief overview of the basic features of performance accountability systems on the basis of existing academic and policy literature in the subject.

Performance accountability systems are often classified on the basis of the directness of the link between institutional performance and state resource allocation. When public higher education institutions are mandated to report their performance in several dimensions of teaching and research to the state legislation but the performance reports have no direct bearing on the amount of public funds each institution receives, the accountability system is called performance reporting. In the case of performance budgeting, institutional performance is considered as one of the many factors that determine the amount of funding from the state.

However, the link between performance and resource allocation is not direct; it is typically at the discretion of state legislators and other officials to determine the extent to which institutional performance is taken into consideration when allocating resources. In the case of the third variant, performance funding, the relationship between performance and resource allocation is non-discretionary: the amount of public funding is determined by funding formulas set by the legislation (McLendon et al. 2006).

In the case of performance reporting, professional accountability as well as public and peer pressure hold higher education institutions accountable for results. Performance budgeting and performance funding policies have their theoretical foundation in resource dependency theory: the state is using financial incentives to sustain, or improve, institutional performance (Barnetson and Cutright 2000). Performance budgeting and funding policies are characterized by outcome-orientation and a centralised, regulated approach (Jongbloed 2008). These policy instruments can be viewed as "a form of legislative oversight of the public higher education bureaucracy", with their specifications representing "efforts by legislators to monitor the activities of higher education for purposes of learning about the bureaucracy's behaviour and, possibly, of remedying deviations from legislative preferences" (McLendon et al. 2006, p. 18). The degree to which state legislatures wish to steer higher education institutions towards desired outcomes vary, just as the outcomes that each state finds desirable may vary.

Indeed, one of the most important features of any performance funding system is the set of indicators that are used to measure performance. Indicators may be related to input, process, output, or outcome measure (Burke 1998). Inputs include the resources, human, financial and physical, that are used to support the educational, research and administrative activities of higher education institutions. Process measures provide information on how a certain activity is carried out. Output indicators provide information on the quantity of products that are the result of the institution's activity; in the case of higher education institutions, output indicators may include measures such as the number of credits earned, or the number of degrees awarded. Finally, outcome indicators measure the impact of the institution's activity on its environment. For example, how many of those holding a degree from a given college find a job within a year after graduation? Are graduates of a given program more or less productive in their jobs than graduates of a similar program offered at another institution?

In the US, institutional instructional performance is measured by "diverse indicators such as graduation rates, graduates' satisfaction of their college education, student transfer rates, licensure test scores etc." (Shin 2010, p. 52). Choosing the indicators is as much of a political decision as it is a practical one. A concern common to all policies that involve some form of indicator-based performance assessment is that the choice of indicators is due "more to the availability of data and ease of measurement than to their importance of policy concerns" (Burke 1998, p. 53). Quantifiable inputs (e.g. number of enrolled students) and outputs (e.g. number of degrees conferred) are easier to measure with precision than, say, the economic impact of a graduate engineering course on the local economy. Outputs may be easier to measure than outcomes, but the assumption that increasing output will improve outcomes may only hold true under specific circumstances.

Measuring what matters rather than what can easily be measured is but one of the many challenges associated with the design of a performance funding system. In the US, state legislatures tend to include more than one indicator in their performance funding systems. The number of indicators seems to vary quite widely: Burke (1998) reported that it ranged from a minimum of 3 in Florida to a maximum of 37 in South Carolina. The pattern is somewhat dissimilar in Europe: states appear to prefer a single performance indicator. Consider the examples of Norway, which funds universities based on the number of graduates (Frøhlich et al. 2010) or Italy, which allocates resources to universities on the basis of exams passed (Bagues et al. 2008).

One issue that arises when choosing which indicators to use is whether to use the same indicators across the board, or to introduce some level of differentiation. The US examples include examples of both universalism and differentiation. The state of Louisiana mandated the same indicators for all public higher education institutions under its jurisdiction. Other states, such as Florida or Washington, chose different indicators for their 2-year and 4-year colleges (Burke 1998).

Once stakeholders arrive at an agreement on which indicators to use, the question of indicator weight arises. Two basic approaches prevail: the use of equal or differential weights (Serban 1998). The use of differential weights may involve the setting of fixed weights, or the funding system may entail the use of funding ranges associated with each range. Equal indicator weights are rare, which may be due to the fact that this approach does not encourage diverse institutional missions and hence unpopular among institutional stakeholders.

Number, kind and weights of indicators aside, there are at least two more key features of any performance funding system: success criteria and funding levels. Serban (1998) differentiates between three basic approaches to setting success criteria: comparisons with peer institutions, institutional improvement over time, and comparisons against pre-set targets. Each approach has its advantages and disadvantages.

The comparative approach is based on the average performance of all institutions, rewarding those institutions that perform above average. The downside of this approach is that in a multi-faceted higher education sector, comparing the performance of institutions with markedly different missions amounts to comparing apples to oranges. To adjust for differences in institutional missions, some states in the US use the same indicators for 2-year and 4-year institutions but compare institutional performance to the average performance of the peer group only. However, in the comparative system not everybody can be a winner, which is bound to trigger institutional opposition. Furthermore, the state may want all of its public institutions to succeed (i.e. improve along certain dimensions) – in which case pitting institutions against each other in a race for resources is not a desirable strategy.

To mitigate the potentially negative effects of a competitive funding system, states can reward improvement in the performance of each individual institution compared to its own previous performance (Serban 1998). In such a system, each institution can focus on maintaining its own strengths and improving on its own weaknesses. Since this approach allows for the maintenance of diverse institutional missions, it tends to be popular among institutional stakeholders.

A performance-over-time approach may unduly penalize those institutions which are already performing well but this can be addressed by specifying that maintaining high levels of performance is sufficient for those among the top performers.

Comparison against pre-set targets is a possible, albeit not particularly popular, method of defining success (Serban 1998). The lack of popularity of this method is mainly due to the fact that regardless of where the performance targets are set, the link between improved performance and funding will be compromised. If the targets are too high, the system will fail to reward legitimate improvements in performance if they fall short of the target. Low performance targets, on the other hand, would not incentivise high-performers.

Last but not least, the level of funding associated with measured performance is a critical feature of any performance funding system. Funding levels are important, since the impact of financial incentives typically varies by the size of the reward (or penalty). Overall, funding directly related to institutional performance makes up a very small share of public funds that higher education institutions receive. For example, among the six states whose performance funding systems Dougherty et al. (2010) analysed, the state of Illinois allocated only 0.4% of the total public funds to the higher education sector based on institutional performance. The highest share of total state appropriations allocated on a performance-basis was found in South Carolina. When South Carolina introduced its performance funding system in 1996, it aimed at gradually increasing the share of public funds allocated on the basis of performance, with the goal of a fully performance-based funding by 2000. However, funding levels peaked at 38% in 1999. Typically, states in the US allocate around 2–5% of public funds to the higher education sector on the basis of institutional performance.

Comparable statistics from Europe suggest that although the use of performance funding for teaching may not be as widespread as in the US – examples of output-based funding of university instruction include the Czech Republic, Denmark, Finland, the Netherlands, Norway, Sweden and Spain (Midwestern Higher Education Compact 2009) –, those countries that do use it devote a relatively higher share of resources to performance funding. Frøhlich et al. (2010) estimate that about 25% of the institutional budget of Norwegian higher education institutions is based on their performance of a single output-indicator: the number of students they graduate. The Midwestern Higher Education Compact (2009) report cites that 30% of Finnish university resources are allocated based on the number of graduates; public funding to universities that is allocated on the basis of the number of diplomas awarded may take up 50% of total allocations in the Netherlands.

In short, there are several basic features of any performance accountability policy that one needs to consider when investigating the origins, adoption, and impact of such a policy instrument. Performance accountability may or may not be associated with financial incentives. In those variants where financial incentives are used (performance budgeting and funding), the link between institutional performance and financial reward may be more or less direct. Indicators of performance typically vary from state to state, and so may indicator weights and success criteria differ. Last but not least, the proportion of public resources allocated on the basis of performance may also vary considerably.

37.3 Empirical Research on Performance Funding – Findings from the US and Europe

The previous section offered a definition of performance accountability and an overview of the basic features of performance accountability systems. Descriptions of US performance accountability systems are numerous (e.g. Burke 1998; Burke and Minassians 2003; Dougherty and Reid 2007; Harnisch 2011; Midwestern Higher Education Compact 2009; Serban 1998). As for Europe, a major international survey on performance funding in higher education was conducted in 11 OECD countries, 7 of them European (Jongbloed and Vossensteyn 2001). A more recent description of the higher education funding systems of select European countries is available through an OECD working paper (Strehl et al. 2007); the country studies make reference to output-based funding and its perceived impact among stakeholders where applicable.

Empirical studies of performance accountability systems have been relatively scarce but have been more numerous in the past 5 years, possibly due to a renewed interest in performance funding among state legislators and non-governmental organizations in many states of the US in the late 2000s (Harnisch 2011; Rabovsky 2011).

Empirical research conducted in recent years approached performance accountability systems from many angles. Some studies tried to determine the factors that contributed to the introduction of performance accountability systems across states (Dougherty et al. 2010; McLendon et al. 2006). Other studies carried out multi-level stakeholder analyses to assess stakeholder perceptions of performance accountability policies (Frøhlich et al. 2010; Huisman and Currie 2004). In certain cases, researchers aimed at exploring the impact of performance accountability policies on various higher education outcomes within one state (Martinez and Nilson 2006), while others chose multi-state approaches to assess the impact of performance accountability on graduation rates (Hicklin-Fryar 2011; Shin 2010; Volkwein and Tandberg 2008). One study (Rabovsky 2011) explored the relationship between performance accountability policies, state higher education budgets and institutional priorities; another studied the effects of output-based funding policies through an analysis of university grading standards and labour market outcomes (Bagues et al. 2008).

Studying the origins of performance accountability in higher education is a challenging task, due to the multiplicity of stakeholders in the higher education sector, as well as to the highly diverse economic and political environments in which such systems emerged. Assessing the impact of performance accountability systems is similarly challenging. There are numerous economic and political factors that may influence the same higher education outcomes that performance accountability policies target (e.g. institutional size, state appropriation levels), making the design of comprehensive statistical models a daunting task. In addition, performance accountability systems do not come in one size: the number and type of performance indicators, indicator weights, success criteria, funding levels may vary from state to state, as well as over time. Last but not least, the success of any empirical study is dependent on the availability of high-quality data, which may not be readily available.

This section offers a select overview of recent empirical research on stakeholder perceptions of various performance accountability systems and on the impact of these systems on institutional behaviour and performance. It highlights recent trends of performance accountability research and compares and contrasts findings where applicable.

37.3.1 Exploring Stakeholder Views of Performance Accountability Systems

Dougherty and Reid (2007) observed that while many states in the US expressed interest in performance funding over the past 30 years, only half of them ended up adopting some form of performance funding for higher education. A follow-up study by Dougherty et al. (2010) probed into the reasons why certain states were more likely to adopt this form of accountability system than others. Six states – Florida, Illinois, Missouri, South Carolina, Tennessee, and Washington – were selected for an exploratory study of the origins of performance funding in the US. The authors selected the cases with the aim to represent as large variation along various features of each state's higher education system (e.g. governance structure, or the proportion of state appropriations to higher education that was based on performance) as possible. Collecting data through semi-structured interviews and document analysis, they mapped the perceptions of higher education stakeholders concerning performance funding.

One of the most important finding by Dougherty et al. (2010) is that performance funding in the US had its champions from within the higher education sector. Their analysis revealed that 2-year colleges (a group of public higher education institutions in the US whose mission typically involves teaching and vocational training rather than research) were found to be in strong support of performance funding in three out of the six states examined. Opposition to performance funding from within higher education came from leaders of public research universities. In addition to community colleges, state officials and business stakeholders were identified as being supportive of performance funding. The study found that the key opponents of performance funding in each case study were public research universities.

In addition to identifying the key supporters and opponents of performance funding in the states studied, Dougherty et al. (2010) also probed into the beliefs and motivations of each stakeholder group to better understand their reasons for opposing or supporting performance funding in higher education. Institutional supporters of performance funding, whether from 2-year or 4-year colleges, were found to regard performance funding as a means to secure additional funds and a way to increase the legitimacy of their institutions. The dominant perception of performance funding among the key opposing group, i.e. public research universities, was that the indicators used in such funding models are "not making sufficient distinctions among research universities, other state 4-year institutions, and community colleges" (p. 82). Public universities also voiced concerns about performance funding serving as an excuse to cut back state funding, as well as about the curtailing of institutional autonomy.

A study similar in scope and methods to that of Dougherty et al. (2010) was conducted in Europe in 2007, as part of the Institutional Management in Higher Education (IMHE) programme of the OECD. Frøhlich et al. (2010) present the findings of this multinational, comparative research, the purpose of which was to explore, through multilayer stakeholder analysis, the differences and similarities in the higher education funding systems of Denmark, Norway and Portugal, and how the differences in funding models may influence institutional behaviour. A wide variety of stakeholders ("HE rectors, managers, administrators and board members, funding organisations, trade and industry organisations, labour and student organisations, ministries and academic staff", p. 8) were surveyed through an online questionnaire in 2005–2006; in-depth interviews and document analyses supplied additional data. The authors used Jongbloed's typology of funding approaches; in this typology, the program oriented model (centralised-regulated approach, oriented toward outcomes) corresponds most closely with the performance funding concept of US higher education policy. Out of the three countries examined, the higher education funding systems of Denmark and Norway were found to belong in this category.

Regarding the perceptions of academic stakeholders, Danish academic staff expressed agreement with the principle of per-exam-funding (also called "taximeter" system), arguing that it "has clear advantages because it stipulated direct requirements for quantity" and, by assigning different rates to different types of institutions and fields of study, it stipulates "indirect requirements for quality" as well (p. 12). However, the execution of the policy was perceived as problematic by academic stakeholders, partly because the taximeter rates have undergone cuts over time, raising concerns about budget security, and partly due to the politicised nature of rate setting by institutions and fields. Though Danish stakeholders bemoaned the lack of budget security due cuts to the taximeter rates, they welcomed the fact that institutions were not mandated to spend their performance-based allocations on instruction-related expenses only, thereby strengthening their managerial autonomy.

In Norway, faculty members reported that after the introduction of the per-teaching-credit funding formula, they spent considerably more time on teaching. Faculty reported to have developed closer contact with their students as a result of the funding reform, which was manifest in them giving more feedback on the written work of students. This was interpreted as evidence that performance funding for teaching, which in average made up 25% of institutional budgets in Norway at the time the survey was conducted, had a positive impact on teaching quality. At the same time, the authors pointed out that the increase in time spent with students was perceived by faculty members as a loss from the vantage point of research, voicing the concern that "giving priority to credit production will result in less time and energy being devoted to research activities" (p. 14). These concerns from European university faculty seem to imply a less than enthusiastic support of performance funding among those higher education institutions that undertake both undergraduate teaching and graduate instruction and research – a pattern also observed in the US.

Similarly to academic stakeholders in the US, Norwegian interviewees saw "result-based funding" as an opportunity to increase institutional revenue in the long run (given that institutions were not made to compete for a set amount of funding but could plan to expand their teaching portfolio in hopes of attracting more funding). However, faculty members were concerned that the funding model makes institutions more efficient but the focus on "churning out graduates" will eventually lower educational quality (p. 16).

The stakeholder analyses of Dougherty et al. (2010) and Frøhlich et al. (2010) highlight two patterns that American and European higher education sectors have in common. First, stakeholders from institutions with a joint teaching-research mission (public research universities in the US, "Humboldtian" universities in Europe) tend to be less supportive of performance accountability systems than other academic and non-academic stakeholders. Secondly, academic stakeholders in both regions tend to perceive performance funding as a way to attract additional institutional revenue, rather than to increase efficiency and do more with the same (or less) resources.

37.3.2 Assessing the Impact of Performance Accountability Policies on Institutional Behaviour

An important question to answer when trying to assess the impact of any performance accountability system is whether the accountability policies, as outlined by the legislation, are reflected in state resource allocation practices. Rabovsky (2011) set out to answer this question. The study uses data from the Integrated Postsecondary Education Data Source (IPEDS), a database maintained by the National Center of Education Statistics of the US government which aggregates higher education data from all states. The study investigates the relationship between state higher education funding (measured as state appropriations in a given year) and the performance of 4-year public institutions (measured as graduation rate), hypothesising that in those states where performance funding was adopted, higher graduation rates will be associated with higher levels of state appropriations. Rabovsky (2011) finds that higher graduation rates are correlated with higher levels of state appropriations even in those states that did not adopt performance funding policies. The author also finds that the interaction term between graduation rates and the adoption of performance funding is negative, implying that "states with performance funding have a somewhat weaker link between student outcomes and institutional funding" than in other states (p. 14).

In addition to exploring the impact of performance funding policies on state resource allocation practices, Rabovsky (2011) also probes into the impact of these policies on the internal resource allocation practices of higher education institutions.

He analyses the relationship between the adoption of state-level performance funding policies, and the instruction-related and research-related expenditures of institutions in each state. Given that state-level performance funding policies in the US tend to focus on instruction-related outcomes, he hypothesises that, *ceteris paribus*, colleges in states with performance funding policies would be more likely to spend on instruction and less likely to spend on research. He finds statistically significant evidence for these hypotheses but notes that the effects are minor in each case: colleges in states with performance funding policies are found to be only 0.22% less likely to spend on research, and only 0.89% more likely to spend on instruction than their peers in states without performance funding policies.

Rabovsky (2011) interprets his findings as evidence that "performance funding policies have not been successful in transforming state budgets when it comes to higher education" (p. 15) and have been only very moderately successful in influencing the internal resource allocation of institutions. He argues that the latter is likely due to the small size of the financial incentive that performance funding systems in the US provide. He writes:

> [P]ublic universities face strong financial incentives to increase graduate student enrolments and improve their research capacities. Given these powerful market forces, performance accountability mechanisms may need to be much stronger than is currently the case if they are to result in substantial shifts in institutional priorities. (p. 19)

He concludes that more research is needed to understand why current formulations of performance funding in the US public higher education sector seem to fail to substantially impact institutional behaviour, and proposes to explore "the considerable variations in the nature and content of the performance funding policies that states have adopted" (p. 19) and how these differences may influence the impact of these policies.

A working paper from the Fundación de Estudios de Economía Aplicada (Spain) on institutional grading policies in Italy provides indirect evidence that output-based funding policies may influence institutional behaviour but the effect may not be what the policymakers intended (Bagues et al. 2008). The study investigates the relationship between students' exam grades with their labour market performance. Exam grades are relevant from a higher education policy perspective because funding is allocated to universities on the basis of the ratio of exams that enrolled students in the given academic year should have passed, over the number of exams that the students actually passed (commonly referred as the full-time equivalency or FTE). This allocation mechanism is performance-based in the sense that it assumes that the higher the FTE, the more effective the given institution is in instructing its students.

Bagues et al. (2008) use data from a university-to-work transition survey that was conducted in 1998, 2001, 2004 and sampled around 25% of total Italian university graduates each year. Using the ordinary least squares (OLS) method, the authors compare students' exam grades with their labour market performance (obtained from the surveys). Having made adjustments for students' academic ability and socioeconomic status, the study finds that higher average grades in a given university or department are significantly and negatively correlated with lower labour market outcomes, such as employment rate, for students from the given university or department. The authors interpret this as a sign that some universities inflate grades and let more students pass in order to increase their FTE.

Bagues et al. (2008) point out the weakness of the FTE as a performance indicator: "[I]n the absence of quality assurance mechanisms, the FTE might capture both the students true quality and the easiness (or grading standards) of a given institution" (p. 9) and emphasize that allocating public funds on the basis of such a problematic indicator may induce undesirable institutional behaviour, such as grade inflation or the undue filtering of university applicants based on academic ability and socioeconomic status, which goes against Italy's commitment to open access to higher education.

37.3.3 Assessing the Impact of Performance Accountability Policies on Institutional Performance

A prominent share of recent empirical research on performance accountability addresses the issue whether performance accountability policies are, in fact, effective in increasing institutional performance. Volkwein and Tandberg (2008) take a comprehensive approach to the issue. They choose state grades published in *Measuring Up* (a state-by-state report card for higher education prepared and published bi-annually by The National Center for Public Policy and Higher Education in the US), as indicators of aggregate institutional performance. The *Measuring Up* report cards grade performance along five dimensions: college completion, participation, preparation, affordability and benefits in each state. The study by Volkwein and Tandberg (2008) investigates the relationship between these grades and state characteristics and regulatory practices. One such regulatory practice they include is the adoption of some form of performance accountability system; the categories are based on Burke's threefold typology of performance reporting, budgeting and funding.

Using cross-sectional time series analysis, Volkwein and Tandberg (2008) find that

> [t]he things that states have little control over (their demographic and economic characteristics) are many times more influential in determining the Measuring Up grades than the things that they have relatively more control over (their governance, accountability, and regulatory arrangements). (p. 191)

This finding seems to be in line with the conclusion of Rabovsky (2011): performance accountability policies seem to have no, or minor, impact on institutional performance which is likely due to the typically minor share of performance-based allocations in state and institutional budgets.

Choosing college graduation rate as a proxy for instructional performance, Shin (2010) studies the impact of performance funding on institutional performance in American public 4-year colleges in the period of 1997–2007. He uses three categories for performance accountability, also based on Burke's typology: states with performance budgeting, states with performance funding, and states with both performance budgeting and funding. He includes several covariates in his hierarchical linear regression model, including state financial support to higher education, state unemployment rate as a proxy for each state's economic condition, and averages of student qualification factors (ACT or SAT scores) for each institution. When including the performance accountability variables in the model, Shin (2010) finds that those states that adopted some form of a performance funding system display higher growth rates in graduation rates during the examined period.

The hierarchical linear model Shin (2010) uses allows him to separate the variance in graduation rates that is caused by institutional effects from variance that is associated with state effects. He finds that 76% of total variance in graduation rates is attributable to differences in institutional characteristics, while 15% is attributable to state-by-state differences. He emphasizes that "a considerable proportion of state variance is accounted for outside the model – by state demographics and economic conditions that states might not easily control" (p. 57). This finding is in line with the conclusion of Volkwein and Tandberg (2008) that the leverage of higher education performance funding policies, especially compared to the impact of the economic environment, appears to be rather limited in the US.

While studies discussed so far focused on whether or not performance accountability policies impact institutional performance across the board, a recent study by Hicklin-Fryar (2011) asks the question whether performance funding has disparate impact on different groups of institutions. Hicklin-Fryar (2011) hypothesizes that institutions that enrol higher shares of minority and low-income students would be negatively affected by performance funding policies, whereas institutions with a lower share of disadvantaged students would perform better in states with performance funding policies. As a first step, she tests the relationship between performance funding policies and graduation rates and finds a small, but significant, negative correlation between the two variables.

The other studies discussed above found either no, or very modest positive, impact of performance accountability policies on graduation rates. Hicklin-Fryar (2011) is the first to find a negative effect:

> But why would we find any support for negative outcomes? Institutions could very well ignore these policies, but why would they produce negative results? Usually, in these situations, we might expect endogeneity to be the culprit, but the work on the adoption of performance funding policies (McLendon et al. 2006) finds no link between educational attainment in a state and the adoption of these policies. (p. 11)

Dismissing endogeneity as a possible explanation for the negative coefficient is not fully convincing, since educational attainment and graduation rates are not the same. Educational attainment levels capture the share of total graduate-aged population that has 4 years or more of college and is thus a state-level indicator. Graduation rate is defined as the share of those students who started college and completed it in 6 years or less and hence it provides institution-level information. Depending on features of the higher education sector that may vary from state to state (e.g. access, share of private higher education providers), it is possible that state educational attainment is relatively low, while institutional graduation rates within the state are high, or the other way round. More research is needed on the relationship between state-level graduation rates and the propensity to adopt performance funding policies.

Regarding the potentially disparate impact of performance accountability systems, Hicklin-Fryar (2011) tests the relationship between performance funding and graduation rates for advantaged and disadvantaged institutions separately, advantage being defined by the share of Pell grant recipients the institutions enrol. She finds no evidence in support of her hypothesis that more advantaged institutions would benefit more from performance funding policies: the adoption of performance funding has a small but significant negative correlation with graduation rates across the board, even among those institutions where less than 40% of the student body receives Pell grants.

37.4 Discussion and Avenues for Further Research

The review of recent empirical research on performance accountability has revealed commonalities in the perception of performance- or output-based funding policies in the US and Europe. Multi-level stakeholder analyses by Dougherty et al. (2010) and Frøhlich et al. (2010) provide evidence that higher education institutions with a joint teaching-research mission are more likely to oppose performance funding measures than other academic and non-academic stakeholders. These studies also suggest that academic stakeholders in the states and countries studied tend to consider performance funds as additional revenue source; a finding indicative of the fact that none of the states currently tie all, or even most, of their appropriations to institutional performance. Further research is warranted to explore how performance accountability systems may affect the various missions of higher education institutions.

Research by Rabovsky (2011) provides preliminary evidence that performance accountability policies have the potential to influence institutional behaviour: colleges and universities in states with performance funding are slightly more likely to spend on instruction, and slightly less likely to spend on research, than their peers in other states. However, the size of impact detected is very small. This result, similarly to the perception of performance funding as a source of additional rather than core revenue source, may be attributable to the low share of performance funds in total state appropriations. Nevertheless, there is considerable variation in the relative share of performance based funds in state higher education budgets. Future research could develop a new classification of performance funding systems based on funding levels and investigate whether states with higher shares of performance-based funds have a more substantial impact on institutional behaviour.

The finding of Bagues et al. (2008) that grading standards vary considerably within the Italian higher education system suggests that output-based funding policies may have adverse effects: institutions with lower grading standards may be behaving opportunistically in order to obtain more resources, at the risk of lowering instructional quality and decreasing access. The exploration of intended as well as unintended effects of performance accountability systems merits further attention.

As far as the relationship of performance accountability systems and institutional performance is concerned, research findings suggest either modest positive, slight negative, or no effect of performance accountability. Volkwein and Tandberg (2008) find that institutional performance as captured in the *Measuring Up* grades is not correlated with the adoption of either forms of performance accountability. Rabovsky (2011) finds that the positive link between graduation rates and state appropriation levels is weaker in those states that adopted performance funding. Shin (2010) finds that states with performance accountability policies display higher growth rates regarding the graduation rate. Hicklin-Fryar (2011) finds a slight negative relationship between state graduation rates and the adoption of performance accountability policies, and notes that endogeneity might be the reason for the negative coefficient.

These findings suggest several potential avenues for further research. First of all, the indication that the models used to assess the impact of performance accountability policies might be affected by endogeneity highlight the need for a better understanding of why certain states or countries adopt, or do not adopt, performance accountability policies. Studies by McLendon et al. (2006) and Dougherty et al. (2010) provide useful insights to the economic and political factors that might have influenced the policy adoption in the US. Further research could build on these findings, potentially by extending the scope of inquiry to Europe, too.

Furthermore, existing research does not address the issue of variance that pertains to performance accountability systems. Collecting data on state policies, indicators and budgets in a way that allows for meaningful qualitative and quantitative comparison is a daunting task but the insights gained from such a research would have important implications for state-level policymaking and institutional management alike. One feature of performance accountability systems that certainly merits further attention is the proportion of performance based funds in state higher education budgets, but indicator numbers, indicator weights, success criteria and many other features should also be considered.

Finally, the review of recent scholarly literature also reveals a shortage of recent empirical research in the European context. No doubt this is partly due to the fact that despite the ongoing integration of the European higher education area, significant differences remain between higher education systems of European countries. This makes comparative studies even more challenging than in the US, where regional accreditation boards and federal policies lend a certain level of homogeneity to the higher education landscape. However, those European countries that adopted some form of output-based funding seem to have higher proportions of their state appropriations allocated on the basis of performance. This provides additional opportunities to explore the relationship between the size of performance funds and the effectiveness of performance accountability policies. Differences in higher education systems notwithstanding, comparing data from groups of countries may still be possible: for example, Norway, Denmark and Sweden all allocate a certain share of public higher education funds based on the number of credits earned. Individual country studies relying on longitudinal data may also be of use in assessing the impact of output-based funding policies.

In short, future research on performance accountability in the US and Europe has many interesting avenues to explore, and it can rely not only on theoretical works and descriptive studies but also on the insights gained from empirical research conducted on both sides of the Atlantic in recent years.

References

Bagues, M., Labini, M. S., & Zinovyeva, N. (2008). *Differential grading standards and university funding: Evidence from Italy* (Fundación de Estudios de Economía Aplicada Working Paper 2008-07). Retrieved from http://www.fedea.es/pub/papers/2008/dt2008-07.pdf

Barnetson, B., & Cutright, M. (2000). Performance indicators as conceptual technologies. *Higher Education, 40*, 277–292.

Burke, J. C. (1998). Performance funding indicators: Concerns, values and models for state colleges and universities. *New Directions for Institutional Research, 97*, 49–60.

Burke, J. C., & Minassians, H. (2003). *Performance reporting: "Real" accountability or accountability "lite"* (Seventh annual survey 2003). Albany: SUNY. Retrieved from http://www.rockinst.org/pdf/education/2003-performance_reporting_real_accountability_or_accountability_lite_seventh_annual_survey_2003.pdf

Dougherty, K., & Reid, M. (2007). *Fifty states of achieving the dream: State policies to enhance access to and success in community colleges across the United States* (CCRC Working Paper). Retrieved from http://www.achievingthedream.org/_images/_index03/DoughertyReid_Fifty_StatesofPolicy4907.pdf

Dougherty, K. J., Natow, R. S., Hare, R. J., & Vega, B. E. (2010). The political origins of state-level performance funding for higher education: The cases of Florida, Illinois, Missouri, South Carolina, Tennessee and Washington. *Teachers College Record, 114*(3), 2012. http://www.tcrecord.org. ID Number: 16313.

Frøhlich, N., Kalpazidou Schmidt, E., & Rosa, M. J. (2010). Funding systems for higher education and their impacts on institutional strategies and academia. *International Journal of Educational Management, 24*(1), 7–21.

Harnisch, T. L. (2011). *Performance-based funding: A re-emerging strategy in public higher education financing*. American Association of State Colleges and Universities, Higher Education Policy Brief, Washington, DC, June 2010. Retrieved from http://www.aascu.org/uploadedFiles/AASCU/Content/Root/PolicyAndAdvocacy/PolicyPublications/Performance_Funding_AASCU_June2011.pdf

Herbst, M. (2007). *Financing public universities. The case of performance funding*. Dordrecht: Springer.

Hicklin-Fryar, A. (2011). *The disparate impacts of accountability – Searching for causal mechanisms* (Conference Paper). Syracuse, NY. Retrieved from http://www1.maxwell.syr.edu/uploadedFiles/conferences/pmrc/Files/HicklinFryar_TheDisparateImpactsofAccountability SearchingforCausalMechanisms.pdf

Huisman, J., & Currie, J. (2004). Accountability in higher education: Bridge over troubled water? *Higher Education, 48*, 529–551.

Jongbloed, B. (2008). Creating public-private dynamics in higher education funding. In J. E. Enders & B. Jongbloed (Eds.), *Public-private dynamics in higher education: Expectations, developments and outcomes* (pp. 113–138). Bielefeld: Transcript Verlag.

Jongbloed, B., & Vossensteyn, H. (2001). Keeping up performances: An international survey of performance-based funding in higher education. *Journal of Higher Education Policy and Management, 23*(2), 127–145.

Martinez, M. C., & Nilson, M. (2006). Assessing the connection between higher education policy and performance. *Educational Policy, 20*(2), 299–322.

McLendon, M. K., Hearn, J. C., & Deaton, R. (2006). Called to account: Analyzing the origins and spread of state performance-accountability policies for higher education. *Educational Evaluation and Policy Analysis, 28*(1), 1–24.

Metz, T. (2011). Accountability in higher education: A comprehensive analytical framework. *Theory and Research in Education, 9*(1), 41–58.

Midwestern Higher Education Compact. (2009, February). *Completion-based funding for higher education* (Working Paper). Minneapolis: Midwestern Higher Education Compact. Retrieved from http://www.mhec.org/pdfs/0209completionbasedfunding.pdf

Rabovsky, T. (2011). *Accountability in higher education: Exploring impacts on state budgets and institutional spending* (Conference Paper). Syracuse, NY. Retrieved from http://www1.maxwell.syr.edu/uploadedFiles/conferences/pmrc/Files/rabovsky_Accountability%20in%20Higher%20Education%20Exploring%20Impacts%20on%20State%20Budgets%20and%20Institutional%20Spending%20Patterns.pdf

Rhoades, G., & Sporn, B. (2002). Quality assurance in Europe and the U.S.: Professional and political economic framing of higher education policy. *Higher Education, 43*, 355–390.

Romzek, B. S. (2000). Dynamics of public accountability in an era of reform. *International Review of Administrative Sciences, 66*(1), 21–44.

Serban, A. M. (1998). Performance funding criteria, levels, and methods. *New Directions for Institutional Research, 97*, 61–67.

Shin, J. C. (2010). Impacts of performance-based accountability on institutional performance in the U.S. *Higher Education, 60*, 47–68.

Strehl, F., Reisinger, S., & Kalatschan, M. (2007). *Funding systems and their effects on higher education systems* (OECD Education Working Papers, No. 6). Paris: OECD Publishing. Retrieved from http://dx.doi.org/10.1787/220244801417

Trow, M. (1996). Trust, markets and accountability in higher education: A comparative perspective. *Higher Education Policy, 9*(4), 309–324.

van Damme, D. (2009). The search for transparency: Convergence and diversity in the Bologna Process. *Mapping the Higher Education Landscape – Higher Education Dynamics, 28*, 39–55.

Volkwein, J. F., & Tandberg, D. A. (2008). Measuring up: Examining, the connections among state structural characteristics, regulatory practices, and performance. *Research in Higher Education, 49*, 180–197.

Zumeta, W. (1998). Public university accountability to the state in the late twentieth century: Time for a rethinking? *Review of Policy Research, 15*(4), 5–22.

Chapter 38
European Universities Diversifying Income Streams

Enora Bennetot Pruvot and Thomas Estermann

38.1   Introduction

Financial sustainability is one of the key challenges for Europe's universities today.[1] Despite the tremendous diversity that exists in Europe, all higher education systems are increasingly under pressure due to rising student populations and mounting costs of teaching and research activities, and therefore face the same challenge of designing sustainable funding models.

Since 2006 the European University Association (EUA) has been conducting ambitious research on the topic of financial sustainability. The first study on this topic explored the development of full costing in European universities and the ways to improve their capacity to identify better the full costs of all their activities. Maintaining an appropriate degree of diversity in the funding structure is another important step for universities to achieve financial sustainability. This was the focus of the EUDIS project ("European Universities Diversifying Income Streams") which EUA undertook with its partners HUMANE (the Heads of University Management and Administration Network in Europe), the Bavarian State Institute for Higher Education Research and Planning, and the University of Bologna.

The study builds upon previous work developed by EUA on university financial sustainability and governance, and has involved major data collection over

---

[1] This paper draws from the report *Financially sustainable universities II: European universities diversifying income streams* published by EUA in 2011. The present contribution is an adaptation of the paper first published in *Beiträge zur Hochschulforschung*, 2/2011 available at: http://www.eua.be/pubs/Beiträge_zur_Hochschulforschung.pdf

E.B. Pruvot (✉) • T. Estermann
Unit Governance, Autonomy and Funding, European University Association (EUA),
Avenue de l'Yser 24, 1040 Etterbeek, Brussels, Belgium
e-mail: enora.pruvot@eua.be; thomas.estermann@eua.be

A. Curaj et al. (eds.), *European Higher Education at the Crossroads:*
Between the Bologna Process and National Reforms,
DOI 10.1007/978-94-007-3937-6_38, © Springer Science+Business Media Dordrecht 2012

27 European countries. Quantitative data were collected through several questionnaires to university representatives and public authorities and qualitative data through site visits to universities and in-depth case study contributions at seminars and conferences.

This paper aims to provide the reader with an overview of the study while exploring some of the key findings of this research.[2] It provides a concrete definition of income diversification, analyses its drivers and the current state of play in Europe. It further explores the challenges that universities face today in relation to the way they are funded, which framework conditions are needed for a successful diversification of funds, and finally details a "roadmap" for universities to develop such a strategy.

38.2   Income Diversification

What does income diversification mean in the higher education sector?

In the framework of this research project, income diversification is understood as the generation of additional income (through new or existing funding sources) that contributes to balancing the income structure of the institution. It is a tool to achieve financial sustainability, if the conditions in which the universities operate allow and require it. In turn, financial sustainability aims to ensure a university's academic goals are reached by guaranteeing that the institution produces sufficient income to enable it to invest in its future academic activities.

The EUDIS study considers the distribution and diversification of funding sources in general and in particular within the categories of public funding and of additional (other) funding sources. The latter includes income generated from contracts with the private sector (research contracts and education-related activities), philanthropic funding, income generated by the provision of services – rental of facilities, residences, catering, consultancy, libraries, museums... – and income through financial activities. The figure below shows the diversity of entities/institutions from which universities may receive funds and the variety of how these funds may be delivered to the university (Fig. 38.1).

38.3   Drivers to Income Diversification

Why do universities seek to diversify their funds?

Universities face external challenges, such as pressures on public budgets, globalisation and internationalisation of higher education, which increase competition

---

[2] The report "Financially sustainable universities II: European universities diversifying income streams" is available on EUA's website: www.eua.be/eudis

Income sources and funding modalities

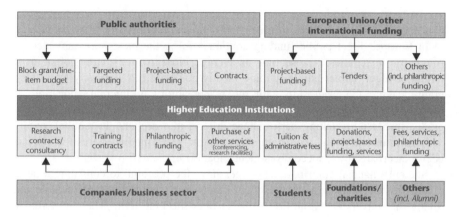

Fig. 38.1 Income sources and funding modalities

but also provide new opportunities for activity expansion. These evolutions also drive institutions to seek additional funding from other sources. Income diversification may be strategically used to develop activities and respond to new missions, as it may reinforce the position of an institution on the local, national or international stage by supporting its competitiveness.

Risk management constitutes one of the major drivers for income diversification for universities in Europe. The perception that it is necessary to spread financial risks is commonly shared among universities, especially in the light of the consequences of the economic crisis[3] and on the basis of pessimistic expectations regarding future trends in funding coming from "traditional" sources. Developing additional funding streams becomes necessary to mitigate negative consequences of a sudden drop in income or to fuel further growth of the institution's activities.

Universities also tend to approach income diversification as a means to gain more flexibility in their internal financial management, as public funding often comes with complex administrative requirements. Different public funders tend to establish various, and at times incompatible, rules and modalities. Income generated through commercial or fundraising activities is perceived as being comparatively easier to manage and has the advantage that it can be allocated internally without restrictions.

Although some additional income sources do offer this type of flexibility, it is evident that contracts with private partners can be just as demanding as public funding programmes. Often, the private sector works according to funding modalities that limit the company's contribution to partial funding of these activities.

---

[3] See below "the impact of the economic crisis".

38.4   State of Play

How are universities funded in Europe? Are universities diversifying their funds?

In Europe, direct public funding continues to be the most important income source for universities, representing, on average, close to three quarters of an institution's budget. Direct public funding mostly comes to the university as a block grant, leaving the leadership with the responsibility of internal allocation of resources. Public authorities tend to resort to funding formulae to determine these grants, increasingly taking performance criteria into account. In parallel, public authorities use more and more competitive and targeted funding, a trend which has been exacerbated by reduced investment capacities.

Student financial contributions or fees have the potential to constitute a large income source, considered by those who can charge them as fairly predictable and giving the university the ability to invest over the long term. Their importance varies greatly however depending on the legal framework in which universities operate. In some countries like England (25% on average) or Spain (13% on average), they represent a significant income source. Although in many European countries universities can charge fees for some groups of students, their level is often regulated by the state and in some cases contributes only a small percentage to a university's income. Student populations are often segmented according to academic level or different criteria (national origin, on-campus or distance studies, part-time or full-time, language of classes, etc.), painting a complex picture across Europe. Although different perceptions and traditions exist across Europe on the inclusion of fees in the funding model for higher education, the debate is gaining relevance in most countries – especially in view of the economic downturn – and will continue to be at the heart of the discussion around funding models for higher education in the coming years.

Additional sources represent almost 20% of the budget of a majority of universities. In some cases, this type of funds amount to between a fourth and a third of the institution's income structure. Contracts with private partners represent the largest additional source with an average of 6.5%. It varies significantly between institutions though, ranging from 1% to 25% of the income structure. Philanthropic funding amounts on average to 4% of the total income of a university, with some universities generating close to 10% of their income from this source. While universities in the United Kingdom are generally more successful in their fund-raising activities, the study also found successful examples in other countries (Motion and Beney 2011). Foundations are the universities' main partner in this context, but companies and alumni are also getting more involved. Income raised from the provision of services averages 4% of a university's income structure, but the ability to generate such funds is highly differentiated across Europe. Some British universities receive between 10% and 25% of their total income from this type of activities.

Financial and staffing autonomy experience and expertise to provide consultancy or facility-related services play an important role in the institution's capacity to generate such income. Management of conference facilities, catering and accommodation

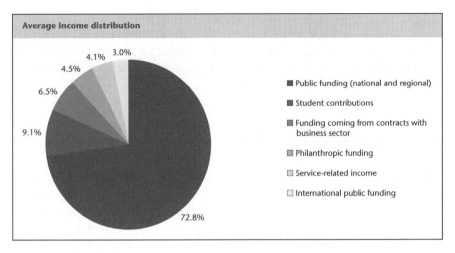

Fig. 38.2   Average income distribution

(including student residences) represent the largest part of this income source, followed by consultancy services, educational services and commercialisation of research results.

International public funding is almost exclusively made up of European funds, such as the Structural funds, the European research framework programme and the Lifelong Learning Programme (Fig. 38.2).

The EUDIS study also asked university leaders how they expect the institutions income streams to evolve in the near future. A clear majority expects public funding for teaching to decrease over the coming years. They also expect to receive more income from more sources and in particular anticipate that the smallest sources (European and philanthropic funding) will grow.

38.5   Funding Challenges

The study highlights a number of challenges related to public funding that need to be overcome if Europe's universities are to continue to provide high quality teaching and excellent research.

38.5.1   Complex Financial Management

Developing new funding streams often translates into complex financial management. Some universities have well over 100 different income sources, which have, in many cases, very diverse accountability regimes. Nor does the higher education community expect this trend to slow down or reverse. A majority of the respondents in the project's survey actually believe that the overall number of sources will increase. Universities therefore need to invest a lot both in time and resources if they want to obtain these funds, which application, contractual, reporting and reimbursement procedures often differ widely. In reality, "small income sources" can often generate a disproportionate amount of paperwork and administration which in turn raise the operational costs for universities.

38.5.2 Increasing Co-funding Requirements

The increasing trend to resort to co-funding requirements is probably the most underestimated challenge to universities' financial sustainability. Co-funding requires that a university raise a proportional amount of the full cost of the activity or project being funded, from its own budget or from another public or private source. Data from the EUDIS study showed that a majority of universities deal on a daily basis with co-funding requirements, whether for most or part of their public funding. Both European and national public funders increasingly use co-funding requirements by either funding only a certain percentage of the direct costs or just a part of the indirect costs of an activity (especially in competitive funding schemes).

This is a threat to the universities' financial sustainability, especially if it affects a significant part of their public funding. Indeed, co-funding does not necessarily lead to leveraging funds from other sources; in most cases, universities have to resort to using resources from their core budget. The EUDIS survey revealed that 65% of the respondents co-funded these activities from core public funding, while 35% resorted to a mix between public and private funds.

The reason for this is clear – it is very difficult to raise funds from private funders to cover a part of the indirect costs of a project whose core activities are already funded. This, in turn, reduces the university's capacity to invest in its future, diminishing the amount of "unconstrained" funds available to finance facilities, equipment or staff.

This issue is all the more relevant as there is a strong link between the frequency of co-funding and the degree of diversification. Additional income sources rarely fund activities on a full cost basis.

Universities that have been very successful in attracting additional funds through competitive research funding schemes face major problems as a result. Thus, co-funding has become a risk associated with income diversification which needs to be solved through appropriate funding schemes.

38.5.3 European Funding Schemes

The European Union offers non-negligible income to many universities, who widely expect to receive more income from this source in the future, although substantial increases of the amounts available are unlikely to occur in the coming years.

Competition among universities for this funding will therefore become more acute, in a context where traditional income sources are expected to stagnate or decrease.

European funding schemes are an important, but also among the most complex, funding programmes available to universities. European structural funds and the Framework Programme for Research and Innovation are the two main sources of European funds for higher education institutions and present similar characteristics. The diversity of instruments and associated rules, the heavy administrative processes and accountability requirements, and finally the systematic use of co-funding deter a growing number of universities from participating in these programmes. However, in a context of stagnating national funding, not many universities can afford to disregard such schemes, even under unattractive funding models. This, in turn, will broaden the funding gap of their research activities.

In some countries, public authorities have developed mechanisms to support universities applying to European funding programmes, for instance funding the preparation phase of a project or by providing the missing part of the funding. However, if such schemes are not coordinated among member states, they may contribute to creating an unlevel playing field for universities across Europe, with some countries providing more comprehensive support than others. Simplification of rules and procedures and moving towards funding on a full cost basis of these schemes appears as the only sustainable solution in the long run.

38.5.4   Impact of the Economic Crisis

EUA has been monitoring the evolution of the economic crisis and its effects on higher education systems in Europe since its onset in 2008. The continuous feedback from various sources provided up-to-date reports of the situation and highlighted the evolving nature of the effects the crisis has had on higher education across Europe. One should note that the varying availability of data, the different ways in which it is calculated and communicated, and the constantly changing situation are significant challenges to this comparative exercise. However, trends can be identified.

Public funding is not only diminishing in many countries, but also changing in the nature and form in which it is provided to universities. It is increasingly subject to conditions for its allocation or accompanied with growing accountability requirements. This has given public authorities increasing steering power over universities, which can have counterproductive effects as it can significantly contribute to reducing universities' autonomy and their capacity to manage their own funds freely. Such developments are worrisome as they can hinder universities' capacity to successfully overcome the crisis. The universities' ability to respond effectively to the ongoing economic situation has largely depended on the level of their institutional and, more especially, their financial autonomy.

Major cuts to public funding of higher education were first observed in Latvia, where an initial cut of 48% at the beginning of 2009 was followed by a further cut of 18% in 2010 stemming from the recommendations of the International Monetary Fund and the World Bank to reduce public funding of higher education drastically. Although they follow nearly 7 years of increases in university budgets, the cuts have put serious pressure on the Latvian higher education system, demanding major changes and structural reforms to be introduced in the forthcoming years. Academic salaries have been significantly cut down (according to some estimates, staff salaries are now about 53% of their 2008 level).

In Italy, the 2010 financial law which refers to the years 2011–2013, plans for a cumulative decrease of 14% in comparison with the funds allocated in 2010. However, the cut will also have the effect of mechanically diminishing universities' income from tuition fees, which are limited to a maximum of 20% of their total public funding. The situation appears critical as some 25 universities already face a default risk in the near future. At the same time, a wide-ranging reform of the higher education system is being passed, which is to impact the way funding is delivered to universities.

The situation is also critical in Greece, where the student population is increasing while the government has been implementing cuts of about 35% in 2010 and 2011. In Hungary, the government decided in February 2011 to implement cuts of 11%, following the cancellation of plans announced in 2007 to increase overall university funding. The intention to proceed to a further 4% cut has been made public in September 2011.

England is also undergoing major changes at system level, following the release of the 2010 Comprehensive Spending Review. The higher education system is being re-engineered around a student-centered approach. The move is intended to foster the efficiency of the system. While funding for research is stabilising, teaching funds will be essentially removed as of 2012. This follows previous cuts in 2010 in teaching budgets and in capital funding. Clearly this has serious long-term consequences for the future funding of English higher education. But the situation in England is somewhat different from the other countries in this category. The reduction in public funding is meant to be covered by private contributions from students (up to £9,000 per year), following the recommendations of the Browne Review in October 2010. Under the new system, students would benefit from loans backed by the public authorities, repayable after graduation on an income-contingent basis. While the public authorities have committed to transfer the funds from calculated tuition fees directly to universities, there remains much uncertainty as to how this will work and what the consequences for higher education institutions will be over the long term.

Scotland has not remained unaffected and has also announced cuts of about £67 million for 2011, with an 11% cut in the Scottish Funding Council's teaching budget.

In Ireland, despite a growing student population, universities have been facing a cut of 9.4% in 2010 followed by a 7% cut in the universities' grant for 2011. In addition, the capital grant has been halved for 2011, reducing drastically the amount of funding available for infrastructure maintenance.

In Iceland, the sector has suffered from a series of budget cuts of about 18% in total in the last three years.

Cuts between 5% and 10% have been introduced in several countries.

In the Netherlands, Dutch universities are confronted with a cut up to 10%. Romania has cut funding to higher education by 10% and Lithuania by 8% in previous years. State-commissioned higher education institutions in Estonia have seen their public funding decrease by just under 7% between 2008 and 2010. In Spain, the National Rectors' Conference estimates the drop in funding between 5% and 10% over the period 2008–2011.

Cuts up to 5% have been observed in many countries of Eastern and South Eastern Europe, including the Czech Republic (where the cut for 2012 is estimate at 5% of public funding), Slovakia, Croatia, Serbia and the Former Yugoslav Republic of Macedonia.

So far, **no direct cuts or minor cuts only** have been reported by the Nordic countries, including Sweden, Finland and Denmark, or by Poland and Switzerland. Nonetheless, many universities across these countries give accounts of facing indirect impacts on their funding structure. In some cases, financial pressures seem to stem especially from increased student numbers, the cost of which is already having an impact on universities' financial sustainability. Such increases in the student numbers may also affect the universities' different activities, if the increases are not reflected in correspondingly higher budgets.

In many countries, **governments have discarded previous commitments to increase funding**. Both communities in Belgium have also reported that their regional governments have abandoned previous plans to increase funding. In the Flemish community of Belgium, universities are coping with a 3-year funding freeze which has replaced a previously promised increase of approximately 10%; while the French speaking community has seen the investment of 30 million EUR planned to be invested over 8 years now extended over 15 years. Similarly, in Austria, plans by the government to increase higher education expenditure by 2% between 2013 and 2015 have now been scrapped, as negotiations have clearly shown that a budget cut will be inevitable for this same period.

In contrast, some European **governments have upheld their commitments**, or indeed provided new investments to fund higher education, like in Norway.

France's announcement of the "Grand Emprunt" (national loan) has seen a significant increase in overall higher education funding, which comes as part of a large investment in key priority areas, especially teaching and research. In 2010, 11 billion EUR were foreseen for investments to improve the overall quality of higher education and 8 billion EUR invested towards developing research. A further 8 billion EUR had been foreseen to create new university campuses of excellence or go towards restructuring existing ones. The prospect for 2011 remains positive, as a further increase of the budget by about 4.7 billion EUR, mainly to raise the attractiveness of career personnel, support of university reform, student social policy and increased resources for research, has been foreseen. However, since a major part of the investments foreseen by the "Grand Emprunt" consist of capital contributions, this means that the actual amount received by universities ultimately depends on the financial markets and is likely significantly smaller.

Another case where funds for higher education have been raised over recent years is Germany. Though higher education funding in Germany is largely provided by Länder authorities, the federal government has been increasing investments to support the financial security of German higher education and research institutions. The investments will provide an additional 800 million EUR under the renewed Higher Education Pact which will support growing student numbers until 2015.

The federal government will also invest a further 2.7 billion EUR from 2012 to 2015 through the German Excellence Initiative, as well as provide additional funding through the 5% per year increase for the Innovation and Research Pact until 2015. Federal authorities with state support will also guarantee further financial resources over the next 10 years as part of a Pact to Increase the Quality of Teaching; which comes in parallel to a 2% increase in current levels of student support via the Federal Student Finance Act. On the other hand, it seems that these developments may also have an impact on the structure of the German higher education funding model in the future. As it becomes apparent that some Länder plan to cut or have already cut their higher education funding for 2011, the increases in federal funding will, to some extent, alleviate this loss while also shifting the balance in the provision of funding between the Länder and the Federal authorities.

In the case of Portugal the situation is mixed, as a recent agreement between the government and rectors will provide a greatly needed investment of 100 million EUR for higher education which will alleviate the burden of cuts from previous years. The situation is however evolving rapidly and this positive development may be halted by expected salary cuts in public administration that will affect university staff. In addition, in 2012, the sector also expects cuts up to 14% of total public funding.

38.6 Creating the Adequate Conditions for Successful Diversification

Public authorities have to play a key role in helping universities overcome all of these challenges. Governments need to provide the right framework conditions and remove barriers that prevent universities from unlocking their full potential. Funders and public authorities in particular, should also set appropriate incentives and support mechanisms to build up the capacity of universities to respond to these new opportunities.

38.6.1 The Importance of Adequate Regulatory Frameworks: Autonomy

The capacity of universities to generate additional income relates to the degree of autonomy granted by the regulatory framework in which they operate. This relation was tested for the organisational, financial, staffing and academic dimensions of autonomy (Estermann and Nokkala 2008). The data collected revealed that financial autonomy, which is perceived as the lowest of these four aspects, is the most correlated with the capacity of the universities to attract income from additional funding sources. Autonomy in staffing matters, and in particular freedom in recruiting and setting salary levels of academic and administrative staff, is also positively linked to the degree of income diversification.

However, while policymakers themselves see autonomy reforms as an important driver to foster income diversification, university leaders consider autonomy more as a pre-requisite. Conversely, diversified income structures may also contribute to enhancing the autonomy of an institution, mitigating the risks associated with dependence on a given funder. Additional resources enable universities to invest strategically in otherwise overlooked areas, helping to unbind institutional priorities from external objectives.

Universities identify a number of hurdles in their regulatory framework that hinder income diversification. Inadequate governance structures and the inability to change them, financial restrictions as to the funding cycle or inflexible staffing regulations impede universities from exploiting their potential and developing new funding streams.

38.6.2   Funding Modalities

Inadequate funding modalities may have a negative effect and create powerful disincentives for universities to seek additional funding sources. An excessive administrative burden and uncertainty associated with these sources – whether public or private – is one hurdle, which is especially relevant in the context of competitive funding schemes. Simplification of administrative processes and requirements associated with funding programmes are therefore of key importance. Simplification of rules will ensure that both financial and human resources are released for the primary objectives of excellent teaching and research. This should be underpinned by proportionate accountability measures as well as consistent rules and terminology across programmes.

Public authorities also influence income diversification strategies through the modalities under which they deliver funding to the universities.

Incentives may include the inclusion of specific criteria in funding formula, encouraging external funding, or the extended use of competitive funding. It is important though that if such criteria are used to include mechanisms to counterbalance the effects of co-funding, for example to set up top–up grants. Funding formula may have a direct, intended effect (through the inclusion of the amount of external funding received by the institution in the funding formula), or a knock-on effect due to the attraction of international staff and students as a result of successes in excellence initiatives.

38.6.3   Smart Incentives and Support Measures

38.6.3.1   Matched Funding Schemes

Matched funding schemes, whereby public authorities reward universities for their success in raising funds from the private sector, are an innovative incentive mechanism to foster income diversification. In such a scheme, public authorities may provide funds either to a full or proportional amount to the funds raised from the private sector by the university itself. These additional public funds may be granted to the general budget of the university, without necessarily being attached to the completion of a designated activity. These schemes are or have been used in countries such as Canada, the USA, New Zealand, but remain the exception in Europe. Only the United Kingdom, Norway and Finland have used such funding incentives. Modalities may be diverse but these measures have often proved their effectiveness in increasing the participation of the private sector in higher education through philanthropic funding. Key principles for success include simplicity of rules, broad definition of university activities and types of donors eligible for matched funding and a guarantee not to reduce core funding. Accompanying tax incentives and capacity-building funding are desirable for an even higher leverage effect.

38.6.3.2 Development of Full Costing

Appropriate strategic tools play a crucial role in achieving financial sustainability. Universities must be able to identify the full costs of all their activities, to assess the degree to which these costs are covered by the funding source, and whether engaging with a given partner results in a profit or a loss for the institution. This should inform the decision without conditioning it: pursuing an activity may be relevant if other sources can be found or if a return of investment can be foreseen in the long term. The information provided by full costing systems also further allows universities to adopt appropriate efficiency measures.

EUA's work on the topic has shown that universities need support to implement full costing systems. Through the EUIMA project,[4] EUA organises a series of country workshops throughout Europe designed for university management, funders, research councils and governments to foster the development of full costing initiatives within universities and also to support coordinated approaches at the national level. Although this topic is increasingly considered as relevant for higher education in a number of countries, there remains a lack of awareness around the need to support the development of full costing. In this respect, it is crucial that national governments step up their efforts to support the development of full costing in order to improve the sustainability of the system.

38.6.3.3 Support to Leadership Development and Professionalisation of Management

Leadership, management and skill development matter enormously when developing a successful income diversification strategy, in view of the transformations reshaping higher education in the last decade. Facing the challenges of today and

---

[4] European Universities Implementing the Modernisation Agenda – EUA project co-financed by the European Commission under the 7th Framework Programme for Research and Development (2009–2011).

tomorrow requires university leaders and managers to acquire new skills to engage in new activities and reach out to new partners. At operational level, this also demands the integration of new staff profiles, in particular in the areas of research management, fundraising, human resources, communication and financial management. Public authorities can support this transition by providing, directly or through intermediaries, management development programmes. However the United Kingdom is the only European country that has invested significantly in the creation of a dedicated structure which promotes a culture of organisational learning and champions examples of excellent governance and management in British universities. National and European funders need to step up efforts to support universities in developing adequate training programmes towards this end.

38.7   Universities: Roadmap for Successful Diversification

Universities themselves need to continue to seek to further diversify their income. This requires a proactive approach on several levels. To position themselves in an increasingly competitive environment, universities need to identify their strengths and specificities, allowing them to develop an adequate branding strategy. This should be complemented by an analysis of their activities in relation to the potential for income generation. To turn the strategy into reality, universities will also need to invest in the development and professionalisation of their support staff. None of this is possible, though, without the university leadership's experience and commitment to the process.

38.7.1   Embedding Income Diversification in the Institutional Strategy

Diversification should begin with a strategic analysis of the status quo, the institutional strengths, specificities and opportunities, as well as a scan of the competitive environment. Pre-existing additional income streams should be included in the overall evaluation. Apart from undertaking an appropriate analysis of cost effectiveness and risk of various activities, institutions need to assess the appropriateness of these activities in relation to the universities' mission and culture.

The university leadership's commitment to this process is of crucial importance. The leadership is best placed to project a vision and build the case for diversification activities, as well as engage the broader university community in the process. University leaders also play an important role in shaping the necessary change processes related to diversification, be it a cultural change or an organisational change.

Many activities to increase and generate new income sources need new expertise, which does not necessarily always exist within the institution. Universities may recruit professionals from outside the sector or invest in the development of staff to acquire these skills. When external staff is recruited, it is important that they understand the specificities of the research and education environment or are integrated in an established team. Professionalisation is relevant at all levels, including human resources management, knowledge transfer activities, research administration, financial management, etc. A gradual approach to structured development of staff capacity may be best adapted considering the fact that the potential to invest in human resources is reduced in times of financial constraints. Given the high relevance of building up these skills for successful income diversification however, targeted support from governments towards this end would have a high leverage effect.

The success of income diversification strategies largely depends on the ability of the institution's leadership to communicate effectively with the university community as well as with external stakeholders. Universities need to reinforce awareness around the range of activities they undertake and the added value they create for society, helping potential partners to evaluate funding options. External communication should also contribute to reinforcing the image and specific profile of an institution. Communication can also usefully be undertaken at sector level, upholding the value of higher education for the wider economy.

Those universities that have adopted a broader approach to income diversification have usually accompanied this with structural changes in the institution – creation of specific teams or dedicated structures, including sometimes streamlining governance bodies for more efficient decision-making. These processes are informed by adequate tools including accounting and costing data. Finally, the leadership, on the basis of all of the above, may embed appropriate incentive mechanisms in its strategy, focusing on staff or faculty level (consultancy credits, income-sharing terms, modalities of spin-off creation).

38.7.2   Illustrations from European Universities

As demonstrated above, income diversification consists of multiple aspects and calls for universities to design coordinated approaches based on a strategic vision. The examples below are only a few illustrations of the various dimensions of income diversification strategies, developed by universities with different institutional profiles.

38.7.2.1   Maastricht University

Maastricht University offers a telling example of how to exploit the institution's specificities to develop a strong diversification strategy. As a university founded in the 1970s, Maastricht has been seen as an "outsider" to the established group of Dutch research-intensive universities, and has therefore had to develop a differentiation strategy from the onset. This has resulted in two academic innovations: the adoption of "problem-based learning" approaches (which privileges small study groups over lecturing) and the creation of a series of "niche" interdisciplinary fields. Thus Maastricht has built a specific academic offer which has contributed to increase its visibility amongst a wider student population.

The other specificity of the university is its geographic location, at the periphery of the Dutch decision-making centres, but strategically placed to attract both German and Belgian students, which quickly became key target groups for the university. The increased presence of "regional" international students and staff has also pushed Maastricht to become a fully bilingual university. This early orientation towards internationalisation has helped the university to further build on this to identify "focus" countries outside the EU and create an integrated approach to international student recruitment.

Importantly, the Dutch government stopped subsidising places for non-EU students in 2006, which triggered the implementation of differentiated fees for this part of the student population. This has resulted in significant risk mitigation for the university as a large part of its students (about 40%) does not depend on financial support from the Dutch government.

These developments are therefore underpinned by a consistent strategy to which the university leadership is strongly committed. This in turn is supported by coherent financial planning driven by expectations (such as the reduction of public funding available and the need to enhance additional funding).

38.7.2.2   Loughborough University

Loughborough University's income generating activities strongly underpin the institution's ethos and academic mission.

As a financially sound university, Loughborough University's financial target is to deliver a 3% surplus on an annual basis. However, on the basis of expectations regarding cuts in public funding, the university's management is engineering a large operation aiming at reshaping the institution into more cost-effective and academic-focused structures. This includes rationalizing the number of academic structures into larger cost centres (merging departments) and looking for saving and investment opportunities across the university's services. Expected funding cuts have nevertheless not been driving the agenda for income diversification, as a long-time target has been to increase, in absolute terms, public funding while reducing it as a proportion of LU's total income.

This is strongly embedded in the institution's budget process through the direct involvement of the deans in the drafting of the development plans of their faculties. The deans are asked to identify and prioritise saving and investment opportunities. This process is "locked in" by assuming a certain level of enterprise and fundraising growth in all development plans. Transparency is also key to success, while important work has been conducted on keeping academics informed and making them aware that surpluses are needed to sustain development.

In terms of income potential, the University does not expect a big growth in terms of additional international students, as market opportunities become more limited and dependence towards large student-providing countries is not desirable; similarly, the university does not seek to increase its offer in undergraduate programmes, as the local population does not provide a sufficient pool to tap into. Distance-learning programmes however provide an interesting form of additional revenue generation. Therefore, as teaching activities are expected to remain rather constant in the near future, balance must be achieved by increasing revenue generated by enterprise and commercial activities, as well as by contractual research.

38.7.2.3 Istanbul Technical University

The leadership of Istanbul Technical University (ITU), faced with declining public funding, increasing student population and a need to upgrade research and teaching infrastructure in the 1980s, saw a need for additional income generation to solve these issues. Part of the strategy designed by the institution consisted in developing a multi-stage fundraising effort. The university chose to focus first on student and academic support facilities as well as the teaching environment in general. In a second phase, fundraising was targeted at improving research infrastructures and supporting research activities. Finally, in the third phase, priority was given to the creation of an endowment that in turn ensured the sustainability of the mechanisms created in the first two phases.

Success factors were identified in a triangle "Strong reasons – Devoted people – Committed stakeholders". On the side of the university, assets included a new administration with a clear vision and mission statement; a capacity for change and reform; a commitment to restructure the system to put external funding to best use and to control external constraints. The institution carefully designed the projects and advertised their benefits for ITU's reforms. It set up efficient and progressive task forces to implement the projects. Finally, and perhaps most importantly, the leadership took care of maintaining transparency in all the processes.

The institution also benefitted from a strong alumni community in the industry and business sectors, who felt strongly committed to ITU's projects. The university further structured this community through setting up integrated alumni networks (foundations, associations).

The leadership sought to involve alumni more closely by spreading alumni councils at departmental and faculty levels, to increase interactions and therefore extend donations. The media also contributed to publicising the fundraising campaign.

The strategy brought unprecedented funding for investments for R&D and infrastructure obtained from alumni and other resources (industry, additional state funds).

38.7.2.4 Trinity College Dublin

The College has a fair degree of diversification but is, according to the institution's own feeling, still too dependent on inflexible state funding, which is allocated on a yearly basis. The abolition of tuition fees for undergraduate students has increased this inflexibility and is seen as a reduction in the College's financial autonomy. The institution has also been affected in multiple ways by the economic crisis. Severe reductions in public funding within the last years are accompanied by a decrease in trust from the funders towards universities. As a consequence, the degree of autonomy has diminished on various aspects and accountability measures have grown disproportionately.

The introduced "Employment control framework" through which universities need to get permission from the state authorities to hire staff particularly hinders the institutions' autonomy. Staffing autonomy is perceived as low because of a lack of options to create incentives to attract high level staff and reallocate people or change their duties. All of this also impacts on the implementation of a diversification strategy.

In the last years, Trinity College has step up its internal mechanisms to diversify income. More financial autonomy for faculties, and a higher percentage of generated income from diversification activities that goes to the faculties, are two measures that have helped in increasing the level of diversification activities. The institution also has a sophisticated strategy to generate income through its estates activities. It includes leveraging the value of its facilities and sites through strategic cooperation with developers, combining their know-how with the College's purchasing power and good rating to provide good funding conditions.

The change from financial management being a "compliance function" to an "enabler function" has generally had a high impact on the College's implementation of diversification. In recent years, it took a strong proactive approach in bringing forward new initiatives of diversification. The finance function has played an important role in three activities related to diversification: new income generation, cost management and treasury management by placing cash in strategic investment.

38.8   Conclusions and Recommendations

The study revealed that many universities in Europe have already diversified their income structure to some degree. The collected data showed that additional funding sources such as contracts with the business sector or indeed philanthropic funding represent a higher percentage of a university's income structure than commonly assumed. Although the extent to which the income structure is diversified varies widely across institutions, there is evidence that income diversification is not the prerogative of a few countries. However, the regulatory framework in which universities operate does have an important influence on their ability to diversify income.

Public authorities play a key role in supporting income diversification by providing the right framework conditions, removing barriers and setting incentives. Granting extended autonomy to universities is an essential step forward in this context. The findings show that financial and staffing autonomy especially foster diversification. The ability to generate additional funding streams requires flexibility and autonomy for universities to manage their organisational structure, their finances and staff. However, this only creates the background against which public authorities need to provide additional support.

Universities, in turn, need to integrate income diversification in their institutional strategy. That involves applying a proactive approach in diversification and identifying opportunities; incorporating partnerships with broader implications across the whole institution; and engaging the academic community in the diversification strategy and its actions.

Universities, supported by public authorities, must invest in people to improve further capacities and competences to engage in income diversification. This is conditional on the establishment of strong leadership and management. Universities can also design internal incentives to foster the involvement of faculties and staff in income diversification, in particular via favourable resource allocation models.

Finally, smart interaction with external stakeholders is crucial, through enhancing the awareness that the university is creating value for external stakeholders and identify areas of mutual benefit with local and regional partners.

All actors – whether public authorities, private funders, EU institutions and universities – have to foster a culture of trust, through which it becomes possible to work together towards the improvement of the legal and funding frameworks in which higher education institutions operate, with a view to enhance the sustainability and efficiency of the system in the long term.

References

Estermann, T., & Bennetot Pruvot, E. (2011). *Financially sustainable universities II: European universities diversifying income streams*. Brussels: European University Association.

Estermann, T., & Nokkala, T. (2008). *University autonomy in Europe I: Exploratory study*. Brussels: European University Association.

Motion, J., & Beney, A. (2011). Income diversification through philanthropy in UK higher education. *Beiträge zur Hochschulforschung*, vol. 2, 58–67.

Chapter 39
Who Is to Pay for Mobile Students?

Marcel Gérard*

39.1   Introduction

In most European countries, higher education tuition fees are especially low if not zero. This does not mean that university studies are free goods. Indeed, graduates are expected to get higher wages than less skilled people and, therefore, to pay higher taxes, especially in those countries where labour income tax is progressive. In that sense, students receive implicit loans from the government during the time of their studies that they later repay possibly with an interest, in a way contingent to the income generated by their studies. One could conclude from that simple reasoning that the current system of financing higher education is close to a contingent loan mechanism, namely a system where the students receive money covering the cost of studies and sometimes the cost of living, and pay back that amount after their graduation, in line with their income.

That reasoning holds in a world where the graduates pay their tax in the country where they graduated. However, it no longer holds in a setting where people graduate in one jurisdiction and then have their career in another one or in some other

* This paper is part of IAP Project 6/09, financed by the Belgian Federal Services for Scientific Policy, Belspo. Its content expands that of Chevalier and Gérard (2009, 2010). The author is especially grateful to Cédric Chevalier and Jérôme Hubert for their helpful research assistance. He is also indebted to Liviu Matei and Magnus Malnes for comments and suggestions.

M. Gérard (✉)
Louvain School of Management and Institut d'Etudes Européennes, Université catholique de Louvain, Chaussée de Binche 151, B-7000 Mons, Belgium

College of Europe, Bruges, Belgium

CESifo, Munich, Germany
e-mail: marcel.gerard@uclouvain.be

A. Curaj et al. (eds.), *European Higher Education at the Crossroads:*
Between the Bologna Process and National Reforms,
DOI 10.1007/978-94-007-3937-6_39, © Springer Science+Business Media Dordrecht 2012

Table 39.1 Imbalance in the mobility of students within the EU (2008)

Countries	Foreign students (%)	Balance of mobility (%)	Countries	Foreign students (%)	Balance of mobility (%)
Austria	11.36	−8.02	**Hungary**	1.20	0.36
Belgium	6.98	−4.62	**Italy**	0.54	1.06
United Kingdom	4.06	−3.63	**Finland**	0.74	1.37
Czech Republic	5.21	−3.01	**Poland**	0.11	1.43
Netherlands	4.17	−2.41	**Portugal**	0.68	2.50
Denmark	2.70	−1.18	**Greece**	0.15	4.06
Sweden	2.03	0.11	**Ireland**	1.92	7.47
Germany	2.61	0.26	**Slovak Republic**	1.59	9.73
Spain	0.75	0.30	**Luxembourg**	37.00	232.70
France	1.60	0.33			

Source: Eurostat and own computation

countries. In such a setting, one country pays for the cost of studies and other countries benefit from the skill, the contribution to the local GDP and tax revenue.

In today's European Union we are in some sense moving from the first to the second setting even if the first one still extensively dominates. However, the second setting may no longer be ignored; on the one hand, it corresponds to an emerging single market for high skilled labour, and on the other hand, it creates spill over effects or externalities which call for internalisation if one wants to improve the efficiency of the higher education system in Europe.

The latter issue is addressed in this paper. In other terms, our research question is 'who is to pay for mobile students?' By 'who' we mean which jurisdiction, as well as which individual. In other terms, we plan to investigate a key missing character in the Bologna Process: its financing side.

Prior to go ahead with that issue, we may usefully document on the mobility of students in Europe and the relevance of the issue we cope with; this is done in Sect. 39.2 where the contemplation of Table 39.1 especially deserves interest since it motivates our investigation[1]. Based on the examination of those stylised facts, with a focus on the imbalance in student migration, the research question actually becomes: 'how to internalise the negative externality imposed to Austria, Belgium and similar countries by their large neighbours'?

Then, in Sect. 39.3 we briefly examine, based on the existing literature, the impact of student mobility, including on economic growth. Section 39.4 is the core of the paper. It presents, in words, a series of models that we elsewhere develop more formally (Gérard 2007, 2010a, b), which set forth the relative inefficiency – or degree of efficiency – of alternative ways to finance mobile students. We first describe the system currently operated in Europe based on a host country principle; we then turn to another system based on the alternative origin country principle. Then we relate to the latter model the use of two-part vouchers – shown to be also

---

[1] The table is explained in Sect. 39.2.4 below.

instruments to direct students towards some fields of study and to favour some targeted groups within the population –, of a Bhagwati tax and of contingent loans. In Sect. 39.5 we highlight those developments by three country cases referring to Norway, Australia and Switzerland, respectively. Policy suggestions conclude the paper in Sect. 39.6.

The literature on the subject of this paper includes Mechtenberg and Strausz (2008, 2009, 2010) and their references. For those authors 'the most stable result (…) is that although increasing mobility (…) will lead to higher private investment in education, public provision will decrease. The government will tend to free-ride on the education system of other country'. Similar results might be read in Buettner and Schwager (2004); next to the free riding effect, Kemnitz (2005) sets forth the competition between governments to provide education to mobile students.

39.2   International Student Mobility

International student mobility is not a new phenomenon. To make an example, let us mention that, for a long time, German students were known for their travelling across German states for the purposes of studying. Also, many professors currently teaching in EU universities have spent one or more years in US institutions. The importance of the phenomenon, however, is sharply growing and it is encouraged by the European higher education system through fellowships like Erasmus or the European Research Council (ERC) scholarships, and by the approximation of the degrees and information of supplements to diploma set up by the Bologna Process.

Student mobility is now regarded as part of the European culture, as a means to favour peace, prosperity, and employment through the raise of a single market for graduates or high skilled labour. Moreover, many governments consider the mobile students as future ambassadors; they contribute to a positive recognition of their own country abroad, and when they come back home, to a positive recognition of the host jurisdiction.

39.2.1   Who Is an Internationally Mobile Student?

In this contribution, international student mobility relates to higher education, sometimes also called tertiary education. We may use the definition suggested by Kelo et al. (2006); for them, mobile students are 'students who crossed a national border to study or undertake other activities relating to the studies, for a part or less than one syllabus or for a certain period of time, in the country in which they moved'.

We understand that international student mobility implies a physical move, inducing a cultural contact with the country in which they study; that rules out e.g. distance learning.

Considering three main criteria for mobility, Chevalier and Gérard (2010) propose a useful diagram to understand the concept – see Fig. 39.1. In that figure,

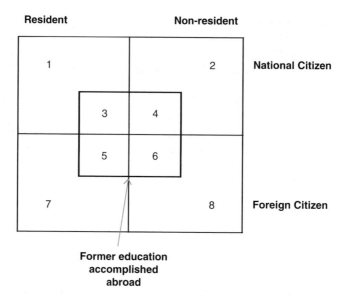

Fig. 39.1 Criteria for determining an internationally mobile student (Source: Chevalier and Gérard 2010)

a (non-) resident means an individual who is (not) a permanent resident of the country in which the individual is studying; and a national (vs. foreign) citizen refers to an individual who does (not) have the nationality of the country in which the individual studies.

Students located in box 6, who study in a country whose they are neither citizens nor permanent residents and where they did not obtain their previous degree (say, the degree received for secondary education) are the sole ones to be regarded as truly mobile. That definition will be taken into account in the theoretical and policy sections of this paper, though it is more severe than the concept used in many statistics where the citizenship plays a major role.

39.2.2 Which Are the Main Host Countries for Internationally Mobile Students?

According to OECD data, the number of internationally mobile students enormously increased in the recent past. Indeed, in little more than 30 years, it was multiplied by four, to reach approximately 3.3 million individuals in 2008.

Figure 39.2 enables us to observe the distribution of student mobility across host countries. It is to be noticed that a little more than 40% of the mobile students move to Anglo-Saxon countries and that more than 30% move to EU Member States. More generally, nearly three quarter of the mobile students are concentrated in 17 countries. These countries are all among those with the highest GDP per capita.

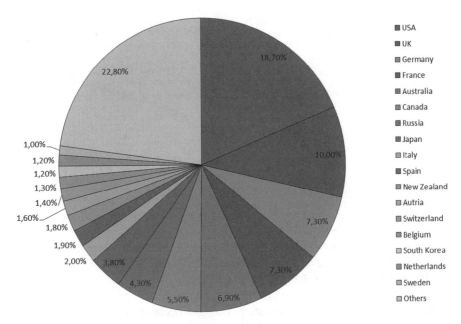

Fig. 39.2 Market share of the main host countries in international student mobility (Source: OECD 2010)

Though not illustrated here, the distinction made by Rivza and Teichler (2007), who suggest two types of mobility, deserves interest; those two types are: the 'vertical' mobility, which primarily concerns flows of students going from developing to developed countries, and the 'horizontal' mobility which corresponds to students moving between similarly developed countries, say between European countries, respectively.

39.2.3   The Erasmus Programme and the Bologna Process

The European Union started 60 years ago. Its main objective was to build up a union organised around the coal and steel industries. Today, one of the objectives of the EU Member States is to set up a single European labour market, a condition for a monetary union to function. Another objective is to make the EU the most advanced area in research, development and innovation – see the Lisbon Agenda (European Council 2000), the Sapir Report (Sapir et al. 2003) and more recently the Europe 2020 Strategy (European Commission 2010a), especially the flagship "Youth on the move".

Both the Erasmus Programme and the Bologna Process might be read today in that prospect. In 1987, the ERASMUS Programme was launched, encouraging EU students to spend a term or a year of their higher education in an institution located

Fig. 39.3 Number of students in the ERASMUS programme (Source: European Commission 2010b)

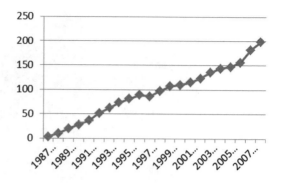

in another Member State. This programme has been especially successful, as we may observe in Fig. 39.3.

The Bologna Process was not an initiative of the EU itself, when launched in 1999; its initial goal was to build up a European educational space by 2010. Although it was signed by the Ministers in charge of higher education of 46 European countries, this process does not rest on an intergovernmental arrangement. Its philosophy is well summarised in the Bologna's Declaration (Bologna Declaration 1999). That declaration states that 'A Europe of Knowledge is now widely recognised as an irreplaceable factor for social and human growth and as an indispensable component to consolidate and enrich the European citizenship, capable of giving its citizens the necessary competences to face the challenges of the new millennium, together with an awareness of shared values and belonging to a common social and cultural space'.

Then participants recognise the 'Importance of education and educational co-operation in the development and strengthening of stable, peaceful and democratic societies' and the 'Universities' central role in developing European cultural dimensions'. They promote the 'creation of the European area of higher education as a key way to promote citizens' mobility and employability and the Continent's overall development'.

In line with this philosophy six main goals were to be implemented,

- Adoption of a system of easily readable and comparable degrees in order to promote European citizens employability and the international competitiveness of the European higher education system.
- Adoption of a system essentially based on two main cycles.
- Establishment of a system of credits as a proper means of promoting the most widespread student mobility.
- Promotion of mobility by overcoming obstacles to the effective exercise of free movement.
- Promotion of European co-operation in quality assurance.
- Promotion of the necessary European dimensions in higher education.

Since then, those goals have turned into action lines, work plans and objectives which have evolved with time.

Though both the Erasmus Programme and the Bologna Process favour students' mobility, a main difference exists between those two features. The Erasmus

Programme is an exchange programme; a student staying abroad in that framework remains enrolled in the institution of his/her country of origin and is just 'in exchange' in the host institution, where he/she is not asked to pay a tuition fee; usually Erasmus students do not appear in statistics of foreign students. Unlike that, within the Bologna framework, a student enrols in the school where he/she actually attends classes for a term, a year or more, pays a tuition fee in that institution and is permitted to impute the credits obtained abroad – the so-called ECTS – on the programme he/she follows in her original country.

39.2.4 Imbalance in Students Migration

Table 39.1 completes this section and provides the data which eventually motivate this paper. The second and fifth columns represent the share of foreign students of European nationality enrolled in the tertiary education of the host country. The third and sixth columns represent the difference between the number of nationals going abroad for the purpose of higher education (HE) and the number of incoming foreign EU HE students, divided by the total number of HE students in the country. A negative (viz. positive) figure of that balance means that the country hosts more (viz. less) EU foreign students than it sends nationals to other EU institutions.

In other terms, countries like Austria, Belgium, United Kingdom, the Czech Republic, Netherlands and Denmark are thus net importers of students and net exporters of enriched human capital. Such imbalances deserve investigation and are at the root of a challenge for the financing of higher education in Europe. However, the cases of those countries are far from being identical.

Belgium and Austria share a common border and a similar language with a large neighbouring country where *numerus clausus* is at work in medical and paramedical disciplines. Moreover, they charge low tuition fees to local students and, therefore, are bound to charge similar low fees to nationals from other EU countries. Then, numerous students not accepted in German and French schools go to Austria or Belgium.[1] The same kind of argument holds for the Czech Republic, Netherlands and Denmark who also have a common border with Germany; the Czech figures have also to be related with the Slovak ones. One can say that, in those countries, immigrant students are not the top ranked graduates of secondary schools. Further, due to the low tuition fee charged, the human capital of EU immigrant students is enriched at the expense of local taxpayers.

The British situation is very different. It is attractive for foreign students because it provides higher education of good quality taught in the most international language. Those characteristics are sought by talented students who regard the high tuition fee charged to both British and EU students as an investment in their future.

---

[1] According to OECD (2010), there are 16,650 French students in tertiary education in Belgium against 2,768 Belgian students in France; similarly, there are 17,464 German students in Austrian tertiary education against 6,419 Austrians in Germany.

In the rest of the paper we leave aside the case of the UK while we consider that of the other net student importing countries as the stylised fact motivating this investigation. The research question then becomes: "how to internalise the negative externality imposed to Austria, Belgium and similar countries by their large neighbour"?

39.3 Evaluation of the Impact of Student Mobility

The economic literature recognises various effects on international student mobility. Among them, it sets forth a positive link between mobility and economic growth. More generally, studying abroad generates individual and collective positive impacts. Individual effects include access to a foreign culture which may help finding a job in a foreign country after graduation; that opportunity, however, still needs extra empirical evidence. Collective impact stems from mobility making it possible to bring closer different cultures and nations, and then favouring peace among them.

If we focus on the economic effects, two groups appear: simultaneous and direct effects on the one hand, and differed and indirect effects on the other hand.

39.3.1 Simultaneous and Direct Effects

The direct economic effects are quite clear. They relate to the economic impact of hosting foreign students on the territory. Like national students, international students contribute to the expansion of the real estate market and spend money in local stores. But, on the other hand, they generate a cost for the local community due to the hosting related expenditures, namely in terms of teaching and support staff. Since most foreign students do not remain in the host country after completing their studies, that cost is a sunk cost.

Direct economic effects also occur for the country of origin of the students since there is some probability that those students will not come back home after their stay abroad or not have their career at home, which means a loss of skill and of contribution to GDP.

According to Throsby (1999), all in all the impact for the host country is neutral. For the country of origin that impact is more ambiguous. In the case of Germany, it seems that there exists a direct cost in terms of student support, and also in terms of lost output and less social contributions; in Sweden however, the effects seem to be balanced.

39.3.2 Differed and Indirect Economic Effects

A stay abroad also improves human capital indirectly. The economic literature stresses that human capital obeys a process of accumulation. In that respect, a stay abroad, like other features of life and education, is an experiment which may add to the accumulation of knowledge and help improving productivity. This is so because, next to making it possible for an individual to attend classes in another, possibly better, university, staying abroad means being confronted to a new environment. This environment may include the use of another language and the adaptation to a different culture. Such an experiment is positive in terms of productivity; indeed, the mobile students acquire concepts harder to get domestically and they expect that their future employer will recognise that they have a larger capacity in terms of integration and practice of a foreign language.

Moreover, mobility enables creating cross border networks. Former mobile students will be able to propose new outlets for trade to their employers. A good example is reported by Hsu and Saxenian (2001); they set forth the important links woven by a community of Taiwanese people which had settled in Silicon Valley, California. That network effect seems particularly important, though not easily measurable.

The following two questions are especially relevant for our purposes:

– Do studies abroad influence the geographic area in which current mobile students evolve? and
– Do studies abroad influence the geographic area in which former mobile students will evolve?

Large numbers of foreign students could affect the structures that host them. In that respect, Ward (2001) proposes to study the following four questions: What is the nature of the interaction and relations between the international students, the local students and the host institutions, respectively? What is the difference in terms of use of the institutional support between the international and local students? What is the impact of the mobile students on teaching and training? And what are the conditions so that positive effects of internationalisation appear?

These questions led the author to note that the interactions between local and foreign students are weak, even non-existent. It also seems that the impact of the foreign students on the local teaching habits is very weak and that the internationally mobile students have very little influence on the functioning of the institutions in the host country.

One of the most important impacts of student mobility consists in a shift of human capital. If one admits that studying abroad increases the probability of working abroad later in the career, one can easily imagine that international student mobility will allow the creation of an efficient EU wide job market which would permit a better allocation of resources and thus a stronger growth.

Oosterbeek and Webbink (2009) study the impact of a subsidy on the cross border mobility of individuals who pursue higher education in the Netherlands. Their first results, using ordinary least squares, show that the subsidy increases the probability of studying abroad from 25% to 30% and the number of months spent abroad from 5 to 8 months. They also show that recipients of the help have the probability of living in the Netherlands during the first years of their professional career decreased by 30%. Further, second results based on instrumental variables reinforce the first findings: studying abroad increases the probability of settling abroad by 100%, each month spent abroad decreasing the probability of living in the Netherlands at the beginning of the career by 4–5%. This study confirms the intuition issued above; however it refers to the sole case of the Netherlands and it would be interesting to see similar studies for other countries.

Jahr and Teichler (2001) summarise the results of a study undertaken by the Center for Research on Higher Education and Work of the University of Kassel in Germany, over the 1989–1994 period of time. The goal of this study is to analyse the impact of a temporary stay abroad during the studies. The investigation reveals that the students who studied abroad think that their stay was positive for their personal development and the learning of other cultures and foreign languages. However, the majority of the students estimate that the stay abroad did not have a decisive impact on their future job from the point of view of the qualification or remuneration. On the other hand, the authors mention that, among the students actually employed 5 years after the stay, 18% work abroad (9% in the country which hosted them during their Erasmus stay, and another 9% in another country), a figure which is 2–3% higher than the European average. Five years later, a new questionnaire addressed to those individuals reveals that half of them frequently use the language of the country which hosted them; and that approximately one-third always use competences acquired abroad. And even for those who do not work abroad, the knowledge acquired during their stay is important for their employment.

That new study tends to confirm the effects that we anticipated above. For the authors, however, it is likely that the study is biased. Indeed, it is pretty sure that the most mobile people have also little time for filling-in a questionnaire. In the same way, one can think that some competences had already been acquired in the country of origin – like mastering the language – or that the students who left had already an experience of living abroad.

The work of Parey and Waldinger (2011) tries to avoid the above bias. Through a more complex econometric methodology, their first conclusion is that granting more subsidies involves larger student mobility and increasing professional mobility. Then, using a large database on German students, they investigate the causality between student mobility and professional mobility; their results show that studying abroad increases the probability of working abroad from approximately 15–20%. Moreover, it seems that students tend to migrate to the countries where they stayed during their studies.

39.4 Theoretical Analysis

The developments above were devoted to the presentation of stylised facts motivating this study (Sect. 39.2) and to that of results from the economic literature able to highlight some aspects of the topic (Sect. 39.3). Now we turn to a theoretical analysis based on Gérard (2010a, b). It assumes a deliberately simplified world in order to set forth some results that may eventually be turned into policy propositions.

We first assume that higher education is entirely financed by local taxpayers and we call such feature an application of the *host country principle*. Then we turn to an alternative principle: studies are financed by the country where students got their previous degree; in such a system, studies are paid by the country from which the student comes and we can name that an application of the *country of origin principle*.

In order to circumvent the difficulties of implementing the latter system we explore close specific designs like a system of two-part vouchers granted by the country of origin government. In that case, the first part of the voucher is dedicated to cover the cost of the studies either at home or abroad provided it is in an institution whose quality has been recognised by the issuer of the voucher. The second part of the voucher aims at providing a *student wage* which might be also an incentive for attracting students to higher education in general, through an extra wage for students belonging to targeted groups, or to specific fields of study.

39.4.1   The Host Country Principle

Let a Union consisting of two countries. Each wants to maximise the social welfare of its population which depends on the number of graduates from higher education who work in the country, producing GDP. Resident students educated abroad and foreign students hosted in the country and remaining in the territory after completing their studies might be more productive than purely domestically educated residents. This is why countries have to decide on the degree of international opening of their workers, represented by the number of credits (or ECTS) that they intend to deliver to students coming from abroad; such a mechanism encompasses the *quotas* of foreign students introduced by Austria and Belgium in some fields of study. There is no tuition fee charged to students and the costs of providing higher education are supported by local tax revenue. Furthermore, there is no difference in costs between national and international students, or between countries.

Externalities are clearly at work in such a setting. Indeed, a country only cares about students who will work on its territory and thus only includes those people in its objective function neglecting the human capital represented by foreign students educated in its territory but who go back home after completing their studies; those students will increase the GDP in their country of origin.

This model makes it possible to build up a two country infinitely living non-cooperative game and to draw two main conclusions from the obtained Nash equilibrium. On the one hand, too few credits, or seats in the auditorium, are proposed to foreign students as compared with an efficient benchmark where the governments – or a supranational authority – jointly maximise the social welfare of their two countries taken together. On the other hand, the number of credits supplied to foreign students decreases when the probability that they return home at the end of their studies increases; indeed those students will not contribute to local the GDP in the future.

The policy lesson driven by this model is that using quotas to limit the number of foreign students is an inefficient option; we come back below on that issue.

39.4.2   The Country of Origin Principle

Let us suppose the same theoretical framework as in the previous model. But studies of foreign students are financed by the country where they come from; that country is termed their country of origin and it has to finance the studies of its students. Henceforth, each government has to choose the quantity of credits permitted to be obtained by the students it sends abroad or, more simply, to decide on the number of students it sends abroad.

One can show that, although it is still inefficient compared with the efficient benchmark above, the outcome of this design is more efficient than the previous one provided that the probability of returning home after completion of the studies is higher than a given threshold. By 'more efficient' we mean that the number of credits or of foreign students is closer to that generated by the efficient benchmark. The reason of the efficiency gain is that countries now decide on their provision of seats in the auditorium or of ECTS based on the domestic students expected to return home after their studies abroad instead of the foreign students supposed to stay in the host country after those studies, the share of the former being larger than that of the latter.

We may conclude from these two models that the country of origin principle supports a more efficient solution than the current application of the host country principle, even if neither of those principles makes it possible to eliminate the free-riding phenomenon at work: a country might have the studies of the further contributors to its own GDP financed by taxpayers of the other country.

However, the implementation of that second model raises some issues. A simple solution should be that the two countries agree on jointly implementing that design. They may do that through, say, a bilateral treaty like treaties existing on tax or social security matters; or through a directive decided by the EU authorities. In that case, each country commits to pay the actual costs of studies – not the nearly or actually zero tuition fees – of its origin students to the other country, provided that the students enrol in schools agreed by the country of origin, by which it is meant that the quality of their education is recognised by the country of origin. That recognition might be based on a principle of mutual recognition or on the use of a quality certification process.

However, we may question the reasons why a country of origin is prepared to pay for studies in another jurisdiction. In other words, will Germany or France be ready to approve a treaty or a directive implying that they have to pay for the studies of their residents in Austria or in Belgium? Of course, we cannot rule out such possibility, e.g. in the framework of a policy package or in that of a more integrated higher education policy; nevertheless, for the time being, it is hard to imagine such policy design being easily adopted. Therefore, we should consider other, possibly close, designs. The first one comes out to be a good proxy for the just above described mechanism, the other two potentially involve a more efficient outcome. The first one is based on vouchers delivered by the country of origin; the second one, on a Bhagwati tax and the last one on contingent loans.

Please note that, within the European Union, the country of origin principle currently applies for health care abroad: a Belgian citizen hospitalised in Spain will have his/her health care eventually paid to Spain by Belgian social security. In higher education matters, the principle applies in Switzerland – see Sect. 39.5 below – where a canton without a university pays the cantons with a university that host its students.

39.4.3   A Two-Part Voucher System

Rather than explicitly transferring means to partner country, one may imagine a European or Bologna area reform of higher education financing based on a system of vouchers; and, if possible, a system of two-part vouchers.

39.4.3.1   First Part of the Higher Education Voucher: Covering the Cost of Studies

By that system, we first mean that the government of the country of origin provides its prospective students with vouchers that they may use to pay the actual cost of their studies, i.e. the cost supported by the teaching institutions; and you may imagine that the voucher value corresponds to 1 year of studies or 60 ECTS, either at home or abroad, again, provided that students enrol in schools whose quality is recognised by the issuer of the voucher. For those students who keep studying domestically, nothing is changed by the reform. For those who prefer studying abroad the voucher is to be passed to the authorities of the foreign university.

The efficiency of such a mechanism first calls for a pre-condition – that higher education institutions across the participating area – the EU or the Bologna area, or a larger geographic area – do not accept students unable to produce such a voucher, although we hardly rule out that they accept them for a tuition fee higher than actual cost.

That condition being fulfilled, the system exhibits the important property to allow each country to expand its area of sovereignty over its nationals, in terms of higher education, especially if the vouchers are specified by field of study.

To take the example of medical studies, Germany or France might decide to grant a given number of vouchers for first year studies in Medicine; French or German students who get those vouchers may use them in their country or abroad; those who fail to obtain a voucher are no longer permitted to enrol either at home or abroad. Therefore the *numerus clausus* decided by France or Germany hold for students from those countries even if they decide to study in another jurisdiction.

Table 39.2 below is based on Belgian figures and provides values for the vouchers at stake.

Table 39.2 Budget allocated by the French-speaking community of Belgium

University higher education	Euros per student
Any year of Bachelor and Master's degree in Philosophy, Theology, Humanities, History, Art and Archaeology, Architecture and Urban Planning, Information and Communication, Political and Social Sciences, Law, Criminology, Economics and Management, Psychology and Sciences of Education	5,597.50
1st or 2nd year of Bachelor degree in Medical Sciences, Veterinary Medicine, Dental Sciences, Agronomic Sciences and Biological Engineering, Engineering, any year of Bachelor or Master's degree in Art or Sciences of Art	11,195.00
3rd year of Bachelor degree or any year of Master's degree in Medical Sciences, Veterinary Medicine, Dental Sciences, Sciences, Agronomic Sciences and Biological Engineering, Engineering	16,792.50
Non university higher education	
Short-type economic studies	4,665.63
Long-type economic studies, short-type technical studies	5,132.19
Short-type agronomy, social studies	5,365.48
Applied arts (industrial engineer…)	5,598.76
Translator-interpreters	6,765.16
Paramedical	6,998.45
Education (teachers, …), long-type agronomy, long-type technical	7,698.29

Source: Gérard and Vandenberghe (2007b)
Estimates by field of study, based on the 2005–2006 budget of the French-speaking Community of Belgium

39.4.3.2   Second Part of the Higher Education Voucher: Covering the Cost of Living and Providing Incentives to Targeted Students

The second part of the voucher, though not a necessary condition for the system to operate, would relate it to the financing of the student's life during the studies, providing her with a so called *student wage*.

Such a student wage could pursue two goals. One goal is to encourage students to undertake studying fields which, though especially needed by the society, are less attractive, maybe because they are less rewarded in money terms, or because they are less prestigious. Another goal is to favour some targeted groups like women, low income or immigrant families. That second part of the voucher actually makes it a tool for education – or labour market – and social policy.

39.4.4   A Baghwati Tax

So far the government of the country financing the improvement of mobile students' human capital takes into account a return on investment only if the graduates stay in the country after completing their studies – under the host country principle – or if they return home after such completion – under the origin principle.

Now let us investigate more efficient policy designs where countries investing in higher education either benefit from the contribution of graduates to their own GDP or social welfare, or are compensated for non-benefiting from such a return. The first such design is based on the *Bhagwati tax*. That tax has been suggested by Economist Bhagwati in order to offset developing countries whose students, after completing their education in developed countries, decided to stay and work there rather than to return home (see Bhagwati 1976; Wilson 2008); the tax is levied on the income of graduates remaining abroad and paid to the sending country.

Suppose, therefore, a graduate who studied in country H – for host – with vouchers financed by country O – for origin. After graduation, he/she decides to stay in country H and to have his/her career in that country. If a Bhagwati tax is at work, that person will have to pay a tax to his/her origin country in order to compensate it for the financing of his/her studies. One can show that this design is efficient if the compensation relates to both the financing cost and the opportunity cost incurred by the origin country.

That compensation might be organised through the local tax system and the local tax administration provided an international arrangement be in place. Should the career of the person at stake be shared between countries H and O, the compensation should be *pro rata temporis*. In the same line, extension of the reasoning to the case of a career distributed among various countries is straightforward.

In the introductory section above we wrote that 'graduates are expected to get higher wages than less skilled people and, therefore, to pay higher taxes, especially in those countries where labour income tax is progressive. In that sense, students receive implicit loans from the government during the time of their studies that they later repay with an interest, in a way contingent to the income generated by their studies.' We added that 'that reasoning holds in a world where the graduates pay their tax in the country where they graduated. However, it no longer holds in a setting where people graduate in one jurisdiction and then have their career in another one or in some other countries. In such a setting, one country pays for the cost of studies and other benefit from the skill, the contribution to the local GDP and tax revenue.' The Bhagwati tax set forth in this section is precisely a remedy to that difficulty since, in any case, the graduates compensate the country which provided them with such an implicit grant. Provided the income tax system is progressive, the Bhagwati tax may be made so and thus the investigated design is a form of contingent loan mechanism. One – important – difference, however, is that the size and timing of the refund of a contingent loan is limited while the payment of the tax is not limited over time; however, an equivalence in discounting terms between the two mechanisms might be computed.

Please note that such a Bhagwati tax exists for professional soccer players; a tax is levied on their gains and paid out to the clubs which supported their initial training in junior categories.

39.4.5 Contingent Loans

In the previous section we assumed that the cost of studies was initially paid by public authorities and later recovered through the tax system by means of either a traditional income tax or a Bhagwati tax; such a mechanism looks like a contingent loan where the lender is the government of the country of origin.

One can make a step further and imagine that the lender is the government of either the host or the origin country. To keep the exposition simple consider again the stylised facts which motivate this study and suppose that any European student hosted in a Belgian institution of higher education located in the French-speaking Belgian Community, including Belgian residents, is proposed a loan by the government of that jurisdiction. They will pay that money back during their career, depending on their income.

The lender could be a private institution as well, like a bank or an insurance company, at least in theory. Numerous authors, however, – on contingent loans in general see Barr (1989, 1998) and Chapman (1997, 2005) and on the particular issue investigated here Del Rey and Verheyden (2011) – consider that such a loan is too risky for the private sector, but in some fields like a Master in Business Administration, especially because students are not able to provide the bank with enough collateral. This means that the financial risk has to be partly or totally socialised, by which is meant, that private loans – supposing them feasible – will need a public guarantee. Such public guarantee could be provided by the host country or by the country of origin or eventually by an international institution like the European Investment Bank. Please note that the latter already has some experience with contingent loans as a lender to organisations dedicated to that end.

This system still deserves at least two remarks. The first one is to mention that, in some countries, like Australia, the reported income for tax purposes is used to assess the income taken into account to compute the size and timing of the refund.

A second remark makes a link between the contingent loan and the vouchers depicted above. As we have seen, the vouchers can be used as incentive tools for higher education, labour and social policy. In the same way as granting extra amounts to students undertaking especially needed fields of study, though little rewarded, or belonging to targeted social groups, the size and timing of the refund might be modulated in line with the desirability and the social value of the studies and the socioeconomic group to which the – prospective – student belongs. And some loans might be turned into grants accordingly, e.g. if you become a teacher or a civil servant paid by the government.

More generally, like vouchers were twofold – a voucher to cover the costs of studies, and a voucher to support the cost of living – a contingent loan may aim at both covering the cost of studies and providing the student with a monthly amount equivalent to a student wage. As noticed by Barr in an exposition of contingent loans, that system makes studies costless for the student during the time of the studies.

Before turning to policy suggestions, we still want to highlight the topic under investigation by the examination of some national experiences.

39.5   Some National Experiences

Let us consider three national experiences that we consider as especially relevant for our purposes.

39.5.1   Norway: A Combination of Loans and Grants

In Norway there is generally no tuition fee for higher education. Therefore, the Norwegian State Educational Loan Fund, a public institution, has not been created to help students finance the cost of studies. This Fund intends to support the student's life costs, and thus to provide them with a kind of student wage. Though it primarily aims at Norwegian students, it may be also accessible to foreign students, under some conditions. The amount of the help does not depend on the student's family means; it is presented, initially, as a loan varying between 10,000 and to 14,000 Euros, according to whether or not the student lives in her parents' house and if he/she validates all the examinations. Later, these loans might be turned, partly or totally, into grants.

That aid is also accessible to students who decide to study abroad, though then subject to several conditions, like the similar quality of the host institution, the equivalent level of the studies and the attendance to the courses. These students benefit from the same financial help as the other Norwegian students, and might receive an extra amount related to additional costs implied by the studies abroad, like travelling costs and learning of the local language, and also in the event of very high tuition fees.

This system is generous towards both national and international students and the goal of Norway is twofold and well in line with the ideas developed in the previous section. The first objective is the free access to higher education for all social classes of the country. The second one is more international: by such a system, Norway makes it possible to give an international dimension to its project. It makes it possible to stimulate the Norwegian students to study abroad and it supports the integration of the foreign students in Norway so that they remain in the country at the end of their studies.

For a more detailed description of this system, we suggest to refer to Levy (2004).

39.5.2   Australia: A Contingent Loan System

In Australia, higher education is financed by the government – the Commonwealth contribution – and by the students – student contribution. The history of that system might be read, e.g. in Maguain (2005). Tuition fees are differentiated based on the differences in the costs of studies and the expected future returns on those studies; the latter are left to the appreciation of the institutions.

Australia was the first country to introduce contingent loans, called FEE-HELP or Fee – Higher Education Loan Program. That program is accessible to Australian citizens and, under some conditions, to foreign students. Moreover, students with limited means may also call for this kind of loan in order to finance the cost of living. The loans are not charged a real interest rate and their refund is subject to future income: the refund is carried out from a certain income threshold and little increases in income.

Another system was set up for the mobile students, called OS-HELP. It makes it possible to finance the cost of the studies abroad. It obeys the same principle as the FEE-HELP; it is provided for a 6-month period and is renewable only twice; to receive that help, students must be affiliated with an Australian institution.

39.5.3 Switzerland: A Centralised Cantonal Management

Switzerland is a confederation of 26 cantons which have an executive and a legislative power. Competences in terms of higher education are distributed between the confederation and the cantons.

Since higher education is financed partly by cantons, a system called 'Inter-cantonal University Agreement' aims at coordinating the university policy. It allows each Swiss student to benefit from an equal treatment in terms of access to the university. A canton cannot operate a selection at the entrance of its universities based on the canton of origin of the student. On the other hand, if a canton is debtor with respect to another canton, in terms of student flow, it will have to pay compensation to that latter, in line with the cost of the studies in that canton.

Notice that such a system also exists among Scandinavian countries. That system of inter-cantonal – in Switzerland – or international – in Scandinavia – compensation is an illustration of the origin country principle depicted above.

39.6   To Conclude: Policy Suggestions

Our research question was: "how to internalize the negative externality imposed to Austria, Belgium and similar countries by their large neighbours".

Such a question is a true challenge that Belgian – and Austrian – authorities have tentatively responded by imposing *quotas* to the number of first year foreign students, including European students, in some fields of studies.

That system of quotas, however, has been considered by the European Court of Justice – see European Court of Justice (2010) –, the ultimate custodian of EU principles, as not compatible with EU Law. For the Court indeed, 'Articles 18 and 21 TFEU (the Treaty founding the EU) preclude national legislation, such as that at issue in the main proceedings, which limits the number of students not regarded as resident in Belgium who may enrol for the first time in medical and paramedical courses at Higher Education establishments, unless the referring court, having assessed all the relevant evidence submitted by the competent authorities, finds that that legislation is justified in the light of the objective of protection of public health'. Moreover, although 'the Belgian Government, supported by the Austrian Government, confirms that the legislation at issue in the main proceedings is necessary to attain the objective of ensuring the quality and continuing provision of medical and paramedical care within the French Community', the Court adds that 'it follows from the case-law that a difference in treatment based indirectly on nationality may be justified by the objective of maintaining a balanced high quality medical service open to all, insofar as it contributes to achieving a high level of protection of health. Thus, it must be determined whether the legislation at issue in the main proceedings is appropriate for securing the attainment of that legitimate objective and whether it goes beyond what is necessary to attain it (...). That being the case, it is for the competent national authorities to show that such risks actually exist. According to the settled case-law, it is for those Authorities, where they adopt a measure derogating from a principle enshrined by European Union Law, to show in each individual case that that measure is appropriate for securing the attainment of the objective relied upon and does not go beyond what is necessary to attain it. The reasons invoked by a Member State by way of justification must thus be accompanied by an analysis of the appropriateness and proportionality of the measure adopted by that State and by specific evidence substantiating its arguments'.

As far as we know, the position of French-speaking Belgian Authorities is to justify the quotas 'by the objective of maintaining a balanced high quality medical service open to all'.

Our conclusion, at the end of this analysis, is quite different. We entitled one of our papers (Gérard and Vandenberghe 2007a) «Mobilité étudiante en Europe: une idée qui mérite mieux que des quotas» (*Student Mobility in Europe: an Idea Which Deserves More than Quotas*). That is to say that an alternative avenue does exist and we have explored some of its possible designs in this paper; mostly based on the country of origin principle.

The basic idea is that each EU government, when it decides its higher education policy, should take into account the welfare of the whole European Union, not to say of the entire world, and not the sole welfare of its territory or its taxpayers. For a government to behave such, one needs to compensate it for the loss of local welfare generated by students not returning to, or not remaining in, the jurisdiction which has financed their studies.

Therefore, if a government pays for the studies of its resident, either at home or abroad – provided it is in an institution of recognised quality – it will deserve getting a return, either a contribution of the graduate to the local welfare or a pecuniary compensation paid by this graduate in line with his/her means – because he/she would have contributed to the local welfare accordingly. The latter may take the form of a tax either paid directly or paid through his/her country of residence; this is the idea of a Bhagwati tax. Otherwise that payment for studies might take the form of a contingent loan provided by a financial institution with public guarantee; in that case the compensation eventually goes to that institution; in that case there is no need that the lending institution be from the origin country.

Practically both the public grant and the contingent loan may take the form of a two-part voucher, one part to cover the actual costs of studies, another part to provide the students with a student wage. Though it is not a pre-condition for the operation of the system, the student wage is an important block of the financing of higher education – see above the Norwegian case – which allows the whole system to be used to direct students towards higher education in general as well as towards specific fields, like those which are especially needed from a social viewpoint though less rewarded in terms of money; and to incentivise some targeted groups of people of the population like low income people or immigrants.

In that respect, the possibility to turn loans into grants is also an interesting opportunity. We mention the case of Norway providing loans to students from developing countries and turning those loans into grants if those people return home after their studies, contributing to the development of their country of origin.

Although the externalities at the very root of this paper are currently limited, they are expected to grow in the future, not only in Europe but also worldwide. Studies predict an important increase of student flows from Asian countries such as China, India or Indonesia. International mobility covers more than ever a current and future policy issue. That also justifies that the European Union committed to build up a true European space of higher education.

Among the final remarks let us note that, obviously, from the point of view of eliminating externalities, centralising, say at EU level, the organisation and financing of higher education should be an efficient device; however, there is no room in today' s EU agenda to make higher education a EU centralised competence or even a shared one. Should that latter opportunity emerge in the future, we should subject it to a test of subsidiarity (see Pelkmans 2005; Gérard 2008).

Moreover, international mobility of students is not only a question of externalities and free-riding. Other reasons may preside on the decision of an active policy of hosting foreign students. For example, France has recently decided to launch a plan to increase its capacity of hosting foreign students; this country considers that such an action is a real geopolitical investment – a foreign student can be an excellent ambassador of the French culture when he/she returns in his/her country of origin – and an economic investment as well – he/she will be able to create links with France.

Finally, please note that, throughout the paper, we have considered higher education as a sector mainly State financed. We have to be aware, however, that mobility or globalisation are likely to reduce the size of the public sector in that field – which is externality related – and to increase that of the private sector (Justman and Thisse 1997, 2000; Mechtenberg and Strausz 2008, 2009; Buettner and Schwager 2004; Poutvaara and Kanniainen 2000).

References

Barr, N. (1989). *Student loans: The next steps*. London: Freedom Press.

Barr, N. (1998). *The economics of the welfare state*. Oxford: Oxford University Press.

Bhagwati, J. (1976). *Taxing the brain drain, Vol. 1: A proposal and the brain drain and taxation, Vol. 2: Theory and empirical analysis*. Amsterdam: North Holland.

Bologna Declaration. (1999). *Towards the European Higher Education Area*. Conference of Ministers responsible for Higher Education in 29 European countries, Bologna, Italy.

Buettner, T., & Schwager, R. (2004). Regionale Verteilungseffekte der Hochschulfinanzierung und ihre Konsequenzen. In W. Franz et al. (Eds.), *Wirtschaftswissenschaftliches Seminar Ottobeuren 33*, University of Tubingen, Tubingen.

Chapman, B. (1997). Conceptual issues and the Australian experience with income contingent charging for Higher Education. *The Economic Journal, 107*, 1178–1193.

Chapman, B. (2005). *Income contingent loans for higher education: International reform* (Discussion Paper 491). Canberra: Australian National University.

Chevalier, C., & Gérard, M. (2009). La mobilité étudiante est-elle facteur de croissance? In M. Castanheira & R. Veugelers (Eds.), *Education et Croissance, Rapport de la Commission 1 au 17ème Congrès des Economistes belges de la langue française*. Charleroi: Cifop.

Chevalier, C., & Gérard, M. (2010). Effets et financement de la mobilité étudiante en Europe. In F. Degavre et al. (Eds.), *Transformations et innovations économiques et sociales en Europe: quelles sorties de crise ? Regards interdisciplinaires*. Louvain-la-Neuve: University Press of Louvain. *Cahiers du Cirtes, 4*, 239–256.

Del Rey, E., & Verheyden, B. (2011). *Loans, insurance and failures in the credit market for students* (CESifo Working Paper Series 3410). Munich: CESifo Group.

European Commission. (2010a). *Europe 2020, a strategy for smart, sustainable and inclusive growth*. Communication from the Commission, COM (2010) 2020, Brussels.

European Commission. (2010b). *The ERASMUS Programme 2008/2009; A statistical overview*. Brussels: European Commission.

European Council. (2000). *Presidency conclusions, Lisbon European Council 23 and 24 March 2000*. Brussels: General Secretariat of the European Council.

European Court of Justice. (2010, April). *Nicolas Bressol and Others, Céline Chaverot and Others vs. Gouvernement de la Communauté française*.

Gérard, M. (2007). Financing Bologna: Which country will pay for foreign students? *Education Economics, 15*, 441–454.

Gérard, M. (2008). Higher education, mobility and the subsidiarity principle. In G. Gelauf, I. Grilo, & A. Lejour (Eds.), *Subsidiarity and economic reform in Europe*. Berlin: Springer.

Gérard, M. (2010a). Le financement de la mobilité des étudiants Bologne. *Revue Economique, 61*, 577–588.

Gérard, M. (2010b). *Financing Bologna students' mobility* (Taxation Papers 26). Brussels: EU Commission, DG Taxud.

Gérard, M., & Vandenberghe, V. (2007a). *Mobilité étudiante en Europe: une idée qui mérite mieux que des quotas* (Regards Economiques No. 54). Louvain-la-Neuve: IRES.

Gérard, M., & Vandenberghe, V. (2007b). Financement de l'enseignement supérieur et mobilité du capital humain en Europe. In F. Docquier & F. Thys-Clément (Eds.), *Education et Force de Travail, Rapport de la Commission 1 au 17ème Congrès des Economistes belges de langue française*. Charleroi: Cifop.

Hsu, J. Y., & Saxenian, A. (2001). The Silicon Valley-Hsinchu connection: Technical communities and industrial upgrading. *Industrial and Corporate Change, 10*, 893–920.

Jahr, V., & Teichler, U. (2001). Mobility during the course of study and after graduation. *European Journal of Education, 36*, 443–458.

Justman, M., & Thisse, J. F. (1997). Implications of the mobility of skilled labor for local public funding of Higher Education. *Economics Letters, 55*, 409–412.

Justman, M., & Thisse, J. F. (2000). Local public funding of higher education when skilled labor is imperfectly mobile. *International Tax and Public Finance, 7*, 247–258.

Kelo, M., Teichler, U., & Wächter, B. (2006). Toward improved data on student mobility in Europe: Findings and concepts of the Eurodata study. *Journal of Studies in International Education, 10*, 194–223.

Kemnitz, A. (2005). *Educational federalism and the quality effects of tuition fees* (IVS Discussion Paper Series 617). Mannheim: University of Mannheim.

Levy, J. S. (2004). *Student finance schemes in Norway: A case study*. Paris: UNESCO/IIEP.

Maguain, D. (2005). Les prêts contingents aux étudiants dans les pays de l'OCDE. *Revue française d'économie, 20*, 51–71.

Mechtenberg, L., & Strausz, R. (2008). The Bologna Process: How student mobility affects multicultural skills and educational quality. *International Tax and Public Finance, 15*, 109–130.

Mechtenberg, L., & Strausz, R. (2009). *Internal migration and immigration of the highly skilled in Europe: How the Bologna and Lisbon Process can target the transferability of human capital.* mimeo.

Mechtenberg, L., & Strausz, R. (2010). *Migration of the talented: Can Europe catch up with the U.S.?* mimeo.

OECD. (2010). *Education at a Glance 2010: OECD indicators*. Paris: OECD.

Oosterbeek, H., & Webbink, D. (2009). Does studying abroad induce a brain drain? *Economica, 78*, 347–366.

Parey, M., & Waldinger, F. (2011). Studying abroad and the effect on international labour market mobility: Evidence from the introduction of Erasmus. *The Economic Journal, 121*, 194–222.

Pelkmans, J. (2005). *Testing for Subsidiarity* (BEEP Briefings 13). Bruges: College of Europe.

Poutvaara, P., & Kanniainen, V. (2000). Why invest in your neighbor? Social contract on education investment. *International Tax and Public Finance, 7*, 547–563.

Rivza, B., & Teichler, U. (2007). The changing role of student mobility. *Higher Education Policy, 20*, 457–475.

Sapir, A., et al. (2003). *An agenda for a growing Europe*. Brussels: European Commission.

Throsby, D. (1999). *Financing and effects of internationalisation in higher education, the economic costs and benefits of international student flows*. Paris: OECD, Center for Educational Research and Innovation.

Ward, C. (2001). *The impact of international students on domestic students and host institutions*. New Zealand: Export Education Policy Project of the Ministry of Education.

Wilson, J. (2008). Taxing the brain drain: A reassessment of the Bhagwati proposal. In E. Dinopoulos, P. Krishna, A. Panagariya, & K. Wong (Eds.), *Trade, globalization and poverty*. London: Routledge.

Chapter 40
Entrepreneurialism and Financing for Improved Academic Enterprise[1] in Higher Education: Coaching for Leadership and Innovation Reflecting True Demand[2]

James A. Powell and Beliz Ozorhon

40.1 Introduction

A recent report by the EU Committee on the Regions (CoR 2011) outlines the 'need for renewal of societal and industrial structure and processes.....Old practices and structures are not enough to achieve the goals EU political leaders have in their minds for improving welfare and quality of life of its citizens'. This Committee goes on to say 'it is time to re-invent the future for Europe, but the gap between latest research knowledge and real life practice is huge'. Markku Markkula, advisor to CoR and actively involved in leading university led societal innovation at Aalto University, believes 'cities and regions must become real implementation fields for

---

[1] The words 'Reach-Out', 'Outreach' and 'Academic Enterprise' are used interchangeably in this paper to represent what is called, in Britain, the 'Third Stream' of a University Mission. You will realise from the text that we see this as an equal 'First Mission' for Universities and not a lower level activity. For us it represents a rich form of relationship between Universities and their external partners from business, industry, the civil and voluntary services and the community. We prefer the term Academic Enterprise as the key term for this activity because it suggests universities becoming more enterprising in their ways of Reaching-Out/Outreach, where knowledge sharing between all parties in any partnership is virtuous, so Academic Enterprise is the main one used this through the text, but Reach-out and Outreach are also used in the writing for variety and to add colour.

[2] Eleanor Jackson, Professor Powell's doctoral student, has provided significant thinking in this paper and her findings are appropriately referenced.

J.A. Powell (✉)
Academic Director of the PASCAL International Programme on Universities
for a Modern Renaissance, UK Ambassador for Social Enterprise in Higher Education,
Director of Smart City Futures and UPBEAT, Ambassador for the Leonardo European
Corporate Learning Awards, & Member of the New Club of Paris
e-mail: james@jamesapowell.com

B. Ozorhon
Civil Engineering Department, Bogazici University, 34342 Bebek, Istanbul, Turkey
e-mail: beliz.ozorhon@boun.edu.tr

A. Curaj et al. (eds.), *European Higher Education at the Crossroads:*
Between the Bologna Process and National Reforms,
DOI 10.1007/978-94-007-3937-6_40, © Springer Science+Business Media Dordrecht 2012

the EU's strategy, creating platforms for change where universities, public bodies and those from private and third sectors must operate together in a new and creative mood'. In the UK, the Coalition government similarly believes university Academic Enterprise can play its part in the global knowledge economy. Universities themselves must also recognise how their work can be turned into sustainable products and processes which are demanded by society, creating not simply wealth, but also positive improvement for all.

So increasingly across the world, and particularly in Europe, governments now demand greater university engagement in all their Academic Enterprise activities. This is because society expects Universities will work with all citizens and communities to enable them to flourish, thereby creating workable improvements for a knowledge economy that currently has huge economic, social and environmental problems. Universities engage in outreach in interesting and novel ways, playing to their strengths as they attempt to enact their role, as they see it, in coping with today's global crises, major societal challenges, in order to help citizens in general and to improve their income in harsh economic times. Indeed, Gibbons et al. 1994 indicates that in future all universities "will be judged, and learn to judge themselves, by the variety and vitality of their interactions with society", the very essence of Bologna principles.

These new demands require universities to become opportunity managers, reaching out to marshal new resources from a pluralism of sources, not simply from the public purse – from private sponsors and funders, through regional development agencies, from the European Commission, from Research Councils, from philanthropic organisation, through co-funding. They are all learning to get better at such funding acquisition, however, in spite of significant recent positive pressure, and financial support from European governments and their Higher Education Funding Councils, and especially in Britain with its novel Higher Education Innovation fund, Academic Enterprise has still failed to become the third major stream, equal to teaching and research, of university missions in terms of importance, recognition, size and status. Moreover, while almost all universities now claim they are reaching-out to their local partners, rarely does this rhetoric translate through implementation into real 'impact' (Powell 2011). So they have to learn to work more closely with local business and their communities to co-create solutions to real world challenges leading to high impact. Our research shows when they do this entrepreneurially and creatively, on projects demanded by society, then it is relatively straightforward to acquire development funding and co-create solutions leading to socially inclusive wealth creation, in the richest sense of the word wealth. Concentration of determining needs alone is not sufficient.

If Universities are to diversify their activities to ensure financial stability in this new harsh economic world, they must learn how to become involved in deep and meaningful conversations with potential external partners and a new range of potential funders, sponsors and financial supporters. In recognising this, the PASCAL International Observatory has developed a new project known as 'Universities for a Modern Renaissance', where an evaluation matrix, known as UPBEAT, is used to coach potential academic entrepreneurs into becoming creative leaders of high quality

Academic Enterprise. By co-identifying worthy challenges, co-creating sensible solutions and co-producing them for the real world, academics can work with external partners to satisfy demand creating solutions for mutual benefit. In short, this paper describes a more creative way of universities sharing knowledge with strategic partners, coaching their academics to become entrepreneurial leaders and thus achieving success in a global context. Examples of universities achieving early success with such smarter ways of working are portrayed to give colour and understanding to the developing strategies of the most effective Institutions.

40.2 Time for Change: Extending Traditional Ways of Academic Working – A Strategic Perspective

This paper firstly charts the contemporary history of University Reach-out by refocusing on the engagement of academe with business and the community over the last decade. In short, it has developed from a one way process known as 'technology transfer', through 'knowledge exchange', towards 'virtuous knowledge sharing'; the latter shown in summary diagrammatic form on the left of Fig. 40.1. The figure diagrammatically portrays how an innovative idea, developed by the academic, used to be simply handed over to external partners, often by way of a formally specified contract, as a patent or licensing agreement; originally it was felt this technology transfer alone was enough to enable an external partner to design, develop and produce innovative new products or processes. At the turn of this century, it was increasingly recognised that there must be a deeper engagement between academe and business/industry than this suggests, that is if innovative university enterprise projects are to be taken up seriously by external partners enabling them to sustainably develop that idea into a useful deliverable; only then would university and external partner to flourish, thereby creating a real improvement, for real impact. It was also recognised that more than 'an idea' had to be transferred out from the university. Successful implementation in the real word also required deep systemic knowledge, not just the technology, about any new product or process, its design and development, and this, in turn, further required 'know-how' to be developed jointly with the strategic partners involved in any Academic Enterprise. Full design and development protocols, rather than simple conceptual ideas, have to be transferred or more likely exchanged between industry and academe in sustained dialogues, with regular feedback, or rather feed-across, between each part of any collaboration – this is shown in the central column of Fig. 40.1. Finally, even this, while necessary, is not sufficient. The fullest collaboration between all partners in any Academic Enterprise is required to enable an effective and sustainable solution, as expressed in the last column of the figure. The process we go on to suggest has shown the advantages of this even deeper collaboration with business and the community, where facilitated interactions with partners, mutual coaching and mature conversation enables real and lasting improvement and high impact.

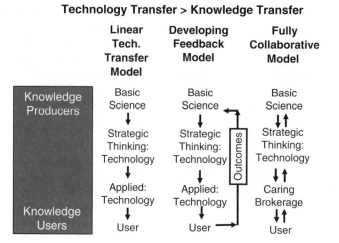

Fig. 40.1 Different modes of university business/community interaction. This model clearly indicates the kinds of innovative and trans-disciplinary ways of working for success in the global knowledge economy – what we call 'virtuous knowledge sharing'. But before we discuss the improved ways of university-business-community engagement in more detail, it was felt necessary to highlight the importance of innovation as the underpinning requirement for success

40.3 Open Innovation and Academic Engagement: A Deeper Strategic Perspective

Innovation is regarded as one of the key factors contributing to national economic growth, competitiveness, and higher living standards. Without this key underpinning component Europe will not be competitive in the global knowledge economy. So, as far as the strategic role of intangible assets is concerned, innovation must be at the heart of the knowledge-based economy of our countries, and companies, as well (OECD 2005). Innovation in general terms is the creation and adoption of new knowledge to improve the value of products, processes, and services. Department of Trade and Industry (DTI) in the UK states that innovation is "the successful exploitation of new ideas" and that "it is the key business process to compete effectively in the increasingly competitive global environment" (DTI 2007).

The importance of innovation and knowledge transfer to both the regional and national economy, and the crucial role of Higher Education in delivering to this agenda, and the changing role of universities is highlighted, for instance in the UK, where its Government's Science and Innovation Investment Framework 2004–14 (DIUS 2008), the Higher Education Funding Council for England (HEFCE) Strategic Plan 2006–11 (HEFCE 2006), and the Northwest Regional Economic Strategy (RES-NWRDA 2006) all play a part. The importance of developing effective mechanisms for HE-business engagement and knowledge sharing between them is paramount to achieving this as all in Europe are beginning to accept. A possible vehicle that has been identified to support this is Britain's Innovation Platform (BERR 2008), but other countries are following this lead. Such a platform provides an integrated approach between key organisations thus coherently linking different elements of the innovation eco-system (Turville 2007).

As the previous section alludes, the traditional, internally focused model for innovation must be replaced by an open innovation system with the aim of strategically leveraging both internal and external sources of ideas (Powell et al. 2009) that enables the fullest knowledge exchange and sharing with a range of strategic partners (Higher Education Institutions, customers, supply chains, etc.) at regional, national and international levels. There must also be a drive to move away from the "ivory tower" approach of academe to more meaningful modes of co-production where teams recognise that a university simply developing 'an idea' is not an end in itself, but it must have a role to play in wider systems of open innovation (Chesbrough 2003). Chesbrough (2003) coined the term 'open innovation' to describe how companies combine externally and internally developed technologies in a flexible way to develop new businesses. Coordination across several organisations is necessary to facilitate innovation and so companies can no longer afford to rely entirely on their own ideas to advance their business.

Research by Ozorhon et al. (2010) has shown the importance of 'knowledge sharing' in developing innovation through a range of innovation case studies conducted within the construction industry. In their work, they adopted the Innovation Value Chain (IVC) view (Hansen and Birkinshaw 2007) that presents innovation at the firm-level as a sequential, three-phase process that involves idea generation, idea development, and the diffusion of developed concepts. On the other hand, Roper et al. (2008) model IVC suggests a recursive process which has three main links: such as 'knowledge sourcing' to assemble knowledge necessary for innovation; 'knowledge transformation' to translate knowledge into physical innovation; and finally 'knowledge exploitation' to improve the enterprise performance. Ozorhon et al. (2010) applied the principles of IVC approach in the cases she investigated and the flow of knowledge to create innovations in a number of construction projects. This work revealed that effective knowledge sharing, and then its management, are essential for achieving innovation; not only in bringing the right ideas into a project, but also to ensure that these ideas are known by the entire project team and are diffused to following projects. In most of the cases, innovation throughout the supply chain was enabled through the trust created by the partnering approach. In one of the cases, knowledge sharing was initiated within the organisations and extended beyond the organisation through an action learning approach (Revans 1983) known as 'Innovation Circles' (Lu et al. 2007) that bring together the supply chain in an open approach to sharing ideas and tackling problems. The use of extensive public consultation and knowledge exchange between project participants also helped generate ideas and transform them into viable products, processes, and services.

40.3.1   The Key Role of Universities in Necessary Innovation Eco-systems

Another emerging concept for improved innovation reflecting university capabilities is the eco-system approach that involves the complex inter-linkages amongst the variety of participants (including individuals, companies and universities) in an innovation economy. It accepts that the system is not fixed, but will grow and evolve according to new needs, circumstances and policies (Wessner 2006). The 'systems of innovation' approach (Edquist 1997) argues that innovation should be seen as an evolutionary, non-linear and interactive process, requiring intensive communication and collaboration between different actors, as portrayed diagrammatically in the right hand side of Fig. 40.1. Howells (1999) identifies at least four overlaid innovation system including sub-regional, regional, national and international level. Initially, the concept of innovation system has been applied to the national level (Lundvall 1992; Nelson 1993; Niosi et al. 1993; OECD 1999). The notion of the National Systems of Innovation (NSI) (Freeman 1987; Lundvall 1992; Nelson 1993) expresses the importance of establishing links between the various networks related to innovation in increasing the innovation capability at the national level and studies innovating firms in the context of the external institutions, government policies, competitors, suppliers, customers, value systems, and social and cultural practices that affect their operation (OECD 2005).

The literature on NSI emphasizes the importance of strong linkages among these various institutions in improving national innovative and competitive performance, and this emphasis applies in particular to universities within national innovation systems (Nelson 1993). Universities and research institutes provide platforms for knowledge creation and diffusion through basic and applied research. Since knowledge is the crucial component of innovation, universities play a major role in the innovation process (Van Looy et al. 2003; Marques et al. 2006) especially through collaboration with industry (Tijssen and van Wijk 1999). The extent and intensity of industry-science relationships is considered to be a major factor contributing to high innovation performance, either at the firm-level, industry-level or country-level (OECD 2002).

University-industry links and their impact on innovation processes have been a longstanding object of analysis in various scholarly communities in management studies, the economics of innovation, industrial organisation, the sociology of science and science studies and science and technology policy (Agrawal 2001; Poyago-Theotoky et al. 2002; OECD 2002; Mowery and Nelson 2004; Hall 2004). So for instance, the Lambert Review (2003) identified possible positive outcomes of engagement which will include industry access to a supply of skilled graduates and post-graduates; highly skilled scientists and researchers; the latest research and cutting-edge technology; international networks of academics; and continuing professional development opportunities for employees. Furthermore, a wider and more extensive role of universities in the innovation ecosystem was first highlighted in the Sainsbury Report (Turville 2007) within which the "*innovation rate depends on inter-linked activities which include: industrial research; publicly funded basic research; user-driven research; knowledge transfer; institutions governing intellectual property and standards; supply of venture capital; education and training of scientists and engineers; innovation policies of government departments; science and innovation policies of RDAs; and international scientific and technological collaboration".* The Innovation Nation (DIUS 2008) is another report that focuses on universities as part of the innovation system.

40.3.2   Towards Enterprising Universities – Structuring an Improved Approach

Universities are being pushed by their governments to operate more entrepreneurially, commercializing the results of their research and spinning out new, knowledge-based enterprises (Kirby 2006). Additionally, academic research has according to Debackere (2000) become "endogenised and integrated into the economic cycle of innovation and growth." "Mode 2" research (after Gibbons et al. 1994) and "triple helix" (Etzkowitz and Leytesdorff 1997) frameworks conceptualize the role of the universities within the innovation processes of knowledge-based economies. "Mode 2" research (Gibbons et al. 1994) is associated with a focus on interdisciplinary, pluralistic, "networked" innovation systems and ways of real world working/research, in contrast to previous 'Mode 1' systems thought where major corporate or academic research institutions often worked in isolation and were less closely linked with other institutions; this resulted in "uni-directional transfer of previously created knowledge" (Dooley and Kirk 2007). Furthermore, the triple helix framework emphasizes the increased interaction among all major institutional actors in industrial economies' innovation systems. Etzkowitz et al. (1998) assert that "in addition to linkages among institutional spheres, each sphere takes the role of the other. Thus, universities assume entrepreneurial tasks such as marketing knowledge and creating companies even as firms take on an academic dimension, sharing knowledge among each other and training at ever-higher skill levels". As the triple helix model suggests, innovation is generated by the combination of relations and inter-relations between universities, industry and the government; we would go further, see next section, and suggest the need to involve communities, clients and end-users as another important part in any innovative development. Furthermore, universities have recently been thinking about their role in building clusters, connecting to the national and international economies and bringing together thinking, practice, and finance. This model of the 'connected university' holds the key to further economic growth (NESTA 2009). It has also been suggested (Powell 2011) that another dimension to the helix should be the end user, client or community in order to ensure all innovative solutions are fit for purpose.

As we suggested earlier, some research (Agrawal 2001; Bonaccorsi and Piccaluga 1994; Grossman et al. 2001) points out the multi-faceted nature of university-industry links are in contrast to the traditional links that focus on the transfer of intellectual property (patenting, licensing, commercialisation). There is an increasing amount, and many different types of engagement that occur, which facilitate knowledge transfer between the higher education sector and industry (Lambert 2003). Santoro (2000) defines these engagements in four broad categories (1) research support, (2) technology transfer, (3) knowledge transfer, and (4) co-operative research. This later phase leads to the formation of deeper relationships with examples including personal contacts and staff exchanges such as visiting professors/guest lecturers or industry secondments; business support and consultancy; collaborative and contract research; and establishment of joint ventures, licensing agreements and spinout companies. Cohen et al. (2002) distinguish between the following channels relevant to industrial innovation: patents, informal information exchange, publications and reports, public meetings and conferences, recently hired graduates, licenses, joint or cooperative research ventures, contract research, consulting, and temporary personnel exchanges. Based on another classification proposed by Schartinger et al. (2001), there are 16 types of 'knowledge interaction' grouped into 4 overarching categories being (1) joint research (including joint publishing), (2) contract research (including consulting, financing of university research assistants by firms), (3) mobility (staff movement between universities and firms, joint supervision of students) and (4) training (co-operation in education, training of firm staff at universities, lecturing by industry staff).

Furthermore, the Kellogg Commission (1999) issued a report calling for "engaged institutions" that build collaborative and mutually beneficial relationships with communities, government, and the private sector for the purposes of identifying and solving real world problems and generated a list of seven qualities that characterize the engaged institution as follows: responsiveness; respect for partners; academic neutrality; accessibility; integration of engagement into institutional mission; coordination, and adequate resources. As the Lambert Review (2003) so rightly recognized, while many universities engage well, there are many systemic and cultural issues within universities which created barriers to effective engagement with industry, as well as a lack of demand from industry. This impression is supported by the DTI occasional paper (DTI 2006) which showed that according to the 2005 EU Wide Community Innovation Survey, universities are one of the least important direct sources of information for companies.

40.3.3 The Role of Clients in Driving Greater Collaboration for Real Impact

One of the best ways to get academe and industry together is through pressure exerted by clients acting in a more professional role than hitherto. For instance, research by Ozorhon et al. (2010) has shown how clients can effectively drive innovation throughout the life cycle of a construction project. They report that the clients have played an exemplary role in producing collaborative project teams, through the procurement mechanisms that have ensured an integrated approach in meeting end user needs. The cases reported in this work were notable for their use of a 'client-driven' approach to innovation and idea generation. The clients all asked for, and some demanded, continuous improvement and sustainability to be incorporated to the construction and operation process. This led both the contractors and suppliers to work on innovative, but at the same time, cost effective solutions to achieve higher operational and environmental performance. Ozorhon et al. (2010) concluded that without professional clients, with a deep knowledge of their users, this situation is unlikely to occur. So when developing the right partnerships for success in Academic Enterprise projects, professional clients ought to be considered as members of the team.

Once the client, or others, drive the need for improved ways of innovative working with universities, there is still a need to ensure universities themselves understand how to act in valued ways, and this is where UPBEAT finds its place, since it drives a structured way of: developing 'virtuous knowledge sharing'; team-work development and intelligent partnering to maximize innovation for systemic improvement: recognition of demands as well as needs; and harnessing individual talent, by developing it to the full, in all successful academically enterprising ventures.

40.3.4   Importance of Measuring Academic Engagement Activities

Embedding research activity within an overall innovation platform can serve to increase the impact of research. In the UK, the Research Councils do not only support the creation of new knowledge, but also increasingly look into how dissemination and engagement can be supported (EPSRC 2009a). The result of this is that funding proposals now ask applicants to complete economic impact statements (EPSRC 2009b) projecting the improvements, outputs and outcomes their proposed projects will achieve. These changes are part of a wider agenda within higher education whereby universities are being asked to move away from traditional "ivory tower" perspectives to take a more engaged role as drivers of prosperity and job creation (DFES 2003) which has been followed through in the Higher Education Funding Council Strategy 2006–11 (HEFCE 2006) and the Government's Science and Innovation Strategy (DIUS 2008). Universities must now consider their research, not only from a perspective of academic impact, but also the value that is placed upon them by their end-user communities. It is clear from the research (Todtling and Trippl 2005) and the debates within the Research Councils, that there is a growing understanding that the relationship between research and its implementation/innovation is non-linear and complex (Swan et al. 2009).

Lambert (2003) identified possible positive outcomes of engagement which will include industry access to a supply of skilled graduates and post-graduates; highly skilled scientists and researchers; the latest research and cutting-edge technology; international networks of academics; and continuing professional development opportunities for employees. Thus, the university engagement extends human intellectual reach. The extent and intensity of industry–science relationships is considered to be a major factor contributing to high innovation performance, either at the firm-level, industry-level or country-level (see OECD 2002) as far as the role of science in fast-growing knowledge-intensive industries is concerned. As Polt et al. (2001) emphasized, rather than cutting-edge research, consulting and contract research tends to provide more common, yet specialised, expertise required especially at the latter stages of the innovation cycle, such as product differentiation and improvement.

As indicated in the literature, university-industry links and their impact on innovation processes have been a longstanding object of analysis in various scholarly communities in management studies, the economics of innovation, industrial organisation, the sociology of science and science studies and science and technology policy (Agrawal 2001; Hall 2004; McMillan and Hamilton 2003; Mowery and Nelson 2004; OECD 2002; Poyago-Theotoky et al. 2002). On the contrary, it has been documented that many university administrators are unaware of the level of community engagement in their institutions (Goedegebuure and van der Lee 2006).

40.3.5   Realising a Collaborative Process for Real Benefits and Impact for All – Developing a Shared Space for Future Development

So, to us, innovation is key to Europe being surviving and hopefully flourishing in the global knowledge economy. Our universities have to develop leading edge thinking, processes and products that will make a difference to society and create impact. However, the benefits of innovation can only be realised by fully understanding the components of the whole innovation process that is based on knowledge acquisition, transformation, and diffusion. Academia and industry must develop *a shared space* whereby the work being undertaken by the research community must have meaning in both the academic and industrial worlds. Co-production of research, with high levels of engagement around a real world problem between industrial and academic partners, provides the basis for much of this engagement, but this requires in turn the incremental development of deepening relationships between all partners through a range of developing engagements. The outputs of research need not only to have meaning to the academic community, but also to the end users (Star and Griesemer 1989) if the relationship is to be perceived as valuable in the longer term.

Despite all these initiatives, as a recent Innovation and Productivity Report (Abreu et al. 2009) revealed, the objectives of 'Industry and Academia' are still often distinctly different. What 'industry and the community want' from academia are 'ideas and talent, rather than a cheap way of outsourcing R&D activities'. Academics, on the other hand, it suggested, still tend to pursue objectives from their own discipline with their studies 'underpinned by research-oriented rationales, rather than by the desire to commercialise technology or create impact or improvement in the real world'. There are also additional challenges in the form of the differing cultures and differing timescales of universities and industry, the conflicting desire of academia to publish and industry to be secretive due to IP, issues to do with IP ownership, and problems associated with strategic responses to the external environment of organisations (Dooley and Kirk 2007). The following sections suggest a pragmatic way of developing workable university-business collaborations enabling all to flourish.

40.4   Successful Practices for Innovative Academic Engagement – An UPBEAT Approach

40.4.1   Different Models for Monitoring and Managing Academic Engagement

We had found a number of useful approaches to improving the engagement of universities with business and the community in order to ensure leading edge research is actually implemented for mutual good as the European Commission would wish. They all require the sensible and sensitive measurement of the progress in any collaboration for innovation, and its formative evaluation, leading to continuous improvement. A new volume on 'Engaged Scholarship' by Fitzgerald et al. (2011) from Michigan State University provides a good summary of best practices in this respect to date. Most models are designed to make universities more properly and deeply engage with business and the community and are focused on monitoring and managing university-business-community engagement or outreach project for mutual benefit. They are all typically aimed at university academics, and their support staff. For instance, Tracking and Improving Community Engagement (**TICE** 2010) from University of Western Sydney uses a variety of methods, including a website to show examples of quality community engagement, the marketing and public relations events related to them and both documentation and presentations to drive for more innovative, sustainable and relevant community-academe interactions. **REAP** (Reciprocity, Externalities, Access and Partnerships, 2008), from University of Bradford, also focuses on managing and measuring community engagement, but with its emphasis being more on the projects being developed, rather than the academic involved. It was developed as a qualitative self-assessment tool, useful for creative planning, monitoring and review. It is not intended to be a tool that has to be complete for every engagement project or that cannot be changed for adapted in the future. Rather, it has been designed as an approach "...which leads to developing a culture of community engagement in the University..." by gathering "...evidence based learning" which demonstrates indicators of achievement, milestones, analysis of the University and the Community input. **Four Points of Distinction**, and the connected **Outreach Measurement Instrument** from Michigan State University (Michigan 2005, 2008) proposes key human values must be embedded in any successful outreach activity; this includes mutuality and partnering, equity, developmental processes, capacity building, "communityness," cross-disciplinary approaches, scholarship and pragmatism and, integrity. Michigan State University looks to help guide the planning and evaluation of outreach across faculty as there were no uniform definitions, designs or values placed on the activity. They have developed a matrix for evaluating, planning, and assessing and scoring outreach activity which uses four dimensions (significance, context, scholarship and impact) to reflect four fundamental characteristics of any outreach activity in a higher education context. **The ACBEE ENGAGEMENT MODEL** (2009) monitors and manages engagement between a University and its industrial partners and is an initiative for improving dialogue and communication between higher education and industry. **The University Partnership Continuum** from Hewlett Packard (2003), like the ACBEE work, is interested in examples of university engagement with industry, and as a consequence considers university academics and also targets industrial partners. They are all useful tools, but we chose to develop, from their best practices and others, **UPBEAT** (Powell 2007) – also highlighted in Fitzgerald et al.'s (2011) *Engaged universities guidance book* – is the one we now focus on since it portrays the strengths of all other models and is particularly suitable for European Universities which are interested in benchmarking their best practices and using such comparisons across universities to prescribe future development approaches that stand a better chance of success. It is a model of sharing knowledge virtuously between like minded universities.

40.4.2   The UPBEAT Approach

In short, UPBEAT was designed to provide a framework for academics and their partners to consider their activities in a way that would create a "real world" improvement. UPBEAT stands for the University Partnership for Benchmarking Enterprise and Associated Technologies and as the name implies it is based on sensible benchmarking. UPBEAT is a simple, intuitive, and highly effective self evaluatory approach to help academic leaders understand and improve their creative leadership of their own creative Academic Enterprise teams. The governance process developed by UPBEAT was shown to be essential by some 25 British and 10 other European Universities who observed their own best working practices. The detailed UPBEAT approach was based on their robust case studies of a total of 185 project reports from cases deemed successful from the Universities undertaking them, especially in terms of a range of socially inclusive wealth creating impacts; these cases can be explored on the www.upbeat.eu.com database, under 'resources. The majority of projects reported there fall under the Business Support and Community categories (58 projects and 42 projects respectively), and are as varied as ones which 'support the introduction of new technology' to those which 'monitor container shipments at the Port of Liverpool', and 'running summer schools which introduce young people to life at University'. Other categories include creative

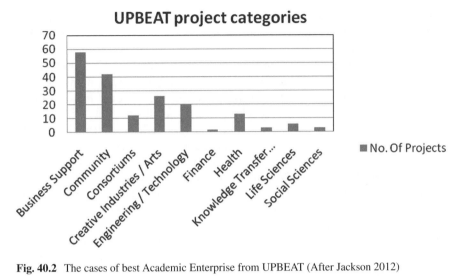

Fig. 40.2   The cases of best Academic Enterprise from UPBEAT (After Jackson 2012)

industries/arts, health, engineering and technology and Knowledge Transfer Partnerships; the full range of cases is shown in Fig. 40.2.

The tool was developed under significant funding from the Higher Education Funding Council for England, has been written up in detail elsewhere (Powell 2008, 2009, 2010, 2011); it can be accessed at either www.upbeat.eu.com/ or in its newer form in www.pumr.pascalobservatory.org for those who want to use it as a tool to develop their own the creative leadership of their own entrepreneurial academics. Both websites describe the detail of the tool, present a range of short case studies showing the types of partners universities involved in its development, and reveal detailed 'success stories' showcasing use of the tool. In this paper, we simply try to suggest how universities need to develop key enterprise skills in their staff to ensure potential innovations become a reality. Such an approach should not be considered a threat to curiosity-based (Royal Society REF) or "blue skies" research, rather it is a complementary model that drives those projects which operate at the boundaries between academia and the end users (Williams et al. 2008). UPBEAT has relevance for engaged scholarship (Van de Ven 2007), as well as business or community focused projects that may operate outside of the boundaries of traditional perceptions of knowledge transfer (Abreu et al. 2009).

The basis of UPBEAT analysis is a structured interview of the project leaders of any Academic Enterprise. They are asked to "tell the story" of the project in which they are engaged against a fourfold of thematic themes. The project "story" is digitally recorded and then written up based on the best principles of narrative theory (Powell and Khan 2008). Narratives are common to all humans as everyone tells stories and hears stories. Narratives are therefore "…a universal tool for knowing as well as telling, for absorbing knowledge as well as expressing it" (Abbott 2003) and therefore, at face value, perhaps the simplest theory to understand. Narrative in simple terms is "...the representation of an event or series of events" (Abbott 2003) and, depending on viewpoint, these events have to occur one after another or have to be causally related.

Central to the UPBEAT narratives is firstly a recognition of the DEMAND for any potential solution; academics normally concentrate their explorations on determining problems and the needs to constructive change; demand also forces academics to think about how they will acquire resources to undertake any project from quite different sources to normal. In parallel with this, both the academics and their partners involved in any Academic Enterprise focus on determining a solution to any problem or issue in a systemic way. Then the interviews thirdly determines how academic project leaders coach their talented staff to success and finally builds a creative interdisciplinary team that can make a real difference in co-designing and co-producing sustainable and workable solutions. In order to determine that innovation is usefully occurring firstly the transcripts are read in order to determine the overarching themes, and then these are grouped and considered with regard to an UPBEAT matrix which shows the progress of an Academic Enterprise at that time.

40.4.3 Questioning Framework

The UPBEAT analysis then uses the focused narratives mentioned above, to create a questioning framework which contains the critical success factors of any successful engagement. This is done through an iterative analysis of the case studies which are then categorised into a set of skills. Our research on successful Academic Enterprise cases shows that UPBEAT should be used to identify and develop a fourfold of complementary entrepreneurial skills for any academic enterprise leader: new business acumen, solution enabling, individual talent and intelligent partnering shown diagrammatically below in Fig. 40.3. These skills are critical components for effective engagement activity by any academically-driven enterprise projects and should be honed in parallel to get the best from a creative enterprise team.

40.4.4 The Fourfold of Enterprise Skills

As previously mentioned in Fig. 40.3, the UPBEAT framework considers four main enterprise success factor areas. Solution Enabling addresses the issues of ideas, need, creativity and solutions. Individual Talent addresses concepts of leadership, motivation, skills and capabilities. Intelligent Partnering looks at team development, networks and the governance and operational principles that make these relationships work. New Business Acumen focuses on making the ideas applicable in the real world, considering not only the "product", but also the mechanisms by which the product is delivered to the end user and the resources and processes which are marshalled to ensure that the idea is effectively delivered. Each of these skills can

Fig. 40.3 UPBEAT's four
underlying skills

be linked to different aspects of innovation. Table 40.1 shows the broad definitions for UPBEAT that are included in the UPBEAT Handbook.

40.4.5 Developing the Skills in Some Detail to Ensure the Successful Completion of Any Academic Enterprise

In this section we simply explore the detail of each of this fourfold of academic enterprise skills, why they are important in the context of this conference and, in particular to the financial aspects of developing sustainable university Academic Enterprise enabling 'financially sustainable universities'. One of the key aspects of this is for the developing entrepreneurial academics to become 'street wise' about how they acquire the funding to undertake such work, which is quite different from their other modes of teaching/learning and research funding. They must therefore learn to work in close collaboration with their external partners to acquire the funding necessary to truly identify demanded solutions, co-design sustainable solutions and co-produce worthwhile new products and processes.

40.4.5.1 New Business Acumen

New Business Acumen is a skill which must be developed by Academics to give them sufficient understanding of business (enterprise) language – including social entrepreneurship – to ensure success when working with external partners. For probably the first time in their lives, when they work in this way with business and the community, academics must co-identify problems that both they and their external partners consider worthy of exploration and development; they must learn how

Table 40.1 Descriptions for sub-skills

Skill	Theme	Description
Solution enabling	Understanding need	This describes how the team or individual has developed their understanding of the need for the solving of a particular real world problem. They recognise deep needs, but also how to turn the need into a solution demanded by a significant audience. This can range from basic recognition to a deep understanding of the problem based on multiple iterations of a possible range of solutions. 'The real problem is to know what the real problem is…and then keep extending and refining it so that solutions reach a wider audience, to a higher level, with greater impact
	Developing solutions	This describes how the team or individual has developed ideas, created solutions and tested them in the real world to refine and further develop newer and improved solutions with more generic and far reaching impact. Higher levels of enterprise engagement suggest increasing levels of innovation and creativity applied to the problem domain with greater effect and impact
Individual talent	Leadership	This looks at the role of leadership within the project, how it is developed and articulated with regards to the project
	Skills and capabilities	The skills and capabilities to deliver the ideas or projects must be considered. This looks at the necessary functional components of the skills necessary to cope with the best solutions satisfying both the needs and demands of the project
	Coaching and learning	Coaching and learning looks to how the talent of the individuals chosen to be in the creative team are being developed and the processes that are in place to manage these; this is both functional, managerial, leadership and creative team working skills
	Motivation	Motivation considers the understanding and meeting of the drivers for individuals to be engaged within the project and how the leaders of the academic enterprise project build on these

Intelligent partnering	Teamwork	This considers how the team is understood and managed. This considers issues such as team roles and responsibilities, shared objectives and processes to manage these interrelationships; how the team moves from a recognition of the need for collaboration, through creative team-working, to innovative partnering and to forming strategic alliances
	Networks	This addresses how the team works with and communicates with appropriate networks related to the problem domain at both an academic and non-academic level
	Communication >> conversations	This addresses how the team communicates with each other and their wider stakeholder groups to make them aware of the activity that they are engaging with; then onto the development of an appropriate discourse and useful conversations
	Co-identification of the final problem, co-creation, and co-production	This looks at how teams work together in terms of jointly determining the development of solutions and ideas. This can range from very loose association from industry participation on steering groups, joint development of solutions and strategic partnerships
New business acumen	Demand	This is concerned with the process of understanding and designing solutions that meet demand of the target group. This means solutions that not only meet the need, but are also understood and appropriable by the end users
	Impact	This addresses the issue of understanding, measuring and maximising the level of impact of the solution. This requires robust approaches that feedback into the solution
	Resources	Recognition of cost in use and development. The difference between cost and price is critical. Furthermore resources must be effectively acquired and managed to ensure that solution delivery is possible. Entrepreneurial academic leaders must therefore learn ways of acquiring funding from a pluralism of sources, not just the traditional ones
	(Business) management	These are the processes that are concerned with effective management of (business) process issues which support the effective performance of the team. This may include basic issues such as invoicing, or more complex issues such as spin out companies

to co-create and co-design acceptable solutions; and then actually work to co-produce appropriate end product and processes. So, at the basic level of engagement with their business or social enterprise partners, they must begin to become both market and business aware and demand driven. Understanding DEMAND is truly a key new skill academics have to learn.

Universities are indeed becoming more diversified in the ways they seek funding (Estermann and Bennetot Pruvot 2011), but only a few have embraced the pluralism of available financial sources to ensure financial sustainability, developed the funding teams required to access a wider range of funding and learned the intricacies of university governance procedures to make new funding streams easily accessible. In a parallel study to the one reported here dealing with Academic Enterprise leadership by Powell and Clark (2012), most academic leaders, by and large, stressed financial difficulties in working in this arena as a problem for them and a real barrier to progress – this was because they had never learned properly how to acquire funds from a pluralism of sources alongside a lack of readily available funding to pursue Outreach. Furthermore, as one academic said to us *'the limited financial rewards made available internally in Universities were often insufficient to promote a greater uptake in Academic Enterprise'*. However, the best leaders observed in the Powel and Clark study indicated their own success as resulting from their ability to find money, where others have not necessarily thought to look: *'finding the resources to make the enterprise work just became one of the challenges, but increasingly a very important one'*; *'leaders take on the pain and marshal the resources to actually get to our required destination'*.

Successful leaders of such new ways of working see funding as just another challenge, and not a barrier to progress, and many have worked with senior colleagues earlier in their careers to develop the skills necessary to acquire continuous funding. It is therefore important for universities to coach junior Academic Enterprise leaders in the processes of funding acquisition to enable their successful future developments. The Powell/Clark paper (ibid.) also indicated universities need to create governance structure and funding teams able to work toward gaining funds from a rich panoply of sources – those with the new academic business acumen leave 'no stone unturned' or potential funders asked, each with their own nuances of being approached and considered. The ones the present authors have shown to be the most useful in terms of Academic Enterprise are: private sponsors, businesses and industries as entities, business and industry clubs and Chamber of Commerce; regional development agencies, business enterprise agencies, the European Commission and its many parts, the Research Councils, philanthropic organisation, the civil and voluntary serves, banks and even communities and groups of citizens themselves. Furthermore, much of funding acquisition now has to be focused on what is called either co-funding and matched funding. Again this is a funding arrangement that often puts traditional academics off, but it is a skill that can be learned and for those who follow the UPBEAT approach, they will already have the willing and able partners to develop such funding arrangement. None of this work or collective action is 'rocket science' but it does require academics to engage in quite a different way with potential funders, for universities to coach them in how to do it and for fast acting management process to be set up in the university to handle funding and the deliverables that relate to it.

So, New Business Acumen is concerned with the practical issues of addressing the 'demand' side of the commercial equation. 'Need', as we have said many times throughout this paper, is differentiated from 'demand' within the UPBEAT model. 'Need' is driven by an understanding of the problem domain which may generate a number of contingent responses. 'Demand', on the other hand is concerned with addressing need in such a way that the solution might be adopted by real end-users who will then be prepared to pay for the solution. I academic terms, this can be viewed as requiring a new range of philosophical stances and following up with practical actions. The meeting of demand requires the development of effective processes, such as properly considering supply issues, management, invoicing, and marketing, for example. And, the academic team needs to be able to marshal the appropriate resources and apply them effectively, if it is going to genuinely innovate (Edwards et al. 2004), rather than just talk about it. This does not necessarily mean the academic team does all these commercial things themselves, but they must have appropriate partners or support to ensure these actions are undertaken.

It is not sufficient for enterprising academics to know how to express better what their external partners need to know, but also how to get into a deeper, meaningful and maturing conversation with them. So, they also need to get a demand side view of any problem, or potential solution, when developing any Academic Enterprise. This capability also considers how teams manage the practicalities of engaging with end user groups. In short, these include the themes of demand, measurement and understanding of impact, marshalling resources and management issues. We have provided an extended discussion of this Enterprise Skill development because it is central to the discussion in this part of the conference and because without financial sustainability no Academic Enterprise stands any chance of flourishing.

40.4.5.2 Solution Enabling

While any Academic Enterprise development depends upon someone recognizing a real need and then its real demand, there is the complementary skill of turning an innovative idea into an implementation of real impact. Solution Enabling is the skill of repositioning imaginative research concepts into a successful working reality; this requires taking research and translating it into foresight that enables a team to undertake the work necessary to form a successful and sustainable solution. It is made up of two main sub-skills within the skill; the recognition of the problem and the capacity to identify workable solutions to those problems.

At the core of any innovation is an idea. It is driven by a number of antecedents (Lesseure et al. 2004) in a particular context which drive a need for an innovative that identify a specific need. These may be enormously variable depending on the approach. Academic engagements, such as Knowledge Transfer Partnerships, may have very specific drivers that affect a specific organisation, but equally, they may be driven by antecedents that are sector specific, national or global issues.

This considers the ability of the group to understand, engage with and potentially change the knowledge base that may drive specific innovations. This also requires a capacity to link with knowledge and define a solution within that space (Roper et al. 2008).

Another consideration is the nature of the innovation itself. As we define it, it must ideally be a boundary object, but as such it is the meaning attributed to it by the end user group that is critical. The developed solution must fulfil one of the definitions of an innovation, to improve things, or create value, for that end user (Edwards et al. 2004). We have discussed how the processes of co-creation and co-production can help an academic team create something with end users to create the boundary object, again showing the effective linkages between the quadrants. The innovation must be able to fit within the real world context, not only understanding the needs of the end users, but also recognising that a specific innovation may link with or compete against other innovations and their supporting infrastructures (Afuah and Bahram 1995); ideas that meet a need can fail because they do not effectively understand the context of the demand.

40.4.5.3 Individual Talent

The key aspect of the skill of Individual talent is self development with a view to becoming 'best in practice' in your discipline and then acquiring the confidence of your knowledge and 'know-how' to work effectively in trans-disciplinary teams whose complementary talent is also 'top-notch' – so key in this skill development is awareness of own talent and capability, honing it to the highest level, being coached to reveal your best and then coaching others to success. This enterprise skill is therefore concerned with the issues connected to individuals within the team. This includes leaders and core team members both within and outside the Academic context. The key themes within this skill are leadership, skills and capabilities, coaching and learning and motivation.

Key in developing this talent is *leadership*. In our context, leadership is defined as "defining the reality of others" (Smircich and Morgan 1982) especially in terms of a purposeful and innovative vision, and must be linked clearly to the development of a creative context of a team as identified under the Partnering skill. The role of leadership was clearly identified through the case studies as being a core critical success factor. While there are a number of different approaches to innovation that may require different leadership approaches (Dechamps 2005), such as varying levels of control and deferring of authority (Krause 2003; Jung et al. 2003), the requirement of some form of leadership to drive innovation is considered as vital to the UPBEAT model. Leadership is not just in the hands of one person – so called 'hero leaders' – it should be shared across the creative enterprise team with different members taking the lead at different times and a sort of democratically empower leadership.

The coaching and learning role of leadership was seen as a key component if the effective development of teams within the UPBEAT framework. Leadership is seen as an essential component of driving a culture of mutual coaching between individuals (Hargreaves and Dawe 1990), but it is about how an individual connects with others. While individual talent considers the development of an individual's skills, the issues of coaching and learning can be seen to expand into issues of the wider effectiveness of the team (Showers and Bruce 1996; Powell and Clark 2012).

The ability of leaders to motivate is also important in driving teams to innovate (Jung et al. 2003; Jackson 2012). However, there are both intrinsic and extrinsic factors which may drive individuals towards or from innovation (Amabile 1998). For the academic context these may be career progression, desire to make a difference or monetary rewards. The UPBEAT model proposes that we make these skills as explicit as possible and understand that they need to be addressed for effective engagement. It also has implications for the wider University in terms of the supporting structures it puts in place to enable innovation (Jung et al. 2003).

Existing competences and capabilities shape the ability of a group to respond to a problem and successfully innovate (Leonard-Barton 1995; Amabile 1999). A competence is defined as a proven skill set which is evidenced by activity. A capability is an underlying capacity to develop a competence. In defining the skills required the UPBEAT team must recognise not only the skills have and potential skills that they may grow, they must also recognise where there is neither competence nor capability required to deliver the innovation.

40.4.5.4   Intelligent Partnering

This Partnering skill is where teams utilise joint strengths to energise enhanced change with systemic outreach and continuing improvement. It also recognises that problems and challenges are now so complex that individuals cannot longer solve them and that academics need to be intelligent in their development of networks of partners for tackling different projects and become more sensitive to the social needs of such partnerships. So, it is concerned with how the individuals work together as a team. Within this skill are the themes of team work, networks, modes of communication and co-identification, creation and production of innovations.

Partnering is concerned with co-operative behaviour, ranging from specific issues of projects teams, to wider engagement in networks and communities of practice (Storck and Hill 2000). The UPBEAT model addresses a range of questions within this context. The first is to address the explicit shared space between the participating group members. This is of particular relevance when considering the issues of academic and external engagement. Developing a shared meaning (Nonaka and Konno 1998; Swan 2000) is often seen as a key factor in sharing and developing ideas and this can often be complex between academia and external parties (Gann 2001). UPBEAT teams need to consider how they engage, such as through the development of boundary spanner skills (Aldrich and Herker 1977). 'This is esential if genuine co-production' (Jasanoff 2004) or 'co-creation is to take place' (Powell and Clark 2012) is to take place. Co-production/creation could be considered an essential component of the developing of outcomes which may have meaning in both the academic and end user worlds; a boundary object that has meaning in both academia and to end users (Star and Greisemer 1989) as innovation outcome.

Partnering also addresses issues such as team building and the various roles and responsibilities of team members. The model asks questions to make some of these issues explicit, with team identifying relevant functions and actions and effectively linking them back to the identified skill sets. This looks at the close relationships of what might be defined a core project team which would include key stakeholders from both within and outside the University.

At the broader level Partnering considers the networks which the group may be involved in. As noted previously, these networks and communities of practice help in both the determination of the problem space, under the Solution Enabling Quadrant, and provide diffusion networks for any innovation (Lrson et al 2005). Effective linking into networks can clearly drive both of these success factors for the innovation. This also links into Chesborough's concept of Open Innovation (2003) where the academic team would be a partner in a wider innovation process, rather than the locus.

It is important to understand the linkages between the four skills and the way they must be developed in parallel for a successful Academic Enterprise. The model defines a balance between the skills required for successful activity. Looking at the ability to both scan relevant issues and define solutions within the Solution Enabling Quadrant, we can see that there is a requirement for domain specific knowledge for internal idea generation (Hansen and Birkinshaw 2007; Amabile 1999), but, as we said earlier, this has to be done while differentiating between the need for any solution and whether it will then either be demanded or a demand developed. In the UPBEAT model it is recognized that Individual Talent has to be recruited and coached to cope with the systemic nature of any problem. Then the interdisciplinary group chosen to undertake any project has become a creative team through Intelligent Partnering. Additionally, as a project grows in stature, the importance of networks (Owen-Smith and Powell 2004), or communities of practice (Storck and Hill 2000), become important to the richer generation and wider diffusion (Larsen and Ballal 2005) of knowledge. The four skills are inherently linked and success in one is co-dependent on development of the others. Those who wish to be coached in the development of this fourfold of skills is encouraged to work with the PASCAL International Observatories Universities for a Modern Renaissance programme which has a structured and intuitive approach to help academics learn to become more innovative using the model mentioned above (www.pumr.pascalobservatory.org).

40.4.6 Qualities and Levels of Engagement – The Drive for Innovation

The previous section highlights the four essential skills an academic has to develop in order to turn his traditional skills into 'enterprising' ones. In this respect, as the academics strive for continuous improvement in these skills and processes taken both individually and collectively, they should strive to improve the "Qualities and Levels" of their engagements with their enterprise development team partners, their client, and end users, etc. For any new project they need to start by recognising how, and with whom, they need to engage in order to initiate a sound, yet innovative, enterprise development. They then need to start building necessary capacity to properly undertake the projects from a broad range of perspectives. At a higher engagement they need to improve their creative team's development as they come to handle their project more competently. Once a team is competent, it should then strive to sufficient mastery of its roles that they can properly negotiate an overall solution from a position of strength, where each team member knows when to 'give and take' for the benefit of the overall team performance.

At the highest engagement levels and academic enterprise, development is working really well, and this is where the creative team, or at least some of its members, are seen to become creative leaders in their own right. Such leaders often extend the scope of any existing project, spin off new sub projects or perhaps even start completely new projects. At the top level of engagement, the team, or some of its leaders, start to act as stewards in a global context, having respect from almost anyone as they become world authorities of their chosen enterprise topic or agenda.

Within UPBEAT, the skills are expressed in terms of capability levels showing high levels or qualities of professional engagement. It is recognised that a group is not either innovative or not, but can show varying levels of skill. As the team improve it is also recognised that real impacts then result.

40.5 New Policies and Practices for Constructive Change – A Radical Challenge, Especially of Those from East European Countries

40.5.1 The Need for Change

It is clear that those unfamiliar with the fairly radical approach proposed here, especially those from more traditional universities and/or ones in Eastern Europe, may well be alienated by its major thrust in asking universities, rather than the State, to mainly 'own' their acquisition of funding for the development of enterprising projects which engage, and then empower, their local businesses, industries and communities. For, at present, many are so used to the State providing funds for all such change developments, that they may feel, if such enterprise activities were necessary, the State would, and should, pay for them. So they often actually feel what is being suggested is unnecessary, unworkable or even impossible for their context. Unfortunately, this situation is compounded by how States assess the quality of their HE, i.e. normally in terms of academics' refereed publications and citations; and this in turn drives HEIs towards these fairly narrow indicators, rather than encouraging them to deeply engage with external stakeholders, with little space for a more differentiated quality approach.

However, the State no longer has the funding for such new developments in a world changed, beyond recognition after the latest 'Economic Crises' and the more ardent societal responses such as the 'Arab Spring' or the 'African Spring'. As a result, there is now an urgent demand for a radically new way of working by all, including universities, driving them towards humanly centred approaches which ensure universities work closely with their communities and businesses on a shared journey of innovation and constructive development. So, like Josef Konvitz, former Head of Regulatory Policy at the OECD (2011), the present authors are keen 'to take the relationship between universities and regions out of the conventional framework based on utilitarian considerations, and to reflect better what universities uniquely are' and how they could best help. Furthermore, in times of stringent economic hardship, part of this challenge for universities must be to become major managers of all opportunities and, with respect to this section of chapters on financing, with their own acquisition of funding necessary to undertake research leading to sustainable innovation for good in the real world. To put it bluntly, if business and the community want universities to help them they will find a way of paying, but only if universities respond to real needs and demands of clients and users; universities need to create the managerial and leadership capacity to deliver demanded projects. Our research clearly shows that if they do this many positive outcomes will result. However, in this section we add to the foregoing discussions just a little to ensure academic managers who had to lead in this area have the appropriate knowledge to convince those with more traditional approaches to university management.

In particular, we will not ignore the challenges that our proposed approach brings to those traditional universities who decide to adopt it and we will also suggest the need for State Policies to support universities who go down this more self depending path. We will also try to answer the concerns of those brought up in a different era of State provision and also indicate, in slightly more depth, why and how such an innovative and foresightful approach is now necessary. Taking the argument to greater depth, four things drive the present authors forward in trying to convince universities and academics to want to develop in a new way: firstly, the complex and uncertain challenges posed by the present economic and social crises requires the sort of reasoned understanding only possible on the basis of sound academic reasoning; secondly, we have found (Powell and Clark 2012) and most academics do have a strong human awareness, high values and truly want to make a difference in the real world; thirdly, there is now a demand from society for universities to do something to help make a real difference for society in its handling the increasingly 'wicked' problems of today and the future (Rittel 1972); and finally, because the best practices of those academic/universities trying to work within the principles recommended here (and reported at http://pumr.pascalobservatory.org), show them to be both effective in developing constructive change and efficient in the co-creation of solutions which actually do lead to innovative improvements for sustainable change in the real world. While the suggested approach may appear 'idealistic', we hope we have shown earlier that it is both systemically and systematically grounded, with the changes proposed resulting in pragmatic deliverables. So we believe we have shown ways and means of universities and their academics working differently.

So, let us now turn to these particular challenges, for, to ignore the questions normally confronting our proposed changes, would lead them not to be dismissed, out of hand. The following small sub-sections will therefore take on just some of the key challenges facing the adoption of our approach in turn, show that the approach has been developed in some rich and quite different context, for quite different cultures, and wherever used is still found to be useful. Furthermore, limiting problems will also be addressed and ways found for sensible implementation:

40.5.2   The Role of National Policy and Its Present Limitations

Unfortunately, some of the existing European Policies are limiting, rather than enabling, in driving constructive change for improved collaborations between external partners trying to work jointly with universities, and furthermore the funds available often seem to push towards traditional directions, as opposed to the innovative ones proposed here. And, for instance in CEE Countries, like Romania (the host of the conference at which this chapter was first presented) States do not presently seem to encourage universities to opportunistically fund-raise (such as leveraging private funding with public money); such States also lack a relevant policy framework which encourages universities to get involved in local/regional partnerships (as they do exist in the UK for instance). Furthermore, a question often now asked is 'why a university which has always been supported by the State for nearly all of its developments would want to act differently'. And further, especially in Eastern European contexts, there are few Public Policies, except at the local level, to provide incentives for the kind of approach suggested. Quite simply the State now has so little funding for Higher Education that developments not thought to be key to the future of universities are seen as dispensable for State funding. While the present authors do not agree with this situation, they recognise it is a reality.

That is not to say that the State, and the EU, cannot help to make a real difference in this arena by adopting the 'right' policies. This has been shown to be successful in the UK, where national policy has led to university led projects of true impact with associated socially inclusive wealth creation; led to a recognition this area to be important, and help given to promote a university processes which drive greater creativity and enterprise, to complement academics traditional roles in teaching, learning and research; provided 'pump priming' resources to begin the necessary constructive cultural change. Indeed, the first named author of this chapter worked for many years while a member of the Higher Education Funding Council of England's 'Business and Community Committee' to improve national policy and implementation processes, thereby ensuring better university practices in the creation of enterprising academic activity across the whole of the UK. And as Adrian Day (2011) has shown, in his successive evaluations of these developing UK processes of Academic Enterprise, there has been much encouraging progress on this front and the UK is now often cited as a widely respected leader of such enterprising university behavior. So we would clearly encourage all European States, and the EU itself, to become more supportive of those universities which truly want to be innovative and enterprising; want to co-identify problems worthy of consider and co-create working solutions leading to real impact; which want to co-produce deliverables that can become sustainable; and which want Academic Enterprise to be seen as a 'noble art' of equal, but different, value within and to society. However, this imperative is not just about funding, but about a change in university culture, supported by the Nation State, and enacted by an empowered local Higher Education. This is where CEE Countries need to follow the UK's lead and perhaps we need a new European programme, the equivalent of PHARE (1989) to assist European accession countries learn to become more enterprising.

If State and EU policies accepted our approach, it would lead to a proper diversity of provision, where not every university would strive to be traditionally research dominated, and where everyone was not similarly seeking to become a Harvard or Oxford, or simply becoming an advanced teaching organisation. For us, at least, some would be enterprising universities where good research and advanced learning would be complemented by Academic Enterprise leading to deliverables of sustainable impact. In such a world, academics would then be known not just by their refereed papers and awards, but also for the innovative solutions they had developed with strategic partners for social good. Our proposed processes assume this aspiration and have been designed, developed and evaluated to provide an intuitive and workable approach in making traditional academics, *enterprising ones*. And, as Garlick (October 2011, 'The Future of Higher Education', from PASCAL discussion by E-mail with James Powell, private communication) so poignantly points out, 'if we are to use higher education as a means to create 'livable' cities and regions, and not just places that we live in, we need to work to quite different systems' *and quite a different approach*....This is a real challenge in a rapidly changing global society that seems to be moving at a pace and gives us no time to take in wisdom. *But we must try!!* The oft stated phrase by universities and regions is to say 'what we are good at'...but rarely they say 'what are we good for'. This kind of wisdom is missing from many higher education institutions and their leaders slavishly following neoliberal principles as they respond to central government funding arrangements'.

Garlick's recent visit to the EU Open days 9th European Week of Regions and Cities – he is an Australian academic – also startled him with a focus that appeared completely devoid of the role of people and instead it seemed to emphasise what he believed was the dressing up of old approaches with new language (e.g. 'smart specialisation' sounds remarkably like business clustering). So Garlick believes an approach is needed that is humanly centred, answering his (S. Garlick, October 2011, 'The Future of Higher Education', from PASCAL discussion by E-mail with James Powell, private communication) 'key questions of: what kind of learning is being developed?; what it is for?; who is the learning for?; and how it will be done?'. But typically these questions are generally ignored in favour of improved structures and processes. This is why the approach suggested here is so important, because it strives to answer his key questions and to properly develop sound relationship between universities and their city regions.

40.5.3   Constructive Developments Can Occur Across a Europe That Has Supportive Policies

It has been suggested that those from the UK are luckier with respect to implementation of improved university Reach-out to business and the community because the UK has a government that has been shown to care and, as mentioned in the previous section, has provided extra funding to 'pump prime' change. This is true, but if the European Commission were to properly understand the strength of the UK's successful development, which is positively endorsed by the researched findings of recent EUA (Pruvot 2011) and Gupta (2011) studies, they would surely encourage other parts of Europe to do likewise.

Furthermore, even in the UK and elsewhere in the world, where universities have initiated approaches similar to the one suggested here on their own account, but with little State support, a gradual growth in alternative sponsored projects, which are both of high impact and wealth creating, seems to have occurred. The key to success in this respect is to start slowly, but act purposefully, continuously and methodically in developing an alternative enterprising culture; recent papers by Powell (2011) and Powell and Clark (2012) show much success in those universities in England which became enterprising even before the new UK change. While good national Policies undoubtedly help, the key driver is the 'will' of the universities themselves, and their enterprising academics, to want to develop in this arena.

40.5.4   Motivating Academics to Commit to the Academic Enterprise as a Complementary Way of Working

Research by the present authors, [Powell et al. (2011) and by Powell and Clark (2012)] and by Jackson (2012) also shows that many academics truly want to become involved in the Academic Enterprise. Actually, they seem to be 'intrinsically motivated in wanting to Reach out to business and society, engage with real citizens and to co-design solutions with them'. However, academics can soon become de-motivated by university policies that do not recognise the kinds of approach suggested here or where there is lack of academic career progression for those who wish to be more enterprising. Unfortunately, all too often, internal policies are poor in the way they motivate and reward those academics who can attract private funding for enterprising behaviour. Very often academics do get rewarded for research reflected in publishing and not necessarily for doing other type of services to the university. This is the problem.

However, those at the conference from Eastern Europe indicated to us that, unfortunately, HEI senior management in CEE was typically collegiate, with systems based on the 'will' of the majority; this tends to be traditional in style and aspiration, and may not be open to entrepreneurial spirit. So, this needs to be confronted and university management has to become more receptive and progressive to necessary future enterprise change. Our research shows that if they do, much constructive impact follows. There is no 'rocket science' required here – the situation simply needs to be handled with a sensitive reward and incentive scheme, and tender loving human care where enterprising academics are encouraged, not just to 'look', 'see' and 'write', but to 'look', 'see' and 'do' something. Furthermore, successful Academic Enterprise leaders are already driven by a strong personal sense of motivation. So, the leaders of cultural change and creative development must work to keep this motivation high. Those academics who want to do – and lead – Outreach should be encouraged to do so; however, academics should not be forced to undertake Academic Enterprise, because of any university's mission statements, but only if they want to. The exemplary academic leaders who Powell and Clark (2012) interviewed talked of a desire to add 'real meaning' in how they help people *better* their *own* lives, and particularly in the way they engaged with external partners. Many such leaders also talked of their passion about their chosen area of Academic Enterprise, as well as a determination to achieve something 'real'. Here are quotes from the interviews given by just two academic entrepreneurial leaders:

> *I'd always been bothered by social issues and the things happening to communities....*
> *I needed to do something about it*

> *I began to realise I could make real changes for myself in outreach for academe*

40.5.5   The Harmonious Co-existence of Traditional and Enterprising Academics – Allowing All to Flourish

Most traditional academics 'are' their refereed papers and awards, but entrepreneurial academics do act differently and must be differently known by their outputs, outcomes and impacts. So how can universities which want to embrace both kinds of approach cope with the fact that conventional academics, doing traditional research, will now have to work alongside entrepreneurial academics that are doing more applied and implementation work? Two potential problems are often thought to cause frictions inside a university:

- traditional academics, because of the high status of research, may be seen to be looking down at the new entrepreneurial academics and this can create bad atmosphere
- entrepreneurial academics seem to make extra money from their work which often then goes into the budget of the HEI for redistribution – hence the entrepreneurial academics may feel like they make money for the Institution and the others, who are not investing time and energy in similar projects, benefit from it.

So the basic question we are often posed here is how do these two types of academics co-exist under one roof?

The key of coping with this potentially problematic situation is firstly to understand it exists, then to design team working into any future project, to recognise traditional and entrepreneurial skills are complementary, and finally to provide appropriate leadership reflecting the power, to all, of intelligent partnering. Once upon a time, the first cause of this potential friction was a regular occurrence, but our research for this chapter firstly shows this to have become a lesser effect, especially in those universities which truly engage with their local businesses and communities. In an earlier era, all academics would strive to be first and foremost researchers trying to understand the real world and develop strong theories to reflect this. Ideally they would have worked but themselves, often rather secretly, in their 'ivory towers', but such is now the complexity, uncertainty and often 'wickedness' of any topic for research, that systemic answers require collaboration. So even traditional academics now live in a world of trans-disciplinary working, where people have to work in a systemic way collaborating with those from quite different cultures. Adding to such team-working those with entrepreneurial skills simply extends the systemic understanding possible and can even ensure much needed funding to develop any R&D to a higher level. Good academic leadership of differently creative teams can also be shown to resolve this first friction, as those with different capabilities realize they have complementary skills of equal academic value to research capability alone. Finding such leaders is not trivial, especially in countries not used to undertaking Academic Enterprise, but we always find academics who can, and want, to become enterprising, but you have to look hard to find them; furthermore for those unused to this kind of development, the PASCAL Universities for a Modern Renaissance programme has educators with skills to coach the appropriate ways forward. As an important aside, encouraging academics to become involved in this area can be further supported by an academic career progress system that recognizes this – see later comments.

The second friction mentioned above, potentially caused by the entrepreneurial academics either gaining enhanced salaries for this work or developing funds used elsewhere by the university, can again be resolved by a good leadership and a 'fair deal incentive scheme' open to all – one where non financial rewards come to the fore. Indeed for academics, recognition of career enhancement seems just as important, if not more so, than extra finances (Powell and Clark 2012). Firstly, any financial rewards and incentives should only be given on the basis of work undertaken 'beyond the call of duty'; and when enterprise funding is taken by the University for alternative use, this action must be transparent and lead to a fair alternative allocation, ideally with those involved in generating funding being involved in the process – failure to do this will cause friction to those raising the funding; in this latter respect, we return to the issue of the fairly traditional collegiate management which does not redistribute resources according to 'fair' criteria, but according to the number of votes in a senate/collegiate body where the decisions of the traditional majority may ignore the aspirations of entrepreneurial academics On the other hand, traditional academics must be allowed to become involved in intelligent teams chosen to create new enterprises and solutions; in this way they can share sponsorship income equitably. However, the best way of avoiding friction from this problem is to focus returns to all academics on the basis of non-financial rewards, such as university recognition of any development and career advancement. The enhanced funding of additional sponsored projects can also lead to larger scale and more relevant research for all at a time when there is a paucity of traditional funding.

40.5.6   Academics Willing to Seek Enterprise Development Funding from a Variety of Sources

It has been argued by others that academics are loath to seek funding to progress their enterprise projects. However, doing this continuously to gain their research funding and our 'studies of exemplary academic leaders (Powell and Clark 2012), who want to work constructively with business and the community, is that they are more than happy to take on the funding acquisition role for their projects as well. Indeed, they nearly all see this as a key part of being an enterprising academic. They have often learned such a skill from senior academics that have done this from early in their careers and have now been coaching their junior staff of their own creative enterprise teams to do likewise. Many also noted that being able to locate the necessary resources was a key skill for Academic Enterprise and went on to say that they were prepared to coach their junior staff in funding acquisition showing the value of working with a variety of potential sponsors'.

Here are another two examples of what exemplary academic enterprise leaders say about this:

> Finding the resources to make the enterprise work just became one of the challenges, but increasingly a very important one

> I think it's very hard in a university because ... a budgetary requirement is so overwhelming now, [and...] most of our money doesn't come from government anymore, it comes from being astute in a commercial and corporate world... [leaders] have got to be Janus faced

Our research also shows that academics can be easily coached to seek funding from a pluralism of sources and if they willingly accept this role, they become very competent at doing it. Furthermore, for those interested in learning how to do this, the PASCAL Programme for Universities for a Modern Renaissance has designed an approach to coach the coaches (http://pumr.pascalpbservatory.org).

A powerful independent example showing the willingness of traditional academics to take on the marshalling of new funding, can be seen in academics from the Veterinary Clinical Sciences section of the University of Edinburgh (Gupta 2011). Having taken part in the University's 'Commercial Breakthrough Programme', and learning to understand relevant customer facing business environments, these academics became effective deal makers increasing clinical income and funds enabling the development of a new Veterinary building to house their School; they quickly learned to develop a commercial mind set, influencing and negotiating skills, and opportunity spotting, screening and testing skills relevant to the new funding environment. 'And what is more, by learning how to do this well and owning the problem for themselves', they began to enjoy this as an addition capability – one then open for use in many future developments. They also learned to become the new and successful leaders of reach-out for their own university.

Again for CEE Universities, with middle management brought up under communism, there may be a greater need to bring in those from other parts of Europe, with the skills to coach for the new ways of working, and to build necessary capacity and develop appropriate cultural change. The European Mobility programme could also be used to help in stimulating international R&D teams so that academics across Europe can mutually coach each other to greater capabilities suitable for the global knowledge economy.

40.5.7 The Time to Develop Cultural Change

Some argue that the approach we have in mind would not happen because of the time required for the necessary cultural change, which is often fairly lengthy. However, it should not put any university off from trying to change because the future will be very different from the past and universities have to prepare for it. Sustained cultural change takes years and not months. For instance, it took the first named author of the present chapter nearly 8 years to get significant and meaningful change at his university Powell and Dayson (2012), but if he had not started, that university would never have got so far as it has today in becoming renowned for its Academic Enterprise prowess. Even here, this university now recognises it is in the middle of a 15 year change programme, with improved empowerment processes being developed to ensure deeply engrained ways of working (Hall 2009) are properly embedded.

40.5.8 There Is Presently a Lack of Entrepreneurial Spirit and Thinking in Universities

Academics have always been enterprising in the way they undertake their research and develop innovative ways of teaching and learning, especially in times of financial restraint where face-to-face contact hours are continuously being reduced. So there is a natural tendency for academic to be creative and innovative, wanting to make a difference. However, there is also a clear lack of entrepreneurial education in the universities to help coach academics who want to be more enterprising in engaging, co-creating and co-producing demanded solutions of value to business and the community. The presently suggested approach provides a basis of just one way, shown by the PASCAL International Observatory to be a workable approach and thus turned into a learning programme for necessary change (http://pumr.pascalobservatory.org)

even on a self managed learning basis. However, there are other private providers, such as Educators UK and the National Council for Graduate Education (both in the UK), and the Kauffman Foundation with its Cross Campus Initiative in the US, providing constructive alternative learning on enterprise for academics. Whoever provides it, such learning is undoubtedly needed.

State actors also need to play a greater role in making higher education institution change their organisation culture, driving academics to become the 'opportunity managers and leaders' for the future. If they do this, especially using the simple and intuitive approach proposed here, the present authors confirm that enhanced university funding will result for projects based on high academic values developed in intelligent partnership with external partners; such work may also improve the quality and range of future research and the applicability and effectiveness of teaching and learning for the university. Whatever else, we must support those in academe who want to be entrepreneurial to be so, to do it with effect and not feel they are thwarted by more traditional approaches.

40.5.9 Proof That Such an Approach Is Truly Productive

The present chapter has already revealed the 130 cases of best Academic Enterprise practice (to be seen at http://pumr.pascalobservatory.org or in Powell (2007, 2010)); the 49 other cases of creative universities and their creative city regions (EUA study, Powell et al. 2011); other studies associated with recent interviews with exemplary Academic Enterprise leaders (Powell and Clark 2012); the EUA's other work as portrayed by Estermann and Bennetot Pruvot (2011); and the PASCAL international observatories interest in developing the PUMR project. All stand testimony to the applicability, value and impact of the developed process. Those adopting the approach come from quite different context and culture, so these strong evaluations make us believe the approach to be proven. However, those who doubt the process ought to study the practices fully written up above.

40.5.10 Ethical Considerations Alone Should Drive Us Towards the Approach Suggested

The belief of the present authors is in the development of a 'modern university' – one that strives to prepare people for a 'Modern Renaissance'. Such a university will answer Garlick's (October 2011, 'The Future of Higher Education', from PASCAL discussion by E-mail with James Powell, private communication) "key question: 'What are you good for?' This provides an edge for the proposed research policy centre over others which are still trying to squeeze out more from the 'what are you good at' approach of universities and their places. There is no doubt a 'what are you good for' culture does present short term funding challenges, *some of which we hope we have answered above* (our words in italics). However, sometimes this is the cost of investing in wisdom and paradigm change... Furthermore, in such a university there has to be a focus on ethical and moral purpose so we have a meaningful and purposeful framework based on goodness for our programmes of learning, social capital, knowledge transfer, human capital, the environment, etc. There is too much learning for all the wrong reasons... That some of the big issues in communities around the globe are taken on (social, economic, cultural and environmental) by universities working with their communities... *and in such a university*:

- There would be a focus on people rather than on structures and processes
- There would be a focus on academics being 'enterprising' about getting the job done and not just theorising about it.
- That learning would be seen to begin at very young ages and that the region and city provide a context for the development of cognitive and non-cognitive ability.
- That humans will not be seen as the only ones capable of adding to our stock of knowledge for solving the problems of communities throughout the world.

That the leadership of the university extend well beyond the campus and embrace other sectors of formal and informal learning and their engagement with the community."

40.5.11 Leadership Is Critical

What is proposed in this chapter is not trivial. It requires a total change in the culture of many universities. However, we have shown academics can be coached into becoming enterprising ones and the leaders of creative enterprise teams (Powell and Clark 2012). However, where should they lead? We want to conclude this part of the discussion by sharing a view, expressed in a recent PASCAL discussion, proposing the way forward. It has been suggested by the aforementioned Josef Konvitz (October 2011, 'The Future of Higher Education', from PASCAL discussion by E-mail with James Powell, private communication). He has recently made a number of linked proposals in talking about universities development in the face of the present crisis. Firstly, in his view, this 'crisis – which will continue for at least a couple of years – is loosening many long-established institutional relationships in multi-level governance. Part of this is driven by fiscal conditions, part by shifts (reductions really) in overall national sovereignty. Hence a situation in which the position of regions, relative to other large governing units whether at the metropolitan/urban or nation-state level, is increasingly difficult to predict, and could well exhibit greater variation country-to-country. Regions that want to take advantage of this flexibility will need a broader range of options than the livability/competitiveness set which has dominated the past two decades. Monitoring of trends needs to be wedded to more imaginative exercises, simulations, reflection-setting seminars which emphasize that we are, as I am now saying with greater confidence, at a point of rupture.

We should resist pressures to be very short-term in our views: we can be most helpful in the short term by looking toward the future, not the past. Second, the OECD reports Regions at a Glance (2009, 2011) continue to reflect the macroeconomic theory of locally specific advantages based on human and physical capital articulated along a range of outcomes often defined as a scale between leading and lagging regions. The virtue of the scale is to show bottom will vary. The main focus remains on competitiveness, looking at output, GDP and component factors. The analysis generates a list for research, comparing the composition of high-tech manufacturing to overall manufacturing, for example, the relative importance of public sector expenditure to performance, the interdependency among regions which are doing relatively well or are hard-hit, and how to attract young people who help make a region more resilient but are more likely to be unemployed in a downturn. On page 50 of the 2011 report, the OECD calls "for policies that support training and human capital formation to respond to regional specificities." On migration, the analysis highlights the importance of networks that help immigrants integrate, suggestion that regional development policies need to take more notice of "soft infrastructure" that could affect integration. Given the selectivity of an OECD report of this kind and its rigorous methodology, the results can be used with confidence – there is also an electronic means to set up thematic comparisons among regions – but the question remains open what the indicators of tomorrow could be, given the direction of change. OECD data is "incontrovertible", necessary but probably not sufficient. 'But development of new or alternative indicators is itself a long-term process. It is worth recalling for the record that the data set of today has its origins in some of the work undertaken in the 1990s for the OECD report, Cities and Regions in the New Learning Economy (2001)'.

40.6 UPBEAT, PUMR and Innovation – A Final Short Discussion

UPBEAT has elicited the best principles of previous academic enterprise assessment and development approaches to provide a simple tool to helps traditional academic become more enterprising in the way the engage with their external partners in a trans-disciplinary way that promotes true innovation. It recognises the creative skill that each member of a talented team can bring to the innovation and drives them to continuously work for more systemic solutions of greater impact. There is nothing unique about the need for the four enterprise skills or the way the process strives to ensure the qualities of engagement relating to them continuously should be improved. The uniqueness lies in the fact that this fourfold of skills must be integrated across teams of different skills, all differently talented, with the whole striving for continuous improvement. The evidence from the cases shows that it is in this way that leading edge university research can truly make a real impact, in the real world and lead to the development of new creative academic enterprise teams that make a real difference. It is the deepening working practices and 'virtuous knowledge sharing' between all partners that makes for innovation in the first place and then on to higher levels of innovation, both within the original domain of the initial academic enterprise and then in supplementary areas. It is the simplicity of the process that can make the difference.

The UPBEAT model can be seen to embed many of the principles of successful innovation, as it addresses issues of potential antecedents (Lesseure et al. 2004), organisational innovation infrastructure such as networks and knowledge (Dewar and Dutton 1984), the processes of innovation (Edwards et al. 2004) and the ultimate outcomes that demonstrate innovation. While an individual project, or range of projects, may not address all of the issues outlined in UPBEAT, it is essentially in any situation to "beg the question" as to whether all key or critical issues have been considered; so UPBEAT simply prompts academics to ask the right questions of themselves in a structured, but flexible, way. It is up to the creative academic-industry teams involved to consider what must be addressed. In this sense, *innovation* is applied in its broadest sense as "the successful exploitation of new ideas". Much of the literature tends to focus specifically on technical and process innovations within a business context (Ettlie et al. 1984; Dewar and Dutton 1986; Edwards et al. 2004), but many of these factors are still applicable when applied to any community of individuals and the improvements that innovations may bring to their lives.

UPBEAT has now been adopted as the assessment and driving process for a new programme, known as the 'PASCAL Universities for a Modern Renaissance' (or PUMR for short). This is now being developed under the auspices of the PASCAL International Observatory for *place management, social capital and learning regions* as a major thrust of their future work with Universities and to work across the globe with those universities desiring to work to the following principles:

Universities harnessing global imagination and unlocking the talents of all people, throughout the world, to co-identify, co-create and co-produce flourishing futures with external partners from business, industry, civil and voluntary services and the community

PASCAL wants to encourage like minded universities to want to become part of their PUMR network and to take part in a deep and meaningful discussion in order to develop the nature of its programme of joint working and knowledge sharing. The immediate desire, through the development of a focused social networking site, is to get Universities to reveal their best practices in this respect, through providing access to case studies illustrating 'virtuous' knowledge sharing leading to mutual benefits, sustained improvements and significant impacts for all – please read further on www.pumr.pascalobservatory.org.

40.7   Conclusions

This paper has described an innovation approach which enables traditional academics to become more enterprising and, as a result, for University Reach-out or Academic Enterprise to become more successfully innovative. It is known as

UPBEAT and while it is not unique in its desire to examine the context and impacts of academic engagement, it does offer a successful method for assessing the impact of innovative academic engagement, and on a global scale. Detailed consideration of the approach highlights how academics must themselves learn how to acquire funds from a pluralism of resources.

The paper also analyses the success of the approach through the lens of innovation theory; we also identify how different perspectives of innovation can underpin our understanding of how such a model supports the "stage management" of leading edge ideas in to the real world. Relevant to this financial section of the overall debate, it requires academics to understand how to develop solutions to real word problems reflecting user DEMANDS by society, as well as their needs.

This paper has drawn some important comparisons between the different models of University Reach-out by focusing on areas of commonality such as methodology, outcomes and impact measurement, guiding principles, modes of innovation and motivation to use the model for managing and measuring academic engagement. It goes on to show the strengths of the UPBEAT model in driving Academic Enterprise in a cost effective way. There are now literally hundreds of examples of enhanced enterprise in academic enterprise across the world – www-upbeat.eu.com. It is a simple, intuitive and easily implementable approach which has stood the test of time in a number of situations. Recently it was highlighted in the new Michigan Handbook for 'Engaged Scholarship' by Hiram Fitzgerald and his colleagues (2011). As a result it has recently been adopted by the PASCAL International Observatory for place management, social capital and learning regions as its sole tool for assessing its 'Universities for a Modern Renaissance' programme – www. pascalobservatory.org.

Finally, it has also tried to deal coherently with comments and challenges put to those developing the UPBEAT approach. These consider policy and practice issues surrounding the cultural change within universities that truly want to become more enterprising. We all are now aware of where we 'need to be in terms of global achievement, but' as Garlick (October 2011, 'The Future of Higher Education', from PASCAL discussion by E-mail with James Powell, private communication), so rightly says 'the old map we are using (innovation) and the old map reading skills we are teaching (human capital) cannot get us there now when the environment we are encased in has so many new questions and unusual twists and turns. The current economic constraints have caught us napping, but as you say have brought it out into the open. This presents fundamental questions of relevance for universities and regions if they are to have a key role, and they should'. We hope this chapter begins to show a constructive way forward.

For those universities that find a way of becoming deeply engaged with their local businesses and communities will also become the champions of future economic growth and social inclusive wealth creation.

Acknowledgement We are deeply indebted to Professor Liviu Matei, Renata Kralikova' and Pusa Nastase, whose detailed and critical questioning prompted the sub-chapter on 'New Policies and Practises for Constructive Change – A Radical Challenge'.

References

Abbott, H. P. (2003). *The Cambridge introduction to narrative* (2nd ed.). Cambridge: Cambridge University Press.

Abreu, M., Grinevich, V., Hughes, A., & Kitson, M. (2009). *Knowledge exchange between academics and the business, public and third sectors.* Cambridge: Centre for Business Research, University of Cambridge.

Afuah, A. N., & Bahram, N. (1995). The hypercube of innovation. *Research Policy, 24,* 51–76.

Agrawal, A. (2001). University-to-industry knowledge transfer: Literature review and unanswered questions. *International Journal of Management Reviews, 3*(4), 285–302.

Aldrich, H. E., & Herker, D. (1977). Boundary-spanning roles and organizational structure. *Academy of Management Review, 2,* 217–230.

Amabile, T.M. (1998), "How to kill creativity", *Harvard Business Review, 76*(5), 76–87.

BERR (The Department for Business, Enterprise and Regulatory Reform). (2008). *Supporting innovation in services.* London: BERR-DIUS.

Bonaccorsi, A., & Piccaluga, A. (1994). A theoretical framework for the evaluation of university-industry relationships. *R&D Management, 24*(3), 229–247.

Chesbrough, H. W. (2003, Spring). The era of open innovation. *Sloan Management Review, 44*(3), 35–41.

Cohen, W. M., Nelson, R. R., & Walsh, J. P. (2002). Links and impacts: The influence of public research on industrial R&D. *Management Science, 48*(1), 1–23.

Day, A. (2011). *Higher education – Business and community surveys (2009–2011).* Higher Education Funding Council of England. Available on line at www.hefce.ac.uk/pubs/hefce/2011

Debackere, K. (2000). Managing academic R&D as a business at KU Leuven: Context, structure and process. *R&D Management, 30*(4), 323–328.

Dechamps, J. P. (2005). Different leadership skills for different innovation strategies. *Strategy and Leadership, 33*(5), 31–38.

Department for Education and Science. (2009). *The Leitch report: Prosperity for all in the global economy – World class skills.* London: HMSO.

Dewar, R. D., & Dutton, J. E. (1986). The adoption of radical and incremental innovations: An empirical analysis. *Management Science, 32*(11), 1422–1433.

DIUS (Department for Innovation, Universities & Skills). (2008). *Innovation nation.* London: DIUS.

Dooley, L., & Kirk, D. (2007). University-industry collaboration: Grafting the entrepreneurial paradigm onto academic structures. *European Journal of Innovation Management, 10*(3), 316–332.

DTI (Department of Trade and Industry). (2006). *Innovation in the UK: Indicators and insights.* London: Department of Trade and Industry.

DTI (Department of Trade and Industry). (2007). *Innovation in services.* London: Department of Trade and Industry.

Edquist, C. (1997). *Systems of innovation: Technologies, institutions and organizations.* London: Pinter/Cassell.

Edwards, T., Battisti, G., & Neely, A. (2004). Value creation and the UK economy: A review of strategic options. *International Journal of Management Reviews, 5/6*(3–4), 191–213.

EPSRC. (2009a). Tait, J. (2009). Upstream engagement and the governance of science: The shadow of the genetically modified crops experience in Europe. *EMBO Reports: Special Issue on Science and Society, 10,* S18–S22.

EPSRC. (2009b). Boaz, A., Fitzpatrick, S., & Shaw, B. (2009). Assessing the impact of research on policy: A literature review. *Science and Public Policy, 36*(4), 255.

Ettlie, J. E., Bridges, W. P., & O'Keefe, R. D. (1984). Organization strategy and structural differences for radical versus incremental innovation. *Management Science, 30,* 682–695.

Estermann, T., & Bennetot Pruvot, E. (2011). *Financially sustainable universities II: European universities diversifying income streams.* Brussels: European University Association.

Etzkowitz, H., & Leytesdorff, L. (1997). *Universities in the global economy: A triple helix of academic-industry-government relation.* London: Croom Helm.

Etzkowitz, H., Webster, A., & Healey, P. (1998). Introduction. In H. Etzkowitz, A. Webster, & P. Healey (Eds.), *Capitalizing knowledge.* Albany: State University of New York Press.

EU Committee of the Regions (CoR). (2011, May 22). Working Document entitled *'The role of local and regional authorities in achieving the objectives of the Europe 2020 strategy'.* Brussels.

Fitzgerald, H. E., Burack, C., & Seifer, S. (2011). *Handbook of engaged scholarship: Contemporary landscapes, future directions: Vol. 1. Institutional change.* East Lansing: Michigan State University Press.

Freeman, C. (1987). *Technology policy and economic performance: Lessons from Japan.* London: Pinter.

Gann, D. (2001). Putting academic ideas into practice: Technological progress and the absorptive capacity of construction organizations. *Construction Management and Economics, 19,* 321–330.

Gibbons, M., Limoges, C., Nowotny, H., Schwartz, S., Scott, P., & Trow, M. (1994). *The new production of knowledge: The dynamics of science and research in contemporary societies.* London: Sage.

Goedegebuure, L., & van der Lee, J. (2006). *In search of evidence. Measuring community engagement a pilot study.* Brisbane: Eidos.

Grossman, J. H., Reid, P. P., & Morgan, R. P. (2001). Contributions of academic research to industrial performance in five industry sectors. *The Journal of Technology Transfer, 26*(1–2), 143–152.

Gupta, S. (2011). Professionals in management and leadership. In *Beitrage zur Hochschulforchung* (Vol. 2). ISSN 0171-645X.

Hall, B. H. (2004). University-industry partnerships in the United States. In J.-P. Contzen, D. Gibson, & M. V. Heitor (Eds.), *Rethinking science systems and innovation policies. Proceedings of the 6th International Conference on Technology Policy and Innovation.* Ashland: Purdue University Press.

Hall, M. (2009). *University of Salford strategic plan – 2009/10 to 2017/18.* University of Salford, December 2001.

Hewlett, P. (2003). Johnson, W. C. (2003). University relations: The HP model. *Industry and Higher Education, 17,* 391–395.

Hansen, M. T., & Birkinshaw, J. (2007). The innovation value chain. *Harvard Business Review, 85*(6), 121–130.

Hargreaves, A., & Dawe, R. (1990). Paths of professional development: Contrived collegiality, collaborative culture and the case of peer coaching. *Teaching and Teacher Education, 6*(3), 227–241.

HEFCE (Higher Education Funding Council). (2006). *Strategic plan 2006–2011.* Bristol: HEFCE.

Howells, J. (1999). Regional systems of innovation? In D. Archibugi, J. Howells, & J. Michie (Eds.), *Innovation policy in a global economy* (pp. 67–93). Cambridge: Cambridge University Press.

Jackson, E. (2012). *Motivation in academic enterprise,* in preparation for a doctorate at the University of Salford, England, UK.

Jasanoff, S. (2004). The idiom of co-production. In S. Jasanoff (Ed.), *States of knowledge in the co-production of science and social order* (pp. 1–12). London: Routledge.

Jung, D. I., Chow, C., & Wu, A. (2003). The role of transformational leadership in enhancing organizational innovation: Hypotheses and some preliminary findings. *The Leadership Quarterly, 14*(4–5), 525–544.

Kellogg Commission. (1999). *Returning to our roots: The engaged institution.* Third Report of the Kellogg Commission on the future of State and Land-Grant Universities. Washington, DC: National Association of State Universities and Land-Grant Universities.

Kirby, D. A. (2006). Creating entrepreneurial universities in the UK: Applying entrepreneurship theory to practice. *The Journal of Technology Transfer, 31*(5), 599–603.

Konvitz, J. (2011). *The Great Contraction.* Glasgow: Adam Smith Research Foundation, Glasgow University.

Konvitz, J., & Bruhat, T. (2011). *'Inventing the Future Cities'* private communication from josef@ konvitz.com.

Krause, D. E. (2003). Influence-based leadership as a determinant of the inclination to innovate and of innovation-related behaviours: An empirical investigation. *The Leadership Quarterly, 15*(1), 79–102.

Lambert, R. (2003). *The Lambert review of business and university collaboration.* London: HM Treasury.

Larsen, G. D., & Ballal, T. M. A. (2005). The diffusion of innovations within a UKCI context: An explanatory framework. *Construction Management and Economics, 23*, 81–91.

Leonard-Barton, D. (1995). *Wellsprings of knowledge.* Boston: Harvard Business School Press.

Lesseure, M., Bauer, J., Birdi, K., Neely, A., & Denyer, D. (2004). Adoption of promising practices: A systematic review of the evidence. *International Journal of Management Reviews, 5/6*(3&4), 169–190.

Lu, S., Abbott, C., Jones, V., & Sexton, M. (2007, March 26–27). The role of innovation circles in stimulating innovation in small construction firms. *Proceedings of 4th International SCRI Research Symposium.* Lowry Theatre, Salford, UK.

Lundvall, B. A. (1992). *National systems of innovation: Towards a theory of innovation and interactive learning.* London: Pinter.

Macmillan, G., & Hamilton, R. (2003). The impact of funded basic research: An integrative extension of Martin and Salter. *IEEE Transactions on Engineering Management, 50*(2), 184–191.

Marques, J. P. C., Caraca, J. M. G., & Diz, H. (2006). How can university–industry–government interactions change the innovation scenario in Portugal?: The case of the University of Coimbra. *Technovation, 26*, 534–542.

Michigan. (2005). *Points of distinction: A guidebook for planning and evaluating the quality of outreach.* East Lansing: Michigan State University. Available at http://www.msu.edu/unit/outreach/pubs/pod.pdf. [Zimmerman, D.]

Michigan. (2008). *The outreach measurement instrument.* East Lansing: Michigan State University. Available at http://ncsue.msu.edu/measure.aspx. [Fitzgerald, H., & Zimmerman, D.]

Mowery, D. C., & Nelson, R. R. (Eds.). (2004). *Ivory tower and industrial innovation: University-industry technology before and after the Bayh-Dole Act.* Stanford: Stanford University Press.

Nelson, R. R. (1993). *National systems of innovation: A comparative analysis.* Oxford: Oxford University Press.

NESTA (National Endowment for Science, Technology and the Arts). (2009). *The connected university.* London: NESTA.

Niosi, J., Saviotti, P., Bellon, B., & Crow, M. (1993). National systems of innovation – In search of a workable concept. *Technology in Society, 15*, 207–227.

Nonaka, I., & Konno, W. (1998). The concept of the 'Ba': Building a foundation for knowledge creation. *California Management Review, 40*(3), 40–54.

NWRDA (Northwest Regional Development Agency). (2006). *Northwest regional economic strategy.* Available online. www.nwda.co.uk/PDF/RES06v2.pdf, 02/05/2010.

OECD (Organisation for Economic Co-operation and Development). (1999). *Managing national innovation systems.* Paris: OECD.

OECD (Organisation for Economic Co-operation and Development). (2002). *Benchmarking industry–science relationships.* Paris: OECD.

OECD (Organisation for Economic Co-operation and Development). (2005). *Oslo manual* (3rd ed.). Paris/Luxembourg: OECD/Eurostat.

OECD Report. (2001). *Cities and regions in the new learning economy.* Paris: OECD.

OECD Report. (2009). *Regions at a glance.* Paris: OECD.

OECD Report. (2011). *Regions at a glance.* Paris: OECD.

Owen-Smith, J., & Powell, W. W. (2004). Knowledge networks as channels and conduits: The effects of spillovers in the Boston Biotechnology Community. *Organization Science, 15*(1), 5–21.

Ozorhon, B., Abbott, C., Aouad, G., & Powell, J. (2010). *Innovation in construction: A project life-cycle approach.* Salford: University of Salford.

PHARE. (1989). *'The Phare programme'* – one of the three pre-accession instruments financed by the European Union to assist the applicant countries of Central and Eastern Europe in their preparations for joining the European Union, European Union in Wikipedia Free Encyclopedia.

Polt, W., Rammer, C., Gassler, H., Schibany, A., & Schartinger, D. (2001). Benchmarking industry-science relations: The role of framework conditions. *Science and Public Policy, 28*(4): 247–258.

Powell, J. A. (2007, October). Creative universities and their creative city regions. *Industry and Higher Education, 21*(5), 323–335.

Powell, J. (2008). Elaborating academic enterprise for the University of Salford. In K. Lane, P. van der Sijde, M. Lahdeniemi & J. Tarkkanen (Eds.), *Higher education institutions and innovation in the knowledge economy*. Helsinki: ARENE Publishing, ISBN 978-952-67165-0-3.

Powell, J. A. (2009). *The role of universities in knowledge sharing and real world problem solving.* Proceedings of the National Conference on Developing design learning and research to tackle real world problems held by the Design Council, at the University of Northumbria, 22 October 2009.

Powell, J. A. (2010). University knowledge through knowledge sharing – UPBEAT: University engagement through virtuous knowledge sharing and academic staff development. In H. E. Fitzgerald, C. Burack, & S. Seifer (Eds.), *Handbook of engaged scholarship: Contemporary landscapes, future directions: Vol. 1. Institutional change* (pp. 1–29). East Lansing: Michigan State University Press.

Powell, J. A. (2011). University knowledge through knowledge sharing – UPBEAT: University Engagement through Virtuous Knowledge Sharing and Academic Staff Development. In H. E. Fitzgerald, C. Burack & S. Seifer (Eds.), *Handbook of engaged scholarship: Contemporary landscapes, future directions: Vol. 1. Institutional change* (pp. 1–29). East Lansing: Michigan State University Press.

Powell, J. A., & Cooper, I. (2011). *Universities for a modern renaissance – Towards co-creation and co-design between universities and society*. Proceedings of the EAIR 32nd Annual Forum. Valencia, Spain, 1–4 September 2010.

Powell, J., & Clark, A. (2012). *Leadership for improved academic enterprise*. UK: Leadership Foundation for Higher Education.

Powell, J. A., & Dayson, K. (2012). Engagement and the idea of the Civic University. In P. Benneworth (Ed.), *University engagement with socially excluded communities: Towards the idea of 'the Engaged University'*. London: Springer.

Powell, J. A., & Khan, S. (2008). *Towards better leadership, governance and management – Practice in support of university reach out to business & the community – An UPBEAT approach*. Salford: University of Salford.

Poyago-Theotoky, J., Beath, J., & Siegel, D. (2002). Universities and fundamental research: Policy implications of the growth of university–industry partnerships. *Oxford Review of Economic Policy, 18*, 10–21.

REAP (Reciprocity, Externalities, Access and Partnerships). (2008). Pearce, J., Pearson, M., & Cameron, S. (2008). The ivory tower and beyond: Bradford University at the heart of its communities. *Participatory Learning and Action, 58*, 82–86.

Revans, R. W. (1983). *ABC of action learning*. Bromley: Chartwell-Bratt.

Rittel, H. (1972). Wicked problems. *Design Studies, 2*(1).

Roper, S., Du, J., & Love, J. H. (2008). Modelling the innovation value chain. *Research Policy, 37*, 961–977.

Santoro, M. (2000). Success breeds success: The linkage between relationship intensity and tangible outcomes in university-industry collaborative ventures. *The Journal of High Technology Management Research, 11*(2), 255–273.

Schartinger, D., Schibany, A., & Gassler, H. (2001). Interactive relations between universities and firms: Empirical evidence for Austria. *The Journal of Technology Transfer, 26*, 255–268.

Showers, J., & Bruce, J. (1996). The evolution of peer coaching. *Educational Leadership, 53*(6), 12–17.

Smircich, L., & Morgan, G. (1982). Leadership: The management of meaning. *The Journal of Applied Behavioural Science, 18*(3), 257–273.

Star, S. L., & Griesemer, J. R. (1989). Institutional ecology, 'Translations' and boundary objects: Amateurs and professionals in Berkeley's Museum of Vertebrate Zoology, 1907–39. *Social Studies of Science, 19*(3), 387–420.

Storck, J., & Hill, P. A. (2000, Winter). Knowledge diffusion through strategic communities. *Sloan Management Review, 41*(2), 63–74.

Swan, W., Powell, J. A., Jackson, E., & Abbott, C. (2009). The UPBEAT approach in supporting academics to create "Real World" change. *The Proceedings of the International Research Symposium* (pp. 487–506). Salford, UK.

TICE (Tracking and Improving Community Engagement). (2010). A web based *Outreach Assessment tool* v17 n6 p391-395 originally designed for the University of Western Australia, by Jarvis K and held on University of Western Australia's Server.

Tijssen, R. J. W., & Van Wijk, E. (1999). In search of the European Paradox: An international comparison of Europe's scientific performance and knowledge flows in information and communications technologies research. *Research Policy, 28*, 519–543.

The ACBEE ENGAGEMENT MODEL. (2009). Underwood, J., Williams, A., & Thurairajah, N. (2009). Improving performance through HEI-industry engagements in the built environment. *Industry & Higher Education, 23*(1), 39–49.

Todtling, F., & Trippl, M. (2005). One size fits all? Towards a differentiated regional innovation policy approach. *Research Policy, 34*, 1203–1219.

Turville, L. S. (2007). *The race to the top*. London: HM Treasury.

Van de Ven, A. (2007). *Engaged scholarship*. Oxford: Oxford University Press.

Van Looy, B., Debackere, K., & Andries, P. (2003). Policies to stimulate regional innovation capabilities via university-industry collaboration: An analysis and an assessment. *R&D Management, 33*(2), 209–229.

Wessner, C. (2006). *Entrepreneurship and the innovation ecosystem, policy lessons from the United States*. New York: Springer.

Williams, L., Turner, N., & Jones, A. (2008). *Embedding universities in knowledge cities: An ideopolis and knowledge economy programme paper*. London: The Work Foundation.

Chapter 41
Relating Quality and Funding: The Romanian Case

Adrian Miroiu and Lazăr Vlasceanu

41.1 Introduction

In the past two decades, a growing number of countries implemented non-traditional, innovative solutions to the considerable shortcomings and challenges they faced in financing higher education (Salmi and Hauptman 2006). Governments have used funding schemes for higher education institutions (HEIs) to reach specific policy objectives. Promoting equity in higher education, increased autonomy and accountability of HEIs or increased quality of university programmes are arguably examples of such objectives. At the same time, a funding scheme may also attempt to offer the actors in higher education (HEIs, students or teaching staff) both positive and negative incentives in order to eventually curb their behaviour. These financial incentives may consist in general rules for funding universities, such as funding formulas or even more specific procedures. One may thus see certain relationships between higher education public funding and its outcomes.

The demand for tertiary education in most countries around the world grew to levels one could hardly imagine 30 or even 20 years ago. On the other hand, developing quality programmes and attempting to create top (or world-class) universities adds a new pressure on governments. However, in many countries the governments failed to provide public resources that are adequate to meet any demand. The disparity

A. Miroiu (✉)
Department of Political Science, National School of Political and Administrative Studies, Bucharest, Romania
e-mail: admiroiu@snspa.ro

L. Vlasceanu
Department of Sociology, University of Bucharest, Bucharest, Romania
e-mail: lvlasceanu@sas.unibuc.ro

A. Curaj et al. (eds.), *European Higher Education at the Crossroads:*
Between the Bologna Process and National Reforms,
DOI 10.1007/978-94-007-3937-6_41, © Springer Science+Business Media Dordrecht 2012

between available public resources and the growing demand for tertiary education prompted governments to develop a series of policies. The most frequent response has been to provide incentives for a more efficient use of the public funds, for example by increasing the university autonomy. Another response has been to extract more resources from stakeholders as a way of increasing cost sharing: introducing or raising tuition fees, seeking additional private resources, initiating various loan schemes for students etc. Some governmental actors decided to provide funding schemes consisting in the preferential allocation of funds to the universities which were regarded as offering high quality programmes.

The main hypothesis of this paper is that the funding mechanism generates a set of incentives, behavioural patterns and specific institutional processes (i.e. at university level) that are pivotal both for the understanding and the management of an education system. Given its importance, it is one of the key reform tools in higher education reform processes. We argue that many of the changes that may be identified in the behaviour of the public universities in different countries could be traced back to the incentives and constraints provided by the funding mechanism in use. We shall focus here only on one example, the Romanian case. This case may be of interest by considering a comparative analysis of funding mechanisms with respect to their consequences and the institutional dynamics they set in motion (e.g. the traditional and various types of formula-based allocations). The paper presents various elements of evidence in this respect.

We will focus on the relation between university quality and budgetary allocations. Are they related or need they be related? Is the policy of adjusting funding to the quality of the programmes and to the ranking of the universities defensible?

One important point, related to the Bologna Process, should be mentioned here. The Bologna Process has indeed provided the wider framework for the changes and configurations of higher education funding mechanisms. This framework has increased the opportunities for a more intense transnational exchange of information and policies as well as for specific cross-national comparative analysis. However, the Bologna framework as such has had little direct influence, if any, on national funding mechanisms. These have been mostly oriented towards the introduction of market-based instruments by paying attention to such specific issues like diversifying funding sources, formulas of budgetary allocations, accountability and maximisation of social return of public investment. Among the objectives and principles of the Bologna Process almost no reference was made to higher education public funding with the exception of such general recommendations like the need for an increased budgetary allocation to higher education, considered as a "public good". Higher education funding mechanisms seem to be mostly a domestic national affair, meant to increase competition both within and between systems and institutions. For this reason, we are primarily interested in highlighting those institutional configurations in which national higher education actors operate when confronted with strategic interactions related to funding and quality.

41.2 A Short History of Romanian Higher Education Funding

History does matter in most of the public affairs, and not only in this area. When adopting an institutional perspective of analysis (North 1990), the historical "path dependence" is very much at work. It is for this reason that we choose to refer shortly to the recent history of Romanian higher education funding.

Immediately after 1989, the Romanian higher education experienced huge changes. First, the structure of the university programmes was previously unbalanced: nearly 70% of the new places allocated for students by the government were in the field of Engineering while Social Sciences, Economics, Business or Medicine were severely undersupplied. Secondly, the public universities enrolled a very small number of students compared to the demand for higher education. The economy of queues and shortage, characteristic to Socialist societies, had as its counterpart in higher education a fierce competition among candidates for one of the few places in a university programme. Five to fifteen candidates for one place represented the normal state in the case of Medicine, Law, Humanities, Business or Economics programmes. From this perspective, the changes in the 1990s were drastic, but not surprising. With an economy in deep restructuring, the demand for Engineering fell down dramatically. Technical universities continued however to offer a large number of government-subsidised places, but often less than one candidate competed for one place. However, in absolute terms, the number of places offered by them did not decrease significantly, while in relative terms, in 1999 the proportion of students enrolled in technical programmes dropped to 36.5%. The number of state-subsidised places offered in the fields of Medicine, Social Sciences, including Economics and Business increased, but the lack of public resources prevented public universities from coping with the demand. As one can easily imagine, the newly established private higher education institutions succeeded in attracting a large number of students, most of them in these fields.

However, despite these changes, until 1999, public universities were funded according to principles more or less inherited from the Socialist period. Roughly, the mechanism could be described as follows: the largest part of the State funds was distributed according to the number of faculty and auxiliary staff positions. Other funds were distributed on predetermined destinations like utilities, investments, etc. The level of funding for each university was dependent upon historical funding and to a large extent the officials in the Ministry of Education had a discretionary control over it.

One of the most interesting institutional consequences of this incentive system was that not all teaching positions were filled; actually, the universities preserved a large number of them vacant. The reasons were complex, but all can be accounted of in a rational-actor framework: first the staff could be better paid, on a cumulative scheme, when a person occupied more than one position. Secondly, in case of budgetary cuts, universities dispensed with vacant positions, and avoided firing their employees. A third, and compelling, reason was that, since the university budget coming from the State budget was highly correlated with the number of staff positions, university officials tried to expand it. However, the Ministry of Finance limited the total number of positions in the higher education system; the interests of university officials to maximise their budget competed with the interests of the officials of the other universities, as well as with the interests of the officials in the central Ministries.[1]

A noteworthy institutional dynamics took place in the area of increasing the number of university positions allowed by the State authorities. One way to increase them was to propose a new study programme (The procedure was in fact complex: the university had to proceed to authorising the new programme, by presenting it to the National Council for Academic Evaluation and Accreditation[2]). Then the university asked for some new budgetary places for students to be enrolled in the new programme; it entailed the need to cover the courses, and this resulted in new teaching positions the Ministry was forced to accept. Second, universities argued that the existing programmes did not overlap significantly new courses and that similar courses and other teaching activities must be counted separately, in different teaching positions. For example, the same introductory course in Mathematics was taught for each and every specialisation in a technical university, but counted separately. Third, the pressure to make larger and larger the weekly number of courses and seminars a student was required to take was difficult to resist; and these larger numbers translated into new teaching positions, etc. The number of non-teaching positions expanded mostly when related to student services. Most governments in the 1990s tried to assure the support of the students' associations and therefore did not hesitate to accept their demands on the side of the universities.

Universities appealed to student flows criteria, but only in an instrumental sense, since larger flows resulted in more university positions. But the number of students enrolled could be increased in two ways: first, by getting more places the costs of which was supported from the State budget; and second, by offering new places for students who were willing to pay the tuition fees themselves. The competition for more students became very fierce. More important than that, a "public choice" type of pressure (Buchanan and Tullok 1999) was set into motion under the form of an intense lobbying and interest group action. On the one hand, public universities tried to prevent the private, newly established, universities from attracting too many competitive candidates. The instrument they used in this sense was to block them from being accredited and hence get a higher legal status. Two examples could offer a good illustration in this respect. First, for more than 4 years, Medicine programmes in private universities were all blocked from being even temporary authorised to enrol students. On the other hand, although many private universities satisfied all

---

[1] For analytical purposes the budgetary funds used to cover the personnel expenses can be conceptualised as a common-pool resource (Ostrom et al. 1994). The increase in the number of teaching and non-teaching positions resulted at the end of the 1990s in the 'overgrazing' of the budget. In many respects the introduction of the new, formula-based funding mechanism could be seen as a response to the coordination problems raised in this framework.

[2] In 2006 the National Council for Academic Evaluation and Accreditation was replaced by another institution: the Romanian Agency for Quality Assurance in Higher Education (ARACIS).

legal criteria, set as conditions for their accreditation process, the decision was postponed by the accreditation agency for more than 3 years (*i.e.* from 1998 to 2002). Conversely, private universities lobbied to block a Cabinet Ordinance according to which public universities could enrol students who paid their own fees. As a result, given that State-supported places in higher education were limited, a large number of higher education candidates could thus be directed towards private universities. As it happened, public universities were allowed to enrol fee paying students only beginning with 1998, roughly in the same period when the Parliament passed the law according to which the new funding mechanism was established.

In this institutional setting related to the distribution of both public and private financial resources to higher education, quality provision became not only a secondary matter. Its standards fell dramatically. Securing a higher number of students and, thus, more financial resources meant also diminishing quality standards. Discussions about "diploma mills" multiplied. It became clear that higher education funding mechanisms had unintentional effects related to a diminishing quality provision in most of the HEIs and study programmes.

41.3 A New Formula-Based Funding and Its Consequences

Starting with 1999, a new formula-based funding scheme has been enforced. It may be seen as a solution to two basic problems: (a) the pressure on the budget generated by a "common pool resource" over-usage logic, and (b) the self-impairing dynamics created by the lobby competition between public and private universities acting in a typical "public choice" logic.

Let us explain this. The funding mechanism is based on a few simple principles. The funds Romanian universities received from public sources are divided in two large categories: basic or core funding and complementary or additional funding (Dinca 2002). Complementary funding covers the subsidies for student accommodation, equipment, investment and general overhaul, and funds for academic research. The complementary funding can only be obtained on a competitive basis (except subsidies for student accommodation, which were mainly established by taking into account criteria like the number of students who lived in student residence halls). Basic funding is meant to cover all staff costs and material expenses (without general overhauls). This sum is allocated under a formula. The formula includes general, widely considered input criteria (Kaiser et al. 2001; Jongbloed 2001). The most important criterion is the number of students enrolled in different (Bachelor or Master) programmes. The Ministry of Education offers yearly a number of student fellowships for undergraduate and graduate studies. In the past decade, this number was settled to about 60,000 for new entrants in undergraduate programmes; given the Bologna process, the number of fellowships for students enrolled in Master programmes has increased to more than 30,000.

Besides the number of students enrolled, the main parameters taken into account by the formula are: (adjusted) cost coefficients by field of study and type of

Table 41.1 Funding coefficients for types of university programmes, 1999

Type of programme	Coefficient (1999) for personnel expenses	Coefficient (1999) for material expenses	Aggregated coefficients (1999) (material expenses: 20%)	Aggregated coefficients (2010) (material expenses: 20%)
Social-humanities	1.000	1.000	1.000	1.000
Experimental sciences (physics, chemistry)	1.472	2.000	1.578	1.650–1.900
Psychology	1.280	1.280	1.280	1.000
Applied mathematics	1.280	1.280	1.280	1.650
Economics and business	1.000	1.000	1.000	1.000
Engineering	1.472	2.000	1.578	1.750–1.900
Agriculture	1.643	1.643	1.643	1.750
Medicine	1.708	2.500	1.866	2.250
Sports	1.838	1.950	1.860	1.860
Music-arts	2.477	2.477	2.477	3.000–5.370
Theatre-film	5.374	5.374	5.374	5.370–7.500

Source: Miroiu and Dinca (2000, p. 52), also see Nica (2001) and CNFIS (2009)

programme, the lump sum (approved by the State budget law) that establishes the level of funds the Ministry of Education can allocate to all the universities for basic funding. In order to determine the amount of funds allocated to a university, the number of (State-supported) students enrolled is weighed according to the field and the level of the programme (Bachelor or Master). The root formula used to compute the funding of a public university is:

$$N_{se} = \Sigma_{i=1} \left(N_{fi} \cdot K_i \right)$$

where N_{se} is the number of weighted (or 'equivalent') students of the university, N_{fi} is the (average) number of (State-supported) students enrolled in a programme of type i, and K_i is the weighted coefficient corresponding to the programme i. The weighting coefficients took into account different levels of personnel costs and material costs (Miroiu and Dinca 2000; CNFIS 2009). Table 41.1 exemplifies these coefficients (when the ratio of material expenses is 20%). It is important to note that in more than one decade these coefficients have not changed significantly.

Besides these coefficients, the level of programme is also pivotal. Comparisons have appealed to the so-called equivalence coefficients. Taking a standard Bachelor programme as basic, i.e. with an equivalence coefficient 1.000, other types of programmes (e.g., Master or doctoral programmes or programmes in a language other than Romanian) were correspondingly weighted. Table 41.2 presents the main equivalence coefficients.

So, for example, a student enrolled in a standard social science Bachelor programme was translated into one equivalent student; a student enrolled in a standard social science Master programme was translated into two equivalent students. But a student enrolled in a Bachelor programme in Engineering offered in English was to

Table 41.2 Equivalence coefficients in the funding formula

Bachelor programmes	
Bachelor programme in Romanian	1.000
Bachelor programme in a foreign language	1.500
Bachelor programme in Hungarian (native language)	2.000
Bachelor programme in German (native language)	2.500
Bachelor programme in campuses abroad	2.500
Master programmes	
Master programme in Romanian	2.000
Master programme in a foreign language	3.000
Master programme in campuses abroad	3.000
Doctoral programmes	
Doctoral studies in engineering, agriculture, science and medicine	4.000
Doctoral studies in other fields	3.000

Source: CNFIS (2009)

be translated into, e.g., $1.750 \times 1.500 = 2.625$ equivalent students and a student enrolled in a Master programme in Engineering offered in English was to be translated into, e.g. $2.625 \times 3.000 = 7.875$ equivalent students.

The funds are directed towards universities on a block scheme. As a result, under the new funding mechanism, their autonomy increased. The State authorities lost their control over the number of teaching and non-teaching positions in universities. The 49 public universities got full control over the use of their facilities and over their investment policies. Since funding is based on a formula, allocations became more transparent. To ensure transparency and accountability, the formula is applied by a buffer organisation, the National Council for Higher Education Financing (CNFIS).[3]

The funding process proceeded as follows: first, the Ministry of Education allocated for each university a number of State-supported student places. The university was allowed to distribute these places among its study programmes. After receiving the university distribution, CNFIS computed: (i) the total number of equivalent students for each university; (ii) the total number of equivalent students at national level; and (iii) the value of a grant per equivalent student. Given the number of equivalent students for each university, the total amount of money for the so-called basic funding was easily computed.

This formula-based funding scheme provided quite simple incentives for university leaders. First, it allowed universities to autonomously use their budget. Universities could design and implement their own policies of institutional development.

---

[3] However, the State authorities maintained a powerful instrument to influence universities: the Ministry of Education strictly controls the student flows, in that it establishes the number of State-supported students in each field and for each university. This entails that the Ministry of Education retains the control on the size of university budgetary funding. It is important to add that for more than a decade, under all cabinets, there were no transparent criteria for establishing the number of State-supported students each university is allowed to enrol. In this respect, the discretionary power of Ministry officials was retained.

Secondly, universities developed strategies to reduce costs. They usually included: increasing the student/staff ratio by enrolling more students in the same classes; increasing the ratio of the vacant teaching positions (according to the Romanian legislation, the costs associated with the vacant positions are much lower); overuse of the teaching facilities; reducing the offer for other facilities offered to students (dormitories, student restaurants, sport facilities etc.), changing curricula by reducing the weekly number of courses, laboratories and seminars required for students and offering the same courses to students enrolled in different study programmes; reducing the number of programmes for which the costs were very large; enrolling much more students who pay the fees themselves.[4] Let us underline that this funding mechanism has been applied under the conditions of shrinking public allocations to higher education.

In the first years after the new funding formula was enforced, the incentives to minimise costs resulted in an increased capacity of the State universities to cope with the chronic lack of financial resources. The changes were even more beneficial, given that the level of funding from the State budget was critically low. Some examples may be useful. First, under the historical funding mechanism, the academic curriculum became excessively loaded. The reason was that it translated in a more teaching and non-teaching positions which had to be financed from the budget. At a time when the ratio students-staff was 15–18 students to one teacher in many European countries, in the Romanian universities the ratio was about 5 students to one teaching position. Although dysfunctional when judged according to academic standards, these transformations represented, however, the rational response of the universities to the historical funding framework. With the new funding scheme, cost rationalisation became one of the driving policies of the universities. The existing data confirm this dynamics. The number of students per teaching position was in 1998 as low as 4.85. In 2001, 2 years after the new funding mechanism was implemented, the total number of teaching positions in Romanian public universities was 44,949, while the total number of students was 254,675 (ratio student/teaching position: 5.66). In 2004 the number of teaching positions reached a peak of 45,201, but in 2007 it fell to 42,299 and in 2010 it was 43,029. But, in this period, the number of students increased very much. Not taking into account the students in Master and doctoral programmes, the number of students enrolled in Bachelor programmes increased from 485,371 in 2004 to 515,593 in 2007, while in 2010 it decreased to 447,660. So, the ratio students in Bachelor programmes/teaching staff climbed to 10.73 in 2004, 12.18 in 2007 and then went down to 10.40 in 2010.[5]

---

[4] The Academy of Economic Studies in Bucharest offers a stark example. In 1997 it enrolled a number of about 21,500 State-supported students. However, as soon as the university was in a position to enrol students who paid their fees, the number of State-supported students decreased. In 1999, their number was less than 16,000, while the number of students who paid their tuition fees reached more than 5,800. Two years later the number of self-paying students increased to nearly 15,500.

[5] There are more reasons why the number of students enrolled in bachelor programmes decreased. First, we have demographic trends; secondly, the Bologna system reduced the length of bachelor programmes (usually with about two semesters). But in this period the number of students enrolled in master programmes increased very much.

Fig. 41.1 The number of specialisations offered by the West University of Timisoara

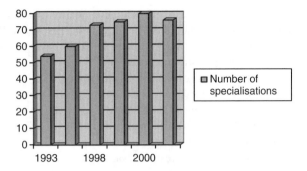

Secondly, the historical funding mechanisms provided the universities with an incentive to offer a larger and larger number of programmes. The list of academic specialities in the long – and short-term educational offer extended dramatically. In Romania there are 49 public universities (this number does not include military and similar HEIs), where approximately 570 specialities are being studied. In just 4 years (1994–1998), the National Council for Academic Evaluation and Accreditation temporarily authorised or fully accredited these specialities, on request. In other cases, academic subjects such as Mechanical Engineering, Energy or Chemical Engineering have been further divided into tens of specialisations across 5 years of study with apparently different curricula, when it was obvious that (at least in the first 2 or 3 years) the teaching was almost identical. The diversification of academic specialities at the undergraduate level has been generated to a great extent by the historical funding, in conjunction to the deans and department chairs' need to fulfil personal or group projects, rather than by a needs analysis of the labour market or by a mere reaction to the labour market. This is why the number of narrow, strictly disciplinary specialisations has been growing at a spectacular rate. One expects that in a formula-based funding mechanism the strategic option should be moving towards broader specialisations for the initial academic training, so that graduates could access, through continuing education, various academic modules and thus this problem could be functionally solved. An example is instructive. The West University of Timisoara is a medium-sized university. It enrolled a number of 9,351 students in 1999, and 11,988 in 2001. But the number of teaching positions decreased from 2,640 in 1999 to 2,054 in 2001. Figure 41.1 shows how the number of academic specialisations offered evolved from 1993 to 2001. One can see that 2001 was the first year when some specialisations were not offered anymore, although they were accredited; hence the decision not to enrol students in those programmes belonged to the university itself.

The formula-based funding formula provided important incentives to the State universities to reduce costs. Not surprisingly, the quality of the educational programmes suffered most. Moreover, there were no *prima facie* incentives to contravene this propensity. However, starting with 2003, the Ministry of Education and CNFIS have introduced a mechanism to urge universities to take quality into account. The idea was to use so-called quality indicators which would account for the allocation of a part of the funding. In the first years, 10% of the budget allocated according to the formula was distributed by taking these indicators into account, and then the proportion reached 30%. The better a university satisfies the quality indicators, the larger the sum of funds it received.

Quality indicators concerned most domains of university activity: human resources (accounting for 8.5% of the funding[6]); research (accounting for 9% of the funding); facilities (3.5%); university management (9%). Each group of indicators included at least two, and sometimes one indicator had an extremely complex structure. To give an example, university research was evaluated by means of three indicators:

IC6: quality of research
IC7: the proportion of Master and doctoral students in the total number of students
IC8: the proportion of funding from research in the total university budget.

But IC6 is a very complex indicator (CNFIS 2008). It included ten simpler indicators, grouped in five categories.[7]

Now, it is well-known that a larger number of criteria used to measure a variable result in extremely flat results. Universities could rank well on some dimension, but worse on another. For example, the fact that more students pay the tuition fees themselves may induce a higher proportion of funding attracted from other sources than the State budget, but would also generate a higher ratio student-teaching staff. If both indicators are taken into account, they would mutually eliminate influences. The result is that although 30% of the funding was allocated according to quality indicators, no university succeeded in scoring more or less than 11.6 than the ground zero, with most universities receiving the same funding as if no quality indicators were used. Table 41.3 documents this. So the incentives were not very strong to contravene the tendencies we already mentioned. Universities could well balance the level of fulfilling the quality indicators in order to maximise their benefits. For example, increasing the number of students enrolled in distance learning programmes remained very cost-efficient. All public universities acted in this way, as Table 41.3 shows.

41.4   On Institutional Homogeneity and Isomorphism

Funding schemes were not then successful in increasing the quality of Romanian higher education. They did not discriminate much on the basis of quality or performance indicators, and instead promoted an equalitarian funding. The incentives to increase quality and to develop specific strategies were ineffective.

---

[6] We refer to the 2010 allocations (CNFIS 2009).

[7] University management was measured by taking into account 14 simpler indicators.

Table 41.3 Budgetary allocations to HEIs with and without quality indicators included in the formula

	Budgetary allocation without the influence of the qualitative indicators	Budgetary allocation according to quality indicators			The influence of the quality indicators (no influence = 30%)
		Total	Budgetary allocation given the number of equivalent students (70%)	Budgetary allocation weighted by quality indicators (30%)	
University Politehnica Bucuresti	165,027,913	184,269,492	115,519,539	68,749,953	41.66%
University "Babes – Bolyai" Cluj	123,647,465	124,786,657	86,553,226	38,233,431	30.92%
University "Al. I. Cuza" Iasi	87,356,878	86,838,754	61,149,815	25,688,939	29.41%
University of Bucuresti	107,667,721	108,635,809	75,367,405	33,268,404	30.90%
University "Constantin Brancusi" Târgu Jiu	8,804,737	7,911,039	6,163,316	1,747,723	19.85%
University Politehnica Timisoara	75,944,654	77,679,590	53,161,258	24,518,332	32.28%
University "Eftimie Murgu" Resita	8,280,336	7,449,443	5,796,235	1,653,208	19.97%
University "Lucian Blaga" Sibiu	52,806,832	49,981,614	36,964,782	13,016,832	24.65%
University of Arts in Bucuresti	13,453,015	12,032,425	9,417,111	2,615,314	19.44%

Our argument is that the egalitarian allocations brought about by these funding schemes had quite different consequences. Not only did they not help increase quality of the study programmes offered and the differentiation in the mission and activities of the Romanian universities, but acted in a quite contrary direction. This is a typical case of unintended consequences of a funding mechanism which rationally intended to provide incentives for enhancing HEIs autonomy and accountability.

One striking characteristics of the Romanian higher education system is its homogeneity, or at least the existence of a powerful process of weakening the differences between State and public universities, between old and new ones, between large and small universities, between comprehensive and highly specialised universities. Their mission (as codified in the university Charts) is quasi-identical, their organisational structures, types of study programmes and their organisation, as well as content, procedures and practices related to teaching and research, the internal regulations are all similar (if not simply copied from one another) and at most incrementally different.[8]

For institutionalist scholars, the process which resulted in these consequences should be no surprise. As DiMaggio and Powell (1991) argue, in highly structured organisational fields like higher education, incentives exist to produce homogeneity. According to DiMaggio and Powell (1991), isomorphic forces are powerful in the field of higher education mainly due to three characteristics. First, its objectives (such as getting knowledge or producing educated graduates) are difficult to measure. Secondly, the technology used (teaching activities) is largely unclear. And third, the organisational actors are extremely professionalised.

The two authors identify three mechanisms through which institutional organisational change occurs: mimetic, normative, and coercive. First, mimetic mechanisms express a propensity of some universities characterised by a lack of legitimacy to imitate universities perceived as traditional and highly performing. In Romania, the establishment of new universities in the past decade, as well as the appearance of private universities provided a strong impetus in this direction. Institutional mimetism consisted in adapting the organisational structure to existing traditional patterns, in developing new study programmes similar to those existing in prestigious universities, etc. The result is the increase of legitimacy on the part of the new (and private) universities, although not necessarily correlated with an effective better quality.

Normative mechanisms had an important role: in the past decades, the impact of the norms defined at national level with regard to the access to faculty positions was quite extensive. The process of professionalization of the persons who populate both old and new universities resulted in their tendency to be more and more similar in the educational activities carried on in the universities employing them, as well as in the type of research they performed. The quality assurance legislation also contributed to

---

[8] The process of institutional isomorphism also characterizes other educational systems (Birnbaum 1983; Morphew 2009). A similar process can be met when we move across national boundaries: as argued in Dobbins and Knill (2009), the Bologna process brings about institutional isomorphism across European higher education systems.

this process. The Romanian Quality Assurance Agency for Higher Education (ARACIS) provided evaluations for about 4,000 study programmes (Bachelor and Master) by appealing to more than 700 evaluators. Their joint activities impacted the way in which standards of quality assurance are defined and applied in Romanian universities, as well as the routines and practices developed in them.

However, the most important mechanisms that led to institutional isomorphism were the coercive ones. Regulations issued by the State authorities played a core role. Laws, Cabinet decisions, decisions of the Ministers of Education brought about stricter requirements on the organisation and structure of universities, on the types of study programmes offered, on the human resources policies. The financial incentives provided by CNFIS stimulated the Romanian universities to adopt quite similar policies and structures. The example of the quality indicators, which did account for 30% of the core financing of the State universities, is relevant: if they wish to fulfil these indicators, the best strategy for State universities is to become similar. In our view, the main reason why the universities try to satisfy the quality indicators is not that they get larger funds in this way; for, as we argued above, the differences resulting by taking into account the quality indicators are in general less than 10%. But, by better satisfying the performance indicators, universities enjoy a higher legitimacy and a better external perception of the quality of their activities. This expectation determined universities to be increasingly organised around rituals of conformity.

To conclude, the incentives provided by regulations on quality assurance and funding have largely contributed to enforcing a process of homogenisation of the Romanian higher education system. While this process contributed to an increased conformity with general regulations and some good practices, to a higher legitimacy of many, especially new, universities, it has also had a negative side. The race for conformity is not necessarily a move towards greater efficiency and higher and higher quality standards. On the contrary, in an institutional framework, the propensity to align to a median position is accompanied by the downwards shift of this position. On a medium term, homogenisation is strongly correlated with lower quality standards. The reason is simple: homogenisation, as well as the legitimacy it displays, is a public good. Therefore, if they attain a certain level, organisational actors have strong incentives to free-ride. And free-riding brings about worse result for all the actors involved (see also Miroiu and Andreescu, 2010).

41.5   Looking Ahead for a New Funding Mechanism

A growing concern in the academic world about the decreasing quality performance of the Romanian universities brought about fierce debates for nearly a decade. Something had to be done – but no way out was reached for quite a while. Both an adequate conceptual picture of the state of affairs and feasible policy recommendations were missing. However, by the end of 2009 a comprehensive report (currently known as the "Miclea Report") on the state of Romanian education and research was made public and widely and controversially debated. In this context, a new law on education was enforced at the beginning of 2011.[9] The new law sets the objective to classify all universities, both State and private, in three classes based on their quality in research, teaching, relations with environment and institutional capacity. The legally stated classes are: universities focused on teaching, universities focused on teaching and research, and research intensive universities.

The classification is not intended to provide a university ranking, but rather to support them in defining different missions and developing differentiation strategies. The law clearly states that universities in all classes must be supported according to the way in which they succeed in achieving performance with respect to their stated objectives. In the summer of 2011 the Ministry of Education published the first, if provisional, classification. A number of 12 universities were included in the class of research intensive universities, and 15 in the class of universities focused on teaching and research (www.edu.ro). The classification was completed by a ranking of all study programmes in five hierarchical categories.

The two processes had an immediate consequence: the magnitude of the resources distributed by the Ministry of Education to the public universities faced a sudden, and sometimes dramatic, change.[10] Thus, the universities which were classified as research intensive received more grants for students enrolled in Master programmes (approx. 20% more), and more grants for doctoral students; while the teaching and research universities roughly retained the same number of grants for students enrolled in Master programmes, they received smaller numbers of grants for doctoral students and only for those programmes that were highly ranked. But the teaching-focused universities received a drastically diminished number of grants for doctoral and Master students. Since the formula-based funding scheme is still in place, this fact immediately translates into much smaller budgetary allocations for the core basic financing.

CNFIS is currently preparing a new funding scheme to be in use from the financial year 2012. It assumes two driving principles. First, in line with university classification, funding aims at supporting their differentiation. Secondly, in line with the programme ranking, funding would take into account the classification of the universities and the ranking of their study programmes.

As for the first aim, the general view on differentiation is that it would be: (1) multi-dimensional; (2) inclusive; (3) non-hierarchical; (4) flexible, and (5) non-compulsory (also see Van Vught 2007). Multidimensionality is non-reductionist. For example, it should not favour just one aspect of university performance (e.g. research or ability to attract funding). Inclusiveness implies that it should apply to all Romanian universities, regardless of their being public or private. The non-hierarchical character is required in order to attract the positive action of the universities: for any differentiation that ends with top-positioned and bottom-positioned

---

[9] http://www.edu.ro/index.php/base/frontpage

[10] It is worth noting that in the past decade the formula-based funding mechanism was implemented in such a way so that changes in the size of allocations from the state budget were always incremental.

universities creates frustrations and perverse actions to undermine the criteria proposed and the effects of the resulting hierarchy. Non-compulsory differentiation means that the universities themselves have the crucial role in defining their position as members of a cluster or another; and flexibility entails that differentiation is not static, but dynamic. This immediately entails that there is not a single, universal, policy proposal. Differentiation can be induced by using a large number of types of incentives. A standard example in this regard is provided by the Higher Education Funding Council for England. Among the incentives the Council appealed to we may note: institutional flexibility in the use of block grant funding, with freedom to determine resource allocation internally; dual support for research, enabling universities to plan their own research profiles; institutions freedom in determining the form of engagements with businesses and community; student premiums, which recognise differing costs between levels and modes of study; specialist institution premiums, especially for small and mono-subject institutions; special funding incentives for particular purposes; supporting institutions in developing their own missions and strategies, by taking into account performance indicators which recognise the variety of institutional types and allow benchmark comparisons to be made, etc. (HEFCE 2000; see also Taylor 2003).

How would funding take into account the ranking of the study programmes? First, the number of grants allocated to study programmes should not be left at the arbitrary decision of the ministerial bureaucracy, but computed according to: (i) the domain in which it is offered (is it a priority for the government public policies of the time?); (ii) the capacity of the universities to enrol a number of students without decreasing the quality of the programme, and finally (iii) the way that study programme is ranked. However, as we already mentioned, quality needs to be regarded in a non-reductionist way: the number of grants allocated to a university would vary according to its capacity to reach its mission and objectives.

Secondly, the new law requires that a sum representing at least 30% of the core funding be allocated to the universities on the basis of quality. Quality indicators are then expected to be so constructed that they would differentiate HEIs much more than they did before. The idea is that this policy would determine them to be much more careful in developing new programmes, and on the other hand, direct resources to the higher quality programmes and departments in research and/or teaching. Third, a new so-called funding for institutional development would be established. In our view, this new type of funding may be the vehicle to be used by the Ministry of Education, and CNFIS, to propose and enforce policies of institutional change. One example may be envisaged: one policy objective of the authorities may be that of reducing the number of universities. In Romania there are 49 State universities (to which we can add 7 military universities), and more than 60 private universities. Among the State universities, some have a few hundreds or thousands students. The Ministry repeatedly expressed its view that university merging would contribute to more efficiency in the use of public resources, as well as to more competitive universities in the present European and globalisation context. Funding incentives are, in our view, extremely appropriate: if merging, universities would receive funds to strengthen their managerial, research, and/or teaching capacity.

How would the actors (universities, staff, and students) respond to this new set of (different) funding incentives? This is a question for the future. In the meantime, we are looking for a way to better specify and then implement the new funding mechanisms.

41.6   Conclusion

It is a truism to say that funding mechanisms hold a key position in any explanation of the higher education system and organisational developments. However, we are far from fully understanding the institutional matrix at work. By looking more closely, from an institutionalism perspective, at the workings of higher education funding mechanisms in Romania, we intended to highlight how these mechanisms generated certain consequences in areas like student flows, staff recruitment and promotion, quality assurance and organisational structures.

Funding mechanisms are historically "path dependent" in their functioning. Their generating consequences are also dependent on the contextual institutional matrix existing at both system and organisational levels. For this reason, whatever purposive actions and objectives might have been designed in a funding mechanism, many unintended consequences are induced by its very contextual and institutional context. Some of these consequences may prove to be quite detrimental at both system and HEIs levels, while others are associated with quality. In order to prevent some negative unintended consequences of the existing funding mechanisms, a new policy of higher education public funding should be periodically envisaged while also anticipating and monitoring its intended and unintended consequences. This is particularly important when considering the growing diversification of higher education provision on public/private axis, but also the changing ties among the polity, economy and civil society, the institutional embeddedness of academic markets coupled with an increased demand for higher education qualifications and a higher pressure for public accountability. Organisational changes are thus viewed as interest-based actions constructed in the context of specific institutional and historical parameters, but also with regard to the wider system level parameters.

Government regulations targeting the institutionalisation of new funding and accountability schemes have both intended and unintended consequences on the "inner" organisational structures of HEIs and also on the ways the higher education system functions as a whole. Coupling the endogenous and exogenous institutions at work (Meyer and Rowan 2006) also calls for an analysis of the issues of power in the process of institutional change in higher education.

References

Birnbaum, R. (1983). *Maintaining institutional diversity*. San Francisco: Jossey-Bass.
Buchanan, J.M., & Gordon, T. (1999). The Calculus of Consent: Logical Foundations of Constitutional Democracy, Indianapolis, IN: Liberty Fund, Inc., (1958).

CNFIS. (2008). *Analiza evoluției indicatorului de calitate IC6 privind "nivelul performanțelor în cercetarea științifică din universități" și influența acestuia în repartizarea alocațiilor bugetare destinate finanțării de bază.* http://www.cnfis.ro/documente/011508-analizaIC6-draft.pdf

CNFIS. (2009). *Metodologia de repartizare pe instituții de învățământ superior a alocațiilor bugetare pentru finanțarea de bază în anul 2010.* At http://www.cnfis.ro/fb2010/ MetodologieFB2010.pdf

DiMaggio, P. J., & Powell, W. W. (1991). The iron cage revisited: Institutional isomorphism and collective rationality. In W. W. Powell & P. J. DiMaggio (Eds.), *The new institutionalism in organizational analysis.* Chicago: The University of Chicago Press.

Dinca, G. (2002). *Financial management and institutional relationship with civil society.* Bucharest: UNESCO-CEPES.

Dobbins, M., & Knill, C. (2009). Higher education policies in Central and Eastern Europe: Convergence toward a common model? *Governance: An International Journal of Policy, Administration, and Institutions, 22*(3), 397–430.

HEFCE. (2000). Diversity in higher education: HEFCE policy statement, HEFCE Publications 2000: 00/33.

Jongbloed, B.W.A., & J.J. Vossensteyn (2001). Keeping up Performances: an international survey of performance based funding in higher education, In: *Journal of Higher Education Policy and Management, 23*(2), 127–145.

Kaiser, F., Vossensteyn, H., & Koelman, J. (2001). *Public funding of higher education. A comparative study of funding mechanisms in ten countries.* Enschede: Center for Higher Education Policy Studies.

Meyer, H.-D., & Rowan, B. (Eds.). (2006). *The new institutionalism in education.* Albany: State University of New York.

Miroiu, A., & Dinca, G. (2000). *The policy of higher education funding in Romania.* Bucharest: Paideia Publishing House.

Miroiu, A., & Andreescu, L. (2010). Goals and Instruments of Diversification in Higher Education, *Quality Assurance Review, 2*(2), 89–101.

Morphew, C. C. (2009). Conceptualizing change in the institutional diversity of U.S. colleges and universities. *The Journal of Higher Education, 80*(3), 243–269.

Nica, P. (2001, June 11–13). *The current status and problems related to design and use of system – Level indicators for higher education: Romanian perspectives* (Invited Paper). Hiroshima: Higher Education Management Roundtable.

North, D. C. (1990). *Institutions, institutional change, and economic performance.* New York: Cambridge University Press.

Ostrom, E., Gardner, R., & Walker, J. (1994). *Rules, games, & common-pool resources.* Ann Arbor: The University of Michigan Press.

Salmi, J., & Hauptman, A. M. (2006). *Innovations in tertiary education financing: A comparative evaluation of allocation mechanisms* (Education Working Papers Series, #4). Washington, DC: World Bank.

Taylor, J. (2003). Institutional diversity in UK higher education: Policy and outcomes since the end of the binary divide. *Higher Education Quarterly, 57*(3), 266–293.

Van Vught, F. (2007). *Diversity and differentiation in higher education systems. Challenges for the knowledge society.* www.uhr.no/documents/Fran_van_Vught_text.pdf

Part VII
Diversification of Higher Education Institutions Missions as a Response to Global Competition

Chapter 42
Refocusing the Debate on Diversity in Higher Education

Sybille Reichert

42.1 Introduction

Responding to the growing demands of knowledge societies, higher education institutions are expected to fulfil an expanding range of roles and tasks well beyond the traditional functions of teaching and research. Higher education institutions are supposed to adapt their offer so as to allow an increasing proportion of an age cohort to access higher education and to cater also to those that return to higher education from the professional world to update their knowledge and broaden their range of competences. They are supposed to contribute to business innovation and knowledge transfer by providing relevant graduate competences and research collaboration. They are supposed to conduct research that may feed into regional and national core sectors as well into an increasingly fierce international competition. And, last not least, they are supposed to raise interest and understanding among citizens for the opportunities, implications and challenges posed by new global developments. In general, higher education activities should reflect regional anchoring and commitment, as well as international orientation and market prowess. In view of stagnating higher education budgets, many higher education representatives observe that no institution can possibly do justice to such a wide array of demands. Indeed, to avoid 'mission stretch' (Scott 2007), spreading institutional efforts too thinly over too wide a gamut of activities, the institutional leaders and policy makers are increasingly pushing for a diversity of institutional profiles which would allow for more institutional coherence and efficiency. Under the heading of 'institutional diversity', the need for

S. Reichert (✉)
Reichert Consulting: Strategy and Policy Development for Higher
Education, Zürich & Bamberg, Schützenstr.54, 96047 Bamberg, Germany
e-mail: sybille@reichertconsulting.ch

A. Curaj et al. (eds.), *European Higher Education at the Crossroads:*
Between the Bologna Process and National Reforms,
DOI 10.1007/978-94-007-3937-6_42, © Springer Science+Business Media Dordrecht 2012

diverse profiling of higher education institutions has become a new focus of national and European policy debates.[1] 'Diversity' in this context is synonymous to 'differentiation' and would be discussed under the latter heading in an American higher education discourse where diversity is reserved for the composition of an institution's student body or staff with respect to its ethnic, religious or gender variety.

Higher education institutions (HEI) find themselves caught in a web of contradictory forces and conflicting calls from academics, students and stakeholder groups. On the one hand, they are to live up to the challenge of international competition, where narrowly measured institutional reputation has become a key asset for attracting students and researchers. On the other, they are to respond to the wide range of expectations of their regional and national knowledge societies. Such conflicts and ambivalent institutional choices are also reflected in the conflicting approaches to institutional diversity at macro-level, where policy makers, regulators and funding agencies choose different ways of promoting a particular range of tasks to be fulfilled by HEIs, sometimes targeting some types of institutions more than other, in other cases addressing them indiscriminately. To understand the different national approaches to institutional diversity, and as an introduction to the theme of institutional diversification in this volume, the following article reviews some key concepts and normative pre-conceptions of the European debates on institutional diversity, analyses values attached to different dimensions of institutional diversity in a range of European countries (Sect. 42.2) and explores the forces which influence institutional behaviour (Sect. 42.3). Finally, some key distinctions, which have structured research and policy discussions of institutional diversity, will be re-evaluated.

The analysis is based on a recent comparative study conducted by the author for EUA (Reichert 2009, called the EUA diversity study henceforth) which explored the values, conditions and methods with which higher education systems and institutions in England, France, Norway, Slovakia, and Switzerland promote or undermine institutional diversity. In competing for limited resources with other institutions, and in responding to their key stakeholders and to their own norms and values, institutions (or units within them) prioritise those dimensions that they feel will most easily provide access to resources and other rewards. Quite often, such institutional choices may increase homogeneity rather than diversity, even in those countries where explicit diversity policies and instruments exist. The study showed how such choices are brought about by the array of conflicting reward structures at system and institutional levels. Unlike most previous literature on institutional diversity or diversification, which often take the term as a positive value that any higher education system should pursue, such value judgements become the object of inquiry in

---

[1] In an American higher education policy or research context, similar discussions would be termed institutional differentiation instead, while institutional diversity would be associated with staff or student profile. In contrast, there does not seem to be much of a national debate or widespread concern regarding institutional differentiation, given the highly diverse higher education landscape and funding sources.

the study, revealing interesting divergences within systems and institutions. The study also differs from previous literature on institutional diversity in taking a broad view of a whole range of aspects of diversity, rather than just focusing on one aspect of institutional diversity and tracing changes over time. Values, policies and implementation measures are compared at system and institutional levels, with special focus on tensions and inconsistencies in the approaches to institutional diversity, in particular between explicit policies and funding instruments. The data sources of the study comprised an online survey of institutions of all types (from research-intensive internationally visible universities to regionally oriented, more purely professionally oriented higher education institutions) in the five countries (with return rates ranging from 33% to 70% of the public higher education sectors) as well as in-depth interviews with higher education representatives with different functions at national and institutional levels, including institutional leaders, academic staff, presidents and general secretaries of rectors conferences, directors of quality assurance agencies, funding authorities and research councils.

42.2   Diversity Concepts and Values

42.2.1   Dimensions of Diversity

To put the current European higher education policy debates into perspective, it should be noted that the term 'institutional diversity' or 'diversification' is most often used rather restrictively, referring, first, only to external diversity, i.e. the divergent profiles of higher education institutions, rather than the diversity which institutions have to address within their institutional boundaries (internal diversity). Second, European diversity discussions most often refer to diversity of missions, which is understood to signify the varying institutional emphases on particular types of higher education activity, such as research, teaching, innovation or continuing education. Curiously, other possible dimensions of mission and institutional identity are not discussed under the heading of mission diversity or mission stretch.

Currently, the most prominent preoccupation with mission diversity concerns the intensity and form of research engagement as criteria for institutional differentiation. This concern has gained urgency in recent years with the rise of international rankings since the latter focus primarily on the measurable research activities which are registered in internationally accepted data sources (Hazelkorn 2008; Rauhvargers 2011). The mono-dimensionality of this research orientation has given rise to intense discussions, but has not yet led to more differentiated approaches to mission diversity (see also Chaps. 19 and 43 by Hazelkorn). There is a growing number of institutions, however, which define their missions well beyond the rhetoric of research intensity even though they would describe themselves as research-intensive and teaching, e.g. highlighting their teaching or curricular approaches, such as Maastricht University in the Netherlands or Jacobs University or Leuphana University in Germany. Moreover, the self-confidence of institutions which see themselves as research-oriented in alternative ways, e.g. more responsive to regional needs and business innovation concerns, is on the rise in some national contexts where sufficient symbolic and financial incentives have been set, as, for example, in Finland or the Swiss Fachhochschul sector. The transparency instruments such as the U-map and its relatives in Norway and Estonia (see Chap. 45 by Kaiser and colleagues and Chap. 46 by Skodvin) have been designed to reveal the diversity of institutions also in different functional respects in order to ensure that the institutional engagement in functions that have not gained sufficient attention in public or policy debates is receiving a new prominent data-based recognition. The hope is that they would also serve as a basis on which more differentiated financial incentives could be designed so as to promote more diverse forms of excellence orientation.

Another differentiating dimension that has receded into the background in the last two decades consists in institutions' regional orientation. This dimension of institutional diversity was a prominent concern in the wave of institutional expansion in the 1970s and 1980s all over Europe. After the fall of the Iron Curtain, the expansion of higher education systems in Eastern Europe has also valued regional distribution as a key criterion for institutional diversification, as documented in the Slovak case study of the EUA study, as well as in the Slovak research system evaluation of 2008. More recently, the regional role of higher education institutions and the concurrent need for diversification has been highlighted in a major OECD study (OECD 2007) as well as in the EUA study on knowledge regions (Reichert 2006). With the shift of attention to internationally visible research as a politically wanted criterion for institutional differentiation, regional distribution seemed to have receded from policy attention. Political attention is focused on critical mass and concentration of resources rather than on regional distribution. However, recently, an interesting new development can be observed, where regional cooperation between HEI and other research institutes, enterprises, NGOs or other public interest organisations is increasingly highlighted as a comparative advantage in research funding selection criteria for project grants. Likewise, the political actors voice concerns regarding an increasingly perceived bias toward internationally oriented fundamental research to the detriment of national and regional educational and innovation aims, e.g. the German Science Council (Wissenschaftsrat 2011) in its recent recommendations on institutional differentiation.

Other dimensions of diversity could concern the composition of academic and administrative staff or of the student body. This is the key concern with diversity in the US, resulting in diversity offices and diversity management. In the comparison of the five European countries of the EUA study, this dimension of diversity was shown to have only played a significant role among policy makers and institutional leaders in England. Likewise, student selection is a criterion of differentiation that plays a large role in some countries, such as the US and England, while it is currently of only minor importance as a differentiating feature among institutions in others, such Norway, Switzerland or Germany. Interestingly, in these systems where secondary school diplomas give theoretically widespread free access and even the right of access to higher education institutions, institutional methods of selecting students are also on the rise wherever they are legally possible, e.g. at the level of graduate education or for certain subjects that are in high demand. Nevertheless, given the internal differentiation of institutions in these systems, the degree of selectivity with which students are admitted is still not regarded as one of the primary characteristics of institutions as it would be in the US, where College guides or rankings group institutions according to this criterion.

Last not least, institutions could be and often are differentiated on the basis of perceived quality differences with respect to overall research or teaching performance. These judgements are sometimes based on national evaluations, such as the Research Assessment Exercise and National Student Survey in England or the ARRA reports in Slovakia, but are also often based on partial or reputational data, as is the case in some rankings. While partly corroborated through data on some aspects of institutional performance, such summative judgements are often based on subjective perceptions and reputation. Some rankings, such as US News and World Report and Times Higher Education Supplement Ranking use reputation explicitly as a criterion of ranking institutions, ignoring the tautological error thus committed (US News &World Report) or implicitly through their peer review scores (former Times Higher Education Supplement Ranking) where 'experts' in a particular field are asked to pass judgements on institutions as a whole, i.e. on performance well beyond their field of expertise, thus having to refer to their own subjective impressions and familiar institutional reputations (Rauhvargers 2011). With the various excellence initiatives in continental Europe, quality or institutional performance differentiation is also gaining ground in national funding schemes (Table 42.1).

42.2.2   Diversity Values

It is not only the quality dimension of institutional diversity that implies value judgements. The varying prominence of a particular dimension in policy attention and funding schemes reflects that all dimensions are subject to culturally and historically bound value judgements.

From the beginnings of a diversity discussion in higher education, the term 'diversity' has been valued positively. It was associated with adaptive behaviour toward environmental conditions, comparable to the dynamics of biological populations, which is often used as a basic analogy for the investigation of diversity in higher education (Birnbaum 1983; Huisman 1995). Using the analogy of adaptive behaviour of populations, Birnbaum provides a first list of arguments in favour of diversity that many later studies have adopted and built upon. According to Birnbaum, institutional diversity within a higher education system is a normative value since it allows it to:

1. meet students' needs
2. provide opportunities for social mobility
3. meet the needs of different labour markets (with an increasing variety of specialisations)

Table 42.1 Dimensions of diversity

Institutional size	Usually described in terms of student numbers, also number of academic staff and support staff. Budget volume or third party funding is also sometimes used to differentiate institutional volume
Subject profile	From comprehensive universities, covering all subject groups, to universities with only groups of subjects (e.g. technical universities) or specialised, single subject higher education institutions (e.g. management schools)
Emphases on types of activity	Conducting curiosity-driven research, identifying new problems and challenges
	Conducting application-driven research, in collaboration with external partners
	Contributing to social and economic innovation and addressing societal challenges
	Teaching the next generation, forming subject-specific and transferable competences to succeed in a wide variety of working lives and in different biographical phases
	Continuing education and professional development, updating of knowledge and skills
	Educating citizens and providing informed discussion platforms for citizens on issues of public concern
Teaching approaches and methodologies	Variety of teaching methodologies from traditional lectures to interactive incl. project-based learning, student-centred learning
	Distance and blended learning
Student clienteles	Different student profiles (school leavers, mature students, students of different ethnic, national and social backgrounds, professional part-time learners, adult education for citizens)
Student selectiveness	From highly selective to non-selective in student admissions. Used as an institutional differentiating criteria in the US and England
Regional distribution	Distribution of higher education institutions across the national system, as motors of regional development, incl. responsiveness to regionally relevant sectors
Target communities/ stakeholder orientation	Orientation toward values and interests of different target communities, e.g. academic disciplinary communities, professional communities, industry, business and public service, civil society, alumni and student community, regionally, nationally or globally
Reputation/quality standards	Implicit or explicit judgements of the overall quality of research and teaching of an institution as conveyed in summary rankings, implying a stratified system, as, for example, in the English RAE and National Student Survey in England, or the CHE Excellence Ranking in Germany

4. serve the political needs of interest groups
5. combine elite and mass higher education (cf. also Trow 1979)
6. increase the level of higher education institutions' effectiveness
7. offer opportunities for experimenting with innovation in a few institutions, thus limiting the high risks connected to the failure of such an experiment

Most studies and policy approaches to institutional diversity in higher education have espoused this positive value attached to diversity and have linked it to the positive performance of a higher education system (Huisman 1995, 2000; Meek et al. 1996; Van Vught 2008). Only few researchers have attempted to present institutional diversity more critically by analysing conflicting motivations and forces of convergence and divergence in higher education systems (Kivinen and Rinne 1996) or pointing to additional systemic features which are needed in order to ensure the responsiveness of HE systems (Neave 2000; Douglass 2004; Guri-Rosenblit et al. 2007; Teichler 2008).

In contrast to the majority of studies on institutional diversity, this author's study for EUA made the values associated with institutional diversity themselves an object of inquiry. Taking a closer look at the normative dimension of national approaches to institutional diversity, a comparison of the five countries investigated reveals, first of all, that institutional diversity is not valued positively without exception or without any conditions attached in any national context. The high level of diversity of institutional types in France, for example, is felt by many policy makers and institutional representatives to produce a lack of transparency for users and a high degree of fragmentation. In most countries, the diversity of institutional types or profiles seems to be valued positively only if it goes hand in hand with sufficient transparency as regards the definition of access criteria to different institutional types or profiles, as well as with sufficient flexibility, cooperation and exchange between the different types of institution. Indeed, three of the five countries (England, Norway and Switzerland) have paid considerable attention in recent years to improving flexibility and mobility between institutional types. This is the case for the transition from the so-called Foundation Degrees to university degrees in England and for transfer from University Colleges or Fachhochschulen in Norway and Switzerland. Moreover, to prevent the institutional diversity from leading to fragmentation, wasteful duplication and unexploited synergies or economies of scale, most national systems have introduced incentives to promote cooperation in teaching and research between HEIs. In institutionally diverse contexts, cooperation is meant to achieve several aims at once:

- to exploit the complementarity of diverse institutional profiles with respect to disciplines, functional emphases and student and staff profiles,
- to increase flexibility by facilitating recognition and transfer between institutions for students and staff,
- to share costly infrastructures and cost-intensive research. With rising science costs, the latter concern is becoming a key issue for national funding agencies, regional ministries or development agencies, which promote inter-institutional cooperation arrangements to justify development of major research emphases and to ensure sufficient critical mass and international visibility.

A widely discussed example of the alignment of institutional diversity and inter-institutional cooperation can be observed in the French introduction of the PRES (*Pôles de recherche et d'enseignement supérieur*), in which institutions of different profiles are grouped together at regional level to exploit complementary expertises and share research investments and infrastructures (such as Doctoral schools or major research facilities). Cooperation is also a key concern of policy makers and funding agencies in Switzerland, where substantial research funds have been made available to encourage inner-Swiss cooperation in areas with high scientific or innovative potential. Support for Doctoral schools is made available on the condition of inter-institutional cooperation in order to facilitate complementary research portfolios and critical mass. In Slovakia, inter-institutional cooperation has become a concern with respect to the relations between universities and the institutes of the Academy of Sciences, to new funding instruments developed to promote closer links. Only in England does inter-institutional cooperation not seem to be a prominent policy issue. It was only in some research councils that some research funds have been made available for cooperative research infrastructures. However, industry has called for more efforts to complement institutional diversity through closer inter-institutional cooperation (CIHE 2003).

In this context, the recent Excellence Initiatives in Germany and France are also a good case in point. While the Excellence Initiatives are designed to promote internationally oriented research capacity, select particularly research-intensive institutions for prioritised support and, thus, fostering vertical differentiation in the system, both funding programmes also emphasise cooperative structures between research-intensive universities and other types of institutions, be they public research institutes outside of the university sector (Max Planck or Helmholtz in the German case or the CNRS institutes in the French one) or other higher education institutions in the region that are not primarily research-driven (e.g. the PRES regional pole cooperation in the French context).

Hence, the value of institutional diversity is increasingly being linked to the value of inter-institutional cooperation, creating structures that soften the rigidity of inter-institutional boundaries and make the HE system internally more osmotic and synergistic.

42.2.2.1 Functional Diversity as a Priority

The largest transnational consensus with respect to institutional diversity values concerns the desirability of functional diversity, i.e. varying emphases on the different functional dimensions of HE activities, such as research, teaching, services aiming at business innovation or continuing professional development. Such functional diversity is also the focus on most public debates on mission diversity in recent years. At system level, judgements and choices diverge considerably not only with respect to the overall distribution of functional emphases, but also as to how big the mission overlap between the different institutional profiles should be, and what hierarchy of values should be attached to the various functions. Functional differentiation within the overall HE sector has become a key concern of institutional steering, at system as well as at institutional levels. In public debates and media, such functional debates seem to focus on the role, orientation and intensity of research activities, particularly internationally oriented basic research. Thus, it may come as a surprise to see that the survey of institutional leaders in the author's EUA study revealed that teaching and applied research are placed highest in priority: teaching is found to be a vital function by 61% of all institutions and an important one by another 31%, and applied research is declared a vital function by 52% of institutions and important by another 40%. Applied research is valued significantly more highly than basic research. Interestingly, in the formally differentiated sectors, institutional functional preferences with respect to research diverge more than the formally integrated so-called unitary systems. In the formally differentiated systems, universities prioritise basic research significantly more highly, while the other higher education institutions limit their research activities to applied research, most often with a regional focus. Such differentiation is also reflected in staff hiring criteria. In the integrated systems, preference is less clearly differentiated in this respect.

The author's EUA study also confirmed that the value of internationally visible research for the competitive profile of an institution has risen in the perception of policy makers and institutional leaders in all five countries, as well as in Romania (Chaps. 44 and 50 by Andreescu et al.) and Germany (Wissenschaftsrat 2011). The expansion of the research capacity of HEIs plays a differentiating role in all five national contexts, but in very different ways. In England and Slovakia, research has become the key criterion for vertical differentiation among institutional types – formally, through legislative definitions and accreditation criteria in Slovakia, and informally or implicitly through the weight of the funding instruments in England. In Norway and Switzerland, increasing research capacity is also associated with the applied research functions of the university colleges or *Fachhochschulen*, thus allowing for more horizontal differentiation in this regard. In France, research seems to become a new differentiating principle, cutting across the old divide between the elite professional sector and the freely accessible, largely egalitarian university sector. But, in all five countries, one can observe internationally oriented research exerting a homogenising effect on institutional profiles. Where international research is the most decisive determinant of funding flows, as is the case in England, the mainstreaming effect is stronger than in national contexts such as Switzerland or Norway, where multiple types of research funding sources exist to sustain research with different orientations, from international and basic to regionally oriented and applied research.

The positive value associated with functional differentiation is not just associated with external diversity between institutions but also with increased internal diversity. At institutional level, functional diversity is often emphasised in declared missions or strategy documents, although such declared priorities are not always fully reflected in staff hiring and promotion criteria or resource allocation criteria. But some degree of functional diversity with varying emphases on teaching, research, innovation, continuing education and institutional administration is promoted through differentiation of contracts and promotion criteria for other academic staff positions. But, while two thirds of all responding institutions prioritise diversity in academic staff's relative inclinations to contribute to research, teaching, innovation or service to society, institutional attempts to differentiate are often undermined by homogeneous career patterns at national and international levels. Only in those countries where some differentiation of staff profiles for different types of institutions is laid down by law (such as in Norway or Switzerland), did the institutions show more differentiated staff conditions (including hiring and promotion criteria, task descriptions and salaries).

In contrast with the American diversity discussions, the examination of values attached to diversity in Higher Education in the EUA study also reveals that European institutional diversity approaches rarely focus on the diversity of staff or student composition in terms of ethnic, religious, social or even national or gender composition. With respect to gender diversity, institutional policies rarely include respective prioritisation of gender as part of hiring criteria of academic staff. Likewise, ethnic, social or international diversity of the student body is a priority only for a few English HEI. Diversity is an issue only with respect to qualification profiles among the student body.

42.2.2.2   Horizontal vs. Vertical Differentiation

In any system of values, some values are emphasised more than others and prioritised in their guiding force for action. With respect to institutional diversity values, the research literature distinguishes 'vertical diversity' and 'horizontal diversity' to describe value systems which prioritise highly or hardly. The terms 'vertical diversity' or 'vertical differentiation' of institutions describe those higher education systems which clearly favour one type of institution over others. Conversely, 'horizontal differentiation' would describe systems in which equal value is attributed to different types of institutional profiles. With all attempts to create diverse institutional profiles and attribute some value to all types of institutions, some types of institutional orientations seem to be more highly valued than others in all higher education systems, according to the dominant social norms. Indeed, some degree of vertical differentiation, whereby some types of institutional emphases receive more support than others, seems to be present in any national system. But, in some systems, the values attached to different institutional choices diverge more strongly than in others, the EUA study reveals. Indeed, some systems openly foster vertical differentiation, as could be observed in Slovakia, where research intensity is rewarded more than any other dimension of institutional engagement. Moreover, even those systems that explicitly claim to foster horizontal differentiation in their policy documents, where different types of institutions would be valued equally, will find their explicit policies undermined by reward systems, especially funding instruments and sources and quality assurance criteria.

The clearest case of vertical differentiation to be found in the EUA study may be said to be the Slovak higher education system. The Slovak system has been expanding rapidly over the last two decades and has developed a high degree of horizontal differentiation in the first phase of expansion in the 1990s, with different institutional profiles emerging in different parts of the country, largely in support of regional needs. While some of these portfolio differences have subsisted, institutions have expanded further, often moving toward a model which was found to be more advantageous in the competition for students, namely that of the comprehensive university. During the process, given that resources were not sufficient to support the expansion, quality problems emerged. Moreover, the 'university' title began to be used indiscriminately for any institution, regardless of size, portfolio, or the presence of any research activities. Meanwhile, the pressures for research competitiveness have increased, pushed by national attempts to implement the Lisbon Agenda and increasing visibility of research-biased rankings. Under these pressures, the value system has adapted, resulting in calls for a higher education system which would apply quality standards more rigorously, would differentiate funding accordingly, and which would strengthen the research capacity of its universities. Ultimately, the national policy solution became a blending of these calls into a new form of institutional differentiation, which would use the volume and quality of research as its sole differentiating criterion. This policy took several years to implement, but it was conceived from the beginning as a model of vertical differentiation using a formal method of differentiating institutional types while clearly setting one type (that of the research-based university) above the others. In the meantime, with the first phase of implementation, where the classification of institutions were revealed, the government bent under the pressures of the influential institutional representatives and abandoned the system before it was fully implemented. The Romanian reform outlined in the chapters of Andreescu et al. (Chaps. 44 and 50) in this volume seems to follow a similar logic of the original Slovak vertical differentiation approach.

An internally conflicted case of vertical differentiation can be found in the English system. Here, values and national as well as institutional policies seem to make a strong case for horizontal differentiation, with equal values being attributed publically to different mission types of institutions. The dividing lines are mostly soft and self-organised, rather than regulated, and follow criteria of research intensity and attention to diverse student clienteles, discriminated positively according to quality of qualifications and social background (less privilege receiving special promotion). At the same time, however, the dominance of funding for research and the strong visibility of research performance for the reputation of institutions creates a strong vertically differentiating force within the system.

France is an interesting case, since one model of vertical differentiation seems to currently be succeeded by another, although a more horizontal broadening of values attached to HE adds further complexity to the picture. Traditionally, the French system is highly vertically differentiated, with clear lines drawn between a selective elite sector (the professionally oriented *grandes écoles*) and free access universities. In neither did research play a decisive role, since research capacity and its most highly performing functions were largely associated with the CNRS, which was linked to the universities, but separately run. However, with the growing importance of research for national competitiveness and reputation, research has recently become an important vertical differentiating criterion for institutional position. Most institutions, universities and *grandes écoles*, are expanding their research strengths in their most promising areas to attract public recognition, funds, students and regional support. Given the accompanying promotion of cooperation (e.g., PRES, etc.), a new landscape is emerging, in which new forms of vertical differentiation are combining with new forms of horizontal differentiation (e.g. again through the PRES).

Norway has had, so far, a largely horizontally differentiated system, with formally differentiated types, universities and university colleges, performing different functions. In recent years, the system has been transforming into a more vertically differentiated one, with research and research training intensity again the differentiator. The traditional emphasis on regional diversity is increasingly over-shadowed by the concern with institutional positioning through competitive research funding successes. Some higher education researchers would traditionally have called such a shift 'academic drift', but it should be noted that the research which plays the differentiating role is no longer just academic basic research, but contains a wider range of different types of research, including research which is not only applied, but even often explicitly oriented to the needs of the businesses. Thus, the term 'research' has become more inclusive in its scope while its practice has become more exclusive through its differentiating function. Instead of 'academic drift', the label 'research drift' would be more fitting. As Teichler (Chap. 47) shows in this volume, the academic profession, its values and practices, reflect the omnipresent increase of research orientation. While the result seems to be a convergence of insti-tutional types in the traditional sense (and the formal boundaries have been rede-fined to enable them to be more easily crossed), new institutional types may be emerging, as Skodvin is suggesting in this book.

Finally, Switzerland could, perhaps, be seen as the most horizontally and least vertically differentiated system of the five. While research also plays a high role on the national agenda, the distinction between more internationally oriented research and more regionally responsive research and innovation, which serves to support the dividing line between the two sectors, is not associated with a strong difference of social status or public recognition. The two types of research are catered for through separate funding channels, as are the institutional types in which they are conducted, thus allowing for the comparatively horizontal form of differentiation noted above. The high esteem in which the *Fachhochschulen* are held is embedded in a tradition which attributes comparatively high social status to high-level voca-tional education and which confronts academic education with a comparatively high degree of scepticism unless it is seen to serve as a foundation for innovation in the long run. As a result, the binary line seems relatively stable and rooted in the national value system, although boundaries are significantly more blurred in some subject areas (such as engineering and pedagogical training) than in others. In addi-tion, within each institutional type, an increasing internal differentiation can be observed with respect to expanding missions and functional emphases.

The EUA study clearly showed that there are two conditions upon which hori-zontal differentiation and parity of esteem must be built: first, it needs visible, strong and different reward structures which to help sustain the differing orientations and value systems on which they feed. Second, and as a consequence of the first, hori-zontal differentiation needs relatively high levels of expenditure in order to provide sufficient incentive to support the diversity sought. Without considerable funding, any parity of esteem will dissolve in the face of limited resources and prioritised activities. With this conclusion, we have moved into the heart of the discussion on the drivers of diversification.

42.3   The Interplay of Forces Driving Diversification or Convergence

For policy makers and institutional leaders who wish to promote particular aspects of diversity, the key question is what the key drivers of diversification or convergence are in a higher education system, so that they may design effective methods accordingly. In the research discussion of such drivers, the following have been identified:

1. *Scientific developments*, which involve a growing complexity of bodies of knowledge and, consequently, also the emergence and growth of new disciplines as well as increased fragmentation within and among HEIs (Clark 1983, 1998). This often results in attempts to build bridges between disciplines, programmes and institutions.
2. The *regulatory framework*, which may lay down distinct missions of institutional types, as is the case in formally diversified systems. These missions may differ legally not just in the scope of functions attributed to different types of institutions as core dimensions of their institutional missions (often differentiating the role regarding research, research training, or continuing education). They may also regulate access, recruitment and contract conditions for exercising particular functions in higher education, e.g. the status of professors or other groups of academic staff.
3. *Funding instruments*, such as:
   - institutional grants, which are usually distributed on the basis of some input or output indicators, which may act as strong incentives for institutional behaviour
   - additional development grants for special purposes or projects, e.g. widening participation, introducing new learning technologies, particular reforms
   - competitive research grants distributed after open calls for projects
   - scientific infrastructure resources granted ad hoc or competitively
4. *The expansion of changing composition of the student body.* This could involve the emergence of new clienteles, with a wider range of talents and qualifications, and socio-economic and educational backgrounds. Hence, programme orientation, pedagogical methods and support services may diversify to respond to the various needs. Diversification may also result from changed or increased demand with respect to a particular student group, as has been the case for doctoral candidates in recent years or professional mature learners updating the knowledge and skills.

5. *Societal and stakeholder demands.* Such demands influence institutional policy choices, programme development, as well as student and staff orientation. As a recent study showed (Kaiser et al. 2007), governance changes in HE in many countries in Europe have most often implied an increase of direct influence of stakeholder and societal demands on HE development, through stakeholder boards or external members on executive boards at institutional level, and even at the level of individual programmes. Indirect influence is being exerted through the perception of such societal needs by academics and students, which informs their teaching or study choices.

6. *International developments* in higher education or its environments. One obvious example is the Bologna Process, which proposes and imposes a number of structural convergences on the European national HE systems. While there have been some studies on policy convergence through the effect of the Bologna reforms (Bleiklie 2001; Huisman and van der Wende 2004; Witte 2006), its effects, convergent or diversifying, on programme definition, student clienteles or institutional profiles, is still unclear. Only the effect of convergence between institutional types has been noted (Witte 2006). Another example is the emergence and growing influence of international ranking schemes, and of global markets for researchers, research training and research products at least in some scientific areas (such as the Natural Sciences and Medicine). These have had profound effects on the perception of HEIs on their possibilities, as well as on the characteristics needed to sustain a 'competitive' HE system.

7. *Quality assurance and accreditation criteria and standards.* These affect diversity in so far as they may or may not take account of different institutional missions and profiles. Thus, the recommendations arising from institutional or programme evaluations may contain assumptions about mission emphases or programme orientation which could promote convergence, some quality assurance methods may be more neutral with respect to diverse missions, such as fit-for-purpose quality evaluations, which take the missions and aims of an institution as a point of departure. Indirectly, convergence could also be pushed through attitudes of the peers (see 8.). But fit-for purpose evaluations could also recommend institutional developments that would strengthen the uniqueness of institutional profiles and, thus, promote differentiation. Accreditation often imposes particular standards of institutional structures, size, staff profiles and even curricular content and, thus, is likely to result in more convergence.

8. *Academic norms and values.* These have been recognised as key factors contributing, most often, to convergence, since the reproduction of the professoriate tends to follow homogeneous selection and reward criteria. According to several researchers (Riesman 1956; Birnbaum 1988; Clark 1993, 1996), faculty members tend to identify more closely with their discipline than with their institution and department. Success for academic staff is, thus, achieved primarily through behaviours and success that are nationally and internationally recognised by their peers in their fields or disciplines.

42.3.1   Formal vs. Informal Methods of Diversification

With respect to the second and third of the above-mentioned drivers, higher education researchers have emphasised the distinction between formal and informal methods of promoting institutional diversity (i.e. external diversity in this context). Formal methods of promoting diversity emphasise the role of State regulation for sustaining the separate institutional types, including legal definitions of the institutional types, their often separate funding authorities and instruments, as well as respective accreditation and quality assurance criteria. Such formal diversity approaches are realised in binary systems but also in the new HE classification systems of Slovakia (since 2008) and Romania (2011, see Chaps. 44 and 50 by Andreescu et al.). Informal methods of promoting diversity focus on inter-institutional competition for resources and, thus, on appropriate funding instruments. The underlying assumption of such approaches usually liken HE systems to markets in which institutions compete for resources. If these resources are limited, each institution would seek to identify the market niches in which it would have the best capacity to increase its resources (according to resource dependency theory). Funding instruments have to be designed in such a way that different financial sources would respond to the core strengths of different mission mixes or institutional groups.

Higher education research is divided over the question as to which approach, formal or informal, would ensure or develop institutional diversity most effectively. While Birnbaum (1983) makes government regulation (formal approach) responsible for convergence in several higher education systems between 1960 and 1980, finding diversification of institutional types hampered by centralised State planning and rigid accreditation criteria, Huisman, in his study of the effect of Dutch government policies on institutional diversity, observes that such policies, or the second-guessing of government policy, contributed to increasing programme diversity (Huisman 1995, 1996; Rhoades 1990). Conversely, Skolnik (1986), Huisman (1998), Morphew (2000), Codling and Meek (2006), and others point to the convergence effects informal methods of differentiation, which rely only on competitive resource allocation without mission regulation. In both cases, the focus is on the dangers of either restricting institutional autonomy through regulation or of allowing institutional types to converge by dropping regulatory differences between institutions. Such institutional convergence or 'mission creep' most often refers to the academic drift of formerly professionally oriented HEI, but could also occur through the vocational drift on the side of the university sector, e.g. in the context of the Bologna reforms with the emphasis on employability as a key goal of higher education. As the discussions in this volume show (Chaps. 19 and 43 by Hazelkorn, Chaps. 44 and 50 by Andreescu et al., and Chap. 46 by Skodvin), the discussion is still ongoing.

The author's diversity study showed that the opposition between formal and informal methods of promoting diversity or between binary and integrated higher education systems may not be as clear-cut as is often suggested in policy debates, with rigidity associated with the former, or flexibility associated with the latter. With respect to the dynamics of institutional development and shifting mission mixes, an informally differentiated system which gives institutions unlimited autonomy to orient itself in any direction, such as the English one, may not be more flexible than a formally differentiated one, such as the Swiss one. There are two main reasons why this harsh juxtaposition is misleading. One reason is that the flexibility of development of regulated types has been underestimated. Even regulatory distinctions are adaptable, as has been shown in the expansion of the research function of the Fachhochschulen or university colleges in all binary systems, which reflects mission development without necessarily implying mission creep. In all binary HE systems, the research mission of professional HEIs emphasises the applied character and orientation toward regional needs, in particular of small and medium enterprises. As Lepori observes, the introduction of an explicit research mandate to professionally oriented, non-university higher education institutions has added complexity at system and institutional levels which cannot be simply reduced to the notion of academic drift. Rather, a dynamic of specialisation and differentiation concerning research that could lead to either convergence or to stronger differentiation or even reinforcement of the binary divide, depending on the implementation methods, can be noted (Lepori 2008). This may even diverge between subject areas within the same national context or institution. With the introduction of research into the sector, new institutional profiles have emerged, some of which are even experienced as institutional types. The UAS7 in Germany see themselves as a mission group, for example.

A second reason why the juxtaposition between formally or informally regulated systems is exaggerated concerns the limits of institutional flexibility in the informally differentiated integrated systems. Even though institutional autonomy should theoretically allow development in all directions, in policy debates, as well as in some of the research literature, the assumption is often made that the degree of institutional diversity is linked to the degree of institutional autonomy in the system. It is supposed that greater institutional autonomy would allow institutions to adapt to varying needs more flexibly and, thus, to explore and occupy varying institutional niches. This assumption cannot be confirmed in this unconditional formulation by the findings of the EUA study. The reality is clearly more complex and less linear. First, while it may appear that institutional autonomy in a given area opens a wider field of choice in institutional orientation, the choice may be restricted by many other factors, such as the values or prestige associated with different options, or the opportunity costs connected with one line of action compared to another. These restrictions are not just set by academic values, though these may indeed act as a counterforce, but may be a more subtle combination of contextual and institutional forces such as career structures, financial instruments and conflicting market opportunities, as is illustrated by the English case study. Moreover, the relationship between institutional autonomy and diversification is not linear because systems which are formally differentiated, i.e. which regulate institutional types, do not necessarily prohibit institutional autonomy altogether, but rather set limits to developments, while other forms of differentiation may still be allowed, foreseen and even promoted through incentives, as is illustrated by the research funding incentives for Fachhochschulen in the Swiss case study.

In short, if the diversification of institutional profiles is to occur within or between the legal or other boundaries between different institutional types, incentives and values also have to be diverse enough to sustain such diversification. The dynamics of diversification are not necessarily hindered by formal boundaries and not necessarily helped by their absence. Rather, they are defined by the interplay between regulatory factors and a whole array of other forces. Institutional autonomy and inter-institutional competition only promote differentiation if values and rewards (symbolic and financial) are supportive. The choice to define some institutional types through regulation is one way of creating a framework which supports alternative reward structures. The choice between formally differentiated systems (binary or multi-partite) should not be misrepresented as either/or a decision between deregulation of institutional mission and institutional autonomy on the one hand, and regulated missions and no institutional autonomy on the other. Formal and informal methods of promoting diversity are not diametrically opposed choices, but part of an overall set of factors which, together, define the degree of support available for institutional choices, and in which institutional autonomy is not present or absent absolutely, but by degrees. If alone and unsupported by other factors, the institutional autonomy will have little effect on differentiation; but supported by other factors, it allows for more possibilities. Where institutional autonomy is very restricted, institutional development will not be able to adapt to changing conditions and new challenges. Where institutional autonomy is permitted, institutions will adapt in those directions for which the greatest symbolic and financial rewards are granted.

42.3.2   Academic Values

The last-mentioned driver of diversification of the above list has also received prioritised attention by higher education researchers, ever since Riesman's study of imitating behaviour of universities and isomorphism (1956): universities push for prestige by emulating the most highly regarded. This orientation is driven by the norms of faculty members who identify primarily with their academic communities rather than with their own institutions and who are anxious to create structures and programmes which correspond to their image of the ideal university environment, which is not necessarily related akin to their own university's mission and resources. Thus, competition between higher education institutions should not be seen only as competition for resources but also, through the value system of academic staff and leadership, as competition for stature, prestige and legitimacy, which encourage 'conformity to prevailing models rather than attempts to distinguish themselves from their competitors' (Rhoades 1990, p. 191). The consequent academic drift reduces the diversity of institutional types and programmes, even if the latter are incentivised through government funding measures. To illustrate such norm-inspired academic drift, one may point to the dominance of internationally visible research publications as the primary measure of institutional and individual success in a majority of countries all over Europe, as confirmed by our study (see also Chaps. 27 and 47 by Teichler's and Chaps. 19 and 43 by Hazelkorn). Academic staff's attitudes affect research funding choices (through peer review), institutional orientation (through self-government) and higher education policies (through consultative bodies). The hegemony of such academic values, if given free reign (i.e. in the absence of other strongly regulatory forces sustaining the diversity of institutional profiles), is found to be the prime cause of academic drift by a whole range of researchers (Rhoades 1990; Meek 1991, 2000; Skolnik 1986; Huisman 1995; Huisman and Morphew 1998; van Vught 2008).

While our study confirms the dominance of some academic values (the international research bias) and its influence on academic career decisions and, indirectly, also on national career structures, it still shows a slightly more varied picture than it is often assumed. Both interviews and survey data showed that the academic values do diverge between different institutional and national settings and have undergone considerable changes in the last decade. In particular, the increased interest and recognition of contributing to business innovation through relevant research and teaching orientation can be noted in England, Norway and Switzerland. In this volume, Teichler (Chap. 47) will shed more in-depth light on the variety of academic values and working conditions, shifting the diversity discussion from its primary institutional focus to the importance of other influential social settings. But, in spite of the larger than expected variety of academic staff values, funding and career structures are still largely dominated by the recognition of more narrowly-defined types of research performance, either because the traditional research-biased values still determine the majority or most influential group of academics, or because these values are not strong enough as drivers of behaviour when compared with funding and career opportunities found (resource-dependency overriding norm-dependency in this respect). Whichever the case may be, we can conclude that academic values are not the decisive impediment to institutional diversification in the national contexts investigated.

42.3.3 Conflicts of Forces

The study raises the question whether the forces influencing the overall movement to institutional diversification (or convergence), when looked at across the cross-national sample, are found to be aligned or in conflict with one another. The most obvious recurrent conflict of forces found is the inconsistency between national attempts to diversify HE missions (through regulated institutional definitions, explicit policies or funding instruments) and the homogenising effect of national career regulatory frameworks, which tend to be more conservative and hierarchical and favour particular kinds of research products as the main hiring or promotion criterion. The homogenising effects of traditional academic career patterns dominated by research performance are often reinforced by the internationalisation of academic careers. By contrast, strong regional orientation (e.g. in Norway or Switzerland) helps to raise the importance of other criteria of academic success, e.g. in research that is relevant for business innovation, or continuing education achievements.

In all countries, national and institutional policies were in conflict with one another with respect to programme or subject diversity. In general, institutions have an interest in expanding their portfolios to meet new student and scientific demands, e.g. through interdisciplinary Master or Doctoral programmes which explore new interfaces between subject areas, while national policies are more interested in cost-saving concentration effects.

In general, institutional diversity results from a complex interplay of different, often conflicting forces which include explicit national regulations, policies and funding instruments, but also, other rewards and incentives, which are sometimes too easily ignored in national approaches to diversification, such as quality assurance standards, career advancement practices, stakeholder values and support, regional policies and support as well as international and scientific developments and academic values. Policy makers and institutional leaders who wish to develop proactive policies with respect to any aspect of institutional diversity should take into account the whole array of such forces if they wish to be effective.

42.4 External vs. Internal Diversity – Institutional Boundaries Revisited

Higher education research literature on institutional diversity has primarily focused on external diversity, on the diversity of institutional profiles or types at the level of the overall system, rather than on the internal diversity of institutions. Indeed, little attention has been paid to the motivations and attempts of institutions to differentiate internally, with respect to their programmes, clienteles and audiences, their services, policies, services and other organisational responses to diverse stakeholder needs or student profiles. Within one institution, different units and individuals may pursue, and are often even encouraged to pursue different emphases regarding their types of activities, their primary types of students, their external partners. Some departments may be primarily geared toward an international academic community, while others seek their successes in relation to industrial innovation and the training of business leaders. Continuing education may be regarded as core business in one unit and as marginal in another. While such internal differentiation and diversity could be seen as part of mission stretch, it could, at least theoretically, also be seen to create more flexible learning, teaching and research environments and, hence, to release creative potential. Indeed, it is hardly self-evident that diverse societal expectations would have to be met by a wide variety of different types of institutions that should be relatively coherent internally and homogeneous in their missions, as is so often assumed, rather than by diverse institutional responses which vary mostly within institutions. Why do most diversity discussions simply assume the desirability of external diversity of institutions, rather than at least also considering the advantages and disadvantages, and challenges of internal diversity?

The EUA diversity study noted many institutional attempts to address and even to promote diversity internally, not just in terms of diverse student profiles, but also disciplines, functional orientation, stakeholder emphases, many of which were seen to be not just tolerable but even beneficial forms of internal differentiation.

Of course, there are areas where external diversity and institutional coherence would seem to be obviously preferable. With regard to institutional visibility and marketing, institutional coherence helps position the institution in its most advantageous market niche, and is clearly more efficient and effective if it addresses a more homogeneous range of students and staff in terms of qualifications and expectations. In light of the increasing pressures to promote institutional reputation internationally, it calls for increased external diversity, thus most often supported by those who want to position their institutions or systems on international markets. Too wide a range of student qualifications may result in unrewarding or even frustrating learning and teaching experiences in many cases, as has been confirmed by the data gathered in our study.

In all other respects, however, it is simply an assumption that external diversity would provide a better answer to the challenge of diversifying demands and achieving maximum institutional responsiveness, an assumption that has been repeated enough to become a common belief. Moreover, given that the primary identification of most academics lies with their disciplinary or interdisciplinary community, well beyond the boundaries of the institution, the emphasis on institutional coherence may seem curiously exaggerated. It results, one may surmise, from the discovery of the institution as coherent actor in European higher education. This has been achieved through institutionally oriented governance reforms, which have increased strategic and central steering capacities searching for institutional coherence. It has also been pushed through higher education reforms such as the Bologna reforms, which have required a lot of internal coordination and communication, increasing the institutional sense of community and common purpose. Moreover, the European-wide exchanges on policy changes and institutional reforms have strengthened communication channels between policy makers and institutional leaders alike, creating a European-wide consensus regarding the necessity of stronger institutional steering mechanisms (De Boer et al. 2008) and the desirability of recognisable, more coherent institutional profiles. As beneficial as the increased steering capacity, visibility, and coherence of institutions as actors in the higher education systems may be for many aspects of innovation and institutional positioning, it is not as clear as current policy debates make it sound that it is equally needed for optimal institutional diversity. The latter does not have to be achieved primarily through relatively coherent institutions diverging from each other. Such a bias may even become outdated sooner or later as institutional coherence is being simultaneously undermined through many new incentives for institutions to cooperate or even to form consortia or merge. As cooperative networks become increasingly intertwined, strategic developments aligned and common structures formed, institutional boundaries soften and often even dissolve. The ideal of HE institutions as coherent actors in the system is becoming more and more difficult to uphold in today's densely networked world of co-authored science, open innovation, joint curricula and common institutes. In the future, debates on institutional diversity may, thus, have to revise such key assumptions. Inter-institutional thematic networks may become the recognisable units positioning themselves, rather than the nebulous holdings calling themselves institutions from which they emerge. But, today, we still live in a historical phase where the problematic sclerotic effects of formerly highly de-centralised institutions can be experienced all over Europe, so that institutional steering capacity is appreciated much more than an array of chaotic clouds of un-steerable networks with an indomitable array of external partners. And yet, the future is not so far away. The diversification of funding sources and partnerships and the wide-reaching effects this has on institutional steering have already become an object of study and policy concern (Estermann and Pruvot 2011). How important will institutional boundaries remain in tomorrow's world of global challenges and networked solutions?

To conclude, the author proposes that external and internal diversity be jointly looked at, taking account of the increasingly fuzzy boundaries between institutions. This study has shown how often diversity is valued and approached in conjunction with different kinds of cooperative arrangements. Hence, the understanding and measurement of institutional diversity in any higher education system only in terms of external diversity – that is, by looking at the number of units, programmes and institutions of different profiles, target groups and orientations – falls short of recording the complexity of real institutional responses.

42.5 Conclusions from the Bologna Higher Education Researchers' Conference Discussions on Diversity in Higher Education

In response to the previous reflections and the five papers on institutional diversity presented in this volume, the three sessions on diversity in higher education at the Bologna Higher Education Researchers' Conference highlighted four central concerns as areas for more differentiated policy attention:

1. Current policy debates on institutional diversity are strongly influenced by increasing preoccupation with international competitiveness, visibility and position in rankings, which favour one institutional model and one dimension of higher education activities over others, thereby undermining the sort of diversity which is needed to respond to the wide range of demands which society expects higher education institutions to meet. It should be recognised, for example, that a wide variety of different forms and orientations of research are needed, not just those expressed in terms of international high impact journal publications but also problem-solving research which may fuel business and societal innovation. In teaching, institutions have to compete not just for the most highly qualified students but should also cater to the diverse demands of students with a wide range of qualifications and of diverse backgrounds. Instead, one has seen, in recent years, a concentration of public resources on a narrow notion of research

performance accompanied by a decreasing investment in a whole range of higher education tasks, including teaching quality and innovation which would be necessary to take such Bologna reform goals as student-centred or competence-based teaching and learning seriously. Thus, the competitiveness agenda which originally helped to justify the Bologna reforms is now undermining its meaningful realisation.

2. Institutional diversity is often too narrowly discussed in terms of external diversity, i.e. in terms of diversity of institutional types and profiles. This overlooks, firstly, the fact that institutions of one type vary widely among each other and that the differences between individual parts of one institution may be greater in terms of primary missions than those between different institutions or institutional types. Secondly, this internal variety has not been proven to be necessarily problematic or inefficient. Internal functional diversity is even needed to provide educational and research breadth. Policy makers and institutional leaders have to distinguish more clearly for which aspects of institutional orientation one needs internal institutional coherence and for which internal diversity would be more beneficial. And thirdly, it does not take account of the fact that academics are increasingly densely cooperating with external partners, softening the boundaries of institutions, so that the institution should not be the only unit of focus for dealing with diversity in higher education.

3. The development and implementation of new transparency instruments (such as U-Map) do not just reveal a surprising degree of diversity of intensity with respect to dimensions of institutional activity. They also show how important it is to find more differentiated descriptors for HE activity in order to develop differentiated incentives to underpin diverse systems of higher education. Multidimensional indicator-based descriptors can help the dialogue between national policy makers and institutional leaders if they are complemented by other kinds of qualitative information.

4. Recent HE research does not confirm that academic values are a mainstreaming force in higher education systems. There is more diversity in this respect than is often assumed. But national and institutional reward systems, especially with respect to funding instruments and hiring or promotion criteria, do not give academics the change to follow diverse career orientations and paths. National policy makers have to develop more diverse reward systems if they want to prevent homogenisation in their higher education systems.

References

Birnbaum, R. (1983). *Maintaining diversity in higher education*. San Francisco: Jossey-Bass.

Bleiklie, I. (2001). Towards European convergence of higher education policy? *Higher Education Management, 13*(3), 9–29.

CIHE (The Council for Industry and Higher Education). (2003). *Diversity and co-operation in higher education – A contribution to the debate*. London.

Clark, B. R. (1983). *The higher education system*. Berkeley/Los Angeles: University of California Press.

Clark, B. R. (1993). The problem of complexity in modern higher education. In S. Rothblatt & B. Wittrock (Eds.), *The European and American University since 1800*. Cambridge: Cambridge University Press.

Clark, B. R. (1998). *Creating entrepreneurial universities: Organizational pathways of transformation*. Oxford: Pergamon Press.

Codling, A. P., & Meek, V. L. (2003). The impact of the state on institutional differentiation in New Zealand. *Higher Education Management and Policy, 15*(2), 83–98.

Codling, A., & Meek, V. L. (2006). Twelve propositions on diversity in higher education. *Higher Education Management and Policy, 18*, 1–24.

De Boer, H., Jongbloed, B., Enders, J., & File, J. (2008). *Progress in higher education reform across Europe. Governance reform*. Brussels: European Commission.

Dill, D., & Teixeira, P. (2000). Program diversity in higher education: An economic perspective. *Higher Education Policy, 13*, 99–118.

Douglass, J. A. (2004). The dynamics of massification and differentiation: A comparative look at higher education systems in the United Kingdom and California. *Higher Education Management and Policy, 16*(3), 9–35.

Fairweather, J. (2000). Diversification or homogenization: How markets and governments combine to shape American higher education. *Higher Education Policy, 13*, 79–98.

Geiger, R. L. (1996). Diversification in US higher education: Historical patterns and current trends. In V. L. Meek, L. Goedegebuure, O. Kivinen, & R. Rinne (Eds.), *The mockers and mocked. Comparative perspectives on differentiation, convergence and diversity in higher education*. Oxford: Pergamon.

Goedegebuure, L., & Meek, L. (1997). On change and diversity: The role of governmental policy and environmental influences. *Higher Education in Europe, 22*(3), 309–319.

Guri-Rosenblit, S., Sebková, H., & Teichler, U. (2007). Massification and diversity of higher education systems: Interplay of complex dimensions. *Higher Education Policy, 2007*(20), 373–389.

Hazelkorn, E. (2008). Learning to live with league tables and ranking: The experience of institutional leaders. *Higher Education Policy, 21*, 193–215.

Hazelkorn, E. (2011). *Rankings and the reshaping of higher education. The battle for world-class excellence*. Houndmills/Basingstoke: Palgrave Macmillan.

Huisman, J. (1995). *Differentiation, diversity and dependency in higher education*. Utrecht: Lemma.

Huisman, J. (1996). Diversity in the Netherlands. In V. L. Meek, L. Goedegebuure, O. Kivinen, & R. Rinne (Eds.), *The mockers and mocked. Comparative perspectives on differentiation, convergence and diversity in higher education*. Oxford: Pergamon.

Huisman, J. (1998). Differentiation and diversity in higher education systems. In J. C. Smart (Ed.), *Higher education: Handbook of theory and research* (Vol. XIII, pp. 75–110). New York: Agathon Press.

Huisman, J. (2000). Higher education institutions: As different as chalk and cheese? *Higher Education Policy, 13*, 41–54.

Huisman, J., & Kaiser, F. (Eds.). (2001). *Fixed and fuzzy boundaries in higher education. A comparative study of (binary) structures in nine countries*. Den Haag: Adviesraad voor Wetenschaps- en Technologiebeleid.

Huisman, J., & Morphew, C. C. (1998). Centralization and diversity: Evaluating the effects of government policies in US and Dutch higher education. *Higher Education Policy, 11*(1), 3–13.

Huisman, J., & van der Wende, M. (2004). The EU and Bologna: Are supra- and international initiatives threatening domestic agendas? *European Journal of Education, 39*(3), 349–357.

Huisman, J., & van Vught, F. (2009). Diversity in European higher education. In *Mapping the higher education landscape. Towards a European classification of higher education*. Dordrecht: Springer.

Huisman, J., Meek, L., & Wood, F. (2007). Institutional diversity in higher education: A cross-national and longitudinal analysis. *Higher Education Quarterly, 61*(4), 563–577.

Jenniskens, I. (1997). *Governmental steering and curriculum innovations: A comparative study of the relation between governmental steering instruments and innovations in higher education curricula*. Maarssen: Elsevier.

Kivinen, O., & Rinne, R. (1996). The problem of diversification in higher education: Countertendencies between divergence and convergence in the Finnish higher education system since the 1950s. In V. L. Meek, L. Goedegebuure, O. Kivinen, & R. Rinne (Eds.), *The mockers and mocked. Comparative perspectives on differentiation, convergence and diversity in higher education.* Oxford: Pergamon.

Kyvik, S. (2004). Structural changes in higher education systems in Western Europe. *Higher Education in Europe, 29,* 393–409.

Larédo, Ph. (2003). University research activities: On-going transformations and new challenges. *Higher Education Management and Policy, 15*(1), 105–123.

Lepori, B. (2008). Research in non-university higher education institutions. The case of the Swiss universities of applied sciences. *Higher Education, 56,* 45–58.

Lepori, B., & Attar, L. (2006). *Research strategies and framework conditions for research in Swiss Universities of Applied Sciences.* Report to the Federal Office of Professional Education and Technology. Lugano.

Meek, V. L. (1991). The transformation of Australian higher education: From binary to unitary system. *Higher Education, 21,* 461–494.

Meek, V. L. (2000). Diversity and marketisation of higher education: Incompatible concepts? *Higher Education Policy, 13*(1), 23–39.

Meek, V. L., Goedegebuure, L., Kivinen, O., & Rinne, R. (Eds.). (1996). *The mockers and mocked. Comparative perspectives on differentiation, convergence and diversity in higher education.* Oxford: Pergamon.

Meek, V. L., Goedegebuure, L., & Huisman, J. (Eds.). (2000). Diversity, differentiation and markets. *Higher Education Policy,* Special issue, *13*(1).

Morphew, C. (2000). Institutional diversity, program acquisition and faculty members: Examining academic drift at a new level. *Higher Education Policy, 13,* 55–78.

Neave, G. (1996). Homogenization, integration and convergence: The Cheshire cats of higher education analysis. In V. L. Meek, L. Goedegebuure, O. Kivinen, & R. Rinne (Eds.), *The mockers and mocked. Comparative perspectives on differentiation, convergence and diversity in higher education* (pp. 26–41). Pergamon: Oxford.

Neave, G. (2000). Diversity, differentiation and the market: The debate we never had but which we ought to have done. *Higher Education Policy, 13,* 7–22.

OECD. (2007). *Higher education and regions: Globally competitive, locally engaged.* Paris: OECD.

Rauhvargers, A. (2011). *Global university rankings and their impact.* Brussels: European University Association.

Reichert, S. (2006). *The rise of knowledge regions: Emerging opportunities and challenges for universities.* Brussels: European University Association.

Reichert, S. (2009). *Institutional diversity in European higher education: Tensions and challenges for policy makers and institutional leaders.* Brussels: European University Association.

Rhoades, G. (1990). Political competition and differentiation in higher education. In J. C. Alexander & P. Colony (Eds.), *Differentiation theory and social change* (pp. 187–221). New York: Columbia University Press.

Scott, P. (2007). Back to the future? The evolution of higher education systems. In B. Kehm (Ed.), *Looking back to look forward. Analyses of higher education after the turn of the millenium* (Werkstattberichte 67). Kassel: W. Jenior.

Siegel, D. (2003). *The call for diversity, pressure, expectation, and organizational response.* New York: Routledge.

Skolnik, M. L. (1986). Diversity in higher education: The Canadian case. *Higher Education in Europe, 11,* 19–32.

Sörlin, S. (2007). Funding diversity: Performance-based funding regimes as drivers of differentiation in higher education systems. *Higher Education Policy, 20,* 413–440.

Teichler, U. (2003). The future of higher education and the future of higher education research. *Tertiary Education and Management, 9,* 171–185.

Teichler, U. (2008). Diversification? Trends and explanations of the shape and size of higher education. *Higher Education, 56*(3), 349–379.

Teixeira, P., Jongbloed, B., Amaral, A., & Dill, D. (Eds.). (2004). *Markets in higher education. Rhetoric or reality?* Dordrecht: Kluwer.

Trow, M. (1970, Winter). Reflections on the transition from mass to universal higher education. *Daedalus, 99*(1), 1–42.

Trow, M. (1979). *Elite and mass higher education: American models and European realities, research into higher education: Process and structures.* Stockholm: National Board of Universities and Colleges.

Trow, M. (2005). Reflections on the transition from elite to mass to universal access: Forms and phases of higher education in modern societies since WWII. In P. Altbach (Ed.), *International Handbook of Higher Education.* Norwell: Kluwer.

Van Vught, F. (1996). Isomorphism in higher education? Towards a theory of differentiation and diversity in higher education systems. In V. L. Meek et al. (Eds.), *The mockers and mocked: Comparative perspectives on differentiation convergence and diversity in higher education.* Oxford: Pergamon.

Van Vught, F. (2008). Mission diversity and reputation in higher education. *Higher Education Policy, 21*, 151–174.

Van Vught, F. (Ed.). (2009). *Mapping the higher education landscape. Towards a European classification of higher education* (Higher education dynamics series). Dordrecht: Springer.

Warner, D., & Palfreyman, D. (Eds.). (2001). *The state of UK higher education. Managing change and diversity.* Buckingham: SRHE & Open University press.

Witte, J. (2006). *Change of degrees and degrees of change. Comparing adaptations of European higher education systems in the context of the Bologna Process.* Promotionsschrift. Enschede: CHEPS/Universität Twente. www.utwente.nl/cheps/documenten/2006wittedissertation.pdf

Chapter 43
"Everyone Wants to Be Like Harvard" – Or Do They? Cherishing All Missions Equally

Ellen Hazelkorn

> Diversity has been identified in the higher education literature as one of the major factors associated with the positive performance of higher education systems. (van Vught 2008, 154)

> Diversity is not necessarily desirable particularly if, in the name of differentiation of resources, one lets slide into penury those institutions which bear the brunt of mass teaching and learning whilst creating poles of excellence for the fortunate few. How does diversity of resources for instance, square with the notion of equality of access to public service across the national territory? (Neave 2000, 19)

43.1 Multi-dimensional Diversity

Institutional diversity is seen as a basic norm of higher education policy because it best meets educational and societal requirements (Birnbaum 1983). It is considered a "necessary consequence of the rapid growth in tertiary education enrolments and the movement of many tertiary education systems from elite to mass systems" and beyond (Santiago et al. 2008, 76). A diverse range of higher education institutions (HEI), with different missions, allows the over-all system to meet students' needs; provide opportunities for social mobility; meet the needs of different labour markets; serve the political needs of interest groups; permit the combination of elite and mass higher education; increase the level of HEI effectiveness; and offer opportunities for experimenting with innovation. However, despite its prominence within the policy lexicon, pursuit of diversity (it is argued) is continually undermined by countervailing

E. Hazelkorn (✉)
Directorate of Research and Enterprise, and Higher Education Policy Research Unit (HEPRU),
Dublin Institute of Technology, 143-147 Rathmines Road, Dublin 6, Ireland
e-mail: ellen.hazelkorn@dit.ie

A. Curaj et al. (eds.), *European Higher Education at the Crossroads:*
Between the Bologna Process and National Reforms,
DOI 10.1007/978-94-007-3937-6_43, © Springer Science+Business Media Dordrecht 2012

tendencies (Riesman 1956; Birnbaum 1983; Huisman 1998; Meek 1991; van Vught 2008; Rhoades 1990).

The lack of diversity or de-differentiation or isomorphism occurs because of a combination of market, policy and professional factors which contribute to increasing convergence or homogeneity within the higher education system leading to "academic" or "mission" drift. This process may occur when the "nature, number and distribution of organisations at any given time is dependent on resource availability and on competition within and between different species of organisations" (van Vught 2007, 9). It may also arise if, for example, research is perceived by government, HEIs and/or the public as more highly valued than teaching, or if some institutions are portrayed as second- or third-class citizens. The image presented is of a hierarchically differentiated higher education system in which "institutions lower in prestige try to emulate higher status institutions (often the status of the university)" (Huisman 1998, 92).

Globalisation and the quickening pace of competition, exemplified by the arrival and popularity of global rankings, can also contribute to this phenomenon by norming perceptions of prestige and excellence. Institutions and nations are constantly measured against each other according to indicators of global capacity and potential in which comparative and competitive advantages come into play. While government had often been a guarantor of diversity, these factors are driving governments to reify a particular higher education model; for many European countries, this has meant overturning policies which previously treated all HEIs equally. Indeed, this situation is often used to explain perceived poor performance in rankings:

> ...we have not concentrated funding on a few universities. Rather the policy has been to have many good universities but not many excellent ones. (German government official quoted in Hazelkorn 2011, 167)

The "world-class" research university, modelled after the characteristics of the top 100 globally-ranked universities, has become the panacea for ensuring success in the global economy. As a result, governments around the world have embarked on significant restructuring of their higher education and research systems; many HEIs have also revised strategies and policies to fit the image promulgated by rankings.

These developments expose a major and growing tension at the heart of higher education policy. The cost of pursuing the "world-class" model are straining national budgets just as the demands on and requirements for universal higher education are rising.

> We want the best universities in the world ... How many universities do we have? 83? We're not going to divide the money by 83 (Nicolas Sarkozy, President, France, quoted in Enserink 2009).

> European countries are going to have to become much more selective in the way they allocate resources. There are nearly 2,000 universities in the EU, most of which aspire to conduct research and offer postgraduate degrees. By contrast, fewer than 250 US universities award postgraduate degrees and fewer than 100 are recognised as research-intensive (Butler 2007).

At the same time, the emphasis on research, which is given disproportionate weight in most global rankings, is forging a wedge between HEIs, according to whether they excel in research or teaching. By preferring to concentrate resources in a few universities, governments are choosing to emphasize vertical and reputational differentiation between institutions, which is translated in policy terms into greater hierarchical differentiation between research (elite) universities and teaching (mass) HEIs. In so doing, diversity is portrayed as a one-dimensional concept with two rival characteristics: teaching and research. The policy tension arises because the pressures of and responses to globalisation and rankings are emphasizing elite forms of higher education, while the demands and needs of society and the economy are urging horizontal differentiation with wider participation and diversified opportunities.

In contrast to this narrow prism, the history of higher education suggests an alternative perspective in which diversity is more complex. The last decades have witnessed a transformation in the role, number and mission of higher education. Rather than institutions attended by a small intellectual or social elite, attendance is now more or less obligatory for the vast majority of people in order to sustain democratic civil society and most occupations. A distinguishing feature of this history is the way higher education has evolved over time to take on a diverse set of functions and niches within and between institutions (Clark 1978); indeed, some of the most well-known universities nowadays began life as much more modest institutions (Marcus 2011). Describing the US system, Julius (2011) wrote:

> Small sectarian colleges educating clergy have become large secular universities; local teachers colleges have become regional and in some cases national universities. The land-grant institutions themselves have undergone a transformation unimagined by their founders: from colleges focused on finding cures to oak smut and better mining or agricultural techniques to international conglomerates with budgets in the billions elective admission standards, thousands of faculty … and branch campuses throughout the world.

Or "doctoral programmes … once rare or non-existent in many universities have expanded to their present scale only in recent decades and research as a major component of universities is a relatively modern phenomenon" (Skilbeck 2003, 13).

Today, HEIs provide education from associate degree to PhD level, conduct research, participate in outreach initiatives, and are a source of innovation and entrepreneurship. They are emblems of nation-building; to some they are the engine of the economy, to others a critical partner in the ecosystem. Beyond imparting education, they are the source of human capital; act as a regional, national and/or global gateway attracting highly-skilled talent and investment, actively engaging with a diverse range of stakeholders through knowledge and technology transfer, and underpinning the global competitiveness of nations and regions. Many have medical schools, museums, theatres, galleries, sports facilities and cafes – all of which play a significant role in their community, city and nation. As a group, they sit within vastly different national context, underpinned by different value systems, meeting the needs of demographically, ethnically and culturally diverse populations, and responding to complex and challenging political-economic environments.

From the vantage point of the real-time observer, it may appear that HEIs have engaged in mission creep, but this may be due to the similarity of language. Adopting a longer timeframe shows that HEIs and systems have evolved in response to what Neave (2000) has called a further step in the democratisation of the "Humboldtian ethic". Macro-level descriptors of teaching, research and service do a disservice to the diversity of educational ethos and pedagogy, research focus and fields of specialisation, student profile, engagement with stakeholders, etc.; as Clark says, "at best they function as useful ideologies that throw a net of legitimacy over diverse activities" (Clark 1978, 242). In contrast to a time when institutional boundaries reflected a relatively simple understanding of society, knowledge systems and labour markets, as knowledge has become more complex and society more demanding, diverse higher education models have developed. The transformation from elite to universal higher education has given birth to multi-dimensional diversity.

This article aims to re-define diversity for the twenty-first century. There are three main sections. Section 43.2 provides an overview of the drivers of change in higher education, illustrating how the growing complexity of knowledge production and concepts of research and scholarship, and the trend for universal higher education has driven greater diversity. If new ideas/methodologies are produced by an array of knowledge producers ranging from curiosity-driven to use-inspired and from blue-sky to practice-led, shouldn't higher education reflect this wider diversity of perspectives? To what extent can this be portrayed as "mission evolution" rather than "mission creep"? Section 43.3 presents a new approach for profiling diversity – one that seeks to illustrate the great complexity of the higher education landscape. Finally, Sect. 43.4 asks: if the goal is institutional diversity – what are policies? Despite objectives to encourage greater diversity, public and policy discourse promotes a simplistic understanding. To what extent does the policy environment undermine its own goals? Do funding initiatives and assessment/evaluation schemes reinforce traditional definitions and differentiations? Does everyone really want to be like Harvard – or do they just want to be loved? What policy or institutional practices could support a new direction for higher education?

43.2 When Systems and Institutions Evolve

43.2.1 Emerging Missions and Purpose

The first degree-granting university in Europe, and the world, was the University of Bologna (established 1088). Remaining aloof from commercial activity and focused primarily on the liberal arts, the early university nonetheless believed society would benefit from the scholarly expertise generated by the university. Over the next centuries, universities were created across Europe to help satisfy a thirst for knowledge, and provide the basis for resolving difficult problems. The modern European university was strongly influenced by the scientific revolution and Wilhelm von Humboldt (1767–1835, founder of the University of Berlin, 1810) and Cardinal John Henry Newman (1801–1890, inspiration for establishment of Catholic University, Ireland, 1852–1858). While the latter saw the university as the place for teaching universal knowledge, the former viewed the university as a training ground for professionals underpinned by a close nexus between teaching and research.

About the same time, the US Morrill Act (1862) established the Land Grant University and created the first set of mass institutions. With their focus on the teaching of agriculture, science, and engineering, it sought to meet the needs of a changing social class structure rather than simply concentrate on the historic core of classical studies. The American Graduate School of the early twentieth century played a similar role for the next generation of scholar-researchers, albeit knowledge was still pursued for its own sake and research agendas were set by individuals. This began to change in the post-Sputnik era when the Bayh-Doyle Act (1980) signified the official shift of attention, with respect to university research, from curiosity-driven investigation to being an arm of economic development. At the same time, community colleges, with their origins in the early twentieth century, began to "provide job training programs as a way to ease widespread unemployment" in response to the depression of the 1930s (Kasper 2002–2003, 15). These developments facilitated the massification of higher education and intensification of research, and marked the dismantling of the boundary between "town" and "gown".

While the US expanded and diversified its system, developments in Europe and elsewhere were slower, and tended to be regulated or engineered by the state which, with few exceptions, remains the primary paymaster. Vocational schools and colleges, polytechnics and new generation universities were established to cater for a wider range of socio-economic and learner groups, educational requirements and rapidly expanding careers in "technical, semi-professional, and managerial occupations" (Trow 1974, 124). Many emerged from the transformation of workingmen's or technical institutes. To contain institutional ambitions and costs, statutory instruments and other regulations were created to maintain differentiation, creating what is referred to as the binary system, while traditional universities continued to cater for a small number of elites and the growing middle class. In subsequent years, new educational models and arrangements including distance learning, franchising and over-seas campuses, alongside a proliferation of new private (not-for-profit and for-profit) institutions, have emerged catering for specialist and socio-economically diverse learners of all ages. Figure 43.1 illustrates the extent to which the decades after 1970 marked a watershed in higher education growth across the OECD. Demand is continuing to grow (Vincent-Lancrin 2008), and at least "one sizeable new university has to open every week" over the next decades (Daniel 1996).

Historically, the demarcation between institutional types was more pronounced; universities taught the classical canon of subjects, including philosophy, language and theology or *basic knowledge*, while *Hochschule*, etc. taught natural and engineering sciences or *applied knowledge*. As labour markets evolved, demand expanded and the social and commercial worlds impinged more and more on higher

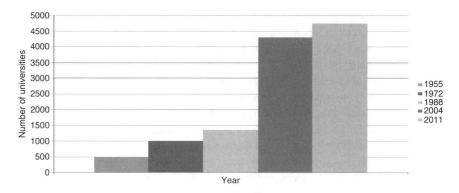

Fig. 43.1 HEI growth in OECD countries 1955–2011 (Source: IMHE/OECD, from *World List of Universities and other HEIs*, IAU, 1995, 1971–1972, 1988–1989, 2004; Universities Worldwide http://www.univ.cc/)

education, traditional universities have been unable to meet all the demands and requirements of the global knowledge society (Neave 2000; Clark 1983; cf. Geiser and Atkinson 2010). Globalisation, the Bologna Process and more recently global rankings have all helped create a single world market for knowledge and talent. Professional education is no longer a feature solely of vocational institutions; rather, the number of such programmes has risen substantially in universities compared with traditional liberal arts type programmes which have declined absolutely (CFAT 2011). Today, boundaries between classical and technological disciplines have blurred, leaving institutional nomenclature often owing more to political than accreditation concerns. The terms "unitary" and "binary" are similarly becoming out-dated. What was once decried as mission creep may more accurately be described as mission evolution (Guri-Rosenblit et al. 2007).

43.2.2 Aligning Knowledge Production and Higher Education

In the elite system, higher education was about shaping the ruling class, while research was something conducted in a secluded/semi-secluded environment. Research was curiosity-driven and focused around pure disciplines in order to increase understanding of fundamental principles with no (direct or immediate) commercial benefits; as a consequence, research achieves accountability from within the academy and through peer-review (see Table 43.1). Gibbons et al. (1994) called this Mode 1 knowledge production. As higher education evolves to being more or less obligatory for a wide range of occupations and social classes, it is increasingly a knowledge-producing enterprise rather than simply a people-processing institution (Gumport 2000). The number of actors has grown alongside the breadth of disciplines and fields of inquiry in pursuit of understanding principles and solving *practical problems* of the modern world; thus, research achieves

Table 43.1 From elite to mass to universal higher education

	Elite	Mass	Universal
% relevant age cohort	0–15%	16–50%	Over 50%
Attitudes to access	Privilege of birth or talent or both	Right for those with certain qualifications	Obligation for the skilled working, middle and upper classes
Functions of higher education	Shaping mind and character of ruling class; preparation for elite roles	Transmission of skills; preparation for broader range of technical elite roles	Adaptation of "whole population" to rapid social and technological change
Curriculum and forms of instruction	Highly structured in terms of academic conceptions of knowledge	Modular, flexible and semi-structured sequence of courses	Boundaries and sequences break down; distinctions between learning and life break down
Institutional characteristics	Homogeneous with high and common standards; small residential communities; clear and impermeable boundaries	Comprehensive with more diverse standards; "cities of intellect" – mixed residential/commuting; boundaries fuzzy and permeable	Great diversity with no common model; aggregates of people enrolled but many rarely on campus. Boundaries weak or non-existent
Research and knowledge transfer	Pursuit of understanding of fundamental principles focused around "pure disciplines" and arising from curiosity, with no (direct or immediate) commercial benefits. Conducted by a limited number of research actors in a secluded/ semi-secluded environment. Achieves accountability via peer-review process **Mode 1** (Gibbons et al. 1994)	Pursuit of understanding of principles in order to solve practical problems of the modern world, in addition to acquiring knowledge for knowledge's sake. Broad range of research actors across breadth of disciplines/ fields of inquiry. Achieves accountability via a mix of peer and social accountability **Mode 2** (Gibbons et al. 1994)	Research is focused on solving complex problems via bi-lateral, inter-regional and global networks, not bound by borders or discipline. Knowledge production is democratised with research actors extending/involving "beyond the academy". Emphasis is on "reflective knowledge" co-produced with and responsive to wider society, with an emphasis on impact and benefit. Achieves accountability via social and public accountability **Mode 3** (author's own term)

Source: Adapted from Brennan (2004) and Trow (1974, 2006)
Highlighted section indicates author's contribution

accountability through a mix of peer review and social accountability or Mode 2. In the universal phase, the inter-connectedness between higher education and society is further deepened; education is concerned with ensuring that the majority of the population has the knowledge and skills to adapt to rapid social and technological change. Research is co-produced and exchanged, focused on solving complex problems through bi-lateral, inter-regional and global networks, not bound by either national, institutional or discipline borders. Mode 3 (author's own term) occurs when research "comes increasingly to the attention of larger numbers of people, both in government and in the general public, who have other, often quite legitimate, ideas about where public funds should be spent, and, if given to higher education, how they should be spent" (Trow 1974, 91; Lynton 1995). Mode 3 knowledge production achieves accountability via social and public accountability.

Trow's elite, mass and universal "phases" of higher education are ideal types, and may occur in tandem at the institutional level or represent sequential stages at the system level. Likewise, the transition from Mode 1 to Mode 2 and then Mode 3 display additional complexities in the knowledge production process. They may co-exist symbiotically within institutions depending upon discipline and research problem and not simply across different institutions; nevertheless, a progression is occurring. The essential point is that if the Enlightenment was characterised by a "model of knowledge produced for its own end in the splendid isolation of the academy – the ideal of liberal education" (Delanty 2001, 154), recent decades have borne witness to a closer alignment between higher education and society. The civic or publicly engaged scholar is one way of describing the transformative process that has brought the end user into the research process as an active participant shaping the research agenda, and an assessor of its value, impact and benefit. Translational research, traditionally applied to medicine ("from bench to bedside") is now appropriate to other fields. Knowledge is ceasing "to be something standing outside society, a goal to be pursued by a community of scholars dedicated to the truth, but is shaped by many social actors under the conditions of the essential contestability of truth" (Delanty 2001, 105).

This is changing not only how the work is organised but the status of the work, the people doing it, the fields and disciplines, and the institutions themselves (Ellison and Eatman 2008, 7). While higher education may always have been a source of intellectual know-how for society, this was usually indirect; walled campuses express this sense of distance. Today, for better or worse, the inter-relationship between higher education and society, but more particularly the economy, is direct. Critics have denounced this progressive penetration of the market into fields of inquiry and their application as "academic capitalism" (Slaughter and Leslie 1997), but the process has helped underpin the democratisation of knowledge, and facilitated the emergence of more diverse roles and models of higher education. Table 43.2, read vertically, illustrates the historic alignment between the research-innovation spectrum and different educational models. Today, the strict demarcations between pure basic or fundamental, use-inspired basic, problem-solving or goal-oriented, pure application or market-oriented and technology/knowledge transfer have become porous. The linear model of research has been replaced by a dynamic

Table 43.2 Alignment between the research-innovation spectrum and higher education

Higher education framework	Pure basic or fundamental	Use-inspired basic	Problem-solving or goal-oriented	Problem-solving or goal-oriented	Pure application or market-oriented	Development and technology transfer	Knowledge transfer
Indicative outputs and impact	Peer articles Books and monographs Books chapters	Peer articles Policy and technical reports Patents Creative work	Peer articles Policy and technical reports Patents Creative work	Peer articles Policy and technical reports Patents Creative work		Licenses Contribution to standards New products and services New companies and employment	
Accountability	Peer review citations	Peer review citations Social and market accountability	Peer review citations Social and market accountability	Peer review citations Social and market accountability		Social, public and market accountability Peer, user and stakeholder esteem	
Educational models	Academic	Professional	Professional	Vocational		Entrepreneurship	

understanding of innovation (Rothwell 1994). Boundaries between educational models have also faded. As traditional boundaries fade, all HEIs are entrepreneurial – to paraphrase Clark (1998).

43.3   A New Way to Profile Diversity

43.3.1   Defining Diversity

Diversity is usually described using macro-level generic categories, such as institutional size, form of institutional control, range of disciplines offered, degrees awarded, and modes of study (Huisman et al. 2007). The US Carnegie Classification system has had a major influence on how institutions are described and describe themselves. While the system was changed in 2005 to embrace more characteristics with opportunity for customisation and multi-listings, its early rendition identified six main criteria and institutional categories/missions (McCormick 2006; see Table 43.3). Unfortunately, the system was read hierarchically and used accordingly by governments and institutions thereby confusing classification and identity (McCormick and Zhao 2005, 55). This in turn influenced, for example, the way *US News and World Report* subdivided its ranking of universities into tiers, of which Tier One is the most favoured – becoming the focal point for both political and institutional ambitions (USNS 2010). Both Reichert (2009, 122) and the EU-sponsored U-Map project (van Vught 2009) have endeavoured to overcome the problems encountered by Carnegie by identifying 5 and 14 dimensions, respectively.

Moving beyond distinction by level (e.g. BA, MA, PhD), the OECD (Vincent-Lancrin 2004) envisioned post-secondary education as "a collection of specialised HEIs carrying out several missions or functions for different groups of the population and for different kinds of knowledge". Read at either the system or institutional level, institutional missions are seen to be complex and meeting a wide range of socio-economic requirements. Duderstadt (2000) proffered another variation assigning indicative descriptors much like a car-showroom might display a range of different models. Clark (1998, xiv) coined the term "entrepreneurial" university to describe universities which "took chances in the market"; Lynton's "metropolitan university" (1995) has similarities to Bleiklie and Kogan's "stakeholder" university (Bleiklie et al. 2007, 371) or Goddard's "civic university" (2009, 4), the latter denoted by the way universities "engage (as-a-whole and not piecemeal) with wider society on the local, national and global scales, and … do so in a manner which links the social to the economic spheres." The engaged institution fulfils Delanty's observation that "the university is the institution in society most capable of linking the requirements of industry, technology and market forces with the demands of citizenship" (2001, 158; see also Sturm et al. 2011).

Differences may exist within institutions or between them; indeed, different units of an HEI may operate in different ways depending upon the discipline, orientation, business/financial model, etc. and the overarching historic/socio-economic context

Table 43.3 Different ways to describe institutional missions

Carnegie Classification System (1973, 2005)	Duderstadt (2000)	OECD (Vincent-Lancrin 2004)	U-Map (van Vught 2009)	Reichert (2009)
Doctoral-granting institutions	World university – international focus	Tradition – catering to relatively small share of youth for credentials	Types of degrees offered	Institutional clienteles or target communities
Comprehensive universities and colleges	Diverse university – social/ethnic diversity; pluralistic learning community	Entrepreneurial – teaching, research and service are well balanced	Range of subjects offered	Missions and functional emphases, i.e. research, teaching, research training, CPD, etc.
Liberal arts colleges	Creative university – university of the arts, media, architecture	Free market – market forces drive specialisation by function, field, audience	Orientation of degrees	Programme or subject profiles, e.g. academic, professional, etc.
Two-year colleges and institutes	Division-less university – interdisciplinary approach to learning	Lifelong learning and open education – universal access for all ages w/less research	Involvement in life-long learning	Staff profiles
Professional schools and other specialized institutions	Cyberspace university – open and distance learning	Globally networked – teaching/training institution in partnership with other orgs.	Research intensiveness	Student profiles
Instructional program	Adult university – advanced education and training	Diversity of recognised learning – disappearance of formal institution – distance, "open course" education	Innovation intensiveness	
Enrolment profile	University college – undergraduate provision; the lifelong university – programme provision throughout lifetime		International orientation: teaching and staff	
Size and setting	Ubiquitous university – new "life-form" linking/connecting social institutions		International orientation: research	
"Elective" classifications	Laboratory university – new "green-field" site experiment in learning		Size	
			Mode of delivery	
			Public/private character	
			Legal status	
			Cultural engagement	
			Regional engagement	

and governance model. Traditional collegial or federal models tend to tolerate greater internal differences than newer or managerial models which favour a unitary approach. Greater similarity in practice may be a feature of single-discipline institutions or highly unionised environments. Socio-cultural, economic and historic context are always important influencers (Codling and Meek 2006).

A difficulty with these approaches is the level of granularity is insufficient to fully appreciate the extent to which differentiation exists. This occurs because it depends upon an indicator being present or not, and differences between institutions are usually recorded quantitatively by the level of intensity, e.g. the greater number or proportion of an activity. Quantification appears to be scientific – objective and not subjective – but it has led to some perverse effects of ranking and classification systems.

> Colleges and universities are complex organizations that differ on many more dimensions than the handful of attributes used to define the classification's categories, and of course the very act of asserting similarity among institutions runs counter to the rhetoric of distinctiveness on our campuses. More important, the host of intangibles that constitute institutional identity could not possibly be incorporated into an empirically based classification system. (McCormick and Zhao 2005, 55)

In other words, by using a limited number of macro-level characteristics, many of the distinctive features of higher education remain hidden. Institutions and the system-as-a-whole look fixed in time, so change is greeted disapprovingly. Terms such as "mockers and mocked", "institutional chameleons" and pseudo-universities are used to describe what is considered imitative or "striving" behaviour (Meek and O'Neill 1996; O'Meara 2007).

43.3.2 Multi-dimensional Diversity

One way to address the problem of complexity is depicted in Fig. 43.2; it superimposes the European Union's concept of the knowledge triangle of teaching, research and innovation (European Commission 2010) onto different institutional missions and distinguishes particular foci from each other. Kerr's (1963) "multiversity" described higher education at the intersection of an expanding and multifaceted set of objectives and stakeholders, interpreted and prioritised in different ways by HEIs rather than in a bipolar world of teaching and research. Figure 43.3 updates this scenario using quadrants, whereby institutions position themselves in varying proportions to meet different socio-economic and policy objectives. Figure 43.4 displays two different institutional types – one with a strong teaching and societal commitment and the other more focused on traditional academic research. By visualising institutional profiles in this way, resembling the sun-bursts used by both U-Map and U-Multirank (van Vught 2009, 2011; van Vught et al. 2010), *some* differences can become more apparent to each other and other stakeholders. However, because, terms such as "education", "research" and "innovation" – which dominate most mission statements – operate at the macro level, they cannot adequately showcase diversity. Thus, it appears all institutions are pursuing the same objectives

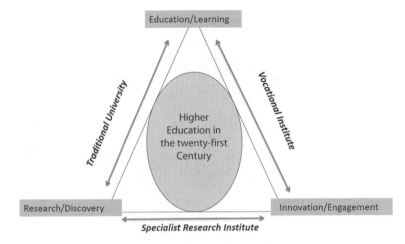

Fig. 43.2 New model of higher education (Source: Adapted from Hazelkorn 2005, 43)

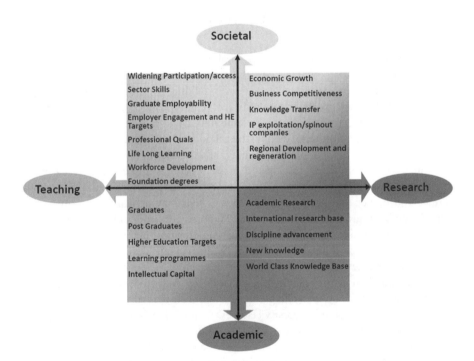

Fig. 43.3 Some agendas and expectations of higher education (Source: Wedgwood 2004, 10)

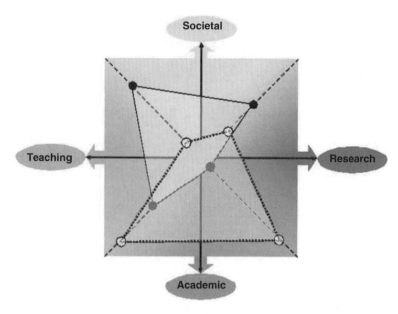

Fig. 43.4 Mapping diverse HEI profiles (Source: Wedgwood 2004, 11)

in the same way. The new multi-dimensional approach to diversity (see below and Fig. 43.5) aims to overcome these perceptual limitations and misunderstandings by moving to the next level of granularity – and providing a useful vocabulary.

As knowledge systems and institutions evolve, it is possible to "envisage a larger and still more varied array of providers, both public and private, national and international, global and corporate, campus-based and virtual" (Skilbeck 2001, 58–71, 2003) or to identify institutions which may straddle the line between categories – specialist art schools which also award masters degrees and conduct research or dual-sector institutions of Ireland, Australia, Africa, and Canada which offer both further and higher educational programmes. There may appear to be substantial duplication in programme provision but this ignores differences in pedagogy, use of work-based or on-line learning, case studies, internships, etc. which provide very different learning environments. Similar difficulties plague descriptions of research. This is because research is usually measured in terms of "intensity", e.g. the number of papers and citations per faculty, the ratio of research students/faculty, research income, patents/licenses, etc. The greater the number, the more a particular HEI is designated as a research university. However, quantification fails to distinguish between approaches to knowledge production and critical inquiry, and ignores field specialisation. Measuring activity at the macro-level may also exaggerate the extent to which de-differentiation and isomorphism or "striving" is occurring.

The *Multi-dimensional Diversity Framework* (Fig. 43.5) adopts a different approach. It displays multiple sub-characteristics, below the macro-level, to showcase the complex terrain of higher education. It also provides the necessary vocabulary – the set of key words – required by policymakers and HEIs to better express diversity. The characteristics/sub-characteristics are divided into four groups: mission,

Mission

Traditional Academic; Civic/Engaged; Liberal Arts; Technological; Entrepreneurial; Vocational/Professional; Specialist
International; National; Regional; Metropolitan; Community
Research-Intensive; Research-Informed; Teaching-Led
Religious; Non-Religious

Students

Elite; Mass; Universal
Selective; Recruiting; Open Access
Doctoral; Masters; Bachelor; Associate; Certificate; Dual Sector
Homogeneous; Multi-Ethnic/Diverse
Local; Domestic; International
18-22; Mature; Part-Time; Distance Learning; First-in-Family; Up/Re-Skilling; LLL; All Learners

Academic

Multi-Disciplinary; Specialist Disciplines; Mono-Discipline
Classical Canon; Professional; Technological; Vocational; Entrepreneurship
Lecture; Seminar; Case-Studies; Problem-Oriented; Work-Based; Practice-Based; Community Engaged Learning; Internships; Service Learning; Study Abroad; Blended-Learning;
Pure Basic/Fundamental; Use-Inspired Basic; Problem Solving/Goal-Oriented; Pure Application; Market-Oriented
Technology Transfer; Knowledge Transfer; Community Engagement

Organisation

Residential; Commuter; ODL
Old; Young
Wealthy; Humble
Collegial; Managerial; Corporate
Wholly Public; Public Dependent; Private Not-For-Profit; Private For-Profit
Government/Public Controlled; Regulated; Semi-Autonomous; Autonomous
Unitary; Federalist
Colleges; Faculties; Schools; Departments
City; Town; Suburban; Rural
Large; Medium; Small
Single-Campus; Multi-Campus; International Campuses; Franchise

Fig. 43.5 Multi-dimensional diversity framework

students, academic and organisation, albeit, this is simply an indicative list. Each characteristic/sub-characteristic is treated independently so they can be mixed accordingly. For example, an institution may be urban-based, disciplinary focused with strengths in use-inspired basic research while another may be specialist but focused primarily on problem-solving/goal-oriented research. In this way, HEIs can be shown to be more diverse than would be the case by simply describing them as teaching vs. research or world-class vs. regional suggests. While data is an important strategic tool, relying on quantification to determine diversity may actually reduce complexity to a few pre-selected categories – effectively undermining the purpose of the exercise. The *Multi-dimensional Diversity Framework* is proposed as a strategic tool for policymakers and higher education for, inter alia, benchmarking or quality assurance purposes to help define and profile institutional diversity.

43.4 Moving Forward: Recommendations

The evolution of higher education reflects the growing complexity of peoples, society and knowledge systems. As ways of thinking and doing expand beyond the preserve of a small elite to embrace a wide array of knowledge creators and end-users, higher education has changed to reflect this wider diversity of perspectives and requirements. But, while policy declares support for diversity, the methodologies used to assess, measure, evaluate and fund higher education are often at variance.

> Institutional diversity will thrive only if both the system of regulation and funding as well as the values which underpin institutional development do not favour a particular profile or particular dimensions of institutional activity over others. (Reichert 2009, 8)

So, if the goal is institutional diversity – what are the policies?

The literature on diversity points to a broad range of factors which have either encouraged/discouraged differentiation between HEIs. While it is difficult to ascertain a single cause, the policy environment is certainly a critical factor. Three areas of complexity which pose particular challenges to policy development are addressed briefly below: government steering methods, conceptualising research and third-mission activities. Finally, a process for embedding diversity into performance assessment for institutions and individuals is proposed.

43.4.1 Diversity and Government Steerage

In Europe, governments commonly sought to impose differentiation through regulatory mechanisms, what is known widely as the binary system. It assigned distinct roles/missions to universities and Hoschule, etc. in ways which mirror the US California model (Douglass 2000). Top-down regulation of mission often coincided with government micro-management of the institutions, including budgets and expenditure at the operational level, curriculum, and academic appointments. In recent decades, there has been a shift from control to regulation to steering, not least because it is widely argued that successful institutions are those most able to direct and strategically manage their own affairs (Estermann and Nokkala 2009; Aghion et al. 2008). At the same time, governments want to retain control, especially with respect to publicly-funded or -dependent institutions. Driving change from a distance may include promoting common comparability frameworks at either a national or international level, e.g. qualifications frameworks, global rankings, assessment of learning outcomes. While these initiatives are promulgated in response to pressure for greater accountability, they could undermine diversity by endorsing common standards (Eaton 2011). The challenge is how to balance autonomy and accountability with diversity.

One approach gaining traction is university contracts or compacts. This seeks to engage HEIs in a service-level agreement to provide teaching, research, services, etc. appropriate to mission in return for funding. Australia has been an early mover, and has sought to tie the "unique mission of each university to the Government's goals for the sector". From the government's vantage point, compacts enable a more "coordinated response to the … goals for higher education, research and innovation" (Evans 2010) while linking funding to performance. Denmark, the Netherlands, Norway and Ireland have adopted similar approaches. The Irish *National Review of Higher Education to 2030* recommended the introduction of a "strategic dialogue" between the Higher Education Authority (the buffer agency) and individual institutions, and occasionally at a sector-wide level, as a means of "aligning the strategies of individual institutions with national priorities and agreeing key performance indicators (KPIs) against which institutional performance will be measured and funding decided" (Review Group 2011, 91). Aside from ensuring that HEIs meet societal needs, the emphasis is on ensuring "a diverse range of strong, autonomous institutions." The process involves a formal conversation at which

> each institution will be required to define its mission and decide how it can best contribute to achieving national goals, as determined by the government. In defining mission, institutes should avoid playing catch-all – this is a formula for blandness and dissipation of energy and resources – and ultimately will not be funded … They need to find a balance between their own development as institutions and the development of the sector as a whole; between competition in quality and standards, and due regard to the strategic objectives of others, and national objectives. (Boland 2011)

The process is described as "directed diversity"; while there may be some opportunity for institutions to self-define their mission, it will not be open-ended. This means the choice of KPIs is critical. The key questions are whether government can resist the temptation to micro-manage, and whether this approach can provide a legitimating ideology for each mission (Clark 1978).

43.4.2 Diverse Research Missions

Research and teaching are often seen as oppositional attributes; an institution can excel at one but not both. Governments often express policy options in terms of "world-class research universities" vs. "world-class teaching institutions" or university vs. **non**-university; sometimes the former is shortened to "world-class university" where the word "research" is implicit. Another formulation is "world-class university" vs. "regional university" – whereby the distinctions are also understood in terms of status not only mission. In the rush to criticise the obsession with "world-class", commentators have argued that

> …what we really need in countries everywhere are more world-class technical institutes, world-class community colleges, world-class colleges of agriculture, world-class teachers colleges, and world-class regional state universities. (Birnbaum 2007; Salmi 2009, 3)

While the sentiment is worthy, it does not get around the fact that the drive for "world-class" status is usually made on the basis that "steep vertical diversification of higher education is desirable" and sustained by an unquestioning correlation between quality and elite universities (Guri-Rosenblit et al. 2007, 381).

Table 43.4 Indicative list of diverse research outputs/impact

Journal articles	Peer esteem/citations
Book chapters	Impact on teaching
Computer software and	Improved productivity, reduced costs
databases	Improvements on environment and
Conference publications	lifestyle
Editing of major works	Improving people's health and quality
Legal cases, maps	of life
Major art works	Increased employment
Major works in production or	Informed public debate
exhibition and/or award-	New approaches to social issues
winning design	New curriculum
Patents or plant breeding rights	Patents, licenses
Policy documents or brief	Policy change
Research or technical reports	Social innovation
Technical drawings, designs or	Stakeholder esteem
working models	Stimulating creativity
Translations	
Visual recordings	

Research presents a policy dilemma for diversity. First, research is generally interpreted as homogeneous – institutions either engage in research or they do not. This simple distinction can be modified by distinguishing between basic and applied research, in which the former is generally perceived, in status terms, as *real* research implicitly associated with big science and fundamental bio-medical discoveries. But, as Boyer reminds us

> the word "research" actually entered the vocabulary of higher education [recently]....schol-arship in earlier times referred to a variety of creative work carried on in a variety of places, and its integrity was measured by the ability to think, communicate, and learn. What we now have is a more restricted view of scholarship, one that limits it to a hierarchy of functions. (Boyer 1990, 15)

Second, this over-simplification of research activity is driven quantitatively by bib-liometric practices which count productivity principally by journal articles, and impact by citations or rather what one academic has written and another read. But this is only a fraction of research activity; Table 43.4 shows that what is measured (above the line) represents a fraction of the breadth of activity (below the line; cf. Ellison and Eatman 2008, 1; Sandmann et al. 2009). Unfortunately, this narrow conception informs most rankings, classification systems and policy (Hazelkorn 2009, 2011a, b). At a time when society has a growing need for new methodologies and interdisciplinary research to explore and resolve major societal and scientific challenges, the simplicity and limitation of data collection and analysis obscures important understandings (see McCormick and Zhao 2005, 56), and leads to distortions in policy and resource allocation, and hiring, promotion and tenure (CFIR 2004, 2).

43.4.3 Engagement and Third-Mission Activity

Another area of complexity concerns "third-mission" activities; this has replaced the traditional concept of "service" which usually referred to membership of in-house or professional committees – arguably a Mode 1 understanding of higher education. Today, sustained, embedded and reciprocal engagement is defined as learning beyond the campus walls, discovery which is useful beyond the academic community and service that directly benefits the public. Different programmatic models and initiatives are emerging which bring together actors from civil society, the state and state agencies, and higher education to mobilize and harness knowledge, talent and investment in order to address a diverse range of problems and need through co-ordinated action. While these objectives are lauded, policy and academic practice has done little to formally reward such endeavours beyond paying lip-service to counting patents and licenses. Carnegie's Community Engagement classification draws upon institutional documentation (Driscoll 2008, 41) while U-Multirank uses a limited set of pre-selected indicators (van Vught 2011). In contrast, the EU-funded E3M project (2011) has developed an extensive range of continuing education, technology transfer and innovation, and social engagement indicators (Table 43.5).

43.4.4 Aligning Diversity with Performance

For diversity to be meaningful, these complexities need to be captured and reflected in policy and public discourse, and the systems that incentivise and reward institutions and individuals. However, there is little doubt that diversity breeds complexity – and potentially undermines another government objective of cost containment and efficiency. To be fair to both the goal and the process, a multi-faceted process that meets the different objectives needs to be developed. One solution is to change the assessment and reward system, for institutions and individuals, to better align it with policy intentions rather than "systems that distort academic investments and produce inequality ..." (Calhoun 2006).

Because academic norms and values can be a road-block to diversity, new forms of academic credentialism and assessment that recognise the diversity of research outputs and impacts as part of the "continuum" of scholarship should be adopted.

> The term continuum has become pervasive because ... it is inclusive of many sorts and conditions of knowledge. It resists embedded hierarchies and by assigning equal value to inquiry of different kinds. (Ellison and Eatman 2008, ix)

Some research assessment exercises are beginning to reflect Mode 2 and even Mode 3 realities, shifting focus away from simply measuring inputs (e.g. human, physical and financial resources) to looking at outcomes (the level of performance or achievement including the contribution research makes to the advancement of scientific-scholarly knowledge) and impact and benefits (e.g. the contribution of research

Table 43.5 Indicative list of Third Mission indicators

Continuing education (CE)	Technology transfer & innovation	Social engagement
CE included in HEI policy/strategy	TTI included in HEI policy/strategy	SE included in HEI policy/strategy
Existence of CE institutional plan	Existence of TTI institutional action plan	Existence of SE institutional action plan
Existence of quality assurance procedure for CE activities	Number of licenses, options & assignments (active & executed, exclusive & non-exclusive) to start-ups or spin-offs & existing companies	Budgetary assignment to SE
Total number of CE programmes active in year for implementation	Total budget coming from commercialisation revenues	Percent academics involved in volunteering advisory
Number of CE programmes delivered which have a major award under higher education system	Number of start-ups/spin-offs	Number of events open to community/public
Number of partnership with public/private business CE programmes delivered in year	Number of creative commons & social innovation projects HEI employees involved in	Number of research initiatives with direct impact on the community
Percent international CE programmes delivered in year	Number of R&D sponsored agreements, contracts & collaborative projects with non-academic partners	Number/cost of staff/student hours made available to deliver services & facilities to community
Percent funded CE training projects delivered in year	Percent HEI budget from income of R&D sponsored contracts & collaborative projects with non-academic partners	Number of people attending/using facilities
Total number of ECTS credits of delivered CE programmes	Number of consultancy contracts	Number of projects related to educational outreach
Number of ECTS credits enrolled	Percent postgraduate students & postdoctoral researchers directly funded or co-funded by public & private businesses	Number of faculty staff & students involved in educational outreach activity
Number of registrations in CE programmes in year	Number of created (co-funded) or shared laboratories & buildings	Percent HEI budget used for educational outreach
Percent CE ECTS enrolled referred to the total ECTS enrolled	Number of companies participating in CPD courses	
Percent qualifications issued referred to total CE registrations	Number of HEI employees with temporary positions outside of academia	
Student satisfaction	Number of non-academic employees with temporary positions	
Key stakeholder satisfaction	Number of postgraduate theses or projects with non-academic co-supervisors	
Completion rate for all programmes (in average)	Number of joint publications with non-academic authors	
Percent CE programmes with external accreditations	Number of academic staff participating in professional bodies, networks, organizations & boards	
	Number of external organizations or individuals participating at advisory, steering, validation, review boards to HEIs, institutes, centres or taught programmes	
	Number of prestigious innovation prizes awarded by business & public sector associations or funding agencies (national & international)	

Source: Adapted from E3M Project (2011)

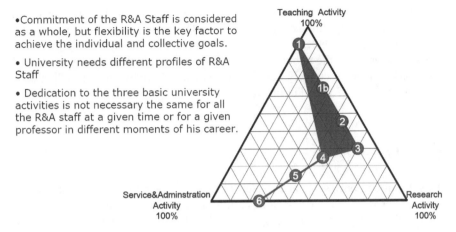

•Commitment of the R&A Staff is considered as a whole, but flexibility is the key factor to achieve the individual and collective goals.

• University needs different profiles of R&A Staff

• Dedication to the three basic university activities is not necessary the same for all the R&A staff at a given time or for a given professor in different moments of his career.

Fig. 43.6 Flexibility in task assignments (Source: Vidal 2006)

outcomes for society, culture, the environment and/or the economy) (European Commission 2010, 36–37). As the UK Research Assessment Exercise (RAE) developed, it became more inclusive of disciplines and methodologies but was undermined by protestations about the level of "bureaucratic" intrusion. Arguably this came loudest from those universities which gained the most and saw little point investing more time and money into the exercise. The result in the UK and Australia was to push for metrics-based assessment but this process simply amplified the distortions identified above (Corbyn 2010; Rowbotham 2011).

Another approach is to align resources to the different elements of the knowledge triangle or quadrants (Figs. 43.2 and 43.3 above). Units and individuals would be expected to develop provision/activity which reflects education/teaching, discovery/ research and engagement/innovation – relevant to the academic discipline – with resources or rewards based upon meeting thresholds in at least 2 of these areas (e.g. 40%+40%+20%). One such example is the Research and Academic Staff Commitment Agreement (CA) developed by the Universitat Rovira i Virgili (Spain); modelled on the knowledge triangle concept, the CA is described as an "instrument that makes it possible to manage the time that the academic and research staff (PDI) of the Rovira i Virgili University (URV) spend on the activities they carry out: teaching, research, technology transfer, continuous training, management, etc." (Vidal and Xavier 2006; Fig. 43.6). Dublin Institute of Technology (www/dit.ie) uses a similar approach for its professorial appointments; candidates must show outstanding achievement in at least one of the three principal criteria: Research, consultancy, scholarship and/or creative achievement, Professional standing and Academic leadership. Other examples can be found most readily in the US where the concept of the engaged-scholar has become more established (see Saltmarsh et al. 2009; Ellison and Eatman 2008).

Variations of these latter models can work at the individual, institutional and system level – and combined with the Multi-Dimensional Diversity Framework further amplified by Tables 43.4 and 43.5 – can facilitate better profiling of institutions and clarity for the public. They can be used to help develop the vocabulary necessary to more accurately describe institutional diversity without falling back onto simplistic macro-level terminology.

43.5 Conclusion

This discussion only snips at the heels of possible ways forward. Its value is not simply to broaden our understanding of diversity but to begin to develop what Clark calls (1978) a "legitimating ideology" to anchor diversity in response to other pressures, e.g. rankings, which juxtapose teaching with research. Arguably, the battle over mission descriptors is really about wealth and status in an environment of increasing competition. Yet, many pre-selected indicators and categories are a disservice to diversity; they end up controlling rather than profiling differences between institutions (McCormick and Zhao 2005, 52). Research and teaching, and globally-facing and regionally relevant are often portrayed as contradictory or oppositional rather than complementary characteristics. This is because there are obvious difficulties associated with profiling complexity – but acknowledging these limitations is one thing, understanding their ideological impact and implications is another. In the rush to provide simple cost-effective solutions, we risk distorting higher education to meet the terms of the indicators or stylised models. There is already substantial evidence from the experience of the Carnegie Classification system and global rankings that measuring the wrong things produces distortions, leading to profound and often perverse affects on higher education and society – far beyond those envisaged by the producers.

The European Commission (2011) says "Europe needs a wide diversity of higher education institutions … with more transparent information about the specific profile and performance of individual institutions …" This is where the *Multidimensional Diversity Framework* (Fig. 43.5 above) could be helpful, facilitating governments and institutions to go beyond macro-level terminology of teaching vs. research, basic vs. applied, comprehensive vs. specialist, school leaver vs. mature, etc. It carries the arguments of the OECD, Wedgewood, U-Map and U-Multirank a step further. It embraces a deeper understanding of diversity by moving away from a reductive set of dimensions. Saying everyone wants to be like Harvard is an easy quip. As long as higher education is perceived in terms of a status hierarchy, as long as governments react to rankings by valuing particular institutions and disciplines over others, then all developments and change, whether at the individual, institutional or system level, will be portrayed as a "snake-like procession" (Riesman 1956) – and "parity of esteem is not likely to occur" (Clark 1978, 250). Because these views have become ingrained in our status system, overcoming these preconceptions requires strong leadership and vision.

Acknowledgments This is based on a presentation to the EAIR conference, Iceland, 2011. Thanks also to Siobhan Harkin, Brian Norton, Sybille Reichert, Jacqueline Smith and Elaine Ward for their helpful comments and suggestions at various stages in the development of this paper, to participants at the Bologna Process Researchers Conference, Bucharest, 2011, and to Evin McCarthy for helping design the *Multi-dimensional Diversity Framework*.

References

Aghion, P., Algan, Y., Cahuc, P., & Shleifer, A. (2008). *Regulation and distrust*. Unpublished paper, Harvard University.

Birnbaum, R. (1983). *Maintaining diversity in higher education*. San Francisco: Jossey-Bass.

Birnbaum, R. (2007). No world-class university left behind. *International Higher Education, 47*, 7–9.

Bleiklie, I., Laredo, P., & Sörlin, S. (2007). Introduction. *Higher Education Policy, 20*, 365–372.

Boland, T. (2011). *Hunting for treasures: A vision for an excellent higher education sector in Ireland*. Paper at opening of first academic year at Limerick Institute of Technology following the integration with Tipperary Institute, Higher Education Authority, Ireland.

Boyer, E. L. (1990). *Scholarship reconsidered. Priorities of the professoriate*. Princeton: Carnegie Foundation.

Brennan, J. (2004). The social role of the contemporary university: Contradictions, boundaries and change. In Center for Higher Education Research and Information (CHERI) (Ed.), *Ten years on: Changing education in a changing world* (pp. 22–26). Buckingham: The Open University. http://www.open.ac.uk/cheri/documents/ten-years-on.pdf. Accessed 5 June 2011.

Butler, N. (2007). Europe's universities – Time for reform. *Centrepiece*, Autumn 10–11. http://cep.lse.ac.uk/pubs/download/cp233.pdf. Accessed 29 Aug 2011.

Calhoun, C. (2006). The university and the public good. *Thesis Eleven, 84*, 7–43.

CFIR – Committee on Facilitating Interdisciplinary Research. (2004). *Facilitating interdisciplinary research*. National Academy of Sciences, National Academy of Engineering, Institute of Medicine. Retrieved July 31, 2009, from http://books.nap.edu/openbook.php?record_id=11153&page=2

Clark, B. R. (1978). Academic differentiation in national systems of higher education. *Comparative Education Review, 22*(June), 242–258.

Clark, B. R. (1983). *The higher education system: academic organization in cross-national perspective*. Berkeley, California: University of California Press.

Clark, B. R. (1998). *Creating entrepreneurial universities. Organizational pathways of transformation*. Oxford: IAU Press/Pergamon/Elsevier.

Codling, A., & Meek, V. L. (2006). Twelve propositions for diversity in higher education. *Higher Education Management and Policy, 18*(3), 31–54.

Corbyn, Z. (2010, April 1). Nervous HEFCE 'edging out' of REF citations. *The Times Higher Education*.

Daniel, J. (1996, August 9). The world cuisine of borderless knowledge. *Times Higher Education*. http://www.timeshighereducation.co.uk/story.asp?storyCode=99628&sectioncode=26. Accessed 11 Sept 2011.

Delanty, G. (2001). *Challenging knowledge. The university in the knowledge society*. Buckingham: SRHE/Open University Press.

Douglass, J. (2000). *The California idea and American higher education, 1860 to the 1960 master plan*. Palo Alto: Stanford Press.

Driscoll, A. (2008, January/February). Carnegie's community engagement classification. Intentions and insights. *Change*, 38–41.

Duderstadt, J. J. (2000). *A university for the 21st century*. Ann Arbor: The University of Michigan Press.

E3M PROJECT. (2011). *Final report of Delphi study.* European Indicators and Ranking Methodology for University Third Mission, Universidad Politécnica de Valencia and the Universidad de León, unpublished.

Eaton, J. (2011). *Does quality assurance threaten institutional autonomy and academic freedom?* Paper to the XXIII Anniversary of the Magna Charta Universitatum conference. Bologna.

Ellison, J., & Eatman, T. J. (2008). *Scholarship in public: Knowledge creation and tenure policy in the engaged university.* Syracuse: Imaging America.

Enserink, M. (2009, December 9). Sarkozy to French universities: We're going to invest massively. *Science Insider.* http://news.sciencemag.org/scienceinsider/2009/12/sarkozy-to-fren.html. Accessed 28 May 2010.

Estermann, T., & Nokkala, T. (2009). *University autonomy in Europe I. Exploratory study.* Brussels: European University Association.

European Commission (2010). *Assessing Europe's university based research.* Expert Group on the Assessment of University-based Research. Brussels: European Commission. http://ec.europa.eu/research/science-society/document_library/pdf_06/assessing-europe-university-based-research_en.pdf. Accessed 4 Apr 2010.

European Commission (2011). *Supporting growth and jobs – An agenda for the modernisation of Europe's higher education system.* COM (2011)567/2, Brussels.

Evans, C. (2010). *University compacts to reward high performance.* Joint Media Release. Canberra: Department of Education, Employment and Workplace Relations. http://www.deewr.gov.au/ministers/evans/media/releases/pages/article_101026_140947.aspx. Accessed 11 Sept 2011.

Geiser, S., & Atkinson, R. C. (2010). *Beyond the master plan. The case for restructuring baccalaureate education in California.* http://cshe.berkeley.edu/publications/docs/ROPS.Geiser.Atkinson.BeyondMP.11.18.10.pdf. Accessed 30 Oct 2011.

Gibbons, M., Limoges, C., Nowotny, H., Schwartzman, S., Scott, P., & Trow, M. (1994). *The new production of knowledge.* London: Sage.

Goddard, J. (2009). *Re-inventing the civic university.* London: NESTA.

Gumport, P. J. (2000). Academic restructuring: Organizational change and institutional imperatives. *Higher Education, 39,* 67–91.

Guri-Rosenblit, S., Sebkova, H., & Teichler, U. (2007). Massification and diversity of higher education systems: Interplay of complex dimensions. *Higher Education Policy, 20,* 373–389.

Hazelkorn, E. (2005). *Developing research in new institutions.* Paris: OECD.

Hazelkorn, E. (2009). *The impact of global rankings on higher education research and the production of knowledge* (UNESCO Forum on Higher Education, Research and Knowledge Occasional Paper No. 16). http://unesdoc.unesco.org/images/0018/001816/181653e.pdf. Accessed 3 May 2010.

Hazelkorn, E. (2011a). *Rankings and the reshaping of higher education: The battle for world class excellence.* Houndsmills: Palgrave Macmillan.

Hazelkorn, E. (2011b, August 16). The futility of ranking journals. *Chronicle of Higher Education.* http://chronicle.com/blogs/worldwise/the-futility-of-ranking-academic-journals/28553. Accessed 25 Sept 2011.

Huisman, J. (1998). Differentiation and diversity in higher education systems. In J. C. Smart & W. G. Tierney (Eds.), *Higher education: Handbook of theory and research.* Norwell: Kluwer Academic Publishers.

Huisman, J., Meek, L., & Wood, F. (2007). Institutional diversity in higher education: A cross-national and longitudinal analysis. *Higher Education Quarterly, 61*(4), 563–577.

Julius, D. J. (2011). When systems evolve. *Inside Higher Ed.* http://www.insidehighered.com/views/2011/06/03/essay_on_the_evolution_of_flagship_universities

Kasper, H. T. (2002–2003, Winter). The changing role of community college. *Occupational Outlook Quarterly,* 14–21. http://www.bls.gov/opub/ooq/2002/winter/art02.pdf

Kerr, C. (1963). *Uses of the university.* Godkin lectures. Harvard University. (Reprinted as *The uses of the university* (5th ed.) by C. Kerr, 2001, Cambridge, MA: Harvard University Press).

Lynton, E. A. (1995). What is a metropolitan university. In D. M. Johnson & David A Bell *Metropolitan Universities: An Emerging Model in American Higher Education,* (pp. xi–xxi). Denton, Texas, University of North Texas Press.

Marcus, J. (2011). Old school: Four-hundred years of resistance to change. In B. Wildavsky, A. P. Kelly, & K. Carey (Eds.), *Reinventing higher education* (pp. 41–72). Cambridge, MA: Harvard Education Press.

McCormick, A. C. (2006). *The Carnegie classification of institutions of higher education*. OECD Workshop on Institutional Diversity. Paris. http://www.oecd.org/dataoecd/9/41/37800086.pdf. Accessed 25 Sept 2011.

McCormick, A. C., & Zhao, C. M. (2005, September/October). Rethinking and reframing the Carnegie classification. *Change, 37*, 51–57.

Meek, V. L. (1991). The transformation of Australian higher education from binary to unitary system. *Higher Education, 21*(4), 461–494.

Meek, V. L., & O'Neill, A. (1996). Diversity and differentiation in the Australian unified national system of higher education. In V. L. Meek & A. O'Neill (Eds.), *The mockers and mocked: Comparative perspective on differentiation, convergence and diversity in higher education* (pp. 60–78). Issues in higher education. Oxford: IAU Press/Elsevier Science Ltd.

Neave, G. (2000). Diversity, differentiation and the market: The debate we never had but which we ought to have done. *Higher Education Policy, 13*, 7–21.

O'Meara, K. (2007). Striving for what? Exploring the pursuit of prestige. *Higher Education: Handbook of Theory and Research, XXII*, 123–124.

Reichert, S. (2009). *Institutional diversity in European Higher Education. Tensions and challenges for policy makers and institutional leaders*. Brussels: European University Association.

Review Group. (2011). *National strategy for higher education to 2030*. Report of the Review Group. Dublin: Department of Education and Skills.

Rhoades, G. (1990). Political competition and differentiation in higher education. In J. C. Alexander & P. Colomy (Eds.), *Differentiation theory and social change. Comparative and historical perspectives*. New York: Columbia University Press.

Riesman, D. (1956). *Constraint and variety in American education*. Lincoln: University of Nebraska Press.

Rothwell, R. (1994). Towards the fifth-generation innovation process. *International Marketing Review, 11*(1), 7–31.

Rowbotham, J. (2011). Kim Carr bows to rank rebellion over journal rankings. *The Australian*. http://www.theaustralian.com.au/higher-education/kim-carr-bows-to-rank-rebellion/story-e6frgcjx-1226066727078

Salmi, J. (2009). The challenge of establishing world class universities. In *Directions in human development*. Washington, DC: The World Bank.

Saltmarsh, J., Giles, D. E., O'Meara, K.-A., Sandmann, L., Ward, E., & Buglione, S. (2009). Community engagement and institutional culture in higher education. An investigation of faculty reward policies at the engaged campus. In B. Moely, S. Billig, & B. Holland (Eds.), *Creating our identities in service-learning and community* (pp. 3–29). Greenwich: Information Age Publishing, Inc.

Sandmann, L. R., Thornton, C. H., & Jaeger, A. J. (Eds.). (2009). *Institutionalizing community engagement in higher education: The first wave of Carnegie classified institutions* (New directions for higher education, No. 147). San Francisco: Jossey-Bass.

Santiago, P., Tremblay, K., Basri, E., & Arnal, E. (2008). *Tertiary education for the knowledge society, 1*. Paris: OECD.

Skilbeck, M. (2001). *The university challenged. Review of international trends and issues with particular reference to Ireland*. Dublin: Higher Education Authority.

Skilbeck, M. (2003). *Towards an integrated system of tertiary education: A discussion paper*. Unpublished.

Slaughter, S., & Leslie, L. (1997). *Academic capitalism. Politics, policies and the entrepreneurial university*. Baltimore: Johns Hopkins University Press.

Sturm, S., Eatman, T., Saltmarsh, J., & Bush, A. (2011). *Full participation: Building the architecture for diversity and public engagement in higher education*. http://www.fullparticipation.net/download/the-catalyst-paper. Accessed 30 Oct 2011.

Trow, M. (1974). Problems in the transition from elite to mass higher education. *In General Report on the Conference on Future Structures of Post-Secondary Education*, OECD, Paris, 55–101. (Reprinted in M. Burrage (Ed.), 2010, *Martin Trow. Twentieth-Century Higher Education. From Elite to Mass to Universal*, Baltimore, MA: Johns Hopkins University Press, 88–143).

Trow, M. (2006). Reflections on the transition from elite to mass to universal access: Forms and phases of higher education in modern societies since WWII. In J. F. Forest & P. G. Altbach (Eds.), *International handbook on higher education* (pp. 243–280). New York: Springer (Reprinted in M. Burrage (Ed.), 2010, *Martin Trow. Twentieth-Century Higher Education. From Elite to Mass to Universal*, Baltimore, MA: Johns Hopkins University Press, 556–610).

van Vught, F. A. (2007, November 16). *Diversity and differentiation in higher education systems*. CHET Anniversary Conference, Cape Town.

van Vught, F. A. (2008). Mission diversity and reputation in higher education. *Higher Education Policy, 21*(2), 151–174.

van Vught, F. A. (Ed.). (2009). *Mapping diversity. Developing a European classification of higher education institutions*. Dordrecht: Springer.

van Vught, F. A. (2011). *A user-driven and multi-dimensional ranking tool in global higher education and research*. Paper to the UNESCO Global Forum on Rankings and Accountability in Higher Education: Uses and Misuses, Paris.

van Vught, F. A., Kaiser, F., File, J. M., Gaethgens, C., Peter, R., & Westerheijden, D. F. (2010). *U-Map. The European classification of higher education institutions*. Enschede: CHEPS.

Vidal, G. (2006). *The URV research and academic staff commitment agreement*. Presentation to the 1st European Forum for Quality Assurance: Embedding quality culture in higher education, Munich.

Vidal, G., & Xavier, F. (2006). *The URV research and academic staff commitment agreement*. Tarragona: University Rovira i Virgili.

Vincent-Lancrin, S. (2004). Building future scenarios for universities and higher education. An international approach. *Policy Futures in Education, 2*(2). Paris: OECD-CERI.

Vincent-Lancrin, S. (2008). What is the impact of demography on higher education systems? A forward-looking approach for OECD countries. In CERI (Ed.), *Higher education to 2030: Vol. 1. Demography* (pp. 41–104). Paris: OECD.

Wedgwood, M. (2004). *Higher education for the workforce: Barriers and facilitators to employer engagement*. London: Department of Innovation, Universities and Skills. http://www.bis.gov.uk/assets/biscore/corporate/migratedD/publications/D/DIUS_RR_08_04. Accessed 7 Sept 2011.

Webography

CFAT – Carnegie Foundation for the Advancement of Teaching. (2011, January). *Updated Carnegie Classifications™ show increase in for-profits, change in traditional landscape*. http://www.carnegiefoundation.org/newsroom/press-releases/updated-carnegie-classifications. Accessed 11 Sept 2011.

European Commission. (2010, June). *Era in the knowledge triangle*. http://ec.europa.eu/research/era/understanding/what/era_in_the_knowledge_triangle_en.htm. Accessed 11 Sept 2011.

U-Map – http://www.u-map.eu/. Accessed 31 Aug 2011.

U-Multirank. http://www.u-multirank.eu/. Accessed 31 Aug 2011.

USNS – U.S. News Staff. (2010, August 17). Frequently asked questions: College rankings. *US News and World Report*. http://www.usnews.com/education/articles/2010/08/17/frequently-asked-questions-college-rankings#8. Accessed 11 Sept 2011.

Chapter 44
Institutional Diversification and Homogeneity in Romanian Higher Education: The Larger Picture

Liviu Andreescu, Radu Gheorghiu, Viorel Proteasa, and Adrian Curaj

44.1 Introduction

Two decades after the regime change in 1989, Romanian higher education is still institutionally homogenous.[1] The relative lack of diversity is obvious in institutional structures, professional norms and the structure of the professoriate, in the design of academic programs and in educational contents. More surprisingly, perhaps, even after two decades of privatization and substantial expansion – in terms of the number of students, staff, and institutions – homogenization is also apparent in the system's low tuition fees.

---

[1] A number of analyses on recent developments in and future challenges for Romanian higher education, together with a vision for 2025 which purports to address some of the latter, are available at http://www.edu2025.ro/

L. Andreescu (✉)
Spiru Haret University, Bucharest, Romania
e-mail: andreescul@gmail.com

R. Gheorghiu
Institute for World Economy, Bucharest, Romania
e-mail: gheorghiu.radu.cristian@gmail.com

V. Proteasa
Viorel Proteasa is a benefiter of the programmes "Doctoral scholarships for the development of a knowledge based society - BDSC", and "Restructuring doctoral research in the fields of political sciences, public administration, sociology and communication", co-funded by the European Union through the European Social Fund, Sectorial Operational Programme Human Resources Development 2007-2013.

National School for Political Studies and Public Administration, Bucharest, Romania
e-mail: viorel.proteasa@gmail.com

A. Curaj
Politehnica University, Bucharest, Romania
e-mail: adrian.curaj@uefiscdi.ro

A. Curaj et al. (eds.), *European Higher Education at the Crossroads:*
Between the Bologna Process and National Reforms,
DOI 10.1007/978-94-007-3937-6_44, © Springer Science+Business Media Dordrecht 2012

863

The genuine concern with the absence of institutional and program diversity in Romanian higher education (HE) is a quite recent trend. It was most likely triggered by two no less recent developments, one domestic and one external. The former consisted of a set of measures which came into force with the National Education Law adopted early in 2011, specifically: the introduction of a system of classification for higher education institutions (HEIs) and an accompanying ranking of academic programs. The non-domestic development was an explicit pan-European concern with classifications and rankings, a concern which manifested itself quite bluntly in such initiatives as U-Map and U-Multirank, but also in a more diffused manner. Perhaps just as significant for the sudden surge of interest in diversification is the (also recent) effort to change the image of quality assurance in Romania – from a heavily accreditation-biased system to a more service-oriented one, and therefore, to a system which is more sensitive to institutional particularities (Vlăsceanu et al. 2011).

Given the recent nature of this concern with institutional diversity among both policy-makers and students of educational policy, the treatment of this subject in a Romanian context remains meager. As far as the latter group is concerned, like other scholarly attempts to understand differentiation/diversification in higher education – for our purposes, these concepts are sufficiently similar to be used interchangeably –, this treatment has been particularly indebted to neo-institutionalism, and especially to studies of institutional isomorphism (DiMaggio and Powell 1983). Consequently, legitimization strategies and professional norms have been generally identified as the main sources of homogenization in the Romanian academe. Our goal in this article is to offer an additional explanation to complement this neo-institutionalist perspective. Specifically, we argue that, until very recently, the pressure for diversification has not been sufficiently strong to generate a more diverse academic system. In other words, the institutional incentives for diversification have not been strong enough in this country so as to overcome those for imitating flagship universities or adhering closely to established professional norms.

In the first section below we offer a rundown of theories of diversification and a brief outline of how these theories have been applied in a Romanian context. The section following it provides a summary statement of our hypothesis as to the causes for the current homogeneity, as well as some necessary conceptual clarifications and delimitations. In the subsequent section we provide a more detailed analysis and some factual data in support of our hypothesis. We conclude with a discussion of recent relevant developments and a few predictions.

44.2 Theories of Diversification and Romanian Higher Education

Diversification has been a persistent concern of organization theorists over the past decades, both in general and in higher education specifically. The process has been explained in a variety of ways by a variety of theorists, and these explanations are rarely mutually exclusive. (The opposite seems to be the case.) Most initial theories were concerned with diversification *within* organizations (what has been occasionally defined as internal differentiation). In a well-known set of articles and larger studies (e.g., Blau 1970), one of which was devoted specifically to "the organization of academic work" (Blau 1994), Peter Blau tied internal differentiation to organizational size, analyzing the broader implications of his theory that diversification increases with size at decelerating rates. Blau found this to be the case in firms, governmental organizations and universities, though some of the consequences of his general rule were, it was argued, different depending on the type of organization.

Another one of the more notorious conceptualizations of diversification construes it as a strategy to avoid constraining resource dependence. As Pfeffer and Salancik (2003, p. 127) explained,

> Diversification can be viewed as another organizational response to the environment. It is a strategy for avoiding interdependence. Diversification buffers the organization against the potential effects of dependence by putting the organization into another set of relationships that are presumably different. Diversification is a way of avoiding the domination that comes from asymmetric exchanges when it is not possible to absorb or, in some other way, gain increased control over the powerful external exchange partner. Diversification is most likely to be used when exchanges are very concentrated and when capital or statutory constraints limit the use of merger or other strategies for managing inter-organizational relationships.

According to this view, internal differentiation is likely to occur in environments where exchanges are concentrated while relationships are asymmetric and usually involve dominant organizations. Organizations adjust themselves in order to reduce dependence on a single provider of essential resources and to enhance autonomy. Organizations intensively doing business with governments are, for these reasons, particularly liable to engage in diversification.

This theory of diversification lends itself more directly than Blau's to an interpretation in terms not only of internal but also of institutional diversity. Organizations diversify not merely their products, but sometimes also their broader strategies and their goals. Consequently, they may ultimately become less similar to organizations in the same environment, as in cases in which diversification consists of expansions into other markets or economic sectors. This view has been relatively popular with higher education theorists, who predicted increased differentiation in environments where universities are heavily dependent on certain types of resources, usually provided or controlled by governments (Huisman 1995).

Based on the claim that organizational forms are isomorphic to environments (Hannan and Freeman 1977, p. 939), organizational ecology provides a more nuanced view of diversification. Standardization is the result of the interaction of organizations in the same environment and of environmental selection more generally, so that sometimes a more diversified environment does tend to breed more diverse organizational forms. However, depending on the specific environmental circumstances, constraints – such as coercive norms – or the elimination thereof may act both to diminish and to enhance diversification. Sometimes constraints are put in place precisely in order to generate or maintain diversity. Conversely, while the elimination of constraints may initially enhance diversity, it sometimes indirectly limits it on the longer term by creating more competitive pressure in the environment – a view, it should be noted, often at odds with the prevalent wisdom in higher education studies (e.g., Birnbaum 1983). Competition for scarce resources may thus strengthen homogeneity rather than encourage diversity.

Neo-institutionalists accept the broad notion of the isomorphism of organization and environment, insisting nevertheless on the likelihood of homogeneity in strongly institutionalized fields (such as higher education). According to this view, institutional isomorphism is the product of a number of factors which fall into three broad categories – coercive, mimetic, and normative (DiMaggio and Powell 1983). The three types of isomorphic factors are in practice sometimes difficult to disentangle (a fact the two authors above, for example, openly acknowledge), but by and large the first type involves pressures exercised by other organizations on which the organization analyzed is dependent – whether through laws and regulations or more subtly; the second type involves voluntary copying or "modeling" by an organization of others which are perceived as successful, chiefly as a response to uncertainty, while the third is induced by professionalization processes, whereby an occupational community standardizes the goals or processes of its work. Neo-institutionalists make a number of predictions about homogeneity in organizational fields. They claim isomorphism increases in fields where organizations are dependent upon a single source of support for vital resources; where organizations transact mainly with State agencies; where technologies are uncertain or goals are ambiguous; as well as in highly institutionalized fields (DiMaggio and Powell 1983, pp. 155–156).

Higher education evidently meets all these criteria, so it is unsurprising that this strand of neo-institutionalism has proven popular with HE theorists studying diversity. Thus, the current homogeneity on the Romanian academic market has been attributed to a combination of the following factors (Miroiu and Andreescu 2010). First, there have been noticeable legitimization strategies on the part of more recent (public[2] or private) institutions competing with the traditional universities. In particular, given the high uncertainty in Romanian higher education, especially in the first part of the final decade of the last century, newly emerging institutions copied the older, high-reputation universities. Second, the past two decades have also seen an accelerating process of professionalization in higher education in this country. The process involved a considerable restructuring of professional norms and is, as a matter of fact, still far from being over. This process has yielded professional standards, practices, and forums which have strengthened institutional isomorphism.

Third, regulations in the field of quality assurance, funding, or professional academic titles have exerted a strong isomorphic force on institutions. Accreditation was introduced as a Procrustean quality control mechanism which forced all academic programs to look like the established ones in older, highly-regarded universities; subsequently, quality assurance was conceptualized primarily as accreditation (Vlăsceanu et al. 2011). A uniform set of professional standards essential for academic promotion were imposed across the entire system. The funding system that

---

[2] In this article we use the terms "State" and "public" interchangeably to refer to the formal ownership of HEIs.

changed about a decade ago but preserved historical levels of allocation was – except for factors reflecting these historical standards – undifferentiated and thus encouraged organizations to behave in like manner and not unlike the ways they did in the past. Coercive isomorphism of this type was judged to be the most important driver of homogeneity in Romanian higher education (Miroiu and Andreescu 2010, p. 91).

As a general picture, this assessment of the causes of persisting homogeneity seems to us largely correct. Whether the prevailing, dominant isomorphic mechanisms were the coercive ones, or rather the mimetic and/or the normative ones is somewhat debatable – but also less relevant for our purpose here, which is not to dispute the explanation outlined above but to expand on it. In so doing, we shift the perspective from institutional isomorphism to resource dependence in order to argue that, until very recently, the pressure exercised by resource scarcity has not been substantial enough to foster institutional diversification in Romanian HE. This being said, our broader explanation remains within the ambit of neo-institutionalist theory.

Before we proceed further, some methodological clarifications are in order; first, with respect to our unit of analysis. In this article, we seek to explain a *systemic* phenomenon: homogenization in higher education as a distinct sector. In our explanation, we focus on *individual* organizations (HEIs) as the key actors of this sector. In so doing we are indebted to the concept of an "organizational field", defined by DiMaggio and Powell (1983, pp. 2–3) as the organizations that, "in aggregate, constitute areas of institutional life: key suppliers, resource and product consumers, regulatory agencies, and other organizations that produce similar services or products". An organizational field – such as that of higher education – is "structured" by clearly defined inter-organizational patterns of domination and coalition formation, mutual awareness of a common enterprise, an acceptance of the institutional logic, an intuitive sense of the fields' limits, the institutionalization of norms through regulations, the establishment of market niches, as well as by the symbolic re-creation of the environment (DiMaggio and Powell 1983; Păunescu 2006). Though interactions in an organizational field are complex and involve a variety of actors, in the discussion below we pay a comparatively limited attention to, for instance, such intra-organizational structures as the quasi-autonomous (and therefore usually powerful) faculties. We occasionally consider the role of such actors, but only in order to contextualize our broader explanation. In choosing this strategy, we do not claim that professional or non-professional, supra- or sub-organizational or individual actors are not relevant or that they do not substantially complicate in practice the actual dynamics of the institutional diversification in Romanian higher education. Our claim is rather that, by focusing on the HEIs as the main resource-dependent actors, we offer an explanation for the predicament of higher education in this country, which complements the analyses already on the table. We also have a more pragmatic argument, familiar to organizational ecology (Singh and Lumsden 1990): for legislative reasons which, in turn, determine the substance of official statistics, but also due to difficulties in conceptualization, the entities whose birth, development, and death are most easily traceable are the universities.

Second, diversity in higher education systems is not easy to define. Attempts to clearly delimit concepts such as "diversity", "differentiation" and "diversification" (e.g., Huisman 1995) rarely manage to move beyond generic suggestions that the former is a static concept and the latter two (which, we repeat, are used here interchangeably) are dynamic. Furthermore, institutional diversity, perhaps more than internal organizational diversity, is notoriously difficult to quantify. As suggested by older and more recent attempts to measure diversification as a process within national HE systems (e.g., Morphew 2009), depending on how diversity is conceptualized and measured it may have different relationships with environmental factors such as governmental coordination or the magnitude and degree of strictness of regulations in the field. Diversity in higher education may simultaneously increase by some criteria or standards and stagnate or decrease by others, so that much of it is in the eyes of the beholder. For example, the emergence of a small sector of confessional universities in Romanian HE is, surely, a sign of increasing diversity. But, by the same token, the fact that these universities are subject to criteria of institutional and program accreditation uniformly applied across the organizational field, or that they are forced to imitate secular universities in their structuring of programs and research or in hiring and promotion standards can be judged as a sign of homogeneity. We (conveniently) ignore such complications here, though in the next section we offer a summary of the differences between the organizational forms subject to our analysis.

Third, we do not attempt in this article to provide support for our claim that Romanian higher education is relatively homogenous. Not only would this be a complex task in itself, but as implied above, exactly what "homogenous" means in this context is itself a matter of dispute (though hardly impossible to defend for this reason). Is Romanian HE today not sufficiently diverse if judged by the EU, OECD, US or some other international standard (if any)? Is it, rather, merely less than ideally diverse? Or perhaps is it not as diverse as it would be expected after two decades of reform? We do not engage these questions here, though they may be relevant, but rather take existing claims of considerable homogeneity on educated common sense.

This being said, it is important to qualify the two clarifications immediately above. As it will hopefully become clear from the argument developed below, when we discuss differentiation and homogeneity in Romanian higher education in terms of resource dependence we draw chiefly on the impact of resources on "programmatic diversity", that is, on "what is taught, at what level, and in what combinations … their integration into both a major mission orientation and an emphasis that may in some institutions become [their] single most identifiable characteristic" (Birnbaum 1983, p. 43). In other words, we approach the (systemic) issue of diversity in higher education by looking closely at how resources influence (individual) organizational behavior in terms of academic programs. This is largely because academic programs can be persuasively related in a more direct manner to resources and to demand generally. Consequently, when we refer to homogeneity in the Romanian higher education, as we repeatedly do, we *primarily* have in mind programmatic homogeneity. This is not to say, however, that our argument could not be expanded to cover other types of diversity as well, (at least) on the assumption that, in time, product differentiation also generates diversification in terms of missions, structures, constituencies, and so on. Indeed, this view is generally implicit in our argument.

44.3 The Larger Picture: Homogeneity and Diversification in Romanian Higher Education Since 1990

Besides the "natural" isomorphic trends in the Romanian academe, the high level of homogeneity in our higher education system may also be explained by the absence, until very recently, of conditions fostering institutional diversification. In particular, the financial pressures for differentiation have not been substantial enough. The very low rates of access to higher education in Communist times – the lowest in Europe – created a strong demand for academic degrees. This demand enabled post-1990s HEIs to focus on matriculating as many students as possible given the conditions on the academic market, such as initially very selective admission exams, the increasing competition created by the emergence of new institutions, limited infrastructure, the economic status of the population, and so on. Constantly rising enrollment rates (Fig. 44.1) have ensured for both State and private universities a steady income, which until not long ago was sufficient to enable the perpetuation of the existing "academic business model". The latter involved not only the uniform organizational structures (faculty-centered universities in which these schools enjoy considerable autonomy from the organizational center), but also a strong vocational inclination of the studies (even in Humanities and Social Sciences), as well as limited investments in infrastructure and teaching staff. Perhaps nowhere has

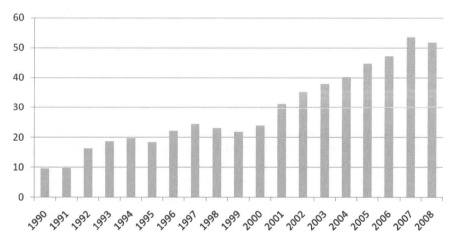

Fig. 44.1 Rate of participation to higher education in Romania, 1990–2008 (Source: National Institute of Statistics and Encyclopedia of the Nations. Data for the year 1998 could not be found so it was interpolated)

homogeneity been more apparent than in the structure and substance of academic programs, which have been very similar within the same field of study irrespective of institutional coordinates (large or small, local or regional, public or private, nationally renowned or undistinguished). Furthermore, while academic programs naturally differed in substance from one field of study to another, they have always been similar in terms of their structure and of their goals.

Resource dependence theory predicts growing diversification as competition for resources gets tougher. In the case of higher education in this country, relevant resources consist primarily of funding from State allocations (which in Romania are exclusively accessible to public HEIs), student fees (which State universities have been legally entitled to charge only since 1999), rents and commercial services (relatively limited in size), as well as research financing (which has come mainly from the State, has been usually meager,[3] as well as not limited to the university sector given the large number of research institutes inherited from the Communist era). Such material resources, which are often the prime focus of resource dependence theory, are complemented by less tangible ones, on which they sometimes depend. Access to funding, for instance, has depended on a number of other factors, in particular legal status (specifically public/private ownership) and perceived academic prestige (reputation), both of which play a significant part in our argument below. Other resources, which we occasionally allude to but not place at the core of our explanation are authority over professional standards or power to influence political processes which determine, for example, the size and patterns of state allocations to institutions.

When universities come to depend on scarce resources and, moreover, these resources are controlled by a few dominant organizations (such as the government), organizations are expected to differentiate by offering new products, seeking novel markets, and expanding into economic sectors. At least in Europe, with its tradition of public universities, private HEIs are more vulnerable to diminishing resources (Teixeira et al. 2011) and therefore are often also the organizations most likely to engage in diversification under conditions of resource scarcity. However, the constantly increasing size of enrollments in Romanian higher education has delayed such a development. Rather, the per-capita funding model for public universities introduced in 1999, the social pressure for "massification", and the historically low rates of participation to HE have encouraged virtually all universities to focus on enlarging student intake by recruiting from the traditional student pool (young adults fresh out of high school), while paying considerably less attention to other constituencies, such as somewhat older adults or professionals. Given the relatively uniform expectations of this group and its overwhelming representation in the recruitment base, universities have not been under considerable pressure to change their business (no need, for instance, to adapt to the constraints imposed by new constituencies). This also explains the very low rates – by European standards – of

---

[3] With the exception of one recent and unfortunately short period, briefly discussed later on in this article.

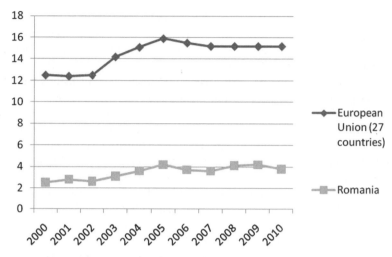

Fig. 44.2 Participation in education and training in the EU and Romania as a percentage of population, 25–35 age group (Source of data: Eurostat)

engagement in lifelong learning (LLL) in Romania (Fig. 44.2). (But on this point see the discussion further down of matriculants in private universities by age.)

The paragraphs above provide a rough sketch of our explanation for the persisting homogenization – or, perhaps, the delayed diversification – in the Romanian higher education. However, given the changing environmental conditions within short time frames (anarchic deregulation in the first years of the 1990s, increasing professionalization and constraints on private providers in the second part of that decade, a change in the funding system around the turn of the millennium, an enrolment plateau recently) it makes sense to discuss the question of resources, institutional strategies, and their impact on institutional diversification in terms of several distinctive periods, roughly 1990–1995, 1995–2000, 2000–2005, and post-2005.

The first post-revolutionary quinquennial was characterized by several processes relevant for our topic. First, there were substantial transformations in academic staff and programs after the change of regime at the end of 1989. This involved the introduction of new programs and specializations, many of which could not exist for ideological reasons under the Communist ruling. New curricula were designed for the existing disciplines and programs, a development which was particularly intense in the social sciences and the humanities. This entailed a substantial process of uncontrolled diversification directly encouraged by the hands-off approach of the Education Ministry, which preferred to remain aloof. More broadly, after decades of strict control, universities naturally claimed substantial levels of institutional autonomy and the government initially obliged.

A second relevant development during the same period concerned the founding of new universities, both public and private. The new public universities mostly emerged as local or regional institutions, either as new establishments or by building on the structures of existing post-secondary schools. Other "revitalized" local HEIs expanded from minor non-university tertiary institutions into proper universities. Still others capitalized on former local university structures in order to acquire a truly comprehensive regional dimension.

Besides these local and regional State universities, most of them small at the time, there emerged a number of private institutions of higher education whose legal status remained unclear for a while (initially, they were legally registered as NGOs) and which introduced numerous new programs and courses, many of them contested at the time. Thus, within the first post-revolutionary year the number of *new* institutions increased from 44 to 56, while the number of faculties and schools doubled (Eismon et al. 1995). This phase of new establishments and expansions, which was subsequently described as anarchic (Miroiu et al. 1998) and even as a "post-revolutionary psychosis" (Reisz 1994), naturally increased the level of diversity in the Romanian higher education, which was a "massification"-induced rather than a post-"massification" phenomenon.

The third relevant process in this period, closely related to the two above, is therefore precisely the take-off of "massification". Demand for academic degrees was extremely high given the historically very low levels of access to a university education, which was regarded in the Communist era as the province of either the highly successful scholastically or the highly privileged politically. In 1989, the country's student population was roughly at 1970 levels and had decreased by some 15% since the beginning of the decade. After 1989, the number of available places in universities, while undergoing an important expansion, remained limited due to the restricted facilities available, undersized teaching corps, and the prevalent norms of a profession which regarded high selectiveness as a badge of honor. As a result, competition for a place in the university continued to be very intense, reaching peaks such as the infamous 25 candidates per place in the University of Bucharest Law School. In fact, these relatively substantial limits to student intake in the traditional state universities enabled institutional expansion in the Romanian higher education, as well as the unavoidable diversification which came along with it. By the same token, however, the degrees offered by the old, reputable universities remained the real object of desire. The new universities typically matriculated students who had failed to gain admission in one of the traditional, prestigious State institutions, so they mostly offered the same programs and courses, and often similarly designed – but less rigorous – admission tests. As a result, the academic processes and goals in traditional State universities constituted the norm in terms of which most of the new or renewed HEIs defined their business, although it must be emphasized that, for a while, private universities experimented with (frequently very contested) programs and admission practices (hence the label of a "post-revolutionary psychosis").

The anarchic period identified here as the first half of the 1990s – partly for the sake of symmetry and because the first post-Communist law on education was promulgated in 1995 –, came to a halt with an equally strong phase of standardization and consolidation promoted by an interventionist Education Ministry. This stage of coercive dedifferentiation, which initially encountered some resistance from the academic community but was more broadly accepted as the latter was co-opted, led to the formal standardization of fields of study and academic programs, down to curricula and course names. The first half of the decade was also the time when several national councils for higher education were established as buffer organizations. Among them, the National Council for Academic Evaluation and Accreditation (CNEAA) was created under the new law on accreditation, which set tough authorization and accreditation standards for private HEIs, while exempting the traditional public universities from the process. For better and for worse, private universities were forced by the new regulations to closely mimic the structure and processes, and ultimately the goals, of traditional State universities. Moreover, they were compelled to hire many full and associate professors from public universities, who afterwards commonly taught in at least a couple of private academic establishments as well. Naturally, the presence of such senior State-university academics in private HEIs strengthened programmatic and curricular standardization across the higher education system.

Diversification remained on the agenda of both academia and government (Birzea 1995, 1996), but this interest targeted primarily the creation of new fields of study, new departments, and new programs following the model and structure of the existing ones. Other diversification strategies – changes in the missions and functions of HEIs, reaching out to new constituencies, new types of degrees[4] – were comparatively neglected or downright ignored.

As far as enrollments are concerned, State and private universities expanded in both number and size. Traditional State universities continued to enjoy high reputation (some relevant comments and figures are provided later in this section) and remained relatively selective, at least in part because they had no other option: they could matriculate only a limited number of students; since public higher education was free, universities could not charge tuition, and the Education Ministry only approved a limited number of places after a negotiation process. The funding system was based on detailed budgets (a combination of line-item financing with earmarked funds for infrastructure) and, in practice, covered the difference between the funds generated by institutions and their estimated financial needs. This system naturally discouraged institutional initiatives aimed at acquiring funds from other sources in order to expand financial autonomy. It kept enrollments at a sufficiently low level to conserve the selectiveness and reputation of traditional universities and to supply the new ones with unsuccessful candidates.

Another effect of the funding system was the substantial lack of transparency in the allocation of resources. The number of students allocated to the academic programs in State universities was relatively arbitrary, as was the number of teaching loads funded by the Ministry, the relation of which to the number of students remained rather capricious. The size of historical allocations was a constraint in these respects, but it left considerable room for arbitrariness. Under these circum-

---

[4] Short-term "collegiate" degrees did briefly surface before being abandoned with the introduction of the "Bologna" system.

stances, the newly emerging academic oligarchies – the several "national councils" established as buffer organisms – naturally became the focus of power struggles and did little to enhance transparency in higher education.

Around this time, possession of an academic degree became a condition for hiring or promotion in the oversized public sector; demand for HE received an additional boost. The limited capacity of State universities to respond to such high demand, partly mitigated by fields without much appeal but which nevertheless managed to expand enrollment by lowering standards, put the pressure for "massification" on private universities. Consequently, despite the reduction in their number as a consequence of the academic accreditation law, the remaining private institutions expanded enrollment substantially (from 85,000 to 114,000 students between 1992–1993 and 1994–1995, and again from 83,000 the following year – after the implementation of the accreditation law – to 130,000 by 1998–1999) (Georgescu 2011, S12).

The third important phase in our story started at the turn of the millennium, more specifically in the late 1990s. The process of professionalization accelerated, especially as academic reforms in Europe and elsewhere were officially accepted as a model of domestic endeavors. University autonomy was increased, not least in the administration of personnel. On the other hand, the domestic implementation of the Bologna Process enhanced standardization, as alternative academic programs were discarded (the short "collegiate" degrees disappeared) and, with the exception of a few professional fields, virtually all universities adopted the 3-2-3 degree structure.

Arguably the most important change in higher education, at least from the perspective of the subject of this article, was the change in the funding system. In a nutshell, the latter consisted of two essential developments: the former line-item funding was replaced by a per-capita allocation scheme function of the number of State-sponsored students matriculated and for their specializations (a number set by Ministry negotiations with HEIs); and the introduction of uncapped tuition fees in public universities for students not supported from the State budget.[5] Given the still elevated demand for academic degrees, the new funding system made possible a very substantial expansion of enrollment in State institutions. Within 6 years, between 1998–1999 and 2003–2004, the number of students in public universities almost doubled, from 277,000 to 521,000, the large bulk of this increase coming from tuition-paying students (Georgescu 2011, S12, S13) (Fig. 44.3).

In our view, this moment at the turn of the century, and particularly the major changes in the funding system, were crucial in easing the pressures for institutional diversification. Under the new funding schemes, high-reputation State universities engaged in a strategy based on economies of scale – playing the card of marginal cost and low prices. One factor which rendered this strategy possible was the absence

---

[5] We overlook the performance-based funding coefficients, both because they are less relevant to our argument and because they were slow to be implemented and, indeed, have so far remained mostly theoretical.

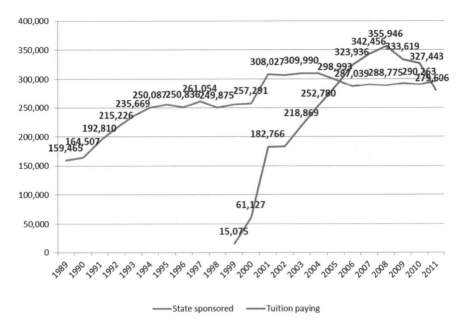

Fig. 44.3 Number of state-sponsored and fee-paying students in State Universities, 1989–2011 (Source: Data compiled from the Ministry for Education, Research, Youth and Sports and National Council for Higher Education Funding; adapted from Georgescu 2011, Slide 13)

of any meaningful competition from "non-traditional" academic players which could have increased the stakes in the struggle for quality. Such players might have been foreign university branches, which unfortunately remained absent on the domestic higher education market, notwithstanding a few MBAs. Or they could have been renowned foreign or domestic companies entering the HE sector without much of the newcomer's reputation handicap and with other reputational assets instead. Either way, such a presence would have likely heightened the competition on reputation by threatening the categorical ascendancy of traditional State universities. The absence of any such pressures has provided the latter with a convenient reputational slack.

To support a strategy based on economies of scale, in public HEIs the per-capita State allocations were "re-distributed" to cover tuition-paying students, as indicated by a comparison of allocations with charged tuition fees (see Fig. 44.4a–d).[6] In most fields, the vast majority or all public and private universities charge tuition fees below the amount of the State per-capita allocation for the respective field. In many

---

[6] Unfortunately we only have data for the current academic year. The data was compiled by the authors from academic websites and promotional leaflets, since it is absent from publicly accessible statistics. In the figures below we also provide, besides minimum and maximum levels of tuition per academic field in public and private universities, a breakdown for four specific fields, as this illustrates more clearly the disparities between fees and State allocations, as well as the relative homogeneity of tuition across the system.

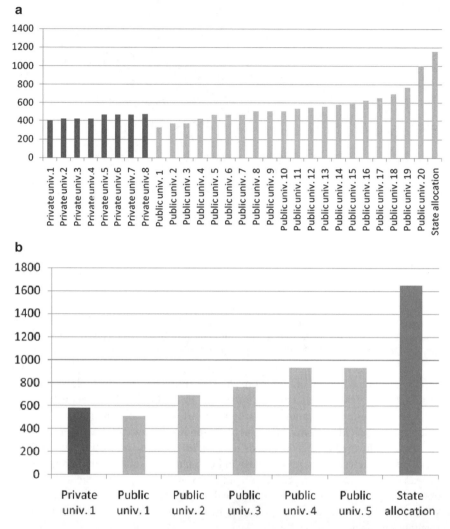

Fig. 44.4 (a) Tuition fees for technical fields (other than physics and chemistry), 2011–2012 academic year (in Euro, average per university) (Source: Data compiled by the authors from 2011 university leaflets and websites. Several public and private universities are represented, as well as several technical programs within the same institution). (b) Tuition fees for architecture, 2011–2012 a.y. (in Euro, average per university) (Source: Data compiled by the authors from 2011 university leaflets and websites). (c) Tuition fees for business and economics fields, 2011–2012 a.y. (in Euro, average per university) (Source: Data compiled by the authors from 2011 university leaflets and websites). (d) Minimum and maximum tuition fees per fields of study, 2011–2012 a.y. (in Euro) (Source: Data compiled by the authors from 2011 university leaflets and websites)

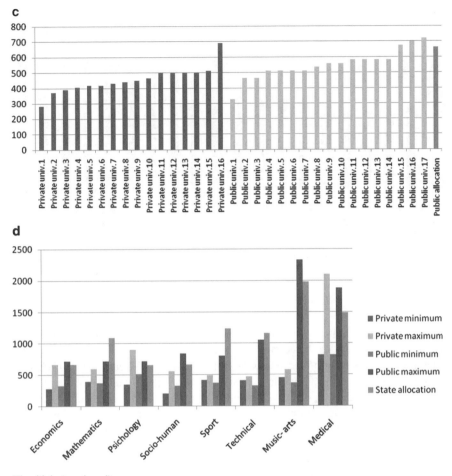

Fig. 44.4 (continued)

cases, the fees are substantially lower and, in a few exceptional cases, as much as a fraction of the State disbursement. (Medical studies in a private institution are an interesting exception.)[7] As a consequence of the effort to achieve economies of scale, enrollment exploded during this period. The rate of participation to HE, a metric which considers only the 19–23 age bracket disproportionately represented in the Romanian higher education, reached a peak of 53.6 in 2007–2008 from just 31.2 in 2001–2002 (MECTS 2010). Institutions boosted enrollment often in the absence of the necessary material and academic infrastructure, some still capitalizing on the limited investments in capacity made during the days (1990–1995) of high demand for fields such as Law and Economics.

---

[7] We surmise this is because medical studies and the medical profession in general are tightly regulated fields, so any successful entrant will be able to claim high quality solely by virtue of being admitted to the field.

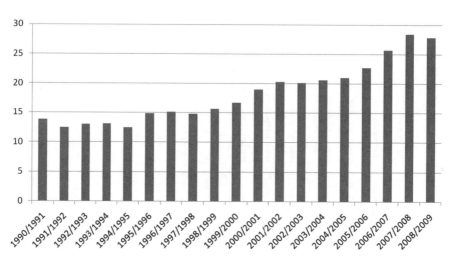

Fig. 44.5 Number of students per teaching staff in tertiary education, 1990–2008 (Data source: National Institute of Statistics)

The State universities' low-tuition, large-enrollment strategy may be explained by other factors besides the economies of scale adopted by these institutions. One factor that comes to mind is the low flexibility in salary differentiation. (Whether this low flexibility is due to public regulations and/or the difficulty of managing pay disparities due to the organization of interest groups inside Romanian universities is a question we will not approach here.) As wages in public HEIs remained quite low – except for full professors, who took care of themselves through the national Parliament in which they were so generously represented –, one way to pay higher wages without violating the rule of uniform payment for each academic rank and without increasing the nominal salaries was to give academics several teaching loads (Fig. 44.5). This planned, deliberate "overloading" became a national epidemic, teacher-student ratios be damned.

Beyond such contextual details, the important matter remains that the low tuition levels practiced by high-reputation universities severely limited the strategies of private and of new, local State HEIs, which could not compete on price except to a very limited extent. (However, geography may have provided a break to local universities, as many students could now study in their home city.) As a result, private and local institutions, and perhaps especially the larger private institutions in the country's main academic centers, competed mainly on opportunity costs, promising students formally identical degrees with little academic effort. This promise was certainly appealing to older students, who represented a larger proportion of matriculants in private and local universities (Fig. 44.6). But it also impeded diversification based on the new constituencies attracted to higher education, as private universities continued to offer the same kinds of easily recognizable and therefore economically "safe" programs and degrees.

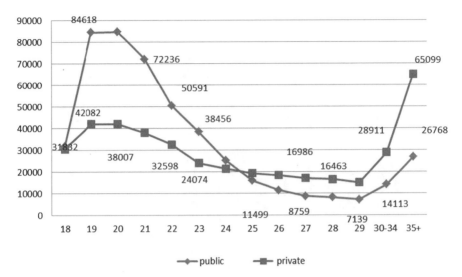

Fig. 44.6 Distribution of student numbers in public and private universities by age/age bracket, 2008–2009 academic year (Adapted from Georgescu 2010) (Source: National Institute for Statistics)

We have repeatedly referred above to the question of reputation, in particular to the advantage enjoyed by traditional State universities as far as the public perception of academic quality is concerned. Our main argument above hinges on the claim that high-reputation State universities acted as drivers on the academic market by setting a low-tuition strategy and thus severely limiting the practical options of the other players. Alternative strategies, such as high-selectivity, high-tuition were not pursued by these trusted institutions (whatever the reasons). This reputational advantage is undisputed and has remained substantial through the period(s) discussed here. As late as 2007, only 26% of faculty and 47% of students agreed with the statement that private academic education is at least as good as that provided in public institutions (though considerable higher percentages of 58 and 71, respectively, agreed with the statement that faculties in private HEIs are competent) (Soros 2007). In 2010, State universities clearly dominated the Top 5 of Romanian HEIs in the perception of faculties in both public and private institutions, as well as among students in public universities. In the same year the average grade (on a ten-point scale) for the quality of education in public HEIs was 8.0 in the view of faculty and 7.4 in the view of employers, compared to 5.3 and 5.8, respectively, for private academic institutions (Vlăsceanu et al. 2011, pp. 157–158, 161). Last but not least, in this year's institutional classification exercise, which was almost entirely based on the quality of academic research, all private universities were classified as teaching-intensive, the least research-proficient category of the three defined under the new law on education.

It is time to summarize our argument: after the introduction of tuition in public universities and the switch to lump-sum per-capita public funding, the Romanian

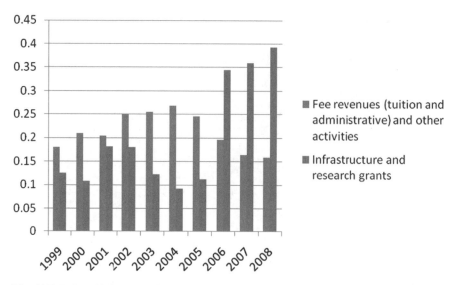

Fig. 44.7 Fees and infrastructure and research grants as a ratio of total public university revenues (Source: Ministry for Education, Research, Youth and Sports. Fees do not include public allocations for state-sponsored students)

higher education system reached a temporary equilibrium based on increased enrollments, low tuition, and a lowering of academic quality generated both by decreasing selectiveness and by matriculation beyond what the existing material infrastructures and academic personnel would have reasonably permitted. Yet the number of students increased sufficiently rapidly so as not to compel universities to cater for new constituencies in ways that would also generate new types of academic programs and, subsequently, the new organizational structures or the professional stratification to accompany them. Simply put, the conditions for institutional diversification, and program diversification in particular, were not there.

After 2005, the enrollment curve in State universities started to flatten. For the HE sector as a whole, enrollment peaked in 2007–2008, decreased slightly the following year and substantially by 2009–2010. One of the main causes is demographic and has been a familiar topic of concern among educators and educational policy-makers. The school population (all levels) for the 2009–2010 school year decreased by 3.4% compared with the previous year and by 4.2% compared with 2005–2006 (INS 2010, pp. 154–155). In our view, this diminution of the enrollment base heralds pressures for diversification. As predicted by resource dependence theory, these pressures would lead to the creation of new market niches and new types of products offered by HEIs. A temporary respite from the academic financial crisis which this development could have triggered was offered by a concomitant – and coincidental – dramatic increase in research funds (Fig. 44.7). But the financial slack was short-lived: the economic recession put an abrupt end to this new source of money, so at this point the old strategies seem increasingly difficult to sustain given the demographic strain.

44.4 Steps Forward

It is difficult to predict how institutional diversification will proceed in the coming years, but we can advance a few suggestions (with a whiff of recommendation). Firstly, new constituencies will probably be sought. As we have repeatedly noted, tuition fees in Romanian higher education have stayed quite low, almost irrespective of field, so there is room for an increase. The rise of the high-income class, the young members of which often go to study and live abroad, suggests this could be a potential target for universities if high tuition is backed by high academic standards and by an accompanying high reputation of the degrees offered. There is already a considerable demand for private lower-level schools, where fees are typically higher than in universities. A private kindergarten in Timișoara, one of the country's premier academic centers, costs between 1,300 and 3,000 Euro a year, up to six times a year of academic education in the same city (Hnyatek 2011). The same is true in Bucharest and most of the countries' major urban/academic centers. This is hardly an uncommon occurrence. Consequently, one possible diversification strategy is for some HEIs – perhaps including new entrants on the academic market, some with ties to large corporations – to offer special high-tuition, high-reputation programs competing directly not so much with the domestic programs but with those provided by prestigious universities elsewhere.

Besides the high-income bracket, universities might also look into other niches, such as professionals and older students, two categories that are still under-represented in higher education in this country. Here the best strategy is probably to provide shorter-term programs, perhaps organized in modular fashion in order to keep open the opportunity of eventually advancing to a BA degree and beyond. Since such programs do not have much of a tradition in Romanian higher education, public perception could be a barrier and discourage institutional initiatives in this direction. On the other hand, we already know that employers place more value on work experience than on either academic performance or the university which provided the degree (Vlăsceanu et al. 2011). With proper marketing and formal backing from the State, these programs could succeed. Such formal backing would include recognition and promotion of short programs by the government and professional associations.

Special mention needs to be made of students from lower socio-economic groups. The chief obstacle to enrolling in higher education for these groups is, right now, the cost of living. There is a real danger that such students will not be targeted unless the government acts more proactively. This would entail installing the necessary incentives for HEIs to reach out to them through need-based support and assistance schemes. Short-term academic programs would be convenient here too, as they would lower the costs of a degree, be easier to provide by local institutions or branches, and enable students to start work earlier and perhaps complete a traditional BA subsequently, while employed.

In the scenario above, programmatic diversification is triggered by universities' tapping into new constituencies. But program differentiation is appealing for other reasons as well, both academic and economic. By introducing short-term programs universities could comply better and more easily with accreditation standards, which have become a hassle for many institutions, as they are usually designed rigidly, with the best programs in mind. HEIs with a diploma-mill strategy could "migrate" some of their no longer accreditable or borderline-accreditable BA programs into short-term ones, though, as noted above, here the main handicap would be the likely widespread suspicion of non-traditional programs. As for the economic argument, the introduction of short-term programs would be a standard product differentiation strategy, enabling HEIs to charge a range of tuition fees, from more expensive BA- and higher-level programs to progressively less expensive shorter programs.

We briefly mentioned in the introductory sections of the article that diversification may receive some top-down impetus from new regulations in the field of higher education, and particularly from the recent classification of Romanian universities and the projected rankings of academic programs. Whether and to what extent these measures will enhance diversification depends a lot on the uses which the classification and rankings will be put to. The classification of Romanian universities into three pre-established categories – roughly research-intensive, teaching-and-research, and teaching-intensive institutions – was based mainly on research output and, as a result, appears to enhance vertical diversity. The immediate consequences of the three classes of universities will be that the bulk of doctoral and many master's programs will be allocated to the leading, research-intensive HEIs while the teaching-intensive ones will get only a small portion of the advanced degrees, based on the high quality of some of their programs, or will be forced out of postgraduate education entirely. It is noteworthy that State subsidies for masters' programs are twice as large as the allocation for bachelor programs in the same field of studies, while doctoral allocations are three times as high. As it has been observed, one of the best predictors of the recent classification is the age of the university, backing up the popular perception of reputation with supposedly hard data, and thus making the less reputable institutions' hunger for legitimacy more acute.

It is unclear at this point exactly how the classification-cum-rankings game will play out. It is somewhat obvious that the drive to classify (and rank) is the product of the persistent anxiety about "quality" in Romanian higher education, an anxiety which has systematically manifested itself in the form of attempts to measure and standardize. It also seems plain, though it is perhaps more difficult to prove, that diversification in higher education has not been among the key concerns of the recent classification and ranking, at least in the form these instruments eventually assumed. A concern for diversity seems hard to reconcile with a rigid list of institutional types such as that provided by the classification. It is also rather incompatible with the short time frame in which the classification was carried out (around half a year since the HE law was adopted, and considerably less since the drafting of the methodology), as this leaves institutions little space to position themselves and to make strategic choices. Neither is genuine interest in diversity compatible with a classification methodology which does not take into account institutional mission (no mention of this notion is even made in the aforesaid document), and which in fact seems to tacitly impose such a "mission" from the top with its three rough and inflexible institutional categories (research-intensive, research-and-teaching, and teaching-intensive). Last but not least, a classification that is not accompanied by a clear and explicit set of policies that presume to act upon it – the funding methodology is still in the works, for example – only makes room for confusion and uncertainty, and is therefore hardly an instrument that serves diversity.

Given the persistent interest in measurement and standardization, and since higher education goals are notoriously hard to define while academic outputs are infamously difficult to quantify, the foreseeable result of the first round of classifications has been a strong focus on research output. Romania has experienced this academic obsession with academic evaluation-by-research for more than half a decade now, and it seems to us that so far the main outcome has been a strengthening of mimetic, professional, and coercive isomorphism. Most Romanian universities, large or small, selective or lenient, local or national, sternly declare in their mission statements and strategic plans that they have great ambitions in research and invest a lot of effort in this claim.

The program rankings are yet to be generated, but the classification is just in and its consequences are, as yet, far from clear. It may well be that the research-oriented rankings which underlie this exercise will be widely accepted (some immediate institutional grumpiness notwithstanding), and the HEIs in this country will acknowledge their fate and start working diligently to prove that they are among the best in their class and, more broadly, that their class is engaged in worthwhile pursuits. Government allocation of funding and support for postgraduate education and research will back up the classification with palpable constraints which may compel some institutions to concentrate on what they are or may become good at. If the government will also back up educational goals which may be best or most efficiently achieved by teaching-intensive institutions with appropriate incentives, it may see its strategy succeed in terms of vertical differentiation. And since teaching-intensive institutions (as well as some of the research-and-teaching HEIs) are typically more dependent on local economies and cultures, vertical diversification may be complemented on the long run by horizontal differentiation within classes as well.

This is the happy scenario. The not-so-happy one we are already familiar with. The bulk of the attention, funding, prestige, and able studentry will go to the research-intensive universities, whose research prowess will also continue to be reflected in and buttressed by the uniform national standards for acquiring professional titles (associate and full professor). The financial slack afforded to research-intensive universities by the new funding system will enable them to keep tuition fees relatively low, while the reputational slack augmented by the boost in prestige effected by classifications and rankings will allow them to moderately lower standards and enroll many students. Every university not fortunate enough to make it into the research-intensive class will secretly aspire to get there and behave as if it was on the verge of succeeding in this enterprise. But the erosion of the legitimacy of institutions in the lowest category could force them into a harsh competition for a less talented ill-prepared studentship, creating a vicious circle that locks them further and further away from the status and modes of operation of a university.

A third scenario – with a retro touch – may also be put forward. Academic drift will gain momentum and, with a new government in power and friendly forces in the relevant ministries, the classifications will be abandoned as a bad, misguided dream or – as with performance-based funding coefficients over the past decade – will remain a formal exercise with little practical import.

44.5 Conclusions

Until very recently, the traditional State universities have been the true drivers of the higher education market in Romania. The constant increase in student numbers encouraged these HEIs to pursue economies of scale, maintaining very low tuition levels – despite the absence of tuition caps –, decreasing selectivity in admissions, and lowering academic standards overall. Since this strategy was employed by virtually all of the larger, older, high-reputation universities, the smaller, newer ones, which started at a reputational disadvantage had to find their own niche. Assuming that they could not compete on price given already very low tuition levels, they could have competed instead on either quality/reputation, or on "opportunity costs" for obtaining a degree. As reputation is costly, the latter strategy is more likely to be adopted in a context such as the one described above. Hence, numerous recent and/ or local public or private HEIs can be suspected of having turned more or less into diploma mills. On the other hand, precisely because they charged only marginally lower prices and suffered reputationally, these institutions were compelled to mimic the traditional HEIs in order to maintain legitimacy, offering identical programs and degrees rather than trying to stake out new markets and cater to new communities. Signaling quality by formally adhering to academic standards as reflected in, for instance, identical program structure and curricula further delayed diversification.

The effects of these strategies across the Romanian HE system were a loss of quality-based competitiveness overall; a lost appetite for innovation in program and curricular design; a hemorrhaging of potentially well-paying and/or very able students who go to study abroad; and arguably a diminished public trust in higher education as a whole. This situation kept institutions from developing their academic and teaching potential, urged them to focus their planning on the short term, and encouraged them to behave mimetically. Some enrolment sources (e.g., the constituencies potentially interested in LLL programs) have not been adequately tapped, so academic programs remained very similar in structure and, within the same fields of study, also in curriculum. Programmatic diversification has been delayed and, with it, many institutional incentives for other forms of diversification have been weakened.

The demographic and economic crises are, however, upon us, and at least the former is here to say. This predicament, which is both domestic and international, may explain the recent interest in institutional differentiation, both in Romania and elsewhere. But, as far as manifest efforts at institutional differentiation are concerned, in this country they have been mostly top-down and supply-driven. It is still not clear how institutions will reach out, or how they will respond to the recent classifications and coming rankings. However, as resources become a pressure it is important that supply-driven diversification should not inhibit the potential demand-driven initiatives.

References

Birnbaum, R. (1983). *Maintaining diversity in higher education*. San Francisco: Josey-Bass.
Birzea, C. (1995). *Educational reform and educational research in central-eastern Europe: The case of Romania*. Paper presented at the IBE International Meeting, Tokyo, Japan.
Birzea, C. (1996). Educational reform and power struggles in Romania. *European Journal of Education, 31*, 97–107.
Blau, P. (1970). A formal theory of differentiation in organizations. *American Sociological Review, 35*, 201–218.
Blau, P. (1994). *The organization of academic work* (Rev. ed.). New Brunswick/London: Transaction.
DiMaggio, P., & Powell, W. (1983). The iron cage revisited: Institutional isomorphism and collective rationality in organizational fields. *American Sociological Review, 48*, 147–160.
Eismon, T., et al. (1995). Higher education reform in Romania. *Higher Education, 30*, 135–152.
Georgescu, L. (2010, February 25–March 1). *Evoluția învățământului superior românesc*. Presented at the conference "Forumul Organizațiilor Studențești din România", Bucharest.
Georgescu, L. (2011, March 30–April 1). *Evoluția finanțări sistemului de învățământ superior din România*. Presented at the conference "Perspective în finanțarea învățământului superior", Bucharest.
Hannan, M., & Freeman, J. (1977). The population ecology of organizations. *The American Journal of Sociology, 82*, 929–964.
Hnyatek, A. (2011, March 6). Scump, doamna, scump! Gradinita privata costa de sase ori cat facultatea, la Timișoara! *Opinia Timișoarei*.
Huisman, J. (1995). *Differentiation, diversity and dependency in higher education*. Utrecht: Lemma.
INS. (2010). *Starea economică a României, 2008-09*. București: Institutul național de statistic.
MECTS. (2010). *Raport asupra stării sistemului național de învățământ, 2010*. Retrieved August 23, 2011, from http://www.edu.ro/index.php/articles/15128
Miroiu, A., & Andreescu, L. (2010). Goals and instruments of diversification in higher education. *Quality Assurance Review for Higher Education, 2*, 89–101.
Miroiu, A., et al. (1998). *Invatamantul romanesc azi*. Iasi: Polirom.
Morphew, C. (2009). Conceptualizing change in the institutional diversity of US colleges and universities. *Journal of Higher Education, 80*, 243–269.
Păunescu, M. (2006). *Organizare și câmpuri organizaționale*. Iași: Polirom.
Pfeffer, J., & Salancik, G. (2003). *The external control of organizations: A resource dependence perspective*. Stanford: Stanford Business Books.
Reisz, R. (1994). Curricular patterns before and after the Romanian revolution. *European Journal of Education, 29*, 281–290.
Singh, V., & Lumsden, C. (1990). Theory and research in organizational ecology. *Annual Review of Sociology, 16*, 161–195.
Soros Foundation. (2007). Sistemul universitar românesc: Opiniile cadrelor didactice și ale studenților. Bucharest: Fundația Soros Romania.
Teixeira, P., et al. (2011, June). *Public-private mix and patterns of program diversification across European Higher Education*. Paper presented at the 24th Consortium of Higher Education Researchers, Reykjavik, Iceland.
Vlăsceanu, L., Miroiu, A., Păunescu, M., & Hâncean, M.-G. (Eds.). (2011). *Barometrul Calității 2010. Starea calității în învățământul superior din România*. Brașov: Editura Universității Transilvania din Brașov.

Chapter 45
U-Map, University Activity Profiles in Practice

Frans Kaiser, Marike Faber, and Ben Jongbloed

45.1 Introduction: The U-Map Instrument

The rationale for developing a European classification of higher education institutions lies in the desire to better understand and use diversity as an important basis for the further development of European higher education and research systems (see also van Vught 2009). In order to reap the full benefits of increasing diversity, a tool is needed to describe this diversity. This is the aim of U-Map – an instrument for mapping the European higher education landscape which enables various groups of stakeholders to comprehend the diverse institutional activity profiles of European higher education institutions. This will contribute to the creation of a stronger profile for European higher education on a global stage and to the realisation of the goals of the Lisbon strategy, the Bologna process, and the Modernisation agenda (European Commission 2011).

45.2 Classifications and Rankings (Diversity and Transparency)

Global rankings intend to *judge* higher education institutions and they do so largely by focusing on research performance. They give only limited regard to disciplinary, language and institutional diversity. In addition, global rankings offer composite institutional indicators on the basis of which league tables are constructed. Rankings

F. Kaiser (✉) • M. Faber • B. Jongbloed
Center for Higher Education Policy Studies (CHEPS), University of Twente,
P.O. Box 215, 7500 AE Enschede, The Netherlands
e-mail: f.kaiser@utwente.nl; m.faber@utwente.nl; b.w.a.jongbloed@utwente.nl

A. Curaj et al. (eds.), *European Higher Education at the Crossroads:*
Between the Bologna Process and National Reforms,
DOI 10.1007/978-94-007-3937-6_45, © Springer Science+Business Media Dordrecht 2012

are instruments to display vertical diversity in terms of performance by using quantitative indicators. Most existing rankings in higher education take the form of a league table. A league table is a single dimensional, ordinal list going from 'best' to 'worst', assigning to the entities unique, discrete positions seemingly at equal distance from each other (from 1 to, e.g., 500).

The critique on rankings is well known[1]: rankings

- focus on 'whole institutions' (ignoring internal variance)
- concentrate on 'traditional' research productivity and impact and neglect the performance on other dimensions of activity
- focus on 'comprehensive research universities', and neglect the bulk of higher education institutions
- aggregate performance into composite overall indicators, without clear rationales regarding the weighting of the spate indicators
- use constructed 'league table' that may suggest clear rank orders based on insignificant absolute differences between institutions
- imply cultural and language biases, favouring English language publications
- imply bias against humanities and social sciences

Classifications are intended to do something very different. Rather than ignoring or limiting diversity, these instruments intend to make diversity transparent. Classifications are tools that try to describe and visualise the diversity of institutional activity profiles.

45.3   The Development of U-Map

U-Map was developed in three stages, all subsidized by the European Commission. In the first stage (van Vught et al. 2005), the conceptual framework for the study was drafted and the basic design principles were developed in an intense consultation of various stakeholders. These design principles were in short:

The classification is

- based on empirical data: it should be based on activities not on normative mission statements
- based on a multi-actor and multi-dimensional perspective. There is not one single user of the classification but a range of users (policy makers, higher education institutions, employers, students).
- based on a multi-dimensional perspective. The activities of higher education institutions are too complex to be captured in only one dimension.
- non-hierarchical; it addresses the horizontal diversity in higher education, the richness of the landscape.

---

[1] See van Vught et al. (2011), Rauhvarges (2011) and Hazelkorn (2011).

- relevant for all higher education institutions in Europe; U-Map is focused on individual European higher education institutions that are recognized as separate and legally identifiable organisations in their own national systems and that offer accredited higher education degree programmes.
- descriptive, not prescriptive; the indicators and the way the results on the indicators are presented should be non-normative, passing no judgment on quality or performance
- based on reliable and verifiable data
- parsimonious regarding extra data collection; response fatigue among higher education institutions should be avoided.

Using these design principles, the conceptual frame was further elaborated and dimensions and indicators were selected and defined in the second stage of the development of U-Map (van Vught et al. 2008). In advisory board meetings and stakeholder conferences the users were actively involved in this stage. A first version of the data collection instrument was tested among nearly 75 higher education institutions and the results indicated that U-Map is a feasible transparency instrument. Based on that result, the instrument was further developed. Indicators and dimensions were reassessed and instruments to analyse and visualize the results were developed and tested (van Vught et al. 2010). The current version of U-Map was presented in October 2009.

In the current version of U-Map six dimensions and 25 indicators are used to characterize the activities of a higher education institution (Table 45.1):

Once the indicators are defined, empirical information could be collected. The main data-gathering instrument is the on-line U-Map questionnaire for higher education institutions. International databases comprising comparable data at the institutional level do not exist or they cover only a very limited part of the data needed. In Europe the prime data provider will be higher education institutions through country-specific questionnaires that can be pre-filled the information with that is available from national databases. The questionnaire is organized around seven sections:

1. General information
2. Students
3. Graduates
4. Staff
5. Income
6. Expenditure
7. Research and Knowledge Exchange.

An online Glossary and Help Desk are provided to facilitate consistent and comparable data-collection across institutional and national settings.

U-Map offers the option to have the questionnaire partly pre-filled using existing data from national databases provided by statistical agencies, rectors' conferences or ministries of education. This can reduce institutional data collection burdens and provides standard data definitions.

Table 45.1 U-Map dimensions and indicators

Teaching and learning profile	Student profile	Research involvement
Degree level focus (1–4): % of degrees awarded at doctorate, master, bachelor and sub-degree level	**Mature students (13)**: % of mature (30+) students	**Peer reviewed academic publications (22)**: Number of peer reviewed academic publications per fte academic staff
Range of subjects (5): Number of large subject fields (ISCED) in which at least 5% of degrees are awarded	**Part time students (14)**: % of part time students	**Professional publications (23)**: Number of professional publications per fte academic staff
Orientation of degrees (6–7): % of degrees awarded in general formative programmes vs. programmes for licensed/ regulated and other career oriented programmes	**Distance learning students (15)**: % of students I distance learning programmes	**Other research output (24)**: Number of other peer reviewed research outputs per fte academic staff
Expenditure on teaching (8): Expenditure on teaching activities as % of total expenditure	**Size of student body (16)**: Total number of students enrolled in degree programmes	**Doctorate production (25)**: Number of doctorate degrees awarded per fte academic staff
		Expenditure on research (26): Expenditure on research activities as % of total expenditure

Involvement in knowledge exchange	International orientation	Regional engagement
Start-up firms (9): Number of start-up firms (new in last 3 years) per 1,000 FTE ac staff	**Foreign degree seeking students (17)**: Number of students with a foreign qualifying diploma as a percentage of total enrolment	**Graduates working in the region (27)**: % of graduates working in the region (NUTS2)
Patent applications filed (10): Number of new patent applications files per 1,000 fte academic staff	**Incoming students in exchange programmes (18)**: Number of incoming students in exchange programmes as % of total enrolment	**New entrants from the region (28)**: Percentage of new entrants coming from the region (NUTS2)
Cultural activities (11): Number of concerts and exhibitions (co-) organised by the institution per 1,000 fte academic staff	**Students sent out in exchange programmes (19)**: Number of students sent out in exchange programmes as % of total enrolment	**Importance of local/regional income sources (29)**: Income from local/regional income as % of total income

(continued)

Table 45.1   (continued)

Involvement in knowledge exchange	International orientation	Regional engagement
Income from knowledge exchange activities (12): Income from knowledge exchange activities (income from licensing agreements, copyrights, third party research and tuition fees from CPD courses) as % of total income	**International academic staff (20)**: Number of non-national academic staff (headcount) as % of total academic staff (headcount)	
	Importance of international income sources (21): Income from international sources as % of total income	

(1 to 29) refers to the number of the indicator in the Table 45.1 and the number of the element of the sunburst chart (see Fig. 45.1)

Institutional data is validated by the U-Map project team in consultation with individual institutions and, where possible, comparing data with existing national and international databases.

The questionnaires have been piloted with more than 50 institutions while the concept of pre-filling has been tested in the case of the Norwegian higher education system. Several other European higher education systems have shown interest in a similar process.

The final step is to determine the position of the institutions on the indicators in the different dimensions. The data provided by the higher education institutions are used to calculate indicator scores. These scores are presented in a categorised way in a graphical chart (a sunburst chart, see Fig. 45.1). The indicator scores are grouped into four categories, where the boundaries between the categories are determined by *cut-off points* that depend on the distribution of the indicator scores across the sample. At the moment, quartile scores are used to guide the choice of the cut-off points.

To communicate the results of the U-Map classification process, a web-based application was developed that allows the user to explore the results in an interactive way.

The web-based application consists of two instruments, the *Profile-Finder* and the *Profile-Viewer*. These tools allow the user of the classification to first select and then compare institutions. Through the *Profile-Finder*, the user selects HEIs by filtering out those institutions that have the same values on user selected indicators (e.g. the selection of the two institutions in Fig. 45.2 is based on their score on 'peer reviewed academic publications' and 'mature students'). With the *Profile-Viewer* the user may zoom in on the indicators of the profiles of the institutions selected with the *Profile-Finder.*

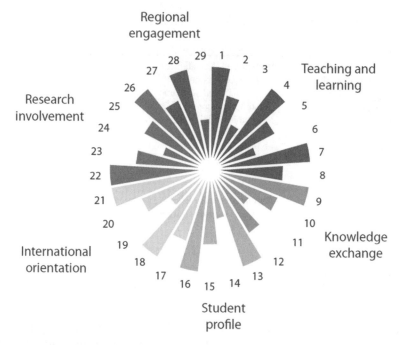

Fig. 45.1 U-Map activity profile (sunburst chart)

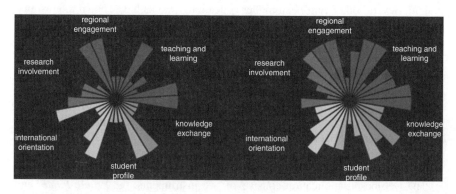

Fig. 45.2 U-Map profile-viewer

U-Map is a flexible tool continually being improved in a dynamic environment. Indicators, data elements and underlying definitions are held under constant review. User suggestions are collected and improvement options are studied and discussed.

This process results in adaptations in the U-Map tool (every 4 or 5 years). Notwithstanding this dynamic evolution, U-Map remains consistent to its founding principles.

45.4   The Implementation of the U-Map Tool

One of the limitations of the U-Map tools so far has been the number of higher education institutions that have submitted data. Because of this constraint, it is not methodologically sound to present the results in the intended way. The institutional activity profiles are presented in a fully functional way (see www.u-map.eu/finder) but the profiles cannot be linked to a specific institution (i.e. the name and country). This restricted demo mode limits the full potential of the U-Map instrument. Although it allows the user to experience the functionality of the instrument, it does not allow comparison of real identifiable higher education institutions. In order to make the next step towards a fully functional classification tool, the number of data submitting higher education institutions needed to be expanded.

In 2010 a fourth stage was added to the U-Map project sequence. The objective of this project, subsidised by the European Commission under the Lifelong Learning programme, was to further the implementation of the European classification of higher education institutions (U-Map) and to enhance its impact on transparency in the EHEA. The focus of activities was on the expansion of the number of participating institutions.

Two approaches have been used so far for recruiting higher education institutions:

- A national approach, combined with pre-filling. In this approach, one or more national organisations (be it a ministry of education, or a rector conference) take the initiative to invite all higher education institutions to participate in the classification project. Participation is on a voluntary basis (see Box 45.1: The U-Map Protocol). Analyses are made of existing national data bases. The analyses comprise the coverage, the definitions used and the constraints in data delivery. Relevant data from these national databases are used to pre-fill the on-line questionnaires of the institutions. Relevant data from these national databases are used to pre-fill the on-line questionnaires of the institutions.
- Bilateral filling refers to the submission of data by an individual higher education institution on the institution's own initiative. There is no third party involved, other that the institution and the U-Map team, assisting in the process.

More than 70 institutions in two countries (Estonia and Portugal) and 20 individual institutions were recruited. This project, as well as a project initiated by the Dutch government, has provided insights in the feasibility and relevance of U-Map in a cross-national perspective. In the following part the implementation of U-Map in three national systems will be discussed.

Box 45.1 The U-Map Protocol

(a) U-Map accepts all higher education institutions provided that they offer at least one degree programme that has been accredited by the relevant national agency.

(b) The official contact person for the higher education institution will receive a username (which is the same as the email address of the contact) and a password.

(c) With this access information the questionnaire can be accessed. The contact may distribute the access information to other persons in the higher education institution who may contribute to the completion of the questionnaire. Changes to the data may be saved at any time.

(d) If the data pre-filled by the U-Map team are not correct, these data may be changed. If pre-filled data are changed, a short explanation in the comment box at the bottom of the page is required.

(e) Once all questions are answered (all items on the starting page are checked) the data may be submitted to the U-Map team. Submitting the data implies that the higher education institution has certified the information as being accurate. To verify that the official contact person has submitted the data, that person receives a verification code that is needed for completion of the data submission.

(f) The data submitted will be analysed by the U-Map team. Outliers, unexpected results and inconsistencies will be reported back to and discussed with the contact person. If these discussions result in the need for adjustment of the data, the adjusted data can be resubmitted.

(g) Once the submitted data are approved, the contact person will receive a message with a link to the U-Map activity profile of the higher education institution. The contact person has to confirm that the profile has been inspected and that there is no objection to publication.

(h) Once the U-Map team has received this confirmation, the profile will be published on the U-Map website.

(i) The U-Map team will use the information provided only for classifying the higher education institutions. The U-Map team will not provide the information to third parties or use it for different purposes, unless the higher education institution has given its explicit written permission for this.

45.5   Estonia

The Estonian higher education system is a small system (around 55,000 students), comprising 6 public universities, 4 private universities and 22 institutions of applied higher education. The larger institutions have branch campuses in different parts of the country. The institutions differ widely in size (from 50 to 17,500 students) and scope of activities and disciplines.

45.5.1   U-Map Implementation

The recruitment of institutions was organised in close cooperation with the Estonian Ministry of education (department of higher education). Representatives from the Estonian higher education institutions and potential other data providers joined in to discuss procedures regarding pre-filling and the data provision by the institutions. Based on those discussions data were extracted from national existing data sources and used to pre-fill parts of the institutional questionnaires.

After pre-filling, a technical workshop was organised with the participating higher education institutions. Issues regarding the definitions of indicators and data-elements and practical issues regarding the questionnaire were discussed. Based on these discussions the decision was made to change the reference year (from 2008 to 2009), as well as further clarification could be given regarding the definition and use of region and temporary staff data. Data collection using the on-line questionnaires was concluded 4 months after the technical workshop and the verification process took another month.

At the end of the project, 28 higher education institutions (out of 32) provided data, and U-Map profiles were generated.

45.5.2   The National Policy Context

The Estonian government is rethinking the higher education system. In 2005 a higher education strategy was outlined for the period 2006–2015 (Estonian Ministry of Education and Science 2005). Internationalisation of higher education, increasing participation, especially in science and technology, increasing the production of doctoral graduates, realigning the higher education system to become more compatible with the European systems, reform of the quality assurance system and more attention to the social dimension of higher education were the main objectives in that strategy (Estonian Ministry of Education and Science 2010). Currently (2011), a higher education reform plan is drafted. The aim of that plan is to increase the fairness of the higher education system for students, enhance the efficiency of the system and increase the autonomy and accountability of higher education institutions (see also Estonian Ministry of Education and Science 2011).

The international economic hardship and the national demographic situation (an upcoming drop in secondary school leavers) are major challenges for realising the plans.

Progress is made regarding the legislative frameworks facilitating reform, but the limits on state funding have kept the system from making progress in terms of participation and doctorate production (student support systems and scholarship programs could not be implemented). Important changes have started regarding the institutional landscape and further changes are planned. A few vocational educational institutions have been transformed into institutions of professional higher education and more institutions are to follow. This transformation of the non-university sector is seen as an important way to upgrade participation and quality of education in that sector. There are plans to change the strong central steering of higher education institutions. According to the draft reform plans, the concept of state commissioned education will be abolished and institutions will have to decide how many students places will be created, based on their profile and function. Profile and mission oriented performance contracts between the ministry and individual institutions are envisaged as major instruments for steering the system. As for the internationalisation objectives there are ambivalent results. Estonian students are internationally mobile, Erasmus mobility is well balanced, but there are far more students leaving the country for studying abroad than students coming in.

The dynamic character of higher education in Estonia became apparent in the discussions regarding the reference year. There was a strong feeling among the institutions that the reference year should be as recent as possible, since things changed very rapidly in the Estonian higher education landscape. The fact that there was an intense discussion on staff and how to count staff on short and part time contracts can be related to a particular characteristic of the higher education system: the large number of small institutions.

The resulting U-Map profiles are to a large extent in line with the expectations of the Estonian institutions and the Ministry. The fact that there are five or six larger institutions with significant research involvement and a large number of small highly specialised institutions did not surprise the Estonian audience. The strong regional engagement in most institutions was also not seen as a surprise as Estonia is considered to be one NUTS2 region and most of the larger institutions have branch campuses across the country. Most interesting differences/diversity could be found in the 'international orientation' dimension and the dimension 'knowledge transfer'.

Estonian institutions have started comparing their profiles and questions regarding the various scores have emerged. These questions will be used in a next stage to improve the interpretation of the definitions and the consistency of data provision across the Estonian institutions. It became also clear that some of the small institutions with a 'small' profile were already in some way under scrutiny. The doubts regarding their viability were expressed before the profiles were created. This touches upon a crucial point of the use of U-Map. U-Map is an instrument that describes the activity profiles of an institution. If that activity profile is 'small' it does not mean that the performance of that institution is low. It may hint at viability issues but that needs to be firmly embedded in the institutional and national context. U-Map may give a signal, but most certainly not the only signal.

45.6 Portugal

The Portuguese higher education (around 400,000 students in 2010) comprises a large number of institutions: 93 private (thereof 10 universities) with around 88,000 students in 2010 and 40 public institutions (thereof 14 universities) with a total of more than 300,000 students (slightly less than 200,000 in universities).

45.6.1   U-Map Implementation

In February 2011 meetings were held with the Portuguese Ministry of Education and representatives from the three associations of higher education institutions. During these meetings the procedures regarding pre-filling and the data provision by the institutions were discussed. The databases of the Ministry and the associations were used to pre-fill parts of the institutional questionnaires (mainly student and graduate information). Seventy-five institutions were invited by the associations of higher education institutions to participate in the project. 63 institutions responded and 55 provided a full dataset.

In April a technical workshop was organised in Lisbon, where 53 representatives of institutions, rector conferences and ministry discussed the details of the online questionnaire. Based on the discussions, a country specific FAQ section was created on the website, and a country specific page was created on the website. Main issues at that workshop were the position of the associated research institutes at universities, the exclusion of short post-secondary degrees for the project, the definition of publications and the breakdown of government funding by teaching and research.

The process of data-collection continued into September 2011, whereas the verification process was concluded early October.

45.6.2   The National Policy Context

Portugal is 'modernising' its higher education system. Following up on the 2006 OECD review of tertiary education (OECD 2007), Portuguese government has implemented a number of reforms. The higher education institutions need to become more responsive to the needs of society and the economy. More autonomy and more accountability are keywords in this context. The issues that have been addressed since 2006 are new legislation, system diversity, quality assurance, loans schemes to facilitate more student participation and international partnerships in teaching and research (Ministry of Science, Technology and Higher Education, Portugal 2011).

The new legislative framework is intended to facilitate an outward focus of institutions. Public universities are allowed to acquire an independent legal status. To what extent this will help to create more effectively university industry links is to be seen. Modernisation of the higher education system is interpreted also as strengthening and expanding the polytechnic sector. The main rationale is the stronger orientation of the polytechnic degrees towards the profession. This and the regional dispersion of polytechnics and other non-university HEIs are supposed to enhance knowledge transfer, regional engagement and social inclusion.

U-Map has some clear benefits to offer in the Portuguese policy context. The focus on system diversity is most interesting. Diversity is seen as a strengthening of the binary system. U-Map may help in bringing more nuances to this discussion. Although the responsiveness to the (local/regional) economy and society is a key element in the Portuguese modernisation agenda, there are other dimensions in the reform agenda that go beyond the traditional binary divide. The international orientation and regional engagement are issues that may cut across the binary divide (as becomes apparent in other countries). The divide between both 'types' of institutions regarding their activities in these areas may not be as sharp as suggested: universities may be active in 'professional' fields, polytechnics (and other non-university institutions) may be more internationally active than some universities etc.

U-Map has a clear potential relevance in the Portuguese policy discussions as there were lively discussions regarding degrees (especially the short technical oriented degrees), discussions regarding the role of professional publications and the emergence and character of research in the polytechnics.

Preliminary results show, not surprisingly, that there is diversity on the relevant issues (regional engagement, international orientation, research orientation), but is also clear that this diversity does not follow the binary divide in all dimensions. The closest 'fit' is in the dimensions 'Research involvement' and 'Teaching and Learning Profile'. University have in general a higher involvement in research and have a more doctorate/master level and general formative focus. In other dimensions, like international orientation' and 'student profile' it is quite difficult to find traces of the binary divide. Although it is difficult to predict the impact of the outcomes (as the government has no official part in the project), it is clear that U-Map points out that the current discussions regarding institutional diversity and responsiveness should be broadened beyond the binary divide.

45.7   The Netherlands

The Dutch higher education system is a binary system with the UAS (40 public ones, 415,000 students) on the one side of the divide and the 14 public universities (165,000 students) on the other side. In addition, there is a private sector where CPD courses and programmes as well as recognized degree programmes are offered. There are more than 60 private institutions, with a wide diversity in size and scope.

45.7.1   U-Map Implementation

The Dutch U-Map project was initiated by the Dutch Ministry of Education and Science. It was interested in having the U-Map profiles for all Dutch higher education institutions. Early 2010 preliminary meetings with the associations of UAS and universities (HBO-Raad and VSNU) were held, discussing the protocol to follow. All higher education institutions (119: 40 public UAS, 14 public universities) were invited by the Dutch Ministry of Education and Science to participate. Sixty-three responded positively and 46 (of which 13 public universities) provided a full data set. Most of the small specialized teacher training colleges decided not to participate; workload and lack of relevance were reported as the main reasons for that decision. As for the private sector, the umbrella organization of the private institutions informed its members of the project and invited them to participate as well. In total 10 responded and 4 provided a full dataset.

The process of implementation in the Netherlands is still ongoing. Prior to the technical workshop, in which the definitions of the indicators and data-elements were discussed with the participating institutions, the HBO-Raad had started a discussion on the indicators in the research dimension. They argued that the indicators selected did not represent the (practice oriented) research activities that are emerging in the universities of applied sciences. Because of this critique, the U-Map profile was changed and the indicator 'peer reviewed publications' was split up in three: 'peer reviewed academic publications', professional publications', and 'other peer reviewed research products'. This eased some of the pain, but there was still some reluctance to participate. Therefore a discussion with experts regarding the issue was organized, as well as a second workshop in which participating institutions could discuss about alternative indicators in the dimension research and international orientation. These discussions lead to a better understanding of the definitions, but did not lead to another change of the U-Map profile. In the university sector a different discussion emerged: how to deal with teaching hospitals? This issue is a problematic issue for already quite some time. The discussion that U-Map started was welcomed by the relevant universities, but the teaching hospitals did not want to participate due to a problem in the alignment of the timing of the discussions. Eventually the universities decided how to take teaching hospitals into account, but it slowed down the process of data collection and verification significantly. Definition issues dominated the discussions during verification, but political sensitivities had an even more significant impact on the process. Both individual institutions and the associations were during the process reluctant to share the resulting U-Map profiles. The protocol was adjusted so that formal approval of the Board of the institution was needed for publication of the profile on the Dutch U-Map website. This additional 'hurdle' was built in on request of the associations and it underlined the political sensitivity of the issue of institutional profiles in the Dutch policy context.

After one and a half year, only 1 out of 4 institutions did allow publication on the Dutch password protected website. Although this may increase in the near future due to an encouragement letter by the associations, it is clear that the policy context has put the U-Map project in a delicate position, forcing the researchers to walk on eggs.

As for the results, they are not very surprising at first glance. The binary divide is clearly visible in the dimensions 'research involvement' and 'teaching and learning profile'. In the other dimensions however, the divide is not that clear and obvious. There are a number of UAS that are equally or even more internationally oriented than the universities. Professional orientation and the indicators in 'regional engagement' show also diversity along different, 'non-binary' lines.

45.7.2   The National Policy Context

The Dutch government has presented its latest plans for higher education in the Summer of 2011. In the Strategic Agenda (Ministerie van Onderwijs and Cultuur en Wetenschap 2011), the focus is on raising the quality and efficiency of the higher education system. Enhancing both horizontal and vertical diversity of the higher education system is key to these policy plans. Higher education institutions need to develop their profiles both in terms of activities (horizontal diversity) and their performances (vertical diversity). The government wants to link the performance profile to a very limited part of funding through bilateral performance contracts comprising performance profile related indicators. The activity profiles are seen by the government as a tool that may help higher education institutions in finding and developing their profiles. The government sees U-Map as a promising way to develop institutional activity profiles and has supported the testing and implementation of U-Map in the Dutch higher education system.

The associations and the HEIs have taken a very cautious position. This has most likely to do with the prominent role institutional profiles play in the aforementioned Strategic Agenda and a previous policy document (Commissie Toekomstbestendig hoger onderwijs stelsel 2010). In the latter report there was a strong call for more institutional diversity. U-Map was mentioned as a promising way to illustrate diversity. This report has been well accepted by the higher education institutions (as it also called for substantially more resources for the higher education sector). The report was an important input for the 2011 policy document (Strategic Agenda) that drafts the outline for the higher education system in the years to come. Institutional profiles play an important part in this new policy. Institutions have to decide on their institution profile (mission) and negotiations will be held to draft performance based contracts between individual institutions and the government. These contractual agreements will have potential financial consequences. In this setting, the development of institutional activity profiles (U-Map) is seen by many as confusing. Not all institutions are easily inclined to fully co-operate in drafting and sharing these profiles in current uncertain times. The ministry argues that the U-Map profiles can be used by the institution internally as a tool in the institutional quest for its profile. Even though the ministry stresses that the U-Map profile will not be used in any way related to financial or structural decisions, institutions remain reluctant.

45.8   Results

In Figs. 45.3 and 45.4 a random selection of institutional profiles from the Estonian, the Portuguese and the Dutch case are presented. Since all three countries have some kind of a binary divide, the profiles are grouped into two groups: the universities of applied sciences (or polytechnics) and the research universities. Within the limited number of 15 institutions per group, the U-Map activity profiles show a remarkable diversity. Least diversity can be seen regarding the teaching and learning

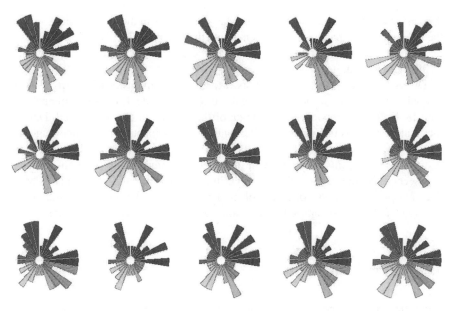

Fig. 45.3 Activity profiles of Universities of Applied Sciences in Estonia, Portugal and the Netherlands

Fig. 45.4 Activity profiles of research universities in Estonia, Portugal and the Netherlands universities

dimension and the research dimension. Many indicators in these dimensions reflect the characteristics that are used to demarcate the binary divide. UAS and universities differ most on these indicators, although there are some institutions that would fit in other group quite well.

Diversity is much stronger with respect to the other dimensions. This diversity is not only between the two groups, but cuts across the divide. If the focus of analysis shift to another dimension, the grouping of the institution change as well. During the final workshops in Estonia and Portugal, the participants were invited to group the activity profiles into an Estonian/Portuguese classification of higher education institutions. All teams came up with different groupings, using different primary and secondary foci. This hands-on experiment underlined the result that U-Map does not provide one classification of higher education institutions but allows the user to generate a personalised classification of higher education institutions.

45.9 Discussion

Enhancing transparency in the European Higher Education Area has been a key objective of the Bologna process. Knowing what the vast number of higher education institutions do is a crucial element in that process. Structural reforms to align certain features of higher education institutions (like degree structures, credit systems, quality assurance) have been a powerful way to push that process forward. U-Map is an instrument designed to add new dimensions to the discussions regarding transparency and diversity and transcend the traditional dichotomies that tend to dominate and in many instances stifle the discussions on institutional diversity.

U-Map is not perfect. The implementation of a new transparency instrument is a complex and labour intensive process. The way the process is set-up, the relations between and roles of individual institutions, associations and the policy makers determine to a large extent the speed and success of the implementation.

U-Map is designed as a European transparency instrument. National higher education issues may be addressed in the analyses of the profiles, but it is clear that U-Map as a European tool is not fully aligned with national institutional needs. Its relevance for national policy discussions may therefore vary between countries.

The implementation of U-Map so far has shown that a national approach is the most promising approach. The availability of national databases and frameworks allow for a more in-depth analysis of those existing data structures and for a better alignment of definitions and data both nationally and internationally. It also provides a better base for verification of the data. U-Map has proven to be a viable transparency instrument, that will improve the more institutions and national systems participate. Further development of the instrument, procedures and protocols and the set of indicators will further improve the relevance of the European classification: U-Map.

U-Map is more inclusive than many other transparency instruments: it comprises more dimensions, is open to more 'types' of higher education institutions and cuts across national borders. This broadened perspective and the clear orientation towards the user to allow for personalised 'classifications' Despite its shortcomings, the U-Map instrument may broaden our understanding of what has happened in the European Higher Education Area since Bologna.

References

Commissie Toekomstbestendig hoger onderwijs stelsel. (2010). *Differentiëren in Drievoud omwille van kwaliteit en verscheidenheid in het hoger onderwijs*, den Haag. http://www.rijksoverheid. nl/ministeries/ocw/documenten-en-publicaties/rapporten/2010/04/13/advies-van-de-commissie-toekomstbestendig-hoger-onderwi.html

Estonian Ministry of Education and Science. (2005). *Estonian higher education strategy, 2006–2015*. http://planipolis.iiep.unesco.org/upload/Estonia/Estonia-Higher-Education-Strategy-2006-2015. pdf

Estonian Ministry of Education and Science. (2010). *Summary of developments of Estonian higher education policy from 2006 to 2009, overview of the activities that have taken place based on the 2008–2010 implementation plan for the Estonian Higher Education Strategy 2006–2015*, Tartu.

Estonian Ministry of Education and Science. (2011). *The five challenges of Estonian education, Estonian education strategy 2012–2020, draft*. http://www.elu5x.ee/public/Haridusstrateegia_ENG_spreads_appendix.pdf

European Commission. (2011). *Communication from the commission to the European parliament, the council, the European economic and social committee and the committee of the regions, supporting growth and jobs – An agenda for the modernisation of Europe's higher education systems*, Brussels. http://ec.europa.eu/education/higher-education/doc/com0911_en.pdf

Hazelkorn, E. (2011). *Rankings and the reshaping of higher education, the battle for world-class excellence*. New York: Palgrave Macmillan.

Ministerie van Onderwijs, Cultuur en Wetenschap. (2011). *Kwaliteit in verscheidenheid, Strategische agenda hoger onderwijs, onderzoek en wetenschap,* den Haag. The Hague: Sdu Uitgevers.

Ministry of Science, Technology and Higher Education, Portugal. (2011). *Science, technology and tertiary education in Portugal, 2011.* A background report based on a seminar with the OEC's Directorates for Science, Technology and Industry and for Education, 20 April 2011 at the OECD headquarters, Paris, Lisbon.

OECD. (2007). *Reviews of national policies for education: Tertiary education in Portugal*. Paris: OECD.

Rauhvargers, A. (2011). *Global university rankings and their impact*. Brussels: EUA.

van Vught, F. (Ed.). (2009). *Mapping the higher education landscape, towards a European classification of higher education*. Dordrecht: Springer.

van Vught, F., & Ziegele, F. (Eds.). (2011). *Design and testing the feasibility of a multidimensional global university ranking*, CHERPA Network, s.l. http://ec.europa.eu/education/higher-education/ doc/multirank_en.pdf

van Vught, F., Bartelse, J., Huisman, J., & van der Wende, M. (2005). *Institutional profiles towards a typology of higher education institutions in Europe*. Enschede: CHEPS. http://www.utwente. nl/mb/cheps/research/projects/ceihe/publications/socratesceiheinstitutionalprofiles.pdf.

van Vught, F., Kaiser, F., Bohmert, D., File, J., & van der Wende, M. (2008). *Mapping diversity; developing a European classification of higher education institutions*. Enschede: CHEPS.

van Vught, F., Kaiser, F., File, J. M., Gaethgens, C., Peter, R., & Westerheijden, D. F. (2010). *U-Map The European classification of higher education institutions*. Enschede: CHEPS. http:// www.u-map.eu/U-MAP_report.pdf.

Chapter 46
How to Measure Institutional Profiles in the Norwegian HE Landscape

The Norwegian 'Institutional Profile Project'

Ole-Jacob Skodvin

46.1 Introduction

All countries have the intention or political goal of having a diverse higher education system. But what do we actually mean with diversified higher education systems? And furthermore, how can we measure it? In this paper, I want to elaborate on these questions, and try to describe and analyse how the Norwegian higher education authorities (The Ministry of Education and Research and the Norwegian Agency for Quality Assurance in Education (NOKUT)) use public registers data to make institutional diversity transparent and to compare the different institutional profiles of the higher education system.

As part of the result-oriented planning, the Ministry of Education and Research annually conducts an individual consultative steering dialogue meeting with each public HEI. This is regarded as an instrument to help promoting a diversified HE sector in Norway. In addition, institutional diversity is measured by different performance indicators along different dimensions. With the so-called flower project, the Ministry employs a new tool to describe the diversity in the Norwegian HE sector.

The classification of higher education institutions into institutional profiles is based on the EU classification project – U-Map. Viewed from the Norwegian policy point of view, the European Classification Project is both exciting and relevant. It is important to have a project that focuses on diversity as well as uniqueness among the HEIs.

O.-J. Skodvin (✉)
Department of Analyses and Development, Norwegian Agency for Quality Assurance in Education, Kronprinsens gt. 9, P.O. Box 1708 Vika, NO-0121 Oslo, Norway
e-mail: ojs@nokut.no

A. Curaj et al. (eds.), *European Higher Education at the Crossroads:*
Between the Bologna Process and National Reforms,
DOI 10.1007/978-94-007-3937-6_46, © Springer Science+Business Media Dordrecht 2012

Norway is in a unique position through the National Database for Statistics on Higher Education (DBH). Statistical information on the institutional level is reported from all the HEIs to the DBH, and with some preparation, it provides almost all the indicators that are required in the classification system (U-Map). (All the dimensions – and most of the indicators in the U-Map project, are covered in our national public statistics). This enables Norwegian higher education to develop a somewhat simplified and modified version of the U-Map project based on statistical register data. The Ministry is responsible for gathering data on the institutional profiles in our HEI system, while NOKUT, in cooperation with the DBH, is now developing profiles of different academic fields (Medicine, Political Science etc.) within the HEIs.

In this paper I will describe the particular challenges with respect to institutional diversity in the Norwegian higher education system and show how the Norwegian implementation of the U-Map methodology helps to make the diversity of different institutional profiles in our HEI system transparent. An important issue is whether the Norwegian HE system is going in a more diversified direction – or the opposite. Finally, I will try to elaborate on responses that have been gathered so far from the sector.

46.2 Institutional Diversity: Concepts and Drivers

From a political point of view, diversity has been seen as something good and valuable, and almost all countries have an intention or a political goal of having a diverse higher education system. This means that it is preferable to have a higher education system where institutions have different profiles, end products and strengths. In principle, a clear division of labour and specialisation should exist among the different types of institutions so that they may provide what society needs in education, research, dissemination and innovation (Huisman 1995; Kogan 1997). In view of this overall goal, classification systems have been developed to display and promote diversity in higher education.

Classifications of higher education are not intended to place the institutions hierarchically, and are thus an alternative to the international rankings. Rankings that compare different types of institutions by using the same criteria may, in fact, undermine the diversity among higher education institutions. If the higher education institutions (HEIs) adapt to the criteria in the rankings in order to score well, the consequence over time can be that HEIs become more similar or homogeneous rather than diversified. An instrument that describes the diversity among HEIs can actually counteract the uniformity or convergence process. The idea is that a typology based on diversity can help the HEIs define and develop their profile. This could, in turn, improve the methodologies of the rankings so as to become more multidimensional by being adapted to different institutional categories and educational needs. In this way, it will not be necessary to only measure HEIs in terms of the characteristics of a research university.

But what do we actually mean by institutional diversity? In organisational studies of higher education (Huisman 1998), different forms of institutional diversity and differentiation are usually distinguished:

Forms	Object of study
External diversity (system level)	Classification, typology, comparison of institutions
Internal diversity and differentiation (programme level)	Classification, typology, comparison of disciplines/ programmes

The Norwegian typology has up to now focused on external diversity, but, at the moment, there is also an ongoing project focusing on the programme level – the internal diversity and differentiation.

We can ask the question why diversity is perceived as positive. There are a lot of reasons and some of the most common are listed below (see Huisman 1995, 1999; Birnbaum 1983):

- Diversity is seen as positive because it:

  - Increases students' options (meeting students' needs and leading to increased social mobility)
  - Increases the overall efficiency of the higher education system:

    - It opens up higher education for the community
    - It facilitates and maintains specialisation within the system
    - It meets the demands of an increasingly complex society and labour market

  - Provides opportunity to use different organisational models
  - Protects institutional autonomy
  - Allows both an elite education and a mass education
  - Provides for division of labour and specialisation in relation to research and development
  - Paves the way for reforms and innovation through institutional competition and comparisons

With respect to the drivers of diversity, it is generally known that two different sources of influence are important: State control and the market. The influence of another driver, namely the underlying value systems (e.g. DiMaggio and Powell 1983; Huisman 1999), is difficult to assess. The authorities are using instruments such as financial regulation and stimulation to achieve differences between the sectors of the HEI system. When we are talking about the public authorities' management of higher education, the metaphor 'Gardener' can be useful in the way that 'he/she' cares for and maintains diversity – (and removes unwanted weeds) (Olsen 1988).

In systems where the government has less influence on higher education, market competition is often believed to encourage institutions to find their own niche.

A recent study on diversity in five national higher education systems – England, France, Norway, Slovakia and Switzerland – focuses on the interplay of factors which are the main driving forces behind diversity and convergence, both at institutional and system levels (Reichert 2009).

The debate in Europe often concentrates on differences in HEI profiles and their ability to respond to different claims and demands from society. The claims and demands are to a great extent connected to the 'massification' of higher education and increased diversity in the student population. The HEIs are to an increasing degree expected to meet other requirements than the traditional tasks of teaching and research, like new requirements connected to the modern knowledge society, innovation, dissemination and lifelong learning. In sum, all these new missions and requirements can result in too fragmented and dispersed resource allocation, in what Scott (2007) calls a 'mission stretch'.

Furthermore, the study distinguishes between vertical and horizontal differentiation. Vertical differentiation means that some types of HEIs are superior to others regarding duties and rights in education and research, either through legislation or different quality standards/accreditation. A horizontal differentiation means that equal value is attributed to different types of HEIs. If different types of HEIs are not regarded or treated as equal, the consequences may be an institutional (academic) drift and overload in dispersal of different tasks. Regarding systems where HEIs are, in principle, regarded as equal (horizontal differentiation), it will be important that the authorities develop incentives that can contribute to the development of different institutional profiles.

The study recommends a mix of funding, legislation and accreditation systems in order to enhance and maintain diversity. It is underlined that funding systems and economic incentives are more important in this respect than institutional autonomy alone. This means that autonomy for HEIs in itself does not necessarily lead to more diversified universities and colleges. Especially if horizontal differentiation is to be established, equal value and rewards, especially economic incentives, should be attributed to promote various roles and tasks.

46.3 Different Higher Education Structural Models in International Comparisons

46.3.1 Higher Education Systems: Different Structural Models

To place the particular challenges which Norwegian higher education is facing with respect to diversity, we should distinguish between the following HEI systems or models (Skodvin and Nerdrum 2000):

- A diversified and multipurpose system: USA and Canada;
- A binary system: A university sector and a specialised college sector – vocationally/ professionally oriented: Germany, Austria, Switzerland, the Netherlands and Finland;

- A unified system: UK and Australia[1]: All institutions have the university name, however – they are in different 'divisions' – clear status differences between the institutions.

46.3.1.1 A Diversified and Multipurpose Higher Education System

The United States of America (and Canada to some extent) are considered to be the prototype of a diversified and multipurpose higher education system. The USA has a hierarchy of both private and public universities and community colleges where the official status of the different institutions is based on an official classification system (see http://classifications.carnegiefoundation.org/). Institutional diversity has always been an important goal in the American higher education system, which is characterised by a multitude of somewhat permeable institutions that are partly overlapping in their function, while being distinctive in their major goals as well as in their academic standards (Birnbaum 1983).

Norway and Sweden have another variant of a diversified and multipurpose higher education system, a kind of transparent binary system with opportunities for 'advancement' (but no 'degradation'/'relegation'),[2] see Sect. 3.1.

46.3.1.2 A Binary System: A University Sector and a Specialised College Sector

A common higher education system in many European countries has traditionally been characterised by a binary division between a traditional 'Humboldtian' university sector, and a more specialised and fragmented non-university sector (Teichler 1996). In countries such as Germany, Austria and Switzerland this higher education system is represented by universities versus 'Fachhochschulen'. In countries like Finland and the Netherlands we find a division between universities and polytechnics, respectively, and 'Hogeschool'. Previously – most of the non-university institutions only offered shorter (2 or 3 years) vocational courses in a limited number of fields of study with loose links to universities. In most of these countries there are still loose links to universities, but today it is common that polytechnics and so-called applied university colleges award both their own bachelor degrees and to some extent also their own master degrees. They are perceived as complementary to the universities.

---

[1] Australia and UK abolished their binary systems in 1988 and 1992 respectively, and replaced it by a unitary one.

[2] Degradation is theoretically possible – but has not happened yet.

46.3.1.3 A Unified System

Australia and the United Kingdom abolished their binary system in 1988 and 1992, respectively, and replaced it by a unified system where all institutions acquired the university name. Nonetheless, the government in both countries insisted that the new systems should not be a unitary one. All the HEIs should be funded for what they do, not for what they are called. The authorities' main intention was to increase the diversity and differentiation through competition among the institutions, especially regarding research funding (Fulton 1996; Meek 1991; Meek and O'Neill 1996). Today all the higher education institutions in both countries are still named universities, but there are clear status differences between the institutions.

46.3.2   National HE-Structural Models and Their Effect on Diversification

The issue of diversity in HE raises several policy relevant questions as well as a number of basic theoretical issues. With respect to theory, both the higher education and organisational literature are divided on the topic of whether HEIs tend 'naturally' to move towards homogenisation or heterogeneity (DiMaggio and Powell 1983; Huisman 1999). Neither is there any consensus about whether diversity is best achieved under conditions of enhanced market competition or direct government intervention (e.g. Reichert 2009).

Several researchers have discussed the importance of the structure of national HE-systems in relation to diversity. Huisman (1997, 1998) did a study on institutional diversity in higher education where he made a comparison of ten national HEI systems (United Kingdom, Australia, Austria, Denmark, Finland, Belgium (the Flemish part), France, Germany, the Netherlands and Sweden). One of the findings in this study was that binary systems seemingly provide a better guarantee to (maintaining) diversity than unitary or unified systems. An explanation for the high level of diversity in binary systems could be that legally mandated boundaries are preserving diversity within the system.

Others point out that the distinction between binary and not binary systems is exaggerated with respect to maintaining or increasing diversity. According to Reichert (2009), it is politics and policy which are the most important factors in maintaining and enhancing diversity; in other words, it is concurrence between regulations, funding and incentives, quality standards, as well as norms and values within academy, employment and society in large.

The Bologna Process is also likely to have an effect on diversity as it shifts the focus from the structure to the content of higher education. The ambition of integrating the European Higher Education Area (EHEA) with the European Research Area (ERA) and the intention for a more integrated Higher Education and Research policy within the framework of the Bologna Process will have implications for the diversification process in European higher education.

This article will not answer these questions, but rather focus on how we can view or 'measure' different institutional profiles in higher education in a technical sense.

46.3.3   Recent Developments

Today, higher education is characterised by increased competition for students, research funding and talent, nationally and internationally. Furthermore, research is changing in the direction of larger cooperative structures and academic communities with the intention to increase higher quality or international competitiveness. Several countries are also establishing elite universities. In addition, we can observe that the interdisciplinary and multidisciplinary approach increases. This competition promotes quality, but can also create unintended barriers to the national cooperation and good use of resources across institutions.

It appears that the structural changes in most European countries follow the general dynamics in the OECD area. The OECD does, to a large degree, relate higher education to economy. At the same time, there is an increasing international competition for talent – that is, the best students and researchers – and the competition becomes increasingly global. One consequence is that higher education institutions are seeking to concentrate the academic, economic and administrative resources into larger, more competitive and powerful units. Moreover, several countries have begun to focus on the creation of elite universities. The USA and UK have had elite institutions for some time, and now several European countries follow (e.g. Germany and France).

46.4   The Norwegian HE System and Its Diversity Challenge

46.4.1   A Short Overview

The Norwegian HE institutions are dispersed throughout the country – and there are great differences between the various HEIs concerning size, academic profile and organisational structure, as well as geographic location (see Fig. 46.1).

The higher education sector in Norway now encompasses: 8 universities; 8 specialised university institutions, out of which 3 are private; 2 are academies of the arts; 23 are State university colleges, and 32 are private university colleges. (In addition, we have the Police Academy and 4 defence university colleges.)

As previously mentioned, Norway has, in reality, a sort of a flexible and 'transparent' binary higher education system, with universities (including specialised universities) on the one side, and university colleges on the other side. However, the university colleges can qualify for university status if they fulfil certain national academic standards and criteria – therefore called flexible and 'transparent binary system'.

Fig. 46.1 The Norwegian public higher education landscape

The Norwegian Agency for Quality Assurance in Education (NOKUT[3]) is responsible for this institutional accreditation.

In total – there are approximately 220,000 students and 30,000 staff (2010). See Table 46.1.

---

[3]NOKUT is the controlling authority for educational activity at all Norwegian universities, special field universities, university colleges and institutions with single accredited higher education programmes. Through an evaluation procedure, NOKUT decides on the recognition of the institutions' internal quality assurance systems and carries out checks to see if their educational provision meets national quality standards.

Controls take account of the fact, as stated in law and Ministerial Regulations, the institutions themselves carry full responsibility for the quality of their educational provision. A Ministerial Regulation sets some national standards and criteria, which are further developed in NOKUT's own Regulation. Together, these documents define the national standard that NOKUT's control activities refer to.

With few exceptions, NOKUT's control mechanisms involve the use of expert panels. The primary aim is to check that the quality of educational programmes is satisfactory. However, the mechanisms have a double function, as NOKUT also provides recommendations as to how the institution can enhance the quality of its educational provision and quality work.

Table 46.1 Registered students in HEI in Norway 2004–2010

	2004	2005	2006	2007	2008	2009	2010
Academies of the arts	842	852	824	796	788	818	816
Private specialised universities	16,292	15,433	15,247	15,395	15,684	16,141	15,954
Private university colleges	8,394	9,036	8,944	8,997	9,159	9,594	9,773
State specialised universities	9,503	7,385	7,137	7,237	7,657	7,787	8,428
State university colleges	98,735	91,956	92,595	91,991	86,553	87,606	89,572
Universities	74,472	82,708	81,815	78,555	86,256	91,783	93,768
Sum	206,238	207,370	206,562	202,971	206,097	213,729	218,311

Source: Database of Statistics on Higher Education (DBH), http://dbh.nsd.uib.no/
Remarks: Registered students on the 1st of October

In the international context, the Norwegian university college sector is unique: no other country spends so much time and resources on research and development work (R&D) in their vocationally oriented higher education sector (Kyvik 2007). There is a huge drive in the university college sector to obtain university status, either alone or most commonly through cooperation and mergers. In 2004 there were four universities in Norway. Today, we have eight. In addition, there is now a series of on-going processes in the university college sector with the aim of a closer cooperation and, in some cases, mergers. The common denominator is that most of these network alliances and mergers want to reach university status.

In 1995, Norway had ten higher education institutions with independent right to award doctoral degrees: the universities and the specialised universities. The corresponding figure today is 22. The increase has mainly taken place in the university college sector. In addition, several other university colleges are at the moment in the process of establishing new doctoral degree programmes.

Seen in an international perspective, with approximately 5 million inhabitants, Norway has a high number of institutions with the right to award doctoral degrees. After the structural reform in Denmark, only eight Higher Education institutions award doctoral degrees. In Finland, we find 16 universities with doctoral law, while, in 2008, Sweden had 21 universities and colleges with doctoral law. In the United States, Wisconsin, with approx. 5.5 million inhabitants, at the moment has two public universities that can award a doctorate, while California with 36 million inhabitants has ten (until recently, nine). These two states are examples of integrated higher education systems with a planned division of labour.

There may be several reasons for this academic drift in the Norwegian HE sector, but some obvious ones may be that the Norwegian HEIs:

- are regulated by the same law;
- have a common job position structure;
- have a joint reward and career system;
- have common academic norms and values;

So, currently there is an on-going discussion on whether this drift will lead to decreased diversity or homogenisation at the system level or not. An important question is, therefore, whether the Norwegian higher education sector is now moving in the 'wrong' direction? Will the new universities be pale copies of the originals? Another option could be to copy the UK-model: all the higher education institutions receive university status. The point is not what they are called – but what they actually do. Alternatively, one could choose to maintain diversity by using incentives that stimulate various forms of institutional profiles that, together, will provide what the society needs in terms of education, research, dissemination and innovation. The slogan should be: 'Different, but equal.'

The authorities' view on this is at least twofold. First of all – they are, of course, in favour of a diversified HE system, and they have several incentives and tools to maintain such a system. They are aware of the academic drift in the HE sector – and the danger of decreased diversity. Secondly, they prefer voluntary processes – the HEIs themselves shall decide their own profile and academic portfolio. To explain and understand this, I will continue with a short description and elaboration of steering and governance of the Norwegian HEIs, and then a short description of the on-going voluntary reorganisation of the Norwegian HE-sector.

46.4.2   Steering and Governance of Norwegian Higher Education

In 2003, Norway implemented a comprehensive reform in higher education, the so-called Quality Reform. There were two main objectives behind the Quality Reform:

- The national needs for quality improvements in higher education and research;
- The Bologna Process and Norway's obligations in that respect.

Briefly, we can say that, in addition to the introduction of the Bologna degree structures and a systematic quality assurance and accreditation system, the reform gave the HE institutions more freedom and academic autonomy, which also has implications for the authorities' steering and governance of the HE institutions (Michelsen and Aamodt 2007). Concentrating on the public sector, we can differentiate three types of steering mechanisms: (1) by law; (2) through the State budget and the budget allocation letter; (3) consultative steering dialogue.

One single law covers both State and private higher education institutions (Act no. 15 of the 1st of April 2005) that have three main objectives relating to: education; research and 'community contact'. The main features are institutional autonomy, academic freedom and 'institutional mobility' following accreditation procedures.

As a part of the Quality Reform, a performance-based funding system was introduced in Norway, and around 40% of the funding is now performance-based (education and research components). More specifically, funding of the HEIs is a grant based on three components: an education component (approx. 25%); a research component (approx. 15%) and a basic component (approx. 60%).

The grants passed by the Parliament are made available to the HEIs through the budget allocation letter, which is individual for each HEI. Various performance objectives are set down in the individual budget allocation letter, and the institutions have to fulfil them.

The third steering mechanism consists in a consultative steering dialogue which the Ministry of Education and Research holds annually with all public HEIs. This is a 'dialogue', or consultative meeting based on reporting and assessments/evaluations of the performance of the HEIs. (The institutions are represented by the leadership, board members, students and staff representatives.) In addition, the Ministry conducts other more informal meetings with relevant stakeholders, for instance with the Norwegian Association of Higher Education Institutions.

We can say that the authorities today in their governance and steering of HE institutions use a type of result-oriented planning (Skodvin et al. 2006).

46.4.3   Reorganisation of the Norwegian Higher Education Sector

A Government Commission for Higher Education (the Stjernø Commission), which was established in May 2006 and delivered their report to the Minister on the 22nd of January 2008 (Norges offentlige utredninger 2008) underlined that the Norwegian HE structure was under pressure. Too many of the institutions are vulnerable – small and academically fragmented – especially those located in rural areas. The Commission stated that the number of HE institutions was too high and recommended a stronger concentration, specialisation and division of labour through mergers (from 38 public HEIs to 8–10 HEIs). According to the Stjernø Commission, the main arguments for the mergers are:

1. Larger units would result in qualitatively stronger academic institutions;
2. Larger units would allow better management and use of administrative resources;
3. Larger units would improve the use of physical resources.

The Commission's recommendation for the amalgamation of institutions was connected to thoughts about the division of labour and collaboration between all the institutions within higher education.

The Ministry of Education and Research (and the HEIs) agreed on the Commission's diagnosis – but not on their solutions: they did not want State-initiated mergers. The Ministry supported an increased focus on cooperation, specialisation, concentration and division of labour among the HEIs – but on a voluntary basis. The Ministry wants to stimulate quality along different axes in a diversified HE-system, which means along the lines of the different types of Higher Education institutions (Norwegian Ministry of Education and Research 2010).

To a large extent, the Ministry's desired development has actually taken place. Several voluntary co-operation alliances, consortia and mergers have occurred in the last 3–4 years in order to enhance the co-operating institutions' position on the regional, national and/or the international HE market. They are searching for the 'right' institutional profile. The Ministry has already supported voluntary cooperation and merger processes through the State budget, and also signalled that they will continue to stimulate such processes. But the common denominator for the

HEIs is the wish to reach university status. This is not necessarily an undesirable development. If the new universities become pale copies of the old universities, then the Norwegian HEI has a large problem. If, however, they complement and represent good alternatives to the established universities, this may be a positive development. But how can the government control or monitor the institutional development of the higher education institutions? How can they measure diversity? Are the HEIs now moving in the 'wrong' direction or not?

46.5   Making Norwegian HE Diversity Transparent – How to Measure Diversity?

As part of result-oriented planning, the Ministry of Education and Research annually conducts an individual consultative steering dialogue meeting with each public HEI. This can be seen as an instrument to help promote a diversified HE-sector in Norway. Diversity is then measured by different performance indicators – but, in addition, they do also try to classify the HEIs institutional profiles. In 2010, the Ministry developed a tool to describe the diversity in the Norwegian HE-sector – the so-called flower project. This is a model for the classification of higher education institutions – their institutional profiles.

The project is based on the EU classification project – U-Map (van Vught et al. 2010; www.u-map.eu), powered by CHEPS (Center for Higher Education Policy Studies) (see Chap. 45 by Kaiser). The starting point for the project is that diversity is the strength of the European higher education system. A multidimensional classification system is intended to illustrate, compare and describe similarities and differences among higher education institutions. The U-Map facilitates this by providing a framework to present and analyse the institutional profiles. An institutional profile is the sum of a HEI's position on different dimensions and indicators in the typology. The classification makes it possible to perform various analyses of institutional profiles. The U-map can be used to compare institutions according to one or more dimensions based on a set of indicators, and to identify institutions that have a specific profile. Institutional profiles are also intended as a tool for higher education institutions in the internal strategy development, external benchmarking, for developing cooperation across institutional boundaries and for use in internal and external communication. Individual countries have already adopted the classification system in use, others are considering it.

Viewed from the Ministry's perspective, the European Classification Project is important because it focuses on diversity as well as on uniqueness among the HEIs. Furthermore, the U-Map Project is important in order to support quality cultures along different axes, to strengthen the HEIs capabilities to formulate clear objectives and strategies, to show the HEIs' profiles and purposes to the outside world, and, finally, to facilitate comparison between similar HEIs (which is difficult with the current ranking systems).

46.5.1   The Norwegian 'Flower-Project'

Inspired by the European U-Map Project, the Norwegian Ministry of Education and Research developed a model or classification system for displaying the individual HEI's profile. Like the U-Map Project, this is a non-hierarchical approach. The purpose is to raise awareness and trigger reflection on institutional characteristics. Each HEI's profile is expressed as a flower, and the typology model is also called 'the flower project'. In cooperation with the DBH,[4] the Ministry presented in spring 2010 the first version of the 'flower' in the report that yearly monitors the situation in the Norwegian higher education system (Norwegian Ministry of Education and Research 2010). The 'Flower Project' is further developed in 2011, but only with minor adjustments.

Norway is in a unique position though the National Database for Statistics on Higher Education (DBH). Statistical information at institutional level is reported from all the HEIs to the DBH, and with some preparation, it provides almost all the indicators that are required in the classification system (U-Map). All the dimensions – and most of the indicators in the U-Map project – are covered in our national public statistics (see http://dbh.nsd.uib.no).

The indicators comprise those that are part of the national funding system, performance indicators that are reported to the Ministry, and other indicators that are part of the quality assurance procedures. The 'Flower Project' shows roughly the institutional profiles we have in the Norwegian higher education system. In our classification system, there will be operated with five dimensions and a total of 20 indicators. The five dimensions and their indicators are presented in Table 46.2.

The visualisation of institutional profiles can be said to be the petals of a flower. Each petal represents a dimension or indicator area with its unique colour. Each dimension has its set of indicators. In our flowers – the 'Education' field has a blue colour, 'Research' is green, 'Economics and Resource Management' is red, 'Relations with Society' is orange, 'Institutional Size' is purple and the "Internationalisation" is brown. The scale used runs from 0 to 100.

It should not be interpreted to mean that something is bad or good. If, for example, a HEI has a clear vocation-oriented profile, many students taking continuing and further studies, a mature student population, etc., then it is just a simple description of what kind of institution this is. The universities have a different institutional profile than State colleges – this is also the intention (larger share of Master's degree students, more doctoral production, publishing, etc.) – they actually have different purposes.

---

[4]The Database for Statistics on Higher Education (DBH) is a data warehouse which holds data on a broad range of topics in the sector of higher education and research in Norway. This includes data about students and PhD candidates, educational institutions, researchers' publication points, staff, finances, building area in square meters, and also the amount of stocks and shares held by higher educational institutions. The DBH is initiated by the Norwegian Ministry of Education and Research and assigned to the NSD (Norwegian Social Science Data Services) in Bergen. It functions as an important steering and decision-making tool by providing quantitative parameters for the use of both the Ministry, as well as the 63 educational institutions in the sector.

Table 46.2 Dimensions and indicators in the 'flower'

Size	Education	Research
Number of students	Vocational-oriented profile	Academic staff profile (share of associate professors and professors)
Number of academic staff	Master's degree students	Doctorate degree production
Size of budget	Continuing and further education students	Academic publication (extent of publication points)
Number of courses	Distance learning students	Research Funds from EU and Norwegian Research Council (NRC)
	Students credit points production	
	Students' age profile	
	Student popularity (number of qualified applicants)	
Internationalisation	Relations with society	
Exchange students, outgoing	Contributions to activities outside the EU and NCR	
Exchange students, ingoing	Contract work (as a percentage of total expenditure)	
Courses taught in English	Business ideas	

Some of our institutions have a specific regional role, others have both a regional and a national role, and others are again responsible for the full spectrum from the regional, national and to the global arena. Nevertheless, comparisons between different institutional 'flowers' can be useful in order to highlight areas for improvement, but primarily as a result of comparisons between institutions with fairly similar institutional profiles.

46.5.2   The Logic of the Classification System

Figure 46.2 illustrates the institutional profile of a hypothetical institution X. Each petal represents a dimension with its unique colour and its set of indicators. The indicators are operationalised somewhat differently; some are in absolute sizes, such as the number of students, while others are in relative sizes, such as student production, which is measured as the number of produced credit points in relation to the number of full-time equivalents. For all indicators, the scale is 0–100 in increments of 10. The indicators are distributed according to the scale so that the entire scale is used.

46.5.2.1   Institutional Size (Purple)

The purple colour in the flower illustrates the institutional size. The purpose of the indicators is to show the institution's size from several absolute sizes. The first indicator

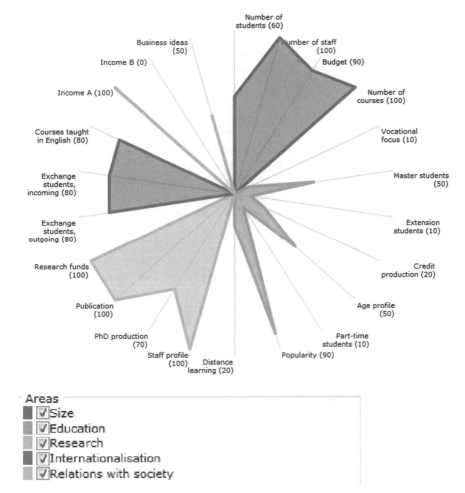

Fig. 46.2 Institutional profile of institution X

shows the institution's size measured in number of students. We can see that the institution X is given the score 60, which here means that it has between 14,001 and 16,000 students, indicating a large institution in terms of numbers of students.

The next indicator shows the HEIs size measured in number of academic staff. We can see that the institution X is given the score 100, which here means that it has more than 3,000 academic staff, indicating that it is a large institution.

The third indicator shows the budget the HEI receive from the Ministry of Education and Research. Institution X is given the score 90, which means that it has received between 2 and 3 billion Norwegian kroner. This indicates again that it is a large HEI.

The last indicator in this petal shows the institution's size measured in the number of study programmes. Institution X has a score of 100, which here means that it has more than 250 study programmes. This confirms that it is a large institution.

46.5.2.2   Education (Blue)

The blue colour in the flower illustrates the educational dimension. The first indicator shows the HEI's vocational- or professional-oriented focus. A high score indicates that it is a vocational-oriented higher education institution (teacher education, engineer education, nurse education etc.). Institution X has a score of 10, which means that the majority of the study programmes are more academically-oriented.

The next indicator shows the proportion of Master's degree students by the total number of students in the institution. Institution X has a score of 50, which illustrates that it has quite a high share of Master's degree students.

The third indicator in the educational dimension shows the proportion of further and continuing education in the institution. Institution X has a score of 10, which illustrates that the institution is not a typical further and continuing education institution.

The fourth indicator – 'Students' credit points production' shows the total study point production per full-time students in autumn 2010. The goal is to show how productive the institution's students are. Institution X is given a low score – 20 – illustrating that the institution has a low throughput and then potential for improvement in this area.

The indicator 'Age Profile' is based on the age median of the registered students. The purpose is to show the students' age distribution. Institution X is given the value 50, which illustrates that the average age of students is 24 and 25 years.

The indicator 'Part-Time Profile' shows the proportion of part-time students in the institution. For institution X, which is given a low score – 10 – it indicates that the institution has few part-time students (and then, in fact, a large proportion full-time students in the institution).

The seventh indicator in the educational dimension is attractiveness, which shows the number of student applicants for the various institutions. This is measured by the number of qualified applicants per study place. The institution X is given the score 90, which illustrates a high attractiveness.

The last indicator is 'Flexible Students', which means the proportion of students following decentralised education or distance education. Institution X is given the score 20, which indicates a low proportion of flexible students.

46.5.2.3   Research (Green)

The green colour illustrates the research dimension. The first indicator is the 'Competency Profile', measured by the proportion of the academic staff employed in Associate Professor or Professor positions out of the total academic staff. Institution X is given the score 100, indicating a very high proportion of the academic staff with top academic qualifications.

The next indicator is 'PhD Production', measured as the number of doctoral degrees per faculty (education and research staff). The intention is for the indicator to provide a measure of how intensive the doctoral education is in the HEIs. Institution X is given the score 70, indicating a good PhD production.

The third indicator is 'Scientific Publication', measured by the number of publication points per faculty in education and research positions. The indicator reflects the extent of publication points in relation to the size of its academic staff, and is a measure of how intensive publishing activities are in the HEIs. The institution X is given the score 100, indicating that the institution is among the institutions with the highest scientific publishing activity.

The last indicator is the allocation of research funding from the European Union and the Norwegian Research Council (NRC). The purpose is to highlight the extent of research funding from the EU and the NRC measured against the size of the academic staff. The indicator provides a measure of how active and successful institutions are in obtaining external research funding. The institution X is given the value 100, which illustrates that the institution is very competitive when it comes to attracting external research funding.

46.5.2.4   Internationalisation (Brown)

The brown colour of the flower illustrates the international dimension. The first indicator shows the number of outgoing exchange students, in relation to the number of registered students. The institution with the highest proportion of outgoing exchange students will score 100. Institution X is given the score 80, which must be classified as high.

The second indicator shows the number of incoming exchange students, in relation to the number of registered students. The institution with the highest proportion of incoming exchange students will score 100. Institution X is given the score 80, which means that it has quite a high share of incoming exchange students.

The last internationalisation indicator shows the number of courses taught in English. All subjects with more than 10 credit points are included in the overview. It shows to which extent the institution is prepared for internationalisation at home. Institution X is given the score 80, which is a high score.

46.5.2.5   Relations with Society (Orange)

The dimension 'Relations with Society' has an orange coloured petal in the flower. The first indicator is 'Contributions to Activities outside the EU and NCR[5]'. This shows the degree of external funding outside the EU and NCR, measured as contribution activities as a percentage of the total operating revenues. Institution X is given the score 100, which means that more than 5% of the total operating revenues are contribution activities.

The next indicator is 'Contract Work', which intends to give a picture of the scope of commissioned business of the institution. The indicator is measured by

---

[5] NCR = the Research Council of Norway.

contract work as a percentage of total expenditure. Institution X is given the score 0, which means that contract work activity is between 0% and 0.49% of total operating revenues.

The last indicator in this dimension is 'Scope of Business Ideas', which intends to give a picture of how active the institution is when it comes to commercialisation and innovation. It is measured in numbers of registered business ideas per institution per 100 academic staff. Institution X is given the score 50, which means seven to eight business ideas per 100 academic staff. The threshold (score) is low on this indicator because this is a relatively new activity in the higher education sector.

46.5.3   Institutional Profiles in Norway

Based on the 'flower typology', one can now look more closely at the different institutional profiles among the Norwegian HEIs and compare profiles among different groups of HEI.

46.5.3.1   State University Colleges

The State university colleges include a variety of different institutional profiles. Broadly speaking, we can make a distinction between the almost 'pure' vocational-oriented university colleges, colleges with an 'academic profile', and mixing models between these two. I will now show some examples of the three different university college categories.

Oslo University College (HiO) is an example of a typical vocational-oriented university. HiO is the largest university college in Norway with approximately 14,000 students (2010). The institution has recently merged with another university college (Akershus University College). Figure 46.3 illustrates the institutional profile of HiO in 2010.

If we look at the educational dimension (blue colour), HiO has a vocational-oriented focus (e.g. teacher, nurse and engineer education), primarily at an undergraduate level, an average age profile among their students and scores high on students credit production. Furthermore, HiO is a very attractive institution for the students and has quite few part-time students.

Compared to other university colleges, HiO is a relatively internationally-oriented institution in the educational area (red colour), and, with respect to the research area – the institution is quite strong on research publication and the academic staff has relatively high research competence.

Figure 46.4 shows the institutional profile of Oslo University College compared to three other public university colleges in the South-Eastern part of Norway (Telemark University College, Vestfold University College and Østfold University College), which can all be categorised as mixed models.

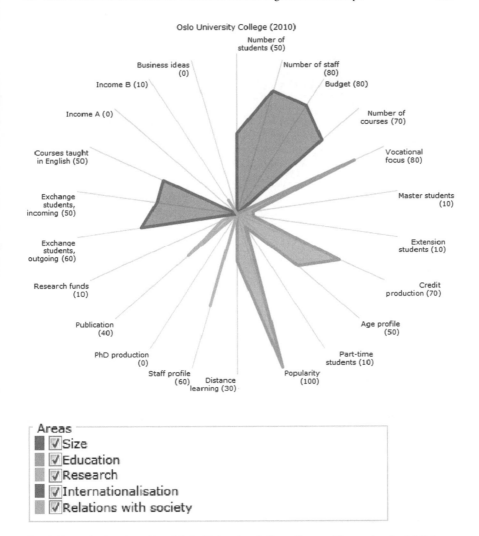

Fig. 46.3 Institutional profile of Oslo University College (Source: Norwegian Social Science Data Services)

Figure 46.4 indicates that HiO is very attractive for students, compared to the three other university colleges. Furthermore, we see that Vestfold University College and, to some degree, Østfold University College, have a strong relation with society (industry).

Bodø University College is a typical university college with an academic profile located in the Northern part of Norway (see Fig. 46.5). The institution was upgraded to university status in January 2011 through an institutional accreditation process carried out by the Norwegian Agency for Quality Assurance (NOKUT). The name of the institution today is University of Nordland.

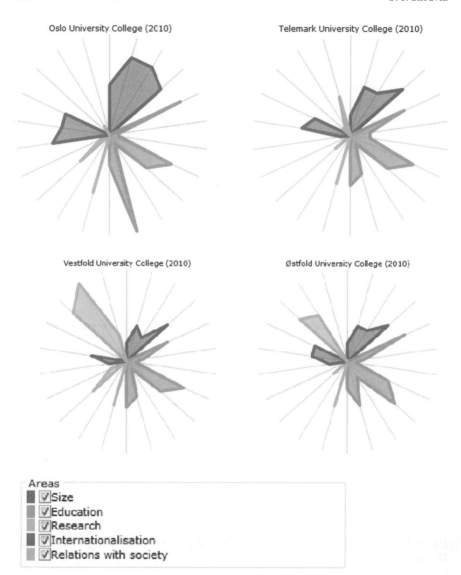

Fig. 46.4 Institutional profile of Oslo University College, Telemark University College, Vestfold University College and Østfold University College (Source: Norwegian Social Science Data Services)

On the educational area (blue colour), Bodø University College is characterised by a relatively high share of Master's degree students, a relatively mature student population and a lot of distance education courses compared to all other HEIs in Norway. Given the student recruitment challenge for the HEIs located in the Northern (and in general more rural parts) parts of Norway Bodø University College manages to attract a fair amount of students.

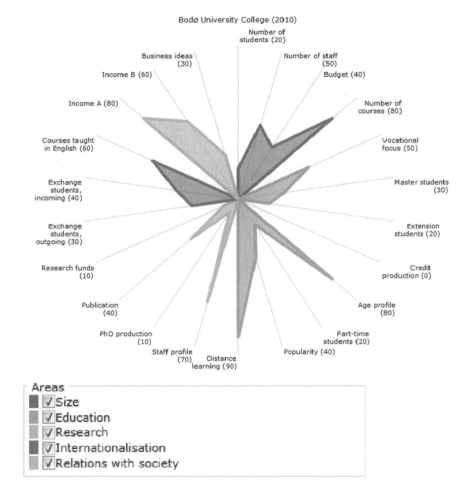

Fig. 46.5 Institutional profile to Bodø University College (Source: Norwegian Social Science Data Services)

Compared to most other university colleges, Bodø University College is performing quite well in the research area (green colour); has a competent academic staff, PhD production, research publication and is competitive with respect to obtaining external research funds.

Figure 46.6 shows the institutional profile of Bodø University College compared to three other public university colleges in the Northern part of Norway (Nesna University College, Finnmark University College and Narvik University College), which all can be categorised as mixed models.

A common denominator in the education area (blue colour), is that they all have a mature student population, and they offer many distance education courses. Furthermore, they struggle in recruiting students to their study programmes.

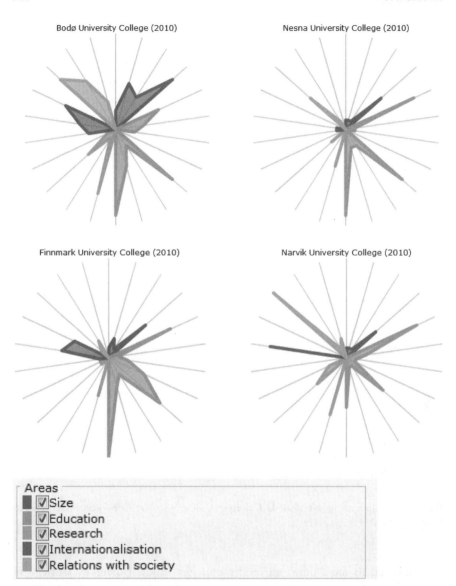

Fig. 46.6 Institutional profile of Bodø University College, Nesna University College, Finnmark University College and Narvik University College (Source: Norwegian Social Science Data Services)

In the research area, there are certain variations between the institutions. Bodø University College has the most visible research profile, but Narvik University College has quite a good score on the research indicators (research competence, publication, and attracting external research funds) also.

46.5.3.2   Universities

Currently, Norway has eight universities[6] (seven in 2010 – which correspond to the data used in this paper) – all of them public. Up to 2005 the number was four. On that basis we can distinguish between the four 'old' universities (University of Oslo, Bergen, Tromsø and Norwegian University of Science and Technology) and the new universities (University of Stavanger, Agder and Norwegian University of Life Sciences[7]). The institutional profiles of the 'old' and new universities are however quite different. 'A university is not a university'.

Figure 46.7 shows the institutional profile of the University of Oslo, which is the oldest (200 years in 2011) and largest[8] of the Norwegian universities.

We can see that the profiles differ a lot compared to university colleges. In short, we can say that the UiO is a very popular and attractive institution for students, it has a large part of the student population on Master's degree level, it offers relatively few distance learning courses, and, finally, UiO is quite strong on student internationalisation.

The University of Oslo is also strong in the research area, and has a high score on all the indicators that are used.

Figure 46.8 shows a comparison between the four 'old' comprehensive universities in Norway. The institutional profiles are relatively similar, especially Universities of Oslo and Bergen.

Figure 46.9 illustrates the institutional profile of one of the new Norwegian universities – the University of Agder (UiA), which was established as a university in September 2007 through an institutional accreditation by the Norwegian Agency of Quality Assurance in Education (NOKUT). Previously it was a university college.

UiA has a quite different institutional profile compared to the 'old' universities. In the educational area it has a more vocational-oriented profile, and a lower share of Master's degree students. Furthermore, the university offers more distance education courses than the old universities.

The research profile is also somewhat less pronounced compared to the established universities, especially with regard to PhD production and the attraction of external research funds.

Figure 46.10 shows a comparison of the institutional profiles of the three new universities (University of Agder, Stavanger and Norwegian University of Life Sciences).

University of Agder and University of Stavanger have quite similar institutional profiles, while Norwegian University of Life Sciences differs, especially having a

---

[6]In addition, we find eight specialised universities, five public and three private. All of them are small, and the common denominator is that they are specialised in one or a few academic fields (e.g. Music, Architecture, Veterinary Medicine, Business Administration, Religion). They are not included in this analysis.

[7]University of Nordland reached university status in 2011, and is not included in this analysis.

[8]In 2010 UiO had approximately 30,000 students and 6,000 staff.

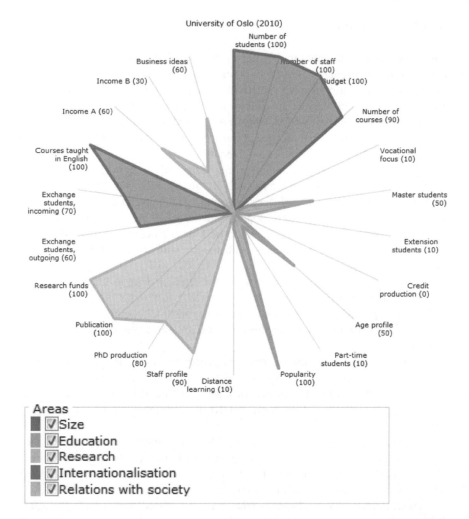

Fig. 46.7 Institutional profile of University of Oslo (Source: Norwegian Social Science Data Services)

stronger research profile. This can be explained by the fact that the latter institution was previously a specialised university college in the field of Agriculture with a relatively strong research base, while the two others where university colleges.

46.5.4 Are We Going in a Direction with More or Less Diversity?

The previous review of institutional profiles showed us that Norway has a relatively diverse higher education system. First of all, there are, as expected, large

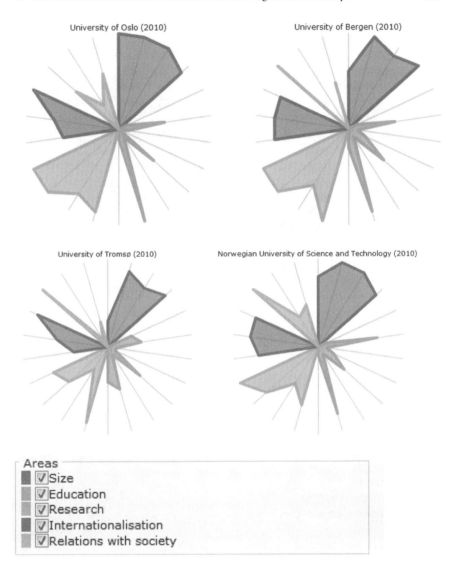

Fig. 46.8 Institutional profile of University of Oslo, University of Bergen, University of Tromsø and Norwegian University of Science and Technology (Source: Norwegian Social Science Data Services)

differences between university colleges and universities. The universities are more research-intensive and have a larger share of its education portfolio at master and PhD levels. Moreover, university colleges are generally more vocationally and practice-oriented than the universities, and there is also a far greater proportion of students who are engaged in flexible learning/distance education.

Second, the review of institutional profiles shows that there are large differences among the group of university colleges or universities. The diversity among the

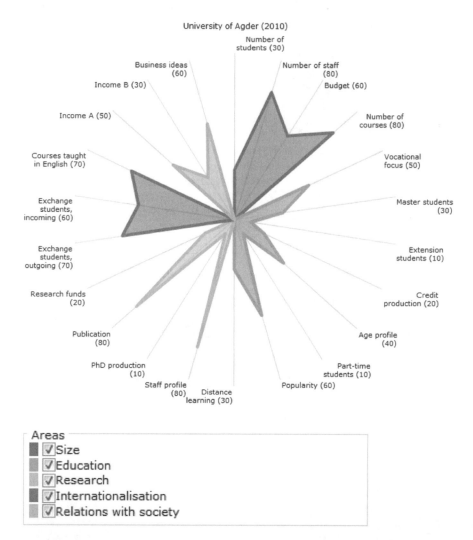

Fig. 46.9 Institutional profile of University of Agder (Source: Norwegian Social Science Data Services)

colleges is large in terms of vocational orientation, international orientation and research and development activities.

When it comes to universities, it is striking that the new universities have a very different profile from the old ones. So far, they do not seem to be pale copies of the old ones, and they have more in common with the most research intensive university colleges than the four old comprehensive universities. But it is important to underline that these institutional profiles do not give us enough evidence to determine whether the different universities complement each other or not. For this we need the different academic profiles within each higher education institution, and developments over a longer time-span. The Norwegian Agency for Quality

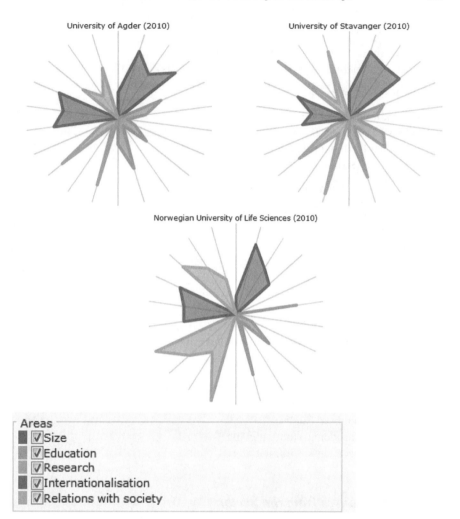

Fig. 46.10 Institutional profile of University of Agder, University of Stavanger, and Norwegian University of Life Sciences

Assurance in Education (NOKUT) is currently developing, in cooperation with Norwegian Social Science Data Services (NSD), a pilot project to view academic field profiles within in the Norwegian universities (Medicine, Political Science etc.). The model will build on the institutional 'Flower Project' (and U-Map). It will operate with six dimension/indicator areas in the 'academic field flowers':

1. Size

    (a) Number of students
    (b) Number of academic staff
    (c) Number of courses

2. Education – admission

   (a) Student popularity (number of qualified applicants)
   (b) Admission quality (quality of admitted students)

3. Education – profile

   (a) Vocational-/professional-oriented profile
   (b) Master's degree students (proportion of Master's degree students by the total
       number of students at the institution)
   (c) Distance learning students

4. Education – performance

   (a) Students credit point production
   (b) Share of students having successfully completed Bachelor's degree at normal
       time
   (c) Share of students having successfully completed Master's degree at normal time

5. Research

   (a) Academic staff profile (share of Associate Professors and Professors)
   (b) Doctorate degree production
   (c) Academic publication

6. Internationalisation

   (a) Exchange students, outgoing
   (b) Exchange students, ingoing
   (c) Courses taught in English
   (d) Exchange academic staff, outgoing
   (e) Exchange academic staff, ingoing

46.5.5   Responses from the Sector

The Norwegian 'Flower Model' became public through publication and web in
spring 2010 (Ministry of Education and Research 2010; NSD 2011). It is used as
a tool for the Ministry of Education and Research to consider the HEIs' profile
and contribution to the diversity of the HE system, in connection with their yearly
individual consultative steering dialogue meeting with each public HEI.

From the Ministry's point of view, the use of institutional profiles is obviously
considered as a useful tool to 'measure' diversity in the Norwegian higher education
sector. It gives a quick overview of what kind of institutions we have in our
HE-landscape, and it is a good starting point for dialogue and discussions with each
public HEI. Moreover, it is a good basis for further inquiry and analysis on relevant
diversity and other policy issues.

The reactions and feedback from both management and academic staff in the
HEIs are also largely positive. It is viewed as a useful tool for the visualisation of

their and other HEIs' institutional profile. It is also to a large extent used in individual institutional strategic work. Second, the use of institutional profiles is also considered as a counterweight to the use of one-dimensional rankings, which is a controversial issue in the Norwegian higher education debate.

For the typical student, the institutional profiles are not known and probably not perceived as relevant and interesting. Nevertheless, the feedback from the National Union of Students in Norway is positive regarding the use of institutional profiles.

In NOKUT's work with accreditation issues and especially in the context of institutional accreditation (from university college to university) and audit, the visualisation of institutional profiles are considered useful instruments. Furthermore, it is a starting point for further inquiry and analysis of different issues. As previously mentioned, the NOKUT and NSD are currently developing a pilot project to view academic field profiles within in the Norwegian Universities. This can be a useful tool to focus on programme level diversity. In addition, used in institutional accreditation and audit, it will also be most useful in the accreditation of new studies and in the reaccreditation of the existing ones.

References

Birnbaum, R. (1983). *Maintaining diversity in higher education*. San Francisco: Jossey-Bass.

DiMaggio, P. J., & Powell, W. W. (1983). The iron cage revisited: Institutional isomorphism and collective rationality in organizational fields. *American Sociological Review, 48*, 147–160.

Fulton, O. (1996). Differentiation and diversity in a newly unitary system: The case of UK. In G. Meek, O. Kivinen, & R. Rinne (Eds.), *The mockers and mocked: Comparative perspectives on differentiation, convergence and diversity in higher education*. Pergamon: IAU Press.

Huisman, J. (1995). *Differentiation, diversity and dependency in higher education*. Twente: University of Twente.

Huisman, J. (1997). *Institutional and programmatic diversity. A comparative analysis of national higher education systems in nine Western European countries*. CHEPS, University of Twente, Position 193.

Huisman, J. (1998). Diversity and differentiation in higher education systems. In J. C. Smart (Ed.), *Higher education: Handbook of theory and research* (Vol. XIII). Dordrecht: Kluwer Academic.

Huisman, J. (1999, July). *Differentiation and diversity in higher education systems*. Workshop on Questions of Institutional Landscape (pp. 75–110). Bohinj: CHEPS..

Kogan, M. (1997). Diversification in higher education: Differences and commonalities. *Minerva, 35*, 47–62, Kluwer Academic Publishers.

Kunnskapsdepartementet (Norwegian Ministry of Education and Research). (2010). *Tilstandsrapport for høyere utdanningsinstitusjoner i 2010*. Oslo. http://www.regjeringen.no/upload/KD/Vedlegg/UH/Sektoranalyse/Tilstandsrapport_2010_versjon-1.0.pdf

Kyvik, S. (2007). *Høyskolesektorens rolle i utdannings- og forskningssystemet i Vest-Europa* (NIFU STEP rapport 37/2007). Oslo.

Meek, V. L. (1991). The transformation of Australian higher education from binary to unitary system. *Higher Education, 21*(4), 461–494.

Meek, V. L., & O'Neill, A. (1996). Diversity and differentiation in the Australian unified national system of higher education. In G. Meek, O. Kivinen, & R. Rinne (Eds.), *The mockers and mocked: Comparative perspectives on differentiation, convergence and diversity in higher education*. Pergamon: IAU Press.

Michelsen, S., & Aamodt, P. O. (2007). *Evaluering av Kvalitetsreformen – Sluttrapport*. Oslo: Norges forskningsråd (Norwegian Research Council).

Norges offentlige utredninger. (2008). *Sett under ett: Ny struktur i høyere utdanning* (NOU 2008:3). Oslo.

NSD (2011). http://dbh.nsd.uib.no/styringsdata/typologi_rapport.action?versjon=2011.

Olsen, J. P. (1988). *Statsstyre og institusjonsutforming*. Oslo: Universitetsforlaget Oslo.

Reichert, S. (2009). *Institutional diversity in European higher education. Tensions and challenges for policy makers and institutional leaders*. Brussels: European University Association.

Scott, P. (2007). Back to the future? The evolution of higher education systems. In B. Kehm (Ed.), *Looking back to looking forward. Analyses of higher education after the turn of the millenium* (Werkstattberichte 67). Kassel: International Centre for Higher Education Research.

Skodvin, O.-J., & Nerdrum, L. (2000). *Mangfold, spesialisering og differensiering i høyere utdanning: Internasjonale erfaringer* (NIFU skriftserie 1/2000). Oslo.

Skodvin, O.-J., Wien Fjell, M., Andre Andreassen, G., & Moi, A. (2006, October 3–5). *Assessing performance within higher education in Norway*. Paper prepared for the joint OECD/ONS/ Government of Norway workshop: 'Measurement of non-market output in education and health', Brunei Gallery, London.

Teichler, U. (1996). Diversity in higher education in Germany: The two type structure. In G. Meek, O. Kivinen, & R. Rinne (Eds.), *The mockers and mocked: Comparative perspectives on differentiation, convergence and diversity in higher education*. Pergamon: IAU Press.

van Vught, F. A., Kaiser, F., File, J. M., Gaethgens, C., Peter, R., & Westerheijden, D. F. (2010). *U-Map: The European classification of higher education institutions*. Enschede: CHEPS. www.u-map.eu.

Chapter 47
Diversity of Higher Education in Europe and the Findings of a Comparative Study of the Academic Profession

Ulrich Teichler

47.1 The Theme "Diversity"

The extent to which higher education is varied or homogeneous or should be substantially varied or only varied to a moderate extent is not only a theme of constant controversial debate. But, also, all observers addressing this thematic area agree that higher education is constantly on the move towards increasing or towards reducing the extent of the previously existing variety.

The issue of diversity of higher education is touched upon in so many analyses that it is impossible to provide a comprehensive overview. However, only a few scholars have addressed this thematic area repeatedly and based on a very broad knowledge of the issue in a multitude of European countries; one might name primarily – in alphabetical order – Jeroen Huisman (1995, 2009), Guy Neave (1989, 1996, 2000), Peter Scott (1996, 2008), and Ulrich Teichler (1988, 2008) in this context. Moreover, two major studies were published in Europe in recent years concerning the issue of diversity in higher education (Teichler 2007; Reichert 2009). They both aim to provide a conceptual map of the issues addressed and give an account of the existing extent of variety in various countries.

Scholars agree that there are concurrently a multitude of forces which either increase or reduce the extent of diversity within national systems of higher education, sometimes favoring international convergence, at other times, promoting specific national options. Meek et al. (1996) argue that explanatory concepts of the causes for the change of higher education systems can be classified into three perspectives: According to *internal perspectives*, dynamics within higher education play a major role (for example, the increase of student numbers or the trend towards

U. Teichler (✉)
International Centre for Higher Education Research (INCHER-Kassel),
University of Kassel, Kassel, Germany
e-mail: teichler@incher.uni-kassel.de

A. Curaj et al. (eds.), *European Higher Education at the Crossroads:*
Between the Bologna Process and National Reforms,
DOI 10.1007/978-94-007-3937-6_47, © Springer Science+Business Media Dordrecht 2012

specialization disciplines, e.g. Clark 1996); according to *systemic perspectives*, powerful actors try to shape it according to their views and values (Neave 1996); according to *environmental perspectives*, external social, political and economic forces affect the configuration of the higher education (van Vught 1996). Teichler (2007, pp. 124–125) identifies four "developmental theories" to explain the dynamics of structural change: the "*expansion and diversification theories*", according to which higher education is bound to get more diverse in the process of expansion in order to serve the diversifying needs (cf. Trow 1974); the "*drift theories*", according to which the majority of actors in higher education is not faithful to the specific "missions" of their sector, but try to imitate those concepts which they consider the most successful ones (Neave 1979); according to the "*flexibilization theories*", higher education seeks soft compromises between contradictory forces; according to the "*cyclical theories*", certain patterns of the higher education system come and go just in response to efforts to counteract the most visible "mistakes" of the last generation of diversity in higher education.

Teichler intends to provide an account on the changing concepts and actual developments in a broad range of economically advanced countries since about the 1960s; his notions and own interpretations are also summarized in the overview article "Diversity in Higher Education" in the International Encyclopedia of Education (Teichler 2010a). According to this most recent account, most of the discourse on "diversity" addresses the quantitative-structural patterns of national systems of higher education: the "shape and the size" of higher education systems. There are exceptions, though, where the term "diversity" is employed to discuss also organizational differences (e.g. the steering and governance), the financial regime (e.g. public versus private higher education), and the modes of educational delivery (e.g. distance education). He points out that the shape of the system customarily is classified *vertically* (according to "quality" or "prestige") or *horizontally* (according to programmatic thrusts), whereby either formal descriptors (e.g. *types* of higher education institutions or types of programs and *levels* of programs) or informal descriptors (e.g. *rankings*) are employed. Moreover, a distinction is occasionally made between diversity *within higher education institutions* (internal, intra-institutional, or program diversity) or *between higher education institutions*.

Teichler, finally, argues that the discourse on "diversity" is often *biased through terminology issues*. The term "diversity" sounds as if a high degree of variety was desirable. Some advocates of steep hierarchical higher education systems even claim that there is only a choice of counterproductive homogeneity or "diversity", thereby assuming that maximum variety is desirable, or – more moderately phrased: "More diversified systems, generally speaking, are thought to be 'better' than less diversified systems" (CHEPS 2008, p. 8). Instead, there is a range of choice between "moderate" and "steep" diversity, whereby the strengths and weaknesses of any position of such a possible spectrum has to be taken into consideration. And he argues that most efforts to measure the existing diversity are disguised efforts to "sell" certain models as desirable or even to put pressure on higher education to move into such a direction (Teichler 2011b).

Second, Sybille Reichert (2009) analyzed the institutional diversity of higher education in some European countries in a study for the European University Association. In this framework, she carefully analyzed the academic and political discourse on diversity, and she voices three directions of critique as regards the dominant inclinations of this discourse:

- First, the persons involved in the debate on diversity advocate *strong normative positions* to attach certain values to different aspects of diversity at different levels in higher education. As a consequence, she considers it necessary that the sound analyses of the issue of diversity in higher education have to make "the values of diversity themselves an object of inquiry" (ibid., p. 12).
- Second, the discussions on the diversity of higher education often suggest that *a certain type of diversity or a certain principle of diversity has to rule*, whereas others have to fade away or have to be given up. This seems to be most pronounced in the concepts in favor of steep vertical diversity of higher education which does not accept any genuine diversity of missions and functions.
- Third, Reichert argues that most studies had "focused exclusively on *external diversity* of institutional types or profiles" (ibid., p. 13). She suggests to take into consideration as well "*internal diversity*, i.e. diversity within higher education institutions" (ibid.) – for example, how individual institutions serve deliberately a broad range of students.

On the basis on five country studies, Reichert clearly shows that there are no moves towards a coherent simple model of diversities. Forces are in play both underscoring the horizontal and the vertical dimensions of diversity. There is a coexistence of pressures and efforts towards growing and reduced diversity (called "convergence" in this study) and towards both an important role of inter-institutional and internal diversity. Change of the higher education systems is underway in all European countries in one way or other, and the mixes of systems eventually emerging are not the product of a single targeted policy, but rather the result of multiple forces.

The author of this article suggests here that there are three highly influential political approaches as regards the extent and the character of diversity in higher education in Europe in the first decade of the twenty-first century. All three are strongly pursued, interact de facto and contribute to increased controversy and tension in higher education in Europe.

The first approach might be named *the Bologna approach*. We identify the following elements of this approach: (a) An increasing international similarity of the patterns of national higher education systems is taken for granted or/and it is advocated. (b) The levels of study programs are believed to be a very important dimension of the institutional patterns of higher education; they obviously are expected to overrule the strong role types of higher education it was expected to play in the preceding decades (cf. OECD 1991; Scott 1996). (c) The Bologna approach implicitly opposes any steep vertical and any extreme horizontal mobility, because the "zones for mutual trust" for student exchange and intra-European partnerships would be extraordinarily small if substantial vertical and horizontal variety was in place (cf. Teichler 2008).

The second approach might be called the *world-class university approach or ranking approach* (cf. its presentation by its advocates in Sadlak and Liu (2007) and its critique in Shin et al. 2011; Kehm and Stensaker 2009). (a) An increasing international similarity of the patterns of the higher education system is taken for granted and certainly is advocated. (b) Institutions of higher education are viewed to be the clearly overarching dimension of diversity; the academic quality of the individual scholar and the individual units of teaching and research is seen to be strongly influenced by the quality of the higher education institution as a whole. (c) This approach concentrates fully on vertical diversity, whereby it might vary according to the number of variables and groupings of vertical diversity. (d) The approach is characterized by the assumption that a steep vertical stratification of the higher education system is beneficial.

The third approach might be named *managerial approach* (cf. Kogan 2004). (a) As in the case of the second approach, institutions of higher education are viewed to be the clearly overarching dimension of diversity. (b) The University management, in reflecting the institutional context as well as the institutional potentials, is free, in principle, to strive for re-allocation of the institution's vertical and horizontal positions on the map of the overall national higher education system or of higher education all over the world and ought to use its power to push the institution of higher education to the desired position on the map. (c) Implicitly, this approach seems to assume that intra-institutional diversity should be moderate.

47.2 The Implications of Diversity of Higher Education in the Academics' Views and Activities

The analyses of the pattern of diversity of higher education systems have concentrated in the past on institutional dimensions (types of institutions of higher education, types of programs, individual institutions and departments, etc.) as well as on the input, process and outputs with respect to the core functions and activities of higher education (number of graduates, graduates' competences, publications, etc.). They have also discussed the roles of policy makers such as governments, external "stakeholders", university management, and the "market" in trying to shape the quantitative-structural patterns. Much less attention has been paid to the academic profession of actors as regards diversity, and hardly any attention has been paid to the views and activities of academics as indications of the actually existing extent and the actually existing modes of diversity in higher education.

The following analysis is an attempt to describe the extent and the modes of similarity or diversity within higher education as reflected in the views and activities of academics. The responses to representative survey questionnaires mostly undertaken in the year 2007 in seven European countries with altogether more than 8,000 respondents will be taken as an information basis for describing the extent and variety of views and activities of the academics who are employed in institutions of higher education. The results are analyzed according the following differentiating criteria:

- *country within Europe*: Are academics alike across European countries or very much distinct by country?
- *status within academic career*; for example: Are junior academics more internationally oriented and active than those in professorial positions?
- *type of higher education institution*; for example: Do professors in other higher education institutions more or less share the same views as university professors about the roles and functions of higher education?
- *inter-individual differences*: Are some professors more strongly research-oriented than others, and how does this affect the character of their academic work in various respects?

The data base for this comparison of seven European countries has been collected in the framework of the study "The Changing Academic Profession (CAP)" covering almost 20 countries from all over the world; actually, surveys were undertaken predominantly in 2007 and additionally in 2008 (according the conceptual basis in Kogan and Teichler 2007; Locke and Teichler 2007; the results published on the selected theme in the Research Institute for Higher Education, Hiroshima University 2008, 2009, 2010; Diversification of Higher Education and the Academic Profession 2010; Locke et al. 2011; first country reports available in Coates et al. 2009; Aarrevaara and Pekkola 2010; Bentley et al. 2010; Jacob and Teichler 2011). In some thematic areas, a comparison can be undertaken regarding the academics' views and activities in the early 1990s, when the Carnegie Foundation for the Advancement of Teaching (Princeton, NJ, U.S.) initiated the first comparative study on the academic profession (see Boyer et al. 1994; Enders and Teichler 1995; Altbach 1996; Teichler 1996). It might be added here that a similar survey has been undertaken in six additional European countries in the framework of the project "The Academic Profession in Europe" (EUROAC). The results of this project, supported by the European Science Foundation (ESF), will be available in 2012.

In this article, about 20 aspects addressed in the CAP survey of the academic profession will be examined to establish the extent of similarity and diversity across countries as well as between and within the dimensions named above. This will provide the basis for a final discussion of the findings: how far is higher education in Europe similar or diverse, what roles do institutional types play, etc. with respect to the individual dimensions?

47.2.1   Career

As regards the academic careers, information will be presented on five aspects: the proportions of the academics having obtained a doctoral degree, the age of the award of a degree, the frequency of inter-institutional mobility, and the extent of part-time and of short-term employment.

A *doctoral degree* is more or less a "must" for an academic career in universities in various, but not in all European countries: more than 90% of university professors have been awarded a doctoral degree in Portugal, Germany and Finland; the respective proportion is somewhat lower in Norway (85%), the Netherlands (83% at present – clearly lower than in 1992: 90%) and the United Kingdom (78%), and, in Italy, only a minority of professors are doctoral degree holders (33%). As regards senior academics in other institutions, however, we note a more polarized situation – with more than 80% doctoral degree holders in Germany, Norway and Portugal and a minority in Finland (41%) and the Netherlands (only 17%).

It is widely assumed that the award of a doctoral degree marks a similar stage of the academic career across Europe. Therefore, we could assume that the average *age at the award of a doctoral degree* does not substantially differ between European countries. The university professors in the seven European countries surveyed were 34 years old on average at the award of the doctoral degree, but this varies strikingly between the relatively low average age of 30 years in Germany and 31 years in the United Kingdom on the one hand and relatively high age of 36 years in Finland and 37 years in Norway on the other hand.

In many countries of the world, the *inter-institutional mobility of academics* is viewed as a healthy phenomenon, and spending the whole academic career in a single institution is often pejoratively called "inbreeding". There are countries as well, though, where spending the whole academic career in a prestigious institution is most highly respected, while inter-institutional mobility might indicate detours on the way to academic success. We note that inter-institutional mobility is more or less a "must" in Germany, and only 8% of the university professors have never worked in another higher education institution. In Norway and the UK, about a quarter, but in Italy and the Netherlands about a half of the professors have never changed the university.

Part-time employment and short-term employment of university professors were exceptional in the early 1990s. This continues to hold true for part-time employment with the Netherlands as the only exception (14% in 1992 and 23% in the most recent study). However, the tradition of permanent employment of professors has been somewhat shaken in recent years in Finland (34% employed on a short-term basis), the Netherlands (16%) and Portugal (13%). The situation of senior academics in other higher education institutions does not differ substantially from that of the university professors in those respects.

Part-time and short-term employment is far more widespread among junior staff in universities than among professors (the former including assistant professors and the latter associate professors). This tends to be viewed as indispensible in highly selected careers; it is often advocated as a beneficial component of an incentive system, and it is often criticized as undermining the motivation of young scholars. Whatever the discourse about the strengths and weaknesses of a less stable situation of academic junior staff may say, one cannot note any common trend of change among the European countries having participated in both surveys. Heterogeneity across Europe persists: in the recent survey, part-time employment ranges from 2% in Italy and 6% in Finland to 31% each in Germany and the

Table 47.1 Part-time and short-term employment of academics[a] in selected European countries 1992 and 2007 (percentage)

		DE	FI	NL	NO	IT	PT	UK
Senior academics at universities								
2007	Part-time	0	4	23	6	3	3	5
	Short-term	3	34	16	4	•	13	2
(1992)	Part-time	(2)	•	(14)	•	•	•	(6)
	Short-term	(2)	•	(3)	•	•	•	(9)
Junior academics at universities								
2007	Part-time	31	6	31	11	2	12	13
	Short-term	80	50	41	75	•	69	29
(1992)	Part-time	(25)	•	(34)	•	•	•	(6)
	Short-term	(79)	•	(44)	•	•	•	(28)
Senior academics in other higher education institutions								
2007	Part-time	6	10	41	10	•	2	14
	Short-term	2	7	11	12	•	16	13
(1992[b])	Part-time	(7)	•	(51)	•	•	•	•
	Short-term	(6)	•	(15)	•	•	•	•

Source: Survey "The Changing Academic Profession" (CAP) (August 2011 data set)

DE Germany, *FI* Finland, *NL* Netherlands, *NO* Norway, *IT* Italy, *PT* Portugal, *UK* United Kingdom

[a]Data on junior staff are not included in the tables and not addressed in the text, because this status is very heterogeneous

[b]1992 data combined for all academics at institutions of higher education

Netherlands. Also, short-term employment differs substantially between 29% in the United Kingdom and 41% in the Netherlands and 75% in Norway and 80% in Germany (see Table 47.1).

Altogether, the information chosen from the comparative surveys of the academic profession suggests that the career settings for academics in Europe are enormously diverse by country, and the comparison between the surveys does not indicate any convergent trend. On the contrary: Some countries moved toward more than exceptional short-employment of university professors, while others did not move in this direction, thereby increasing the European variety of academic career settings.

47.2.2   Academic Work

Four themes of academic work addressed in the comparative study are chosen here for the discussion of diversity: the number of weekly working hours, the academics' preferences for teaching and research, the proportion of time spent on teaching and research as well as the assessment of the infrastructure for academic work.

We could have expected that the actual *weekly working time* of university professors is similar across European countries. The standard working time of employees in the European countries does not differ substantially, and university

Table 47.2 Preferences in teaching and research of academics in selected European countries 2007 (percentage)

	DE	FI	NL	NO	IT	PT	UK
University professors							
Primarily in teaching	5	2	5	2	2	3	8
In both, but leaning towards teaching	20	19	17	18	22	36	23
In both, but leaning towards research	63	61	55	60	67	48	48
Primarily in research	12	18	23	20	10	14	22
Total	100	100	100	100	100	100	100
Junior academic staff in universities							
Primarily in teaching	7	8	5	2	3	6	9
In both, but leaning towards teaching	22	12	17	14	22	41	24
In both, but leaning towards research	38	39	49	44	60	47	37
Primarily in research	33	42	30	40	15	6	30
Total	100	100	100	100	100	100	100
Professors in other higher education institutions							
Primarily in teaching	42	15	16	3	•	11	•
In both, but leaning towards teaching	35	49	33	22	•	43	•
In both, but leaning towards research	22	26	40	58	•	37	•
Primarily in research	1	10	11	17	•	9	•
Total	100	100	100	100	•	100	•

Abbreviations of country and source: see Table 47.1

professors are viewed as being strongly devoted to their professional work task and, thus, could be considered likely to work more than the time usually required. However, the average working hours vary substantially by country: university professors in Germany report 52 h on average, followed by their colleagues in various countries between 44 and 47 h, and, finally, university professors in Portugal with 41 h and in Norway with only 38 h. Thus, we note a range of about 30% if not more at all than lasts the normal work time of an employee. Junior academics in universities as well as both senior and junior academics in other higher education institutions report that they work some hours less than university professors, but the variation between countries is similar.

University professors are in charge of both teaching and research, but it is widely assumed that more professors have a *preference for research* than for teaching. However, according to conventional wisdom, university professors in some European countries tend to be more strongly devoted to teaching than in other countries. Indeed, the study reveals relatively little variety in this respect. Asked about their actual preferences and interests, the proportion of professors stating a clear preference for research varies by country only between 10% (Italy) and 22% (United Kingdom). In summing up the statements of such a clear preference and a somewhat stronger leaning toward either research or teaching (see Table 47.2), we note a stronger research than teaching orientation by about three quarters or more of the university professors in most European countries surveyed, slightly fewer in the United Kingdom (70%) and clearly fewer in Portugal (62%). As compared to the early 1990s, the emphasis on research increased slightly in Germany, remained unchanged in the Netherlands and decreased slightly in the United Kingdom.

Table 47.3 Annual weekly work time spent on various academic functions of academics in selected European countries 2007 (percent, only full-time employed academics)

	DE	FI	NL	NO	IT	PT	UK
Senior academics in universities							
Teaching	28	33	30	33	31	34	31
Research	38	37	40	37	45	38	35
Service	11	5	5	5	8	6	4
Administration	14	17	18	18	11	15	22
Other activities	9	7	7	7	5	8	8
Total percentage	100	100	100	100	100	100	100
Junior academics in universities							
Teaching	21	35	27	16	32	41	25
Research	51	45	56	69	48	42	43
Service	16	3	5	2	8	3	2
Administration	7	9	8	8	7	9	22
Other activities	5	7	5	6	5	5	8
Total percentage	100	100	100	100	100	100	100
Senior academics in other HEIs							
Teaching	41	52	•	38	33	42	•
Research	20	24	•	33	39	18	•
Service	5	7	•	4	8	2	•
Administration	27	12	•	16	13	28	•
Other activities	6	5	•	9	7	10	•
Total percentage	100	100	•	100	100	100	•

Abbreviations of country and source: see Table 47.1

A stronger emphasis on research than on teaching holds true in a similar way for junior academics in universities. The responses of professors and junior staff in the individual countries hardly differ except for Portugal, where an even lower proportion of junior staff puts emphasis on research (53%).

Senior academics in other institutions of higher education, as one could expect, lean to a lesser extent to research. Two countries stand out as contrasts: Germany with a very low quota of senior academics at Fachhochschulen favouring research (22%) and Norway with a very high quota of senior academics in colleges leaning towards research (65%).

The *proportion of the work time* university professors spend – on average of the whole year – on *teaching* is fairly homogeneous. It only varies from 28% in the case of Germany to 34% in the case of Portugal (calculated for full-time employed academics). Correspondingly, the proportion of time spent on *research* varies among most of the European countries surveyed only from 35% to 40% (with an exceptionally high proportion – 45% – in Italy). In all seven countries analyzed, university professors spend somewhat more time on research than on teaching – between 1.1 times and 1.4 times (see Table 47.3).

In contrast, junior staff's involvement in teaching varies substantially by country, i.e. between 16% in Norway and 41% in Portugal. In Norway, the junior staff in universities spends a clearly lower proportion of the work time on teaching than professors; in some countries, this difference is smaller – in Germany, Finland and the United Kingdom; in Italy, no difference exists between senior and junior staff in this respect, while in Portugal and the Netherlands, the junior staff spends a higher proportion of time on teaching than senior staff. In comparing the time taken for research to that for teaching, we note that the junior staff in Norway spends more than four times as much time on research and those in Germany and Finland more than twice as much time, while the junior staff in Portugal spends about the same proportion of the work time on research as on teaching.

The proportion of time spent on teaching by senior academics in other institutions of higher education does not vary as much by country as in the case of junior academics in universities, but more than in the case of university professors. Senior academics in other institutions of higher education in the Netherlands and Germany spend a substantially higher proportion of their time, those in Norway and Portugal somewhat more time, but those in Finland the same proportion of time on teaching as university professors.

The *assessment of the infrastructure of academic work* varies somewhat by the academics' country. Of the eight aspects addressed in the questionnaire (such as technology for teaching, laboratories or library facilities), university professors in Finland rate 5.6 and those in Norway and Netherlands slightly more than 5.0 as positive in contrast to 3.6 in Italy and 3.5 in the United Kingdom. The junior staff in universities rates the infrastructure similarly to senior academics of their respective country. Also, the ratings by academics from other institutions do not differ substantially from those in universities.

In sum, it is not possible to generalize about the extent and the major dimensions of diversity across the four aspects of academic work discussed. We might assume that university professors in most European countries are full-time employees, are expected to care more or less equally for teaching and research, should appreciate both teaching and research as major components of their work tasks and should be equipped to do their work decently. From that point of view, the differences observed are by no means negligible: in one country on the top of the respective ranking, university professors work almost one third more hours on average than in the country on the bottom; similarly, the proportion of those leaning more to research than to teaching, when asked about their preferences, is almost one third higher in one extreme than in the other. The proportion of the work time is about one fifth higher in one extreme than in the opposite extreme. And those most satisfied with the infrastructure of their work name about 1.6 as many aspects of the infrastructure as positive as those who are least satisfied.

The junior staff in universities is most similar to senior staff in the assessment of the infrastructure of academic work. Junior academics – also those employed full-time – spend on average fewer weekly hours on their work than senior academics, and they reserve a higher proportion of their time to research and have stronger preference for teaching on average across the seven countries analyzed. But there are variations across countries in the extent of similarity or difference: in one country, senior and junior academics spend about the same proportion of their time on research; in another country, the time devoted to research by the junior staff is about 1.8 times higher than the time spent by university professors.

In comparing the responses of senior academics in other institutions of higher education with those of university professors, we note a surprisingly similar assessment of the infrastructure of academic work. On average, across countries, academics in other institutions of higher education work fewer weekly hours, and they lean less strongly towards research in their preferences and spend a smaller proportion of their time on research. In considering the prevailing notion of the functional differences between universities and other types of higher education institutions, we might have expected a more striking difference. Just to illustrate: one would not have expected that senior academics of other institutions of higher education spend only 12% less of the weekly work time (27% as compared to 39%) on research – on average across countries – than university professors. Again, however, we note substantial differences by country: in one extreme, senior academics in other higher education institutions spend a similar proportion of their work time on research as those in universities; in other cases, only about a half of the proportion of the work time is spent by the former on research as by the latter.

47.2.3   Teaching

Three aspects of teaching will be addressed: the regulatory framework of teaching, the respondents' attitudes towards teaching and the variety of teaching modes.

In response to the question of how much teaching is *regulated or steered* (for example, by workload settings in teaching, funding according to the number of graduates or considering the quality of teaching in personnel decisions), only one third of the professors note such steering efforts in four countries, but somewhat more in Norway and even about a half in the Netherlands and the United Kingdom. The responses by junior staff are quite similar to those by senior academics. Senior academics in other institutions of higher education in Finland and Germany consider themselves – in contrast to university professors of their respective country – also as relatively highly regulated.

Attitudes towards teaching and teaching-related issues vary substantially by country as well, as Table 47.4 shows. For example, among university professors,

- About three quarters underscore a practice-oriented approach in Germany and Portugal, but only about a half in Norway, four out of ten in the Netherlands and less than one third in Finland.
- About 70% often address issues of values in classes in Portugal and the United Kingdom, but only about 40% in Italy.
- Similarly, almost all professors in the United Kingdom warn against cheating, but only about one third in Norway and Italy.

Again, the responses by the junior staff in universities are similar to those of the professors in the respective countries. As one might expect, scholars in other institutions of higher education underscore more strongly a practice-oriented approach and somewhat less strongly an international approach.

Table 47.4 Attitudes towards teaching and teaching-related activities by academics in selected European countries 2007 (percentage[a])

	DE	FI	NL	NO	IT	PT	UK
Seniors in universities							
Practice-oriented approach	75	31	40	49	54	75	69
International approach	79	63	64	69	62	90	66
Value-oriented approach	57	53	48	45	40	71	69
Honesty approach	53	41	53	36	32	78	94
Meritocratic approach	72	95	54	78	79	55	87
Juniors in universities							
Practice-oriented approach	77	48	42	51	54	77	67
International approach	50	46	60	60	60	82	60
Value-oriented approach	36	41	44	36	34	71	70
Honesty approach	41	38	58	36	28	88	86
Meritocratic approach	59	89	59	71	81	53	79
Senior academics in other higher education institutions							
Practice-oriented approach	93	79	84	57	•	81	•
International approach	60	52	58	61	•	68	•
Value-oriented approach	54	53	71	39	•	73	•
Honesty approach	58	60	67	41	•	72	•
Meritocratic approach	80	98	42	80	•	47	•

Practice-oriented approach: "practically oriented knowledge and skills are emphasized in your teaching"; *International approach*: "in your courses you emphasize international perspectives or content"; *Value-oriented approach*: "you incorporate discussions of values and ethics into your course content"; *Honesty approach*: "you inform students of the implications of cheating or plagiarism in your courses"; *Meritocratic approach*: "grades in your courses strictly reflect levels of student achievement"
Abbreviations of country: see Table 47.1
[a]Responses 1 and 2 on a scale from 1 = "Strongly agree" to 5 = "Strongly disagree"

There are noteworthy differences by country as well regarding the variety of *teaching activities*. In response to a list of seven types of activities beyond classroom instruction (e.g. learning in projects, electronic communication with students and individualized instruction), professors in German institutions mention on average only 2.8 types, while their colleagues in Finland report 4.4 and in the United Kingdom 4.5. The junior staff in universities reports somewhat fewer types of activities and, in contrast, the staff in other institutions of higher education more types of activities, but the variety by country is similar.

Altogether, the teaching scene in the universities in the various European countries does not seem to be more or less alike. According to the university professors' perception, the regulatory conditions for teaching have remained varied by countries. Even though the power of higher education management is widely assumed to have grown in all European countries and even though this seems to be linked with a stronger inclination of those in power to influence the efficiency of academic work through regulations or through incentives and sanctions, academics themselves characterize the extent to which their activities are steered in such a way quite

Table 47.5 Views regarding research and scholarship by academics in selected European countries 2007 (percentage[a])

	DE	FI	NL	NO	IT	PT	UK
University professors							
Original research	**83**	68	80	92	73	81	68
Synthesis of findings	61	69	44	56	45	59	68
Application	62	74	41	59	57	77	69
Societal relevance	61	65	45	50	62	73	58
Junior academic staff in universities							
Original research	69	61	82	86	74	74	66
Synthesis of findings	67	59	41	61	49	62	63
Application	67	84	42	65	64	76	65
Societal relevance	44	58	46	51	61	73	59
Senior academics in other higher education institutions							
Original research	56	54	67	88	•	80	•
Synthesis of findings	72	75	52	68	•	57	•
Application	87	92	63	56	•	88	•
Societal relevance	63	78	74	56	•	66	•

Original research: "scholarships are best defined as the preparation and presentation of findings on original research"; Synthesis of findings: "scholarships include the preparation of reports that synthesize the major trends and findings in my field"; Application: "scholarships include the application of academic knowledge in real-life settings"; Societal relevance: "the faculty in my discipline have a professional obligation to apply their knowledge to problems in society"
Abbreviations of country and source: see Table 47.1
[a]Responses 1 and 2 on a scale from 1 = "Strongly agree" to 5 = "Strongly disagree"

differently according to European countries. They differ also in the way they characterize their basic understanding of teaching and in the variety of teaching modes they employ. Junior staff in universities in the various countries does not differ substantially in their perceptions of the conditions of teaching and their understanding of teaching, but they employ a somewhat smaller spectrum of teaching activities than university professors. Senior academics in other institutions of higher education feel more strongly steered by regulations and incentives than university professors; on the other hand, they employ a broader range of teaching activities.

47.2.4   Research

Academics vary by country in their *views of the tasks of scholarship*, as Table 47.5 shows:

- Even their understanding of scholarships as preparation and presentation of findings of *original research* ranges from 92% in Norway to 73% in Italy.
- More considerable differences are visible regarding the task of *synthesizing findings and trends*: we note a range from less than a half in Italy and the Netherlands to more than two thirds in Finland and the United Kingdom.

Table 47.6 Number of publications completed in the most recent 3 years by academics in selected European countries 1992 and 2007 (index[a])

	DE	FI	NL	NO	IT	PT	UK
University professors 2007	56	38	41	27	40	44	38
(University professors 1992)	(33)	•	(50)	•	•	•	(29)
Junior ac. staff in universities 2007	20	16	27	12	29	23	15
(Junior ac. staff in universities 1992)	(14)	•	(20)	•	•	•	(20)
Senior ac. in other HEIs 2007	19	10	21	41	•	29	•
(Academics in other HEIs 1992)	(9)	•	•	•	•	(8)	•

3 points each for scholarly books (co)authored and co(edited); 2 points each for articles published in academic books or journals and research reports, 1 point each for papers presented at conferences and articles written in newspapers/magazines
Abbreviations of country and source: see Table 47.1
[a]Arithmetic mean

- The emphasis on the *application* of academic knowledge in real life settings even varies from clearly less than a half in the Netherlands to about three quarters in Portugal and the Finland.
- Finally, the *societal relevance of research* is again only emphasized by less than a half of the university professors in the Netherlands, but by three quarters in Portugal.

The responses of junior staff in universities again are similar to those of the professors in their respective country. This confirms the overall impression that junior academics in the individual European countries hardly differ from senior academics as regards their professional views and attitudes.

Altogether, senior academics in other institutions of higher education differ, as far as their understanding of research is concerned, on average clearly from that of university professors. They underscore original research less often and application and societal relevance more often. Again, a substantial variety can be observed by countries. Senior academics in other institutions of higher education in Norway clearly differ from their colleagues in other countries in harboring more or less the same views as professors of their country. As has been shown above, senior academics in Norwegian colleges also spend much more time on research than their colleagues in other countries and are also close in this respect to university professors in Norway (according to the interpretation of the Norwegian case in Kyvik (2009)).

Public debates suggest that academics in all countries are increasingly expected to be visibly productive. One could assume that the volume of publication is generally on the rise. A comparison of the findings of the survey conducted in the early 1990s with those of the most recent survey shows an overall growth trend, but we note a growth of more than half in Germany and of less than half in the United Kingdom and a reduction by about one fifth in the Netherlands. Although the expectation to be more visibly productive seems to be a global phenomenon, publication activities vary substantially. According to an index developed in the framework of the CAP project referred to in this analysis, German university professors publish more than twice as much as their colleagues in Norway (see Table 47.6).

Junior staff in universities publishes only about half as much as university professors. Again, the variety by country is striking: those in the Netherlands publish more than twice as much as those in Norway.

Publications play a completely different role in other institutions of higher education. Senior academics in Portugal and Norway do not publish much less than university professors in their respective country. But their colleagues in the Netherlands do not publish one fifth as much as the university professors in their country. Thus, those publishing most, i.e. senior academics in other institutions of higher education in Portugal, publish more than five times as much as their colleagues in the Netherlands.

University professors in the various European countries seem to differ in their views on the tasks of their research as much as in their views regarding teaching. Although it is widely claimed that increased pressures for visible academic productivity are more or less a global phenomenon, the publication activities vary strikingly by country. As one might expect, senior academics in other institutions of higher education underscore on average application and social relevance of research more strongly and publish less than university professors. But the borderlines between the two types of institutions are not consistent across Europe. In some countries, the university professors are, on average, more application-oriented than senior academics in other institutions of higher education in other European countries. In some countries, senior academics in other institutions of higher education publish more than university professors in other European countries. Finally, junior academics in universities might differ in their activities – in this case in the number of publications – from their seniors, but not in their views.

47.2.5   Internationality

The extent to which internationality varies will be examined with respect to three aspects: the international mobility of the academics, their international activities and the use of foreign languages.

The proportion of university professors who have *migrated* or who have been *mobile* in the course of their academic learning and work varies substantially by country. As the first five lines each show in Table 47.7, this proportion is even higher than one third among university professors in Portugal and one third in Norway, but only one out of seven or eight in Finland, Italy and the Netherlands. We note a similar range among senior academics in other institutions of higher education: on the one hand, more than one third in Norway and about one third in Portugal and, on the other hand, less in Finland and the Netherlands.

University professors in the majority of European countries included in the CAP study report on average a similar degree of *international activities*; only those in the United Kingdom and Italy seem to be less international in their activities. Junior academics in universities are less active internationally than their seniors, and senior academics in other institutions of higher education even less so, but, in both cases, we note a higher variation across countries than in the case of university professors.

Table 47.7 Migration and mobility of academics in selected European countries 2007 (percentage)

	DE	FI	NL	NO	IT	PT	UK
University professors							
Early immigrants	4	1	3	6	1	1	3
PhD immigrants	2	2	0	5	0	0	4
Professional migrants	4	3	6	5	0	0	10
Study mobile academics	9	2	4	9	0	19	3
PhD mobile academics	2	4	2	8	11	16	1
Non-mobile academics	79	88	86	67	87	63	78
Total	100	100	100	100	100	100	100
Senior academics in other HEIs							
Early immigrants	8	2	1	18	•	5	•
PhD immigrants	2	1	0	3	•	0	•
Professional migrants	1	1	1	5	•	2	•
Study mobile academics	5	3	7	10	•	10	•
PhD mobile academics	3	2	0	5	•	15	•
Non-mobile academics	81	92	90	60	•	67	•
Total	100	100	100	•	100	100	•

Mobility during course of study or the doctoral phase of immigrants is not taken into consideration
Abbreviations of country and source: see Table 47.1

Table 47.8 International activities of academics in selected European countries 2007 (arithmetic mean of number of activities)

	DE	FI	NL	NO	IT	PT	UK
University professors	4.3	4.5	4.6	4.2	3.5	4.7	3.9
Junior academic staff in universities	2.6	3.3	4.1	3.1	3.2	3.4	3.3
Senior academics in other HEIs	2.2	2.9	1.9	4.1	•	3.6	•
Junior academic staff in other HEIs	1.0	2.0	1.0	3.0	•	3.0	•

International activities: international content in teaching, teaching many international graduate students, teaching abroad, international research collaboration, international research funding, joint publications with authors abroad, publishing abroad; international scope of research
Abbreviations of country and source: see Table 47.1

For example, senior academics of other institutions of higher education in Norway report on average that they are involved in four of the eight international activities addressed in the questionnaire, while their colleagues in Germany and the Netherlands state only two of those activities (Table 47.8).

Finally, the most dramatic variation across European countries can be observed with regard to the *use of foreign languages in academic work*. 42% of university professors in the Netherlands report that their home country language – Dutch – is neither the dominant language of their teaching nor of their research activities. The respective proportions are: 19% in Finland and 12% in Norway, and only 5% in Italy, 4% in Germany and 2% in Portugal. As one might expect, no British professors report to do their academic work predominantly in a language other than English. The range of responses is quite similar among junior academics in universities.

Teaching and conducting research predominantly in a foreign language is by far less frequent among senior academics in other institutions of higher education. Only 13% of the Dutch respondents report that they teach primarily in a foreign language, and a further 1% mentions that both teaching and research are undertaken in a foreign language. The two figures altogether are considerably smaller in other European countries.

In sum, ironically, one notes the very small extent of international similarity with respect to the visible international character of academia. Migration and mobility, visible international activities and the use of foreign languages varies dramatically in universities by country. Universities in small European countries are most international in those respects, and major English-speaking countries least international, corroborating the findings of an earlier study that the major Anglo-Saxon countries pursue "internationalization by import" (Enders and Teichler 1995).

Junior academics in universities are, in some respects, similarly international as seniors and, in some respects, less international, where they have had fewer opportunities in the course of their career or due to a more limited influence in the university. These findings suggest that there is not any sudden leap forward in the new generations as far as the internationality of academic work is concerned. Finally, we note that academics in other institutions of higher education are clearly, to a lesser extent visibly international than their colleagues.

47.2.6   Institutional Management

It is widely assumed that the institutional management in higher education has substantially changed in most European countries in the recent 2 years. Undoubtedly, the power of the university management seems to have grown to shape and steer the inner life of the institutions of higher education, and various means of evaluation seem to have become omnipresent. This was taken for granted in the survey "The Changing Academic Profession" (see Kogan 2007; Musselin 2007), and the responses to the question about evaluation clearly indicate a growth of evaluation activities as compared to the early 1990s, when the predecessor survey was undertaken.

However, a possibly similar worldwide trend in higher education policy does not necessarily mean that the internal environment within higher education institutions becomes very similar. In the framework of the study "The Changing Academic Profession", the respondents were provided a relatively long list of *characteristics of management style* in their institution of higher education. In one of the subsequent analyses, these items were classified into four groups:

- "the academic university", i.e. the university characterized by a strong influence of the academics,
- "the managerial university", characterized by a strong performance orientation, a strong emphasis on the institution's mission and a top-down management style,

Table 47.9 Perception of the higher education institutions' management style by university professors in selected European countries 2007

University with	+	~	−
Researchers' orientation	DE, US	FI, IT, PT, AU	NO, JP, UK
Management orientation	FI, AU, UK, US	JP	DE, NO, IT, PT
Service orientation	JP, US	DE, FI, NO, AU, UK, US	PT
Collegial orientation	FI, NO	DE, IT, PT, AU, JP, US	UK

Source: Teichler (2011a) (based on the survey "The Changing Academic Profession" (CAP), 2010 data set)
Managerial university: "a strong performance orientation", "a strong emphasis on the institution's mission", "a top-down management style". Collegial university: "students should have a stronger say in determining policy that affects them" (in reverse scale order); "I am kept informed about what is going on in this institution", "collegiality in decision-making processes", "good communication between management and academics", "lack of faculty involvement is a real problem" (in reverse scale order); Supportive university: "the administration supports academic freedom", "a supportive attitude of administrative staff towards teaching activities", "a supportive attitude of the administrative staff towards research activities", "professional development for administrative/ management duties for individual faculty", "a cumbersome administrative process" (in reverse scale order)
Abbreviations of country: see Table 47.1

- "the collegial university", where strong emphasis is placed on good information for everybody, collegiality in decision-making processes and students' participation, and, finally,
- "the supportive university", where the leaderships supports academic freedom, administrative staff shows a supportive attitude towards teaching and research activities and where opportunities are provided for the professional development of the individual academics.

Table 47.9 summarizes the findings for six European and three other economically advanced countries. In summing the responses according to these four dimensions of management style, we note that university professors:

- in Germany consider their university to be shaped by a strong academic emphasis and a weak management,
- in Finland perceive their university as both management-oriented and collegial,
- in Norway view their university characterized by a strong collegial emphasis and low managerial as well as academic orientation in its managerial style,
- in Italy consider their universities not being managerial universities,
- in Portugal note both a low managerial and supportive emphasis, and
- in the United Kingdom consider their universities to have a strong managerial emphasis, while the academic and collegial orientation is viewed to be weak.

Thus, the findings certainly do not support the view that the universities in the various European countries have become very similar in their managerial styles.

One of the major managerial approaches in recent years has been a growing emphasis placed on the individual institution of higher education. University managers tend to develop "mission statements" and "visions" of individual institutions;

Table 47.10 Academics' affiliation to their own higher education institution in selected European countries 2007 (arithmetic mean[a])

	DE	FI	NL	NO	IT	PT	UK
University professors 2007	2.6	2.1	2.6	2.6	2.3	1.8	2.9
(University professors 1992)	(2.6)	•	(2.4)	•	•	•	(2.1)
Junior academic staff in universities 2007	2.8	2.1	2.7	2.6	2.4	2.1	2.8
(Junior academic staff in universities 1992)	(3.0)	•	(2.6)	•	•	•	(2.3)
Senior academics in other HEIs 2007	2.6	2.3	2.5	2.4	•	1.9	•
(Academics in other HEIs 1992)	(2.9)	•	(2.5)	•	•	•	•

Abbreviations of country and source: see Table 47.1
[a]On a scale from 1 = "Very satisfied" to 5 = "Very dissatisfied" in 2007; four-point scale in 1992

often, a development of a clear institutional "profile" is advocated, and popularity of rankings is based, in most cases, on the belief that the quality of individual academic work is strongly determined by the environment of the individual institution. Therefore, one could expect that, if this managerial policy is successful, the academics' commitment to their institution of higher education is growing.

Although there is a difference between the scales employed in the two surveys, Table 47.10 suggests a different direction of the development of the institutional affiliation in the three countries for which information is available at both points. On the one hand, German academics who have had the least feeling of institutional affiliation in 1992, feel somewhat more affiliated to their institution in the meantime. In the Netherlands, we note only a small move into the same direction. In the United Kingdom, however, where the institutional affiliation was relatively strong in 1992, it declined considerably over time.

The most recent data do not suggest any similarity across countries. For example, in reporting the findings in percentages (not in arithmetic means, as stated in Table 47.10), we note that 76% of university professors in Portugal feel strongly committed to their own university, but only 46% of their colleagues in Germany and Norway. Junior academics in universities and academics in other institutions express a similar extent of institutional affiliation to their institution, whereby the variation by country is, by no means, smaller.

47.2.7 Professional Satisfaction

Finally, the degree of variety among academics regarding their professional satisfaction will be shown again differentiated according to different countries, types of higher education institution and career status of the academics. Except for a single country, academics of the various countries are satisfied to a similar degree, as Table 47.11 shows. Or in percentages: between 5% and 10% of university professors express dissatisfaction with their overall professional situation in six of the countries addressed and 15% in the United Kingdom. Among the junior staff in universities,

Table 47.11 Overall professional satisfaction of academics in selected European countries 1992 and 2007 (arithmetic mean[a])

	DE	FI	NL	NO	IT	PT	UK
University professors 2007	2.2	2.2	2.1	2.2	2.1	2.3	2.6
(University professors 1992)	(2.4)	•	•	•	•	•	(2.5)
Junior academic staff in universities 2007	2.5	2.3	2.2	2.3	2.4	2.6	2.8
(Junior academic staff in universities 1992)	(3.1)	•	•	•	•	•	(2.8)
Senior academics in other HEIs 2007	2.3	2.2	2.1	2.3	•	2.4	•
(Academics in other HEIs 1992)	(2.7)	•	•	•	•	•	•

Abbreviations of country and source: see Table 47.1
[a]On a scale from 1 = "Very satisfied" to   5 = "Very dissatisfied"

the respective proportion is somewhat higher and ranges from 8% in Norway to 20% in the United Kingdom. The respective proportion among senior academics in other institutions of higher education ranges from 6% to 13%.

47.2.8   Inter-individual Diversity

The descriptions and analyses hitherto published on the results of the comparative survey "The Changing Academic Profession" have focused on the extent of variety according to country, type of higher education institution and career status of the respondents. The CAP survey data are not suitable to analyze intra-institutional diversity, but they can be employed to analyze the diversity between individuals within the same type of higher education and the same career status. This will be illustrated with a few examples as regards university professors.

Obviously, university professors are quite free to shape their academic role:

- Some of the university professors report that they work more than 60 h per week, while other – full-time employed – professors work even less than the customary working hours in their country.
- Most professors consider both teaching and research as important components of their work, but 17% of them (country mean) point out a clear preference for research and 4% for teaching.
- 18% express a very high job satisfaction, while 3% are highly dissatisfied.

The impact on individual options on academic work has been recently analyzed for university professors in Germany and the United Kingdom with the help of CAP data (Teichler 2010b). Obviously, academics are relatively free to take options as regards their notions and activities with respect to teaching and research:

- 59% of university professors in Germany share their time between teaching and research in a relatively balanced way, but 24% devote clearly more time for research and 17% more time for teaching. Similarly, 43% of university professors in the United Kingdom have a relatively balanced schedule, while 33% spend clearly more time on research and 24% on teaching.

- Strong preferences for research are expressed by 12% of the university professors in Germany and 26% in the United Kingdom. Respective strong preferences for teaching are only expressed by 2% and 5%.
- 33% of university professors in Germany and 39% in the United Kingdom consider themselves as strongly theory-oriented, 25% each as both theory and practice-oriented, 22% and 19% as strongly practice-oriented, and, finally, 20% and 17% as neither strongly theory nor practice-oriented.

The in-depth analysis suggests that neither preferences for teaching and research nor orientations towards theory and practice have a pervasive influence on the university professors' views and activities. However, the time allocation for teaching and research is closely linked to make aspects of the academics' role:

- 75% of professors in Germany spending much time on teaching are involved in curriculum development, but only 46% of them are spending much time on research. The respective figures are 95% and 66% in the United Kingdom.
- In both countries, those spending much time on research publish twice as much as those spending much time on teaching.
- Professors spending much time on teaching believe more often that research and teaching are hardly compatible than those spending much time on research (33% vs. 3% in Germany and 33% vs. 23% in the United Kingdom).
- Those investing much time into research more often perceive a good working environment in their institution than those putting much time into teaching (55% vs. 39% in Germany and 47% vs. 31% in the United Kingdom).
- Professors in Germany spending much time on research believe much more often that they have a strong influence on their university (34% vs. 13%), whereas no such difference can be observed in the United Kingdom (9% vs. 8%).
- Finally, those spending much time on research are clearly more highly satisfied with their job than those spending much time on teaching (84% vs. 45% in Germany and 62% vs. 37% in the United Kingdom).

This analysis, in sum, shows that academics have room for options in their academic role, and we note that many academics do chose so. For example, some of them might only spend 1 h on various teaching-related activities per teaching hour, while others might spend 3 h or more on such activities per teaching hour. According to the above-named analysis, time allocation for research and teaching seems to be a very important issue for many aspects of academic life, but this does not go so far that it shapes all activities strategically. Altogether, however, those spending much time in research consider themselves in a preferable situation and are more highly satisfied than those spending much time on teaching.

47.3   Conclusion

The debate on diversity in higher education suggests that the national systems of higher education are likely to become increasingly similar as a consequence of the efforts to create a convergent European Higher Education Area, of widespread believe in the virtue of certain trends of "modernization" of higher education, and as a consequence of global competition for creating world-class universities according to global rankings. In some respects, comparative surveys on the academic profession confirm such trends, for example, in showing a spread of evaluation activities and in a growth of visible international activities.

However, a survey on the views and activities of university professors in seven European countries undertaken recently in the framework of the study "The Changing Academic Profession" indicates a substantial variety by county. Across the about 20 themes examined, one notes very few cases where differences between countries could be called extreme, and one also observes very few cases where almost common norms and practices prevail across Europe. In most instances, one can note a range of variety which might be called substantial. For example, the proportion of university professors reporting a practice-oriented approach in teaching varies by country between 31% and 75%. And emphasis on applied research – not as the dominant one, but as one of several emphases – ranges from 41% to 77%. Even pressures to be more visibly efficient have different consequences: in some countries, the university professors' working time matches the routine of employees, whereas, somewhere else, 30% more working time is customary. In the respective European country on the top, the number of publications is twice as high as in the country on the bottom in this respect.

The junior staff in universities, first, differs from university professors in some respects which might be explained by the career stage: for example, a less secure employment, a lower number of publications and less research cooperation worldwide. Second, one notes that the research and teaching functions and respective preferences on the part of the respondents are more varied between countries than on the part of university professors. In some countries, their research and teaching tasks seem to be similarly distributed and this is the case for university professors, while, in other countries, they concentrate more strongly on research. Third, the junior staff holds views very similar to senior academics as regards the conditions and the tasks of academic work. There are no indications that a changing understanding of the tasks and functions of higher education discussed publicly and the change of the managerial climate or resources for academic work affect the newer generations more strongly than the elder generations of academics.

Academics in other institutions of higher education, as one should expect, are more strongly devoted to teaching, are less international and publish less than academics in universities. At first glance, the findings seem to confirm conventional wisdom. A closer look reveals that the differences are often smaller than one might expect. For example, senior academics in other higher education institutions spend on average across countries only 10% more of their time on teaching and teaching-related activities. But this cannot be interpreted as a sign of erosion of the divide between institutional types in Europe, for, in some European countries, senior academics in other institutions of higher education spend almost a similar proportion of their work on research as university professors while, in other countries, they spend less than half of the time on research. Again, there seems to be more variety of norms and practices for academic work in other institutions of higher education in Europe than for academic work of university professors.

The study "The Changing Academic Profession" does not provide any information about the extent of variety or similarity of the academic views and activities between institutions of the same institutional types. Therefore, we cannot examine the extent to which the institutional rankings and institutional profiles are mirrored in the academics' views and activities. However, information is available on inter-individual variety. There are norms and practices affecting large numbers of academics, but, obviously, academics have an enormous freedom to shape their individual academic life. For example, more than a third of the university professors do not consider themselves to strike more or less a balance between teaching and research, but rather consider themselves clearly as researchers with some additional teaching tasks or as teachers with, possibly, some additional research tasks. Interestingly enough, those clearly opting for research see fewer problems of compatibility of teaching and research in universities and are more highly satisfied with their overall professional situation than those clearly opting for teaching.

One might draw the conclusion that the debate about the desirable and the actual extent of diversity – substantial or moderate, vertical or horizontal – is too strongly occupied with the shape and the size of the system and with policy and management approaches to higher education. The academic views and practices seem to be shaped to a lesser extent by supranational fashion and pressures than one might expect, and they seem to reflect national cultures of higher education more strongly than the visions of Europe or of global higher education suggest.

References

Aarrevaara, T., & Pekkola, E. (2010). *Muuttuva Akateeminen Profession Suomessa – Maaraportti* [The changing academic profession in Finland – National report]. Tampere: Tampere University Press.

Altbach, P. G. (Ed.). (1996). *The international academic profession: Portraits of fourteen countries*. Princeton: Carnegie Foundation.

Bentley, P., Kyvik, S., Vaboe, A., & Waagene, E, (2010). *Forskningsvilkar ved norske universiteter I et internasjonalt perspektiv* [Research conditions at Norwegian universities from a comparative perspective] (Rapport, 8/2010). Oslo: NIFU STEP.

Boyer, E. L., Altbach, P. G., & Whitelaw, M. J. (1994). *The academic profession: An international perspective*. Princeton: Carnegie Foundation.

CHEPS. (2008). *Mapping diversity: Developing a European classification of higher education institutions*. Enschede: COLOFON.

Clark, B. R. (1996). Diversification in higher education, viability and change. In V. L. Meek, L. Goedegebuure, O. Kivinen, & R. Rinne (Eds.), *The mockers and mocked* (pp. 17–25). Oxford: Pergamon/IAU Press.

Coates, H. B., Dobson, I., Edwards, D., Friedman, T., Goedegebuure, L., & Meek, L. V. (2009). *The attractiveness of the Australian academic profession: A comparative analysis*. Melbourne: LH Martin Institute for Higher Education Leadership and Management, Educational Policy Institute/Australian Council for Educational Research.

Diversification of higher education and the academic profession (special issue). (2010). *European Review, 18* (Supplement 1).

Enders, J., & Teichler, U. (1995). *Der Hochschullehrerberuf im internationalen Vergleich* [The academic profession in international comparison]. Bonn: Bundesministerium für Bildung, Wissenschaft, Forschung und Technologie.

Huisman, J. (1995). *Differentiation, diversity and dependency in higher education: A theoretical and empirical analysis*. Utrecht: Lemma.

Huisman, J. (2009). The Bologna process towards 2020: Institutional diversification or convergence? In B. M. Kehm, J. Huisman, & B. Sensaker (Eds.), *The European Higher Education Area: Perspectives on a moving target* (pp. 245–262). Rotterdam/Taipei: Sense Publishers.

Jacob, A. K., & Teichler, U. (2011). *Der Wandel des Hochschullehrerberufs im internationalen Vergleich: Ergebnisse einer Befragung in den Jahren 2007/08* [Change of the academic profession in international comparison: Results of the survey of the years 2007–08]. Bonn/Berlin: Bundesministerium für Bildung und Forschung.

Kehm, B. M., & Stensaker, B. (Eds.). (2009). *University rankings, diversity and the landscape of higher education*. Rotterdam/Taipei: Sense Publishers.

Kogan, M. (Ed.). (2004). *Management and evaluation in higher education* (UNESCO Forum Occasional Paper Series, 7). Paris: UNESCO.

Kogan, M. (2007). The academic profession and its interface with management. In M. Kogan & U. Teichler (Eds.), *Key challenges to the academic profession* (Werkstattberichte, Vol. 65, pp. 159–173). Kassel: International Centre for Higher Education Research Kassel.

Kogan, M., & Teichler, U. (Eds.). (2007). *Key challenges to the academic profession* (Werkstattberichte, Vol. 65). Kassel: International Centre for Higher Education Research Kassel.

Kyvik, S. (2009). *The dynamics of change in higher education*. Dordrecht: Springer.

Locke, W., & Teichler, U. (Eds.). (2007). *The changing conditions for academic work and careers in select countries* (Werkstattberichte, Vol. 66). Kassel: International Centre for Higher Education Research Kassel.

Locke, W., Cummings, W. K., & Fisher, D. (Eds.). (2011). *Changing governance and management in higher education*. Dordrecht: Springer.

Meek, V. L., Goedegebuure, L., Kivinen, O., & Rinne, R. (1996). Conclusion. In V. L. Meek, L. Goedegebuure, O. Kivinen, & R. Rinne (Eds.), *The mockers and mocked* (pp. 207–236). Oxford: Pergamon/IAU Press.

Musselin, C. (2007). Transformation of academic work: Facts and analysis. In M. Kogan & U. Teichler (Eds.), *Key challenges to the academic profession* (Werkstattberichte, Vol. 65, pp. 175–190). Kassel: International Centre for Higher Education Research Kassel.

Neave, G. (1979). Academic drift: Views from Europe. *Studies in Higher Education, 4*(2), 143–159.

Neave, G. (1989). Foundation or roof? The quantitative, structural and institutional dimensions in the study of higher education. *European Journal of Education, 24*(3), 211–222.

Neave, G. (1996). Homogenization, integration and convergence: The Chesire cats of higher education. In V. L. Meek, L. Goedegebuure, O. Kivinen, & R. Rinne (Eds.), *The mockers and mocked* (pp. 26–41). Oxford: Pergamon/IAU Press.

Neave, G. (2000). Diversity, differentiation and the market: The debate we never had but which we ought to have done. *Higher Education Policy, 13*(1), 7–22.

OECD. (1991). *Alternatives to universities*. Paris: OECD.

Reichert, S. (2009). *Institutional diversity in European higher education: Tensions and challenges for policy makers and institutional leaders*. Brussels: European University Association.

Research Institute for Higher Education, Hiroshima University. (Ed.). (2008). *The changing academic profession in international comparative and quantitative perspectives* (RIHE International Seminar Reports, Vol. 12). Hiroshima: RIHE.

Research Institute for Higher Education, Hiroshima University. (Ed.). (2009). *The changing academic profession Over 1992–2007: International, comparative and quantitative perspectives* (RIHE International Seminar Reports, Vol. 13). Hiroshima: RIHE.

Research Institute for Higher Education, Hiroshima University. (Ed.). (2010). *The changing academic profession in international comparative and quantitative perspectives: A focus on teaching & research activities* (RIHE International Seminar Reports, Vol. 15). Hiroshima: RIHE.

Sadlak, J., & Liu, N. C. (Eds.). (2007). *The world-class university and rankings: Aiming beyond status*. Bucharest/Cluj-Napoca: UNESCO-CEPES/Presa Universitara Clujeana.

Scott, P. (1996). Unified and binary systems of higher education in Europe. In A. Burgen (Ed.), *Goals and purposes of higher education in the 21st century* (pp. 37–54). London/Bristol: Jessica Kingsley Publishers.

Scott, P. (2008). Structural differentiation in higher education. In Kehm, B. M. (Ed.), *Hochschule im Wandel* [Changing higher education] (pp. 169–180). Frankfurt/M. and New York: Campus Verlag.

Shin, J. C., Toutkoushian, R. K., & Teichler, U. (Eds.). (2011). *University rankings: Theoretical basis, methodology and impacts on global higher education*. Dordrecht: Springer.

Teichler, U. (1988). *Changing patterns of the higher education system: The experience of three decades*. London: Jessica Kingsley Publishers.

Teichler, U. (1996). The conditions of the academic profession: An international comparative analysis of the academic profession in Western Europe, Japan and the USA. In P.A.M. Maassen, & F. van Vught (Eds.), *Inside Academia: New challenges for the academic profession* (pp. 15–65). Utrecht: Uitgeverej De Tijdstrom.

Teichler, U. (2007). *Higher education systems: Conceptual frameworks, comparative perspectives, empirical findings*. Rotterdam/Taipei: Sense Publishers.

Teichler, U. (2008). Diversification? Trends and explanations of the shape and size of higher education. *Higher Education, 56*(3), 349–379.

Teichler, U. (2010a). Diversity in higher education. In P. Peterson, E. Baker, & B. McGaw (Eds.), *International encyclopedia of education* (Vol. 4, pp. 347–353). Oxford: Elsevier.

Teichler, U. (2010b). The diversifying academic profession? *European Review, 18*(1), 157–179.

Teichler, U. (2011a). Germany: How changing governance and management affects the views and work of the academic profession. In W. Locke, W. K. Cummings, & D. Fisher (Eds.), *Changing governance and management in higher education* (pp. 223–241). Dordrecht: Springer.

Teichler, U. (2011b). Social contexts and systemic consequences of university rankings: A meta-analysis of the ranking literature. In J. C. Shin, R. K. Toutkoushian, & U. Teichler (Eds.), *University rankings* (pp. 55–69). Dordrecht: Springer.

Trow, M. (1974). Problems in the transition from elite to mass higher education. In OECD (Ed.), *Policies for higher education* (pp. 51–101). Paris: OECD.

Van Vught, F. (1996). Isomorphism in higher education. In V. L. Meek, L. Goedegebuure, O. Kivinen, & R. Rinne (Eds.), *The mockers and mocked* (pp. 42–58). Oxford: Pergamon/IAU Press.

Part VIII
Higher Education Futures and Foresight

Chapter 48
Transmodern Journeys: Futures Studies and Higher Education

Ziauddin Sardar

Futures studies have had a lukewarm reception from the academia. Conventionally, a new discipline is said to have emerged with the publication of a couple of dedicated journals. Futures and foresight have a string of journals devoted to the field – *Futures, Foresight, Technological Forecasting and Social Change, World Futures* and the *Journal of Futures Studies* – yet, it is not seen as worthy of being taught in a university. There are a few courses devoted to this area of enquiry, but, as a whole, futures studies are conspicuous largely by its absence from the university curriculum.

Part of the problem is that the area of enquiry we call futures studies does not see itself as a conventional discipline with well established disciplinary boundaries. Indeed, the problem begins, as I have argued elsewhere, with the name of the field itself (Sardar 2010a). But a bigger hurdle is the interdisciplinary and transdisciplinary nature of the field. Given that it straddles a number of disciplines across the academia, it is not easy to decide what to include or what to exclude from futures studies. However, not all disciplines with 'studies' in their academic prefix (such as cultural studies, women's studies, or philosophical studies), which signifies a heterodoxy of methods and approaches have fared badly. So why has futures studies singularly been neglected so much? An overall problem in teaching futures is the lack of general theories that shape the field of enquiry. And associated issue is the lack of 'Great Men', whose ideas have to be studied. In fields such as cultural studies there are specific theories to focus on and giants in the field whose ideas have to be wrestled with. In contrast, futures studies seem only to have methods.

But these conventional shortcomings of futures studies are set to become its major strengths. In post normal times, when complexity, uncertainty, contradictions

Z. Sardar (✉)
Editor Futures, 1 Orchard Gate, NW9 6HU London, UK

Professor of Law and Society, School of Law, Middlesex University, UK
e-mail: ziauddin.sardar@btopenworld.com

A. Curaj et al. (eds.), *European Higher Education at the Crossroads:*
Between the Bologna Process and National Reforms,
DOI 10.1007/978-94-007-3937-6_48, © Springer Science+Business Media Dordrecht 2012

and chaotic behaviour are the norm, the modes of enquiry grounded on a single discipline are becoming increasingly irrelevant (Sardar 2010b). Complex, wicked problems need to be tackled from a number of different perspectives and requires a host of different methods to understand. Not surprisingly, interdisciplinary and transdisciplinary research is increasingly taking a centre stage in research agendas (Lyall et al. 2011) – providing an opportunity for futures studies to come into its own. Moreover, the exploration of futures spaces acquires a prominent importance in times of uncertainty. Complex problems can only be solved in the future, so an understanding of what the future may look like, or has to offer, becomes paramount. Already, a number of disciplines, from Architecture to Urban Planning, Geography to evolutionary Psychology, Sociology to Economics, have increasingly become concerned with future developments. This trend will not only increase, but would become an essential way of understanding and dealing with problems – making futures studies an indispensible tool in the academia. The universities and academic institutions would, therefore, neglect futures studies at their peril.

There is another reason why futures studies cannot be ignored in the academia. The notion of the future is not something that is limited to the future itself. It is one of the main instruments through which we make sense of the past and understand the present. Educating a student holistically, as Gidley (2012) shows, requires imparting a notion, an image, a vision of the future that equips the student with the relevant insights and skills to think critically and creatively about the future and engage positively in shaping it. We may learn from our past, we may understand the future, but the only arena where we can actually make a difference is the future. Given the current global issues, from climate change to depletion of oil, social unrest to market meltdown, and accelerating rates of change, the future could be a rather uncomfortable and hazardous place. In any case, it would be radically different from the present. A student unable to think about the future, a space that is increasingly becoming all important, will be a truncated individual unsuited to the complexity and plurality of the times to come. And a university that does not tackle foresight and futures in some way would simply not be fit for purpose in the future.

In particular, universities would have to shift from the industrial production model where students are processed from the beginning of their course to graduation as though they were ball bearings. As Alfonso Montuori has argued, universities in the world are still stuck in the industrial age, producing 'reproductive education' and seek to prepare students for a static world of conformity (Montuori 2012). The future, in contrast, requires a different set of competencies. Higher education, notes Marco Rieckmann, now has to 'enable individuals to reflect on their own actions by taking into account their current and future social and environmental effects – from a global perspective – and to intervene productively in shaping them in a sustainable manner'. Students must have the ability to envision better futures and be able to understand links between long term goals and immediate actions. Rieckmann used a Delphi study, involving experts from Europe and Latin America, to identify key competencies crucial for surviving in the future, including systematic thinking and handling complexity, anticipatory and critical thinking, ability to work across disciplines and cultures, and empathy and open-mindedness (Riechmann 2012).

Montuori argues that the future demands that 'learners move from being consumers to creators and from bystanders to participants in the post normal dance of knowledge'. In a world where what we always assumed to be 'normal' is rapidly disappearing, imagination and creative enquiry must be at the heart of scholarship. Montuori offers a very specific take on creativity. 'Creative enquiry', he writes, 'involves the cultivation of a fundamental attitude to the world that actively embraces uncertainty, pluralism, and complexity, and sees them as potential sources of creativity. It recognises that making meaning in such a world is itself a creative act, indeed a co-creative act'. Thus, creativity requires much more than the simple creation of tradition 'products' such as thesis and dissertation. Rather, 'it is a way of approaching the world that recognises the personal and social dimensions that go into our particular understanding of the world (and inform any view of the world), the possibility (and likelihood) of other perspectives, as well as a perceptual choice to remain open to experience with all its ambiguity and complexity rather than immediately superimposing an interpretive framework'. In such a framework, life itself becomes 'an ongoing process of enquiry, creation and exploration. It assumes that understanding is, by its very nature, hermeneutically circular and indeed recursive, beginning not from a God's eye view from nowhere, but in the very middle of existence, viewing learners as participants, not bystanders'.

The kind of creative enquiry that Montuori seeks and Rieckmann is suggesting with his list of future and sustainable competencies require breaking of all artificial borders and boundaries.

Borders have been incredibly useful tools for higher education: they have served to keep disciplines 'pure' and manageable. They have also been used to control and contort the reality of other cultures and to maintain the hegemony of Eurocentric worldview. It is the site at which the dominion over Others and other ways of knowledge has been constructed. All the definitions of borders and transitory states in modern and post modern theorising derive from the same source – the fear-ridden insecurity of Western self identity provoked by the expatriate experience of colonialism and the reverse process of fear of immigration of ex-colonial subjects into the metropolis. During colonialism the fear of 'going native', of contamination by closeness to and engagement with Other societies, was the neurosis encouraging emphasis on borders, boundaries, divisions and hierarchies. Ranked stages in scales of civilisation were everywhere to provide borders between Us and Them, the conceptual distance that enabled, supported and justified domination, dispossession and despoiling Other ways of life and thought. With the end of colonialism, the reverse process begins. When Others arrive on the metropolitan doorstep, they inhabit the transitory world of being required to change as the price of inclusion.

This Eurocentric outlook, as Vinay Lal (2012) argues, is intrinsic into many disciplines. Most of the disciplines taught in universities have evolved from the cultural milieu of Western society and incorporate their concerns and prejudices within them. In a globalised world, where power in the next decades will shift from the West to the East, disciplines anchored in Eurocentricism will have little to say about the rapidly shifting realities. By opening up Social Science and Humanities disciplines to the concerns and outlooks of non-Western cultures, universities can prepare their students for the future. Universities need to ask a few urgent questions. What relevance do borders have in a globalised world? Can societies and cultures exist without borders? How are fluid identities and multiple selves taking us to a different, more permeable, more porous future space? What kind of world would the world of 'inbetweeness' be – the world our students would inhabit? How would we equip them to engage with a pluralistic world of mindboggling diversity? These and other questions cannot be explored from the standard, and failed, perspectives of modernity and postmodernism – we need to go over and above to a new transmodern perspective. What would a transmodern world look like? What new disciplines would we need?

To think beyond borders, to prepare our students for multiple futures, and resolve the awful legacy bequeathed by the twentieth century, we must begin with three basic realisations. First, societies and cultures have seldom been bounded. Identity has largely been a permeable membrane formed by the interpenetration of diversity, the interaction of multiple mutual influences in plural worlds, of multiple conversations – or polylogue – between cultures. Far from existing in splendid isolation, all cultures were surrounded by others with which they maintained and sustained relations. The apparently hermetically sealed cultural borders, particularly of 'the Orient', were, in fact, porous. Second, our discourse has been totally dependent on just one civilisational and historic corpus. We must appreciate that the presumptive universality of our terms of reference are in themselves presumptuous, a false imposition on the lived reality of most non-European cultures. Third, much of the terminology we glibly band around is constructed and forged by a single, questionable discourse and now needs to be rethought: zones of transition, inclusion and exclusion, and especially hybridity, self and other are all ideas that have to go back into the melting pot of redefinition because they are the imposition of one worldview upon many Others worldviews. We need not only new ways of thinking beyond borders, but also, a new vocabulary for shaping new discourses. Borders and boundaries are the instruments that generate the problems of living in heterogeneous societies. We have to un-think borders as we have known them at all levels of conceptualisation if we are to find paths across the no man's lands we create to enter the future domain of plural intermingled worlds.

Disassembling borders, creative enquiry and future competencies all require us to move beyond the dominant conventional and confining frameworks of modernity and postmodernism.

Modernity, a concept abstracted from this experience of Western society, is predicted on the notion of progress. And, as we are discovering, at the beginning of the twenty-first century, progress is but the visible real world success of domination. Modernity is a one way progress following in the wake of the apex of human achievement, a process of Westernisation made in the image and with the defining features of how Anglo-Saxon society and its inheritors became the dominant powers of the globe and took up the burden of teaching the rest of the world how to be properly human. It has been liberalised and democratised. It has been supremely successful in creating the opportunity for more and more individuals to attain material prosperity. But it has also created an unjust, inequitable world where greed, selfishness and short term interests have become the norm. Where non-Western and indigenous cultures, as well as their flora and fauna, are decimated in the name of efficiency and progress. What modernity has delivered is an endless quest for own things shorn of all prudential values and decoupled from any exercise of civic virtue. The age of consumerism was ushered in by a renewed rhetoric of a property owning democracy but one that did not accept the concept of society. Consumerism is the ideology of individual choice, of the personal prerogative to get and to spend; and it is the bedrock of modernity. Its consequence has been to breed insecurity and a proliferating sense of powerlessness. Social worth has come to be evaluated through conspicuous display of what we own. We shop for a lifestyle; we make eclectic choices from merchandised options for everything to define who and what we are. But we live with insipient fear, fear of the collapse of the very systems that have brought us our material well-being. Talk of sustainable future is meaningless in a framework that generates endless wants and desires that have to be endlessly satisfied. Modernity reinforces boundaries, between cultures, between those who are 'modern' and those who are 'traditional' (and by definition backward), between economics and social justice, and between disciplines. As a system of thought and action, modernity is not amenable to complexity or transdisciplinary thinking, to empathy and respect for other cultures, to generating the type of creative enquiry that Montuori argues for.

Postmodernism is what comes after modernity; it is post in terms of time; it is a natural conclusion of modernity. This is why it is sometimes described as 'the logic of late capitalism'; in the subtitle of my book *Postmodernism and the Other,* I described it as 'a new culture of Western imperialism'. It represents a liner trajectory that starts with colonialism, continues with modernity and ends with post-modernity, or postmodernism. It is not surprising than that postmodernism and traditional cultures are like two fuming bulls in a ring: they are inimically antagonistic to each other. Postmodernism states that all big ideas that have shaped our society, like Religion, Reason, Science, Tradition, History, Morality, Marxism, do not stand up to philosophical scrutiny. There is no such thing as the Truth. Anything that claims to provide us with absolute truth is a sham. It must be abandoned. Moreover, postmodernism suggests, there is no ultimate Reality. We see what we want to see, what our position in time and place allows us to see, what our cultural and historic perceptions focus on. Instead of reality, what we have is an ocean of images; a world where all distinction between image and material reality has been lost. Postmodernism posits the world as a video game: seduced by the allure of the spectacle, we have all become characters in the global video game, zapping our way from here to there, fighting wars in cyberspace, making love to digitised bits of information. We float on an endless sea of images and stories that shape our perception and our individual 'reality'. But if all is an image, what happens to real pain and suffering? If grand narratives are meaningless, then what explains the rise of religion? If all is relative, then what happens to ethics and morality, to some notion of objectivity and rationality? In the end, postmodernism has only delivered a world of spectacle, more consumerism, more desires and even more consumption of the Other.

As such, both modernity and postmodernism are unsuitable philosophies for the future. The universities have been the cornerstone of modernity and postmodernism – embedded in these outlooks and perpetuating them. The future demands that institutions of higher learning free themselves from such monolithic, destructive worldviews. We need a new mode of thought and enquiry that takes us trans – over and beyond modernity and postmodernism into another state of being. That framework, I would like to suggest, is transmodernity (Sardar 2006).

We can best understand transmodernity with the aid of chaos theory. In all complex systems – societies, civilisations, eco-systems etc. – many independent variables are interacting with each other in great many ways. Chaos theory teaches us that complex systems have the ability to create order out of chaos. This happens at a balancing point, called the 'edge of chaos'. At the edge of chaos, the system is in a kind of suspended animation between stability and total dissolution into chaos. At this point, almost any factor can push the system into one or other direction. However, complex systems at the edge of chaos have the ability to spontaneously self-organise themselves into a higher order; in other words, the system 'evolves' spontaneously into a new mode of existence. Transmodernity is the transfer of modernity and postmodernism from the edge of chaos into a new order of society. Things change radically; but they also stay the same. Societies and individuals become transmodern while retaining the basic components of their cultural identity. In transmodernity, both sides of the equation are important: change has to be made and accommodated; but the fundamental tenets of culture and tradition, the source of its identity and meaning, remain the same.

This, then, is the ultimate goal of higher education: to prepare their students to move from post normal times to a transmodern future. It is a journey that requires shedding the Eurocentric nature of disciplines and moving towards interdisciplinary and transdisciplinary teaching and research. It is a transformation that cannot be achieved without creative enquiry or future competencies. Or, indeed, without dissolving borders that keep us separate and isolated.

References

Gidley, J. M. (2012). Re-imagining the role and function of higher education for alternative futures through embracing global knowledge futures. In A. Curaj et al. (Eds.), *European Higher Education at the Crossroads, Volume 2: Governance, Financing, Mission Diversification and Futures of Higher Education* (pp. 1018–1037), Heidelberg: Springer.

Lal, V. (2012). The politics and consequences of eurocentrism in university disciplines. In A. Curaj et al. (Eds.), *European Higher Education at the Crossroads, Volume 2: Governance, Financing, Mission Diversification and Futures of Higher Education* (pp. 1038–1055), Heidelberg: Springer.

Lyall, C., et al. (2011). *Interdisciplinary research journeys: Practical strategies for capturing creativity*. London: Bloomsbury Academic.

Montuori, A. (2012, January/February). Creative inquiry: Confronting the challenges of scholarship in the 21st century. *Futures, 44*(1) (in press).

Rieckmann, M. (2012, March). Future-oriented higher education: Which key competencies should be fostered through university teaching and learning? *Futures, 44*(2) (in press).

Sardar, Z. (2001). *Postmodernism and the other*. London: Pluto Press.

Sardar, Z. (2006). Beyond difference: Cultural relations in a new century. In E. Masood (Ed.), *How do you know: Reading Ziauddin Sardar on Islam, science and cultural relations*. London: Pluto Press.

Sardar, Z. (2010a, April). The Namesake: Futures, futures studies, futurology, futuristic, foresight – What's in a name? *Futures 42*(3), 177–184.

Sardar, Z. (2010b, June). Welcome to postnormal times. *Futures 42*(5), 435–444.

Chapter 49
Multiple Futures for Higher Education in a Multi-level Structure

Attila Havas

49.1 Introduction

Universities[1] are among the oldest organisations, and have already shown an immense diversity in terms of their societal and economic role, sources of funding, methods of running them, etc. It is suffice to recall the major differences, for example between the early medieval universities in Europe, set up and run by the church, on the one hand, and the so-called land-grant universities, first set up in the second half of the nineteenth century by various American states to advance agriculture, science and engineering in a highly pragmatic way, on the other. Both the oldest and the more recently established ones had undergone fundamental changes several times in their lifetime (spanning six to nine centuries or just 50–100 years). Yet, due to economic and societal pressures, their mission, teaching and research methods, as well as management structures and financial models need to be renewed yet again, as stressed by policy-makers, analysts, and universities themselves (Aghion et al. 2007; EC 2003, 2007; EG 2010; Georghiou and Harper 2008; LERU 2006; OECD 2006; Ritzen and Soete 2011; STRATA-ETAN 2002; Vincent-Lancrin 2006). Systematic prospective analyses can contribute to these efforts by considering the wide-ranging and complex factors that are shaping the future of the higher education systems and individual HE organisations.

---

[1] The term "universities" is used in this chapter in a broad sense, covering all sorts of higher education establishments, including, for example, the German *Fachhochschulen*, the British *polytechnics* and the French *Grandes Ecoles*.

A. Havas (✉)
Institute of Economics, Hungarian Academy of Sciences,
Budaorsi ut 45, H-1112 Budapest, Hungary
e-mail: havasatt@econ.core.hu

A. Curaj et al. (eds.), *European Higher Education at the Crossroads:*
Between the Bologna Process and National Reforms,
DOI 10.1007/978-94-007-3937-6_49, © Springer Science+Business Media Dordrecht 2012

This chapter argues that careful planning is needed before launching any prospective analysis (or forward-looking activities [FLA])[2] to avoid disappointment. FLA practitioners and FLA clients/sponsors (those decision-makers who are going to launch an FLA project, use its results, and finance these activities) have several choices during the preparation process, and the implications of the decisions made at these 'cross-roads' should be considered thoroughly. The main objective of this chapter is to assist these 'qualitative cost-benefit analyses' by raising guiding questions, indicating likely benefits and costs of different choices made, and offering multiple futures for HE in a multi-level structure. Hence, it is organised around questions to be answered during the planning process: *why* to conduct FLA (Sect. 49.2); *how* to do that (building single vs. multiple futures; conducting single vs. multi-level prospective analyses); and by *whom* (Sect. 49.3).[3] Then, Sect. 49.4 presents multiple futures at various levels, and the concluding section highlights policy implications and offers recommendations.

This chapter follows the systems of innovation approach, or more generally, the theoretical framework of the evolutionary economics of innovation (Dosi et al. 1988; Edquist 1997; Fagerberg et al. 2005; Freeman 1994; Lundvall and Borrás 1999; OECD 1998).

Several caveats are in order. First this chapter is not meant to offer fully-fledged 'futures' or any other type of FLA 'products': that would be a task for an expert team, together with stakeholders (or without them, depending on the approach chosen) – but never for a single author. Rather, the intention here is to pose several guiding questions, as well as examples of futures as illustrations for planning real-life FLA projects. Obviously, real-life FLA would lead to different futures, given the aim of that project, its context, and the main values shared by the participants, clients, and sponsors. Second, it is not aimed at a detailed analysis of the current state and performance of universities. Third, the geographical scope is limited to the European Union (EU) – yet, the proposed method can be applied in other regions, too, by replacing EU-specific trends, policies and governance modes, etc. by the relevant ones. Fourth, the immense diversity across universities and HE systems cannot be tackled here. Just to flag some major differences: (i) the share of HE organisations in research activities vis-à-vis the other research performing sectors is rather high in less advanced countries, while business R&D units play a dominant role in all the advanced ones; (ii) in small and medium-sized countries the national government devises HE policies, and funds HE organisations, while in bigger countries – e.g. in Germany and the UK – regional authorities perform these tasks (Sanz-Menéndez 2007); and finally (iii) the quality of education and research activities also differs significantly across HE organisations both inside a given country and across countries (Bonaccorsi and Daraio 2007).

---

[2]Prospective analyses and forward-looking activities (FLA) are used in this chapter as interchangeable, broad umbrella terms to denote a wide variety of activities to consider future state(s) from different angles, using various approaches/tools/methods, involving different types of participants.

[3]Several other important details should also be considered during the preparation for an FLA exercise, e.g. various methods/tools; timing, budget, communication among the project participants and with those who are affected by the outcome, project management, the need and methods of evaluation (internal vs. external; on-going vs. ex-post), etc. These issues are not tackled here.

49.2   Why to Conduct FLA on Higher Education

Several major trends and driving forces change – or likely to change – the landscape for HE organisations, both in terms of their research and education activities. For centuries, mainly universities produced, validated, and disseminated new scientific knowledge,[4] but this is not the case anymore. Firms and public labs have emerged since the late nineteenth century as important research actors, accompanied by patient groups and other NGOs more recently. Users also play a significant role in the innovation process, and thus contribute to knowledge production (von Hippel 1988; Fagerberg et al. 2005). As for education, new actors have also entered the market, especially since the second half of the twentieth century.

Some of the key trends and likely future changes are highlighted below,[5] but not necessarily in the order of their significance.

49.2.1   Major Changes in the HE Landscape

Universities teach, conduct academic research, co-operate with businesses, and provide scientific advice for policy-makers and societal actors. The *balance between these roles* is changing, leading to different 'portfolios' at different types of universities; e.g. the dominance of undergraduate teaching in some cases, and research – coupled with post-graduate training – in others. Further, *new roles* are emerging, e.g. universities are becoming influential players in local, regional, sectoral, national, and international innovation systems.

The increasingly *intense global competition* among universities, as well as *financial, demographic, technological, and societal factors* also shape the HE landscape considerably. Universities need to improve their international standing in order to raise funds for education and research activities. That requires intense international collaboration, on the one hand, but competition for talents (students and staff members) becomes fierce, on the other. Cuts in public expenditures tighten HE funding, too, leading to ever more intensive competition among universities for the shrinking cake. While scientific instruments become more sophisticated, and more expensive, universities must modernise their equipment; otherwise would be relegated to 'second-league' players due to the fierce and globalising rivalry. Given this extra burden on the already tight budgets of universities, cost-efficiency of education and research is becoming a key factor in decision-making.

---

[4]The role of inventors in advancing knowledge should not be ignored, either: several major inventions have long preceded theories uncovering the scientific laws explaining the operation of technologies (e.g. the steam engine, the first airplanes, semiconductors, etc.). Hence, it would be a great simplification to think of technologies as applied sciences. Indeed, several scientific disciplines evolved given the fundamental questions posed by certain technologies: why they work as they do (Nelson 2004; Rosenberg 1996, 1998).

[5]For more details on trends affecting research and education activities of HE organisations, see, e.g. Havas (2008, 2009), respectively.

Policy measures – introduced by regional, national or supra-national bodies – can alter some of the above driving forces (reinforce, soften or redirect their impacts), or generate new drivers for change e.g. by setting goals for universities or changing their environment. The Bologna Process, for instance, set in force by the EU, has affected universities in a fundamental way.

New types of courses/degrees need to be offered to meet new societal and economic needs, e.g. short(er), more practical courses for job-seekers, regular re-training for managers and policy-makers, as well as researchers (to assist them in life-long learning). In general, courses/curricula should be tailored to students' needs (of different ages, coming from different social backgrounds). More directly articulated demand can be expected from those who provide funding for HE organisations, notably governments, businesses, foundations, alumni associations, and 'consumers' (students and their parents). As an important element of this trend, universities would be required to develop problem-solving skills, underpinned by multi- (trans-; inter-) disciplinary education and training, as well as to prepare for co-operation and communication in multi-cultural teams.

The share of HE students is already fairly high in the age group of 20–29 years old, transforming the HE sector composed of predominantly elite universities to 'mass producers' of degrees. As 28–49% of the relevant age cohort is registered at tertiary education organisations in most OECD countries, students cannot be regarded the 'elite' anymore, and neither is it the major mission of universities to reproduce the academic and societal elite. Hence, teaching and research are increasingly separated, making the Humboldtian model an exception, rather than the rule.[6]

A more intense competition can be expected given the increasing number of globally active players.[7] Currently 'unthinkable' actors might launch HE services and conduct research, relying on radically new or modified organisational forms and 'business models'.

That could lead to the application of new norms and methods when legitimating and validating knowledge. Besides academic researchers, knowledge is already produced by think tanks, commercial labs, consultancy companies, market research organisations, foundations, government bodies, patients' groups, various NGOs, trade associations, interest groups, etc. The knowledge generated is exploited by its producer internally (government agencies, firms' labs), sold to clients (by contract research organisations, consultancies) or used in political/societal processes (by NGOs, trade associations). As knowledge is diffused, it is validated (formally or informally; explicitly or implicitly). The rules of validation are undergoing changes, and thus the traditional peer-review process is not the only method anymore. Various futures might emerge: (a) non-academic sources of knowledge are accepted as fully

---

[6]The Humboldtian model of universities assumes a unity of teaching and research, based on the idea of higher education through exposure to, and immersion in, research activities (Kehm 2006).

[7]Some of the currently national actors, once fundamentally re-structured and strengthened, would enter the global arena, and new types of HE service providers can also be expected. Contributions to Thorne (1999) describe several types of these new players.

legitimate, i.e. academics lose their power to validate knowledge; (b) knowledge – regardless of its source – is only accepted if validated by academic rules and actors; (c) a clear separation between knowledge created by credible academic organisations and non-academic ones, the former with a higher status (Bonaccorsi 2007).

Further, new open-access channels for publishing research results have already opened up, due to the changing behaviour and norms of scientists, assisted by low-cost information technology solutions. This trend is likely to become stronger, spread more widely (in terms of disciplines and geographic coverage), and hence would affect the diffusion and validation of knowledge, as well as the business models of publishing houses, the cost structure of universities (their libraries), and in some cases their revenues, too.

Given the new actors, the HE 'ecology' would be characterised by a more pronounced variety, as well as new opportunities and rules for co-operation and competition. A number of HE actors, or even HE 'species', that would not 'fit' to the new environment, might be wiped out.

The above changes would also bring new evaluation metrics in, to complement the conventional criteria of academic excellence (publications and citations). Evaluators would assess to what extent universities fulfil their societal roles by launching what types of courses (tailored to what groups), at what level of quality, with what share of foreign staff and students, as well as the weight of multi- (trans-; inter-) disciplinary training and research, and the efficiency of using resources. Various types of universities (e.g. the ones focussing on vocational training as opposed to post-graduate teaching and research; or meeting local research needs vs. acting as a global player; etc.) are likely to be evaluated by different sets of criteria.

There are inherent tensions between the interests, values, and goals of different stakeholders, just as between the need to monitor and control the various activities of universities to improve efficiency and the nature of academic activities. Universities are already using a wide variety of governance and management models to tackle these tensions and dilemmas (Kehm 2006). The new players – introducing new business models for universities – would increase variety in this sense, too.

49.2.2   Ways to Respond to the Changing Landscape

In principle, HE decision-makers have three broad options. First, they may decide just to watch these sweeping changes unfolding, and accept the repercussions passively. Several reasons can be behind such a decision. They might believe that an FLA project would be too time-consuming, expensive, and/or too demanding in terms of expertise, or they would not be able to act anyway, given their inability to divert those powerful, global trends and the driving forces behind them. The simple answer to these concerns is that the consequences of this inaction might be severe: unprepared universities – unfit to the new environment – are likely to lose talents, as well as funding, and thus eventually might be taken over by stronger ones, or simply ceased. Moreover, there is a wide array of inexpensive, less demanding FLA tools, too, and hence even relatively small HE systems or single universities can find affordable, and still useful methods for a prospective analysis that would identify relevant strategic responses, e.g. to do something very similar to the next option.

Second, they might decide to launch an FLA project with the intention to thoroughly understand the possible new realities, and thus be better prepared to react e.g. to new types of demand for education and research. In this case the goal is to derive a so-called 'future-proof' strategy, that is, actions that would enable a HE system or a single university to 'weather' different kinds of 'storms'. This is a defensive strategy that can be relevant for many players.

Third, more ambitious HE decision-makers might want to take the initiative e.g. by shaping some of the existing trends, setting new trends (e.g. by introducing radically new teaching methods, competition or co-operation patterns, management and financing techniques) or changing the HE system (at a national or supranational level by performance objectives, funding decisions, IPR regulations, validation rules or quality norms). This pro-active strategy is open to a small number of large, influential universities, national and supra-national policy-makers, and other powerful stakeholders.

49.3   Which Type of FLA to Conduct

Those HE decision-makers or other stakeholders who intend to launch an FLA exercise can choose from a wide variety of methods and approaches. This section considers three fundamental methodological choices by posing guiding questions that need to be answered when planning an FLA project.

First, would devising a single future (an image of a feasible and desired future state) assist the decision-makers to a sufficient extent, or is it more useful to consider multiple futures? Second, what would be the appropriate level of the prospective analysis: to consider a university or a HE system (be it national or regional) on its own, or is a multi-level analysis needed to yield essential insights, given the potential impacts of various driving forces arising from the broader systems, in which a given university or a HE system is embedded in? Third, who should be involved: only a few experts are to be commissioned, or should it be a participatory process, engaging representatives of various stakeholder groups?

Although it might be difficult to make stark choices at a very beginning of an FLA project – especially when it is run for the first time at a university or in a HE system, and thus sponsors and project managers cannot rely on first-hand experience of the many types of difficulties and dilemmas they are going to face – the three guiding questions raised above must be answered at the outset. Otherwise no one would know what sort of FLA project is to be conducted, what the major characteristics are, and hence what can be expected.

One might take for granted – almost needless to state – that HE reforms, or strategies of single universities, just as strategies in any field, need to be informed by a thorough consideration of potential future states. Several proposals or policy documents by prestigious authors or highly influential organisations on the HE sector, however, do not discuss desired or likely futures (Aghion et al. 2007; EC 2003; van der Ploeg and Veugelers 2008). It might be useful, therefore, to highlight the relevance of futures as useful tools in decision-preparatory processes. Futures can be utilised as direct inputs: a desirable future (future state), selected from the feasible ones, can be expanded into a so-called fully-fledged or path scenario. The path(s) leading to that specific future state can be identified via backcasting: the timeline of those actions should be designed, which would increase the likelihood of achieving the desired future. Taking one step back, futures can also be used as detailed, reasoned warnings, urging decision-makers and/or other stakeholders to act: current trends lead to an undesirable future state, and hence swift and decisive measures are needed to change that course.

49.3.1   Single or Multiple Futures?

Considering whether to build single vs. multiple futures,[8] one is essentially making a choice between diametrically different 'world views'. Assuming a 'simple world', in which the major current trends, as well as the likely future ones are easy to grasp, and no major interruptions can be expected,[9] a single future can be devised by extrapolating the well-understood trends. In contrast, when developments are driven by a multitude of trends, among which multifaceted, difficult-to-predict interactions can be observed, and disruptive new trends are also likely to emerge, only multiple futures can provide adequate strategic intelligence to decision-makers.

Apparently it is simpler, less time-consuming, and hence cheaper to devise a single future. Moreover, some participants might favour this approach, claiming that 'we are experts, and hence we are not guessing, but build a sound future, based on scientific methods'. Further, some decision-makers might prefer to be presented with a clear-cut solution, as opposed to reading several futures, and considering the corresponding sets of policy recommendations. They usually are pressed for time, and can only read very brief executive summaries.

The current and likely future trends affecting the HE sector, presented briefly in Sect. 49.2, however, are fairly complex, and thus we cannot assume a 'simple world'. In turn, multiple futures seem to be more appropriate to support HE reforms or strategic responses of single universities.[10] It is rather worrisome, therefore, that key policy documents, for example the EU Green Paper on the European Research Area (EC 2007), do not consider multiple futures.

---

[8]The nature of futures, that is, whether the aim is to explore potential future developments or to set visions (devise normative futures) is not discussed here.

[9]Intentions of policy-makers or other stakeholders to change the current settings can be thought of as driving forces, potentially causing discontinuities. There are no such intentions in 'simple worlds'.

[10]Even when the underlying trends are easy to understand and their impacts can be forecast with satisfactory precision, multiple futures offer a major benefit: without having considered the likely impacts of different policy options, one cannot speak of genuine decision-making.

49.3.2 What Level of Analysis?

FLA projects usually face severe constraints in terms of the time and resources available. Sponsors/clients are eager to obtain results quickly, and not willing to finance an army of analysts, either. Given these constraints, universities usually opt for a less demanding prospective analysis, i.e. ask for devising future(s) at their own level. Similarly, education and science ministries or umbrella organisation for universities commission future(s) at the level of the HE sector, without a fully-fledged, systematic analysis of the potential developments in the broader context, which are likely to affect the HE sector as a whole. Indeed, an impressive number of prospective projects on HE has already been conducted, launched by a wide variety of organisations, ranging from single universities to international organisations (Georghiou and Cassingena Harper 2006), but none of them is based on a multi-level analysis. The 'unit of analysis' is either an existing or a hypothetical university in all these cases.

The advantages of conducting prospective analyses in a multi-level structure seem to be overwhelming and compelling. As universities are embedded in socio-economic systems, one simply cannot afford ignoring the possible developments in these settings, and their likely impacts on universities. Further, as already pointed out, a huge diversity can be observed among the broad HE models across continents, as well as across countries on the same continent. To tackle trends and driving forces emerging from broader systems, and to reflect upon this diversity, an FLA project needs to rely on multi-level analyses.

It is worth considering these somewhat 'abstract' benefits in a more detailed way, too, that is, by various stakeholders. For citizens, as well as for decision-makers in general, a main advantage would be that major strategic decisions – in this case on the overall rationale of the EU policies and on the mission of the European Innovation and Research Area – are taken in a transparent and conscious way. No doubt, the 'small-scale' decisions – made every day, without taking into account the 'broader picture' – would shape these broader systems, too. This 'muddling through' might seem to be preferable for those who would like to spare the time needed for dialogues on clearly formulated multiple strategic options, and/or want to avoid the potential tensions occurring while discussing actions and their consequences. The genuine cost, however, can be a missed opportunity: conscious, well-articulated and broadly supported strategic decisions might lead to much more favourable future state, as opposed to the outcome of 'muddling through'.

A major benefit for policy-makers could be to 'simulate' the likely impacts of their decisions, by changing the various 'parameters', e.g. the overall rationale of the EU or national policies (i.e. 'switching' between different EU and national level futures), or the actual higher education policy tools, as well as the links between HE policies, *per se*, and other policies affecting education, R&D and innovation processes (e.g. exploring the impacts of certain polices on the mobility of researchers and students). As already stressed, a number of drivers are global (or EU-wide) in their character, while decision-making competences are with the national or regional authorities. Thus, multi-level governance should be understood in order to devise appropriate policies (accomplishing what is possible and not striving for unattainable goals). A set of futures, representing the various levels of governance, can contribute to design relevant policies. Further, the diversity of universities can also be taken into account, provided that the appropriate 'ideal types' of universities are identified – and used as 'input data' for this qualitative simulation – for a specific policy design task. EU policy-makers might also use multi-level futures as a tool assisting their initiatives to align national policies. In that case, however, futures at the national level need to be devised.

Stakeholders of universities – their executives, academic and supporting staff, students, businesses, the relevant community around them, be it local, regional or national – would better understand the context they work in, including the potential future states, towards which these broader systems might evolve. Hence, they would be better equipped to devise a 'future-proof', robust strategy: they can explore how their planned strategy would work in different future environments, and thus can adjust their strategy to make it successful in these different futures. They can also 'hold' the environment as given, and study if changing their university's main features would improve (or weaken) their performance. That would be a useful exercise in case they intend to reform their university.

Finally, for innovation policy analysts this multi-level structure offers three advantages: (i) the likely impacts of potential changes in the broader socio-economic systems, in which universities operate, can be analysed; (ii) the observed diversity of higher education systems and/or individual universities can be reflected by identifying relevant ideal types (tailored to specific research questions); (iii) the role of other research actors, and more importantly, the links among universities and those other research players can be discussed systematically.

Section 49.4 of this chapter tries to illustrate that neither sponsors/clients, nor FLA project managers need to be 'threatened': multi-level prospective analysis is not beyond their reach.

49.3.3   What Level of Participation?

Considering the third guiding question, that is, the number and types of participants, two major approaches can be followed: FLA can be conducted by hiring a small group of experts, or by inviting representatives of key stakeholder groups.

As for the latter types, these so-called participatory FLA projects (i) involve participants from at least two different stakeholder groups in structured, face-to-face dialogues; (ii) disseminate their preliminary results (e.g. analyses and tentative conclusions) among interested 'non-participants',[11] e.g. at workshops, via the internet,

---

[11] 'Non-participants' are those persons who have not been members of working groups set up by the programme, and have not been involved directly in any other way, e.g. by answering (Delphi) questionnaires.

or in the form of printed documents, leaflets, newsletters; and (iii) seek feedback from this wider circle. Conversely, if any of these criteria is not met, that activity cannot be regarded as a participatory programme.

An FLA project can be constructed as a university strategy or a HE policy advisory process, tackling a few highly specific, pre-defined issues, commissioning a small group of experts. These exercises can be completed in a relatively short timeframe, and be efficient in terms of resource use. They can be also highly effective, that is, have a strong impact by giving strategic orientations to key decision-makers, helping set agendas, or offering back-up solutions/contingency plans in case of certain events happening. In brief, the main benefits are products (lists of suggested priorities, actions to be taken, analyses of strengths, weaknesses, opportunities and threats, etc.). From a different angle, the so-called process benefits – mobilising key stakeholder groups to consider multiple futures and select a favourable one, channelling resources distributed at various actors towards this shared vision, and thus making the whole system more efficient in using resources, as well as reducing uncertainties – simply cannot be expected from these FLA projects.

Participatory FLA projects usually address a larger number of broad issues, involving a higher number of participants from different stakeholder groups. These projects tend to take more time, cost more, but can be still efficient in using funds and time. Their influence can be both direct and indirect. As to the first one, highly visible impacts can be achieved by compelling recommendations, which are practical enough to be implemented. As to latter ones, those are far less visible, and those impacts might take quite some time to make a noticeable difference.

Participatory FLA projects bring together different stakeholders with their diverse sets of accumulated knowledge and experience, as well as distinct viewpoints and approaches so as to enrich the discussion and analysis. It is particularly important in the case of building futures for the HE sector: given the vital role of universities in generating, transmitting, disseminating and applying knowledge, and hence their contribution to socio-economic development, major stakeholders need to be involved when strategic decisions are made concerning universities. Further, a participatory process aligns the actors around emergent agendas, resulting in a co-ordinated mobilisation of people, resources and actions. The shared vision and policy recommendations, stemming from the dialogue among participants, lead to commitment to joint actions, as well as actions by individual organisations along the lines of the shared vision. This, in turn, offers a basis for faster and more efficient implementation. In contrast, futures developed by individuals can only experiment with new methods, or spark dialogues, by offering food for thought, at best.

A participatory FLA project might have many different outcomes. Following the usual distinction in the literature, one can think of 'process benefits' and 'products'. The first would include more intense, regular communication among the stakeholders even when the process is completed, stronger co-operation, a shared vision, leading to consensus on the actions need to be taken, commitment to act upon the recommendations emerging from the process. The second refers to lists of priorities and proposed actions (for different stakeholders, in this case e.g. university rectors and deans, regional, national and EU policy-makers, businesses and local communities as partners of universities), inputs for strategic planning (again, at different levels). The type of intended outcomes always depends on the objectives of an FLA project, i.e. if it is mainly a process-oriented exercise, a product-oriented one, or a mixed approach is taken. Acting upon the recommendations – e.g. strategy formation for a specific university, strategies for the higher education sector in a region, a country or the EU – is the competence and responsibility the decision-makers.

At a first sight, the so-called process benefits would be relevant mainly for FLA projects on a HE system. Indeed, disseminating a new, participatory, transparent, future-oriented decision-making method; bringing together various stakeholders (building new networks and/or strengthening/reshaping existing ones); facilitating their communication and co-operation, and hence contributing to building trust are important features at the level of larger systems. However, several of these benefits would be important at the level of a single university, too: even the 'internal' stake-holders – the teaching and administrative staff and students – are likely to need new fora, somewhat unusual and relaxed settings to meet and communicate in novel ways, and hence more effectively, let alone the communication and co-operation with the 'external' stakeholders (parents, policy-makers, businesses, NGOs, etc.) Also, implementing a new strategy for the university is likely to be smoother and more efficient when it is shared by its – 'internal' and 'external' – stakeholders.

49.4   'Cascading' Futures for Higher Education and Its Wider Contexts: An Illustration

Using universities in the EU as an illustration, this section offers 'cascading' futures for higher education and its wider contexts to rectify the shortcomings of single futures devised at the level of a university. Several factors shaping the future of universities – highlighted in Sect. 49.2 of this chapter – are international in their nature, while the legal competences to set policies are with the national or (sub-national) regional governments. The European Commission has launched several initiatives to align these regional and national policies.[12] Certainly, the EU itself is constantly evolving; triggered by political, economic, societal, and environmental driving forces, both internal and external ones. The existence and nature of various EU strategies would also affect the number and type of participants to be involved in FLA projects: the role and influence of university staff, students and the civil

---

[12]The most visible ones are the so-called Bologna process, the regular meetings of education ministers, as well as the other channels of the so-called open method of co-ordination. The Spring European Council meetings, assessing the progress towards the renewed Lisbon strategy, using several indicators on HE performance, can also influence national (or sub-national regional) HE policies. In an indirect – and less manifest – way, EC funded projects and expert groups on higher education can also affect these policies.

society at large, policy-makers or businesses might differ significantly in distinct 'futures' for the EU.

The starting point of the proposed multi-level prospective analysis is, therefore, the EU, as the broadest socio-economic context for the EU universities. Then futures are presented for the European Research and Innovation Area (ERIA), as the more direct setting in which EU universities co-operate and compete with other HE actors.[13] The huge diversity of the national (regional) education systems prevents a concise treatment of the national – and sub-national regional – level in the form of devising futures. However, some hints are offered for actual prospective analyses. Finally, futures are devised for universities.

Before building futures in this multi-level structure, the major underlying assumptions are explicated to avoid potential misunderstandings. First, as already stressed, policies can modify – e.g. speed up, slow down or 're-direct' – trends, and can also set off new developments themselves. Second, universities are embedded in their socio-economic environment. For these two reasons, various EU polices are considered here, especially the relative weight of competitiveness[14] and cohesion objectives in the overall strategies, as well as the more specific policies aimed at shaping the ERIA. Third, the interrelations between competitiveness and cohesion can be thought of in different ways: (i) as mutually exclusive goals (a 'zero-sum game', in which these policies are competing for the same set of scarce political, intellectual, organisational and financial resources); or (ii) as mutually reinforcing ones (a competitive, thriving EU generates enough funds to support cohesion regions, while narrowing the gap between advanced and laggard regions would enhance the competitiveness of the EU as a whole). The latter view is taken here, and thus a great significance is attributed to innovation processes in the cohesion regions/countries, as well as to the wide range of policies to promote innovation. Fourth, cohesion is an issue (a) inside the large, advanced EU member states (given the significant differences among their own regions), (b) for the four 'classic' cohesion countries, and (c) for the 12 new member states (the ones joined since 2004). In brief, cohesion has already been a major political and policy issue for the EU15, too, and given the recent and forthcoming enlargement(s) it has (and will) become even more accentuated. Fifth, promoting RTDI efforts in cohesion regions via joint research projects has not compromised scientific excellence (Sharp 1998). Sixth, a pronounced policy emphasis on cohesion does – and should – not preclude competition among universities.

As already stressed, the trends and their driving forces stemming from world regions would be important for non-EU countries, too, e.g. in Latin America, the

---

[13] Several major US and Asian universities are already operating in the EU, and their presence is likely to be more prominent due to the ever more fierce global competition for talents and funds.

[14] There is no widely accepted definition of competitiveness; and economists have dissenting views even on the appropriate level of analysis: if it is products, firms, value chains (production networks), (sub-national) regions, nations, or even larger entities, that is, world regions. This chapter simply accepts that several observers and politicians speak of competitiveness at the level of world regions, too.

NAFTA region, or South-East Asia. The proposed multi-level method, therefore, can also be tailored to these other regions, by identifying the relevant trends, policy initiatives, co-operation and competition modes, etc.

These simple, illustrative futures are presented here having two – somewhat ambitious – aims in mind: (i) to initiate a debate among FLA practitioners on the relevance and the feasibility of the proposed method; (ii) to offer some inputs for real-life prospective analyses.[15]

49.4.1   EU Futures

Several sets of multiple futures for the EU have been devised by various teams, mainly considering governance issues, that is, if the balance of decision-making competences between the members states (national governments) and the EU (the Commission, the Parliament, etc.) (i) remains largely as it is (at the time of writing), shifts significantly towards (ii) the national governments (or especially those of the larger member states), (iii) regions and cities, or (iv) the EU.[16] In some cases a possible shift is due to increased security threats and actual conflicts inside the member states and/or at the border of the EU.[17] That forces the EU to focus its attention and resources on foreign and security policy, and hence the large member states assume control, while the European Commission, the Parliament and other major EU-wide organisations lose importance.

Changes in governance across the levels of the EU, national and regional governments might have significant repercussions on HE, too. It is suffice to mention the Bologna Process in this respect. Hence, these futures for the EU might be relevant starting points for universities, national HE policy-makers or other stakeholders who want to launch FLA projects.

Another possibility to devise futures for the EU would be to consider (i) the substance of its overall policies, that is, its main strategic intention/orientation in terms of putting the main emphasis on cohesion (societal issues) vs. competitiveness, and

---

[15] Clearly, this chapter cannot assess the likelihood of the specific futures presented here. The modest aim is to sketch "consistent and coherent descriptions of multiple hypothetical futures that reflect different perspectives on past, present, and future developments, which can serve as a basis for action. They are tools for thinking about the future, which will be shaped partly through deliberate strategies and actions, partly by factors beyond the control of decision-makers" (OECD 2006, p. 1).

[16] The best known futures have been devised by the Forward Studies Unit of the European Commission (Bertrand et al. 1999), but see also Bertrand et al. (2000) and Labohm et al. (1998), as well as further ones listed at http://www.mcrit.com/espon_scenarios/visions_european.htm#EUROPE

[17] For example, a siege mentality might prevail, given widely spread political instability; regional conflicts, which could turn into civil wars; ethnically motivated guerrilla wars; terrorism; organised crime; and arms-dealing.

(ii) its performance vis-à-vis other major world regions (Havas 2007). Taking these aspects as 'binary variables', and combining their 'values', four fundamentally different futures can be derived:

- Future A) *Double success*: A carefully balanced development strategy of the EU – composed of (i) cohesion/welfare policies pursued in a flexible way, and using appropriate, refined policy tools and (ii) competitiveness policies – leads to an 'externally' successful and cohesive EU.
- Future B) *Successful multi-speed EU*: The already successful EU regions, perceived as 'engines of growth', are heavily promoted by EU policies, making them even stronger, leading to enhanced competitiveness of the EU vis-à-vis the other world regions. In the meantime, the gap between these successful EU regions and the less developed ones significantly widens, even inside the large member states.
- Future C): The EU development strategy is incapable of harmonising the requirements of competitiveness and cohesion; policies meant to support the latter are not effective, take up too much resource, and thus hamper the processes/actions needed to enhance competitiveness. Two 'variations' on this theme can be thought of:

  - Ca) *Shaky cohesion*: Temporary success in terms of stronger cohesion (at the expense of external competitiveness, and thus being shaky).
  - Cb) *Double failure*: Inappropriate strategies, insufficient co-ordination of policies, poor implementation, and/or external factors lead to an overall failure both in terms of cohesion and performance vis-à-vis the other world regions.

- Future D) *Failed multi-speed EU*: A multi-speed EU strategy fails to improve the performance vis-à-vis the other world regions, while it widens the gap between the advanced and less developed EU regions. The reasons for this failure can be numerous: e.g. internal (inappropriate policies and/or poor implementation), external (improving EU performance, but an even faster development of the other world regions). The former case is an 'absolute' failure, while the latter is a 'relative' one. Key players of strong EU regions would act together – probably also with their counterparts outside of the EU.[18]

None of these futures can be dismissed on logical grounds. Their likelihood, however, might differ a lot, and there is no sound method to predict which of them is most likely to materialise. Their main use as decision-preparatory tools is to present stark choices in terms of overall strategic objectives, and explore the repercussions of the strategic choices made now. In that way, these futures can inform present-day decisions, and also show the possibilities of shaping the future.

---

[18] For a more detailed discussion of these futures, see, Havas (2008, 2009).

49.4.2   ERIA Futures

The above different futures for the EU have strong implications for the ERIA, too. In principle, therefore, different types of ERIAs can be derived from them.[19] In practice, however, not all of them are equally relevant from a HE strategy point of view. Thus, to demonstrate the use of the proposed method, it is sufficient here to consider two EU-level futures when building ERIA visions: (a) *Double success* and (b) *Successful multi-speed EU*. Some of the main features of the types of ERIA 'fitting' to these two EU futures are presented in Table 49.1.[20]

Another potentially useful logic to devise ERIA futures is to consider governance issues in the domain of science, technology, and innovation policies, that is, the distribution of decision-making competences across the levels of the EU, the national and regional governments. Four stimulating futures have been built by the Europolis project following this logic: Lampedusian Europe, Swiss Europe, Federal Europe, and Round Table Europe (Europolis 2001). Again, these futures, and their implications, to be derived for – and tailored to the needs of – an actual university or a national HE reform during the respective FLA projects, would be highly relevant.

Table 49.1 Features of the ERIA in two EU futures: "Double success" vs. "Successful multi-speed EU"

ERIA ╲ EU	"Double success"	"Successful multi-speed EU"
Rationale for EU RTDI policies	"Double-track": tackle societal challenges, promote cohesion and enhance competitiveness	Excessive emphasis on enhancing competitiveness
Location of major HE and research centres	Widely distributed across the EU, weaker centres are strengthened, new ones are set up in laggard regions with a specific objective to promote cohesion	Concentrated in already strong, successful regions
Research agenda	An appropriate balance between societal and techno-economic issues	Focus on techno-economic issues; some research efforts to tackle social challenges stemming from the widening gaps between flourishing and laggard EU regions

(continued)

---

[19] ERIA is understood in this chapter as the set of the relevant RTDI actors, as well as their interactions. By making a strong link between the EU strategies on the one hand, and the ERIA, on the other, does not deny the possibility that 'ERIA policies' can enjoy some level of independence from the overall strategy of the EU. Yet, it would go beyond the scope of this chapter to discuss when this potential 'discrepancy' can be seen as a 'healthy, creative' tension, i.e. ERIA policies take the lead into the 'right' direction, and pull other policies, too; and when it is 'destructive' by hampering development and/or leading to waste of public resources.

[20] A more detailed discussion can be found in Havas (2007).

Table 49.1 (continued)

ERIA ⟍ EU	"Double success"	"Successful multi-speed EU"
Mobility of researchers, university staff and students	"Two-way traffic": gaining experience, building contacts in more advanced regions across the Triad, and then exploiting these contacts upon return to 'cohesion' regions via intense, mutually beneficial co-operation Mobility grants explicitly aim at nurturing talents for excellence in RTDI and competitiveness and fostering cohesion	"One-way street": brain-drain from laggard regions to booming ones Policy schemes aim at further strengthening strong regions via mobility grants "Two-way traffic" with strong Triad countries/regions
RTDI collaborations	Widely occurring across the EU and globally; policies aimed at promoting RTDI collaborations have an explicit aim of fostering cohesion, too, among other EU-wide issues	Mainly among strong, successful regions across the Triad, driven by businesses, supported by policies; laggards are left out
Innovation systems, co-operation among key players[a]	Strong, flexible innovation systems in a large number of regions (with their own specific strengths), capable of renewal and adaptation to the external environment, underpinning both cohesion and competitiveness Intense communication among businesses, academia, policy-makers, and the civil society to set RTDI priorities – relevant for cohesion and competitiveness –; strong academia-industry co-operation, mutually beneficial, intense links among large firms and SMEs in a large number of regions (gradually increasing over time) Co-ordinated, joint efforts – supported by EU funds – to strengthen weaker innovation systems, including communication, networking and co-operation among key players inside those regions and across regions	Strong, flexible innovation systems in the advanced regions, capable of renewal and adaptation to the external environment, underpinning sustained competitiveness Intense communication among businesses, academia, and policy-makers to set RTDI priorities relevant for enhancing competitiveness; strong academia-industry co-operation, mutually beneficial, intense links among large firms and SMEs both inside and across flourishing regions Ad hoc, weak communication and co-operation among the key players in laggard regions; weak RTDI policy constituencies Insufficient, half-hearted EU-supported efforts – at best – to strengthen weaker innovation systems of laggard regions/countries

(continued)

Table 49.1   (continued)

ERIA \ EU	"Double success"	"Successful multi-speed EU"
Financial infrastructure	Conscious EU efforts (policies, guidelines, networking, exchange of experience) to improve financial infrastructure across the EU	No conscious EU efforts to improve financial infrastructure in the laggard regions
Policy-preparation methods, practices	Conscious EU efforts (guidelines, networking, exchange of experience) to improve policy-making practices across the EU	No conscious EU efforts (guidelines, networking, exchange of experience) to improve policy-making practices in the laggard regions

[a]Co-operation with the relevant non-EU partners is taken for granted, i.e. not discussed here as a distinguishing feature

49.4.3   Hints for Devising Futures at a National Level

Given the diversity of the EU countries – in terms of the level of their socio-economic development, norms, values, methods and formal rules in their overall decision-making systems, the structure, funding, management and performance their HE system – it is simply not possible to devise HE futures at a national level in an 'abstract' way. Thus, only a few hints can be offered here, highlighting certain aspects, which are likely to be important in different HE systems.

In federal states, with important decision-making competences of the regions (e.g. in the UK and Germany) it is crucial to devise futures both at national and regional levels, giving more emphasis to that level, which is – or might become – more important for HE policies. Actually, multiple futures at these two levels can also explore the repercussions of a planned shift of HE decision-making competences between national and regional authorities, or the impacts of a more general political move (such as the devolution in the UK) on the HE system.

In countries with a centralised – overall or HE – decision-making system, futures at the national level would be sufficient, unless some stakeholders would be interested in exploring the feasibility and the repercussions of a decentralised system.

Advanced, more affluent countries, which are also likely to have an internationally recognised HE sector would benefit from national level futures focusing on different aspects compared to the ones of relevance for follower countries. For example, the role and mission of their universities are likely to be different, as well as the objectives and opportunities of their universities in international competition and co-operation, and hence different types of research infrastructures would be needed. These different needs and options necessitate different policy approaches and tools, and it should be reflected in the futures for these different HE systems.

Finally, there might be important differences between large countries with a broad portfolio of HE activities and small countries focussing their resources on a few universities specialised in certain fields of S&T. Just to take an example, there are relatively limited possibilities to study medicine in Norway. Keeping or changing this type of specialisation might be an important issue for Norwegian stakeholders, to be explored by multiple futures. From a different angle, that type of specialisation can be seen as an opportunity for other countries to attract foreign students (e.g. from Norway), but then the repercussions need to be reflected in their national-level futures (e.g. regulations concerning the admission rules and fees for foreign students, harmonising quality standards, courses, etc. with other countries; and non-HE issues should also be considered, e.g. supporting services, health care and housing for foreign students, and tackling potential cultural clashes).

49.4.4 Futures at a University Level

Taking into account the trends and drivers identified in Sect. 49.2, several futures for universities can be elaborated, depending on the extent to which the diversity of universities is to be reflected. A relevant method to deal with diversity is to identify ideal types. To keep the discussion simple and short, only two types of universities are considered here:

- Universities remain largely unchanged, performing the same functions in roughly the same organisational attributes;
- Universities reform themselves – or are reformed by other actors – radically by transforming their main functions and/or organisational attributes.

In other words, a sort of 'average' university is assumed when discussing *unchanged universities*: neither an extremely inward-looking, inflexible one, characterised by inertia and poor performance, nor a flexible, dynamic, highly successful, particularly active one in various networks – although we can find such universities at the extreme. *Radically reformed universities*, by contrast, are highly flexible, and thus adapt their courses, teaching and research approaches, as well as their organisational structures, managerial practices and other internal processes to the ever changing external environment, expressed by the needs of their 'clients' (that is, students, the wider research community, businesses, policy-makers and the civil society). They possess excellent 'navigation' skills to find their way in this complex world, often characterised by conflicting requirements of the various stakeholders.

In this logic, a third option – to emphasise the possibility for fundamentally different futures, and thus encourage 'outside the box' thinking – could be that universities disappear and their functions are assumed by new players, who perform their tasks/roles in radically novel and diverse ways (Havas 2007).

For an actual prospective analysis, aimed at assisting decision-making either at the level of universities, regional, national or EU (ERIA) policies, a much better refined set of ideal types should be developed. These other ideal types could include e.g. (i) 'elite' universities acting at a global scene, trying to push the boundaries of knowledge (and hence focussing on excellence in research and post-graduate teaching, at the expense of other types of courses and missions); (ii) national 'champions' concentrating on research and teaching relevant for preserving and advancing the national culture, contributing to enhanced economic competitiveness, and addressing other country-specific issues; and (iii) universities mainly serving the regional/national labour market, contributing to socio-economic development in their region via problem-solving projects and knowledge diffusion services, etc. at the expense of other types of research.

The aim of the above 'crude' typology is just to demonstrate that (a) different types of universities would act in different ways in the framework of the same ERIA; and (b) the same type of universities would behave differently – at least to some extent – when they are embedded in different socio-economic systems. In other words, this method can be understood as a sort of qualitative simulation. Thus, the method itself should not be judged by the choice of these simplified types of universities, taken as somewhat arbitrary 'inputs' for this qualitative simulation.

Tables 49.2 and 49.3 identify major changes in the external environment of universities – relying on multiple visions developed for the EU and ERIA – and explore the likely features of unchanged and radically reformed universities under those conditions.

Table 49.2 Driving forces and their likely impacts on universities: "Double success" case

Trends, driving forces	Largely unchanged universities	Radically reformed universities
The role/mission of universities	The main emphasis is on teaching and 'basic research' (science for the sake of science), not much interaction with other players in (regional, national, sectoral, international) innovation systems and with the society	A new balance of the main activities; and a new way to conduct them: intense interactions with other players in (regional, national, sectoral, international) innovation systems and with the society
	Universities do not understand/take on their role in addressing societal issues	New activities to promote cohesion among EU regions and enhance competitiveness in the meantime
	Increasing tensions between these 'traditional' universities and the societal and techno-economic requirements of an ERIA in the *Double success* EU	Universities understand the societal and techno-economic requirements of an ERIA in the *Double success* EU, and able to adapt to this new environment

(continued)

Table 49.2 (continued)

Trends, driving forces	Largely unchanged universities	Radically reformed universities
Competition for talents	Only a few 'world-class' EU universities can attract talents from advanced world regions Mindsets are against competition, measurement and evaluation – beyond the traditional academic indicators Inferior performance and a weakening position vis-à-vis the leading non-EU universities	A large(r) number of EU universities become attractive for talents from advanced Triad regions Universities focussing on serving regional/local needs do not pay attention to attract talents from other countries Competition, measurement and evaluation of performance is widely accepted Strong performance vis-à-vis the leading non-EU universities
Courses/degrees	Mainly 'traditional' courses/ degrees are offered, following a 'pure science' rationale; i.e. societal needs and competitiveness issues are largely neglected Shorter, more practical courses are missing or exceptional Life-long learning is perceived as a challenge to centuries-long traditions, and not taken as a great opportunity	Teaching programmes are balanced in terms of meeting societal and techno-economic (competitiveness) objectives Life-long learning becomes a reality; most universities across the EU are flexible enough to offer the right mix of longer (traditional) and shorter courses, adjusted to the new structure/balance of learning and working
Multi-disciplinary research and education/ training	*As for research:* a widely used practice, but conducted in the rationale of 'pure science': the complexities of societal issues and competitiveness are not addressed; the full potential of multi-disciplinary research is not exploited *As for education:* slowly becomes a more widely used practice, but also limited to the logic of 'pure science'	*As for research:* A widely used practice; particularly relevant for universities to play their societal role by better understanding the close relationships between societal and techno-economic issues, as well as by offering these new types of insights for other actors *As for education:* becomes a widely used practice. Students are trained to understand the close relationships between societal and techno-economic issues/challenges
Integration of RTDI activities (across national borders)	Only a few 'world-class' EU universities can join global networks at the forefront of RTDI activities The majority of universities are only interested in 'basic research' projects, isolated from innovation processes	Widely occurs across the EU and globally; policies aimed at promoting the integration of RTDI activities have an explicit aim of fostering cohesion, too Reformed universities actively participate in these co-operations

Table header: Universities — Trends, driving forces

Table 49.3 Driving forces and their likely impacts on universities: "Successful multi-speed EU"

Trends, driving forces	Universities / Largely unchanged universities	Radically reformed universities
The role/mission of universities	The main emphasis is on teaching and 'basic research', not much interaction with other players in innovation systems and with the society Some of the 'elite' universities put emphasis only on enhancing competititveness	Emphasis on enhancing the competitiveness of businesses; all activities serve this goal; close co-operation with businesses
Competition for talents	Same as in the *Double success* case	Same as in the *Double success* case
Courses/degrees	Same as in the *Double success* case	Teaching programmes put emphasis on meeting techno-economic (competitiveness) objectives at the expense of societal challenges Life-long learning is a daily practice mainly in the advanced EU regions; in the laggard ones it is available for, and requested by, only a tiny share of citizens. Universities located in the advanced regions are flexible enough to offer the right mix of longer (traditional) and shorter courses, adjusted to the new structure/balance of learning and working. Most universities located in the laggard regions are not prepared/flexible enough to offer these "mixes" of courses.
Multi-disciplinary research and education/training	Same as in the *Double success* case	Multi-disciplinary research is pursued in a limited sense: mainly integrating disciplines relevant for tackling techno-economic (competitiveness) issues (i.e. somewhat neglecting societal issues) Multi-disciplinary education: same logic as for research

(continued)

Table 49.3 (continued)

Trends, driving forces / Universities	Largely unchanged universities	Radically reformed universities
Integration of RTDI activities (across national borders)	Same as in the *Double success* case, except: Some EU universities actively participate in cross-border RTDI activities, aimed at further enhancing the competitiveness of the advanced regions	Mainly among strong, successful regions inside and outside the EU, driven by businesses, and supported by EU policies; laggards are left out 'Elite' EU universities are active partners in these processes, the ones located in laggard regions seek partners in the advanced regions (not paying attention to the cohesion needs of their own home region)

49.5   Summary and Recommendations

Sweeping changes are already occurring in the HE sector, and further far-reaching and fundamental shifts can be expected due to financial, technological, and demographic factors, as well as the emergence of new HE and research actors. In the meantime, the broader socio-economic environment of HE organisations is also undergoing thorough and wide-ranging transformations. The very notion of education, knowledge and research is being redefined. Stakeholders are reshaping science-society links, and thus new societal demands emerge for universities. Further, the principles of the so-called new public management (accountability, transparency, efficiency and effectiveness, responsiveness, as well as forward look) are posing new requirements for HE policy-makers and managers.

Universities cannot stand still amidst these sea changes; on the contrary, they need to face new realities, either simply by reacting, or taking the initiative in a pro-active way. Indeed, a strong consensus appears to be emerging on the need for major reforms. These reforms, in turn, should be underpinned by relevant prospective analyses. Hence, the practice observed in some potentially highly influential analyses and recommendations by leading academics, as well as in EC policy documents where no discussion is devoted to describe a desired and feasible future state is not a satisfactory basis for any policy decision.

Given the diversity of HE organisations themselves, as well as that of their broader context, in which they operate, it would be a gross mistake to search for a unified, 'one size fits all' solution. On top of that, the methodologies applied for guiding strategy-building processes are also diverse. Thus a conscious, well-considered decision is needed when selecting methods for prospective analyses. To assist this preparation, this chapter has highlighted three methodological choices to be made when planning FLA projects: (i) single vs. multiple futures; (ii) the level of analysis; and (iii) the level of participation. Having considered the costs and benefits of the various options, it has argued that the advantages of devising multiple futures in a multi-level structure, relying on participatory processes, would outweigh the costs, and thus it is worth taking the extra efforts and time needed.

First, a single future cannot reflect that HE is characterised by intricate interactions among the already visible trends, coupled with driving forces potentially causing discontinuities in the future. In such a world multiple futures are needed to assist decision-making processes. In this way not only the huge diversity of higher education systems and individual universities can be reflected, but the likely impacts of different policy options can also be explored. Second, as universities operate in broader socio-economic systems, and the bulk of trends and driving forces are international in their nature, multi-level – or 'cascading' – futures need to be constructed to explore the potential changes of these wider settings, as well as their impacts on higher education. Third, by involving different stakeholders with their diverse sets of accumulated knowledge and experience, as well as distinct viewpoints and approaches, participatory FLA projects are likely to significantly enrich strategy preparation processes. Further, the shared vision and policy recommendations, stemming from the dialogue among participants, offer a basis for faster and more efficient implementation. Futures developed by small groups of experts cannot possibly lead to these process benefits. Their work, however, could yield novel methods and/or analytical insights on the substance, which, in turn, can be exploited in strategy dialogues.

The proposed method can be of relevance in other world regions, too, considering their own salient features. It can be extended to public research organisations, too, operated either in the EU or other Triad regions.

Prospective activities of universities should be promoted by organising awareness-raising events at regional, national, and international levels. Exchanging experience among FLA practitioners is also desirable, as well as promoting strategic dialogues among the stakeholders, and initiating pilot FLA projects on HE. National governments, international organisations, and associations of universities can provide methodological and financial support for these initiatives.

Finally, a pragmatic observation needs to be stressed. As always, context does matter: countries with a more or less similar history, facing similar challenges on the whole and being broadly at a similar level of development can opt for different FLA approaches. The same applies to universities seemingly sharing major characteristics. It all depends on the perceived strategy challenges and options (e.g. whether multi-level analysis is needed to address them), as well as on the people who are key to the success of an FLA project: if decision-makers strongly favour a certain approach, it might not be a good idea to try to push through a drastically different programme design – even if it might seem to be relevant from an abstract theoretical/methodological point of view.

However, in most cases FLA projects are also learning processes – not only on the methods themselves, but also on the perceived needs to be tackled by FLA, and the values and norms of the participants –, and by definition, learning would change the way of thinking of the participants (to a different degree, and at a different pace, though). Further, as already stressed, participatory processes are likely to trigger systemic changes, too. Keeping these in mind, FLA projects can also be launched pursuing these very broad process benefits as secondary objectives – or even primary ones – besides aiming at deriving strategy advice.

Acknowledgments This chapter draws on a report (Havas 2007) prepared for the expert group on *The Future of Key Research Actors in the European Research Area*, financed by DG Research, EC, two articles based on various parts of this report (Havas 2008, 2009), as well as on discussions on forward looking activities with colleagues, who generously shared their insights. (Naming just a few of them would be unfair, while naming all of them would result in too long a list.) Comments on earlier versions by Andrea Bonaccorsi, Elie Faroult, János Gács, Annamária Inzelt, Fabrice Roubelat, and the participants of various workshops are gratefully acknowledged.

References

Aghion, P., Dewatripont, M., Hoxby, C., Mas-Colell, A., & Sapir, A. (2007). Why reform Europe's Universities? *Bruegelpolicybrief*, issue 2007/04. http://www.bruegel.org/publications/publication-detail/publication/34-why-reform-europes-universities/. Accessed 6 Oct 2011.

Bertrand, G., Michalski, A., & Pench, L. R. (1999). *Scenarios Europe 2010: Five possible futures for Europe* (p. 119). Brussels: Forward Studies Unit, European Commission.

Bertrand, G., Rood, J. Q. Th., Labohm, H. H. J., Michalski, A., Pench, L. R., & van Staden, A. (2000). *Scenarios Europe 2010–2020: Possible futures for the union.* http://webhost.ua.ac.be/psw/pswpapers/PSWpaper%202000-07%20bertrand.pdf. Accessed 7 Oct 2011.

Bonaccorsi, A. (2007). Researchers (Part 2). In *The future of key research actors in the European research area – Working papers* (EUR 22962, pp. 53–70). Luxembourg: Office for Official Publications of the European Communities.

Bonaccorsi, A., & Daraio, C. (Eds.). (2007). *Universities and strategic knowledge creation: Specialization and performance in Europe.* Cheltenham: Edward Elgar.

Dosi, G., Freeman, C., Nelson, R. R., Silverberg, G., & Soete, L. (Eds.). (1988). *Technical change and economic theory.* London: Pinter.

EC. (2003, February 5). *The role of universities in the Europe of knowledge.* Communication from the Commission, COM(2003) 58 final. Brussels.

EC. (2007). *The European research area: New perspectives. Green paper.* COM(2007) 161.

Edquist, C. (Ed.). (1997). *Systems of innovations: Technologies, institutions and organizations.* London: Pinter.

EG. (2010, June 16). *Manifesto: Empower European Universities. Expert group on European Universities.* http://www.chanceforuniversities.eu/images/stories/manifesto_version20100617.pdf. Accessed 7 Oct 2011.

EUROPOLIS. (2001). The European research area: A new frontier for Europe? *la lettre OST* No. 22.

Fagerberg, J., Mowery, D. C., & Nelson, R. R. (Eds.). (2005). *The Oxford handbook of innovation.* Oxford: Oxford University Press.

Freeman, C. (1994). The economics of technical change: A critical survey. *Cambridge Journal of Economics, 18*(5), 463–514.

Georghiou, L., & Harper, J. C. (2006, September 28–29). *The higher education sector and its role in research: Status and impact of future-oriented technology analysis.* Anchor paper for the Second International Seminar on Future-Oriented Technology Analysis: Impact of FTA Approaches on Policy and Decision-Making. Seville. http://foresight.jrc.ec.europa.eu/fta/documents/anchor/HigherEdAnchorPaper.pdf. Accessed 6 Oct 2011.

Georghiou, L., & Harper, J. C. (2008). The higher education sector and its role in research: Status and impact of international future-oriented technology analysis. In C. Cagnin, M. Keenan, R. Johnston, F. Scapolo & R. Barré (Eds.), *Future oriented technology analysis: Strategic intelligence for an innovative economy* (pp. 115–129). Berlin/Heidelberg: Springer.

Havas, A. (2007). Universities. In *The future of key research actors in the European research area – Working papers* (EUR 22962, pp. 87–118). Luxembourg: Office for Official Publications of the European Communities.

Havas, A. (2008). Devising futures for universities in a multi-level structure: A methodological experiment. *Technological Forecasting and Social Change, 75*(4), 558–582.

Havas, A. (2009). Universities and the emerging new players: Building futures for higher education. *Technology Analysis and Strategic Management, 21*(3), 425–443.

Kehm, B. M. (2006, March 23–24). *Governance and strategy.* Paper presented at a workshop on Driving Forces and Challenges for the European University, Brussels.

Labohm, H. H. J., Rood, J. Q. Th., & van Staden, A. (1998). *'Europe' on the threshold of the 21st century: Five scenarios* (p. 58). Den Haag: Clingendael Institute.

LERU. (2006). *Universities and innovation: The challenge for Europe.* League of European Research Universities. http://www.leru.org/files/general/Universities%20and%20 Innovation%20The%20Challenge%20for%20Europe%20(November%202006).pdf. Accessed 7 Oct 2011.

Lundvall, B.-Å., & Borrás, S. (1999). *The globalising learning economy: Implications for innovation policy.* Luxembourg: Office for Official Publications of the European Communities.

Nelson, R. R. (2004). The market economy, and the scientific commons. *Research Policy, 33*(3), 455–471.

OECD. (1998). New rationale and approaches in technology and innovation policy. *STI Review, 22.*

OECD. (2006, June 27–28). *Four futures scenarios for higher education.* OECD CERI, presented at the meeting of OECD Education Ministers, Athens.

Ritzen, J., & Soete, L. (2011). *Research, higher education and innovation: Redesigning multi-level governance within Europe in a period of crisis* (UNU-MERIT Working Papers, #2011-056).

Rosenberg, N. (1996). Uncertainty and technological change. In R. Landau, T. Taylor, & G. Wright (Eds.), *The mosaic of economic growth* (pp. 334–353). Stanford: Stanford University Press.

Rosenberg, N. (1998). Technological change in chemicals. In A. Arora, R. Landau, & N. Rosenberg (Eds.), *Chemicals and long run economic growth* (pp. 193–229). New York: Wiley.

Sanz-Menéndez, L. (2007). Regional governments. In *The future of key research actors in the European research area – Working papers* (EUR 22962, pp. 207–229). Luxembourg: Office for Official Publications of the European Communities.

Sharp, M. (1998). Competitiveness and cohesion – Are the two compatible? *Research Policy, 27*(6), 569–588.

STRATA-ETAN Expert Group. (2002). *Higher education and research for the ERA: Current trends and challenges for the near future.* http://cordis.europa.eu/documents/document library/66638171EN6.pdf. Accessed 7 Oct 2011.

Thorne, M. (Ed.). (1999). *Universities in the future.* London: Foresight, OST, DTI.

van der Ploeg, F., & Veugelers, R. (2008). Towards evidence-based reform of European universities. *CESifo Economic Studies, 54*(2), 99–120.

Vincent-Lancrin, S. (2006). What is changing in academic research? Trends and futures scenarios. *European Journal of Education, 41*(2), 169–202.

von Hippel, E. (1988). *The sources of innovation.* Oxford: Oxford University Press.

Chapter 50
Systemic Foresight for Romanian Higher Education

Liviu Andreescu, Radu Gheorghiu, Marian Zulean, and Adrian Curaj

50.1 Introduction

It appears incontrovertible that change in higher education is today urgently needed, widely desired, or at least insistently and loudly talked about almost all over the world appears incontrovertible. More surprisingly, this seems to be the case in spite of the fact that postwar higher education (HE) has already been going through major structural changes for more than half a century. At the same time, the long process of higher education "massification" has substantially weakened the traditional legitimacy of these institutions (Trow 2006a). For several decades, higher education institutions (HEIs) have been struggling to find the appropriate vocabulary and practices in terms of which to justify their business, while being continuously asked to do more things for more people for less money. This predicament seems to have left universities and their bases scrambling for the appropriate terms in which to define their roles and functions – in the present and, it seems, especially for the future.

The Romanian experience of the last two decades is no different. Despite important and occasionally even radical changes (such as an eightfold increase in student numbers), higher education in this country is still facing a double deficit – a traditional lag by comparison with Western HE, often widening as university systems around the globe strive to adapt to new contexts. After 20 years of inconsistent

L. Andreescu (✉)
Spiru Haret University, Bucharest, Romania
e-mail: andreescul@gmail.com

R. Gheorghiu
Institute for World Economy, Bucharest, Romania

M. Zulean
University of Bucharest, Bucharest, Romania

A. Curaj
Politehnica University, Bucharest, Romania

A. Curaj et al. (eds.), *European Higher Education at the Crossroads:*
Between the Bologna Process and National Reforms,
DOI 10.1007/978-94-007-3937-6_50, © Springer Science+Business Media Dordrecht 2012

reforms, education in Romania was evaluated as excessively homogenous (Miroiu and Andreescu 2010), as well as – and quite bluntly – as "ineffective, irrelevant, and low in quality" (Presidential Commission 2007). While the Bologna Process has provided an important opportunity and some added impetus for systemic change, several of its core elements and principles were implemented incompletely or pro forma. The lack of a systemic approach to change in higher education has generated a mélange of reforms but, more importantly, has resulted in the absence of a clear vision of the future bearings of Romanian higher education.

In this chapter we discuss a systemic foresight exercise on the future of Romanian higher education that was conducted between 2009 and the end of 2011. Our interest is not primarily in the substance of the exercise but in its structure, and in particular in the way the project's design responded to what we refer to herein as the wicked problem of higher education reform. To set the context for this systemic exercise, in Sect. 50.2 we provide a brief outline of this problem in the broader context of contemporary discourse about higher education; and we discuss briefly the state of higher education reform in Romania. Section 50.3 offers a summary justification for the appropriateness of structural foresight, and specifically of a systemic exercise with large participation, as a response to the issues raised by change in higher education. Section 50.4, the most extensive of the article, discusses the structure of the process itself. This ample discussion is followed, in Sect. 50.5, by a brief outline of the main challenges encountered in the process, in particular that of maintaining coherence throughout the exercise, and their broader implications on participatory foresight. The final section offers our succinct conclusions.

Before we proceed any further, it bears repeating that – and explaining why –, on the whole, the article says relatively little about the contents of the exercise at its core. Our chief goal is to outline the design of an intensively participatory systemic foresight exercise on higher education; and to justify the decisions made in this design. For this reason, we discuss the context – ideological and otherwise – of the exercise and its structure, as well as some of the challenges we encountered, but ignore many of its results. We did not feel compelled to explore in additional depth this substance (which, to be sure, was there), because this was considered inessential to our goals, though it may have been interesting for other purposes. This being said, we do occasionally introduce substantive considerations, though mainly in order to explore the manner in which substance affected procedure and, ultimately, turned our exercise into a living, evolving, adapting thing.

50.2 The Wicked Problem of Higher Education Reform in a Changing Society

The discourse on the functions and roles of higher education at the present time remains sufficiently plural, but it seems that a dominant discursive thread has emerged both without and, more debatably, within the academe. The notion that universities must somehow adapt to and/or enable the flowering of the so-called "knowledge society" has become a by now a familiar mantra of higher education reform, embraced by decision-makers and academic administrators alike, as well as by many academics and – presumably, though hardly evidently – by the newly anointed "consumers" of higher education services. The face-value appeal of this discourse, which seems simultaneously forward-looking (it speaks of tomorrow), pragmatic and utilitarian (it invites change now and promises immediate bene-fits), and friendly to universities (after all, it is about "more knowledge") is unde-niable. However, as we claim below, knowledge society discourse about higher education has not sufficiently contributed to the appreciation of the wicked problem(s)[1] of university reform, and, indeed, may have advanced unwelcome simplifications.

The relevance of the concept "knowledge society" to the field of higher educa-tion is immediately obvious in the very wording of the phrase. Traditionally, knowl-edge has been the province of universities more than of any other (Western) institution, so the common and rarely questioned assumption seems to be that in the knowledge society universities must also play a central role – a normative claim which, in this context at least, is all the more problematic because of its intuitive plausibility. A further normative claim is made simultaneously: that in order for higher education institutions to play such a central role, they have to radically rethink the ways they go about their business, particularly since the knowledge soci-ety is said to be significantly different from former societal models. This suggests that the term "knowledge society" is ambiguously descriptive and prescriptive at the same time. Knowledge-society discourse does not simply depict the state of the world at the present time, but also sets policy objectives for nation states as well as supra- and sub-national entities (Välimaa and Hoffman 2008, p. 266). Often cast as "the global panacea to economic policy", universities occupy an increasingly cen-tral position in this imaginary knowledge society and, as a result, "governments

---

[1] A neat definition of a "wicked problem" is offered by Loveridge's (2009, pp. 18–19) discussion of "situations": "Problems are usually presented as being well structured or of becoming so given enough attention; this is typical of the reduction process used in much of conventional science. Reduction has been usurped into other endeavors, e.g. social studies, Economics, Politics, where it has never been appropriate even as its appropriateness in scientific inquiry has been modified. Perhaps the most unfortunate aspect of reductionism … lies in the assumption that a problem solved is a problem 'done with', a product of the application of compartmentalization, typical of the organization of science, teaching, government, companies and much of human societies: it is this defect that directs attention to situations and not problems. Situations are neither solvable nor well structured in the manner expected of problem solving. Instead, situations can be recognized from their many elements and their interrelatedness, and their apparent lack of structure. Well-specified causal relations may be present, but may not dominate, leaving many interrelationships to depend on the appreciative setting or behavioral pattern … of the appreciators. … As a further characteristic, the insoluble nature of situations means they are dynamic, occur in cascades and are never 'done with' (according to problem solving), but simply change their context and content after every intervention, appearing to become unrecognizable from their initial form over a period of time, though the initial form remains buried in the stream of new contexts."

around the world, in both advanced and developing economies, are restructuring education systems, often in transparent terms that reflect the new policy template of the 'knowledge economy'" (Peters and Humes 2003, p. 1).

Higher education reform has therefore been an essential part of knowledge society discourse both because universities are called on to enable and help consolidate the emerging society; and, slightly paradoxically, because higher education institutions are often seen as somewhat resistant to changes in their established modes and patterns of knowledge acquisition, processing, and delivery. It is sometimes asserted and often implied that the new forms of knowledge that underlie the new society (the so-called "know-what" and "know-why", for example) have taken shape largely outside or at the periphery of the academic environment. Similarly, "Mode 2" knowledge (collaborative, inter-disciplinary, pragmatic, reflexive, socially-aware), which is said to be replacing "Mode 1" knowledge (theoretical, abstract, cloistered, generated by autonomous disciplines), is usually perceived as something that has coalesced, in a considerable part, without or at the fringes rather than at the core of the university.

In tandem with these claims concerning the transformation of knowledge, knowledge society discourse also advances several more mundane prescriptions. It calls on HEIs to train the "human capital" on a large scale, a mission in relation to which the "massification" of higher education, an older but ongoing trend, is convenient because it fosters the "democratization of expertise" at the heart of the new society.[2] The universities of the near and more distant future are expected both to embrace new forms of knowledge, including the technologies and principles supporting them (knowledge communities, e-learning, virtual delivery, and so on), and to advance these technologies and forms of knowledge. The "separation of educational content from its delivery" (Williams 2007, p. 519), for instance, is often seen as key to the mass-delivery of customized education, while the scalability of e-learning is regarded as one of the great promises of the new technologies in the field of education for its ability to facilitate lifelong access. As *The Economist* optimistically puts it, technology is poised to be "a core differentiator in attracting students and corporate partners" (*The Economist* 2008, p. 4).

According to this view, higher education should equip the knowledge worker of the new economy with flexible, adaptable skills (rather than with abstract knowledge and overly specialized competencies), and primarily with the ability to "learn

---

[2] This is, of course, a trend as old as industrialized modernity itself. As Ernest Gellner noted several decades ago, "the major part of training in industrial society is *generic* training, not specifically connected with the highly specialized professional activity of the person in question, and *preceding* it. Industrial society may by most criteria be the most highly specialized society ever; but its educational system is unquestionably the least specialized, the most universally standardized, that has ever existed. The same kind of training or education is given to all or most children and adolescents up to an astonishingly late age. … The kind of specialization found in industrial society rests precisely on a common foundation of unspecialized and standardized training." (Gellner 2006, p. 26)

how to learn" – hence the twin concept of a "learning-intensive society" (Miller 2004).[3] HEIs are also expected to recognize that the boundaries between formal and non-formal education are increasingly irrelevant in the knowledge economy and to capitalize on this realization in order to change their traditional structures. Along the same lines, knowledge society discourse typically emphasizes the blurring of the traditional distinction between universities and other organizations providing various types of education, as well as the increasing competition between not-for-profit and commercial providers. This too is expected to disrupt traditional organizational patterns in higher education, and, as a result, an increasing emphasis has been placed on adaptability (Sporn 1999), on the resulting differentiation within academic ecosystems (Huisman 1995; Teichler 2008; Morphew 2009), as well as, in a more prescriptive vein, on the "entrepreneurialization" of the university (Slaughter and Leslie 1997; Clark 2004) as essential for a strong academic environment making crucial contributions to national economies.

As sketchily summarized above, knowledge society discourse has been very convincing as an expression of a general mood, one dominated by the sense that something has to change as far as higher education is concerned. However, beyond conveying this vague imperative, this type of discourse has arguably failed to offer a deeper understanding of the ways in which the wicked problem of higher education reform may be tackled. The outlines of this problem are familiar from organizational theory, which already in the 1960s and the 1970s started paying more attention to educational institutions as an organizational type that, rather than being relegated to the fringes of a field of inquiry fixated on the business firm, provided a useful corrective to the latter in suggesting that all organizations are, in fact, complicated creatures.

It is not the place here to detail the interesting relationship between these trends in organizational sociology and the field's interest in educational institutions, though it bears remarking that many important theories were either directly or indirectly indebted to studies of the latter. More significantly for our purposes, these studies yielded a litany of widely accepted observations that, together, add up to what we have called here "the wicked problem of university reform". In a nutshell, organizations in higher education are characterized by a dual and ambiguous locus of organizational authority (professionals and administrators); by vague and ambiguous organizational goals which command general adherence no further than the point at

---

[3] Miller (2004, p. 43) defines the context of a learning-intensive society thus: "The shift away from uniform products forces the addition, at different points in the production process and drawing on different inputs, of new knowledge (or at least new for those involved). 'Inventiveness' is constantly, as opposed to intermittently, required. Certainly, the work undertaken in the 'industrial era' production processes, characterized by a division between conception and execution, always demanded skill and considerable understanding. What is distinctive about a 'learning intensive economy', should it come to pass, is that the dividing line between conception and execution dissolves."

which they need to be operationalized; by the nebulous nature of organizational technologies; by isomorphic pressures due to professional norms in a strongly institutionalized field; by twin commitments – organizational and disciplinary – on the part of academic professionals, and so on (Birnbaum 1991). The matter is complicated by such hallowed norms as professional autonomy and, specifically, individual and institutional academic freedom, which ensure that the role of government in higher education is perpetually undergoing a crisis of legitimacy. Indeed, this crisis is compounded by the fact that governments are hardly in a better position than universities in their claims to democratically represent, before higher education institutions, beneficiaries' interests in or views on educational matters.

This organizational dimension of the wicked problem of higher educational reform has been exercising thinkers and policy-makers for decades now, and knowledge society discourse has not decisively advanced our understanding on how reforms should reconcile professional norms, broader societal values, individual aspirations, and economic needs. Rather, it seems to have introduced several simplifications, often camouflaged in populist claims of accountability and responsibility (Harvey 2009). In conveniently marrying the administrative philosophy of the New Public Management (NPM), knowledge society discourse has typically urged academic institutions to respond directly to market needs, rely on market mechanisms, accommodate stronger leadership and streamline governance structures, embrace quality assurance systems and a new "culture of accountability" – the very issues at the core of the wicked problem of change in higher education.

While obviously cognizant of these complications, the new managerialism has often glossed over the complex nature of higher education reform. It has perpetuated the knowledge society discourse's ambiguities about universities and society, calling on the former to follow a trend or set of trends which seem to have originated outside them, yet championing their role in the avant-garde of the new society. The tensions inherent in this view of universities both as drivers and as providers of the knowledge society have never been convincingly resolved. (Not even rhetorically: the country which gave us NPM has been scolded for its unfriendliness to its universities (Trow 2006b).) Neither has knowledge society discourse satisfyingly answered the matter of how universities can become more entrepreneurial (more responsive to the needs of "the market") without both vigorous governmental intervention (sometimes euphemistically called "steering" in order to avoid the discredited "planning") and governmental appropriation of the role of defining what the beneficiaries – the "consumers" – actually need. If anything, knowledge society discourse has only helped bring into sharper focus the wicked problem nature of university reform.

Romania's efforts on changing higher education over the past two decades serve as a case in point. Everybody understands there is a need for change and even that change is afoot. But behind the variety of reform discourses, including the knowledge society variety, a sure sense of direction has so far been absent. As a result, some of the major structural problems have been growing in intensity. The relationship of universities to the labor market remains fuzzy and invites a lot of skepticism, especially as many graduates are not active in the profession for which they were trained or, if they are, they rely little on the knowledge and skills obtained during college years.[4] There is a growing discontent with the poor showing of academic research (mention is often made of the fact that this country does not have a single university in the Academic Ranking of World Universities' top 500). And there is growing concern over the loss of some traditional academic market niches, such as that of foreign students coming to study in Romania.

As a result, caught in a special dynamics of rapid "massification" and amplifying competitiveness gap, tertiary education in this country has been trying to respond to two not always consistently tackled reform imperatives. The first has been to catch up with the successful academic systems in (Western) Europe. The second has been to respond to the challenges outlined in the first part of this section, usually with explicit reference to the knowledge society. These imperatives are, of course, hardly conflicting (after all, the most successful university systems in Europe have been pursuing the second goal themselves), but following them at the same time and as if they were indistinguishable may have added to the general confusion and, ultimately, may have contributed to the failure of the reform. For instance, some of the policies pursued in Romania were inspired by Western academic solutions or practices that were themselves in the process of being altered or discarded – a typical effect of the double gap.

As a result, the efforts to change higher education after 1990 have resulted in a lengthy but inconsistent process, lacking sustained, general commitment as well as, in many cases, a systematic approach to change – in short, lacking an all-encompassing vision. Enthusiasm for reform has been waxing and waning, depending on the determination of the ruling parties, on their relation with various factions of the academic establishment, on the country's economic prospects, and, last but not least, on the persona of the education minister. Academic reform over the past 20 years has been characteristically driven by political decision and, indeed, used to buttress the general image of the ruling party as either "reform-friendly" or, by contrast, "anti-reformist" (Miroiu et al. 1998, p. 20).

The systematic reforms proposed as a part of several projects supported by international bodies or programs (the World Bank, PHARE) were either implemented at a relatively slow or uneven pace (the case of funding) or remained perpetual desiderata (the case of academic management). Some may have been too radical for their day, or at least couched in terms that seemed too radical. The reforms were often unaccompanied by an understanding of their likely impact on other areas of academic policy (for instance, per capita funding for universities has been heavily criticized for its allegedly dramatic effect on systemic homogeneity and academic quality). Moreover, periods of relative coherence in and heightened commitment to

---

[4] A study published by the Executive Agency of the National Council for Qualifications and Professional Training for Adults (UECNCFPA) shows that graduates believe that only about one third of their skills and knowledge were attained during their undergraduate studies, as opposed to the 55% obtained at their place of work. Furthermore, for 76% of the employers in this study it did not matter whether a potential employee had an M.A. degree besides the B.A. or not (UECNCFPA 2010, p. 5).

reform, such as the late 1990s, were followed by anti-reform or "reform-of-reform" phases, often freezing old developments in their tracks or toning down the changes. While the Bologna process has provided an important opportunity and added some impetus for systemic change, several of its core principles have been implemented incompletely or pro forma (the case, for instance, of the ECTS – the European Credit Transfer System). All the while, a consistent and widely accepted vision for Romanian higher education has been missing from the picture.

After two decades of failed reform, then, what Romanian higher education needs is a vision of its future that should guide and govern coming changes. The timing for such a vision is right also because, as it has become increasingly evident, the prevalent knowledge society discourse has been successful in creating an expectation of change. Such a change would require, in its turn, an image of the future of higher education which is more specific and more robust than many of the generic "visions" usually put forward by the knowledge society discourse itself. Indeed, a vision for Romanian higher education should be the product of a process enabling its participants to move beyond the confines of said discourse, which by now has been mostly reduced to a set of generic ideas confiscated by the reform establishment. Such a vision would provide an opportunity to do justice to the insights of recent perspectives on tertiary education without becoming their prisoners.

To fulfill this role, a credible vision of Romanian higher education should be future-oriented and set itself a sufficiently generous horizon, so as to inform long-term reforms and guide short- and medium-term policies. It should involve wide participation as a response to the complexity of the higher education system, as a way of moving beyond officially-sanctioned reform discourse, as well as in order to generate the requisite legitimacy for change. The vision should be systemic so as both to rise to the epistemic challenge of the wicked problem of tertiary education reform and to facilitate the complex management of the knowledge generated in the process. And, lastly, the vision should be systematic, that is, translate the systemic approach into a coherent set of consultative exercises and methodologies.

The project blueprint we discuss below was designed to deliver precisely such a vision, on the basis of a systemic foresight exercise. Before introducing the project in more detail, we comment briefly on the advantages of foresight in our specific context.

50.3 The Need for a Systemic Approach

As a policy-making paradigm, foresight has developed out of a growing awareness of the complexities facing decision-makers and of the limits inherent to the common understanding of expertise. Foresight is expected to bring several important contributions to the field, among which to inform policy (by improving the knowledge base and supplying anticipatory intelligence); to facilitate policy implementation (by developing strategy and policy through reflexive learning processes and systemic instruments); to embed participation in policy-making and thus enhance transparency and legitimacy; to support policy definition; to reconfigure the policy system (by highlighting the contradictions between future issues and current mindsets); and to signal to the public that decision-making is based on a rational process (Da Costa et al. 2008, pp. 373–376).

At least in its more recent incarnations – those which Miles et al. (2008) classify as the "fifth generation" –, foresight is frequently conceptualized as a holistic approach to public policy and, as such, it seems well equipped to tackle higher education as a complex system. In the postwar period and especially after its pervasive "massification", higher education has become an all-encompassing system which directly and indirectly touches the life of almost every citizen. As previously noted higher education is multi-layered, relies on a web of intricate relationships between actors claiming a variety of sometimes clashing "stakeholder interests" in the fate of the system, and involves perpetually contested claims of authority over various provinces or processes.

Identifying directions of transformation in higher education is therefore, by its very nature, a problem that is neither well structured, nor susceptible of a tidy rational "solution" (Loveridge 2009, p. 18). With its focus on overcoming some of the key drawbacks of traditional policy-making – the short-term outlook of politicians, the undisclosed agendas of experts, the relevance of expert advice, information overload, or the clash of cultures among policy actors –, foresight's commitment to "transmitting complexity" (Da Costa et al. 2008, p. 372) represents an attractive prospect in the context of higher education reform. Additionally, fifth-generation foresight promises to bring together experts "working alongside stakeholders and those with foreseeing skills" in extensive systemic consultations (Miles et al. 2008, p. 17). The ability to "identify where different bodies of knowledge, different professions, disciplines and stakeholders need to be drawn together" (EFILWC 2003, p. 7) seems particularly relevant given the nature of higher education's wicked problem.

A second reason for the appeal of foresight in the context of higher education derives from the more specific significance of university autonomy and academic freedom – both as entrenched, change-resistant patterns of and limits to organizational governance and as wide-ranging and time-honored principles governing the self-perception and behaviors of academic and extra-academic actors. University autonomy and academic freedom spell out the limits of centralized approaches to reform. However, unlike traditional forms of centralized policy-making which are primarily reactive and/or predictive, foresight promotes an activist approach to the future. On the one hand, it implies "deep understanding" and "the ability to [...] spot developments before they become trends, to see patterns before they fully emerge, and to grasp the relevant features of social currents that are likely to shape the direction of future events" (Tsoukas and Shepherd 2004, p. 2). On the other, foresight encourages creation of the future rather than mere adaptation. It is essentially reflexive, contingency-aware (it probes for weak signals and anticipates responses to unforeseen events), and exploratory, involving an important imaginative, creative component. Foresight blends an element of programmatic disruption designed to release the creative energies often stifled by conventional thinking about the future with the formation of extensive communities of practice.

This combination of extended participation and creative energy seems particularly useful in higher education because it meets a triple condition for change in the field: it acknowledges the pre-eminence of professional participation and lends a bottom-up dimension to the process; it simultaneously challenges the ossification of professional norms and expectations; and it encourages the questioning of the dominant assumptions of policy-makers usually perceived as being engaged in a top-down effort. The collective learning-by-doing component of foresight, which is intrinsic to its participation-intensiveness, thus implies the recognition that systemic change depends on mutually reinforcing transformations at multiple levels, both institutional and social.

Foresight has been used with some success in the past in the case of complex systems in which knowledge and innovation play a central role, in this country too (e.g., in developing Romania's research and development strategy). With its system-view approach to "situations", its reliance on widespread participation and consultation, its potential for creative departures from stock assumptions, and its ultimate goal of a shared vision on higher education, foresight holds an attractive prospect. This being said, the sheer complexity of the task, the inherent intricacy of stake-holder interaction in the context of wide participation, and the limitations of foresighting methods entail a number of challenges, both theoretical and practical. Foresight can only go so far, and both its appeal and some of its limitations are apparent in the project we discuss in the remaining parts of this paper. In the next section we offer the project blueprint as a possible model for systemic foresight for higher education, taking into account the specific nature of higher education's ill-structured problems. In the section after that we comment on some of the main structural challenges encountered in the implementation of the project and on their relevance beyond the project itself.

50.4   A Design for a Systemic, Participatory Approach to Change in Romanian Higher Education

The lack of a systemic approach to change in Romanian higher education has generated not only patchwork reforms (carried out in some domains and delayed or never enforced in others), but also the absence of a clear understanding of the implications of sectoral changes on other policy areas in tertiary education. Moreover, assuming the need for a re-conceptualization of higher education, it is apparent that a traditional systematic approach to reform may not be sufficient at the present time.

The project Quality and Leadership for Romanian Higher Education (QLHE), carried out in 2009–2011 by the Executive Agency for Higher Education, Research and Innovation Funding (UEFISCDI) and its partners,[5] was designed to respond to

---

[5] These partners include the National Council of Rectors (Romania), the Romanian Academy, the Romanian Agency for Quality Assurance in Higher Education, the Fraunhofer-Gesellschaft zur Forderung der angewandten Forschung e.V (Fraunhofer ISI) – Foresight Group, the Institute for Prospective Technological Studies (IPTS), the UNESCO-European Centre for Higher Education, the European Universities Association (EUA). More information is available on the project's portal, www.edu.2025.ro.

both challenges above. It set out to offer a vision of Romanian higher education in 2025 in the hope that a comprehensive approach would ensure both the necessary systemic perspective and the desired freedom to rethink higher education. From the onset, the project was set up as a large-scale dialogue designed to mobilize a critical mass of university representatives and stakeholders in order not only to develop a set of instruments and documents, but also to generate the requisite level of consensus and the energy for transformation. In this respect, the so-called "process benefits" of foresight exercises (Martin 2001) have been envisaged not as an extra, but as a precondition for success.

The focal point of the dialogue has been the Vision meant to provide a desirable – and desired – image of Romanian higher education in 2025 based on explicit value statements and on an associated policy document covering a shorter time horizon (2015). The vision which resulted from the dialogue produced several core values, specifically the personalization of education (as a reflection of persons' modern search for individuality), a diversity of institutions and programs (as the tertiary system's answer to students' and employers' need for personalized services), and transparency and reputation mechanisms (as key elements enabling informed choices and as important feedback instruments for the universities). The ensemble of this desired world is fleshed out in the vision document through imaginary stories from 2025 concerning students, professors, researchers, and universities and university clusters. (Figure 50.1 provides a synthetic description of the main participatory elements and of the flow of knowledge as consolidated by the end of the process. Still, the picture shows little of the dynamics of the dialogue and even less of the extent to which, once matured, the dialogue raised new challenges to the process as originally envisaged.)

In order to better grasp the challenges encountered in this very large participatory process on the future of higher education, we will take a step back and look into the literature exploring the generic, phase-based structure of a foresight exercise. We will then attempt to highlight the problems encountered in each stage and briefly introduce our solutions, which were informed by expertise and a variety of practices from other exercises throughout the world, yet also involved new, fit-for-purpose adjustments and, above all, derived from our involvement with what was, ultimately, a learning process.

As noted, fourth- or fifth-generation foresight exercises are typically divided in phases. For their part, Da Costa et al. (2008, p. 379) propose five: a diagnosis phase wherein experts and policy-makers reflect on the current state of the system; a more participatory phase of scenario-building and "exploration"; a phase of strategic orientation with limited participation; a choice-making phase of public debate, and an implementation phase wherein options are translated into policy. In the specific context of transition management, van de Kerkhof and Wieczorek (2005, p. 736) suggest a somewhat similar policy-making framework: the organization of a multi-actor network; the development of sustainability visions; the exploration of transition pathways (scenarios); and the evaluation and monitoring of the progress, goals, and learning process.

Although the foresight exercise that is the subject of this article is structurally compatible with the blueprints above, we discuss it below in terms of the five principles of systemic foresight defined by Saritas as part of his "Systemic Foresight" method, the aim of which is to generate "a creative inquiry that will be engaged in

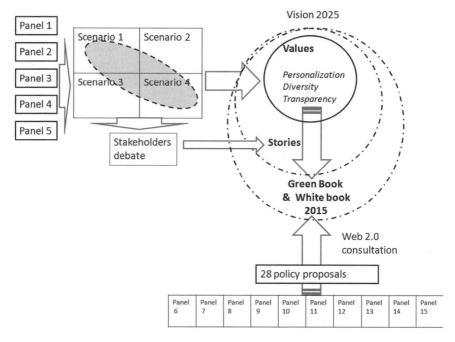

Fig. 50.1 Main participatory and substantive elements generated in the process

designing a future system to fulfill goals and expectations" (Saritas 2006, p. 182). His five "pillars" – which we would more accurately describe as "phases" – of systemic foresight are as follows: systemic understanding (generating a shared understanding and mutual appreciation of the issues at hand by uncovering uncertainties about values, choices and the environment, and clarifying the goals of the activity); systems synthesis (processing the input derived from scanning into conceptual models of the situations involved in the real world); systemic analysis and selection (analyzing and prioritizing alternative models of the future to create a generally accepted model); system transformation (tracing relationships between the future scenario and the present one, with an eye to a future change program); and systemic action ("the operational level, where 'What-how', 'Where-how' and 'Who-how' questions are asked") (Saritas 2006, pp. 183–86).

50.4.1 Systemic Understanding

In our interpretation within the framework of the project, systemic understanding involves chiefly a process of pragmatic positioning towards the system and its problems. In this phase of QLHE, we aimed at rendering explicit fundamental premises and basic assumptions by reaching a more or less general acknowledgement among participants with respect to the sets of issues which Romanian higher education is currently facing. To achieve this kind of "understanding" of the system of higher education two pilot streams were devised which were subsequently integrated in a system diagram. The first involved brainstorming sessions and literature review for the identification of the topics of interest, while the second aimed at the systemic identification of experts and stakeholders. A chief goal of this "scanning phase" was to generate sets of relevant themes which should eventually be inter-correlated and validated by a group of High Level Experts (HLEG).

Three brainstorming sessions involved students, professors, and businesspersons. Each session was based on an electronic communication platform (iLab), was facilitated, and followed established brainstorming methodology: generate a space of creativity through facilitated interaction; generate a flow of creative ideas (group members contributed ideas but no comments were allowed initially); generate a flow of comments (members commented or asked for clarifications); and prioritize ideas through a voting mechanism. The iLab platform ensured close interaction during these stages, as each participant's input was visible to all others (on a screen) while anonymity was fully preserved. Anonymity ensured a smooth voting process in which the most prominent issues among the many generated were selected.

Literature review involved the creation of an online database of relevant literature, which eventually grew to over 600 distinct titles. Some 150 books were consulted in an analysis which sought to identify the key concepts subject to debate according to the volumes' abstracts. A subsequent analysis by means of a combined *Tropes* & *Zoom* software, which offers complex linguistic analysis based on occurrences as well as on linguistic relationships, was used to single out the most frequent and relevant concepts in the literature on higher education.

Finally, a viral questionnaire was designed to serve in the identification of the relevant experts and stakeholders for the project. Respondents were asked to identify other persons and/or institutions which have either an interest in, or the relevant competences for, contributing to debates on the future of Romanian higher education. The nominated individuals were then asked to (co-)nominate other persons or institutions. The viral questionnaire included points such as self-assessment of interest in the issues at hand; institutional involvement in higher education; personal experience in the field; and data on nominated individuals. The questionnaire started from a database of roughly 10,000 names of academic decision-makers, academics, and researchers. The 1,932 respondents[6] nominated a total of 8,845 individual persons and 6,353 institutional representatives. The results of this survey stayed at the core of a comprehensive database, which enabled the mobilization of the community throughout the project (for panels, workshops, focus groups, conferences, online consultations). As it was continuously expanded, the database came to

---

[6] Out of the respondents, 85% held a PhD or equivalent degree, and 26% were high-ranking decision-makers in their respective institutions.

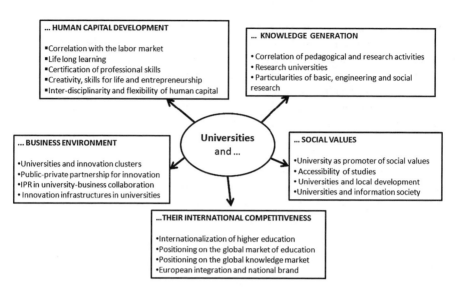

... HUMAN CAPITAL DEVELOPMENT
- Correlation with the labor market
- Life long learning
- Certification of professional skills
- Creativity, skills for life and entrepreneurship
- Inter-disciplinarity and flexibility of human capital

... KNOWLEDGE GENERATION
- Correlation of pedagogical and research activities
- Research universities
- Particularities of basic, engineering and social research

... BUSINESS ENVIRONMENT
- Universities and innovation clusters
- Public-private partnership for innovation
- IPR in university-business collaboration
- Innovation infrastructures in universities

Universities and ...

... SOCIAL VALUES
- University as promoter of social values
- Accessibility of studies
- Universities and local development
- Universities and information society

...THEIR INTERNATIONAL COMPETITIVENESS
- Internationalization of higher education
- Positioning on the global market of education
- Positioning on the global knowledge market
- European integration and national brand

Fig. 50.2 Five broad policy areas relevant to Romanian higher education

comprise, by the end of the process, more than 4,000 persons with complex data, including their involvement into the process.

50.4.2 Systems Synthesis

The second pillar of systemic foresight synthesizes the input derived from scanning into conceptual models of the situations involved in the real world. In our construal, this involved reaching a coherent set of representations of the system of higher education and its parts, and apprehending the relations and causalities therein. The synthesis stage was thus designed to offer an understanding of the current state of Romanian higher education, of its current problems and of anticipated challenges. The input into this process consisted of the list of relevant topics generated during the "system understanding phase" above (and the expert database). Five broad areas germane to the actual state of Romanian higher education were validated by the HLEG (Fig. 50.2) and served as the basis for a set of analyses delivered by five expert panels, each consisting of some 12–15 members of the policy community. The areas/panels were: the university and human capital development; the university and knowledge; the university and the business (eventually, socio-economic) environment; the university and values; the internationalization of the university. The output of each expert panel would later serve as the basis of a debate with higher education stakeholders.

Each panel was asked to deliver a set of documents: a diagnosis of Romanian higher education in the specific context of the panel's area of interest (including a

SWOT analysis and a discussion of internationally relevant issues in the field); an analysis of drivers of change at the horizon 2025 (defined as the manifest, emerging trends expected to influence, in terms of both limitations imposed and opportunities offered, the development of HE); a policy matrix containing a tentative set of policies for each panel's governing theme, and a stakeholder analysis (with stakeholders selected according to an abilities/interest/impact matrix).

Eventually, only four panels delivered the full set of analyses and reports, and these were the only ones to be directly involved in the following stages of the QLHE process. Some of the fifth panel's output was partly integrated into the subsequent work of the other four.

Working side by side with the four panels, a sixth panel of experts strove to provide a systemic picture of the Romanian higher education system, to serve as a general diagram of its structure.

50.4.3   Systemic Analysis and Selection

The third phase involved an apprehension of the dynamics of the system. It has been the most creative stage in the process as well as – and accordingly – the most complex and sensitive, yielding a number of relevant challenges to systemic foresight (to be explored in the following section).

Systemic analysis and selection involved the generation and analysis of alternative models of the future and their prioritization through consultations with actors and stakeholders. The process consisted of a scenario-framework phase (during which scenario frames were created with the involvement of the four remaining expert panels), followed by a debate with stakeholders on the resulting frames and then a final consolidation stage in which the pre-existing output was structured to serve the policy stage.

To generate scenario frames, each of the four expert panels was asked to elaborate, starting from the materials generated during the previous stage, a set of ten challenges for the future of Romanian HE. Challenges were defined either as gaps (relative to the situation in EU or OECD countries) or as future threats and opportunities. These challenges served primarily as an input for a scenario workshop[7] in which the panels and their invited stakeholders developed a 2025 scenario framework each. For the purposes of this exercise, a scenario was defined as a coherent, simplified representation of the higher education system in 2025, specifically as the image of a desirable future (rather than a prediction of what the future would look like). The scenario-making process involved a clarification of the premises (the development of society and the economy in general) and of the role the higher education is expected to play in 2025. The scenario workshop was

---

[7] The workshop was held in Sinaia in December 8–11, 2009.

designed as a collaborative process in which the members of the expert panels and the invited stakeholders worked together and in breakout groups, with more than 70 individuals participating. A number of foreign scenario experts/facilitators were brought in to co-design and facilitate the process partly because of their proven expertise and partly because it was felt that foreign facilitation would help defuse possible tensions among some participants. The workshop served the purpose of generating a set of alternative views of higher education in 2025 which should then be further elaborated; as well as the more diffuse but no less important goal of engendering inter-subjective knowledge which should be assimilated by the participating actors and stakeholders.

This scenario-elaboration phase was followed by a process of consultation with stakeholders. A lot of the knowledge produced during the scenario-framework-development phase remained tacit rather than explicit and diffuse rather than concentrated. The scenarios themselves were designed as simplified and subjective "framework images". Hence the problem of getting stakeholders who had not participated in the scenario-development stage to at least partly buy into and further elaborate the frameworks. To resolve these problems, the scenario-elaboration process, which aimed at an ample debate with the stakeholders, involved some of the participants in previous sessions and, crucially, made use of a few well-established communication techniques designed to generate the desired level of involvement and controversy.

The stakeholder debate took the form of a 4-day workshop in which each panel involved approximately 50 stakeholders.[8] Each group of stakeholders met for a 1-day event to discuss the relevant scenario. To facilitate participant assimilation of the scenario frameworks, the latter were not delivered as such. Rather, a set of up to a dozen key statements were selected from each individual scenario and turned into a set of playing cards (one set for each scenario) to be used in a Scenario Card Game. The game involved debates on each set of cards and then successive augmentation of the set with potentially relevant cards from other scenarios and with custom cards designed on the spot by the participants. To increase interactivity, the card game was combined with the World Café technique (in which all participants except for a table-host repeatedly switch tables to disseminate ideas and viewpoints), as well as with role-playing. Eventually, each group (table) of participants during each 1-day event was asked to elaborate a metaphor describing the universities of the future. Then all participants in each session voted on the metaphors, and the three most desirable ones were subsequently discussed and fleshed out in separate groups. A total of 12 metaphors describing the future of Romanian higher education were generated based on the pre-existing scenario frameworks.

The scenario-building process, which involved several hundred participants, generated a very large amount of material: four scenario frameworks and three corresponding fleshed-out metaphors for each, as well as a lot of considerable

---

[8] Held on January 24–29, 2010 in Bucharest.

additional content (interviews with table hosts, drawings on the paper tablecloths, card arrangements etc.).

It became evident during the process that such a vast amount of material would have to be consolidated in order to provide a consistent basis for the coming "system transformation" phase. As a result, the project team and several international experts reworked the scenarios and the metaphors into one single, coherent, though still simplified framework for the 2025 vision. During this process, one of the four original scenarios served as a meta-scenario providing the bird's eye view, the ecology, and the principles of Romanian higher education in 2025. This so-called "Blue Ocean" scenario envisioned a diverse HE system populated by a multiplicity of "institutional animals" competing not for the "whole ocean" but for a variety of smaller or larger niches. It was, in effect, a scenario of systemic diversity.

The other three scenarios and the associated metaphors described the institutional types populating this system, as well as some general governing principles – such as the integration of life, education and work, and the customization of learning. Three "institutional examples" (tentatively dubbed Scientia, Inovatio, and Regio) for 2025 were eventually described in detail in the form of institutional mini-scenarios, intended to serve together as a framework for the vision and a reference point for the policy actions to be devised in the next phase. While not being institutional archetypes properly speaking, the three stories served as a proxy for the large dialogue around system transformation.

50.4.4   System Transformation

The system transformation stage aimed to trace the relationships between the desirable future scenario and the present. It was part and parcel of the process of designing "specific interfaces for translating outcomes from the collective process into policy options" (Da Costa et al. 2008, p. 378).

The major challenge encountered at this point was that of creating a wide debate on policy issues. The major stumbling block was the lack of expertise in policy development on the scale we envisaged originally. Our solution was to press for a community approach and a gradual expansion of consultations. As a result, we first created panels for policy development whose members were selected on the basis of expertise and representativeness and were supported by training and other assistance in policy formulation. The dialogue between panel members was subsequently expanded through a web 2.0 interaction involving communities of practice identified through a viral survey.

More specifically, a set of ten broad policy areas relevant to higher education today were identified by an initial group of experts. The policy areas were further discussed and refined together with the project's High Level Expert Group, which made a number of recommendations for the members of the ten expert panels associated to the ten policy areas. (Eventually, the number of panels was reduced to nine.[9]) The task of the expert panels was to provide a number of general policy recommendations and to test their relevance in relation to the picture of the desirable future.

Each of the panels consisted of some six experts and a panel coordinator. After receiving training in policy-proposal formulation – which also provided a common policy proposal template –, they were asked to interact online and in a number of policy-setting meetings. Each panel produced three broad policy proposals connecting the present with the desired future; the proposals included justifications and expected impact on the scenario. The policy proposals and justifications served as the basis for an online consultation process roughly taking the form of a Policy Delphi exercise (Turoff 1970) involving a much wider group of experts and key actors in a participatory setup. The goal of the consultation was to optimize the policy proposals of the panels in light of the desirable picture of the future, specifically by evaluating the fit between the former and the latter. The design of the consultation, which we dubbed "eLPHI", involved a set of nine online two-round consultations concerning the nine pre-existing sets of policies elaborated by the panels. The nine questionnaires consisted each of a presentation of the desirable future scenario (in terms of the three institutional mini-scenarios described above, together with a background story of the future HE system); the three policy proposals designed by the relevant panel connecting the present with the desired future; a list of pre-defined values which purported to measure the impact of a policy on an institutional mini-scenario; a field where participants could either introduce a brief argument justifying the selected impact of the relevant policy on an institutional mini-scenario, or select a pre-existing argument; and a field for participants' own policy proposals and other comments. The participants in the Delphi survey were identified by the panels themselves starting from the repository of experts and stakeholders developed during the process. Each panel invited about 600 participants, around a quarter of whom responded.

In the first round of the eLPHI, the participants were asked to evaluate the impact of each policy on the desirable future scenario, specifically on each of the three institutional mini-scenarios, taking into consideration the outline of the broader scenario on the future HE system. This assessment was both quantitative (an estimate of the positive, neutral or negative impact on a scale) and qualitative (justifying of the quantitative assessment by selecting one of the dynamically ranked arguments already in the list or by adding new ones). During the second round, each participant who submitted an online form and whose response was outside a predefined range from the mean was asked to revise or maintain, after consulting the updated list of arguments, the original estimate and to explain the reasons for his or her decision.

After the extended eLPHI consultation, the panels were asked to revise their policy proposals in light of the results of the consultation. The resulting policy

---

[9] The nine panels were Governance, Leadership, Management; Research, Innovation, and Intellectual Property Protection; Academic Profession; Regional and Local development; Knowledge Society; Ethics and Social Values; Globalization/Internationalization; Qualifications and Competences; and Quality of Education. Each of the panel had three or four associated subthemes.

proposals then served, together with the desirable scenario, in the construction of the Vision on Romanian higher education for 2025. This inspirational document outlined three broad principles guiding the future of higher education in this country – personalization, diversity, and transparency.

50.4.5   Systemic Action

The systemic action phase details the plans informing present-day decisions for immediate change aimed at generating structural and behavioral transformations. The QHLE project presented here only makes a few initial steps into the field of systemic action – except, perhaps, if one subscribes (as we do) to the view that, in foresight, the process *is* one of the main outcomes.

Broadly speaking, the systemic action phase consisted of the elaboration of two policy documents with a shorter time-horizon (2015) to accompany the 2025 Vision. These two policy documents are, firstly, a Green Paper on Romanian higher education, designed to serve as an intermediate step in the development – through another round of extensive consultations – of, secondly, a White Paper on Romanian higher education in 2015. The consultations on the Green Book were carried out through an online questionnaire addressed to roughly 14,000 persons (out of which some 400 responded). Just like the Vision, of which it is a short-term operationalization, the White Paper is based on the desirable scenario and the associated set of policy proposals.

In accordance with the principles of the vision (i.e. personalization, diversity, transparency), the White Book proposes a combination of policies meant mainly to generate a functional adaptation of the universities and their stakeholders. On the one hand, it encourages universities to grasp the full potential of the existing systemic freedoms by modulating their services to better target their constituencies. On the other hand, it supports the informed choice of those potentially demanding HE services by developing credible reputation mechanisms. Both dimensions rely not only on immediate coordinated actions, but also on leadership from the part of universities and on active search on the side of beneficiaries. That is why the Vision and the White Book have been complemented by a set of leadership training sessions for university decision-makers, as well as promoted through a Blueprint for foresight in universities (Curaj 2010). In addition, a social networks campaign for the younger generations was created. It includes short movies or profile-based questionnaires inviting respondents to explore options for studying in 2025.

50.5   Challenges and Some Lessons Learned

As far as systemic foresight methodology is concerned, several challenges stood out during the "systemic analysis and selection" (scenario elaboration) and "system transformation" stages of the process. We will briefly discuss below four such challenges. The initial three were raised during the scenario elaboration stage; the fourth problem was generated during the system transformation phase.

One important challenge involved the difficulty of representing a complex system without oversimplification, a problem compounded by the fact that the higher education system is a multi-layered one involving many types of actors. Often, these numerous, diverse actors engaged in various stages of the foresight process do not speak a common language. In order to reach a shared appreciation of the system and its issues, they frequently have to make recourse to substantial simplifications. Participants often select compromise options or solutions, sometimes with the sense that they are *unduly* simplifying, simply because they need to reach some sort of agreement or conclusion, which is thus in a sense forced on them by the process. The newer-generation foresight approaches, with their insistence on widespread and diverse participation and consultation, amplify this problem.

Secondly and directly related to the matter above, it has proven difficult to maintain shared representations of the system while enlarging the circle of participants in consecutive phases. Images of the higher education system were often described in terms that were generic as well as subjective, and the subsequent involvement of additional participants – in order to expand on the existing content, for instance – sometimes seemed to pay too little attention to the subjective meanings of those who generated the original output. More broadly speaking, ensuring the portability of content generated throughout the process to subsequent phases, with considerably more and/or different participants, has been one of the major challenges we encountered.

Given the two issues above, it seems that achieving a degree of inter-subjectivity among participants remains a key issue in a systemic foresight exercise. This usually involves a number of trade-offs: between the extensiveness of the consultations and their intensiveness; between the narrative depth of scenarios and their capacity of being easily assimilated or internalized by successive waves of participants; between descriptive detail and intuitiveness. In the case of QLHE, the management of inter-subjectivity entailed sustaining a strong narrative orientation (relying heavily on stories and especially on stories conveyed through drawings) and on community-oriented communication (World Cafe, Web 2.0 platforms etc.)

A third challenge also emerged prominently in the context of what we have called here the "system analysis and selection phase": given the higher education focus of the exercise, the tertiary education system occasionally seemed to take over the future of society completely. Therefore, the boundaries of the system have often appeared unclear – everything seemed more or less a part of higher education, and higher education itself seemed a part of everything else. Furthermore, the process has been very university-centric in the sense that, for instance, no alternative images of the future society arising from the complex scenario-making exercise assigned higher education as-we-know-it a limited or peripheral role. Very much in keeping with traditional knowledge society discourse, at least in the views of the QLHE participants universities will still be at the core of the knowledge generation process of tomorrow.

This may simply be an accurate reflection of the inexorable role and function of higher education in the future; or it may be a failure of the imagination of those participating in the project (which would be unsurprising given the degree of internalization of knowledge society discourse). Or, more troubling perhaps, it could be an artifact of the projects' design, which may itself have been too centered on the academe. Naturally, it may be that this university-centrism has been a combination of the factors above.

Given the strong path dependencies inherent in such a complex project, decisions to eliminate or compensate for a possible academe-centric bias could not be made after the possibility of such a bias was recognized. But it would be advisable for systemic foresight exercises, at least those involving such pervasive systems as (higher) education, to include "sidetracking" devices or processes that should induce participants to at least envisage or examine a more marginal or limited role for the systems or processes which are the subject of the exercise.

The final stages of the scenario exercise brought to the fore another general methodological issue. The fact that, in a systemic foresight exercise, scenarios are supposed to act normatively generates some confusion concerning the role played by modeling. Models provide an image of the system and its dynamics, but they do not themselves generate the scenarios. The latter are representations of the future achieved at least partly independently of the modeling process. How, then, are we to interpret the relationship between system modeling and scenario construction?

Models suggest possible paths for change and they reduce the number of possible futures to a limited and manageable range. Scenarios, on the other hand, are specifically designed to move beyond the limitations set by the modeling process – otherwise one would simply be doing forecasting according to a number of alternative methods. Scenarios, that is, also require an initial leap of faith. Once this leap of faith is taken, however, systemic foresight typically involves a return to the system model in order to explore the ways in which the future(s) relate(s) to the present. Yet is this not, actually, a way of introducing the constraints of the model – or of modeling more generally – through the backdoor? In seeking robustness in terms of the present, are we not dumbing down supposedly disruptive future scenarios?

50.6   Conclusions

Higher education in Romania, as in virtually all developed societies, has been gradually moving toward the core of socio-economic development. This process not only increases the pressure for delivering, but also multiplies the interconnections with the society, on the one hand, and with the internationalized tertiary education sector, on the other. In response to this growing complexity, systemic foresight provides a framework for a coherent dialogue about future options and the corresponding actions. However, in this context, the systemic approach needs to be understood in terms of the inter-subjective knowledge evolving in the policy community and less in terms of simple representations of the system and its dynamics. Indeed, one of the most telling experiences of the exercise discussed in this article has been the close connection between its structural and procedural design and the substantive content produced.

The participants in the Romanian foresight exercise managed to create a space of shared knowledge, establishing a fairly common language and making explicit a set of challenges as subjects for exploration. The open nature of the dialogue underscored the diversity embedded in the process and diminished the need for a reductionist consensus. Eventually, this procedural diversity spilled into a substantive value at the core of the higher education system itself, and "diversity" was assumed by the 2025 Vision as one of the three functional principles of the future Romanian HE.

The tension between the explorative and the normative dimensions of the scenario-making and visioning processes similarly infiltrated the nature of the recommended policies. Specifically, this tension resolved itself into a natural balance of freedom-oriented, leadership-oriented, and responsibility-oriented policies.

While the process started by following a broadly pre-defined procedural backbone, as the dialogue grew, the nature of the content became more and more constraining for the structure of the dialogue itself. As a result, the latter had to be continuously adapted. Given the large participation, the process has gradually mixed with a communicational campaign based on fit-for-purpose instruments in which positions, stories and mobilization blended. In the end, *the vision is a growing rumor*.

Acknowledgments We wish to thank the several reviewers and respondents to an earlier draft of the article, and particularly Mert Bilgin, Jim Dator, Riel Miller, Fabrice Roubelat, and Ziauddin Sardar.

References

Birnbaum, R. (1991). *How colleges work: The cybernetics of academic organization and leadership*. San Francisco: Jossey-Bass.

Clark, B. (2004). *Sustaining change in universities: Continuities in case studies and concepts*. Maidenhead: Open University Press.

Curaj, A. (Ed.). (2010). *THE FOR-UNI BLUEPRINT: A blueprint for organizing foresight in universities*. Bucharest: Romanian Academy Publishing House.

Da Costa, O., Warnke, P., Cagnin, C., & Scapolo, P. (2008). The impact of foresight on policy-making: Insights from the FORLEARN mutual learning process. *Technology Analysis & Strategic Management, 20*, 369–387.

EFILWC. (2003). *Handbook of knowledge society foresight*. Dublin: European Foundation for the Improvement of Living and Working Conditions.

Gellner, E. (2006). Nations and Nationalism. 2nd ed. Oxford: Blackwell Publishing.

Harvey, L. (2009). Democratising quality. In L. Bollaert et al. (Eds.), *Trends in quality assurance* (pp. 5–9). Brussels: European University Association.

Huisman, J. (1995). *Differentiation, diversity and dependency in higher education*. Utrecht: Lemma.

Loveridge, D. (2009). *Foresight: The art and science of anticipating the future*. New York: Routledge.

Martin, B. R. (2001). Matching societal needs and technological capabilities: Research foresight and the implications for social sciences. In *Social sciences and innovation* (pp. 105–116). Paris: OECD.

Miles, J., et al. (2008). The many faces of foresight. In L. Gheorghiou et al. (Eds.), *The handbook of technology foresight: Concepts and practice* (pp. 3–23). Cheltenham: Edward Elgar.

Miller, R. (2004). Imagining a learning intensive society. In J. Coolahan (Ed.), *Learning in the 21st century: Towards personalisation* (pp. 27–74). Dublin: Information Society Commission.

Miroiu, A., et al. (1998). *Invatamantul romanesc azi*. Iasi: Polirom.

Miroiu, A., & Andreescu, L. (2010). Goals and instruments of diversification in higher education. *Quality Assurance Review for Higher Education, 2*, 89–101.

Morphew, C. (2009). Conceptualizing change in the institutional diversity of U.S. colleges and universities. *Journal of Higher Education, 80*, 243–269.

Peters, M. A., & Humes, W. (2003). Education in the knowledge economy. *Policy Futures in Education, 1*, 1–19.

Presidential Commission. (2007, July 06). *Romania educatiei, Romania cercetarii*. Retrieved August 3, 2011, from http://edu.presidency.ro/upload/raport_edu.pdf

Saritas, O. (2006). *Systems thinking for foresight*. Unpublished Ph.D. thesis, Manchester University.

Slaughter, S., & Leslie, L. (1997). *Academic capitalism: Politics, policies and the entrepreneurial university*. Baltimore: Johns Hopkins University Press.

Sporn, B. (1999). *Adaptive university structures*. London: Jessica Kingsley.

Teichler, U. (2008). Diversification? Trends and explanations of the shape and size of higher education. *Higher Education, 56*, 349–379.

The Economist. (2008). The future of higher education: How technology will shape learning. Retrieved July 2, 2011, from http://www.nmc.org/pdf/Future-of-Higher-Ed-(NMC).pdf

Trow, M. (2006a). Reflections on the transition from elite to mass to universal access: Forms and phases of higher education in modern societies since WWII. In J. J. F. Forest & P. G. Altbach (Eds.), *International handbook of higher education* (pp. 243–280). Dordrecht: Springer.

Trow, M. (2006b). Decline of diversity, autonomy, and trust in British education. *Society, 43*, 77–86.

Tsoukas, H., & Shepherd, J. (Eds.). (2004). *Managing the future: Foresight in the knowledge economy*. Oxford: Blackwell.

Turoff, M. (1970). The design of a policy Delphi. *Technological Forecasting and Social Change, 2*, 149–171.

UECNCFPA. (2010). *Absolventii recenti de invatamant superior si integrarea lor pe piata muncii*. Retrieved October 1, 2010, from docis.acpart.ro/uploads/Fisiere/05__rezumat_ studiu_18_01_2011.doc

Välimaa, J., & Hoffman, D. (2008). Knowledge society discourse and higher education. *Higher Education, 56*, 265–285.

van de Kerkhof, M., & Wieczorek, A. (2005). Learning and stakeholder participation in transition processes towards sustainability: Methodological considerations. *Technological Forecasting and Social Change, 72*, 733–747.

Williams, P. J. (2007). Valid knowledge: The economy and the academy. *Higher Education, 54*, 511–523.

Chapter 51
Re-imagining the Role and Function of Higher Education for Alternative Futures Through Embracing Global Knowledge Futures

Jennifer M. Gidley

51.1 Introduction

Higher education as it currently operates in most of the world is more suited to the nineteenth century industrial era than it is to the twenty-first century. Yet so much has changed in the past 100 years, not just in terms of external developments, but also in terms of how we think and how we know. This paper identifies emergent signs of evolutionary change in human thinking that run parallel with many of the exponential changes manifesting in the external world. Futures studies provide a macro-temporal framing for these changes by exploring the last 100 years in order to prepare for the next 100 years. Weak signals from the early twentieth century indicate the emergence of new ways of thinking and knowledge patterns, which will be key drivers of change in the next 100 years. The new ways of knowing are referred to in the psychological literature as postformal reasoning, and include creativity, imagination, dialogue and the ability to handle paradox.

Throughout the twentieth century, and increasingly in the last 40 years, significant developments can be mapped in most, if not all, of the major academic disciplines. New ways of thinking within the disciplines of science, philosophy, psychology and education will be discussed. In parallel, there is an emerging movement to integrate knowledge, to move beyond the fragmentation of knowledge associated with disciplinary specialisation via inter-, multi-, and trans-disciplinary approaches. Transdisciplinary approaches such as futures studies and planetary/global studies will be discussed. In spite of these strengthening developments within and across many disciplines and knowledge fields, the institution of mass education, designed for the industrial era, has been pretty static since the onset of the industrial revolution.

J.M. Gidley (✉)
Global Cities Research Institute, RMIT University, Melbourne, Australia

President World Futures Studies Federation, Melbourne, Australia
e-mail: j.gidley@planetaryfutures.com.au

A. Curaj et al. (eds.), *European Higher Education at the Crossroads:*   1019
Between the Bologna Process and National Reforms,
DOI 10.1007/978-94-007-3937-6_51, © Springer Science+Business Media Dordrecht 2012

In the current dominant model of higher education, disciplinary and ideological siloism thwart appropriate knowledge transfer—thus limiting the larger project of knowledge coherence so necessary if we are to cope with the complexity we must expect of the next 100 years. I propose that higher education can best be re-imagined through deeply embracing new ways of thinking and new knowledge patterns.

While the remnants of neoliberal capitalism argue for the new "knowledge economy" this economics-dominated thinking perpetuates fragmentation, commodification and instrumentalism. By contrast the new ways of knowing proposed here are grounded in human creativity, innovation and relationship, less dependent on economic and material resources and thus intrinsically more sustainable for a fragile planet.

51.2   Drivers of Change for Higher Education Futures

Over a decade ago, educational researchers with an eye to the future identified several key drivers of change as being key shapers of university transformation: globalism, multiculturalism, virtualization and politicization (Inayatullah and Gidley 2000).

- *Globalism*—the freeing of capital and the taming of labor and nation-states, particularly those in the South;
- *Multiculturalism*—an understanding that while reality is socially constructed and we create gender and culture through practice; cultures, civilizations, and women and men know the world differently, and that a good society must authentically reflect this diversity;
- *The internet*—in all its meanings from the site, the form, the delivery system to the content of the new universities, particularly in the possibility of the creation of the virtual university and decentralized publishing; and
- *Politicization*—in the South this refers to increasing attempts to use the university for repressive measures as well as the university as a site of dissent, and in the North it relates to the university being part of the economic rationalization of society, of the post-industrial problematique.

At the time, globalism and politicization were viewed as fully developed, long-term historical trends, while multiculturalism and the Internet were viewed as more emergent. From another standpoint, the International Commission on Education for the twenty-first century developed four pillars of education—learning to be, learning to know, learning to do and learning to live together. These were aimed at shifting the educational focus from "the local community to a world society", from "social cohesion to democratic participation" and from "economic growth to human development" (Delors 1996).

Just 10–15 years later, some of these drivers have morphed into other forms and some new drivers of change have emerged. While accepting the ubiquity of the above four drivers, this paper expands on some of the more extended impacts of globalism through the globalization of higher education. It also points to the need for higher education to embrace the new ways of thinking and new knowledge patterns and to shift the emphasis from the metaphor of the global knowledge economy to a metaphor of global knowledge future where higher education re-values the importance of imagination, creativity and innovation as ways of knowing suited to the complexity of the twenty-first century. The new drivers of change identified in this paper include:

- Globalization of higher education
- The tension between elite institutions and mass higher education
- Changing views of quality in higher education and social inclusion
- New ways of thinking and systems of knowledge
- The shift from the global knowledge economy to global knowledge futures

51.2.1   Globalisation of Higher Education

As the politico-economic processes of globalisation increasingly impact on socio-cultural spheres, the higher education sector in the twenty-first century is faced with new and more complex challenges across the globe. The tensions between global, national and regional/local interests found in other discourses are spilling over into the higher education literature.

By the 1990s a subtle shift had taken place in Europe by which the previous "national and cultural role" of higher education was being eclipsed by "the economic rationale" (Huisman and Van der Wende 2004). Jeroen Huisman notes that in spite of initial resistance and critique from the higher education sector, the economic rationale was intensified by both globalisation and the rise of information and communication technologies. He argued that "this trend spurred international competition" within higher education (Huisman and Van der Wende 2004, p. 350). This issue of global competitiveness—so central to the functioning of neoliberal economic markets—has penetrated the higher education sector. Indeed,

> This international competitive stance not only relates to the export of higher education, but also to issues of quality. For instance, the Austrian government has established an accreditation mechanism that may be interpreted as a shift towards international competition (instead of cooperation). (Huisman and Van der Wende 2004, p. 354)

Yet the complexity of our times allows new scope for "cross-border initiative and invention in both knowledge and university strategy" (Marginson 2007). Such transversing of borders is exemplified by *The European Commission Bologna Process,*[1] part of the "European agenda towards converging systems of higher education." In this regard Huisman claims that, "in less than 10 years, harmonisation

---

[1] "The *Bologna Process* aimed to create a European Higher Education Area by 2010, in which students can choose from a wide and transparent range of high quality courses and benefit from smooth recognition procedures." http://ec.europa.eu/education/policies/educ/bologna/bologna_en.html

(although preferably called 'convergence') of higher education structures changed from an undesirable objective to a highly advisable aim" (Huisman and Van der Wende 2004, pp. 349–350).

Globalisation has also stimulated mobility (of students, academics and ideas) with the unexpected effect of enabling new insights into the diversity of higher education systems (Lunt 2008). Both established and newer higher education institutions in the North and the South compete for market share in the knowledge economy to prevent "brain drain" (Huisman and Van der Wende 2004), to foster "brain gain", "brain circulation" and global talent flows (Welch and Zhen 2008). Marginson notes that student mobility is asymmetrical whereby "some nations are primarily exporters, others are primarily importers" (Marginson 2004, p. 202). New discourses have emerged on international education, comparative education and global education. The rise of international, transnational and supranational organisations has furthered the drive to restructure.

The rise of the global south in terms of higher education provision is another significant outcome of this process, with China, India, Malaysia, Latin America and Saudi Arabia being new key players in the global higher education sector. The UNESCO-funded International Association of Universities is a leader in this area, with the biennial Global Higher Education Forum (GHEF) in Malaysia being an emerging world-leading event. Notably, GHEF collaborated with the World Futures Studies Federation[2] for a Conference in Penang, December 2011 on "Global Higher Education: Reflecting on the Past, Designing Sustainable Futures."

51.2.2   The Tension Between Elite Institutions and Mass Higher Education

There is little contention that in the last few decades we have witnessed a shift in higher education policy, at least in the Anglo-European context, from universities as elite institutions for the few to higher education as a birthright of the many. This shift is well exemplified in the UK higher education policies of the 1990s. Ingrid Lunt summarised the challenges that the UK higher education system faced at the beginning of the Blair government, noting that similar challenges were arising at the time in the HE systems of all developed countries. Lunt claimed that "the shift from an elite to a mass HE system" led to decreases in public funding to universities creating increased financial challenges. She also argued that the higher education sector felt a need to respond competitively because of beliefs in "the link between the economy and the knowledge and skills of the labour force." The result, she claimed was the so-called "high skills economy" and the "commodification of knowledge" (Lunt 2008, p. 742).

---

[2]This event is a collaborative venture with the 21st World Conference of the World Futures Studies Federation, founded in Paris in 1973. http://www.wfsf.org/

As a counter trend there is evidence in the last few years to suggest the pendulum may be swinging back. While some researchers applaud the concept of the Emerging Global Model (EGM) of the elite twenty-first century research university, claiming that such "top stratum of research universities worldwide" are key to "economic and social development" (Mohrman et al. 2008), this is not the whole picture. Mohrman et al. identify eight characteristics of the EGM: global mission, research intensity, new roles for professors, diversified funding, worldwide recruitment, increasing complexity, new relationships with government and industry, and global collaboration with similar institutions (Mohrman et al. 2008). However, other researchers raise new questions about the impact of such a concentration of resources on higher education more broadly in Europe and Asia (Deem et al. 2008). OECD Analyst Jaana Puuka reminds us that the "new wider mission of higher education institutions, often characterized as a 'third task' or social obligation, can be best mobilized in the context of regions" (Puuka and Marmelojo 2008). This third task is aligned to Boyer's scholarship of application (Boyer 1990).

Marginson claims that the current "transnational markets in higher education are structured as a segmented hierarchy" reflecting dominance/subordination in three aspects: between "developed" and "developing nations"; between English and non-English language universities; and between "the hegemonic power of the United States in world higher education" and higher education in the rest of the world (Marginson 2004, p. 218). He goes as far as to claim that "the old equality of opportunity project is now in terminal crisis, and will continue to be undermined by heightened status competition, markets, cross-border leakages of people and resources, and global commercialisation" (Marginson 2004, p. 234).

In the light of these developments must we conclude that the notion of *quality* in higher education has again been hijacked by elite institutions at the expense of mass education? Or is there a way that quality in higher education may be viewed more systemically, more integrally?

51.2.3   Changing Views of Quality in Higher Education and Social Inclusion

What needs to be discussed here is what is meant by (or what is the identity of) quality in higher education. While the emerging discourse on EGMs suggests that quality in higher education is dependent on research and funding concentration and can be measured by league tables and other performance indicators, it needs to be recognised that this view is underpinned by a particular ideology. The idea of EGMs has emerged from a global knowledge economy based on the free market neoliberal ideology where individual institutions compete with each other. That this ideology, neoliberalism, is the dominant one—and thus invisible in much of the discourse—has been discussed in detail elsewhere (Gidley 2010b).

The UK provides a good case study of the tension between the elite notion of quality in higher education and the social justice ethic towards greater access to higher education. Lunt refers to this as "the trade-off between excellence and equity" (Lunt 2008). She notes "the total increase in participation rates masks a considerable variation by social class" (Lunt 2008) reflecting the paradoxes and tensions even when a government such as that of New Labour attempts to balance the global competitiveness with social inclusiveness and equity. Although Blair's policy rhetoric gave equal weighting to an espoused commitment to "social inclusion and equity", this did not have the significant impact on universities effected by his "enhanced global competitiveness" policy (Lunt 2008). While the prior conservative agenda led to dramatic increases in access to higher education—an increase of one-third in overall student numbers—by 1997, "this expansion had not succeeded in reducing class inequalities" (Lunt 2008, p. 742).

Similar observations have been made in Australia: "the effect of interventions based on this liberal position has been to maintain the status quo of power and privilege with exception proving the rule" (Nunan et al. 2005, p. 252). Marginson claims:

> Neo-liberal marketisation raises sharper questions about social inequality in higher education, in two dimensions: equality/inequality of access to opportunity, and equality/inequality of the opportunities themselves. All else being equal, economic markets are associated with greater social inequalities of access in systems mediated by the private capacity to pay, so that access is more steeply stratified on social lines; and with a steeper hierarchy of institutions, so that what is accessed is also increasingly stratified (Marginson 2004, p. 234).

The default neoliberal idea of quality as a measure of a particular university or a particular nation's competitive edge is not the only measure of quality. Two broader notions of quality in higher education need to be systemically strengthened in the whole domain of higher education globally. From the ideology of *justice globalism,* global networks of higher education institutions would collaborate rather than compete with each other.[3] And from the perspective of *human potential* ideologies, quality in higher education would mean more than global competitiveness or higher levels of access, but would be related to human potential and transformation. These expanded notions of quality have been discussed in more detail elsewhere (Gidley 2010b).

51.3   New Ways of Thinking and Systems of Knowledge

Imagination is more important than knowledge. For while knowledge defines all we currently know and understand, imagination points to all we might yet discover and create.
Albert Einstein

It is not enough for higher education futures to be primarily focused on external "trends" such as globalisation, thus overlooking the major paradigm shifts rocking

---

[3]The latter ideology is reflected in the title of the recent IAU conference: "Associations, Networks, Alliances etc.: Making Sense of the Emerging Global Higher Education Landscape" 2009 Conference of the International Association of Universities, IAU: For A Worldwide Higher Education Community, Mexico.

the foundations of knowledge for the last half-century. This paper argues that the "megatrends of the mind" are as important for higher education futures as the megatrends in the external world (Gidley 2010c). A broad-based global scan of the epistemological developments both within and across disciplines provides considerable evidence that leading thinkers have begun to enact new ways of thinking to such a degree that most major academic disciplines have undergone a major paradigm shift throughout the twentieth century.

51.3.1   Disciplinary Shifts Reveal New Ways of Thinking

Major shifts have occurred within scientific, philosophical and other disciplines since the beginning of the twentieth century.

51.3.1.1   Scientific Shifts

The modernist, formal, scientific worldview, based on Cartesian dualism and classical physics—with its static notions of a mechanical, "building block" universe of atoms—is gradually being replaced by postmodern, postformal worldviews. This paradigmatic shift has arisen from developments in general systems theory, chaos theory and complexity sciences. Within science itself classical physics based on Newtonian mechanics has given way to new physics theories arising from Einstein's theory of relativity and the discoveries of quantum physics (Einstein 1920/2000; Zajonc 2004). In parallel there has been a shift in scientific fundamentals from a dominant emphasis on physics to new biological discourses. The epistemological shift from physics to biology mirrors the difference between the objects of study— the domain of the physical to the domain of life (Bertalanffy 1969/1976). Following the shift from classical to quantum physics there has been a transition from classical biology, including Darwin's theories of evolution to the new biology-based theories of self-organisation and emergence (Deacon 2003; Goodenough and Deacon 2006; László 2007; Russell 2000). The more fluid, life-oriented worldviews arising from this biological turn emphasise life as being "a complex adaptive system" (Swimme and Tucker 2006), "self-organising" (Jantsch 1980; Varela et al. 1993), and "emergent" (Goodenough and Deacon 2006).

51.3.1.2   Philosophical Shifts

A similar transition can also be observed in Western philosophical thought throughout the twentieth century from modernism to postmodernism and poststructuralism. The singular notion of "philosophy"—implying British analytic philosophy, linked to logical positivism—has been increasingly accompanied by a greater "philosophical pluralism"(Mandt 1986). Though more marginalised than the shifts from classical physics and biology to the new sciences, a philosophical turn from static mechanistic metaphors to organic, living, process metaphors of thinking was also emerging in philosophical thought in Einstein's time (Bergson 1911/1944; Steiner 1894/1964; Whitehead 1929/1985). Henri Bergson's *élan vital*, Alfred North Whitehead's *process philosophy* and Husserl's *lifeworld* were all inspired by these shifts. Early twentieth century philosophers, such as Rudolf Steiner, William James and John Dewey, attempted to integrate these emerging organic, natural, biological understandings with the scientific discourses of their day. Interestingly, such ideas were already appearing a century prior, in the leading edge thinking of Goethe's "delicate empiricism" and Schelling's "nature philosophy." Philosophical approaches that point to *constructive* or *reconstructive* postmodernisms tend to draw on the organic, process philosophies of Bergson and Whitehead (Griffin 2002).

More recent philosophical developments include: comparative philosophy, critical social theory, eco-philosophy, hermeneutics, integral theory, postmodernism and poststructuralism.

51.3.1.3   Educational Shifts

The last few decades have also born witness to the beginnings of a transition from formal, factory-model school and university education to a plurality of postformal pedagogies. We are experiencing what I call a *third wave* of impulses to evolve education since the beginning of the twentieth century. The first and second waves have been discussed elsewhere (Molz and Gidley 2008). I refer broadly to these *third wave* approaches to evolving education as "*post*formal pedagogies." Most have emerged over the last decade. I have identified over a dozen emerging pedagogical approaches that reflect new ways of thinking, which facilitate the evolution of consciousness (For references to the literature in relation to these approaches see Gidley (2009)). These include:

- Aesthetic and artistic education;
- Complexity in education;
- Critical and postcolonial pedagogies;
- Environmental/ecological education;
- Futures education;
- Holistic education;
- Imagination and creativity in education;
- Integral education;
- Planetary/global education;
- Post-formality in education;
- Postmodern and poststructuralist pedagogies;
- Transformative, spiritual and contemplative education;
- Wisdom in education.

Lest this list give the appearance that education globally in the twenty-first century is alive and well, creative and innovative, it is worth noting that all of these are relatively small counter-streams to the dominant hegemonic factory model of education. Further there is a neo-conservative backlash within the field of education that seeks to control curricula through the "audit culture" (MacLure 2006). One of my interests is to foster dialogue between these postformal pedagogies, to strengthen their awareness of each other and to increase knowledge transfer among them. Educational futures researchers need to take account of both futures *in* education and futures *of* education.

51.3.2 Beyond Disciplinary Boundaries to New Systems of Knowledge

In parallel with these disciplinary developments, disciplinary specialisation itself is being transcended via inter-, multi-, and trans-disciplinary approaches (Klein 2004; Morin 2001; Nicolescu 2002). Several epistemological approaches have emerged in the second half of the twentieth century that seek to counterbalance the excesses of fragmentation, specialisation and reductionism in the dominant worldview. These include transdisciplinarity, systems theory, integral studies and others. As knowledge breaks the disciplinary boundaries it also moves beyond old conceptions of time and space.

51.3.2.1 Post-disciplinarity as a Knowledge Bridge

New attempts are being made to create *knowledge-bridges* among disciplines. There has been a developing transition from disciplinary specialisation to multi-, inter-, transdisciplinary knowledge creation (Klein 2004; Morin 2001; Nicolescu 2002). The coining of the term transdisciplinarity in the late 1960s has been attributed to Jean Piaget, though others such as Edgar Morin and Erich Jantsch used it around the same time (Nicolescu 2003). Several other developments can be noted in the way that knowledge is constructed in order to be studied. For example, there has been a flourishing of post-disciplinary studies grounded in notions of social justice (such as cultural studies, indigenous studies, queer studies, women's studies/feminism); and other issues of critical importance (such as environmental studies, justice globalism, peace studies, media studies). In relation to the latter the implications of the information age, particularly the world wide web need to be particularly noted for their ubiquitous and controversial effects on other areas of knowledge creation (Gidley 2004; Healy 1998; Steinberg and Kincheloe 2004).

51.3.2.2 Integration of Knowledge

Higher education theorists and practitioners need to seriously consider the emergence of systemic, holistic and integral thinking in various fields of knowledge. At around the same time that transdisciplinarity was first being discussed in France, theoretical biologist Ludvig von Bertalanffy initiated important developments in establishing a theoretical case that the methods of classical physics were not appropriate for studying biological life (Bertalanffy 1969/1976). He developed the theory of *open systems*, claiming that traditional *closed system* models based on classical science were "in principle, inapplicable to the living organism…[and] that many characteristics of living systems which are paradoxical in view of the laws of physics are a consequence of this fact" (pp. 39–40). Systems science is a significant theoretical basis of László's integral theory (László 2007) and Hans Georg Graf's global futures approach (Graf 2002). The importance of knowledge integration was highlighted over 20 years ago by Ernst Boyer (1990).

51.3.2.3 Expanding Space Through Global/Planetary Perspectives

Recent decades have witnessed a political movement from the centrality of nation-states to the rise of the global imaginary, and hybrid concepts of global/local, glocal and even glonacal. The modernist worldview is closely linked with the geo-political unit of the nation-state. Yet there is a growing complexity and urgency of planetary issues from socio-cultural, politico-economic and environmental perspectives— such as increasingly inequitable wealth distribution, climate change, mass extinction of species and water shortages. These require more than piece-meal, fragmented responses and demand a planetary reframing of human relationships with nature and the cosmos. This is also reflected in the relatively recent eclipsing of fields such as *international* studies (grounded in the concept of the nation-state) by the more comprehensive, inclusive and multi-polar field of *global* studies (Sassen 2007). It is also reflected in the increasing reference to global and planetary in relation to consciousness, culture and civilisation (Elgin 1997; Montuori 1999; Swimme and Tucker 2006). This shift is reflected in futures research as an emphasis on planetary, world or global futures.

51.3.2.4 Expanding Time: The Emergence of Futures Studies

Another late 1960s development was the gradual transition from emphasis on the past to awareness of the value of foresight/futures thinking in many discourses, which provided a positive scientific and academic context for futures studies to expand its scope. By *futures studies* I refer to the transdisciplinary, transnational and multi-sectorial field, which includes thousands of academics and practitioners, many of whom operate globally. I take a pluralistic approach to the field, which is detailed elsewhere (Gidley 2010d).

In addition there has been a stretching of time periods that can be "legitimately" studied, e.g. macrohistory (Galtung and Inayatullah 1998) and big history. The concept of linear time itself has undergone significant change since its tripartition into past, present and future by Parmenides (b. 540 BCE) (Gebser 1949/1985). Over the last two millennia, the linear conception of time—which began as the more formal *measurement* of already-recognized cosmic and natural temporal cycles—became rationally conceptualized as the chronological measurement of change. Since the Industrial Revolution, linear, chronological time has further contracted by association with *mechanical* time and *factory* time.

However, the changes to the concepts of time have been even more dramatic in the last century since Einstein. In the early twentieth century significant theoretical developments concerning the notion of time occurred in both the natural sciences and the social sciences. In physics, Einstein's theory of relativity displaced the Newtonian conception of *objective* time as an unchangeable, permanent 'place' upon which the movement or change of things can be measured in discrete, identical fragments (Einstein 1920/2000; Weik 2004). Theoretical attempts have been made to come to terms with these new perspectives on time (Adam 2004; Gidley 2007).

Scientific and technological developments in the last century have seen temporal partitioning become exaggerated by increasingly sophisticated scientific and digital means, from one extreme in radioactive half-life, to the other extreme in nanoseconds. Linear time has also become dominated by politico-economic metaphors, exemplified by such phrases as "time is money," "buying time." This mechanistic and economic colonization of time has increased exponentially in recent decades, contributing to the *speed addiction* of our present age—demonstrated in fast foods, internet, instant global text messaging, accelerated learning, and the three-quick-steps-to-spiritual-enlightenment culture. Just to cope there are drugs to keep up, such as speed and cocaine; and drugs to slow down, such as alcohol and tranquillizers.

51.3.3   The Frontiers of Global Knowledge Futures

Arising from my evolution of consciousness research I became aware of the significance of several discourses that either identify and/or enact new paradigm thinking, including postformal studies, integral studies and global/planetary studies (Gidley 2007, 2010d).

Postformal is the most widely used psychological term to denote higher developmental stages beyond Piaget's *formal operations*. Adult developmental psychologists have been undertaking research into postformal thinking for several decades particularly in the USA. They identify numerous features of postformal reasoning—including complexity, contextualisation, creativity, dialectics, dialogue, holism, imagination, paradox, pluralism, reflexivity, spirituality, values and wisdom (Cook-Greuter 2000; Kegan 1994; Kohlberg 1990; Sinnott 1998). Michael Commons et al. have identified up to four postformal stages of psychological development: systemic, meta-systemic, paradigmatic and cross-paradigmatic (Commons and Richards 2002). *Postformal studies* also includes the work of educational researchers who use the hyphenated form of *post-formal* in relation to critical and postmodern approaches to education (Kincheloe et al. 1999). Educational researcher Joe Kincheloe referred to post-formality as "the socio-cognitive expression of postmodernism" (Kincheloe and Steinberg 1993, p. 309).

Integral is a widely used term by several different schools of thought. The use of the term 'integral' or 'integrative' has become increasingly common in leading edge approaches to many disciplines. Some significant twentieth century and contemporary writers—other than Wilber—who were working from a substantially integral perspective include, Rudolf Steiner, Michael Polanyi, Jean Gebser, Sri Aurobindo Ghose, Ervin László, Ashok Gangadean, and William Irwin Thompson. An important basis of the idea in its varied forms is that the complexity of the present times requires higher-order forms of thinking that go beyond the narrow specialisations of instrumental rationality. Integral approaches include multiples ways of knowing, being and acting in the world. By *integral studies* I include the various discourses that explicitly refer to their theoretical approaches as integral (such as Gebser, László, Sri Aurobindo and Wilber) and also those that can be regarded as integral according to the integrality of their approaches (such as Morin, Nicolescu and Steiner). The first group explicitly identifies integrality and to greater and lesser degrees also enacts it. The second group—while not so explicit about the term—comes close to enacting integrality.

The term *planetary* has been increasing in usage within the evolution of consciousness and futures discourses. The pluralism of its contemporary usage provides a counterbalance to the term, *globalisation*—which has often been limited to politico-economic discourse and processes. Many researchers who use *planetary* have been inspired by Teilhard de Chardin's notion of the *planetization of mankind* (Teilhard de Chardin 1959/2004). The term, *planetary*—which primarily denotes an anthropo-socio-cultural and ecological framing—is gaining increasing currency as a term to characterize important features of the new consciousness, particularly for those theorists who have a critical sensibility in the light of our complex current planetary situation. In addition to its popular use by environmental activists, it is used in academic contexts by a range of philosophers, scientists, educators and sociologists. This critical use of *planetary* has been emphasised in the writings of French philosopher, Edgar Morin who refers to the present times as the *Planetary Era*, which he claims began around 500 years ago (Morin 2001; Morin and Kern 1999). By *global/planetary studies* I refer to the emerging discourses that use the term planetary in the following contexts: critical environmental (biosphere), transcultural (anthropo-socio-sphere), philosophical (noosphere) and spiritual interests (pneumatosphere). I also include the political science and international relations literature that points to the shift from nationalistic to transnational and planetary/global worldviews.

51.4   From Global Knowledge Economy to Global Knowledge Futures

51.4.1   The Global Knowledge Economy

Where is the wisdom we have lost in knowledge?
Where is the knowledge we have lost in information?
(T. S. Eliot 1934, *The Rock*, lines 12–13)

We hear a lot today about the 'knowledge economy' yet this economistic framing fails to attend to the richness and diversity of knowledge creation that is being enacted on a planetary scale. We also hear the term 'information era' as if it were a complete encapsulation of the present phase of cultural evolution. The proponents of the 'information era' generally fail to attend to the evolutionary move beyond mere 'information' to new ways of knowing, new knowledge patterns and the emergence of knowledge integration.

At the close of the first decade of the twenty-first century, some of the most creative, innovative, and dynamic knowledge around the globe is being produced and disseminated *outside* mainstream universities. Academic researchers and research council bureaucrats need to take heed. Now that "knowledge production", "knowledge transfer", and "knowledge dissemination" have become core commodities of the increasingly competitive global knowledge market economy, how will universities and their research centres keep up?

While the juggernaut of old-paradigm thinking keeps its hold on educational institutions the burgeoning of new knowledge "paradigms" is breaking through from the periphery. A plethora of private providers, social movements, niche research institutes, open source resources, edutainment and, of course, the ubiquitous information kaleidoscope of the world wide web, make it increasingly difficult for the former bastions of knowledge production and dissemination—formal educational institutions to compete for "market-share." But is competition the best way forward? Could it be that the leadership of universities and research councils need to listen more deeply to the periphery—to the new, unorthodox developments in the creation and dissemination of knowledge?

51.4.2   Towards Global Knowledge Futures

One of the greatest problems we face today is how to adjust our way of thinking to meet the challenge of an increasingly complex, rapidly changing, unpredictable world. We must rethink our way of organising knowledge. (Morin 2001, p. 5)

Both of these quotes speak of knowledge. The first is from American-British poet, T. S. Eliot, and the second is from French philosopher, Edgar Morin. Eliot bemoans the loss of wisdom while Morin hints at its re-awakening. Perhaps it takes the eye of an artist, a poet, to perceive the loss of wisdom in the stripped-down, prosaic pragmatism of the *Information Era*. Yet it is a philosopher—a lover of wisdom— who actively thinks towards more complex ways of organizing knowledge in the *Planetary Era*.

In my reading of Morin's work it becomes immediately evident through the philosophical and poetic richness of his language and concepts that his notion of knowledge is already filled with the type of postformal, integral, planetary wisdom and foresight that is being gradually articulated in the frontier discourses discussed above. As Eliot indicates, the modern era of hyper-rationality and hyper-specialization has been a reductive process in which the pre-modern unitive world-view of inherited, or revealed, "wisdom" has been superseded by bits—and, more recently,

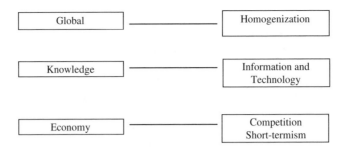

Fig. 51.1 Global knowledge economy—ideological stasis and homogenisation

bytes—of information. In this context, the term "new knowledge" is often used to mean new technologies.

In addition to this fragmentation, commodification of knowledge abounds as a socio-cultural by-product of globalization. Borrowing heavily from industrial era metaphors, education is now marketed as the "product" in a globally competitive "knowledge industry."

The insinuation of neoliberal economic theory into all walks of life—including education—has led to the reframing of education as a subset of the new "knowledge economy." In this new knowledge economy we can witness nations and regions scrambling to grab market-share through creating "science parks", "education cities" and "knowledge hubs." The most disturbing aspect of this "globalization of knowledge" is that it frequently reflects homogenization. This McDonaldization of education transplants outmoded models and approaches as if they were fast-food franchises with little regard to the quality of the learning experience for students or the cultural context in which the model is implanted. In the rush to the top of the globally competitive league tables there appears to be a blind disregard for epistemological and cultural diversity, through alternative ways of knowing. With their embeddedness in the global economy such approaches to global knowledge are also locked into short-termism, stasis and homogenization (see Fig. 51.1).

In contrast to the reductive and economistic ideologies underlying the notion of the "global knowledge economy" my term "global knowledge futures" is intended to unsettle those who use the term knowledge reductively and/or prescriptively. "Global knowledge futures" includes research that eschews the mechanistic, instrumental, reduced versions of knowledge. It seeks to go beyond, to go deeper, to imagine longer time-scales and planetary spaces, to develop and enact more coherent futures of knowledge integration.

My notion of global knowledge futures is framed within the understanding that human consciousness is evolving and for the first time in history we can consciously participate in co-creating our futures through conscious evolution. Although the notion of evolution is frequently attributed to Charles Darwin, the concept was originally seeded by several integrally-oriented German Idealists and Romantics, towards the end of the eighteenth century (Gidley 2010a).

In parallel with the dawning of integral evolutionary thinking in the German states, the Industrial Revolution—a key marker of modernity—was brewing in

Britain, with both progressive and disruptive socio-cultural impact. Grounded in the paradigm of logical positivism, which spawned scientific materialism and analytic philosophy, mechanistic notions of human nature cast a shadow on idealist and spiritual notions of human being and consciousness. Since Darwin—and in spite of his under-appreciated writings on love and moral evolution (Loye 1998, 2004)—the dominant evolution discourse has privileged materialistic bio-mechanical worldviews. More philosophical and spiritual worldviews, e.g. those of the German idealists and romantics, were pushed to the margins being regarded as unscientific. However, several leading thinkers in the early to mid twentieth century carried forward the philosophical and spiritual evolutionary ideas of the idealists and romantics (Aurobindo 1914/2000; Gebser 1949/1985; Steiner 1904/1993, 1926/1966; Teilhard de Chardin 1959/2004). They kept alive the notion that human consciousness is evolving beyond materialistic, instrumental rationality to embrace more complex, creative, integral, spiritual ways of thinking and knowing. Yet overall their work has been largely academically ignored. More recently, evolution of consciousness theories have been picked up and further developed—being ripe for more comprehensive and collaborative articulation through the twenty-first century. Numerous contemporary theorists from a variety of disciplines have begun to research the evolution of consciousness from a more integral perspective (Gangadean 2006; Gidley 2007; Hart 2001; Montuori 1999; Morin and Kern 1999; Swimme 1992; Thompson 1998; Wilber 1980/1996, 1981/1996).

The philosophical and theoretical writings that discuss the emergence of a new movement/stage/structure of consciousness are also supported by some longitudinal research. An emerging change in consciousness was proposed in a study undertaken in the USA over 10 years, reporting on the rise of "integral culture", and identifying almost a quarter of Americans as "cultural creatives" (Ray 1996). In addition, a 43-nation World Values Survey, including Scandinavia, Switzerland, Britain, Canada and the United States concluded that: "a new global culture and consciousness have taken root and are beginning to grow in the world"—the postmodern shift (Elgin 1997).

Building on the evolution of consciousness literature my phrase *global knowledge futures* can be teased out semiotically to clearly distinguish it from the hyper modernist *global knowledge economy*. The cultural pluralism implied in my notion of global, and the ideological diversity in my notion of futures, fold back into the term knowledge, enriching it and opening it up to insights from the frontier discourses discussed above that are central to global knowledge futures (see Fig. 51.2).

51.5   Anticipating Visionary Futures of Global Higher Education

Higher education researchers and practitioners, who move beyond a business-as-usual stance, to embrace new ways of thinking and patterns of knowledge, would benefit from integrating the following 20th century developments in thinking.

- post-classical sciences including quantum physics, chaos and complexity, emergentism, open systems;

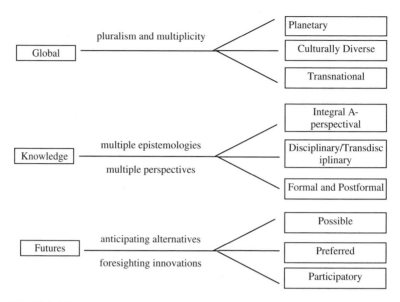

Fig. 51.2 Global knowledge futures—dynamic unity in dialogue with diversity

- postmodern, poststructuralist and comparative philosophies;
- critical, interpretive and contextual theories;
- postformal reasoning, including complexity, creativity, paradox, reflexivity;
- postformal pedagogies;
- global and planetary perspectives;
- systemic, holistic and integral theories;
- inter- and transdisciplinarity.

The following issues also need serious futures thinking and attention from higher education experts:

- Environmental degradation now includes more dramatic climate conditions;
- After the "GFC" the limits to growth discourse is even more pertinent;
- Social and global justice are far from commonplace;
- Cultural pluralism and the needs of the global south require sustained focus;
- The factory model of formal education needs to be "postformalised."

51.6   Reflections

The systemic knowledge shifts of the last century are facets of complex processes that are as yet little understood in terms of their significance for the future of ideas and all that stems from ideas. These diverse, independent, yet interconnected movements pave the way for the emergence of more living and pluralistic approaches to knowledge futures. Higher education researchers, practitioners and policy makers need to take serious account of these dramatic shifts in ideas and ways of organising knowledge. More complex, self-reflective, organic ways of thinking will be vital in re-shaping higher education so young people are better equipped for the complexity, paradox and unpredictability of life in the twenty-first century.

References

Adam, B. (2004). *Time* (Key concepts). Cambridge: Polity Press.

Aurobindo, S. (1914/2000). *The life divine* (2nd American ed.). Twin Lakes: Lotus Press. (Originally published in the monthly review Arya 1914–1920.)

Bergson, H. (1911/1944). *Creative evolution* (A. Mitchell, Trans.). New York: Macmillan & Co.

Bertalanffy, L. v. (1969/1976). *General systems theory: Foundations, development, applications* (Rev. ed.). New York: George Braziller.

Boyer, E. L. (1990). *Scholarship reconsidered: Priorities of the professoriate*. Princeton: Carnegie Foundation.

Commons, M. L., & Richards, F. A. (2002). Organizing components into combination: How stage transition works. *Journal of Adult Development, 9*(3), 159–177.

Cook-Greuter, S. R. (2000). Mature ego development: A gateway to ego transcendence. *Journal of Adult Development, 7*(4), 227–240.

Deacon, T. W. (2003). The hierarchic logic of emergence: Untangling the interdependence of evolution and self-organisation. In B. Weber & D. Depew (Eds.), *Evolution and learning: The Baldwin effect reconsidered* (pp. 273–308). Cambridge, MA: MIT Press.

Deem, R., Mok, K. H., & Lucas, L. (2008). Transforming higher education in whose image? Exploring the concept of the 'world-class' university in Europe and Asia. *Higher Education Policy, 21*(1), 83–97.

Delors, J. (1996). *Learning: The treasure within*. Report to UNESCO of the International Commission on Education for the Twenty-first Century. Paris: UNESCO.

Einstein, A. (1920/2000). *Relativity: The special and general theory* (R. W. Lawson, Trans.). New York: H. Holt and Company. Available from http://www.bartleby.com/173/

Elgin, D. (1997). *Global consciousness change: Indicators or an emerging paradigm*. San Anselmo: The Millennium Project.

Eliot, T. S. (1934), The Rock, London: Faber & Faber, from http://en.wikipedia.org/wiki/T._S._Eliot.

Galtung, J., & Inayatullah, S. (1998). *Macrohistory and macrohistorians*. Westport: Praeger.

Gangadean, A. (2006). A planetary crisis of consciousness: From ego-based cultures to a sustainable global world. *Kosmos: An Integral Approach to Global Awakening, V*, 37–39.

Gebser, J. (1949/1985). *The ever-present origin*. Athens: Ohio University Press.

Gidley, J. (2004). The metaphors of globalisation: A multi-layered analysis of global youth culture. In S. Inayatullah (Ed.), *The causal layered analysis (CLA) reader: Theory and case studies of an integrative and transformative methodology*. Taipei: Tamkang University.

Gidley, J. (2007). The evolution of consciousness as a planetary imperative: An integration of integral views. *Integral Review: A Transdisciplinary and Transcultural Journal for New Thought, Research and Praxis, 5*, 4–226.

Gidley, J. (2009). Educating for evolving consciousness: Voicing the emergency for love, life and wisdom. In *The international handbook of education for spirituality, care and wellbeing*. New York: Springer.

Gidley, J. (2010a). Evolving higher education integrally: Delicate mandalic theorising. In S. Esbjörn-Hargens, O. Gunnlaugson, & J. Reams (Eds.), *Integral education: New directions for higher learning* (pp. 345–361). New York: State University of New York Press.

Gidley, J. (2010b). From access to success: An integrated approach to quality higher education informed by social inclusion theory and practice. *Higher Education Policy, 23*, 123–147.

Gidley, J. (2010c). Globally scanning for megatrends of the mind: Potential futures of "futures thinking". *Futures: The Journal of Policy, Planning and Futures Studies, 42*(10), 1040–1048.

Gidley, J. (2010d). An other view of integral futures: De/reconstructing the IF brand. *Futures: The Journal of Policy, Planning and Futures Studies, 42*(2), 125–133.

Goodenough, U., & Deacon, T. W. (2006). The sacred emergence of nature. In P. Clayton (Ed.), *Oxford handbook of science and religion* (pp. 853–871). Oxford: Oxford University Press.

Graf, H. G. (2002). *Global scenarios. Megatrends in worldwide dynamics.* Zurich: Verlag Rüegger.

Griffin, D. R. (2002). Introduction to SUNY series in constructive postmodern thought. In *Process and difference: Between cosmological and poststructuralist postmodernisms* (pp. vii–xi). New York: SUNY Press.

Hart, T. (2001). *From information to transformation: Education for the evolution of consciousness.* New York: Peter Lang.

Healy, J. M. (1998). *Failure to connect: How computers affect our children's minds—And what we can do about it.* New York: Touchstone.

Huisman, J., & Van der Wende, M. (2004). The EU and Bologna: Are supra- and international initiatives threatening domestic agendas? *European Journal of Education, 39*(3), 349–357.

Inayatullah, S., & Gidley, J. (Eds.). (2000). *The university in transformation: Global perspectives on the futures of the university.* Westport: Bergin & Garvey.

Jantsch, E. (1980). *The self-organising universe: Scientific and human implications of the emerging paradigm of evolution.* New York: Pergamon Press.

Kegan, R. (1994). *In over our heads: The mental demands of modern life.* Cambridge, MA: Harvard University Press.

Kincheloe, J., & Steinberg, S. (1993). A tentative description of post-formal thinking: The critical confrontation with cognitive theory. *Harvard Educational Review, 63*(3), 296–320.

Kincheloe, J., Steinberg, S., & Hinchey, P. H. (Eds.). (1999). *The post-formal reader: Cognition and education.* New York: Falmer Press.

Klein, J. T. (2004). Prospects for transdisciplinarity. *Futures, 36*(4), 515–526.

Kohlberg, L. (1990). Which postformal stages are stages? In M. Commons, C. Armon, L. Kohlberg, F. A. Richards, T. A. Grotzer, & J. D. Sinnott (Eds.), *Adult development: Vol. 2. Models and methods in the study of adolescent and adult thought.* Westport: Praeger.

László, E. (2007). *Science and the Akashic field: An integral theory of everything.* Rochester: Inner Traditions.

Loye, D. (1998). *Darwin's lost theory of love: A healing vision for the new century.* Lincoln: iUniverse Inc.

Loye, D. (Ed.). (2004). *The great adventure: Toward a fully human theory of evolution.* Albany: SUNY Press.

Lunt, I. (2008). Beyond tuition fees? The legacy of Blair's government to higher education. *Oxford Review of Education, 34*(6), 741–752.

MacLure, M. (2006, November). *'The bone in the throat': Some uncertain thoughts on baroque method.* Paper presented at the Engaging Pedagogies, AARE 2006 International Education Research Conference, Adelaide.

Mandt, A. J. (1986). The triumph of philosophical pluralism? Notes on the transformation of academic philosophy. *Proceedings and Addresses of the American Philosophical Association, 60*(2), 265–277.

Marginson, S. (2004). Competition and markets in higher education: A 'glonacal' analysis. *Policy Futures in Education, 2*(2), 175–244.

Marginson, S. (Ed.). (2007). *Prospects of higher education: Globalization, market competition, public goods and the future of the university.* Rotterdam: Sense Publishers.

Mohrman, K., Ma, W., & Baker, D. (2008). The research university in transition: The emerging global model. *Higher Education Policy, 21*(1), 5–27.

Molz, M., & Gidley, J. (2008). A transversal dialogue on integral education and planetary consciousness: Markus Molz speaks with Jennifer Gidley. *Integral Review: A Transdisciplinary and Transcultural Journal for New Thought, Research and Praxis, 6*, 47–70.

Montuori, A. (1999). Planetary culture and the crisis of the future. *World Futures: The Journal of General Evolution, 54*(4), 232–254.

Morin, E. (2001). *Seven complex lessons in education for the future.* Paris: UNESCO.

Morin, E., & Kern, A. B. (1999). *Homeland earth: A manifesto for the new millennium* (S. Kelly & R. Lapoint, Trans.). Cresskill: Hampton Press.

Nicolescu, B. (2002). *Manifesto of transdisciplinarity* (K.-C. Voss, Trans.). New York: SUNY Press.

Nicolescu, B. (2003). Definition of transdisciplinarity [Electronic version]. *Rethinking Interdisciplinarity.* Retrieved March 8, 2008, from http://www.interdisciplines.org/interdisciplinarity/papers/5/24/1/language/en

Nunan, T., George, R., & McCausland, H. (2005). Inclusive education in universities: Why it is important and how it might be achieved. In K. J. Topping & S. Maloney (Eds.), *The RoutledgeFalmer reader in inclusive education.* Oxford: Routledge.

Puuka, J., & Marmelojo, F. (2008). Higher education institutions and regional mission: Lessons learnt from the OECD review project. *Higher Education Policy, 21*(2), 217–245.

Ray, P. (1996). The rise of integral culture. *Noetic Sciences Review, 37*(Spring), 4.

Russell, P. (2000). *The global brain awakens: Our next evolutionary step.* Melbourne: Element Books.

Sassen, S. (2007). *Deciphering the global: Its scales, spaces and subjects.* New York: Routledge.

Sinnott, J. D. (1998). *The development of logic in adulthood: Postformal thought and its applications.* New York: Springer.

Steinberg, S., & Kincheloe, J. (Eds.). (2004). *Kinderculture: The corporate construction of childhood.* Boulder: Westview Press.

Steiner, R. (1894/1964). *The philosophy of freedom: The basis for a modern world conception* (GA 4, Rev. ed.) (M. Wilson, Trans.). Spring Valley: The Anthroposophic Press. (Original work published 1894.)

Steiner, R. (1904/1993). *Knowledge of the higher worlds: How is it achieved?* (GA 10, 6th ed.) (D. S. Osmond & C. Davy, Trans.). London: Rudolf Steiner Press. (Original German work published 1904.)

Steiner, R. (1926/1966). *The evolution of consciousness as revealed through initiation knowledge* (GA 227, 2nd ed.) (V. E. Watkin & C. Davy, Trans.). [13 Lectures: Penmaenmawr, N. Wales, August 19–31, 1923]. London: Rudolf Steiner Press. (Original published work 1926.)

Swimme, B. (1992). *The universe story: From the primordial flaring forth to the ecozoic era celebration of the unfolding cosmos.* New York: HarperCollins Publishers.

Swimme, B., & Tucker, M. E. (2006). The evolutionary context of an emerging planetary civilization. *Kosmos: An Integral Approach to Global Awakening, V,* 7–8.

Teilhard de Chardin, P. (1959/2004). *The future of man.* New York: Image Books, Doubleday.

Thompson, W. I. (1998). *Coming into being: Artifacts and texts in the evolution of consciousness.* London: MacMillan Press Ltd.

Varela, F., Thompson, E., & Rosch, E. (1993). *The embodied mind: Cognitive science and human experience.* Cambridge, MA: The MIT Press.

Weik, E. (2004). From time to action: The contribution of Whitehead's philosophy to a theory of action. *Time & Society, 13*(2–3), 301–319.

Welch, A. R., & Zhen, Z. (2008). Higher education and global talent flows: Brain drain, overseas Chinese intellectuals, and diasporic knowledge networks. *Higher Education Policy, 21*(4), 519–537.

Whitehead, A. N. (1929/1985). *Process and reality.* New York: Free Press.

Wilber, K. (1980/1996). *The Atman project: A transpersonal view of human development* (2nd ed.). Wheaton: Quest Books.

Wilber, K. (1981/1996). *Up from Eden: A transpersonal view of human evolution* (2nd ed.). Wheaton: Quest Books.

Zajonc, A. (Ed.). (2004). *The new physics and cosmology: Dialogues with the Dalai Lama.* New York: Oxford University Press.

Chapter 52
The Politics and Consequences of Eurocentrism in University Disciplines

Vinay Lal

52.1 Prologue

The second half of the twentieth century might have been as distinctive an epoch in world history as any, even if, in many respects, for instance in its appetite for war, it resembled the previous decades and centuries. The two world wars had taken an immense toll of human lives, destroying tens of millions of livelihoods, displacing many more people from their homes, and reducing entire cities, in much of Europe and portions of Asia, to rubble. The destruction that Europe had brought to the rest of the world in preceding centuries, much of it on the pretext that the lands which were laid hollow were *terra nullis* – empty territory, without any owners or claimants – or inhabited by savages, lesser developed peoples, or by people shorn of the blessings of Christianity or bereft of the faculty of reason, had now been visited upon other Europeans. True, there was always another Europe within Europe, the Europe that even the supreme figures of European Enlightenment, men such as Voltaire, Diderot, and Condorcet spoke of with disdain – the Europe, that is, of the Slavs, Poles, Russians, gypsies, and many others who furnished, as Larry Wolf has remarked, Western Europe "with its first model of underdevelopment", a concept that, in time, would travel around the globe (Wolff 1996:9).

The wholesale destruction of the first half of the twentieth century is what "civilization" had wrought and stands forth as a stinging rebuke to the narrative of Eurocentrism, which has insisted upon seeing the world through the template of European history and categories of thought on the grounds that Europe is the fount of modern civilization and the home to all those values that are most cherished around the world. Yet, despite the barbarism in the heart of Europe, the advocates of Eurocentrism have persisted in the belief that Europe, or rather, Europe and the

V. Lal (✉)
Department of History, University of California, Los Angeles (UCLA),
6265 Bunche Hall, 405 Hilgard Avenue, Los Angeles, CA 90095-1473, USA
e-mail: vlal@history.ucla.edu

A. Curaj et al. (eds.), *European Higher Education at the Crossroads:*
Between the Bologna Process and National Reforms,
DOI 10.1007/978-94-007-3937-6_52, © Springer Science+Business Media Dordrecht 2012

United States, are the lodestar of human history. For the moment, however, let us return to the aftermath of World War II. Reconstruction was the task that lay ahead, but the peace that followed the elimination of Nazism and Japanese militarism was short-lived. The atomic bombs dropped on Nagasaki and Hiroshima, whatever the intent to compel the unconditional surrender of the Japanese, were a signal message to the Soviet Union that the United States aimed to exercise full spectrum dominance, and that the war against fascism would now be taken to the communists. So ensued what in common parlance became known as the "Cold War", with most states aligned to either the United States or the Soviet Bloc, and merely 5 years after the end of World War II, hostilities would break out in the Korean peninsula. The fall of the Berlin Wall, the break-up of the Soviet Union, and the dismantling of the Warsaw Pact are commonly viewed as the most reliable signs of the decisive end of the Cold War. The last decade of the twentieth century, in this narrative, is supposed to have ushered in a new period in the midst of which we are still living, characterized by the universal triumph of the idea of the free market, the apotheosis of liberal democracy as the supreme political achievement of human societies, the enshrinement of the individual as the bearer of certain inalienable rights, and the unprecedented flow of goods, ideas and information, all encapsulated under the term "globalization".

The twentieth century that came into shape at the conclusion of the Second World War would, to a scholar from the global South, have had some other distinctive features, often overlooked by those who write world histories. From the standpoint of colonized nations, the second half of the twentieth century was most significantly marked by the fact of decolonization. Indonesia, India, and Ceylon were among the countries that gained independence in the near aftermath of the end of hostilities between Japan and the United States, and, throughout the 1950s, liberation struggles continued to free countries from the grip of colonial powers. At the same time, the new geopolitical order that was coming into shape saw much of the world coming under the sway of American culture, even in countries where the reach of Marxist ideology was not insignificant. The case of India is illustrative in this respect: though Jawaharlal Nehru, who became free India's first Prime Minister and held on to that position through several general elections until his death in 1964, had committed the country to a position of non-alignment, he continued to entertain the hope that the Soviet Union would show the way to genuine socialism. The relations between India and the United States remained testy, and under Mrs. Indira Gandhi India, which suspected that the Americans had much of the same attitude towards India as displayed by its former colonizers, unquestionably showed signs of leaning towards the Soviet Union. Yet, even though the Soviet Union made a concerted attempt to win over the Indian middle class and intellectuals by marketing in nearly all of India's cities highly subsidized editions of Marx, Lenin, Pushkin, Gorky, and other Russian writers, India's educated elites had long since gravitated towards the ideals associated with the West. It is not only that the American Center, the cultural wing of the American Embassy, was more successful in the aggressive promotion of American consumer goods, ideas of success, or notions of liberty. A degree from an American university, particularly one with something of a desirable reputation, was calculated to make one the object of envy and increase one's price in the marriage market.

In the first half of the 1970s, as I recall my adolescent years in New Delhi, the most widely sold books were the novels of Ayn Rand and a set of books by H. J. Eysenck with titles such as *Check Your Own I.Q.* and *Test Your I.Q.* Though I barely knew it then, it is not without immense significance that these were the books that found favor in middle class Indian homes. Ayn Rand's novels – *The Fountainhead* (1943) and *Atlas Shrugged* (1957) – which still command a good share of the market, unabashedly celebrated the ideas of naked greed, rugged individualism, and unhindered self-aggrandizement. In her world, those capable of defending their interests would rise to the top; others would deservedly fall by the wayside. A related form of Social Darwinism informed the work of Hans Eysenck: though his books appeared to be innocuous and even engaging exercises in testing one's "intelligence", he was among those who helped consolidate the idea that one could judge, evaluate, and rank people not, as was once the case, according to the shape of their nose or the distance between their nose and the navel, but in accordance with their "intelligence", much of which was allegedly inherited.

Writers such as Rand and Eysenck had a worldwide following, and their presence points to the three themes that undergird the central arguments of this paper: first, though decolonization was the overwhelming fact of life for most people in Asia and Africa, this meant little more than the physical emancipation of people from the yoke of colonial rule. The Union Jack or the French flag would have been lowered and the national flag raised in this or that country, but the colonized could not then comprehend the degree to which they would continue to be colonized, most of all in the mind, after the last of the colonial rulers had left their shores. Second, if the United States, the dominant power in the post-World War II period, renounced the idea of a formal empire, it would, nevertheless, reign sovereign over a new imperium of knowledge. Several hundred years before, Spain and Portugal had set out in search of riches and carved up the world between themselves, their efforts sanctified by more than one Papal Bull; now, requiring no such legitimation from the church, nor seeking the approbation of anyone else, the United States sets out to carve up the world in accordance with its own conceptions of knowledge and self-interest. One can barely understand many of the social science disciplines, such as Economics and Political Science without some dim awareness of how they were molded under the American dispensation; and "Area Studies", whatever its slight antecedents in the European colonization of much of the world, grew out of the American interest in facilitating knowledge of different regions of the world, in all of which the Americans claimed a strategic interest, if for no other reason than the fact that communism itself was allegedly set on a course of world domination. Third, building on both the Enlightenment project of encyclopedic knowledge of the world as well as the colonial project of mastering the world and achieving a long-lasting conquest of knowledge, the advocates of globalization, whether in the US, Europe, or elsewhere, never shirked from the fact that, more than consumer goods, lifestyle choices, or aesthetic preferences, what had to be globalized were the knowledge systems of the modern West.

52.2   The Disciplinary Structure of Knowledge and Western Modernity

The ethnography of modern disciplinary knowledge must begin with the principal site of production of such knowledge. Much has been written about the university, its origins and ideals, its structure and place in the global economy. Curiously, one central contradiction at the heart of the modern university has received comparatively little attention, namely the fact that the modern university, which claims everything as the proper object of its attention, is very much circumscribed in its ambitions to be the haven of free inquiry and the repository of the world's knowledge by a host of considerations, among them its relationship to the nation-state, its dependency on donors who are driven by ideological agendas that reflect the interests of the ruling elites, and even the fragmentary nature of knowledge itself. Other, more recent, developments have considerably altered the nature of the university in the last few decades: to name two, we might ponder over the extraordinary degree of corporatization of the university and the manner in which many university administrators, who now strut around like princes of little fiefdoms, have managed to effect a *coup d'état* by pushing faculty into the second tier. Above all, however, it is the university's reputation as an "ivory tower" which demands scrutiny, all the more so because the university is, in principle, the entire universe. The words *university* and *universal*, both of them cognate with *universe*, have grown far apart, though the *Oxford English Dictionary* informs us that, at one time, *university* meant not merely an institution of higher education, but "the entirety of something; all things, all creation". That meaning has become just as archaic – and the obsolescence is, in fact, noted by the OED – as its other related meaning – "the whole world; the universe". The commonsense of popular culture understood the university professor as an ivory tower intellectual, someone who lived in a world of his/her own devising; at the same time, knowledge became more fragmentary, reflected in the manner in which universities over time developed new disciplines, sub-disciplines, and even minute specializations. We might say that the universal in the university has been largely eviscerated. The public intellectual, then, is a figure who attempts to build bridges between the university and the universal or, in another language, return the universal to the university.

The story of the demarcation of the disciplines in the university is a familiar one, at least in its broad contours, and needs not be rehearsed at this juncture at any length, though some of its features are not without interest with respect to the arguments of this paper. The academic disciplines, we should recognize at the outset, became disciplines in more than the commonly accepted sense of the term: if they represented the division of knowledge, such that the world might apparently become a more manageable, comprehensible, and ordered place, they also sought to perform the work of disciplining recalcitrant elements of society, often endorsing and justifying inequality, creating new forms of oppression, and stifling dissent. Indeed, the academic disciplines have so disciplined the world – one has only to think of the extraordinary legitimacy granted to "economic science" and the role of economists as the pundits of our times, whose very word, when dispensed through such conduits of the imperial financial architecture as the World Bank and the IMF, is law to beleaguered developing countries – that any intellectual, social, cultural, or economic intervention outside the framework of modern knowledge appears to be regressive, a species of indigenism, the mark of obdurate primitives, and certainly futile. The received view, which practitioners of the social sciences embrace with only marginally varying degrees of fidelity, stipulates that, within the frame, elements can be arranged and rearranged, but that there is only one framework for doing "real" science or social science. "The laws of economics" – and that there are such laws is not doubted by the "real" economists – are the same everywhere, irrespective of the political system, cultural traditions, norms of trading and exchange, and conceptions of the "market"; similarly, there can be a sociology of India, or of China or Nigeria, but we cannot intelligibly speak of Indian, Chinese, or Nigerian sociology. There is no such thing as Japanese science, though, of course, even the positivists recognize that the practices of science in Japan may have their own distinct cultural history, or that nations may have different priorities of research.

It is all the more remarkable, then, how far the prodigious discussion around globalization has occluded the recognition that, in our era, nothing is more global than the formal frameworks of knowledge which have bequeathed to every corner of the globe a universal and supposedly tested and verifiable recipe for development, technological progress, successful management, and democracy – the last enshrined in the idea of "free elections" (first cousin to "free inquiry" and "free markets"), and further guided by the magical incantation of "one man, one vote", though in that very bastion of electoral and yet oligarchic democracy, the United States, some of the principles of even that impoverished notion of democracy appear to have been controversial in a number of Presidential elections. Many gestures against globalization – the revolt in Chiapas against the North American Free Trade Agreement; the widespread opposition to the gigantic agro-business Monsanto, which has been a leader in attempting to introduce genetically modified food; the protests in Seattle against the WTO – are captured in popular memory, but it is useful to recall that American-style management schools are being embraced around the world, that for well over one generation the economics textbooks of Paul Samuelson reigned dominant around much of the world, and that no one protested when social science in the American or British idiom began to prevail in the "developing" and "under-developed" world. No commentator on globalization has noted the yet greater reach of formal modeling and other mathematized forms of social science (Solow 2005). The very ideas of "development" and "poverty" with which economists, social planners, sociologists, and politicians in the non-Euro-American world work are sanctified by several generations of Western experts. One such expert, the celebrated economist Peter [later Lord] Bauer, a close associate of Friedrich von Hayek and advisor to Margaret Thatcher, gave it as his considered opinion that "some of the attitudes in India which are most adverse to material change are indeed unique to the country and are especially pronounced there, such as the operation of caste system, the veneration of the cow, the reluctance to take animal life, and contemplative, non-experimental outlook" (see Alvares 1992). Thus, to become "developed", comparable to men of more sturdy stock and daring thought like Bauer himself, Indians ought to give up the churlish idea that all life is to be venerated and understand that meat is the rip-roaring adrenalin of life.

Long before the founding of formal academic frameworks, knowledge had been divided into such (usually opposed) categories as natural and revealed, useful and idealistic, practical and speculative, and so on. These divisions have by no means disappeared, as the mutual disdain with which traditional and positivist-minded social scientists and those scholars who are animated by post-structuralism, post-Marxism, and other comparatively recent theoretical trends think of each other amply suggests. The story of the emergence of modern social science disciplines, and their subsequent professionalization, has a relationship both to the growth of European power and the advent of industrial civilization. Geography acquired prominence in the age of discovery and exploration, and the rapid expansion of European power into the hinterlands of the great continents of Asia and Africa, which brought forth new responsibilities, including the surveillance of the land and the collection of revenues, ensured that geography would have a long lease of life. History similarly marked its advent after the modern nation-state system began to be put into place following the Treaty of Westphalia; history validated the nation-state. Classical Greek thought had wrought a distinction between "history" and "myth", though the two remained intertwined; and it would devolve upon the Enlightenment to banish myth from the provenance of history, to excise what was manifestly false from what carried the potentiality of truth. As for Anthropology and Sociology, in popular parlance they have been seen as complementary: if the true subjects of anthropological inquiry were the primitives and the exotics, whose "otherness" was construed as offering Europeans with the firmest evidence of their own inalienable superiority, the underclass back home furnished sociologists with the subject matter for an exploration into the lifestyles of others, who were not so far removed and whose very proximity introduced a discomforting instability.

Professionalization of these fields of study, which would turn them into formal academic disciplines, and give rise to new careers, entailed their location in the university, the creation of new standards for certifying a professorate, a prescribed course of study, the formation of scholarly societies, the founding of specialized journals, and the publication of monographs. The *Academie des sciences morales et politiques* in France, set up in 1832, was the first of the national organizations to take the enhancement of the social sciences as its mandate; the British followed suit, in 1857, with the National Association for the Promotion of the Social Sciences, and the Americans were not far behind with the American Social Science Association (1867). But one can think of a good deal else that went into the institutionalization of the social sciences and the development of a critical apparatus. One scholar has described, for example, the pivotal role of the research seminar, first perfected in German universities and then exported to Johns Hopkins and other American universities, in decisively shaping the disciplines: it "was the prime mover behind the multiplication of specialist societies and journals", she avers, and it is the research seminar that taught students method, the mastery of "esoteric techniques" of interpretation, the necessity of meticulous devotion to detail, and the value of diligence as well as collective discussion (Daston 1998:78, 82).

The story of the growth of the disciplines, and their subsequent fragmentation – whether into other disciplines, or into numerous sub-fields and sub-disciplines – plays a central role in the development of research universities, and has most often been told in the vein of neutrality, as a gradual unfolding in each instance of a field of study whose practitioners built upon their predecessors. The disciplines grew incrementally, and the principal narrative encouraged the belief that the practitioners of any discipline, relentlessly committed to the pursuit of truth, discarded falsehoods along the way. One could argue, as an illustration, that the vast majority of contemporary sociologists, evolutionary biologists, and historians have rejected the claims of eugenics and racially motivated science that their predecessors in the nineteenth century were so widely predisposed towards accepting. If one were charitably inclined, one could even go along with the view that it is not merely political correctness that has impelled academics and public commentators to jettison a belief in eugenics; rather, some of the more distasteful ideas of racial thinking that inform eugenics have been so discredited that they cannot be embraced without putting one's own reputation in severe jeopardy. But the matter cannot so easily be put to rest: if eugenics is no longer accepted, what might explain the longevity of the idea that one can distinguish people on the supposedly scientific basis of "intelligence quotient" (IQ)? It is not uninteresting that Stephen Jay Gould's vigorous critique of the racism underlying the idea of IQ, which ranks people "in a single series of worthiness, invariably to find that oppressed and disadvantaged groups – races, classes, or sexes – are innately inferior and deserve their status" (Gould 1981:24–25), was well received by the general population but was panned by scholars as less than compelling (Davis 1983). In most matters, one would not be unjustified in concluding, common people display more sensitivity and ethical sense than social scientists.

Concepts often have a long life, taking new and often more innocuous form as we seem to move into less racist and more sensitive times, but we may not have moved very far at all from the time of cranial measurements and the nasal index to our own age of IQ and the Bell Curve. Moreover, many academics have failed to realize that the nineteenth century European discourse of race and eugenics was transformed into a twentieth century discourse of "development", which deploys a similarly evolutionist framework and has been much more insidious in its effects, reach, and acceptability, since no one wishes to be considered anything but "developed". The present of the non-Western world, one surmises from the literature on development, is none other than the past of the West; its future is only the present of the West, and, one suspects, a poor version of that present. That is only another way of saying that the rest – what is not the West, the mere supplement – does not really have a future; its only future is to live the present of the West, or what would have, then, become the past of the West. History, so to speak, already happened somewhere else: that is the history that the under-developed world awaits breathlessly (Lal 2005a).

Once one begins to launch into an exercise of this kind – excavating the origins and past of the disciplines; inquiring into their supposed contribution in paving the way for a good society; probing how ideas that arose within the template of European experience were given the force of universals, or how particularism is positioned as universalism; discerning the complicity of modern knowledge systems arising out of the West with colonialism, the demands of capitalist and consumerist regimes, and the economic and political interests of the elites – it soon becomes transparent that many of the most conventional and cherished assumptions about the various disciplines are, often, little more than embellished fairy tales.

52.3   Eurocentrism and the Imperialism of Categories

Let us put it starkly and categorically, without any hint of equivocation: the disciplines have failed us. One elementary way to understand the failure is to examine the disciplinary contributions to the solution of human ills, to inquire how far the social sciences have aided in the creation of more equitable societies, and to measure the disciplines by their own preferred yardstick of practical success and utility. Someone might well be prepared to argue that the enormous growth in productivity, world trade, national incomes, and individual wealth since the late nineteenth century owes as much to economic theory as it does to material conditions, the exploitation of natural resources, and the enhancements in science and technology, but then, we should be equally prepared to accept the role of economic theory in giving rise to the massive increase in disparities between the nations of the North and the South, the increasing concentration of wealth in fewer hands, and the numerical increase in the number of poors. In the "developed" part of the world, tens of thousands of economists, who generally act with supreme confidence in analyzing economic indicators and predicting the economic outlook, were entirely clueless about the severe "financial downturn" that would send the world economy into a tailspin in 2008. But, as I have already hinted, the indictment of economists runs much deeper. For all the massive investment in empirical inquiry, no one can say that economists have succeeded in furnishing a template for alleviating problems of poverty and deprivation; indeed, as I shall have occasion to suggest, economists may have vastly contributed to aggravating social problems and creating new forms of inequity.

What is true for economics is also true for other disciplines, and Anthropology is a case in point. Anthropology was born in the crucible of colonialism and genocidal violence, as one of its most esteemed practitioners has admitted: in the words of Claude Levi-Strauss, "Anthropology is not a dispassionate science like astronomy, which springs from the contemplation of things at a distance. It is the outcome of a historical process which has made the larger part of mankind subservient to the other, and during which millions of innocent human beings have had their resources plundered and their institutions and beliefs destroyed, whilst they themselves were ruthlessly killed, thrown into bondage, and contaminated by diseases they were unable to resist." Levi-Strauss faces squarely the Eurocentrism that is the bedrock of Anthropology when he further concedes that Anthropology hearkens to "a state of affairs in which one part of mankind treated the other as an object" (see Alvares 1996:140–141). Though anthropology's *raison d'être* was the study of the diverse customs and modes of living of people in parts of the world who shared little or none of the intellectual, social, cultural, and political histories of the Western world, so that Western scholars could form a more comprehensive picture of the diversity of humankind or understand their own past by surveying the present lifestyles of those viewed as "underdeveloped", there can be little doubt that many societies that fell under the anthropological gaze suffered a precipitous decline and, very often, extinction. It cannot be a mere coincidence that the erosion of human social and cultural diversity, whether measured by genocide, the death of languages (Nettle and Romaine 1998), or the increased homogenization of lifestyles, has been in tandem with the growth of Anthropology. For all its repudiation of its colonial past, its turn towards self-reflexivity, and its promise to be responsive to the people it studies, has Anthropology moved at all towards becoming a humane discipline? Is that at all possible under the present conditions of a huge disparity of resources, and the iniquitous state of knowledge, between the global South and global North?

Scarcely any discipline will be found exculpable, but that is, perhaps, not the most productive way of understanding the epistemological shortcomings and political conservatism of the structures of knowledge in the social sciences. Disciplines have generated the categories which have become commonplace in modern knowledge systems. I have alluded to one such category, namely "development", and will now, very briefly, advert to several others – scarcity, poverty, and literacy – that have become nearly sacrosanct in our times, and in which the hand of (especially American) social science is most clearly visible (see Lal and Nandy 2005). Though poverty has always been with us, the contemporary understanding of poverty, almost invariably attached to the economist's notion of a "poverty line" below which someone might fall, has excised from memory the earlier and richer history of this concept. We might begin with the acknowledgment that there have always been people who have chosen to embrace poverty, and the diversity of ideas surrounding poverty is expressed in the fact that in Persian there are more 30 words to describe those who "are perceived as poor", while in Latin there were 40 words to cover the "range of conditions" embraced by the conception of the poor (Rahnema 1992). The saying of Christ, "It is easier for a camel to go through the eye of a needle than for the rich to enter the Kingdom of Heaven", must appear as something of a joke and embarrassment to social planners, economists, and development specialists, since their expertise has no ostensible purpose but to raise the poor into at least the ranks of the reasonably well-to-do. The poor who are the object of social science's inquiry are largely a construct of modernity, and of the gap, which all indices show is increasing, between socially induced needs and the resources required to fulfill those needs. The social scientists' greatest pretense is that a consumer class only emerges when people are lifted out of poverty; and they refuse to countenance the suggestion that consumerism itself aggravates and creates poverty, and not only in the economic idiom. Indeed, linking the idea of poverty to development (which is presumed to lift people out of poverty), the geographer Lakshman Yapa argues that "conditions of deprivation experienced by poor people in the Third World are a form of socially-constructed scarcity induced by the very process of economic development" (Yapa 2002).

Thus, the social science disciplines would find incomprehensible Thoreau's remark, "A man is rich in proportion to the number of things he can afford to let alone." From the point of view of social scientists, it is a self-evident truth that poverty is, fundamentally, an economic problem, arising from the lack of income or (in the economists' jargon) access to entitlements. It is, in like fashion, obvious to them that "literacy" is one of the most important and indisputable criteria by which the progress of a people or a nation-state ought to be judged. Yet, the word "literacy" makes its first appearance in 1883, though the word "literate" surfaced several centuries earlier: one could make a distinction between literates and illiterates. Though *literate* and *literacy* are cognates, they belong to different registers of meaning. *Literacy* properly belongs within that cluster of terms which are used to measure, order, evaluate, hierarchize, and condemn: what, after all, is the meaning of measuring the literacy rates of countries, if not to suggest that, in the scale of civilization, some countries are better than others, and so to chastise those countries that have failed to increase literacy? The political intent of literacy is to suggest that illiterates have no place in the world, no access to power and the social institutions through which it is exercised, indeed, no substantive claim on the attentions of humanity: they exist only to be pitied, a reminder of the darkness, chaos, and poverty from which literates have been rescued. Literacy doubtless opens wide the doors of society to those who enter its portal, but it shuts out many of the ways in which people customarily sought livelihoods and gained the respect of others.

52.4   Eurocentrism and the Study of History

The world entered into a new "millennium" a decade ago. Not everyone reflected upon the fact that it was not a millennium for everyone, even if was celebrated as such. Howsoever dominant the Gregorian calendar has become in the affairs of the world, there are still many people whose lives are not bound by the week, the year of 365 days, the 24-h clock, and, thus, even less by the appointment book which assumes that there are universal and natural units of temporal calibration. It is doubtful that the new millennium meant anything at all to millions of peasants in India, Africa, or the Andes who till the land. Though the calendar and the schedule govern modern lives, there is nothing inevitable about this course of history. The standardization of time was first achieved, and that too, in a rudimentary form, in the eighteenth century with the emergence of industrialization and the factory clock; in like fashion, the Gregorian calendar inserted itself into the history of the heathens and the primitives, as they were then known, with colonization (Lal 2002:16–41). The striking of the millennium might have reminded Muslims around the world how far they had become marginal to the affairs of the world; it is not their second millennium that was being celebrated. Others might have been reminded by the millennium of the extent to which they lagged behind those who are called "developed".

Temporal frameworks bring us to the subject of history, a discipline to which I shall devote the rest of this paper to understand the operations of Eurocentric thinking. As I have elsewhere argued on numerous occasions, history is, in many respects, the preeminent discipline of modernity (Lal 2003, 2005b). The greatest offense that one can make to a people is to suggest that they have no history (cf. Wolf 1982). When people forge themselves into a new nation-state, almost always the first task of cultural and intellectual consolidation that they set for themselves is the creation of an authorized version of the history of their struggle and a narrative record of their (usually glorious) past. It is equally striking that the most intense intellectual struggles of recent years in many nations, conducted very much in the public domain, have been over the content of history textbooks. Advocates of secularism and so-called Hindu fundamentalism in India have fought long and hard battles over the representation of the past, and, in the United States, the National History Standards were bitterly disputed; in China, meanwhile, loud objections were raised over the textbooks approved by the Japanese Ministry of Education, since it was alleged that these textbooks had ignored the atrocities committed by the Japanese in their war of aggression against China. In nearly every country, people who view themselves as having unjustly been located at the margins of the dominant historical narrative, or altogether excluded from it, have made a concerted attempt to get themselves "written into history". The histories of subjugated peoples, among them women, racial, linguistic and religious minorities, outcast or stigmatized groups, and the working poor have mushroomed and have even become part of the institutionalized domain of history pedagogy and research. Most practitioners of history are convinced that their discipline has opened itself up to a plurality of voices, new modes of historical inquiry, and historical viewpoints that were long suppressed, and that the discipline of history, if not of the world, has thus become more ecumenical.

There is but no question, then, that history has established a primacy within the worldview of modernity. But our narrative of the critiques of national history would be woefully incomplete without an account of how the history of European colonization, and its cultural, epistemological, and intellectual consequences for the colonized people (and often for the colonizers themselves, though that came as an after-thought to most scholars), began to be rewritten in the 1970s. A critical narrative of European colonization had always been present in the writings of some of the principal figures in the history of anti-colonial resistance movements, among them Jose Rizal, Mohandas Gandhi, Rabindranath Tagore, Aime Cesaire, C. L. R. James, Frantz Fanon, and others too numerous to mention, but, in the American Academy, the publication of Edward Said's *Orientalism* in 1978 is commonly viewed as having effected a radical transformation in the study of the exercise of colonial power. This is not the place to assess how far this estimation of Said can withstand scrutiny, and whether Said, who by then had already established something of a reputation as a professor in one of the leading universities in the United States, had intellectual predecessors whose work, written at the margins of the metropolis, not surprisingly, received little or no attention (Sardar 1999). It has been argued, for instance, that many of Said's ideas are anticipated in the work of the Egyptian philosopher Anouar Abdel-Malek, the Malaysian scholar Syed Hussein Alatas, and the Indian historian and diplomat K. M. Panikkar (Abdel-Malek 1963; Alatas 1956, 1977; Panikkar 1953). What is significant is not only that Said's critical framework gained wide acceptance, becoming highly influential beyond the US in Britain, India, Anglophone

Africa, and elsewhere; it is even more critical, for the purposes of my argument, that as wide-ranging as was Said's critique of the intellectual practices which informed the European representations interpretations of non-European societies, Said had no epistemological critique of "history" as a category of knowledge. Though Said had little patience for identity politics, and was astutely aware of how the discourses of multiculturalism in the West become assimilative of dissenting trends (Lal 2005c), he unquestioningly accepted the discursive importance of history and, to that extent, at least would have agreed that the various trends in academic and popular history which had led to women's histories, subaltern histories, and so on had played their share in democratizing historical narratives and allowing for the small and silenced voices of history to be heard (cf. Guha and Spivak 1988).

In the arena of colonial history, and in the study of colonial forms of knowledge, where Said's influence was most perceptible, Said was among those who laid bare the presumptions of Eurocentrism. Orientalist scholars appear as the wise and knowing subjects who represent the Orient not merely to the West but to the Orient itself: those who cannot represent themselves must be represented by others. Said himself had anticipated a yet more profound problem, to which he gave the term "second-order Orientalism". A vast edifice of knowledge was created under the rubric of colonialism, giving rise to institutional modalities – in the case of India, for example, the Trignometric Survey, the Geological Survey, the Archaeological Survey, and many others – as well as grammar and dictionaries of Indian languages, besides, of course, histories, ethnographies, revenue studies, catalogues of native customs, and much else (Cohn 1996). Indian scholars inherited many of the assumptions with which the colonial state and its functionaries worked, replicating them in their work – even when they assumed that they were contesting such assumptions. In the meanwhile, two other developments came to the fore: while scholars working on India, Africa, and Latin America began to show an awareness of the acute complicity between imperialist and nationalist histories, in the West itself there would be a resurgence of "world history". Some scholars argue that world history is the best antidote to both colonial and nationalist histories: indeed, the very enterprise, taking the "world" as the object of inquiry, seems dressed in the language of ecumenism, and some of its most well known advocates are certain that a judicious practice of world history is one way of working towards a more equitable world.

The perils of Eurocentric history are, therefore, best gleaned by a brief consideration of the ambitions and practices of world history. I shall not here delve into many of the reasons for its renaissance, and we can, likewise, largely dispense with the mundane objections that one might raise against world history. One could easily ask whether world histories are truly "world" histories, and how many pages of world history texts are devoted to Africa, Polynesia, India, or Latin America. These arguments about "quotas" are not likely to end soon and skirt more fundamental issues. Large narratives are always susceptible to charges of superficial generalization, and most historians are barely equipped to write histories of the nation, much less of the world unless they have mastery over huge bodies of knowledge and are linguistically gifted. Scholars of world history have long had to face these charges, though it is well to recognize that some practitioners of world history – David Landes, Eric L. Jones, and Michael Mann, to name three – are unabashed supporters of the view that Europe rightfully occupies the center stage of world history, and they have expressed indignation at recent attempts, motivated in their view by political correctness, misplaced feelings of guilt at European colonialism, and a failure to recognize the uniquely European contributions to civilization, to dislodge Europe as the center of world history (Blaut 2000). There is also the much more complex question about the location of world histories. World history has its own political economy: this enterprise is housed in London, Chicago, New York, or Los Angeles, but not in Dhaka, Nairobi, Kabul, Tehran, or Kuala Lumpur. In most formerly colonized parts of the world, the struggle to decolonize received narratives and take possession of the past is far from over. The luxury of writing world history remains firmly within the provenance of the Western scholar (cf. O'Brian 2006).

Entirely legitimate as these concerns are, there are more serious objections that come to mind. Consider, for example, how world histories treat what might be described as world historical figures from the global South. To the extent that world history has place for the likes of Jawaharlal Nehru, a pivotal figure of the twentieth century, it is as men of action rather than as originators of ideas. Even Mohandas Gandhi, in many respects the most arresting and original figure of the twentieth century, has suffered the same fate: the world histories have room for a sanitized Gandhi, the "apostle" of non-violence and liberator of India, but none for his brilliant and withering critique of modernity, or his prescient understanding that oppression will increasingly be exercised through categories of knowledge. No world historian has dared to place Gandhi, whose collected writings run to nearly 100 volumes, alongside Marx, Gramsci, or Freud, since the easy supposition is that he is to be counted among the "doers" rather than the "thinkers", and, of course, Gandhi's slim manifesto of 1909, *Hind Swaraj*, is barely known to the torchbearers of Western intellectual traditions. One wonders, indeed, whether world history, even at its best, does not, particularly with reference to history in the 500 years subsequent to the beginning of European expansion, implicitly endorse the crass supposition, which frequently receives succor from scholars and writers who purport to study the big ideas of our times, that the faculties of reason and reflection have been most developed in the West.

One historian, Jerry Bentley, has proposed a world history around "three realities of global experience and the relationships among them": "rising human population, expanding technological capacity, and increasing interaction between peoples of different societies" (Bentley 2003:51). That such a history – for instance, the account of cross-cultural encounters – may still be excessively predicated on nations and certain nation-states is a criticism to which Bentley pays little attention. If world histories take the holocaust perpetrated upon Jews to be paradigmatic of genocide, which appears very much to be the case, and if that holocaust is "the holocaust" standing forth in singular and sinister isolation, then why should we not suppose that European encounters with the world will similarly become the template for cross-cultural encounters around the world? We are asked to accede to the view, following the immense pleasure taken by many in cross-cultural encounters, that, since colonialism led the Europeans to "increasing interaction" with the world, it must have been a good thing – good at least for the Europeans, which is all that matters. When Bentley remarks that, "generally speaking, the intensity and range of cross-cultural interactions have increased throughout history, albeit at irregular and inconsistent rates" (2003:59), he wishes to lead us to the inescapable, if untenable conclusion, that these "interactions" have led the way to progress and a better and more integrated world. That seems a wholly inapposite conclusion when the conduct of European colonial powers is brought to bear on the question of "cross-cultural interactions". On the other hand, most world histories have been quite inattentive to the Indian Ocean world, which, for centuries, furnished multiple sites of extraordinarily fruitful economic, cultural, and social exchanges largely devoid of the violence that characterized colonial encounters (Abu-Lughod 1989; Chaudhuri 1990; Ghosh 1992; Pearson 2005). Is it merely coincidental that these exchanges bypassed Europe and have also escaped the attention of those who practice Euro-American world history?[1]

Well-intentioned and very respectable scholars of world history, such as Michael Adas, have deplored the narrative of American exceptionalism, and he argues that this narrative cannot be reconciled with the "visions of America", which Adas evidently shares, "as a model for the rest of humankind" (2003:139). That the United States – founded on slave labor, perpetrator of multiple genocides, and the best friend to countless despots – should rightfully be a "model" for anyone is itself a species, rather than a contradiction, of American exceptionalism, but let such trivia pass. Other people at other times thought of themselves as divinely ordained to free the world from oppression, or to bring light to the heathens and the blessings of civilization to savages and barbarians, but Adas concedes that Americans have, unfortunately, been more inclined than others to view themselves as people whose thoughts and deeds are guided by God. Considering that American provincialism is proverbial around the world, who would want to disagree with Adas's plea that world history can, perhaps, be the most useful antidote to the American inclination to be "out of step with time"? What place can there be for American exceptionalism in the era of globalization? Yet, the irony of calling for diversity, multiplicity of voices, and polyphonic histories in the United States, even while American culture has done more to homogenize the world than anything else, should not be lost upon us. I see, however, little signs of such awareness in calls for world history, whose proponents appear to work with the notion that good intentions – not that we should grant that they are always propelled by good intentions – make for good outcomes. Thus, when Jerry Bentley argues that critics of world history ignore the possibility that, "through self-reflection and self-correction, scholars can deal more or less adequately with the problem of Eurocentrism" (Bentley 2005:72), he fails to understand that "self-reflection and self-correction" have themselves become the new form of the West's exceptionalism: whatever the faults and sins of the West, we have been assured, the West displays a unique capacity for self-correction and atonement.

---

[1] One world history that is somewhat attentive to Indian maritime traditions is Fernandez-Armesto (2001).

It is not surprising that Bentley goes on to claim that postcolonial critics of world history "have overlooked the point that, like modern science, professional historical scholarship opens itself to examination and criticism from all angles, while myth, legend, memory, and other alternative approaches to the past make little or no space for criticism" (Bentley 2005:75). Here, in a naked form, are mere reassertions of the orthodoxies about modern science and professional history that have held sway for generations. There is not the remotest awareness of the burgeoning literature in science studies that has effectively put into question the claims of modern science to monopolize knowledge, its apparent freedom from ideology, or its supposed fidelity to objectivity and notions of falsifiability. If self-correction amounts to nothing more than this, world history's proponents have given almost every reason one might need to view their enterprise with deep suspicion.

It is another form of American exceptionalism to believe that what is good for America is perforce good for every other nation. The United States doubtlessly requires many antidotes to its ferocious exceptionalism, but that can be no reason for supposing that everyone should be invested in America's problems. World history will now be foisted upon the rest of the world, and the world will most likely not be able to resist this development; those who make the attempt will be castigated as retrogrades, parochial, acting in violation of the spirit of what, with feigned innocence, is termed the "international community". Such is the imperialism of modern knowledge. Advocates of world history might be puzzled that smaller or relatively insignificant nations are not grateful for entering into the horizon of "world history", but one has only to remember the misfortunes of various nations when they fall under the gaze of colonizing powers. World history is also the apposite form of knowledge for our times, taking its place besides multiculturalism, globalization, multilateralism, and the new world order. It is, thus, one of the twenty-first century's preeminent forms of colonizing knowledge – and all the more insidious in that it appears to be as benign and ecumenical an enterprise as one can imagine. An integrated history of one world, our world, sounds appealing, but we need to have a conception of many worlds, not one world.

Thus, in the present circumstances, the enterprise of world history, from whatsoever angle it is attempted, must be disowned and repudiated, certainly viewed far more critically than it has been so far. But let me push the argument further: keeping in mind the enormous inequities in the world system, the vastly different conditions under which research is conducted and produced in the North and the South, and the dominance of modern knowledge systems, there can be no more desirable outcome than to reduce *certain* contacts between cultures and reject *certain* kinds of conversations and exchanges. In the totalizing conditions of modern knowledge, perhaps best encapsulated now in the primacy accorded to historical knowledge, the intellectual and political imperative must remain one of increasing incommensurability. The intellectual project of the disciplines runs contrary to this dissenting politics, and to aim at a better knowledge of the world from within the framework of the categories deployed by the modern sciences is to do little more than to ripen the conditions under which oppression takes place. Even the most radical historians are unable to write the history of the ahistorical except as a form of pre-history, primitivism, or irrational myth-making, just as the most radical economists, while attentive to considerations of distributive justice, minimum wages, and the like, are unable to bring themselves to an acceptance of the view that the entire paradigm of "growth" may have to be rejected. If there is a prognosis for the social sciences in the twenty-first century, which might introduce into the dominant frameworks some dissent that has not already been rendered captive by numerous models that are posturing as dissent, it is this: the historical mode may have to be compelled to pave way for the mythic and the ahistorical; the formalized platitudes of the social sciences will, at the very least, have to be brought into an engagement with folk, vernacular, subjugated, and recessive forms of knowing; and the claims of Western forms of universality will have to be adjudged not only against the strengths of local knowledge systems, but against competing universalisms which are content with a less totalizing reach. Thus might the stranglehold of Eurocentrism on what is taken as "knowledge" be broken.

References

Abdel-Malek, A. (1963). Orientalism in crisis. *Diogenes, 11*, 103–140.

Abu-Lughod, J. L. (1989). *Before European hegemony: The world system A.D. 1250–1350*. New York: Oxford University Press.

Adas, M. (2003). Out of step with time: United States exceptionalism in an age of globalization. In B. Stuchtey & E. Fuchs (Eds.), *Writing world history* (pp. 137–154). New York: Oxford University Press.

Alatas, S. H. (1956). Some fundamental problems of colonialism. *Eastern World*, pp. 9–10.

Alatas, S. H. (1977). *The myth of the lazy native: A study of the image of the Malays, Filipinos and Javanese from the 16th to the 20th century and its function in the ideology of colonial capitalism*. London: F. Cass.

Alvares, C. (1992). *Science, development and violence: The revolt against modernity*. Delhi: Oxford University Press.

Alvares, C. (1996). Humans without rights. In *Human wrongs: Reflections on western global dominance and its impact upon human rights* (pp. 138–150). Penang: Just World Trust.

Bentley, J. H. (2003). World history and grand narrative. In B. Stuchtey & E. Fuchs (Eds.), *Writing world history 1800–2000* (pp. 57–65). New York: Oxford University Press.

Bentley, J. H. (2005). Myths, wagers, and some moral implications of world history. *Journal of World History, 16*, 51–82.

Blaut, J. B. (2000). *Eight Eurocentric historians*. New York: The Guilford Press.

Chaudhuri, K. N. (1990). *Asia before Europe: Economy and civilisation of the Indian Ocean from the rise of Islam to 1750*. Cambridge: Cambridge University Press.

Cohn, B. S. (1996). *Colonialism and its forms of knowledge: The British in India*. Princeton: Princeton University Press.

Daston, L. (1998). The academies and the unity of knowledge: The disciplining of the disciplines. *Differences, 10*, 67–86.

Davis, B. D. (1983). Neo-Lysenkoism, IQ, and the press. *The Public Interest, 74*, 41–59.

Fernandez-Armesto, F. (2001). *Civilizations: Culture, ambition, and the transformation of nature* (pp. 337–342). New York: The Free Press.

Ghosh, A. (1992). *In an antique land*. New Delhi: Ravi Dayal Publishers.

Gould, S. J. (1981). *The mismeasure of man*. New York: Norton.

Guha, R., & Spivak, G. C. (Eds.). (1988). *Selected subaltern studies*. With an introduction by Edward Said. New York: Oxford University Press.

Lal, V. (2002). *Empire of knowledge: Culture and plurality in the global economy*. London: Pluto Press.

Lal, V. (2003). Provincializing the west: World history from the perspective of Indian history. In B. Stuchtey & E. Fuchs (Eds.), *Writing world history, 1800–2000* (pp. 271–289). Oxford: Oxford University Press.

Lal, V. (2005a). The concentration camp and development: The past and future of genocide. *Patterns of Prejudice, 39*, 220–243.

Lal, V. (2005b). *The history of history: Politics and scholarship in modern India*. New Delhi: Oxford University Press.

Lal, V. (2005c). The intellectual as exemplar: Identity, oppositional politics, and the ambivalent legacy of Edward said. *Amerasia Journal, 31*, 39–42.

Lal, V., & Nandy, A. (Eds.). (2005). *The future of knowledge and culture: A dictionary for the twenty-first century*. New Delhi: Viking Penguin.

Nettle, D., & Romaine, S. (Eds.). (1998). *Vanishing voices: The extinction of the world's languages*. New York: Oxford University Press.

O'Brian, P. (2006). Historiographical traditions and modern imperatives for the restoration of global history. *Journal of Global History, 1*, 3–39.

Panikkar, K. M. (1953). *Asia and western dominance*. London: Allen and Uwin.

Pearson, M. N. (2005). *The world of the Indian Ocean, 1500–1800: Studies in economic, social and cultural history*. London: Ashgate Variorum.

Rahnema, Majid. (1992). Poverty. In Sachs Wolfgang (Ed.), *Development dictionary: A guide to knowledge as power*. London: Zed Books.

Sardar, Z. (1999). *Orientalism*. Buckingham: Open University Press.

Solow, R. M. (2005). How did economics get that way and what way did it get? *Daedalus, 134*, 87–100.

Wolf, E. (1982). *Europe and the people without history*. Berkeley: University of California Press.

Wolff, L. (1996). *Inventing Eastern Europe: The map of civilization on the mind of the enlightenment*. Stanford: Stanford University Press.

Yapa, L. (2002). How the discipline of geography exacerbates poverty in the Third World. *Futures, 34*, 33–46.

Chapter 53
Is Bologna Sustainable in the Future? Future Testing the Bologna Principles

Eddie Blass

53.1 Introduction

By 2050, education will have become interdisciplinary as children are encouraged to think from multiple perspectives to solve problems and teachers facilitate the learning of their students through multimedia classrooms where students study at their own pace. The physical setting will allow for groups of peers to learn together and teachers will be team-teaching in learning spaces. Testing will become non-standardized to foster creativity and students' development of interests. Freelance online instruction will increase as laptop learning becomes the norm. In essence, everyone will become a distance learner and shared new meanings will be constructed through the use of collaborative tools via the internet. Global literacy will be redefined away from the 3R's to accessing, analysing, and evaluating communication in a variety of forms (Zolli 2002). The boundaries between school and university will become blurred, as learners progress at different places throughout their lives. This vision is already developing as a reality for some, but it may take until 2050 for it to be the norm for all. Zaharia and Gilbert (2005) argue that universities need to change the conceptions of their mission in society.

The internet has become the first source of information for young people with their studies and also for social networking/meeting new people and downloading music which exceeded sales in shops over 5 years ago (Williams and Rowlands 2007). Books and journals are following suit. However, simply having access to the books and journals is not enough. Students need guidance on how to formulate search terms and carry out rigorous searches rather than simply browsing (Tenopir and Rowlands 2007). They also have difficulty evaluating the relevance of the search find and the quality of the content of literature, power browsing and flicking through

E. Blass (✉)
Faculty of Business and Enterprise, Swinburne University of Technology,
Melbourne, VIC, Australia
e-mail: EBLASS@groupwise.swin.edu.au

A. Curaj et al. (eds.), *European Higher Education at the Crossroads:*
Between the Bologna Process and National Reforms,
DOI 10.1007/978-94-007-3937-6_53, © Springer Science+Business Media Dordrecht 2012

texts rather than reading in depth has become the norm in their studies. They also use older library materials more often than recent publications but whether this is due to poor researching skills is unknown (ibid.).

E-learning differs from the other forms of delivery because it changes the element of tutor-student and student-student interaction such that it occurs through computer-mediated technology, rather than face to face. Margules (2002:3) argues that 'like it or not, the storage and distribution of information and the associated teaching and learning pedagogy aided by technology, is now undermining the more traditional methods of teaching, learning, and research.' Given the focus on knowledge transfer at the expense of behavioural skills currently being witnessed in e-learning qualifications (Birchall and Smith 2002), there is a danger that a proliferation of such qualifications will result in a form of social de-skilling in the workplace. Blass et al. (2007) argue that e-learning offers a new teaching and learning paradigm and as such requires a new qualification system to recognise this difference, proposing a BE (Bachelors by e-learning) to sit alongside the traditional BA (Bachelor of Arts) or BSc (Bachelor of Science).

The Higher Education sector generally is dominated by strategic plans dominated by simple extrapolation future techniques based on current trend data which lead to stereotypes such as: more concentration of research resources in elite institutions; greater competition to work in or with these institutions; difficulty in other institutions to attract and retain high calibre staff; pressure on other institutions to undertake contract research rather than blue-sky research; pressure on them to massificate teaching; teaching focused HEIs becoming less visible; private sector competition for vocational programmes; more pressure for employability of graduates; more pressure for satisfaction with teaching and learning; less public funding per student; increased student fees; more pressure for value for money, and more need for remedial classes in Maths and English at entry points (Lefrere 2007). It implies a war of all against all which does not benefit anyone. It is against this backdrop that this paper seeks to explore the future of the Bologna Process. In exploring the future of the collaborative Accord, the paper looks at the role of the Academe, the purpose of Higher Education, and who the respective stakeholders are and what their agendas are likely to be in the future.

53.2 The Academe

With respect to the sustainability of the Bologna process, there are a number of issues stemming from the nature of the Academe itself that need to be considered. Firstly is the notion of academic freedom and the extent to which it is upheld in the future; second is the issue of institutional autonomy and how any erosion of autonomy could impact the operations of the institution; third is the concept of academic values which in many ways stems from the above two but is worthy of discussion in its own right, and finally are the issues of comparability and compatibility within the Academe.

In 2006, the Committee on Culture, Science and Education of the Council of the European Parliament unanimously adopted the Doc 10943 which addressed, amongst other matters, academic freedom. In part it states:

4. In accordance with the Magna Charta Universitatum, the Assembly reaffirms the right to academic freedom and university autonomy which comprises the following principles:

> 4.1. academic freedom in research and in training should guarantee freedom of expression and of action, freedom of disseminating information, as well as freedom of unrestricted inquiry in the pursuit and distribution of knowledge and truth;
>
> 4.2. the institutional autonomy of universities should be a manifestation of an independent commitment to the traditional and still essential cultural and social mission of the university, in terms of intellectually beneficial policy, good governance, and efficient management;
>
> 4.3. history has proven that violations of academic freedom and university autonomy have always resulted in intellectual relapse, and consequently also in social and economic stagnation;
>
> 4.4. high costs and losses, however, could also ensue if universities moved towards the isolation of an "ivory tower" and did not react to the changing needs of societies that they should serve and help educate and develop; universities need to be close enough to society to be able to contribute to solving fundamental problems, yet sufficiently detached to maintain a critical distance and to take a longer term view (Council of Europe 2006).

It is interesting to note how the broader reach of academic freedom and institutional autonomy in points 4.1 and 4.2 are counterbalanced by the point in 4.4, despite the warning in 4.3. It is achieving the balance between autonomy, freedom, and responsiveness to needs that appear to be presented as the sustainable model here. Perhaps the phrase 'fitness for purpose' is the key to a sustainable model of academic freedom. Provided there is a 'purpose' and this is met by the academic response then the balance shall be reached. The question that arises will be whose 'purpose' it is that needs to be fit: the academics, the institutions, or some external stakeholders? To a degree, it is questionable whether this matters or not. Provided all three are recognised as having valid 'purposes' that might be 'fit'. If all are pursued in combination with, and not at the expense of, each other then the future of academic freedom should be achievable. If one group's purpose were to lose ground or importance to another's then academic freedom would arguably be eroded.

The same, of course, could be argued with regard to institutional authority. If the balance of power shifts too much to the need to meet external requirements, or support the 'ivory tower' in which the academics sit, then the institution in itself will become dysfunctional. There is an imperative for institutional survival and, hence balancing the needs of many stakeholders is a necessity, and this has always been, the case. Who the stakeholders are, what their stake is, and how this drives behaviour may change, but the balancing of stakeholder needs has always been present.

Currently, the major global educational discourses are about the knowledge economy and technology, lifelong learning, global migration or brain circulation and neo-liberalism. The major institutions contributing to global educational discourses and actions are the World Bank, the Organisation for Economic Cooperation and Development, the World Trade Organisation, the United Nations, and UNESCO. International testing, in particular the Trends in Mathematics and Science Study (TIMSS), and Programme for International Student Assessment (PISA) and instruction in English as the language of commerce are contributing to global uniformity of national curricula (Spring 2008). This may serve to 'regulate' the future student intake across Europe, contributing to the Bologna process in terms of comparability of entry requirements, but could serve to lessen diversity and sense of national identity that can be established through the school education system. This may, in fact, be one of the aims of the EU and Bologna; to reduce the influence of the nation state in favour of the European Union.

Knowledge economy policies are currently very powerful drivers of change in contemporary university approaches to research. They typically orientate universities to a national innovation system which both position knowledge as the key factor of economic growth and see the main purpose of knowledge as contributing to such growth. Kenway et al. (2004) argue that this is a narrow, reductionist logic to knowledge economy policies and that the university should have a wider public contract than generating knowledge for those who can pay for it, making a wider contribution to a broad, rich knowledge base which is attentive to social and cultural knowledge as well as traditions. They argue that a vibrant and generative intellectual community is underpinned by a gift economy based on reciprocity according to social and ethical codes and that while commodification creates freedom of the object and subject, it leads to the destruction of the social and the ethical, which in turn leads to a breakdown of communities. Hence, the future of the 'knowledge economy' needs careful managing rather than being left to market forces if the university is to continue in a role of contributing to society, democracy and the longer term health of the planet. Currently in the UK, for example, the government is supporting the sciences at the expense of the arts, cutting funding to arts education resulting in the closure of humanities and arts in a number of universities (Browne 2010). The argument made in the UK questions the value of the arts and humanities in their contribution to future economic wellbeing of the nation over the contribution of other subjects which prejudges what will be of value in the future as well as skewing its development.

Unbundling the notion of academic freedom reveals the issue of who 'owns' the knowledge that is produced within the Academe? Is it the academic, the institution, the journal or publishing house that publishes the work, or is it a shared ownership once it is in the public domain. Forstrop (2007) claims that in a post-industrial society, knowledge will be regarded as a national property or resource and its cultivation and optimization will provide economic security for those at the top of the global knowledge food chain. He sees the West as dominating the knowledge economy in an extension of capitalist colonialism with manual work being transferred to other parts of the world. In many ways the Bologna Process could be evidence of attempts to achieve such Western domination. By achieving some compatibility and comparability between the European Higher Education Institutions, Europe is arguably building competitive advantage at the expense of those outside of the zone. This makes the club both exclusive in terms of what it offers and who can gain access to it, and of limited membership in that it is only open to European HEIs. While this might contribute to the longer term success of the HEIs themselves, is it contributing to creating a sustainable future for the sector globally?

Technological developments are also providing a disruptive force within the Academe. Firstly, models of authorship and costs of production are changing. Academics can publish their own blog without peer-review to express their opinions; journals can publish online to avoid printing and production costs; and access is becoming ubiquitous with open access materials becoming the norm. This is challenging the university as an institution that provides access to knowledge, and is changing the nature of expectations of students, governments, and other stakeholders (Hilton 2006). In many ways the expansive use of technology supports the Bologna ideal in making comparable and compatible resources available across the institutions of Europe, allowing for convergence in content as well as convergence in outcome.

Lefrere (2007) argues that the HE sector is dominated by strategic plans that have been dominated by simple extrapolation future techniques based on current trend data and this has led to stereotypes in action and policy, such as more concentration of research resources in elite institutions (see, for example, Browne 2010), greater competition to work in or with these institutions, difficulty in other institutions to attract and retain high calibre staff (Hakala 2009), pressure on other institutions to undertake contract research rather than blue-sky research (Etzkowitz et al. 2000), and pressure on them to massificate teaching amongst other things. Such plans pit universities against each other with the current elite holding the balance of power. But are these the actors who should be leveraging the future of the sector and its contribution to society? Is the future society they are creating sustainable? Ahmed (2010) offers a compelling argument for change if we are to halt the failure of civil society and maintain a form of civilization in the future. The riots in London that spread throughout the UK in August 2011 serve as a good example of this phenomenon; many of the rioters were educated youths, university students, and young professionals including teachers.

With the global financial crisis resulting in many EU members being bailed out of bankruptcy by other Euro based economies, the sustainability of the HE provision in many EU countries must be questioned. In England, for example, the government has withdrawn funding of undergraduate studies from 2013 resulting in student fees rising from on average GBP3,500 to GBP9,000.

Who owns the Academe could become a very pertinent question in the future of the Bologna process and its long term sustainability. If the Academe is forced to 'privatise' the inevitability of competition within a capitalist framework will make the collaborative nature of Bologna unattractive. This leads us to question the purpose of Higher Education in the future and whether it will continue to serve the ideals that the Bologna Accord intended.

53.3   The Purpose of Higher Education

The original 'Idea of the University' was proposed by Cardinal Newman in 1853 who talked about the development of the 'educated man', providing education for the sake of education in the liberal tradition. Jaspers (1960) argued that the development of a professional cannot be isolated from the development of the individual as a whole and hence supported a more utilitarian purpose, one supported by Birch (1988:38) who claimed that a 'broader academic ethic places weight on both the capacity to create knowledge and to put it to work.' Newman's view of the university was rooted in religion, morality, ethics and values, a sense of self-awareness and psychological well-being (Newman 1853).

Halsey (1995) argues that the liberal idea of the university is a residual model and that the donnish dominion is in decline. Scott (1995) argues that the dominant model is now that of mass higher education. The unification of the system through the Bologna process supports this discourse as it broadens the purpose of HE beyond national boundaries, shifting it away from an education for the elite, to one shared across a range of providers across a range of countries. At the turn of the century, Barnett (2000:12) claimed 'we are at a point where the old has now to be laid, certainly with dignity, to rest. The new awaits; but so does its formation, its definition, and its character. Much lies ahead.'

It is the Leuven and Louvain-la-Neuve communiqué (Bologna 2009) which best outlines the Bologna Accord's commitment to purposes wider than increasing mobility within the EU Higher Education sector. It refers to widening participation as a public responsibility (item 10), for example, as part of the priorities for the decade to come. Mention is made of the 'various missions of higher education, ranging from teaching and research to community service and engagement in social cohesion and cultural development' (ibid.:2). Sentamu (2000:51) argues that we should be valuing cultural diversity in education, presenting a relatively liberal view that offers a more inclusive interpretation of globalisation: 'Education must challenge our complacency, our prejudices and our misconceptions.'

An informed citizenry is key to a healthy democracy and to make educated decisions in a democracy, individuals need to be able to evaluate the validity and reliability of information, synthesize multiple sources and determine a position or plan of action (Crowe 2006). This highlights the role of education in helping people to understand the information they access, and in evaluating the information they access, and in emphasizing multiple perspectives. Becoming active in the political process does not happen due to increased access to the political process alone, education has a role to play. Students who progress their education beyond school are more likely to vote (Torney-Purta 2001).

Education aimed at teaching 'good citizenship' has more to do with voluntarism, charity and obedience than democracy (Westheimer 2008). Good citizenship for many means listening to authority figures, dressing neatly, being nice to neighbours, and helping out at a soup kitchen – not grappling with the kinds of social policy decisions that every citizen in a democratic society needs to understand. This reflects the 'citizenship' curriculum in schools. In Higher Education, the contribution should shift from education for citizenship to education for democracy. Patrick (2005) asks what the characteristics of a good education for democracy are. He makes the case for a verbal cognitive proficiency that enables one to use core concepts to interpret information and act effectively in political and civic life as being the most relevant cognitive ability in relation to democratic citizenship. The Bologna Declaration explicitly states its aims to include the promotion of cultural diversity and equality, but the extent to which this translates into a conformed European citizenry agenda is questionable. The practical reality of a harmonised qualification system may not be encroaching on the curriculum as such, but in determining the unit sizes in which it is delivered, the indirect impact on content and the students' broader development is felt.

Ford (2002) argues that the modern university is arguably participating in the breakdown of human communities and the destruction of the natural world, impoverishing rather than enriching the world, through its adoption of the dominant economic paradigm. By adopting an underlying assumption that Higher Education should help make the world a better place by enabling human beings to live more meaningful and satisfying lives, by helping promote social justice and environmental sustainability, Ford argues for a curriculum focused on the state of the world, sustainable cultures and social movements, which is a huge change to those that argue that there is nothing fundamentally wrong with the university and that the problems are relatively superficial.

The need for societally-connected thinking that involves mandatory interdisciplinary courses at every level of education, systems (non-linear) thinking and commitment to problem-solving is also proffered as a solution by those who argue that our current educational system is not teaching students how to think critically or preparing them for a long-term commitment to solving major societal problems (Louria et al. 2003). Arguably extending the Bologna Process to introduce a compulsory study-abroad semester within the Bologna signatories could help develop this societal engagement and understanding, but as it stands currently, this is not a requirement.

Much of the debate about the type of person the education system should be producing has been framed within a national context (Lauder et al. 2006) rather than a global context. The knowledge base that underpins global development is vast. It includes cultural knowledge, cognitive skills, languages, ICT skills, and the ability to relate to people who hold a different set of assumptions to your own. The task for education therefore is to ensure that children and adults learn and develop the skills, knowledge base and abilities to allow them to function to their optimum within this global environment.

The concept of globalisation appears to have become all pervasive. The relative wealth and power of countries and even continents around the world are an important part of the globalisation concept. Indeed, it is this economic foundation to the analysis of activity that frames it as globalisation rather than internationalisation. Internationalisation is essentially 'between nations'. Globalisation, on the other hand, is about economics, as it is linked in discourse to the concept of the 'knowledge economy' (Eckersley 2007).

The Fielden report (2007) uses Knight's (1994) definition of internationalisation as its starting point, which is the process of integrating an international/inter cultural dimension into the teaching, research and service functions of the institutions. This definition is quite insular as it is about bringing an international element into the university, although it does stretch to include study abroad, exchanges and accreditation of overseas partners. Globalisation may be better defined as both a strategy and an impact, with a more external focus, perhaps 'the promotion of inter cultural dimensions in teaching, research and education service functions in an international market context' (Blass 2008). The extent to which the Bologna process is global or international becomes a question of intent and impact. While it may have started as a global ideal of exchange to support the EU knowledge economy development, it may ultimately end up being international as the practical realities of the process of integration has dominated the progress and development.

The cultural perspective offered by Spring (2008) offers a sustainable future for the development of global Higher Education rather than the post-colonial perspective currently dominating the horizon. If we are to create a model of globalisation that has a liberal, meaningful purpose with regard to pedagogy, curriculum and educational philosophy, we need to move away from a market driven approach and revisit the roots of university as a place of moral development (Newman 1853). Higher Education is in a unique position in that it has the opportunity to contribute to democracy as well as economy. Globalisation is driving the economic agenda over the democratic agenda and this cannot be good in the long term for the health of the planet. The two, of course, need not be mutually exclusive, as economic success can develop from the success of democracy; it is questionable whether or not it can be achieved the other way round.

The force of globalisation has lead to a focus on creating wealth regardless of distribution, which leaves minorities within nation states needing to surrender their cultural identity for economic progress, which in turn leads them to revolt and look to the international community to deliver (Orstrom Moller 2003). As such people around the world are starting to question the mantra of globalisation in search of a set of common values to keep the powerful nations reined in and legitimising intervention. The extent to which the Bologna Process impacts on the surrender of national cultural identity at the strengthening of a European identity is questionable. While the member states have 'signed' the agreement, the method and extent of their harmonisation of practice is debatable.

In summary, the role of the Bologna Declaration and its impact on the purpose of Higher Education is weak. While it may have founding principles of enhancing democracy, promoting cultural diversity and equality, its role in producing a global competitive advantage is dominating the practice of implementation and as global competition increases, there is a danger that the member states' institutions will compete more fiercely with each other than they even do presently. The collaboration required for Bologna to succeed needs to be termed more in gains for individual institutions than gains for the nation states and the EU. Then we might see a change in institutional behaviour.

The changing role of the State in the governance of the University is shifting the funding base of universities in many member states, and the need for the third stream funding is increasing. Third stream funding is that which is not derived from the traditional activities of teaching and research (Jongbloed et al. 2008), but is rather generated from industry and other external funding sources, including community engagement. States support is proving insufficient to sustain universities and, hence, they have to seek funding sources elsewhere. The success or otherwise of universities at achieving this is being labelled as their ability to be 'entrepreneurial' (Soares and Amarala 1999). Such entrepreneurialism has been described as the 'triple helix' by Etzkowitz et al. (2000) where the Academe, industry and government relate.

Nelles and Vorley (2010) argue that every university has an entrepreneurial architecture, whether they pay attention to it or not, as it is a combination of structures, systems, strategies, leadership and culture. The Bologna Process to a degree endeavours to influence all five of these elements. Is its aim, therefore, to give the EU an entrepreneurial advantage in Higher Education over those outside of its boundaries? This was not one of the explicit aims set out in the original Declaration but may be implicit through the combining of original aims and activities that have resulted. Making such an aim explicit may be one means of promoting sustainability within Bologna in the future but would have far reaching implications for national policy which may exceed the level of commitment that exists amongst signatories.

If it were to occur, what would such an entrepreneurial advantage look like? Taking the UK as an example, the need to focus on demand led development rather than supply driven has been identified as key in the UK where the proportion of the population with graduate qualifications and the percentage of GDP invested in education is lower than in Sweden, Canada, and South Korea, for example. Leitch (2006) suggests that the UK has over-targeted young people at the expense of engaging with employer and work-based qualifications, favouring full-time undergraduate students with funding rather than part-time students who are also employees. He notes that they are unlikely to grow the graduate population within the current framework and provision. Over 20% of UK nationals with a degree live in other OECD countries while immigration tends to be unskilled or low skilled workers. By 2010, fewer than 20% of the full time UK workforce will be white, able bodied men under the age of 45 – the historic core of the workforce (ibid.).

This sentiment is echoed by the Chartered Management Institute. Tomorrow's workforce will be increasingly individualistic, older, mobile, international, ethnically varied and far more demanding of their employers (CMI 2008). There is doubt as to whether the higher education system can produce the right number of people at the right skills level in the future – and some would question whether it should. Is this the role of the university that Europe wants within the Bologna Declaration, or is it simply a response to the market pressures of the here and now? Will the ideology behind Bologna be tempered down in the practicalities of sustaining the sector in turbulent economic times?

53.4   Stakeholders

The three main stakeholders discussed in this section are the government both as a beneficiary in terms of contribution to the public good, but also a contributor in terms of providing funding; industry in terms of a beneficiary of research, innovation and students to fuel the knowledge base they need, and as a contributor in terms of funding; and students, benefiting from the knowledge and skills they develop and their increased market value over time.

Funding is the key issue for the future of universities and there is a danger that they will shift too far towards focusing on economic success at the expense of education (Marginson and Peters 2004), shifting the balance of their role more from the public to the private good. The university may be a self-serving corporate, but it could also be a source of major change in teaching, learning and research, a producer of common public goods and a fountainhead of culture and civilisation, amongst other things. Marginson and Peters question the role of the university as it moves away from the liberal idea within the humanities, to one of system organisation, government policy and institutional management from policy specialists; through the modern mass education ideal for a global competitive state, towards the construction of a national culture – an idea which is arguably compromised by globalisation, neo-liberalism and corporatisation; past the post modern idea of the university playing a role in the authorisation of truths, to the imagining of a university as a standalone corporation swinging free of government in their own global marketplace, subjected to the familiar rituals of leadership and management, or the research-intensive, innovative university driven by technology transfer and R&D. There is much recognition of the need for new, or additional, funding sources to become available in addition to the public purse. Whether this should come from increased tuition fees (Vincent-Lancrin 2004), overseas students (CHERI 2007), employers (Blondal et al. 2001), or research funding (UUK 2008) is likely to vary both between member states and within member states according to the structure of their HE sector.

While ever we have a tendency to fund what we can measure, institutions will become better at playing the games associated with the metrics and league tables (Eastwood 2008) rather than attending to their core purpose of public/private good. Social competition in HE and inter-university competition is steepening the university hierarchies, with the formation of a world market elite and a closer alignment of social hierarchy and educational hierarchy at a national level (Marginson 2004). There is a danger that this will lead to the Bologna Process imploding as the divisions within university sector within the member states themselves lead to a breakdown of the operation of the process.

While the public good as a stakeholder has been discussed in the section on the purpose of higher education above, the private good afforded to the individual has been somewhat ignored. A report on measuring and reporting student achievement has already concluded that while the UK honours degree is robust and a highly valued qualification, the classification system itself is no longer fit for purpose

(Burgess 2007). It cannot do full justice to the range of skills, knowledge, attributes, and experiences of a graduate in the twenty-first century and acts as a summative, simple numerical indicator which is at odds with lifelong learning. Given the Bologna Process is endeavouring to standardise the degree across Europe, this criticism may be true for Europe as well as the UK. What do young people want and need from Higher Education in the twenty-first century, and are universities providing it?

Globalisation does not augur any new unity of humanity – it is a partisan political project, designed to commend and legitimate global capitalist hegemony. It includes the shift to knowledge-based post industrialism in the mature economies, a new international division of labour associated with the relocation of production to the developing economies, the dominant role of multinationals aligned with liberalised trade and round the clock round the globe financial markets, a concomitant attrition of national sovereignty, and a digital divide attended by a deepening social cleavage (McEldowny et al. 2009). Cultural diversity based on religion, language, ethnicity, and political ideology, is a policy objective of the new Europe, yet a strong parochialism exists in a duty to provide educational services to a local catchment area. Will this meet the needs of the next generation?

Posnick-Goodwin (2010) introduces us to Generation Z who would rather text than talk, preferring to communicate online – often with friends they have never met face to face. They do not spend much time outdoors unless adults organize activities for them and cannot imagine life without cell phones, preferring computers to books and wanting instant results. They are also growing up in an economic depression and are under tremendous pressure to succeed, and hence they are growing up fast, and exhibiting behavior far beyond their years. Cetron and Davies (2008) found that young people have more in common with each other than their parents do, no matter where they are located, as they communicate globally through social networking within their generation rather than conversing orally across generations. Perhaps it is this that is leading to this local interest within a global context and understanding. They also have an incredibly strong sense of social justice, social values and altruism. Despite this generation just approaching their teens, they are already impacting the philanthropic nature of the economy (Koodooz 2010).

Research carried out by the Launch Group (2009) on behalf of Habbo has found that generation Z are deeply altruistic, care deeply about their environment, their community and global humanitarian issues. They are less concerned about fame and fortune but want to enjoy their work. Walliker (2008) sees them as gaining the most educational qualifications known to a generation as they become the most educated generation yet.

Are we ready to meet the needs of these stakeholders in the future at our Universities? How will they hold us to account? The future generation is likely to see beyond the boundaries of Bologna and wants a truly global education, travelling the world and experiencing life in other countries as part of their educational experience, as much as transferring the credits they gain for formal study as they go. Already students are boycotting lectures as they can learn more from textbooks or the internet and they can choose the place, pace, and time when they do so rather than being confined to the space, pace, and time that the lecturer chooses (Kennedy 2011). What can we teach the future students and how can we teach them? Bologna offers no answers to these questions.

53.5 Conclusions: Future Sustainability

The private goods provided in HE are subject to economic scarcity, and both their production and consumption are subject to competition, students compete for access to status goods and universities compete with each other for the best students and status leadership, and the production of these private goods is readily turned into an economic market. Global externalities arise both in cross border relationships and flows between nations, and in meta-national regional and worldwide regulation, systems and protocols, e.g. the Bologna Declaration. This enhances the potential for global public goods, including both externalities and collective goods. It also enhances the potential for global public bad (Marginson 2007).

The key question Marginson concludes with is 'whose global public good?' The research and knowledge system is culturally dominated by the English language. In the context of globalisation as homogenisation there is the potential for rivalry and excludability between nations, within the production and distribution of global public goods. Hence, the global public good of the Bologna process may operate within the member nation states at the expense of those outside of the Accord. The extent to which such competitive advantage is sustainable is questionable on a global scale. By focusing too much attention inwards there is a danger that the rest of the world will move in and find alternative means of achieving global public good. The extent to which the concept of EU public good is sustainable within the EU itself is equally questionable and depends on the extent to which the EU manages to sustain itself both on financial and political fronts as well as economics.

UNESCO seeks greater co-operation and solidarity within HE around the world and aims to widen participation and access to HE around the world; develop a global approach to quality assurance; mobilize stakeholders to widen the funding base; promote synergy between teaching and research; protect academic freedom and institutional autonomy and respond effectively to the communities it serves (Daniel 2003). They call for reforms with regard to governance, finance, and the balance between public and private Higher Education. The extent to which the EU can cocoon itself within the Bologna Declaration and ignore this wider calling will be limited. Futures students may hold a national identity but the formation of a European identity is yet to occur.

The Bologna Declaration has in essence attempted to create a single HE provision across Europe in terms of the format in which HE is delivered so that students and staff can seamlessly transition between institutions in the furtherance of their education and/or career. From the perspective of Higher Education as a public good, the intention was to benefit the members of the EU nation states, and to provide a greater sense of European unity and identity. However, Higher Education is not simply a public good. The concepts of private and public are not fixed or natural attributes – the work of HE can be public and/or private and manifest either as individual or collective benefit. A public good is non-rivalrous because it can be consumed by any number of people without being depleted and non-excludable because the benefits cannot be confined to individual buyers, such as social tolerance, law and order. Few goods have both of these qualities in full. The extent to which education is therefore a public good becomes a policy choice. The nation is public, the global is a market (Marginson 2007). The Bologna Declaration in its intent extends the concept of 'nation' to 'Europe' to extend the concept of public good. Is this the preferred future for the EU? Probably, yes. Is it the preferred future for the member states? Possibly, yes. Is it sustainable in the longer term future? Probably not, as the globalisation will both increase and decrease the importance of the nation state and the middle ground posed by such Accords as Bologna will offer no benefit either way. We are likely to see a shift to the opposite position than the one we are currently witnessing. In the future, universities will need to contribute to the global public good in order to justify their position on the world stage, while contributing to the local private good in order to sustain their existence financially. By achieving the former they will attract students to achieve the latter.

The longer term sustainability of the Bologna Declaration is therefore in doubt. It does offer a model and process for the rest of the world though in terms of developing a basis for harmonisation of higher education, but the development of credit transfer schemes and local university partnership agreements is by-passing the need for this to be formalised centrally. In trying to control the sector at a national level, the universities within the scope of the Accord have largely ignored it, favouring instead to exert their autonomy in negotiating their own arrangements both within and outside the Euro zone.

It is difficult to see for whom the longer term sustainability of Bologna would be a preferred future? Perhaps the bureaucrats that work within the European democratic process; perhaps the European students who would like to travel through Europe as they complete their undergraduate studies – but the numbers who can afford to do this are few and far between. For the individual HEIs, neither has the Bologna Declaration had a high impact on the reality of their day to day operations, nor has it impacted on their strategic direction.

Is there a future in which the sustainability of the Bologna Process is possible? It is difficult to see one at present as we sit in the depression stemming from the global financial crisis. Was there ever a future in which the Bologna Process could have been sustainable? This is questionable. While the Accord was full of good intentions, it is not possible to isolate Europe from the rest of the world, and as the rest of the world is bigger, Europe could become expendable if it were to exclude itself. As such, the boundaries of Bologna could never be maintained with any long term integrity. While it may make movement for some students and staff easier, it cannot offer anything exclusive and, hence, dissolves into the bigger picture of globalisation and internationalisation of higher education.

Bologna clearly set out a number of declarations that were felt to fundamentally underpin the nature of higher education as it internationalised and developed in the twenty-first century. The extent to which these principles can be sustained will depend largely on market forces. They were principles stemming from the historical development of the Academe, and the idea of the university as it emerged over the past four centuries; whether such principles are sustainable, we can but hope.

References

Ahmed, N. M. (2010). *A user's guide to the crisis of civilization and how to save it*. New York: Pluto Books.

Barnett, R. (2000). *Realizing the university in an age of supercomplexity*. Buckingham: SRHE & Open University Press.

Birch, W. (1988). *The challenge to higher education: Reconciling responsibilities to scholarship and to society*. Buckingham: SRHE & Open University Press.

Birchall, D., & Smith, M. (2002). *Scope and scale of e-learning delivery amongst UK business schools*. London: CEML.

Blass, E. (2008, October 20–21). *From international to global: A future model for the development of higher education*. In InCULT Conference, Kuala Lumpar.

Blass, E., Ettinger, A., & Holton, V. (2007). Recognising differences in achievement: The case for a separate classification for qualifications undertaken by E-learning. In F. Li (Ed.), *Social implications and challenges of E-business*. Hershey: Idea Publishing Group.

Blondal, S., Field, S., Girouard, N., & Wagner, A. (2001). *Investment in human capital through post-compulsory education and training: Selected efficiency and equity aspects*. Paris: OECD.

Bologna. (2009, April 28–29). *Communique of the conference of European Ministers responsible for higher education*. Leuven and Louvain-la-Neuve.

Browne, J. (Chairman). (2010). *Securing a sustainable future for higher education*. At www.independent.gov.uk/browne-report. Accessed 13 Aug 2011.

Burgess, R. (2007). *Beyond the honours degree classification* (The Burgess Group Final Report). London: Universities UK.

Cetron, M. J., & Davies, O. (2008). Trends shaping tomorrow's world (part 1). *The Futurist, 42*, 35–52.

CHERI. (2007). The changing academic profession in the UK: Setting the scene. In U. UK (Ed.), *Research reports*. London: Universities UK.

CMI. (2008). *Environmental scanning: Trends affecting the world of work in 2018*. London: Chartered Management Institute.

Council of Europe. (2006). Doc 10943: Academic freedom and university autonomy. At http://assembly.coe.int/Main.asp?link=/Documents/WorkingDocs/Doc06/EDOC10943.htm. Accessed 1 Aug 2011.

Crowe, A. R. (2006). Technology, citizenship and the social studies classroom: Education for democracy in a technological age. *International Journal of Social Education, 21*, 111–121.

Daniel, J. (2003). Higher education: Past, present and future – A view from UNESCO. *Higher Education in Europe, 28*, 21–26.

Eastwood, D. (2008). *Understanding institutional performance*. London: Department for Industry, University and Skills.

Eckersley, R. (2007). Teaching and learning about globalisation. *Ethos, 15*(1), 10–18.

Etzkowitz, H., Webster, A., Gebhardt, C., & Terra, B. R. C. (2000). The future of the university and the university of the future: Evolution of ivory tower to entrepreneurial paradigm. *Research Policy, 29*, 313–330.

Fielden, J. (2007). *Global horizons for UK universities*. London: The Council for Industry and Higher Education.

Ford, M. P. (2002). *Beyond the modern university: Toward a constructive postmodern university.* Milton Keynes: Lightening Source UK Ltd.

Forstrop, P.-A. (2007). Who's colonizing who? The knowledge society thesis and the global challenges in higher education. *Studies in Philosophy of Education, 27,* 227–236.

Hakala, J. (2009). The future of academic calling? Junior researchers in the entrepreneurial university. *Higher Education, 57,* 173–190.

Halsey, A. H. (1995). *Decline of the donnish dominion.* Oxford: Clarendon.

Hilton, J. (2006). The future for higher education: Sunrise or perfect storm? *Educause Review, 41,* 58–71.

Jaspers, K. (1960). *The idea of the university.* London: Peter Owen.

Jongbloed, B., Enders, J., & Salerno, C. (2008). Higher education and its communities: Interconnections, interdependencies and a research agenda. *International Journal of Higher Education and Educational Planning, 56*(3), 1–22.

Kennedy, D. M. (2011, July 14–15). *Learning on the go: Mobility and social media.* In Social Media in Higher Education Conference, Melbourne.

Kenway, J., Bullen, E., & Robb, S. (2004). The knowledge economy, the techno-preneur and the problematic future of the university. *Policy Futures in Education, 2,* 330–350.

Knight, J. (1994). *Internationalisation: Elements and checkpoints.* Ottawa: Canadian Bureau for International Education.

Koodooz. (2010). *Generation Z: The new philanthropists.* At http://koodooz.wordpress.com/2010/09/09/generation-z-the-new-philanthropists/. Accessed 28 Aug 2011.

Lauder, H., Brown, P., Dillabough, J., & Halsey, A. (2006). Introduction: The prospects for education: Individualization, globalization, and social change. In H. Lauder, P. Brown, J. Dillabough, & A. Halsey (Eds.), *Education, globalization & social change.* Oxford: Oxford University Press.

Launch Group. (2009). *The next generation has landed.* At www.launchgroup.com.au/Blog/GenZFINAL.DOC. Accessed 28 Aug 2011.

Lefrere, P. (2007). Competing higher education futures in a globalising world. *European Journal of Education, 42,* 201–212.

Leitch, S. (2006). *Prosperity for all in the global economy – World class skills.* In HM Treasury (Ed.). Norwich: HMSO.

Louria, D. B., Didsbury, H. F. J., & Ellersbusch, F. (2003). The need for a multi-level education approach for the future. In H. F. J. Didsbury (Ed.), *21st century opportunities and challenges: An age of destruction or an age of transformation.* Bethesda: World Future Society.

Marginson, S. (2004). Competition and markets in higher Educatoin: A 'glonacal' analysis. *Policy Futures in Education, 2,* 175–244.

Marginson, S. (2007). The public/private divide in higher education: A global revision. *Higher Education, 53,* 307–333.

Marginson, S., & Peters, M. A. (2004). University futures editorial. *Policy Futures in Education, 2,* 159–174.

Margules, D. (2002). *University teaching and learning: Why a more flexible approach?* At http://www.ioe.ac.uk/schools/leid/oet%20html%20docs/Margules_D.htm. Accessed 1 Aug 2011.

McEldowny, M., Gaffikin, F., & Perry, D. C. (2009). Discourses of the contemporary urban campus in Europe: Intimations of Americanisation? *Globalisation, Societies and Education, 7*(2), 131–149.

Nelles, J., & Vorley, T. (2010). Entrepreneurial by design: Theorizing the entrepreneurial transformation of contemporary universities. *Industry & Higher Education, 24*(3), 157–164.

Newman, H. (1853). *The idea of a university* (Reprinted in London: Yale University Press).

Orstrom Moller, J. (2003). Globalization: Social disruption right ahead. In H. F. J. Didsbury (Ed.), *21st century opportunities and challenges: An age of destruction or an age of transformation.* Bethesda: World Future Society.

Patrick, J. J. (2005). Content and process in education for democracy. *International Journal of Social Education, 20,* 1–12.

Posnick-Goodwin, S. (2010). *Meet Generation Z*. California Teachers Association. At http://www.cta.org/Professional-Development/Publications/Educator-Feb-10/Meet-Generation-Z.aspx. Accessed 27 Aug 2011.

Scott, P. (1995). *The meanings of mass higher education*. Buckingham: SRHE & Open University Press.

Sentamu, J. (2000). Valuing cultural diversity in education. In D. Puttnam (Ed.), *Education futures*. London: RSA & The Design Council.

Soares, V. A. M., & Amarala, A. M. S. C. (1999). The entrepreneurial university: A fine answer to a difficult problem? *Higher Education in Europe, 24*(1), 11–21.

Spring, J. (2008). Research on globalization and education. *Review of Educational Research, 78*, 330–363.

Tenopir, C., & Rowlands, I. (2007). Age-related information behaviour. In *Information behaviour of the research of the future*. London: JISC & British Library.

Torney-Purta, J. (2001). What adolescents know about citizenship and democracy. *Educational Leadership, 59*, 45–50.

UUK. (2008). *Patterns of higher education institutions in the UK* (Eighth Report). London: Universities UK.

Vincent-Lancrin, S. (2004). Building future scenarios for universities and higher education: An international approach. *Policy Futures in Education, 2*, 245–263.

Walliker, A. (2008, February 25). Get ready, here comes Generation Z. *The Herald Sun*. At http://www.news.com.au/national/get-ready-here-comes-generation-z/story-e6frfkw9-111111 5637544. Accessed 28 Aug 2011.

Westheimer, J. (2008). What kind of citizen? Democratic dialogues in education. *Education (Canada), 48*, 6–10.

Williams, P., & Rowlands, I. (2007). The literature on young people and the information behaviour. In *Information behaviour of the researcher of the future*. London: JISC & British Library.

Zaharia, S. E., & Gilbert, E. (2005). The entrepreneurial university in the knowledge society. *Higher Education in Europe, 30*(1), 31–40.

Zolli, A. E. (2002). *TechTV's catalog of tomorrow*. Indianapolis: QUE.

About the Editors

Adrian Curaj is a Professor with the Polytechnic University of Bucharest (UPB). He holds a PhD in Automatic Systems from PUB and graduated from the EMBA program at ASEBUSS Bucharest and Seattle-Business School. Curaj is the General Director of the Executive Agency for Higher Education, Research, Development and Innovation Funding (UEFISCDI), and was an Advisor to the Prime Minister (2007–2008) on Science, Technologies, ICT and e-Governance. In 2009–2010, he was the President of the National Authority for Scientific Research within the Ministry of Education, Research, Youth and Sports. He was a Consultant for the World Bank, UNESCO, UNIDO, and the European Commission in the field of Third Education, Science and Innovation, as well as Foresight. He is currently a member of the External Advisory Board PEOPLE, European Commission. He published several books and articles on the topics of research management and foresight on important scientific journals. He is a co-author of an invention that won the gold medal at the International Exhibition of Inventions in Geneva. For his significant contribution to Science and Innovation, he received two distinctions from the Romanian President, the National Order for Merit – Knight in 2000, and the National Order for Merit – Grand Officer in 2008.

Sir Peter Scott is Professor of Higher Education Studies at the Institute of Education University of London. From 1998 until 2010 he was Vice-Chancellor of Kingston University London. Previously he was Pro-Vice-Chancellor responsible for external affairs at the University of Leeds. Before becoming a Professor at Leeds he was Editor of 'The Times Higher Education Supplement'. Between 2000 and 2008 he was President of the Academic Cooperation Association, the Brussels-based organisation that brings together national agencies in Europe active in the field of international education. He has also been a member of the board of the Higher Education Funding Council for England which is responsible for distributing state funding to universities, and Chair of the Universities Association for Lifelong Learning in the United Kingdom.

A. Curaj et al. (eds.), *European Higher Education at the Crossroads: Between the Bologna Process and National Reforms*, DOI 10.1007/978-94-007-3937-6, © Springer Science+Business Media Dordrecht 2012

Lazăr Vlasceanu: Professor, Department of Sociology, University of Bucharest. He is also vice-president of the Romanian National Council on Academic Attestation. His recent publications include Sociology and Modernity (Polirom, 2007), Universities and Reflexive Modernity. Institutional Ambiguities and Unintended Consequences (CEU Press, 2010).

Lesley Wilson joined EUA at its creation in 2001 and formally took over as Secretary General in 2002. Previous to this she held a number of senior positions in higher education and research management at European level, in particular as Director of UNESCO's European Centre for Higher Education in Bucharest (UNESCO-CEPES) from 1995 to late 1999, Head of the newly established Science Policy Unit at the European Science Foundation in Strasbourg (1994/1995) and Director of the EC TEMPUS Office in Brussels from 1990 to 1994. A graduate of the University of Glasgow and the Institut des Hautes Etudes Europeennes at the University of Strasbourg she spent her early career as a scientific staff member of the German Science Council in Cologne before moving to Brussels in 1988 to join the newly established ERASMUS Bureau.

About the Authors

Alberto Amaral is professor at the University of Porto and President of the Portuguese Agency for Assessment and Accreditation of Higher Education (2008 to present). He was the director of the Centre for Higher Education Policy Studies, Portugal (CIPES) (1998–2008) and a former rector of Universidade do Porto (1986–1998). He is the author of papers on higher education policy and editor and co-editor of several books, including From Governance to Identity – A festschrift for Mary Henkel (2008); European Integration and the Governance of Higher Education and Research (2009).

Liviu Andreescu is an Associate Professor with the Faculty of Letters, Spiru Haret University, where he teaches American Studies. He authored a book on academic freedom and published articles on higher education, religious policy and church-state issues (in education and beyond), and American culture.

Angele Attard holds a Doctor of Laws Degree from the University of Malta, an Advanced Diploma in European Studies from the European College of Parma and an MSc (Educational Studies) from the University of Oxford. She currently works as the Assistant Private Secretary to the Minister of Education, Employment and Family in Malta. Previously, Angele worked for Education International as a coordinator within the Education and Employment Unit. She has also worked in the Maltese National Commission for Higher Education and the European Students' Union. She is involved in several consultancy projects on higher education reform with international organisations and governments around Europe.

Eddie Blass is a Professor of Leadership Development in the Faculty of Business and Enterprise at Swinburne University of Technology in Melbourne, Australia. She teaches on the Masters of Strategic Foresight and is a foresight specialist in the field of Higher Education. Eddie left the UK to move to Australia at the beginning of 2011 having completed two futures studies in HE for HEFCE (UK) while at the University of Hertfordshire.

A. Curaj et al. (eds.), *European Higher Education at the Crossroads:*
Between the Bologna Process and National Reforms,
DOI 10.1007/978-94-007-3937-6, © Springer Science+Business Media B.V. 2012

John Brennan – Professor of Higher Education at the Open University since 1992. Directed many research projects, national and international, on the changing relationships between higher education and society, with foci on topics such as graduate employment, quality assurance, regional impact of universities, social equity issues, and the social contexts of student learning. Several books on these themes. A sociologist by background.

Anne Corbett is a Visiting Fellow in the European Institute, London School of Economics and Political Science, Houghton Street, London WC2A 2AE. She is the author of Universities and the Europe of Knowledge, ideas, Institutions and Policy Entrepreneurship in European Union Policy-Making, 1955–2005 (Palgrave Macmillan, 2005).

Jeremy Cox is Chief Executive of the Association Européenne des Conservatoires, Académies de Musique et Musikhochschulen (AEC). Prior to this, he had more than 10 years' experience as Dean of the Royal College of Music in London.

Jeremy has been involved in European developments in higher music education since the start of the Bologna Process. He was chief architect of the AEC's 'Polifonia' Learning Outcomes that are now widely used across Europe.

Adrian Curaj is professor at the Polytechnic University of Bucharest (UPB). He holds a PhD from PUB in Automatic Systems and graduated from the EMBA program at ASEBUSS Bucharest and Seattle-Business School. Curaj is General Director of the Executive Agency for Higher Education, Research, Development and Innovation Funding (UEFISCDI), and was Advisor to the Prime Minister (2007–2008) on Science, Technologies, ICT and e-Governance. In 2009–2010, he was President of the National Authority for Scientific Research within the Ministry of Education, Research, Youth and Sports. He was Consultant for the World Bank, UNESCO, UNIDO, and the European Commission in the field of Third Education, Science and Innovation, as well as Foresight. He is currently a member of the External Advisory Board PEOPLE, European Commission. He published several books and articles in important scientific journals, on the topics of research management and foresight. He is co-author of an invention that won the gold medal at the International Exhibition of Inventions in Geneva. For his significant contribution to Science and Innovation, he received two distinctions from the Romanian President, the National Order for Merit – Knight in 2000, and the National Order for Merit – Grand Officer in 2008.

Hans De Wit is Professor (lector) of Internationalisation of Higher Education at the School of Economics and Management of the Hogeschool van Amsterdam, University of Applied Sciences. He is the Co-Editor of the '*Journal of Studies in International Education*' (Association for Studies in International Education/SAGE publishers). Since 2010 he is a visiting professor at the CAPRI, the Centre for Academic Practice and Research in Internationalisation of Leeds Metropolitan University, United Kingdom. In 2005–2006 He was a New Century Scholar of the *Fulbright Program* Higher Education in the twenty-first century, and in 1995 and 2006 a visiting scholar in the USA and in 2002 in Australia. Hans De Wit is founding member and past president of the *European Association for International Education* (EAIE).

He has (co)written several other books and articles on international education and is actively involved in assessment and consultancy in international education, for organisations like the European Commission, UNESCO, World Bank, IMHE/OECD, and ESMU. His latest book is Hans De Wit (2011), Trends, Issues and Challenges in Internationalisation of Higher Education. CAREM, HvA, Amsterdam.

Marina Elias Andreu – Lecture of Sociology of Education at Department of Sociological Theory at Barcelona University and researcher at GRET (Research group of Education and Work) in Sociology Department of UAB. Research about Higher Education, focus on Bologna Process. Consequences for teachers and students: different profiles, dropouts, learning process etc. From February 2011 to July 2011 I did a 6 month post doctorate fellowship at Centre for Higher Education Research and Information, Open University (London).

Thomas Estermann is Head of the Unit Governance, Autonomy and Funding with responsibilities for EUA's work aimed at strengthening universities autonomy, governance, management and their financial sustainability. He is developing EUA's policy on higher education finance and autonomy and has published on both topics ("Financially sustainable universities II: European universities diversifying income sources", 2011; "University Autonomy in Europe I: Exploratory Study", 2009; "Financially sustainable universities: towards full costing in European universities", 2008).

Marike Faber is a research associate at CHEPS and is currently supporting various research projects on educational transitions and higher education reforms. She holds a Master's degree in educational sciences from the University in Groningen where she graduated in 2003. After finishing this masters, she finished a masterstudy in Euroculture in 2004 at both the University of Groningen and the Georg-August Universität in Göttingen, Germany. Here the topic of her master thesis was the open method of coordination in European higher education. Marike is currently finishing her PhD. Research at the University of Utrecht next to her projects at CHEPS. Her current research interests at CHEPS are: Educational transitions and Higher education reforms. She has been working on projects related to the transition processes from the first cycle of higher education to the second cycle, the reforms of higher education systems under the Bologna process and the U-Map project.

Bogdan Florian is currently a researcher at the Institute for Educational Sciences based in Bucharest, Romania. He holds a PhD degree in Political Science and has been involved over the past years in research and public policy drafting in the field of higher education. He is the author of a number of research papers regarding Romanian higher education. His research interests cover a variety of topics including higher education, public policy and various applications of institutional theories in the field of social sciences.

Sacha Garben, fellow in law at the London School of Economics and Political Science, is specialised in EU law with a particular focus on free movement, citizenship and constitutional principles. She has obtained her PhD at the European University Institute in Florence. The thesis was published by Kluwer in 2011 entitled "EU Higher Education Law. The Bologna Process and Harmonisation by Stealth". Sacha can be reached at S.Garben@LSE.ac.uk

Marcel Gérard – Professor of Economics and Taxation President of the Research Council, FUCaM, Universite catholique de Louvain College of Europe, Bruges, FUSL, Brussels CESifo Fellow and Research Professor Ifo.

Koen Geven is a student in Public Policy in the Erasmus Mundus programme (MundusMAPP) at the University of York (United Kingdom) and Central European University (Hungary). He holds a BSc in Political Science from the University of Amsterdam (The Netherlands). Previously, Koen was a member of the national executive of the Dutch National Students' Union (LSVb) and chairperson of the European Students' Union. He also worked as a policy consultant to Education International in the unit on Education and Employment for 3 years. Koen is engaged in several reform processes of higher education in the Netherlands and Europe.

Radu Gheorghiu holds a BA in Economics from the Academy of Economic Studies and a PhD from the National Institute of Economic Research. He has been a researcher with the Institute for World Economy in Bucharest since 1998, where he has been running the Competitiveness and Innovation Department since 2003. Since 2004 he has been working with the Executive Agency for Higher Education in different national and international foresight projects, the most important of which were related to the future the Romanian research and development and the Romanian higher education systems.

Jennifer M. Gidley is a psychologist, educator and futures researcher. She is President of the World Futures Studies Federation and a Research Fellow in the Global Cities Research Institute, RMIT University, Melbourne, Australia. Jennifer's research interests include educational futures, rapid global socio-cultural change, and global knowledge futures. Publications include The University in Transformation (2000), Youth Futures (2002) and Futures in Education (2004) and special issues of the Journal, *Futures* on "Global Mindset Change" (2010) and "Educational Futures" (2011).

Elsa Hackl, Department of Political Science, University of Vienna, Austria. Master Degree in Law, Doctorate in Political Science. Has worked on qualification and occupational research, as a civil servant in a senior position (Director of the Austrian Ministry for Higher Education and Research), was a visiting scholar at the University of British Columbia, Canada and the European University Institute, Florence, and as an expert for OECD, the Council of Europe, the European Training Foundation and Salzburg Seminar.

Gabriel-Marian Hâncean holds a Ph.D. in political science and currently is associated as teaching assistant at University of Bucharest, Faculty of Sociology and Social Work Bucharest, Romania. His research and academic interests include, besides higher education, the broader fields of sociology of organizations, social networks research and public management and public policy analysis. For more details please visit: http://www.gabrielhancean.wordpress.com

Attila Havas is a Senior Research Fellow at the Institute of Economics, Hungarian Academy of Sciences. His academic interests are in economics of innovation, innovation policy, and technology foresight. In 1997–2000 he was Programme Director of TEP, the Hungarian Technology Foresight Programme. He has participated in international research projects on STI policies, innovation, foresight and prospective analyses, and been a member of several EU expert groups.

Professor Ellen Hazelkorn is Vice President of Research and Enterprise, Dublin Institute of Technology, and leads the Higher Education Policy Research Unit (HEPRU). She is Consultant to the OECD, and works closely with IAU and UNESCO. She is a member of the HEA, and chairs the Dublin Regional Higher Education Alliance (DRHEA). Ellen has been a member of higher education and research review teams in Spain, The Netherlands, Australia, Poland, Germany and Finland. She is Visiting Professor at the University of Liverpool, and member of several Editorial Boards, including *Higher Education Management and Policy* (OECD) and *Higher Education Policy* (IAU). *Rankings and the Reshaping of Higher Education: The Battle for World-Class Excellence* was published by Palgrave Macmillan (2011).

Achim Hopbach: Before taking his current post as Managing Director of the German Accreditation Council, he worked as a Research-Assistant at the University of Tübingen and Managing Director of a faculty at Heidelberg University. Afterwards he joined the German Rectors' Conference. He is a member of the Hong Kong Council for Accreditation since 2005, and President of ENQA since 2009.

Michael Huber is Professor of Higher Education Studies at the Institute of Science and Technology Studies at the University of Bielefeld and Research Associate at the Centre for Analysis of Risk and Regulation, London School of Economics. He earned his PhD at the European University Institute in Florence in 1991 and defended his Habilitation at the University of Leipzig in 2005.

Ben Jongbloed holds a Master's degree in Econometrics from the University of Groningen and a PhD in Public Administration (Public Finance) from the University of Twente. Since starting to work for the Center for Higher Education Policy Studies at the University of Twente in 1992, his research and scholarly publications have focused in particular on governance and resource allocation issues in higher education. His work addresses topics such as funding methodologies for higher education, performance measurement in higher education, and university-industry collaboration. He has worked on several international research projects funded by the European Commission, including a recent (2010) study of governance and funding reforms in European higher education.

Frans Kaiser is senior research associate at the Center for Higher Education Policy Studies (CHEPS). His background is in public administration. He has two decades experience in comparative studies in higher education, both from a qualitative and a quantitative perspective. Frans Kaiser is an expert in international comparison of comparison of higher education systems and policies as well as in the design and use of indicators for international comparison and has conducted several international studies and projects on comparative issues and indicators in higher education, including the U-Map project.

Manja Klemenčič is postdoctoral researcher at the Centre for Educational Policy Studies at University of Ljubljana affiliated with a research project entitled "Differentiation, Equity, Productivity: the social and economic consequences of expanded and differentiated higher education systems – internationalisation aspects" (DEP-08-EuroHESC-OP-016) and visiting fellow at Wissenschaftszentrum Berlin fuer Sozialforschung in Science Policy Research Group. Her postdoctoral research broadly focuses on European higher education reform processes, and in particular, on issues of institutional diversification in Southeast Europe and student and other stakeholder participation in HE governance. She has completed PhD in International Studies at University of Cambridge in 2006, and held several research fellowships: at the Center for International Higher Education at Boston College (2010/2011); at Minda de Gunzburg Center for European Studies at Harvard (2007/2008), a Fulbright Fellowship at the Center for Business and Government at Harvard Kennedy School (2004/2005), and, in 2004, a UACES Fellowship at the Centre for European Policy Studies in Brussels. Between 1999 and 2001, she acted as Secretary-General of (now) European Students' Union.

Snežana Krstić has joined Eurodoc in 2004, where she has actively participated in many (policy) activities related to junior researchers. Particularly active she was in Mobility work-group, which has coordinated in 2007–2009. She holds B.Sc., M.Sc. and Ph.D. from University of Belgrade, where she has also worked as a teaching and research assistant. In capacity of independent consultant, her research interests are in interdisciplinary research on intersection between science/technology, policy, society and innovation.

Vinay Lal teaches has taught history at UCLA since 1993 and was Professor of History at University of Delhi, 2010–2011. He has published a dozen books and writes widely on Indian politics and history, historiography, colonialism, the life and thought of Gandhi, the Indian diaspora, the politics of knowledge systems, American politics, globalization, & popular and public culture in India. His work has been translated into Korean, Japanese, Finnish, German, French, Kannada, Hindi, Persian, Spanish.

Author or editor of a dozen books, including Empire of Knowledge (London: Pluto Press, 2002; new ed., Sage, 2005; Urdu translation, 2008); The History of History: Politics and Scholarship in Modern India (Oxford Univ Press, 2003; 2nd ed., 2005); Political Hinduism (ed., Oxford Univ Press, 2009); and (ed. with Ashis Nandy) The Future of Knowledge and Culture: A Dictionary for the Twenty-First Century (Viking Penguin, 2005).

Dr. Åsa Lindberg-Sand holds a PhD in Educational Science. Her position is Senior Lecturer at Lund University, Sweden. She has led several quality projects at the university level. Presently she is working as educational developer in the university's Centre for Educational Development with a focus on research education. Her research focuses two domains: Student assessment in higher education and the implementation of the Bologna Process.

Tia Loukkola, is Head of Unit responsible for EUA's activities related to quality assurance and transparency with the main focus on supporting quality cultures in the association's member universities. Before joining EUA in 2008 she worked at the University of Turku, Finland, for 10 years in various capacities both in faculty and central administration.

Sinéad Lucey is IUA's International Education Manager. Sinéad's role focuses on the development and implementation of a collective universities' international education strategy, and all associated elements, within the broader Irish International Education Strategy 2010–2015 recently announced by government.

Liviu Matei is CEU's Senior Vice President and Chief Operating Officer, and a Professor at the Department of Public Policy. He served as Academic Secretary of CEU from 1999 to 2008.

Liviu Matei studied philosophy and psychology at Babes-Bolyai University Cluj, and Sociology at Bucharest University, Romania. He received his PhD from the latter. He benefited from fellowships at the Institut Superieure de Formation Sociale et Communication Bruxelles, New School University, Universite Paris X Nanterre, Universite de Savoie, and the Salzburg Seminar. He started his academic career as a lecturer of social psychology at Babes-Bolyai University and combined research on ethnic minorities, civil society and higher education with civic engagement and professional work in these areas. He worked with several national and international NGOs, governmental and intergovernmental organizations.

Nina McGuinness holds a Masters in European Studies from the University of Hannover. Her research interests are in the European research policy and in particular the Open Method of Coordination. She is project manager in the EU Liaison office at the Leibniz University, Hannover.

Robin Middlehurst is Professor of Higher Education at Kingston University, attached to the Vice Chancellor's Office. From May 1st 2004, she has also been on half-time secondment to the Leadership Foundation for Higher Education (LFHE) as Director of Strategy, Research and International, being responsible for commissioning the Foundation's programme of research and leading the development of the Foundation's international strategy which supports the internationalisation agenda of the UK higher education sector.

Klemen Miklavič is an assistant researcher at the Centre for Educational Policy Studies (CEPS), University of Ljubljana. He is particularly focused on the nature and discursive meaning of higher education in modern Europe. Prior to joining the CEPS, he has worked as a consultant, expert or freelance researcher for a number of

NGOs, intergovernmental organizations and research centres, dealing with higher education, such as Council of Europe, Centre for Education Policy (Belgrade) etc. During 2008–2009 he was employed at the OSCE Mission in Kosovo as a senior adviser responsible for higher education and ethnic minority issues.

Adrian Miroiu Professor, Department of Political Science, National School of Political and Administrative Studies, Bucharest. He is also the president of the Romanian National Council for the Financing of Higher Education. His recent publications include Foundations of Politics. I. Preferences and Collective Decisions (2006), Foundations of Politics. II. Rationality and Collective Action (2007) and Political Philosophy. An Introduction (2009).

Roberto Moscati – Professor of Sociology of Education at the University of Milano-Bicocca. Has been affiliated to the Universities of Catania, Trieste, Milano. Studied Sociology at Northwestern University (M.A.), and Education at Harvard University (Ed.M.) has been visiting scholar at the University of California, Berkeley, Stanford University and UCLA. Has been member of the editorial board of "Higher Education", "European Journal of Education" and "Tertiary Education and Management". He is currently member of the "Bologna Promoters" (Italian section).

Kai Muehleck works as senior researcher at the Hanover-based HIS-Institute for Research on Higher Education. Currently, he is leading an international research project on equitable access to higher education (EquNet) and an international research project on tracking of students and graduates (TRACKIT!).

Dr. Terhi Nokkala is a Research Fellow at the Finnish Institute for Educational Research (FIER), University of Jyväskylä. Her research focuses on the interplay between higher education policy, technological developments, organisational parameters and networks, and individual experiences in various aspects of higher education, with specific interest in internationalisation, research collaboration and university autonomy. Prior to joining the FIER in June 2010, Terhi Nokkala worked as a Research Fellow at Centre for Research in Social Simulation at the University of Surrey with research related to research collaboration networks. Terhi received her PhD in Higher Education from the University of Tampere in 2007.

Conor O'Carroll is Research Director at the Irish Universities Association (IUA). He is responsible for the coordination of research policy across all seven Irish universities. He is also responsible for the FP7 Marie Curie, Research Potential Programmes and EURAXESS Network in Ireland. He represents Ireland on a number of European bodies responsible for the development of research careers (currently on the SGHRM). He is a physicist by training with a B.Sc./M.Sc. in mathematical physics and PhD in physics from University College Dublin.

Kata Orosz holds a Fulbright-OTP Bank Graduate Student Scholarship at Teachers College, Columbia University. She has a master's degree in public policy with a specialization in higher education management and policy from Central European University, where she also worked as assistant to the Provost. She is interested in institutional responses to changes in the higher education policy environment, especially changes in the funding environment. She can be reached at ko2270@columbia.edu.

Dr. Dominic Orr is a senior researcher at the HIS-Institute for Research on Higher Education in Hannover (DE). He graduated from Southbank University London in the field of applied business studies and holds a PhD in the field of comparative education from Dresden University.

Since 2005, he has been the head of the international coordination team of the EUROSTUDENT project, a large-scale project intended to collate comparable data from 25 countries on the social and economic conditions of students in European higher education. He has been a member of three expert circles of the Bologna Follow-Up Group since 2008, on reporting, mobility and the social dimension.

Dr. Beliz Ozorhon is an Assistant Professor at Bogazici University Department of Civil Engineering, Bebek-Istanbul/TURKEY Telephone: +90(212) 359-6425 Fax: +90(212) 287-2457, +90(212) 265-8488. Her research interests are in innovation management, knowledge management, international construction, project management, risk management, decision support systems. She hold PhD, Ms and BS degrees in Civil Engineering from the Middle East Technical University, Ankara, Turkey. She has been a Research Fellow at the University of Salford, Manchester, UK; a Visiting Research Scholar at the Illinois Institute of Technology, Chicago, USA; and a Researcher and Teaching Assistant at the Middle East Technical University, Ankara, Turkey

Fernando Miguel Galán Palomares (Segovia, 1986) is a medical student at the University of Cantabria (Santander) and has been at the Università Degli Studi di Bari "Aldo Moro" (Bari, Italy), within the ERASMUS programme. Since 2011 he is a member of the Academic Affairs Committee at ESU (the European Students' Union) and member of the Steering Committee of the Institutional Evaluation Programme of the EUA (European University Association).

Catherine Paradeise is currently Professor of Sociology at the University Paris Est- Marne-la-Vallée and member of the research center Laboratoire Techniques, Territoires et Sociétés – CNRS/UMLV/Ecole Nationale des Ponts et Chaussées (LATTS). She chairs the new French 'Research, Innovation and Society Research Institute' (IFRIS). She has held positions as Deputy Director at the CNRS Department of Social Sciences and Humanities and at the Ecole Normale supérieure de Cachan. She is involved as an expert in several journals, programs, French and European agencies. Her current research focuses on research and higher education Policy and organization.

Mihai Păunescu is currently Associate Professor at National School of Political and Administrative Studies, Faculty of Political Sciences, Bucharest. He is the co-author of several studies on the Romanian higher education system from a neo-institutionalist perspective. His fields of academic interest include the new institutionalism in organizational studies, public management and public policy.

Hans Pechar is a professor for higher education at the University of Klagenfurt, Austria. The focus of his research is comparative higher education and economics of higher education. He represents Austria in the governing board of OECD CERI.

Most recently, his publications have addressed topics of policies of access to higher education, governance of Austrian universities, and equity in education.

James A. Powell OBE, DSc, CEng, BSc, MSc, PhD, AUMIST, FIOA, FIMgt, FCMI, FRSA, FCIOB, FASI, MInst D., MInstKT, UK Academic Director of the PASCAL Universities for a Modern Renaissance Programme Ambassador for Social Entrepreneurship in Higher Education and Ambassador for the Leonardo European Corporate Learning Awards, Director of UPBEAT, UPBEAT (Manchester) Ltd and Smart City Futures and Member of the New Club of Paris.

A Chartered European Engineer with specialisation in Design, Academic Enterprise, Human Communications and Team Building. He was managing director of Britain's first commercial videodisc company and a Pro Vice Chancellor (Enterprise and Regional Affairs) responsible for Salford University's "Reach Out" initiatives. He is now Professor Emeritus at Salford, presently working on the *leadership, governance and management* of university Reach-out to business and the community. He is also presently developing his notion of 'Universities for a Modern Renaissance' for, and with, the Board Members of the PASCAL International Observatory for place management, social capital and learning regions; this idea will be used to focus their developing strategy for university engagement. On the 15th June 1996, in the Queen's Birthday Honours list, he was awarded the OBE for "services to science and to engineering research and education".

Viorel Proteasa is doctoral student of Political Sciences at the National School for Political Studies and Public Administration (SNSPA) in Bucharest. His field of research is public policy and his thesis is focused on higher education. He benefits of a scholarship granted within the programme "Doctoral scholarships for the development of a knowledge based society – BDSC", financed through the Sectoral Operational Programme Human Resources Development – POS DRU. He is a member of the 2010–2012 Secretariat of the Bologna Process.

Enora Bennetot Pruvot is Programme Manager for the Unit Governance, Autonomy and Funding at the European University Association. She focuses on income diversification in universities, and is also closely associated to work on autonomy and governance reforms. She contributes to policy development in the field of higher education finances and is co-author of EUA's report "Financially sustainable universities II: European universities diversifying income sources" (2011).

Lewis Purser is director (academic affairs) at IUA. From 1998 to 2005 he was programme manager at the European University Association. A graduate of Trinity College Dublin and of the Graduate Institute of Development Studies at the University of Geneva, he worked from 1989 to 1998 with various higher education institutions in Hungary, Romania and Bosnia-Herzegovina, and with several United Nations agencies in educational, health and social fields.

Sybille Reichert is the director of *Reichert Consulting Strategy and Policy Development for Higher Education* (www.reichertconsulting.ch), a consultancy which focuses on higher education policy development and institutional change processes in an international context. In addition to conducting international comparative studies on developments in higher education for European organisations or national higher education agencies, Reichert accompanies institutions in their self-analyses and evaluations, strategy development and organisational reform processes.

Ziauddin Sardar, writer, broadcaster and cultural critic, is visiting Professor of Postcolonial Studies at School of Arts, the City University, London. He is the author of over 45 books, including his classic studies, The Future of Muslim Civilisation (1979) and Islamic Futures: The Shape of Ideas to Come (1985), the cultish Postmodernism and the Other (1998), and the international bestseller Why Do People Hate America? (2002). A collection of his writings is available as Islam, Postmodernism and Other Futures: A Ziauddin Sardar Reader (2003) and How Do You Know?: Reading Ziauddin Sardar on Islam, Science and Cultural Relations (2006). He is the Editor of Futures, a Commissioner on the Equality and Human Rights Commission. He is widely known for his radio and television appearance.

Ms Chripa Schneller joined the Asia-Europe Foundation (ASEF) as Special Advisor for its higher education initiative, the ASEM Education Hub (AEH), in 2009, with a focus on the development of AEH's overall strategy and outreach. In this capacity, she is assisting ASEF to promote mutual understanding and cooperation in higher education between Asia and Europe. Ms Schneller is currently pursuing a PhD on the participation of students with an immigrant background in tertiary education in Germany. Before joining ASEF, she was Policy Officer at the Academic Cooperation Association (ACA) in Brussels.

Sir Peter Scott is Professor of Higher Education Studies at the Institute of Education University of London. From 1998 until 2010 he was Vice-Chancellor of Kingston University London. Previously he was Pro-Vice-Chancellor responsible for external affairs at the University of Leeds. Before becoming a Professor at Leeds he was Editor of 'The Times Higher Education Supplement'. Between 2000 and 2008 he was President of the Academic Cooperation Association, the Brussels-based organisation that brings together national agencies in Europe active in the field of international education. He has also been a member of the board of the Higher Education Funding Council for England which is responsible for distributing state funding to universities, and Chair of the Universities Association for Lifelong Learning in the United Kingdom.

Ole-Jacob Skodvin is Deputy Director General at the Norwegian Agency for Quality Assurance in Education (2010 to present). He is head of the Department of Analysis and Development. He has previously held a position in the Ministry of Education and Research, Department of Higher Education, as Deputy Director General with responsibility for Policy Analysis and International affairs (2001–2010). In the period from 1987 to 2001 he worked as a researcher at NIFU (Nordic Institute for Studies in Innovation, Research and Education). He has written several reports and articles in the area of mergers and organizational change in higher education.

Hanne Smidt as Senior Adviser at EUA since 2002, Hanne Smidt has been involved in a wide range of EUA projects related to the implementation of the Bologna reforms. The development of the Lifelong Learning agenda and the "European universities charter on lifelong learning" for EUA has been a core issue for her and she has written recently several publications on this topic. As an independent higher education consultant in Sweden, the main focus of her activities has been to follow the introduction of the Bologna process (the Swedish Master Report) and a number of internal quality enhancing projects in Swedish higher education.

Andrée Sursock is Senior Adviser at the European University Association (EUA). She is the author of the 2010 Trends report, which analyses a decade of policy change in European higher education, and is involved in several EUA projects related to quality assurance and lifelong learning. She has participated in over 70 evaluations across Europe, sits on the boards of several QA agencies, and on the editorial board of Higher Education Management and Policy (OECD).

Ulrich Teichler Professor and former director of the International Centre for Higher Education Research (INCHER-Kassel), University of Kassel, Germany; research areas: higher education and the world of work, higher education systems in comparative perspective, international cooperation and mobility, academic profession. Member of Academia Europaea and International Academy of Education, former chairman of the Consortium of Higher Education Researchers (CHER) and former president of EAIR.

Pedro Nuno Teixeira is Director of CIPES – Center for Higher Education Policy Studies and Associate Professor at the Faculty of Economics – University of Porto. His research interests focus on the economics of higher education and in the history of economic ideas. His publications include his book "Jacob Mincer – A Founding Father of Modern Labour Economics" (Oxford UP, 2007) and the following collective volumes: "Markets in Higher Education – Reality or Rhetoric?" (Kluwer, 2004), "Cost-Sharing and Accessibility in Higher Education – A Fairer Deal?" (Springer, 2006), and "Public Vices, Private Virtues – Assessing the Effects of Marketization in Higher Education" (Sense, 2011).

Peter van der Hijden is an official of the European Commission working at the Skills Unit of the Research and Innovation Directorate General. Please note that the European Commission is not affiliated with this publication and the opinions expressed in this interview do not necessarily reflect its position or opinion.

Lazăr Vlasceanu: Professor, Department of Sociology, University of Bucharest. He is also vice-president of the Romanian National Council on Academic Attestation. His recent publications include Sociology and Modernity (Polirom, 2007), Universities and Reflexive Modernity. Institutional Ambiguities and Unintended Consequences (CEU Press, 2010).

Both **Bernd Wächter** and **Irina Ferencz** work for the Academic Cooperation Association (ACA) in Brussels. ACA is an umbrella-association of European and global agencies which support international cooperation in higher education. Bernd

Wächter has been ACA's Director since 1998, and has held previous positions at the University of Kassel, DAAD, the British Council and the Brussels Socrates Office. Bernd has published widely on international matters in higher education, and he is a frequent speaker at European and international education conferences. Irina Ferencz joined ACA as Policy Officer in 2009, after having completed a Master's degree in European Politics and Policies at the Katholieke Universiteit, Leuven. In parallel to her work in ACA, Irina is currently pursuing a PhD at the University of Kassel, Germany.

Magdalena Wislocka is responsible for the EURAXESS bridgehead office based in the IUA. Magda participates in various European Commission funded projects focusing on researchers' mobility (MOREBRAIN, EURAXESS TOP 1 and People Network). Madga is a biologist by training with a M.Sc. in plant ecology and a PhD in Environmental Biology from Wroclaw University (Poland).

Pavel Zgaga is Professor of Philosophy of Education at the University of Ljubljana, Slovenia. During the 1990s he was State Secretary for Higher Education and Minister of Education and Sport. After his return to academe, he co-founded the Centre for Educational Policy Studies (CEPS) at the University of Ljubljana and has been its director until today. He has held several research grants and directed national and international projects on education policy, mainly concerned with development of higher education in the contemporary European context. He was also engaged in the Bologna Process, serving as general rapporteur (2001–2003), as a member of the Board of the BFUG (2004–2005) and as the rapporteur of the Working Group on External Dimension of the Bologna Process (2006–2007).

Marian Zulean, holds a PhD in (Military) Sociology from the University of Bucharest, a Master in International Affairs from the University of Pittsburgh and a postdoctoral Fulbright Scholarship at the University of Maryland. He teaches Public Policy Analysis, National Security Policy Formulation, International Security and Military Sociology at the University of Bucharest. He is a member of, among others, the Inter-University Seminar on Armed Forces and Society (IUS), Brzezinski Scholar Program, RC01 of International Sociological Association and ERGOMAS.

Index

A. Curaj et al. (eds.), *European Higher Education at the Crossroads:*
Between the Bologna Process and National Reforms,
DOI 10.1007/978-94-007-3937-6, © Springer Science+Business Media Dordrecht 2012